P9-DBN-023

About the Author

Dan Gookin has written more than 120 books about technology, many of them accurate. He is most famously known as the author of the original *For Dummies* book, *DOS For Dummies*, published in 1991. Additionally, Dan has achieved fame as one of the first computer radio talk show hosts, the editor of a computer magazine, a national technology spokesman, and an occasional actor on the community theater stage.

Dan still considers himself a writer and technology "guru" whose job it is to remind everyone that our electronics are not to be taken too seriously. His approach is light and humorous yet very informative. He knows that modern gizmos can be complex and intimidating but necessary to help people become productive and successful. Dan mixes his vast knowledge of all things high-tech with a unique, dry sense of humor that keeps everyone informed — and awake.

Dan's most recent books are *Droid X For Dummies*, *Word 2010 For Dummies*, *PCs For Dummies*, Windows 7 Edition, and *Laptops For Dummies*, 4th Edition. He holds a degree in communications/visual arts from the University of California, San Diego. Dan dwells in North Idaho, where he enjoys woodworking, music, theater, riding his bicycle, being with his boys, and fighting local government corruption.

Dedication

To Milton Francis. Thanks for the love and attention. You will be missed.

Publisher's Acknowledgments

We're proud of this book; please send us your comments at http://dummies.custhelp.com. For other comments, please contact our Customer Care Department within the U.S. at 877-762-2974, outside the U.S. at 317-572-3993, or fax 317-572-4002.

Some of the people who helped bring this book to market include the following:

Acquisitions, Editorial, and Media Development

Senior Project Editor: Mark Enochs

Acquisitions Editor: Katie Mohr

Copy Editor: Rebecca Whitney

Technical Editor: James F. Kelly

Editorial Manager: Leah Cameron

Media Development Project Manager: Laura Moss-Hollister

Media Development Assistant Project Manager: Jenny Swisher

Media Development Assistant Producer: Josh Frank

Editorial Assistant: Amanda Graham

Sr. Editorial Assistant: Cherie Case

Cartoons: Rich Tennant (www.the5thwave.com)

Composition Services

Project Coordinator: Sheree Montgomery

Layout and Graphics: Kimberly Tabor

Proofreaders: John Greenough, Bonnie Mikkelson

Indexer: BIM Indexing & Proofreading Services

Publishing and Editorial for Technology Dummies

Richard Swadley, Vice President and Executive Group Publisher

Andy Cummings, Vice President and Publisher

Mary Bednarek, Executive Acquisitions Director

Mary C. Corder, Editorial Director

Publishing for Consumer Dummies

Diane Graves Steele, Vice President and Publisher

Composition Services

Debbie Stailey, Director of Composition Services

Contents at a Glance

Table of Contents

Margaret E. Heggan Public Library
606 Delsea Drive
Sewell, NJ 08080

Introduction

If trouble were predictable, it wouldn't be a problem. The problem with trouble, however, is that it's unpredictable.

You hold in your hands a big ol' book that's all about solving problems with your computer. The topic is troubleshooting. It needs to be covered in so many pages because there hasn't been a computer yet invented that didn't have trouble following it like a shadow on a sunny day.

The computing experience should be a pleasant one. And it can be — if you're informed and able to deal with the troubles you encounter. This book helps you along that journey in an informative and entertaining way. Welcome to *Troubleshooting & Maintaining Your PC All-in-One For Dummies*.

Woe Is Computer

A byte of prevention is worth a megabyte of cure.

My philosophy on troubleshooting is that it's easier to do when you understand how the computer works. This philosophy is the opposite of what most people expect, which is to look up a specific condition and find a specific cure for it. Although many people like that approach, it has two problems.

The first downfall of the look-it-up approach is that you don't master anything. Because there's a method behind PC madness, often the same solution exists for multiple problems. After you understand why things go wrong, it's not only easier to fix them — it's also possible to prevent them in the first place.

The second difficulty of the specific-solution approach is that it would make this book seriously huge. With millions upon millions of potential hardware and software configurations available in all the PCs in the world, it would take not one but several fat books to document every problem and its solution. This book is big enough already!

My approach is simple: Look up the problem, find out a bit about what might have caused it, and then arrive at a solution. The notion is that when trouble arises again later, you will have the experience to deal with it in a practical manner. Because most PC troubles have a common origin, this solution works.

Married to troubleshooting is maintenance. The two topics go hand in hand; with proper maintenance and care, your computer runs better and more reliably, often negating the need for much troubleshooting in the first place!

Before moving on, please be aware that there's a difference between trouble and an event that's merely annoying. For example, if the text you print from an email message is tiny, it's annoying but isn't a bug. Though specific annoying problems such as that one might not be covered in this book, you can still find a solution here. That's the beauty behind my philosophical approach to troubleshooting. After all, using Windows shouldn't be a frustrating experience.

About the For Dummies Approach

As a *For Dummies* title, this book doesn't delve into the technical. It doesn't start out easy and then become immediately technical and cryptic. And this book never disrespects you as a reader.

It's entirely possible to be a smart and clever (and, I might add, attractive) computer owner and not know a darn thing about what a computer is or how it works. That's fine with me. This book doesn't assume that you're a computer expert or that you want to become one. The subject is troubleshooting and maintaining your computer. Anyone who owns a PC can read and understand this book well enough to fix their computer woes.

This book may appear to be overburdened with humor. I admit that writing in an entertaining manner is a weakness of mine. Troubleshooting can be a serious topic, and this book treats serious issues with respect. But there are times when I feel that the amusement value is necessary to keep the mood light. Computer repair and maintenance need not be a grim topic.

Who Are You?

Allow me to make some assumptions about who you are and why you're reading this introduction.

First, I assume that you're human, or at least posing in human form while visiting Earth from the 23rd dimension. If so, welcome. And, if your plans for destroying the earth are imminent, I'd like to suggest that you aim your death ray at Idaho first. Thank you.

Second, you have a PC. That's the generic term for any computer running Microsoft Windows. So, if the computer runs Windows — whether it's made by Dell, made by Joe the Nerd, or it's an iMac — it's a PC as far as this book is concerned.

Even though you're holding a *For Dummies* book, I must make some assumptions about how well you know your computer. The text assumes, for example, that you know how to start the computer, use the mouse, type, and perform other basic computer activities. If you can read and send email or play a game of *Spider Solitaire,* you have enough computer literacy to understand this book and handle the chores I set forth.

Finally, you're using Windows on your PC. It can be Windows 7, Windows Vista, or Windows XP. All these versions are covered here where applicable. You should be aware, however, that Windows XP lacks a lot of the good PC troubleshooting tools available in Windows 7 and Windows Vista.

How This Book Works

This book is composed of six *minibooks*, each of which addresses a computer troubleshooting or maintenance topic. The minibooks are split into traditional chapters, all geared to a specific subject within the minibook topic. Then the chapters are split into sections consisting of paragraphs, words, and then letters. So, as long as you understand the alphabet, you'll understand this book.

Here are some other important things to note about how this book works:

Cross-references: Because this book contains six Chapter 1s and six Chapter 2s and so on, these chapters in other minibooks are referenced by the book they belong to. So, when you read "See Book II, Chapter 2," you know in which minibook to find that Chapter 2. Chapters within the same minibook are referred to as just plain chapters, such as "See Chapter 2."

Windows, Windows, Windows: When this book refers to *Windows*, it means all versions covered in this book: 7, Vista, and XP. Otherwise, specific mention is made to a version of Windows. Because Windows 7 and Windows Vista are very similar, they're often lumped together.

The Control Panel: Many times this book references the Windows Control Panel, a central location for controlling things in your computer. In Windows 7 and Windows Vista, this book assumes that you're using the Control Panel in Category view, also called Control Panel Home. In Windows XP, I assume that you're using the Control Panel in Icon view.

Procedural steps: This book presents numbered steps to accomplish specific tasks. Occasionally, one set of steps is used for all versions of Windows. More often, you see two sets of steps: one for Windows 7 and Windows Vista and the other for Windows XP. Rarely do you find steps listed for all versions of the operating systems. When all three operating systems are referenced in the same set of steps, letters are used within a step when the versions of

Windows differ — for example, Step 2a for Windows 7, Step 2b for Windows Vista, and Step 2c for Windows XP. Then everyone continues with Step 3.

Typing stuff: When you're supposed to type something, the text appears in **bold type**. In the context of a step, where the text is normally bold anyway, the stuff you type appears in regular roman text.

The Enter key: Do not press the Enter key until you're directed to do so. And even then, just to ensure that you typed everything properly, I recommend that you review what you type before you press Enter.

Period: Do not press a period at the end of any text you type, unless I explain that the period is needed. Unlike sentences in English, a computer command doesn't end with a period.

Filenames and text commands: Windows lets you type filenames or text commands in either upper- or lowercase letters. This book uses lowercase, often using `monospaced text` to present the command name or filename.

How the Videos on the Web Site Work

This book features a host of companion videos. In the first edition, the videos were contained on a companion DVD that was supplied with the book. Rather than weigh down this edition with another DVD, and to avoid all that video piracy, this edition's videos can be found on the Internet.

To view a video, enter into your computer's web browser the web page address shown in this book. Type the address on the Address bar, and the video plays on your computer screen.

You can also visit this web page to find an index of all videos:

`www.dummies.com/go/troubleshootingandmaintainingyourpcaio2e`

You'll find two types of videos:

A walk-through of complex steps listed in this book: Sometimes, despite all my flowery prose, it's difficult to explain on paper how something works. So the video shows you, step by step, how to troubleshoot or maintain your PC.

A demonstration of how to do more physical tasks, such as clean a computer or yank out a hard drive: This type of video uses an actor (myself because I'm cheap) to demonstrate the concept.

All videos referenced in this book have a On The Web Site icon, shown in the margin. The videos also have numbers, which appear in the web page address, or *URL*.

Icons Used in This Book

I'd like to think that everything in this book is a tip, but for those special, worthy items, you find this icon lurking nearby.

A reminder of something not to do, something to avoid, or something that can cause serious trouble is flagged by the Bomb icon.

This icon flags text that's important enough to remember or that reminds you of something you may have forgotten that bears repeating.

Extra information on the topic is available in video form. The paragraph next to this icon indicates which video to view, along with a web page URL to use for viewing the video.

When the urge to blurt out something nerdy overwhelms me, I feel the urge to use this icon to supply a warning sign. You're free not to read any technical text near this icon.

Other images are found in the book's margins, including icon images from Windows itself.

Where to Go Now?

Feel free to start reading this book in any minibook, chapter, or section. Everything is self-contained, so there isn't a reason to read one section before another. For the rare times when it helps to know information located elsewhere in the book, I provide a cross-reference. But it's not necessary to read the book from front to back.

Final Thots

I can't believe I wrote the whole thing.

Writing this book has been the most massive undertaking of my writing career. It's not only a big, fat book on PC troubleshooting and maintenance — it's also a big, fat book that covers *three* versions of Windows. In addition to the writing, this book includes videos on many topics presented in the text. All that stuff took time to do, and I appreciate that my publisher didn't lean on me too heavily during the process; I hope to regain full use of my left knee soon.

Here's my email address:

dgookin@wambooli.com

That's my real email address. All the mail you send to me there pops up on my screen, and I read it. I also promise to answer all my email. If you want a quick response, type a *short* email message. The longer or more detailed the message, the longer it takes me to get around to reading and responding.

Although I promise to respond to all email, I can only answer questions regarding this book. I cannot troubleshoot your PC for you. Consider emailing your ISP, software developer, or PC manufacturer or dealer for technical support.

This book also has a companion web page on my own support site:

www.wambooli.com/help/troubleshooting

The web page contains any needed updates or errata, plus answers to common questions, if there are any.

Thank you for choosing my book,

Dan Gookin

Book I

Hardware

Contents at a Glance

Chapter 1: Let There Be PC

In This Chapter

- Powering on the PC
- Diagnosing hardware
- Finding the operating system
- Loading the operating system
- Logging in
- Making personal settings
- Using the computer
- Ending your PC day

*1*f this book were about troubleshooting a computer that isn't turned on, it would be a very short book. Basically, when a PC is turned off, it performs quite reliably. After power is supplied, however, trouble looms like a flatbed truck loaded with loosely packed logs on a pothole-pockmarked road. That's because disaster can happen right away when you turn on the power.

To best understand PC start-up problems, review the full process of how a computer wakes itself from electronic slumber. Though things may become a bit technical, I believe that knowing the start-up sequence of events better helps you pinpoint and fix things that can go awry.

In the Beginning, There Was Power

During the initial power-on phase, your computer transforms itself from a chunk of quite useless expensive electronics into a chunk of quite useful expensive electronics.

What happens

You press the Power button. When the PC is off, pressing the Power button turns on the PC again. It works that way whether the computer was properly shut down, was put into hibernation, or has met an untimely or inopportune demise.

The computer's *power supply* does its job: It starts converting alternating current into direct current. *Alternating current* comes from the wall socket. *Direct current* is used inside the computer to power its circuitry and motors.

What could go wrong

A lack of power from the wall makes your computer remain quiet. To ensure that a wall socket is properly supplying juice, try this test: Plug a lamp into the socket. If the lamp works, the problem lies with the computer's power supply. If the lamp doesn't work, buy a copy of *Troubleshooting Lamps For Dummies*, available at fine bookstores everywhere.

When the wall socket is operating properly, the problem lies with the PC's power supply. Such issues are easy to detect. The power supply on every PC also contains a fan: If you can hear the fan spinning, the power supply is getting power. You may need to open the case to ensure that the power supply is properly connected to the computer's main circuitry, the *motherboard*.

✦ Power supply problems can be random and unpredictable. Their impact is mostly on the heat inside the computer case. The heat causes a number of weird events, but those events don't happen when the computer is in Safe mode. See Book II, Chapter 3 for information on Safe mode.

✦ If the PC is connected to a power strip or an uninterruptible power supply (UPS), ensure that the gizmo is plugged into the wall and turned on.

✦ Check out Chapter 8 for information on opening a computer's case. You can also find information there on replacing a bum power supply.

The First Test: Hardware Self-Diagnostics

When abuzz with electricity, the computer's internal components spring to life. It might be a chaotic ballet of confusion, but one thing is in charge: the processor.

The processor, also known as the *central processing unit* (CPU), is the computer's main chip. It's the boss. The main dude. *El Comandante Supremo.* In a PC, the processor goes by the name Pentium, Athlon, Phenom, or a similar superhero-sounding name.

What happens

When a chip is *in charge,* the processor knows what to do. As it receives power, the processor "jumps" to a location in memory where it begins executing instructions. Those instructions place the computer in a diagnostic, or self-checking, mode. The computer inventories its various components.

A *POST*, or *Power-On Self Test,* is performed, in which the computer basically checks its own hardware. Memory is tested and its quantity determined. Control is passed to various subsystems (network, video, audio, and power management, for example), which also perform their own inventories and tests.

Information may be displayed on the screen as feedback during this stage. Most PCs, however, display a start-up, or *splash,* screen. The screen may or may not divulge what's happening inside the computer. When it does, you may see a memory count or seemingly random numbers or a copyright notice on the display. That diagnostic information is intended for trouble-shooting (*very* nerdy troubleshooting, as in oscilloscope troubleshooting).

✦ One important message revealed at this point is which key or key combination to press to enter the computer's Setup program. See the section "Your PC's Setup program," a little later in this chapter.

✦ Just because hardware passes the POST doesn't mean that everything is well. Computer hardware also needs software to control it. If the software isn't working, there may still be a problem.

What could go wrong

Problems that come up immediately are signaled by using the console's speaker. The pattern of beeps dictates the type of problem, though the pattern isn't consistent across all PC hardware. Generally speaking, the problem indicated by a beeping speaker is either in the power supply or the display adapter (video system).

When the power supply and video system are working, problems with other devices are indicated by messages appearing on the screen.

At this point, the only real way to fix the problem is to identify and replace the defective hardware. The message on the screen indicates what the problem child is, such as the video system or network or another subsystem. Make a note of whatever error message appears. Then deal with the issue by replacing the hardware.

✦ The computer may operate with defective hardware, but that's no excuse to avoid fixing or replacing it.

✦ Replacing internal hardware is covered in Chapter 8.

✦ Refer to Chapter 7 for tips on troubleshooting hardware by swapping it out.

✦ Sometimes, replacing hardware doesn't work, such as when the hardware is part of the motherboard. The motherboard replacement operation is more of a brain transplant than a simple hardware swap.

I recommend that you contact the computer manufacturer or your dealer for help.

✦ Beeping is a normal part of starting many computers. Just because the computer beeps doesn't mean that something is wrong. In fact, an error-related beep generally has a pattern to it, such as three short beeps and then one long beep.

✦ The list of potential beep codes offered is extensive, made all the more complex because of the variety of motherboard types and manufacturers. The number of beeps you can hear when something goes wrong varies from 2 to 11. You might also hear a beep pattern, such as 2 short beeps followed by 1 long beep. Then there's the annoying, continuous beep, which tells you that something is wrong with your computer and annoys everyone else in the office.

Your PC's Setup program

At some point during the start-up process, you can enter the PC's Setup program. I call it the Setup program, though sometimes it's called the Hardware Configuration Menu or the BIOS Jibbity-Jabber. Whatever. A prompt appears on the splash screen, indicating which key or key combination to press to enter the Setup program.

The key to press is often F1, though also common are Del (or Delete), F2, F10 or a key combination, such as Alt+F1. The only way to know for certain is to check the screen when the computer starts or refer to the manufacturer's documentation (scant though it may be).

You use the Setup program to configure your PC's hardware. You can do things such as set the computer's internal clock, set the order in which storage devices are searched for an operating system, enable or disable hardware components, set security options, and perform other technical tasks.

Using the Setup program is simple: Although each program is different, most of them are easily manipulated by using the keyboard. A simple menu system is used to select things, and helpful (or useless) information is displayed to show you which keys you should use to select, choose, or set options.

When you're done changing things, you're given the option to either save the new settings and restart the PC or quit without saving.

✦ Make a note on this book's inside front cover of which keys are required in order to enter your PC's Setup program.

✦ Various other chapters in this book reference using the Setup program.

✦ Some PCs don't display a message telling you which key to press to enter the Setup program. In that case, try F1.

✦ If the PC has a special Support type of button on the keyboard, such as the blue ThinkVantage button on some Lenovo PCs, press that button. Though pressing it may not open the Setup program directly, it may display a menu from which you can enter the Setup program.

The Search for an Operating System

The computer hardware can check itself out, but that's about it. To run a computer, you need software. The final task that the PC's hardware completes, after all that checking and testing, is to find and load an *operating system*, the main piece of software in the computer. This process is called *bootstrapping* or, when you're in a real hurry, you can just use *boot*.

What happens

A program encoded in the computer's hardware works to find an operating system on one of the PC's mass storage devices. Running this program is the last step in the computer's start-up process.

Back at the dawn of the 1980s, the PC looked for an operating system first on a floppy diskette and then on the hard drive. Today, that order can be changed; the computer can load the operating system from whatever storage device you specify, though traditionally it's the internal hard drive.

After the operating system is found, it's loaded into memory. It takes over the computer system, continues to load itself, and sets up the rest of Mr. PC for you to use and enjoy.

✦ Technically, the PC hardware loads and executes the first portion of the hard drive into memory. That portion is the *master boot record,* or *MBR.* You find this term used quite a bit when diagnosing PC start-up problems.

✦ The master boot record may also contain information about disk partitions. See Chapter 4 for a scintillating discussion.

✦ When you have multiple operating systems installed on the PC, you see the *Boot menu,* where you can select an operating system to load. The boot menu is displayed by a Boot Manager program. In that type of PC configuration, the Boot Manager is given control by the hardware when the PC first starts. The *Boot Manager* isn't an operating system; it's merely a program that helps you select and load an operating system. Chapter 2 coughs up more information about the Boot menu and Boot Manager.

What could go wrong

The hardware may be unable to find the master boot record on the hard drive (it could be missing or damaged). That doesn't mean that the operating system is gone — merely that it's lost. Missing operating-system error messages are described in Chapter 2. Fixing the problem depends on the error message, so directions for where to go next are also found in Chapter 2.

When the boot order is changed, your computer may attempt to load an operating system from a storage device that lacks an operating system. An error message may or may not be displayed when that happens. Refer to Chapter 2 to see how to deal with such a situation by changing the boot order.

A damaged operating system or storage media can muck up the works. A fouled operating system is a software problem. Fixing it involves using a recovery disk or the recovery partition of your PC's hard drive. See Book II, Chapter 8 for more information.

When the hard drive is damaged, you can still attempt to recover the operating system. The recovery process confirms whether the storage system can be used or needs to be replaced.

The boot loader

A *boot loader* is a special program that appears just as your PC's hardware is passing the baton of control to an operating system. The boot loader primarily dwells on the start-up hard drive in the master boot record, though it's found on any bootable media. Like an operating system, the boot loader is transferred from the storage device, loaded into memory, and executed. But keep in mind that the boot loader isn't a full operating system.

The job of the boot loader is to help you choose an operating system for your computer. Some boot loaders do nothing more than continue the process of loading the computer's only operating system. But many boot loaders are more complex.

For example, a simple type of boot loader may merely display a menu from which you choose an operating system to use. Other, more complex, boot loaders might offer partitioning and storage management tools.

✦ Windows features the boot loader NTLDR. The *NT* came from Windows NT, where the NT stands for New Technology. I assume that LDR somehow translates into *loader*.

✦ A common boot loader is the LILO, or *Linux Lo*ader. LILO displays a list of operating systems and you choose one, and then the operating system loads.

+ The most popular boot loader is the GNU GRUB. GRUB stands for Grand Unified Bootloader. It's often used after installing Linux on a PC.

+ The GRUB settings file is edited only from the Linux partition for which it was installed. You cannot modify GRUB's menu from within GRUB itself. The configuration file, named either `grub.conf` or `menu.1st`, is found in (or linked from) the `/boot/grub` directory.

+ Running Windows on a Macintosh involves the Boot Camp boot loader.

Operating System Initialization

The operating system loads itself into memory in a multistep process that's way too boring to detail here. Various mystery steps take place until you log in.

What happens

Lots of stuff happens:

Windows begins to load itself into memory and check out the computer's hardware. This investigation isn't completely thorough (Windows is quite forgiving), which is why hardware errors can crop up later as you use the computer.

If you press the F8 key just before Windows loads (the timing is quick), a special start-up menu is displayed. See Chapter 2.

If the system is recovering from hibernation, information is loaded from the storage system into memory as the computer resumes its operation.

What could go wrong

When something amiss is detected in your PC's hardware or in the *driver* software that controls the hardware, Windows places the system in Safe mode. Refer to Book II, Chapter 3 for how to deal with Safe mode.

If anything is wrong with Windows itself, you see an error message specific to the problem. At that point, however, it's fairly certain that Windows itself is the problem. The solution is to repair Windows. Refer to Book II, Chapter 8.

Some problems make Windows seem to take forever to load. It doesn't, of course: The start-up process for Windows has basically hit a brick wall. It might be possible to repair Windows, but only if you can start the computer by using a repair partition. See Book II, Chapter 8.

Log On to Windows

After Windows has successfully forced itself upon your PC, its final act is to run the program WINLOGON.EXE, the *Windows Logon Manager*. The visual effect is that you see a logon window, prompt, or thingy where you can log in to the computer.

It's possible, but not recommended, to configure Windows XP to forgo the login. Refer to Book II, Chapter 5.

What happens

You select or type your account name and then type a password. If multiple accounts are set up on the same computer, you choose your account from a list.

If you wait at the logon screen and the computer doesn't crash, you can be certain that the start-up problem takes place in one of the personalized start-up programs that run after you log in. See the section "Personalized Start-Up," just ahead in this chapter.

What could go wrong

Your account might be missing. In that case, you have a number of choices. The option I recommend is to press the F8 key as Windows starts and choose Last Known Good Configuration from the start-up menu. Refer to Chapter 2.

You can also repair a missing account by using the recovery console, which is covered in Book II, Chapter 8.

The most common mishap is to forget your password. Passwords are covered in Book II, Chapter 5.

Windows XP offers two types of login: a graphical one and one using the more stolid Windows NT–style logon dialog box. Refer to Book II, Chapter 5 for information on changing the Windows XP login style.

Personalized Start-Up

After the prisoner identifies himself to the warden, or, rather, after you log in to Windows, a series of steps takes place to make your computing experience personal. Problems occurring at this point are due to those programs being loaded as the computer starts.

What happens

Logging in confirms who you are. Windows proceeds to load personal information about you and configures itself according to your preferences. Windows then loads the rest of itself into memory; specifically, the parts that deal with user interaction and program management. Any start-up programs are run as well.

When you get to this point, Windows updates the last known good control set. Those settings are used when you choose to restart the computer by using the Last Known Good Configuration. Refer to Chapter 2.

Eventually the dust settles and you start using the computer. Any chaos that ensues at that point is most definitely *not* due to a start-up problem.

What could go wrong

Start-up programs can run things aground quickly, but another issue with a start-up program is how to disable it if you decide that it's no longer needed. Those issues are dealt with in Book II, Chapter 2.

Use Your PC

At some point, the Windows start-up ordeal ends and you're free to use your computer. Ta-da!

What happens

Oddly enough, even when you choose not to do anything with your computer, it doesn't sit still. A PC running Windows is a beehive of activity. Various programs, called *services,* scamper hither and thither. Windows own programs continue to run, such as the Task Scheduler, which help the computer perform tasks like networking, disk maintenance, and other routine stuff.

The Task Scheduler is covered in Book VI, Chapter 3.

What could go wrong

Services can often run amok or die. Worse, some services are entirely unnecessary. Shutting them down, as well as monitoring them, is covered in Book II, Chapter 2.

The most common PC problem is when it runs slowly. Or does that mean that the PC is *walking?* Anyway, a slow PC is caused by a number of odd things; Chapter 4 in Book II dwells on the topic at length.

The Last Thing You Do

After toiling (or playing or wasting time) with your computer, you eventually turn it off. As far as troubleshooting goes, turning off the computer again presents a slate of issues that may crop up. Those are covered in Chapter 3.

The most important thing about any computer isn't its hardware or its software. No, it's the stuff you create — the *data*. No matter what happens to your PC, preserving that data must be your top priority. The best way to ensure that your data stays with you is by creating a secondary, *backup,* copy of all your important creations, settings, savings, and stuff. Refer to Book VI, Chapter 1 for details.

Chapter 2: Birth Pangs

In This Chapter

✔ **Solving start-up hardware problems**

✔ **Dealing with the BIOS password**

✔ **Losing an operating system**

✔ **Changing the boot order**

✔ **Using the boot, F8, and F5 menus**

✔ **Facing the ugly recovery menu**

I'm sure you have your morning routine. Everyone does. Perhaps you keep things interesting by varying what you do; maybe you dither over whether to brush your teeth before or after a morning shower. Or perhaps you stick to a strict schedule, which is reliable and consistently useful in avoiding that "I've left the house without wearing pants" problem that so many people have.

Your computer likes to maintain the same start-up routine every time it's flush with power. When things kilter that schedule, you can turn to this chapter for solutions.

➤ When troubleshooting start-up problems, it helps to understand the process a computer goes through to get out of bed in the morning. Consider reading Chapter 1 for details on the PC's start-up process, if you haven't already.

➤ Book II, Chapter 2 covers information on programs that may run when the computer starts, also leading to high-tech anguish.

The Onset of PC Heartbreak

Nothing beats that feeling when you arrive at your PC, set down a hot cuppa joe, take your seat, and get ready to start a fresh, productive day. Well, nothing except seeing something unwanted on the screen. This section addresses those issues of initial woe.

➤ Initial woe is almost always a sign of hardware trouble. Replacing a bum part fixes the problem.

✦ Unlike other, typical computer trouble, problems occurring during start-up may not be due to a recent change in the computer. Even so, consider what you've changed or modified on your PC or added to it: Have you installed new hardware, modified a software setting, or updated Windows? One of those issues may have caused the problem.

✦ As long as the problem isn't with the PC's hard drive (storage system), your data that's stored in the computer is probably safe. Replacing the bad hardware, such as a video card or power supply, fixes the problem without damaging your data. However:

✦ You risk losing your data by taking your PC into the shop for repair. That's because sometimes the technicians replace or erase the hard drive or primary storage media. Of course, when the hard drive is the problem, it needs replacing anyway. That's why I recommend backups; see Book VI, Chapter 1.

Nothing — I see nothing

The loud sound of nothing when you turn on a PC means that it has a power supply issue. Check the following items in this order:

1. **Does the PC have power?**

You cannot compute when the power is off. Likewise, you cannot compute during a *dip*, commonly called a *brownout*. In that situation, the power is on but running at a low voltage. Lights work, but motors don't. If the lights are on (dimly) but your computer doesn't work, you may be experiencing a dip. Wait it out or check with the power company.

You might be tempted to run your PC from a UPS, or uninterruptible power supply, during a dip. Don't. Use the UPS only to save your stuff and then properly shut down the computer. (If you have a generator, you can run the computer from its power, but not from a UPS.)

2. **Is the power supply on the computer operational?**

Do you hear the fan? Are any console lights on? If not, the power supply may need replacing. See Chapter 8.

3. **Is the monitor on?**

It's an obvious question, and even I have fallen prey to this maddening problem.

4. **Is everything connected?**

Both internally and externally, cables must be plugged in and wires firmly seated. Especially if you just moved the computer, a cable can become unplugged easily.

Inside the PC is a different story: It doesn't happen often, but cables can wiggle loose — especially because of wide variations in the internal case temperature or if you drop the computer or kick it down the hall. See Chapter 8 for more information on venturing inside a PC's case to check the cable connections.

If you complete these steps and still cannot pinpoint the origin of the nothingness, the issue is most likely too large for you to resolve on your own. Before toting the computer into the shop, however, consider its age. Old computers die. They don't start. (Dead computers have a habit of not starting.) If your PC is more than eight years old, it might just have expired. To fix that problem, buy a new computer.

✦ One way to confirm a dip is to check to see whether the refrigerator or furnace fan is running.

✦ Some uninterruptible power supplies (UPSs) beep during a dip. A few models feature digital displays that may graphically show that the incoming voltage level is subnormal.

✦ It's possible to use a laptop when the power is off — well, if the laptop has a charge in its battery and nothing else is awry. Refer to Book III for information on troubleshooting laptop start-up issues.

POST errors

The *POST* is the Power-On Self Test that all computers take when they start up. (Refer to Chapter 1 for the details). A computer that fails the POST has hardware trouble.

Your PC may or may not beep when it starts. If you hear two or more beeps where you heard only one before, the PC may have either a power supply problem or a video system problem. Otherwise, the PC's splash screen is displayed. Any POST errors after that point are displayed on the computer's monitor.

What you can do with a POST error depends on the error message. Some error messages are cryptic. One POST error message that appeared on my PC was 58. *Hmmm.*

Text messages can be just as bad. For example:

```
Resource allocation conflict on motherboard
```

Whatever.

You can choose from two solutions for these puzzling start-up messages:

The first solution to try is to enter the PC's Setup program and determine whether the issue can be resolved there. Often, any errors encountered during the POST are flagged in the Setup program, or at least information is provided to help you resolve the issue; for example, to resolve a hardware sharing conflict. See Chapter 1 for more information on the PC's Setup program.

The second solution is to contact the manufacturer or your computer dealer to see what's up. If the computer is under warranty and the problem is severe, the manufacturer or dealer has an obligation to fix it.

✦ Some PCs sport error feedback on an LCD or by using colored lights on the console. For example, a red light blinking three times on an HP computer might mean that the processor isn't installed or has popped out of its socket.

✦ Don't think that every code you see on the splash screen is a POST error. Many computers display information during start-up that is completely normal and expected.

✦ POST error beeps vary in their number and variety. Generally, they refer to a problem with the power supply, memory, or video system.

✦ A common POST error is a missing input device, such as the keyboard or mouse. In fact, one of the most comical error messages from the early days of the PC went something like this: `Keyboard missing, press any key to continue.`

✦ If you have access to another computer and the Internet, or if your cellphone has Internet access, you can search for specific POST errors. Many PC manufacturers list the lot on their support web sites.

✦ Obviously, audio error messages work only when the PC's internal speaker works.

CMOS errors

A PC that's getting on in years may experience persistent start-up errors relating to a dead motherboard battery.

Yes, your computer has an internal battery. That battery keeps track of the time while the computer is turned off. On ancient computers, it also maintained something called the *CMOS* (say "see moss"). So a telltale sign of a CMOS error, and therefore a dead PC battery, was that the word *CMOS* appeared in the error message. For example:

```
98304K
162-System Options Not Set
163-Time & Date Not Set
The following configuration options were automatically
    updated:
Disk 1: 2428 Mbytes
If you are running Unix, you need to configure your system
    using the COMPAQ User Diagnostics diskette.
```

```
Total memory installed: 98304 Kbytes
Diskette Drives
CMOS checksum invalid, default values loaded
F1: Save Changes Compaq Deskpro 4000
```

To the trained eye, the information in this start-up text error message says a lot. Don't concern yourself with those details; just note the line that says CMOS checksum invalid. That's the clue: The PC needs a new battery.

Refer to Chapter 8 for more information on opening the computer's case.

There's a BIOS password!

I do not recommend setting the BIOS password. If your PC Setup program has this option, you can lock out access to your PC at the hardware level. The password you set is recorded in the computer's nonvolatile memory, along with other system settings. Upon starting the PC, you're prompted to type the password to continue.

The first problem with BIOS passwords is that people forget them. The second problem, related to the first, is that PC motherboard manufacturers have made it simple to reset or work around the password. That effectively renders the thing useless.

If you have forgotten the BIOS password, check with the motherboard manufacturer (or your computer dealer) to see whether a *backdoor* password is available. For example, the Phoenix-brand motherboard has the backdoor password PHOENIX, which you can type at the BIOS password prompt to gain access to the computer.

An ancient solution to resetting the BIOS password was to open the computer's case and then remove and replace the motherboard's battery. Doing so erases the nonvolatile memory and resets the password. That solution may not work on newer PCs that feature flash memory rather than a CMOS.

Some motherboards feature a *jumper*, which can be removed or reset to erase or disable the password. That operation involves opening the PC's case and determining where the jumper is, which is annoying and all the more reason not to bother with the BIOS password in the first place.

✦ To find out which motherboard you use, pay close attention to your PC's splash screen. The motherboard (or chipset) manufacturer, as well as the version number, is often displayed. If that doesn't work, contact your dealer for support and write down on this book's inside front cover the specifics for your computer's motherboard model number or type and the chipset version.

✦ Backdoor passwords are widely known and published extensively on the web. That makes them seriously insecure.

✦ Refer to Chapter 8 for information on opening the PC's case.

✦ I say this in my other computer books, and I repeat it here: *Do not use the BIOS password*. The mere fact that it's so easy to recover from a missing BIOS password means that the thing is utterly useless in the first place. Trust me: Even if you don't know how to recover a BIOS password, the bad guys most certainly do!

"Did my PC secretly restart?"

If you leave your computer on all the time, you may show up one morning and discover that Windows has automatically restarted itself; rather than see the desktop, you see the logon screen.

The main reason the computer has restarted itself is that you have Windows Updates set to install automatically. That's okay. For some updates, an automatic restart is done. You can confirm it by looking at the pop-up bubble that appears in the notification area, indicating that updates were recently installed. No problem there.

✦ If the computer restarted and no updates were installed, it might indicate a restarting problem. See the "Problems with Restarting" section in Chapter 3.

✦ The power company might be to blame: A power outage or dip in the middle of the night can stop or restart your computer.

✦ Refer to Book II, Chapter 1 for information on Windows Update and how to configure Windows to not automatically restart itself for updating purposes.

Operating System Trouble

You can't do squat on a computer until an operating system is loaded into memory. The computer's boot loader handles the process of loading the operating system, which is part of the PC's hardware. The boot loader's job is to transfer information from the computer's main storage media (typically a hard drive) into memory. It sounds simple, but a plethora of things can go awry.

The horrifying, blinking cursor

The screen is dark. In the upper left corner is a flashing bar: off and on. That's the blinking *cursor*. It's a bad sign: The computer is waiting to load an operating system from somewhere, anywhere. It's not the end of the world, though, because it means that the problem might be easy to fix.

First thing to check: Is a memory card sticking out of the console, like a tiny diving board or an impudent tongue? If so, remove the card and restart the computer. The same thing might happen with an MP3 player or iPod: Remove the device and restart the computer. What happened was that the PC (or IPod), because it's stupid, tried to start itself by using the memory card rather than the hard drive. Removing the memory card fixes the problem.

Mostly, when an operating system is missing, it means that that the computer's *boot order* must be changed. See the next section.

Changing the boot order

The *boot order* is the sequence of storage devices that the computer's hardware checks to find an operating system. As luck would have it, an operating system can lurk in several places:

Hard drive: This is the main storage device for most PCs, selected first for reasons of tradition. More than one hard drive may be in your computer, and those hard drives may be *partitioned* into separate, *logical* drives. All of that's okay. The *master boot record* (MBR) on the primary hard drive holds a map that indicates where the operating system can be found or provides a boot menu to select an operating system.

SSD: Eventually, the solid state drive will replace the hard drive as the PC's primary storage device. Internally, the SSD is composed of flash memory, just like a thumb drive or media card, but with a much higher capacity (and price). Externally, an SSD works just like a hard drive with an MBR and partitions and all the traditional garnishes and relish.

Optical drive (CD-ROM/DVD): Even when you don't choose the optical drive as the primary boot device, many PCs automatically detect a bootable disc in the optical (CD or DVD) drive. When that happens, an option is displayed on the screen, something like `Press Enter to boot from the CD or DVD`. By pressing the Enter key, you direct the computer to start from that disc on the fly.

Network (Ethernet): Rather than load an operating system from the PC's own (local) storage devices, the network option directs the computer to load its operating system from the network. On start-up, the network adapter makes a request to a server for an operating system to load, which it then downloads from the server.

USB device: The USB device can be a thumb drive, a media card, or an external disk drive. This option is useful for laptops that lack optical drives, allowing you to install or upgrade your PC's operating system.

You set the boot order in the PC's Setup program. Generally, the steps go like this:

1. **Restart or turn on the computer.**

2. **Press the key or keys to enter the Setup program.**

   Refer to Chapter 1 for information on the PC's Setup program. As a reminder, the most common key used to enter the Setup program is F1.

   Ensure that you press the key to enter the Setup program or menu. Do not press the key to enter the boot menu, which is a different item (and is covered later in this chapter).

3. **Choose the menu option or options to display the boot sequence.**

   The option may not be obvious from the Setup program's main menu, not to mention that the Setup program is in Text mode. Various computers I've researched display the menu that changes the boot order in these ways:

   Startup⇨Boot

   Boot⇨Boot Device Priority

   Advanced BIOS Features⇨(various priority submenus)

   System⇨Boot Sequence

   Figure 2-1 illustrates a typical Boot Sequence screen found in a PC Setup program screen that I made up.

```
                         System Setup
 Main   Advanced   Security   Power   Boot   Exit
 Boot Menu   Boot Sequence


      1. Hard Drive / SSD
      2. Floppy Drive            (not present)
      3. Optical Drive
      4. Network Controller
      5. USB Device

   Do not boot from:

      6. USB floppy drive
      7. USB Flash Drive



      Press F6 to move an item up; F7 to move
      an item down. Press F10 to save,
      ESC to cancel.
```

Figure 2-1:
A typical
Boot
Sequence
screen.

4. **Set the boot order.**

   Use whichever keys or techniques are required in order to set the sequence in which the hardware searches the storage devices for an operating system.

5. **Save the changes and exit the Setup program.**

   The computer restarts with the new settings.

You might see other options in addition to those that set the boot sequence search order. For example, you might see a way to exclude certain devices from being searched. This might be a good idea for USB media cards that may stop up your PC's start-up sequence or for legacy floppy drives.

You may see supplemental or submenus as well: for example, menus for each of the devices — hard drive, optical drive, and external drive. That way, for instance, when multiple optical drives are present, you can choose which to use as boot devices and which to ignore.

Additionally, you might find boot options to turn off or on for each boot device. For example, your PC's Setup program may allow you to disable or enable booting from the optical drive. If booting is disabled, you can't boot from a CD or DVD no matter where the optical drive is in the boot sequence order.

✦ Booting from the network happens only when the network adapter is configured as a boot device. Not all network adapters have this feature. It can also happen only when the network cable is connected, the network is working, the network supports such a thing, and the network's astrological chart looks good.

✦ For the longest time, PCs looked first to the floppy drive to start the computer. That's why the floppy drive was drive A, the first drive. When the floppy drive didn't contain a diskette, the computer then looked to the first physical hard drive for an operating system. (See Chapter 4 for more information on what a first physical hard drive is.)

The no-operating-system sisters

Several start-up error messages have similar causes and solutions, yet each of them has a tendency to induce heart palpitations. These messages appear before an operating system is loaded, and they indicate that the computer is having difficulty in finding the operating system:

```
Invalid Partition Table
Missing Operating System
Operating System Not Found
Non-System Disk or Disk Error
```

A similar issue causes each of these error messages: a faulty Master Boot Record or partition table. You can easily address this situation; Chapter 4 provides a good explanation of the jargon. Fixing the problem is the domain of the Windows Recovery Console, which is covered in Book II, Chapter 8.

"Press any key to boot from the optical disc"

When you insert a bootable disc into your PC's optical drive, you may see a message prompting you to boot the computer from that disc. The message varies, but reads something along the line of

```
Press any key to boot from the CD or DVD
```

This message is *not* a sign of trouble. It merely means that you stuck a bootable disc into the optical drive — and you configured your PC's Setup program to look for an alert to the presence of such a disc. No problem: Wait out the message and the computer starts up normally. Or, if you press Enter (the "any" key), the computer starts by using the optical disc.

Never start your computer from an unknown disc, such as one burned by a "friend" who is "giving away" a "free" copy of Windows or some other software program illegally. (Sorry for all the quotes.) That's how computers become irrevocably infected with malware. See Book IV, Chapter 4 for more information on *malware,* or evil software.

Removing a boot loader

To remove a boot loader, you must rewrite the storage system's *master boot record* (MBR). That's where the boot loader dwells, so all you need is a tool to raze the existing boot loader like a bulldozer would raze a perfectly good old government building to make room for a new, more expensive government building.

Though it would be emotionally satisfying to use a bulldozer on your PC's hard drive to fix the problem, you must use the recovery console. Directions for using it to rewrite the MBR can be found in Book II, Chapter 8.

  ✦ Refer to Chapter 1 for more information on what a boot loader is and how it plays a role in the way your PC starts.

  ✦ If problems persist after fixing the MBR, the boot manager wasn't the source.

  ✦ A corrupt or missing boot loader prevents the computer from starting — well, specifically, starting from the hard drive. You can still boot the computer from an optical disc, a USB drive, or a media card.

✦ I don't recommend removing the Boot Camp boot loader when you're running Windows on a Macintosh. Even when you plan to use only Windows on your Macintosh, it would just be a bad idea to remove the option for starting OS X.

Start-Up Menus

Before your PC can get up and dance, you may encounter, or desire to encounter, one of a multitude of start-up menus and options. Some are for troubleshooting purposes, and others may present options for starting the computer, selecting an operating system, or placing Windows into Safe mode. This section covers many of those menus and choices.

✦ If you're using a boot loader, you see its menu when you start your computer. Refer to Chapter 1 for more information on boot loaders.

✦ Though you don't see a menu per se, you have the option of pressing one or more keys when the computer starts. One key allows you to enter the PC's Setup program (again, see Chapter 1), and the second presents a boot menu, described in the next section.

The boot menu

The first possible menu you can see for starting your PC is what I call the *boot menu*. I don't believe it has an official name, but it's an option available on many computers.

To view the boot menu, you press a special key when the computer starts. The key to press is described on the PC's start-up, or splash, screen. Often it's the F10 key, though it may be another key, such as the blue ThinkVantage button found on many Lenovo keyboards. Pressing that key displays a boot menu, similar to the one shown in Figure 2-2.

Use the menu to select a storage device containing the operating system you want to start. The PC then attempts to load an operating system from the chosen device.

Unlike setting the boot order in a PC, the boot menu is used to select a *temporary* start-up device; the option you choose from the boot menu doesn't become the primary way the computer starts from now on. This is why the boot menu is often called the Alternative Startup Device option on some PCs.

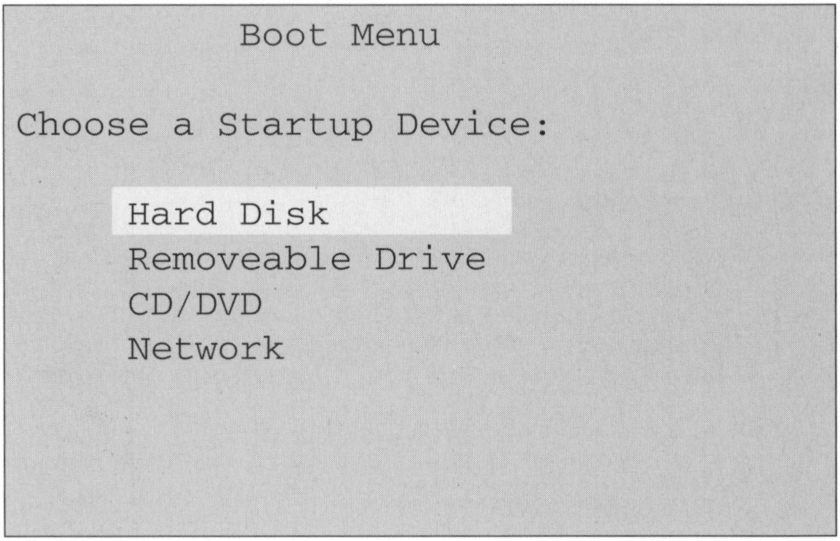

```
                    Boot Menu

Choose a Startup Device:


        Hard Disk
        Removeable Drive
        CD/DVD
        Network
```

Figure 2-2:
A typical
boot menu.

The F8 menu

Perhaps the most well known of the PC's boot-up menus is the Advanced
Boot Options menu, commonly called the F8 menu. That's because the menu
appears when you press the F8 key just after Windows starts. In fact, you
have to be quick: The F8 key must be pressed *before* the Windows start-up
screen (the logo) appears.

Figure 2-3 illustrates what the F8 menu looks like in Windows 7. Windows
Vista and Windows XP feature similar options, as described next.

Repair Your Computer: This option starts up repair and recovery options
on certain PCs, essentially booting the computer into the RECOVERY partition of the main hard drive. See Book II, Chapter 8 to find out how to use this
tool.

Safe Mode: In Safe mode, the computer starts and only Windows is loaded —
no add-on drivers or software. Safe mode is a good tool for tracking down
problem programs, as covered in Book II, Chapter 3.

Safe Mode with Networking: Safe mode is started and networking abilities
are loaded. This option is required when you need to access the network to
assist with troubleshooting.

Safe Mode with Command Prompt: Windows runs in Safe mode but displays
a text-only interface, which is useful for troubleshooting graphics problems
or when you're not completely befuddled by the command prompt and just
enjoy using the computer that way.

```
                        Advanced Boot Options

Choose Advanced Options for: Windows 7
(Use the arrow keys to highlight your choice.)

    Repair Your Computer

      Safe Mode
      Safe Mode with Networking
      Safe Mode with Command Prompt

      Enable Boot Logging
      Enable low-resolution video (640x480)
      Last Known Good Configuration (advanced)
      Directory Services Restore Mode
      Debugging Mode
      Disable automatic restart on system failure
      Disable Driver Signature Enforcement

      Start Windows Normally

Description: View a list of system recovery tools you can use to repair
            startup problems, run diagnostics, or restore your system.

ENTER=Choose                                              ESC=Cancel
```

Figure 2-3:
The F8 boot
menu.

Enable Boot Logging: Selecting this option directs Windows to write detailed information about the start-up process to a file named ntbtlog. txt. See Book II, Chapter 7 for information on reviewing this log file.

Enable Low-Resolution Video (640 x 480): Choosing this option starts the PC in a very low-resolution video mode, but not in Safe mode. This setting is useful for tracking down video problems (see Chapter 6). In Windows XP, this selection reads Enable VGA Mode.

Last Known Good Configuration (Advanced): This item starts Windows by using the most recently saved system configuration information. This option is good for when you experience start-up problems after a Windows update or software upgrade. In Windows Vista and Windows XP, the text (Advanced) doesn't appear on the menu.

Directory Services Restore Mode: Selecting this option is necessary only when using a Windows domain controller. If such a concept befuddles you, rest assured that you'll most likely never need to choose this option.

Debugging Mode: This item is used for programming purposes. It starts something called the Windows kernel debugger. Whatever.

Disable automatic restart on system failure: A gem, this item prevents the vexing and endless issue known as "There's a problem, so I will restart." Refer to Chapter 3 for more information.

Disable Driver Signature Enforcement: This option allows the computer to run drives that don't have proper identification (signatures). Doing so is risky when you're uncertain of the driver software or the developer's reputation, but it's often necessary in order to run a computer when troubleshooting.

Start Windows Normally: Choosing this option continues the Windows start-up process on its merry way, as though nothing ever happened. La-di-da.

When nothing is going wrong, choose Start Windows Normally to continue with the normal Windows start-up procedure. Or, you can press Ctrl+Alt+Delete to restart the computer.

✦ You have to press the F8 key almost *immediately* after the PC's hardware splash screen appears. I often just press and hold F8 to ensure that the menu shows up, though the computer beeps at you when the keyboard's buffer is full (but that's not a bad thing).

✦ An additional item, Reboot, is available only in Windows XP. Choosing Reboot restarts the computer.

✦ The options Repair Your Computer and Disable Driver Signature Enforcement aren't available in Windows XP.

✦ Why the F8 key? I don't know.

The F5 menu

Another start-up menu, though not as popular as the F8 key menu, is the F5 key menu. It works the same way: You press the F5 key just as the computer starts, and hopefully before the Windows logo appears. What happens after pressing F5 depends on your version of Windows.

In Windows 7 and in Windows Vista, the F5 key summons the Windows Boot Manager, which displays a list of operating systems known to Windows. You can choose one from the list. Often, when no other version of Windows is installed, as shown in Figure 2-4, you just choose to start Windows 7.

In Windows XP, the F5 menu looks similar, though it's missing the Tools portion of the Windows 7/Windows Vista menu (refer to Figure 2-4). When only one operating system is installed on the computer, what you see when you press the F5 key looks just like the F8 menu (refer to Figure 2-3) but with the addition of one menu item at the end: Return to OS Choices Menu.

You use the F5 menu to choose an operating system, though the menu itself isn't a boot loader per se. It's more of a way to manage multiple versions of Windows installed on the same PC, which in and of itself is, I think, a nutty concept.

```
                          Windows Boot Manager

Choose an operating system to start, or press TAB to select a tool:
(Use the arrow keys to highlight a choice, then press ENTER.)

    Windows 7




To specify an advanced option for this choice, press F8.




Tools:


    Windows Memory Diagnostic


ENTER=Choose                    TAB=Menu                    ESC=Cancel
```

Figure 2-4:
The F5 menu
in Windows
Vista.

Controlling the F5 menu is done by using the Startup and Recovery dialog box; see the next section.

✦ There's no point in using the F5 menu unless Windows is installed multiple times on your computer. Often, using a boot manager to configure your PC with multiple operating systems is easier.

✦ I last used the F5 menu when I was testing Windows 7 on my Windows Vista machine. In that configuration, the menu appeared automatically every time the computer started; I didn't need to press the F5 key to summon the menu.

✦ In MS-DOS, pressing the F5 key at start-up disabled the AUTOEXEC.BAT and CONFIG.SYS files, preventing them from being executed. Adding the line

        SWITCHES=/N

to the CONFIG.SYS file disabled the F5 key from working when the computer started. Since Windows 98, however, the F5 key has worked as described in this section.

Start-up and recovery options

The options for the various start-up menus are kept in the Startup and Recovery dialog box. Here's how to venture to that dialog box:

1. **Press the Win+Break key combination to summon the System window.**

   The Win key is the Windows key on your keyboard.

2. **Choose the link Advanced System Settings from the left side of the window.**

3. **If prompted with a User Account Control warning, click Continue or type the administrator's password to continue.**

   The System Properties dialog box presents itself.

4. **Click the Advanced tab.**

5. **In the Startup and Recovery area, click the Settings button.**

   The Startup and Recovery dialog box appears. Figure 2-5 illustrates the dialog box for Windows 7; the Windows Vista dialog box is identical.

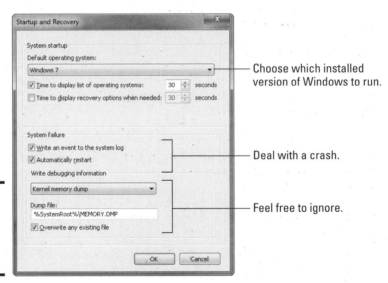

Figure 2-5:
The
Startup and
Recovery
dialog box.

The list of operating systems at the top of the dialog box includes only those that Windows itself knows about — the same items that would appear on the F5 boot menu. (See the section "The F5 menu," earlier in this chapter.) Other options relate to that boot menu as well.

The bottom section of the Startup and Recovery dialog box deals with how Windows handles a crash, including the infamous Automatically Restart option that you might consider deselecting at this point.

6. **Close the dialog box by clicking the OK button, and close any other open dialog boxes or windows.**

If you installed Linux or another operating system on your PC, the computer uses a special boot loader as the computer's start-up menu, not the Startup and Recovery options in Windows.

Don't get excited about the memory dump options; that information is useful only when you're a programmer — specifically, someone working for Microsoft who has a way to fix the Windows code by using the "dump" information.

Windows Error Recovery menu

One ugly start-up menu that you don't want to see is the Windows Error Recovery menu. It has two flavors: One menu shows up for start-up problems and the other for shutdown problems. The shutdown version is covered in Chapter 3, and the start-up version is shown in Figure 2-6.

```
                        Windows Error Recovery

Windows failed to start. A recent hardware or software change might be the
cause. To fix the problem:

   1. Insert your Windows installation disc and restart your computer.
   2. Choose your language settings, and then click "Next."
   3. Click "Repair your computer."

Other options:
If power was interrupted during startup, choose Start Windows Normally.
(Use the arrow keys to highlight your choice.)

     Safe Mode
     Safe mode with Networking
     Safe Mode wth Command Prompt
     Last Known Good Configuration (advanced)
     Start Windows Normally


Description: Start Windows with its regular settings
```

Figure 2-6:
The Windows Error Recovery menu, start-up version.

The first thing suggested by the Windows Error Recovery menu is to use the Windows Recovery Console, as described by the three steps shown in Figure 2-6 (and covered in Book II, Chapter 8).

The bottom part of the window contains commands similar to those on the F8 menu, including Safe mode options.

I recommend first choosing the option Start Windows Normally. If you see the error message again, choose Last Known Good Configuration.

When the problem persists, try Safe mode to determine whether the problem exists in Windows itself or in another program or driver on the computer. See Book II, Chapter 3.

Chapter 3: Death Throes

In This Chapter

↙ **Understanding PC shutdown**

↙ **Controlling the Power button**

↙ **Dealing with shutdown woes**

↙ **Using power management**

↙ **Discovering hibernation**

↙ **Fixing restart issues**

A long time ago, you actually turned a computer off. The console had an on-off switch, and by flipping that switch, you instantly deprived Mr. PC of power, effectively turning the thing off. Those were good times.

Today's computer comes with power buttons, not on-off switches. Furthermore, you don't turn off a PC — instead, the thing methodically plods through what's called a *shutdown process*. That process includes steps that undo all the knots, waves goodbye to all the various processes and services, shakes the rug, tucks in the kids, and eventually turns off the power. That's how it's supposed to work. When things go awry, when the computer smiles the evil grin of a cat that won't stay outside, that's when you turn to this chapter for assistance.

When Will It Stop?

As with starting a computer, understanding the PC shutdown process helps you appreciate where and how things can run amok. Unlike when you start a computer, however, the case of shutting down a computer involves choices: You don't always need to turn a computer off. In fact, I leave my computer on pretty much all the time. I do, however, employ a few, alternative, "almost shutdown" options, described in this section.

Shutting down a PC

When you shut down a PC, the following things happen:

A user check takes place: When other users are logged in to the computer (using another account on the same PC), you're alerted. Do you really want to shut down? Those users may be running programs or have unsaved documents. Clicking No cancels the operation, which is the proper thing to do. (Also see the later section "Someone else is logged in!")

Programs close: Windows shuts down any programs or processes that you've begun or that "belong" to you. It sifts through that list and sends every program the shutdown signal. If a program contains unsaved data, you're prompted to save the data to continue. (Or you can click the Cancel button, which stops the entire shutdown operation.) When a program cannot be stopped, you're prompted to end it, which is discussed later in this chapter, in the section aptly titled "End now?"

Users are logged out: After programs (and processes) belonging to you, the human, are stopped, Windows logs you out, ending your Windows session.

Windows is halted: After you're gone, Windows begins shutting down bits and pieces of itself. These programs, services, and processes are all ended, and Windows ensures that they end properly and have no social issues or gripes.

The shutdown signal is sent: When Windows is done with itself, it sends a signal to the computer's power management hardware to turn off the power. If that feature isn't present, a message appears on the screen, something like `It is now safe to turn off this computer and get back to real life.`

The shutdown process may seem overly formal. After all, a program stops when it's told to stop or when the electricity stops. Even though, years ago, computers were routinely shut down by flipping off the power switch, many users found that method unsettling.

By properly shutting itself down, the computer avoids the issue of *digital detritus*. For example, an improper shutdown causes some programs to leave pieces of themselves lying around like clutter from an explosion. Clutter builds. Rather than deal with the clutter, you should make sure that the tasks the computer does are sanely and systematically shut down.

Another advantage to a proper shutdown is that any looming errors not detected when the computer is running might show up during the shutdown process. Often, that's the only way to identify and troubleshoot an issue, such as a dead or improperly installed program.

Ending your Windows day

You have several choices on the Shut Down menu for quitting your computer duties:

Switch User: You remain logged in to the computer and your programs continue to be open, but choosing this option allows another user to access the computer.

Log Off: You can end your Windows session, save your stuff, and quit programs, but Windows remains on and ready for other people to use the computer.

Lock: Not a complete logout, this option helps you protect your stuff by displaying the Windows logon screen. You must type your password or log in as another user to get into the computer. (Obviously, this option works best when all accounts are password protected; see Book II, Chapter 5.)

Restart: The computer is shut down and then started again when this option is chosen from the Shut Down menu. It's also called a *reset* or, if you want to get nerdy, a *warm boot*.

Sleep: The computer is put into a low-power consumption mode, saving energy. Also known as Stand By, this mode may put the entire computer, or only the monitor or hard drives, into low-power mode. In this power-saving mode, the computer comes back to life quickly, usually with the press of a key or jiggle of the mouse.

Hibernate: Choosing this option, the best power-saving mode, shuts down the computer and turns it off. But information in memory is saved so that when the computer turns on again, you simply resume your former activities (after logging in, of course). Hibernation saves the most power, but it takes longer to restart the computer than either Sleep or Standby mode, because you're literally turning it on again.

Shut Down or Turn Off: When this option is selected, the computer is shut down: You're logged out of your account, which closes your programs and allows you to save your data. Windows then shuts itself down, and eventually the computer turns itself off.

The Switch User, Log Off, Lock, and Sleep options don't turn off the computer. The Restart, Hibernate, and Shut Down options do turn off the system.

See the next section for information on where to access these commands and options.

Also see the section "What is hybrid sleep?" later in this chapter.

Finding the shutdown options

Choosing a shutdown option involves first finding where that option dwells in Windows. For a software shutdown, the location varies, but generally speaking, you need to look to the bottom of the Start button menu.

In Windows 7, the shutdown options are found in the lower right corner of the Start button menu. The most obvious option is Shut Down, shown in Figure 3-1, which turns off the computer. Okay: It *shuts down* the computer. The remaining shutdown options are available on the Shutdown menu, also shown in Figure 3-1.

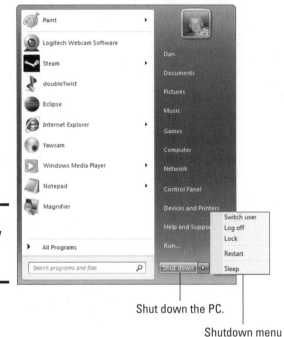

Figure 3-1:
Windows 7 shutdown options.

Shut down the PC.

Shutdown menu

Windows Vista tucks its shutdown options in the same location as Windows 7, in the lower right corner of the Start button menu, as shown in Figure 3-2. Unlike in Windows 7, two special buttons are visible in addition to the Shutdown menu. Also, all shutdown options are displayed on the menu, as illustrated in the figure.

The software Power button (refer to Figure 3-2) can be assigned different functions, so its purpose isn't obvious. Clicking the button activates the functions Shutdown, Hibernate, or Sleep, as described later in this chapter.

Next to the software Power button is the Lock button. Clicking that button does the same thing as choosing the Lock command on the Shutdown menu or pressing the Win+L key combination. (I enjoy how Microsoft occasionally hits you over the head with a command.)

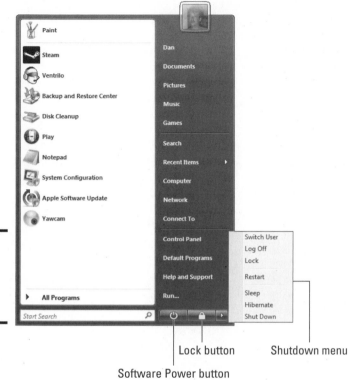

Figure 3-2:
Windows
Vista
shutdown
options.

Lock button   Shutdown menu

Software Power button

You may notice that the Hibernate command is missing from the Shutdown menu in Windows 7 or Windows Vista. If so, you've activated hybrid sleep. When hybrid sleep is on, the Hibernation option isn't available on the Shutdown menu. See the section "What is hybrid sleep?," later in this chapter, for more information on hybrid sleep.

Windows XP sports two options at the bottom of the Start button menu: Log Off and Turn Off Computer. Neither button does what it claims; instead, another menu appears, as shown in Figures 3-3 and 3-4.

Figure 3-3:
Windows
XP logoff
options.

Figure 3-4:
Windows XP
shutdown
options.

Choosing the Log Off options from the Windows XP Start menu displays the Log Off Windows options, as shown in Figure 3-3. Both options allow someone else to use the computer; Switch User suspends your session, and Log Off ends it.

In Figure 3-4, you see the Turn Off Computer window, which contains *four* options. The visible options are Stand By (to enter Sleep mode), Turn Off, and Restart. The fourth option is Hibernate. It becomes visible when you press the Shift key; the Stand By text is replaced by the word *Hibernate*. (Hibernation is available only when it has been turned on, as described later in this chapter.)

The only option not available in either window is Lock. To lock a Windows XP computer, you press the Win+L key combo.

It's normal for the screen background to fade to monochrome when either Windows XP shutdown option menu is displayed.

Setting the Power button function

The poor Power button sits in the real world, often used only to turn on the computer. How sad. But you can use the Power button to turn off the computer as well. That's because the Power button is *programmable*. It can do anything you want it to do, including nothing.

To set the Power button's function, follow these steps for Windows 7 and Windows Vista:

1. **In the Control Panel, choose Hardware and Sound.**

2. **Beneath the Power Options heading, click the Change What the Power Buttons Do link.**

   You see a screen similar to Figure 3-5.

   Unlike in the figure, you may see only one column for Plugged In. The On Battery column (refer to Figure 3-5) shows up only for a laptop, which is battery powered, as well as for a desktop PC connected to an uninterruptible power supply (UPS). For the On Battery power options to appear, your PC must be connected to a UPS by using a USB cable.

Figure 3-5:
Setting
Power
button
functions.

A second row may also appear, When I Press The Sleep Button. That row appears for those few PC models that feature a specific Sleep button.

3. Click a button to choose a Plugged In Power button function.

The button in the Plugged In column, the Power button row, features a pop-up menu with up to four options: Do Nothing, Sleep, Hibernate, and Shut Down. Choose which command you want the PC's Power button to execute when you press that button while the computer is on.

On my PC, I chose the Shut Down option, which is shown in Figure 3-5.

4. Set additional Power button functions.

When your computer features a Sleep button, set its function by clicking the button and choosing a command.

You can also choose functions for the Power button (or buttons) when the computer is on battery power. On my desktop PC, I choose the command Shut Down. On my laptop, it's Hibernate.

5. Click the Save Changes button.

6. Close the System Settings window.

Watch Video 131 to see me work through these steps on your screen:

www.dummies.com/go/troubleshootingandmaintainingyourpcaio2e

Follow these steps to set the Power button's function in Windows XP:

1. Open the Control Panel's Power Options icon.

The Power Options Properties dialog box appears.

2. Click the Advanced tab.

3. **In the Power Buttons area, choose the Power button's function from the drop-down list beneath When I Press the Power Button on My Computer.**

The five options are Do Nothing, Ask Me What to Do, Stand By, Hibernate, and Shut Down.

The Ask Me What to Do option displays the standard Shutdown window (refer to Figure 3-4).

4. **Click OK and close the Control Panel window.**

You must have hibernation activated before you can use hibernation as an option for the Power button. See the section "Activating hibernation," later in this chapter, for the details.

You can assign the Power button to hibernate the computer in Windows 7 or in Windows Vista, even when hybrid sleep is active. See the later section "What is hybrid sleep?"

Setting the Windows Vista software Power button function

Windows Vista features a software Power button on its Start menu, shown earlier, in Figure 3-2. Assigning a function to that button is possible, but it involves following these lengthy, complicated steps:

1. **In the Control Panel window, choose Hardware and Sound.**

2. **Beneath the Power Options heading, click the link Change When the Computer Sleeps.**

The link isn't relevant to setting the software Power button function, but it gets you one step closer to the spot where that body is buried.

3. **Click the link Change Advanced Power Settings.**

The Power Options dialog box appears.

4. **Click the plus sign (+) by the item titled Power Buttons and Lid.**

5. **Click the plus sign (+) next to the option Start Menu Power Button.**

6. **Choose an option for the Start menu Power button.**

The options are Sleep, Hibernate, and Shut Down.

For battery-powered or UPS PCs, set both options: On Battery and Plugged In.

7. **Click OK to dismiss the Power Options dialog box and confirm your choices.**

8. **Close the Edit Plan Settings window.**

TIP

You can, though it isn't easy, determine the software Power button's function by observing the software Power button on the Start menu. An orange Power button means that either Sleep or Hibernation is chosen; a red Power button means that Shutdown is chosen.

Shutdown Malaise

Shutdown problems don't carry the weighty burden of start-up issues, or, really, other typical PC problems. That's probably because shutting down is what you do at the *end* of the day. Also, shutdown issues don't often have an effect on starting the computer. (Well, just hope that's the case.) Regardless, this section contains some good information on dealing with PC troubles and tribulations that happen during the shutdown process.

General shutdown advice

A big reason for shutdown issues in any PC is that the computer's software isn't up-to-date. Old hardware without proper software to support it may work fine when the computer is on. But when you shut down the PC, you have trouble as the older hardware and its equally old software fail to follow proper procedure. So a blanket rule for fixing just about any shutdown issue is to ensure that your computer is using the latest software drivers. Refer to Chapter 7 for information on how to check and update drivers.

Another useful hint: Check the logs. A shutdown problem that causes an error message generates a log entry in Windows. Refer to Book II, Chapter 7 for more information.

Turning off a stubborn PC

The computer's Power button may seem feeble, but you can use a sneaky way to turn it into a true Off switch: Press and hold the Power button for five to eight seconds. After that length of time, the computer turns itself off.

REMEMBER

Using the Power button to forcibly turn off a computer is a desperate measure. Do not use the press-and-hold method as your normal way to turn off the computer. Try to *troubleshoot* shutdown issues, not ignore them.

Slow shutdown

The most common reason that a PC takes a long time to shut down is that it's installing updates. Both Windows 7 and Windows Vista display update information on the screen as those updates are being installed. My advice is to be patient.

How long should you wait? That depends on how much time you have. If you interrupt an update process, at best, you have to repeat the update again; at worst, you corrupt Windows. That's something you don't want: Corrupting Windows is the only problem that forces you to reinstall the operating system.

A good way to determine whether the computer is stuck or just thinking is to examine the hard drive light on the console. When the light is flashing, the computer is simply busy. The light should flash at irregular intervals, however, because a regularly flashing light may indicate that Mr. Computer is stuck in a loop. In that case, force a shutdown as discussed in the preceding section, "Turning off a stubborn PC."

The shutdown process may be slow simply because the PC is slow to begin with. Refer to Book II, Chapter 4 for information on pepping up a slow computer.

Someone else is logged in!

If you're one of the smart folks who bothered to set up multiple accounts on a single PC (one for everyone!), you may have seen a shutdown error message similar to the one shown in Figure 3-6. It's a good message; nothing to panic over.

Figure 3-6: Someone's in the PC with you.

Unless an emergency occurs, click the No button when you're greeted by a message such as the one shown in Figure 3-6. That's because the other person may have open, unsaved files. Only when you *truly* need to shut down or restart, such as during a power outage, should you click the Yes button.

When you click the No button, log out of your account to fix the problem: Use the login screen, which automatically shows up, to determine who else is logged in. Get that person to log out and save their stuff, and then shut down or restart the computer.

A variation on the warning message shown in Figure 3-6 happens when others on the network are using your computer. The message might say something like, `Others on the network are using this PC`. In that case, it's generally okay to proceed.

End now?

The dialog box is titled End Program, but just about everyone I know refers to it by its key button, End Now. One version is shown in Figure 3-7; though a full-screen version also shows similar information but with a big, red End Now button.

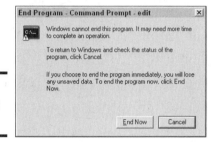

Figure 3-7: Killing off a program.

The End Now prompt occasionally shows up on the computer screen when you shut down or restart the PC. The issue is a program that's stuck or one that's running but that Windows cannot shut down. To continue the shutdown process, click the End Now button. Or, in some cases, you can wait it out and Windows eventually shuts down the program automatically. (I think the program is ruthlessly killed, but I lack the evidence to bring the case to court.)

✦ The full-screen End Now message states something like `The following programs are still running` and then lists the programs. Click the Cancel button to stop the shutdown or logoff operation, or click the red button to continue. (The red button's text varies, depending on whether you're shutting down or just logging off.)

✦ Don't fall into the trap of automatically clicking the End Now button! Occasionally, the message is flagging a program that you must manually shut down, such as the Command Prompt program mentioned in Figure 3-7. In that case, click the Cancel button in the dialog box and then return to the stuck program, save, and quit. You can then shut down or restart the PC.

✦ A common culprit of End Now syndrome is the `Rundll32.exe` process. Don't freak out! In Windows, `Rundll32.exe` is responsible for running (get it?) a number of processes. The problem is most likely not with the `Rundll32.exe` program itself, but rather with whichever process `Rundll32.exe` is running. Refer to Book II, Chapter 2 for information on processes in Windows.

"The computer was improperly shut down!"

Whether it was intended to or not, sometimes the computer crashes. This book would be a lot thinner if computers didn't crash often enough.

In the early days, a computer that was improperly shut down warned you about it the next time it started. A message appeared on the screen, alerting you to the improper shutdown. These days, the computer doesn't display the message; instead, it just automatically checks the disk to fix any problems caused by the improper shutdown.

Face it: Sometimes, you have to "improperly" shut down a computer that has gone haywire. And, sometimes the power just turns off and shuts down the PC immediately. It's okay! Don't freak out! Today's operating systems recognize and recover from these shutdown mishaps.

If you see the message often, you need to troubleshoot it. Often, the culprit is a program that hangs or hogs memory and makes the shutdown process impossible. Refer to Book II, Chapter 2 for information on hunting down such naughty programs.

Windows Error Recovery menu

Sometimes, the boo-boos caused by Windows at shutdown aren't known until you restart the computer. In some of those cases, you see the Windows Error Recovery menu, as shown in Figure 3-8. Yes, this Text mode screen appears as soon as Windows starts to load.

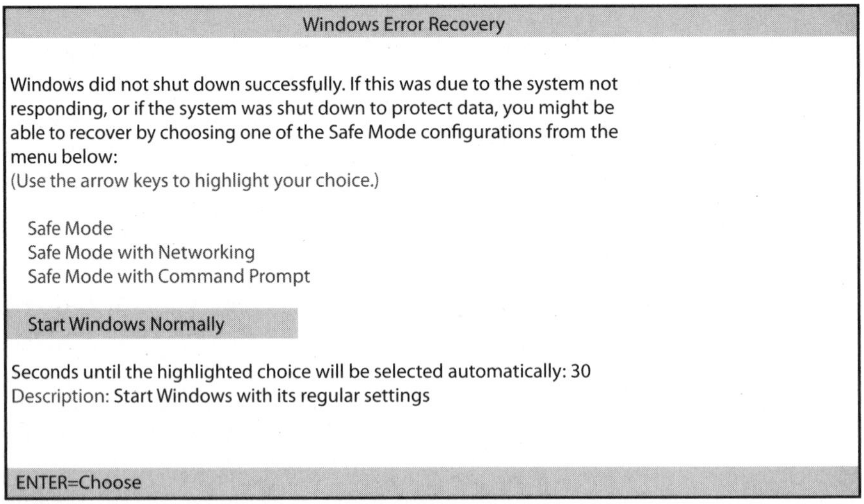

Figure 3-8:
Windows
Error
Recovery
menu,
shutdown
version.

```
                    Windows Error Recovery

 Windows did not shut down successfully. If this was due to the system not
 responding, or if the system was shut down to protect data, you might be
 able to recover by choosing one of the Safe Mode configurations from the
 menu below:
 (Use the arrow keys to highlight your choice.)

    Safe Mode
    Safe Mode with Networking
    Safe Mode with Command Prompt

    Start Windows Normally

 Seconds until the highlighted choice will be selected automatically: 30
 Description: Start Windows with its regular settings


 ENTER=Choose
```

The Windows Error Recovery menu is basically an abbreviated form of the F8 menu; in addition to the standard F8 menu options, it has Safe mode options and the Start Windows Normally option.

✦ If the error appears to be random, select the Start Windows Normally option and, after Windows starts, check the logs to see which program may have improperly shut things down. See Book II, Chapter 7 for information on reviewing the logs.

✦ You can use the Safe mode options to attempt a System Restore operation, but that method works only when you've recently updated hardware or software in your PC. Refer to Book II, Chapter 8 for information on System Restore and to Book II, Chapter 3 for Safe Mode.

✦ When the error is chronic, you need to pay attention to your computer. Something is wrong that needs fixing. Because Windows recognizes the error, it's most likely not a hardware problem. See Book II, Chapter 8 for various Windows recovery options.

✦ The other Windows Error Recovery menu, the start-up version, is covered in Chapter 2.

Power Management Issues

Way back when, hardware engineers set out to enhance the way computers manage power. Various solutions culminated in the set of software protocols and hardware goodness called the *Advanced Configuration and Power Interface (ACPI)*.

Although the ACPI serves many computers well, by managing power, sleeping hardware, and saving lots of energy year after year, it can also be a source of woe. For example, Windows XP often fails to detect ACPI hardware in a computer, so the feature is never installed. Or, worse, the ACPI is improperly detected and you end up with a computer that falls into a coma rather than falls asleep.

This section discusses some common power management messes.

Activating power management in Windows XP

To ensure that Windows XP is taking advantage of your computer's power management prowess, follow these steps:

1. **Open the Control Panel's Power Options icon.**

2. **In the Power Options Properties dialog box, click the APM tab.**

If you don't see the APM tab, your computer is fine and ready to go: Skip to Step 4.

3. **Click the option Enable Advanced Power Management Support.**

4. **Click OK to dismiss the Power Options Properties dialog box, and then close the Control Panel window.**

The computer should now properly manage power options, like Sleep mode.

If you continue to have problems with Windows XP and power management, visit the computer manufacturer's web site to check for new power management driver software. You can also use the Windows Update service to confirm that your computer is using the most current drivers. Refer to Book II, Chapter 1 for information on Windows Update; also see Chapter 7 of this minibook for information on the Device Manager.

Enabling power management for specific devices

Occasionally, you find a Power Management tab in various Properties dialog boxes for devices capable of power management. You can use that tab to enable or disable the power management features of specific devices, such as the networking adapter shown in Figure 3-9.

Figure 3-9:
Power management for specific gizmos.

To find those devices, you use the Device Manager. Heed these steps:

1. **Open the Control Panel.**

2a. **In Windows 7 and Window Vista, choose Hardware and Sound and then click the Device Manager link found under the Devices and Printers heading.**

You may be prompted in Windows Vista to click the Continue button or type the administrator's password to continue.

2b. **In Windows XP, open the System icon, click the Hardware tab, and then click the Device Manager button.**

3. **Open a category to view the devices available in that category.**

4. **Open a device to view its Properties dialog box.**

5. **Click the Power Management tab in the Properties dialog box to control power management for that device.**

Only the gizmos that have power management features sport the Power Management tab in their Properties dialog boxes. When the tab is there, you see an option to enable the power management features, plus maybe other options specific to the device.

6. **Close the various dialog boxes and windows when you're done.**

The devices I've found that have the Power Management tab in their Properties dialog boxes include keyboards, mouse or pointing devices, network adapters, and some system devices. Others may have it as well.

You can configure your PC's mouse or keyboard to *not* wake the computer from Sleep mode. That's done on the Power Management tab of the device's Properties dialog box; simply remove the check mark next to Allow This Device to Wake the Computer. In Windows XP, the command is Allow This Device to Bring the Computer Out of Standby.

Activating hibernation

The Hibernation feature must be activated in Windows before you can use it and, obviously, before it shows up on any Shutdown menu.

When hybrid sleep is active in Windows 7 or Windows Vista, the Hibernation command doesn't appear on the Shutdown menu. You can still assign the Hibernation feature to the Power button; see the sections "Setting the Power button function" and "Setting the Windows Vista software Power button function," earlier in this chapter.

To quickly activate hibernation in Windows 7 or Window Vista, follow these technical but efficient steps:

1. **Pop up the Start menu.**

2. **Choose All Programs➪Accessories.**

3. **Right-click the Command Prompt item.**

4. **Choose Run As Administrator.**

5. **Deal with the User Account warning: Click the Yes button or the Continue button, or type the administrator's password.**

   The Administrator Command Prompt window appears — in all its ugly Text mode glory.

6. **At the command prompt, type** powercfg -h on **and press Enter.**

   That's **powercfg**, a space, a hyphen, the letter **h**, a space, and then **on**.

   There's no feedback for the command.

7. **Type** exit **(and press Enter) to close the Administrator Command Prompt window.**

To deactivate hibernation, repeat these steps but substitute the word *off* for *on* in Step 6.

To activate hibernation in Windows XP, follow these steps:

1. **Open the Control Panel's Power Options icon.**

2. **Click the Hibernate tab.**

3. **Place a check mark by the option Enable Hibernation.**

4. **Click OK and close the Control Panel window.**

After hibernation is active, the next step toward using it is to find the option: In Windows XP, the Hibernation command hides itself behind the Stand By option in the Turn Off Computer window (refer to Figure 3-4). When you hold down the Shift key, the Stand By option changes to Hibernate. Click the Hibernate button to hibernate the PC.

The Disk Cleanup tool can render hibernation inoperable. When using Disk Cleanup, be sure not to remove any hibernation files, such as the Hibernation File Cleaner. Refer to Book VI, Chapter 2 for more information on Disk Cleanup.

What is hybrid sleep?

Somewhere between Sleep mode and hibernation is the *hybrid sleep* feature. It's like hibernation in that information stored in memory (RAM) is saved to disk but the computer doesn't fully turn itself off. Instead, as when it's in Sleep mode, you can quickly resume computer operation by touching a key or moving the mouse.

The advantage of hybrid sleep is that you can quickly resume computer operations *and* avoid the risk of losing data if the power goes out. But to use hybrid sleep, it must be activated. Here's how:

1. **Open the Control Panel.**

2. **Click the Hardware and Sound heading.**

3. **Click the Power Options heading.**

You see a list of power plans for your computer. One of them is selected, which shows the power savings plan your PC uses.

4. **Click the link Change Plan Settings beneath the selected plan.**

5. **Click the link Change Advanced Power Settings.**

The Power Options dialog box appears, similar to the one shown in Figure 3-10.

Figure 3-10:
Activating hybrid sleep.

6. **Open the Sleep item by clicking the plus (+) sign.**

7. **Open the item Allow Hybrid Sleep.**

8. **Click the blue text and choose On from the button menu.**

When your PC has two power sources, such as are shown in Figure 3-10, you need to choose On for both settings.

9. **Click OK to confirm your choice and activate hybrid sleep.**

10. **Close the remaining dialog boxes and windows.**

When hybrid sleep is active, choosing the Sleep command places the computer into Hybrid Sleep mode.

✦ Hybrid sleep isn't available in Windows XP.

✦ If you have disabled hibernation, the hybrid sleep feature may not function properly. Specifically, hybrid sleep may not recover unsaved data if the feature is on and the power goes out. See the preceding section for information on enabling hibernation.

Recovering from a PC coma

Occasionally, a PC may go to sleep and not wake up. It gets stuck. The problem isn't as common as it once was, but the solution is the same: Turn off the computer. Refer to the earlier section "Turning off a stubborn PC."

Yes, it's okay to forcibly turn off a computer when it's in a coma.

When you turn on the computer again, your next task is to update the PC's power management driver software. To complete that task, you can phone your dealer for more information, but you'll probably be directed to the manufacturer's web site. After you're there, look for the Support or Download Drivers link. Find the latest power management driver software for your PC and update it.

You can also use the Windows Update service to ensure that your computer has the latest power management software. See Book II, Chapter 1.

If the problem persists, don't use Sleep mode for your PC. For example, on one of my older, more stubborn computers, I don't use Sleep mode. Instead, I simply turn off the monitor when I'm not using that computer.

Problems with Restarting

Restarting a computer is a common and often necessary task. Even if you're a fan of leaving a PC on all the time, you'll find yourself restarting it every so often for a number of reasons, from installing or updating software to fixing bugs.

Two ugly restart issues may plague you. The first is the random restart, which is unexpected. The second is the automatic restart, or re-restart, which is unwanted. This section covers both.

Restarting Windows often cures many minor ills.

Random restarts

An unexpected restart is a sign of trouble. I'm not talking about the computer requesting a restart — one of those Restart now? type of dialog boxes. Nope. I'm talking about the computer just wandering off into la-la land in a rude and discourteous manner.

Poof!

A random restart is most likely, though not exclusively, a hardware error. The primary culprit is the power supply:

✦ If the power supply lacks the proper wattage to power the PC's hardware, it randomly restarts or dies. The solution is to replace the power supply with a beefier model. See Chapter 8.

✦ If the power supply is just flaky, it needs replacing anyway.

✦ When the power supply's fan fails to keep the computer cool enough, the PC restarts because of the heat. You can buy a power supply with more fans or install a supplemental fan for your PC.

Other hardware glitches may also cause random restarts, so if the problem isn't in the power supply, it can be difficult to pinpoint.

Don't rule out software glitches: Poorly installed and corrupt software can randomly crash a computer. You can use the Windows log files to help determine which programs may be causing random restarts. See Book II, Chapter 7 for more information.

Automatic restarts

For the sake of troubleshooting, an automatic restart is more of a re-restart. What happens is that the computer restarts and then restarts again. Restart, restart, restart. The problem is that you can configure Windows to automatically restart on an error, in which case the computer ceaselessly restarts and coincidentally drives you mad.

You can choose from a couple of solutions for automatic restarts. The first solution is to disable the feature *before* you experience the problem. Obey these steps:

1. **Press the Win+Break key combination to summon the System window or System Properties dialog box.**

The Break key is also the Pause key on some keyboards.

2a. **In Windows 7 and Vista, choose the link Advanced System Settings on the left side of the window.**

In Windows Vista, you click the Continue button or type the administrator's password to continue.

2b. **In Windows XP, click the Advanced tab in the System Properties dialog box.**

3. **Click the Settings button in the Startup and Recovery area.**

4. Remove the check mark by the item **Automatically Restart**.

5. Click OK and close whatever other windows or other dialog boxes linger on the screen.

The second solution is to take advantage of the start-up menu that disables automatic restarts. This solution comes in handy when the restart takes place. For more information, see Chapter 2.

Chapter 4: Mass Storage Issues

In This Chapter

- ✓ Discovering mass storage
- ✓ Adding and removing storage
- ✓ Understanding partitions
- ✓ Reviving a dead optical drive
- ✓ Dealing with disc recording issues
- ✓ Cleaning an optical disc
- ✓ Using professional data recovery

*P*op quiz time! Without reading this chapter's title, can you state which piece of hardware in your PC is the most important? Did you guess the mass storage system? If you did, you probably cheated and read the chapter title. That's okay, but it's wrong.

The most important piece of hardware in a computer is the processor, considering that everything in the computer is geared toward working well with the processor. Even so, because all your stuff — programs, documents, pictures, music, embarrassing videos — is kept on the mass storage system, I would argue that maintaining and troubleshooting your PC's storage devices are much higher on the priority list than anything you can do with that silly old processor.

Mass Storage Overview

It's easy to ignore the basic principles of computer science, so I will. Suffice it to say that storage is a key component of any computer system. This section provides an overview of the PC's storage system. By reading this information, you gain good insight into not only names and functions but also the general storage troubleshooting process.

A computer's storage system has *two* types of components: long term and short term. Both are required. *Short-term* storage is the computer's memory, or RAM. *Long-term* storage, or *mass* storage, is the domain of the disk drives and media cards. That's what's covered here.

Understanding mass storage

Four different types of storage are found on a PC, though similarities and overlaps exist between them. I like to classify them this way:

✦ Hard drive

✦ Solid state drive, or SSD

✦ Optical drive

✦ Removable media

The typical PC comes with hard drive and optical drive storage, which is a form of removable media. The hard drive isn't considered removable storage.

In a few years, the solid state drive, or SSD, will overtake the hard drive as the PC's main storage device. An SSD is superfast and is free of many of the reliability issues that the spinning hard drive bears. Until the SSD price comes down, however, the hard drive remains the mass storage king.

Removable media includes digital media cards and thumb drives but also other types of storage, including external hard drives, oddball drives (magneto-optical and tape drives, for example), and antique floppy drives, which I hear are still used in parts of Cape Cod.

Detailed information about these types of storage is offered in the remainder of this chapter.

✦ The *disk* is the media on which information is recorded. I prefer using the term *storage media* rather than *disk* because computers are now bridging the gap between spinning disk storage and solid-state storage. Solid-state storage doesn't spin, unless you accidentally leave a thumb drive in your pants and put it through the wash.

✦ The *drive* is the part of the mass storage unit that reads the disk. A hard drive contains a hard disk; you insert an optical disc into a CD or DVD drive; a media card is placed into a media drive or media card reader or is connected directly to a USB port.

✦ The PC's hard drive cannot be removed. It's fixed in place, which is why you may see a hard drive referred to as a *fixed drive* in obscure manuals.

Finding mass storage in Windows

Windows provides ready access to storage media in your computer via the Computer window, as shown in Figure 4-1. In Windows XP, the window is titled My Computer, and it looks similar to the one shown in Figure 4-1.

Figure 4-1:
The
Computer
window
shows a
PC's storage
devices.

Windows assigns storage media in your computer by using a letter of the alphabet: a *drive letter*. The main hard drive is usually, though not always, drive C. The drive letters are then assigned to any additional storage media from letters D on up. In Figure 4-1, you see the following items:

Hard drives: Drives C, D, F, and H are classified as hard drives. Drives C and D are two logical drives on a single physical drive, though that's difficult to determine from Figure 4-1. Like most PCs sold today, drive D is used for recovery purposes. Drive F is a second, internal physical drive. Hard drive H is an external backup drive.

Optical drive: Drives E and G are optical drives.

Media drives: Figure 4-1 shows no media drives or thumb drives attached to the computer. If they were, they would be listed in the second area, Devices with Removable Storage.

Network drives: Any drives shared on the local network, or FTP sites on the Internet, appear in the Network Location area. In Figure 4-1, a shortcut to a web site is listed as a network location.

Network drives accessed by your computer can be *mapped* to unused drive letters. They appear primarily in the Network or My Network Places windows, and they have "plumbing" beneath their drive icons, as shown in Figure 4-1.

The number of disk drives available on your computer is different. You may have more, you may have less.

✦ Drive letters are followed by a colon, as in C: or D:.

✦ A single physical hard drive can be divided into multiple *logical* hard drives. In Figure 4-1, drives C and D are two logical drives on a single physical hard drive. See the section "Partitions," later in this chapter, for more information.

✦ You can reassign and change the drive letters, which are covered in Book VI, Chapter 2.

✦ Icons shown for drives can be either generic, such as those used in Figure 4-1, or specific, sometimes even looking like the drive itself or the media read by the drive.

✦ Optical disc icons change depending on the disc's contents. For example, a musical CD uses a custom music icon.

Using the Disk Management console

The Computer/My Computer window is used for file management. To control the PC's mass storage system, you use the Windows Disk Management console. Here's how to summon that window:

1. **Open the Control Panel.**

2a. **In Windows 7, choose System and Security and then Administrative Tools.**

2b. **In Windows Vista, choose System and Maintenance and then Administrative Tools.**

2c. **In Windows XP, open the Administrative Tools icon.**

3. **Open Computer Management.**

4. **In Windows Vista, click Continue or type the administrator's password when prompted by the User Account Control warning.**

5. **Beneath the Storage heading (on the left side of the console window), choose Disk Management.**

The Disk Management console appears, as shown in Figure 4-2.

You can do lots of interesting and wonderful things with the Disk Management console, as covered elsewhere in this chapter. For now, you can close the window, if you like, or keep reading and play with the Disk Management console as the need arises.

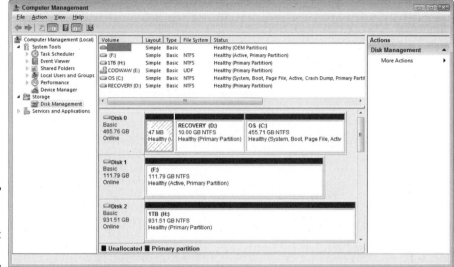

Figure 4-2:
The Disk
Management
console.

Understanding Medea

Jason of *Argonauts'* fame took Medea, princess of Colchis, as his wife. Then he betrayed her. She grew jealous and sought revenge, killing just about everyone, depending on which version of the tragedy you read. But you're probably more interested in *media* than in Medea.

Adding drives and media

You might experience a few issues with adding new items to your PC's storage system. It can be done in two ways.

First, you can insert storage media into the drives that accept removable media: the optical drive and all its various media card readers. Simply stick the media into the drive. After a few moments, the operating system recognizes the media and *mounts* it into the disk system.

In Windows, where drives have preassigned letters, using the drive letter accesses the media you insert. In other words, to use the media card inserted into drive H:, you use the drive H icon in Windows or the designation H: when referring to the drive in this cryptic pathname manner.

Second, you can add storage to a computer system externally by plugging the drive into the PC. You can connect an external drive by using the computer's USB, IEEE, or FireWire port or an eSATA port. After a few moments, Windows recognizes the drive's addition, updates itself to use the drive, and, finally, assigns the drive a letter.

You can confirm that an external drive has properly been added by opening the Computer or My Computer window.

In addition to adding an external hard drive, you can add external removable media drives, such as an optical disc or a media card reader. In that case, you still need to add media to the drive. Although an external, removable media drive is given a drive letter, you then cannot access the drive until you stick some sort of media into the drive.

+ Also refer to the later section "AutoPlay issues" for information on how to handle newly mounted media in Windows.

+ The drive letter doesn't change when you stick new media into the drive. The same drive letter is always used, no matter which media is inserted. An exception to this rule occurs when you stick a thumb drive into a USB port. In this case, the thumb drive is assigned the next available drive letter.

+ Some older PCs running Windows XP may not have USB 2.0 adapters. If so, you cannot successfully use most external USB drives, including flash, or *thumb,* drives. Windows alerts you to the problem. The solution is to buy a USB 2.0 adapter and install it. See Chapter 8 for information on adding expansion cards to your PC.

+ You can attach a drive with media already in it. For example, you can connect a media card reader with a media card already in it and the computer deals with it just fine. Attaching this type of reader works just like adding an external hard drive or attaching a digital camera to the PC; the media reader is added and then the media is read.

Removing media

Windows has no problem recognizing new drives or media, but issues can occur when removing media — especially when the media is still being used.

To properly remove media from a drive, follow these steps:

1. **Open the Computer or My Computer window.**

2. **Click to select the icon for the drive containing the media you want to remove.**

3a. **In Windows 7 and Windows Vista, click the Eject button on the toolbar.**

3b. **In Windows XP, choose the link Eject This Disk from the list of system tasks on the right side of the window.**

For an optical disc, the drive should eject the disc. For a media card, however, you manually remove the card from the reader.

4. **Close the Computer/My Computer window.**

When the computer is still using the removable media, you're warned; you cannot remove media that is being used, has unsaved files on it, or is somehow being accessed by the computer. This warning prevents the data stored on the media from being corrupted.

When you have trouble removing media, close any open applications. Then try ejecting the media again. If that fails, shut down the computer. You can safely remove any media when the computer is turned off.

Removing drives

The media is the thing that stores computer information; the drive is the thing that reads the media. Just as media can be removed (see the preceding section), you can also remove any drives or media card readers attached to your computer. Before you do, you must let Windows know that the drive is going bye-bye or else Windows gets angry at you. To prevent that, follow the appropriate set of steps for your version of Windows:

In *Windows 7,* remove an external drive or media card reader by following these steps:

1. **From the Start menu, choose Devices and Printers.**

   If this item is missing from the Start menu, open the Control Panel and choose View Devices and Printers, found beneath the Hardware and Sound heading.

2. **Click on the drive you want to remove.**

3. **Choose Eject from the toolbar.**

4. **Disconnect the drive from the computer.**

In *Windows Vista,* heed these directions to remove an external storage gizmo:

1. **Open the Computer window.**

2. **Right-click on the drive you want to remove.**

   The drive can be empty, or it can have media attached.

3. **From the pop-up menu, choose Safely Remove.**

4. **After the confirmation message appears, disconnect the drive from the computer.**

In *Windows XP* (as well as in Windows 7 and Windows Vista), you can use the Safely Remove icon in the notification area to disconnect external disk drives or media card readers. Here's how:

1. **Review the Computer window to confirm the letter associated with the drive you want to remove.**

   I urge you to follow this step because today's PCs can sport several drive letters and not always assign the same letter to a removable device.

2. **Point the mouse at the Safely Remove Hardware icon in the notification area.**

   You know that you've found the right icon when the pop-up bubble says Safely Remove Hardware. (Also see the margin art at the end of this section.)

3. **Click the Safely Remove Hardware icon.**

   A pop-up list appears, detailing any removable hardware that's attached to your PC.

4. **Choose the hardware you want to remove from the list.**

5. **When you see the prompt Safe to Remove Hardware, disconnect the device.**

   Windows 7 may not prompt you to remove the hardware, but you can do so.

For an external hard drive, you can either unplug the USB cable or merely turn off the drive's power; it doesn't matter which, at this point.

✦ The Safely Remove Hardware icon in Windows 7 and Windows Vista is shown in the margin.

✦ The Windows XP version of the Safely Remove Hardware icon is shown in the margin.

✦ Even if you don't see the prompt that it's okay to safely remove hardware, Windows plays a "dink-donk" sound whenever a media device has been unmounted from your PC. That is, unless you've configured Windows not to play the sound or your PC's speakers are broken.

✦ There's a difference between removing (ejecting) media and unmounting the drive that reads the media. Ejecting media doesn't disconnect the drive or media card reader.

Hard Drive Stuff

Your PC's main storage device is the hard drive, or *hard disk drive* or *fixed disk* or, if you're over 50, *Winchester drive*. (Boy, does that bring back memories.) For regular PC use, you need to know that the hard drive is the drive C thing people talk about and that you cannot remove it from your computer without using a screwdriver and some C4 explosives. Beyond that, and for troubleshooting purposes, you need to know a bit more about the hard drive. That's why I wrote this section.

Hard drive technical trivia

A *hard drive* is basically a tiny box. It contains the hard disk, which is a stack of disks, or platters. The box also contains read/write heads, which read and record information on both sides of the numerous disks inside the drive. Oh, and the hard drive has a lot more details than that, but for troubleshooting, you don't need to know the trivial stuff.

The hard drive dwells in a *drive bay* inside your PC's bosom. The bay has room for more than one drive; a typical PC can sport up to two physical hard drive units. Larger PCs have room for more; smaller PCs may have room for only one drive.

The drive is connected to the computer via two cables: One is a data cable, and the second is the power cable. Figure 4-3 illustrates the connections and other trivial stuff.

Figure 4-3:
Typical,
naked hard
drive.

Mounting screws (both sides)

Power supply interface

SATA interface

Impressive gibberish

No matter the hard drive internals, the computer treats the hard drive as a single unit — a data storage device. But within this single physical drive can be multiple logical drives. It's important to understand how it works.

To prepare a hard drive for use in Windows, you work these steps:

1. **The hard drive is low-level formatted, which is done at the factory.**

   The low-level format is the basic way a hard drive is formatted. The process merely prepares the disk for partitioning and the high-level formatting done by the operating system.

2. **The hard drive is partitioned into one or more logical drives.**

3. **The partitions are formatted.**

4. **One partition is selected as the active partition, the one that will contain the operating system. (This step is required on only the first physical hard drive.)**

5. **The operating system is installed on the active partition.**

Full detail on using these steps is provided in Book VI, Chapter 2. For now, be sure to note what is a physical hard drive and what is a logical hard drive. The next section covers the details.

✦ The process of formatting a hard drive organizes the disks into individual chunks, where data is stored. A lot of jargon surrounds this process: *cylinder, track,* and *sector,* for example.

✦ The hard drive formatting process explains why the hard drive's rated size is never equal to its formatted capacity. For example, a standard 500GB hard drive formats out to about 465GB. The missing storage space is used by the formatting process and, according to law, some bytes must be given over to the federal government in lieu of taxes.

✦ All information that applies to a hard drive also applies to an SSD. In fact, the SSD usually comes in an enclosure similar to the one shown in Figure 4-3. The SSD has two connectors — data and power — and it's partitioned and formatted, just like a hard drive.

✦ Two types of interface are used to communicate between the hard drive (and optical drive) and the PC's motherboard. Older PCs use the Advanced Technology Attachment (ATA) interface, and newer PCs use the Serial ATA, or SATA interface. Both types basically control how fast data can be moved to and from the hard drive to the processor.

Partitions

A single physical hard drive can become one or more logical hard drives. In fact, it's those logical drives you see in the Computer or My Computer window (refer to Figure 4-1). That's because Windows can use a hard drive only after it's been prepared for use, and part of that preparation includes partitioning and formatting.

To determine how your PC's hard drives are partitioned, refer to the Disk Management console window, covered earlier in this chapter. Open the Disk Management console window and check out the list of drives on your PC.

Every physical hard drive is named starting with Disk 0. (Computer nerds use zero, not one, as the first number.) On your computer, in the Disk Management console window, you see Disk 0 listed along with partitions. One partition is most likely drive C, the main hard drive. Another partition commonly found on today's PCs is drive D, a "recovery" drive. Figure 4-4 shows the relationship between the *partitions,* or logical drives, and the drive icons you see in either the Computer window or the My Computer window.

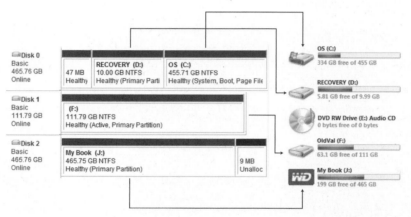

Figure 4-4: From physical drive to logical drive to icon.

If your computer has a second hard drive, you see it listed as Disk 1. This drive may have one or more partitions as well, as illustrated in the Disk Management console window. These logical drives also map out to icons in the Computer or My Computer window.

You can close the Disk Management console window when you're done looking.

REMEMBER

✦ All hard drives must have at least one partition.

✦ Disk 0 is the first physical hard drive inside your computer. Any additional hard drives, internal or external, are numbered Disk 1, Disk 2, and so on.

✦ Each drive is partitioned into one or more logical drives. Those logical drives map out to the drive letters and icons you see and use in Windows.

✦ Each partition has a format type or method, such as NTFS or FAT32, for example. The format type explains how the drive was formatted and how data is written (or stored) to the drive.

✦ Another name for a partition, or logical drive, is *volume*. This isn't a loudness thing; instead, think of a volume in a book.

The master boot record

The most important part of the hard drive is the *master boot record,* or *MBR.* It's the first part of the first physical hard drive (Disk 0) in your PC. The MBR contains two vital items:

✦ A map, or *partition table,* describing how the hard drive is divided into smaller, logical drives

✦ The *boot loader,* or the program used to find and load an operating system from one of the drive's partitions.

A host of errors are associated with a bad, corrupt, or missing MBR. These error messages appear when the computer starts — obviously, before the operating system is loaded. Here's a sampling of error messages, followed by advice about how to deal with them:

Invalid Partition Table: This nasty error message indicates that the partition table is damaged or missing or contains questionable information.

Operating System Not Found: Not a deadly error message, this one might indicate that the partition table has no active partition set: The computer doesn't know which partition to look at for an operating system.

Missing Operating System: This message most likely implies that the partition table is damaged. The MBR is saying that a bootable partition is available, but not any information about where to find the partition.

Non-System Disk or Disk Error: This old error message often surfaced when a nonbootable floppy disk was left in the drive and the computer tried (by default) to boot from the disk.

When you see one of these first three error messages, the solution is to run the Windows Recovery Console. You can use the FIXBOOT or FIXMBR utilities to address the issues, by repairing the MBR and restoring things to normal. See Book II, Chapter 8 for the details.

When a hard drive is damaged beyond repair, it must be replaced. Book VI, Chapter 2 offers details. After installing a new disk, be sure to restore your old files from a backup. See Book VI, Chapter 1 for information on backing up your stuff.

✦ Refer to Chapter 2 for additional information on problems plaguing PCs when they start.

✦ The MBR also contains information identifying the disk — a *disk signature*, which uniquely identifies the disk and may be used by Windows for various and sundry reasons.

Optical Drive Death and Misery

Don't worry: Your PC's optical drive is a robust beast. It's far more reliable than the floppy drives of yore. Hopefully, mankind has kept all the world's floppy drives ready so that we can hurl them at an invading fleet of space aliens. Such a brutal move would devastate any potential galactic foe.

This section contains some hardware troubleshooting tips for your PC's CD or DVD drive, which I refer to collectively as the *optical drive*.

Also refer to Chapter 7 for information on troubleshooting sound problems that might be related to the optical drive.

Is the drive dead?

You can easily determine whether an optical drive is dead: Does the tray eject? If not, the drive could be dead. When the drive has a light and the light isn't lit, it's another sure sign. But the only way to know for certain is to open the PC's case, as described in Chapter 8.

When the drive is getting power and the tray slides in and out, check the media. Is the disc okay? The easiest way to determine the answer is to try the disc in an optical drive that works. If the disc is okay and the drive doesn't recognize it, the drive is probably dead.

✦ In Windows XP, recordable optical drives may seem to vanish from the My Computer window after you uninstall CD/DVD recording software. That's because of a sloppy uninstallation. See this web page for information on how to address the issue:

        http://support.microsoft.com/kb/314060

✦ The good news is that optical drives are cheap and easy to replace. Again, see Chapter 8.

✦ The drive cannot read a disc that has been inserted upside down. Likewise, a nonrecordable drive cannot read blank discs.

A disk is stuck in the drive!

Whether the computer is on or off, you can easily eject a stuck disk. Look for the drive's "dimple" hole. Figure 4-5 helps you find the hole; it's a tiny, pin-size hole, found on the face of every optical drive.

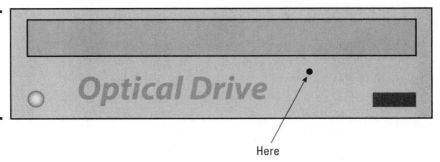

Figure 4-5: Where to find an optical drive's dimple hole.

Here

Insert a bent paper clip into the hole. Push! The drive tray pops out a bit. Then you can remove the disc.

Some PCs feature, on the front of the case, a plastic bezel that can obscure the dimple hole. In that case, you have to pop off the bezel to access the optical drive directly. Or, commonly, if you look closely, you can see a hole in the bezel through which you can access the optical drive's eject dimple hole.

The program doesn't install

When you install a new program, the theory goes that when you insert its optical disc into the computer, the program automatically installs. When it doesn't, follow these steps:

1. **Open the Computer or My Computer window.**

2. **Right-click the optical drive icon.**

3. **From the Shortcut menu, choose the command Install or Run Program.**

If the Install or Run Program command isn't available, choose AutoPlay instead.

The install or setup program on the disk should now run and install the software. If it still doesn't, choose the Open command in Step 3 or just double-click the optical drive icon. From the window that opens, locate an icon named `setup` or `install` and open it to begin installation.

✦ The optical drive isn't always drive D.

✦ Refer to Book II, Chapter 6 for more information on program installation problems.

AutoPlay issues

When you stick a disc into the optical drive, any number of things might happen. When the computer doesn't know what to do, it presents you with a list of options in the AutoPlay dialog box.

Software installation discs have built-in AutoPlay. A file named `autorun.inf` exists in the disc's root folder. It's a text file that Windows reads when the disc is inserted. The file contains instructions that describe which icon to use for the disc, as well as which program to automatically open when the disc is inserted.

When a disc without an `autorun.inf` file is inserted, the Windows AutoPlay function takes over. You've probably seen the dialog box displayed, as shown in Figure 4-6. Basically, you choose a disc type so that Windows can more properly display the information stored on the disc or so that Windows can deal with the disc's contents (music and video, for example).

Figure 4-6:
The typical
AutoPlay
dialog box.

You can customize the AutoPlay settings, creating preset options for various types of discs or controlling whether AutoPlay is used.

In Windows 7 and Windows Vista, configuring AutoPlay is done by carefully following these steps:

1. **Open the Control Panel.**

2. **Choose Hardware and Sound.**

3. **Choose AutoPlay.**

    You see a list of various media types, which Windows identifies for you
    when an optical disc is inserted into the PC's optical drive. Next to each
    media type is a list of actions to take.

4. **Choose an action to take for a specific media type.**

   For example, next to Audio CD you could choose the command Play Audio CD Using Windows Media Player from the button's pop-up list. Or, choose the command Rip Music from CD Using Windows Media Player to automatically copy all the music to your computer.

5. **Click the Save button to confirm your choices and close the AuotPlay window.**

In Windows XP, you control the AutoPlay feature by following these steps:

1. **Open the My Computer window.**

2. **Right-click the optical drive icon.**

3. **Choose Properties from the pop-up menu.**

4. **In the drive's Properties dialog box, click the AutoPlay tab.**

5. **Use the dialog box's drop-down list to choose a disc type.**

6. **Choose the action to take from the Actions area.**

7. **Click the OK button when you're done.**

The goal here is convenience: If you always rip your CDs into Media Player, choosing that AutoPlay option for all music CDs you insert into your PC saves you time.

✦ One AutoPlay option is Take No Action. When you choose it and insert a disc, the AutoPlay dialog box doesn't visually assault you.

✦ One disc type is Software and Games. If you choose the Take No Action item for this type of disc, your software doesn't automatically install.

✦ Another option is Ask Me Every Time or Prompt Me Each Time to Choose an Action. It's the opposite of the Take No Action option in that every time you insert a disc, you see the AutoPlay dialog box.

✦ The AutoRun command on the optical drive's shortcut menu automatically runs whichever program is specified in the `autorun.inf` file.

The drive doesn't record

To make your own optical disc, you need a PC that sports an optical drive that lets you record discs. When you don't have this gizmo, don't expect to be making many of your own discs.

The key to knowing whether your optical drive can record discs is to read the drive's faceplate. Recordable drives often have the word *recordable* or *recorder* on them. If not, you see the common R, +R, -R, or RW labels — or any variations — on the drive.

In Windows XP, you need to confirm that recording abilities have been activated for a recordable optical drive. Mind these steps:

1. **Open the My Computer window.**

2. **Right-click the Optical Drive icon.**

3. **Choose Properties from the shortcut menu.**

The drive's Properties dialog box appears.

4. **Click the Recording tab.**

You should see the dialog box shown in Figure 4-7. If you don't, the drive isn't recordable. Go to Step 6.

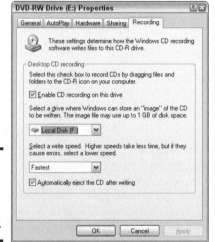

Figure 4-7:
Enabling
recording
goodness in
Windows XP.

5. **Place a check mark in the box next to Enable CD Recording on This Drive.**

6. **Click OK.**

If the drive still doesn't record discs, the drive itself may have a problem. See Chapter 8 for information on replacing a bum optical drive.

✦ When it's difficult to tell whether the drive is recordable, you can rely on the Device Manager to confirm it for you. By opening the DVD/CD-ROM Drives category, you can confirm that you have a CD-R/RW or DVD-R/RW by looking at the device's name. Refer to Chapter 7 for more instructions on using the Device Manager.

✦ For information on recording optical discs, refer to my book *PCs For Dummies*, available only in the fourth dimension.

The disc doesn't record

Optical discs come in many recordable flavors. Always ensure that you get the right disc for your drive. For example, a DL, or Dual Layer, disc cannot be recorded as a DL disc in a non-DL drive. If your recordable drive is older and doesn't recognize the RW format, don't buy RW discs.

In some cases, software might be specific about the type of disc you record to. For example, DVD-making software might prefer that you use the more compatible DVD-R format for a video rather than the more efficient DVD+R format.

 Some discs are duds. When a disc doesn't record, toss it out. Try another. If you end up tossing out all the discs, the problem is most likely with the drive and not the discs (which means that you need to untoss the discs.)

✦ Ensure that any optical disc recording software you're using is up-to-date. That way, you can eliminate any recording problems with older software.

✦ Most television DVD players read the DVD-R format and have trouble reading the DVD+R format. Also note that a DVD must be formatted for playing in a television DVD player; you cannot "play" a DVD with data on it.

On cleaning an optical drive

Before you resort to cleaning an optical drive, consider cleaning the disc: Simply wipe the disc with a damp cloth. Wipe from the center outward; don't wipe around the disc in a circle. If you have a special disc cleaning solution, use it in addition to any special disc cloth. The idea behind cleaning is to remove things that may interfere with the laser reading the disc but not scratch the disc by cleaning it.

Optical disc disposal

You can throw out an optical disc, but check with your local refuse company to see whether optical discs have a special classification. If so, dispose of the discs according to the proper methods.

Never burn a disc. It gives off toxic fumes. The fumes are also present when you microwave a disc, in case that thought has ever crossed your mind.

The most secure way to dispose of an optical disc is to shred it. Many common paper shredders feature an optical disc slot (that can also be used to shred old credit cards). Use a shredder when you're concerned about the disc contents landing in the wrong hands.

When the disc is still unreadable by the optical drive and the drive refuses to read other discs, it's time to clean the optical drive.

Long ago, as in the previous edition of this book, I believed that optical drive cleaners were hooey. Even so, I recently tried one on a laptop's optical drive as a last resort; the alternative was buying an expensive, external optical drive for the laptop or taking it into the shop. Anyway, after a quick spin of an optical drive cleaning disc, the drive worked flawlessly.

✦ Optical drive cleaning discs aren't cheap. Therefore:

✦ You don't need to buy an optical drive cleaning disc unless you're experiencing problems with your computer's optical drive.

Professional Data Recovery

One reason that few people back up their computer data is that they know professional data-recovery services exist. Similarly, the reason that many people back up is that they know how expensive those professional recovery services can be.

Yes, your data is important to you, but how much are you willing to spend to recover it? Big businesses and the government don't seem to mind paying hefty fees to recover data from damaged hard drives. Often times, fees start at $500 just to look at the drive, though the final tally can end up at $10,000 or more.

You have to consider two issues for using a professional data-recovery service: cost and time. Both issues are related, given the old adage "Time is money." In this case, the quicker the time, the more the money.

For an individual, I don't recommend using professional data-recovery services. The cost is just too prohibitive. And, I would never trust any bargain basement data-recovery service. Nope — just back up. Trust me.

Chapter 5: Pain in the Printer

In This Chapter

- ✔ **Understanding the printer**
- ✔ **Locating printer stuff in Windows**
- ✔ **Confirming the printer driver**
- ✔ **Canceling printing**
- ✔ **Dealing with output ugliness**
- ✔ **Unjamming**
- ✔ **Printing the page properly**
- ✔ **Doing envelopes**

A printer is part of your computer system and at the same time is its own, separate device. Indeed, today's printers are little computers in themselves, complete with the basics of computer science: input, output, storage, and processing. It's the stuff that computer-camp songs are made of.

The printer itself is best suited to a specific task: Get information from the digital world onto paper in the real world. When this task falls short, turn to this chapter for some printer troubleshooting.

Marginal Printer Stuff

For good reason, a computer isn't sold with a printer in the same box: Computers and printers hate each other. No, it's stronger than that: My guess is that the printer and computer secretly despise each other — like they were once married or shared a political debate program on a cable news channel.

The result of your digital labors is the printed copy of your stuff. This section covers some of the places in Windows where printing takes place, or where it *should* take place when everything goes well.

Amazing printers

If you're using an older printer with your computer, you're missing out on some of the latest tricks. Although older printers share the fancy displays and full-text messages of today's printers, newer models often sport one of those handy Cancel buttons. Nothing beats that.

The printer connects to your PC with a USB cable. Older printers use a specific printer cable called, remarkably, a *printer cable*. If you have an older printer, ensure that you get a *bidirectional* printer cable, which is more compatible with the printer's features, allowing communications between the printer and computer.

Printers also plug into the wall.

Most printers feature power management abilities, just like your computer does. The printer can be left on all the time and doesn't consume an abundance of electricity. Still, I recommend turning off the printer when you don't plan to use it for great lengths of time.

✦ Yes, there are wireless printers. They can be network printers, which plug into computer networks just like modems or other computers. There are also Bluetooth printers. Troubleshooting these printers involves not only the printer hardware and Windows but also wireless and network communications. That's three things to troubleshoot, not the normal, annoying two.

✦ *All-in-one* printers — the gizmos that combine printing with scanning, copying, and faxing — are popular, though they add extra items for hardware troubleshooting. For example, when the fax component stops working and you have to have it repaired, you then lose its printing and scanning abilities too — unless you go buy a new printer.

✦ Get to know your printer. Discover how the paper goes in: face down or face up, and top edge first or top edge last or whatever. Often, a set of icons on the paper tray describe the paper's orientation. Make a note of it.

✦ If you have an older or a cheaper printer without a text display, know what its lights mean. Perhaps even label the lights with a Sharpie so that you can remember. English beats international icon hieroglyphics every day!

✦ Always have plenty of paper and ink available for the printer.

✦ Some printers feature an *on-line* or a *select* button. It controls communications between the printer and the computer. When the button is on, the printer is ready to print. Taking the printer offline or deselecting the button means that the printer is on and can be configured (or fixed) but nothing can be printed.

Printing in Windows

Because Windows handles all printing duties for you, the printing procedure works basically the same way in every program: Press Ctrl+P to summon the Print dialog box, as shown in Figure 5-1. If need be, adjust settings in the dialog box; otherwise, just click the Print button to print. Or, you can click the Print toolbar button to quickly print a document.

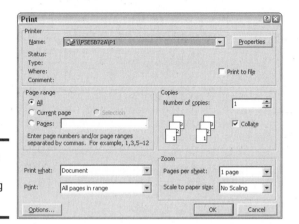

Figure 5-1:
A typical
Print dialog
box.

The printer must be on and ready to print and have plenty of paper and ink for the printing process to be successful.

Here are some general printer notes:

✦ Save paper! Use the Print Preview command before printing. Proof your document. Print only when everything is ready to print.

✦ The Range option allows you to set the starting and ending pages. Some Print dialog boxes (refer to the one shown in Figure 5-1) offer a more flexible plan: You can specify individual pages or a range or a combination of both. Separate individual pages with commas; a range of pages, with a hyphen. For example:

    2,4,9-16

This range prints pages 2 and 4 and then all pages 9 through 16.

✦ When a Selection option is available, only the text or items selected in the document are printed.

✦ Some printers can print on both sides of a sheet of paper — *duplex printing.* When this type isn't available, print all odd pages first. Reinsert the pages in the printers face down, and then print all even pages.

✦ If the stack of paper comes out of the printer in the wrong order (the first page is on the bottom), consider printing in *reverse* order. An option to do so can generally be found in the Printer's Properties dialog box; click the Properties button in the Print dialog box.

✦ The Print to File option is dubious. Rather than send information to the printer, you save the same raw data in a file. There isn't much you can do with the file, sadly. Rather than have you use Print to File, I recommend using the Adobe Acrobat Writer program to create a PDF file. You can also use the Microsoft XPS format, though it's not as popular.

✦ Acrobat Writer is a different program from the widely available and free Acrobat Reader program. See `www.adobe.com/acrobat` for more information.

✦ Color options are often available, but not in the Print dialog box itself: Click the Properties button in the Print dialog box and then use the printer's Properties dialog box to set color options.

✦ Printing a color document in grayscale (no color information) saves color ink. It's a good trick to use for drafts.

✦ When the Collate option is used, multiple documents print one after another. When documents aren't collated, all the first pages print first, and then the second pages, and so on.

✦ The infamous printer error message `PC Load Letter` means that the printer is out of paper. `PC` in this case stands for Paper Cartridge, and `Load Letter` means to load letter-size paper.

Using the Page Setup dialog box

The Print dialog box (refer to Figure 5-1) is where settings are made that affect how things are printed, but it's not the only place to look for printer problems. Another location is the Page Setup dialog box, as shown in Figure 5-2.

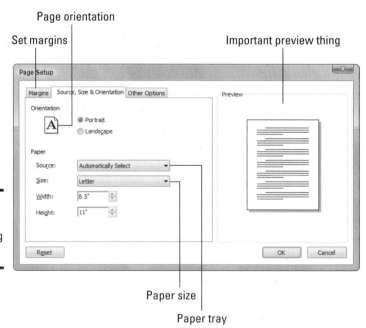

Figure 5-2:
The Page Setup dialog box.

Printing Windows

You can print documents and graphics by using applications in Windows, but what about printing Windows itself? That's a sticky point: Windows own folder windows lack a Print command. If you want to print a list of files in a folder, you have to use a third-party utility or the command prompt to do so.

To print the desktop, press the Print Screen key. It sends a snapshot of the desktop to the Clipboard. Similarly, Alt+Print Screen captures the front (or top) window to the Clipboard. You can then paste that image into any application that accepts graphics, such as Windows Paint. From there, you can print the image.

To access the Page Setup dialog box, choose the File⇨Page Setup command. In certain newer Windows programs, the Page Setup command may be found on the File tab, which is the leftmost tab above the toolbar. The Page Setup command may be on the Print or Publish submenu on the File tab.

Though the Page Setup box may appear to have nothing to do with printing, it has a lot to do with how the page you print is formatted, including some items you might think would fall into the Print dialog box but do not:

Margins: To set your document's margins, you use the Page Setup dialog box. In the Page Setup dialog box example shown in Figure 5-2, you click the Margins tab to specify how far out the text is displayed on the page.

Paper size: When printing on a sheet of paper of a special size, you must use the Page Setup dialog box to set the paper size.

Paper orientation: Whether printing longways (landscape) or normal (portrait), you choose the page orientation in the Page Setup dialog box.

Paper source: When your printer has more than one paper tray, the source is chosen in the Page Setup dialog box, not in the Print dialog box.

Printing is the mechanical job of putting a document on paper with ink. The duties of the Page Setup dialog box are document formatting, not printing.

- ✦ In some applications, the Page Setup command on the File menu might be titled Document Setup.

- ✦ Sometimes you access the Page Setup dialog box by pressing a button — for example, in the Print dialog box.

- ✦ When you choose another paper size in the Page Setup dialog box, don't forget to stock your printer with the new paper size. The printer's display may remind you of the paper swap, or it may not.

✦ Not every printer is capable of printing to the full edge of a piece of paper. Many printers cannot print within a half-inch of the paper's edge. Some printers can go farther, but usually one edge of the page is necessary to help pull the sheet through the printer. On that one edge, you must have a margin.

Dealing with printers

Just as Windows has a location for showing storage devices in your computer (see Chapter 4), it also sports a spot for showing which printers are connected to and used by your computer. For storage devices, the location is the Computer or My Computer window. For printers, the location has different names, depending on your version of Windows.

In Windows 7, the location is the Devices and Printers window. This window, shown in Figure 5-3, lists all devices attached to and used by your computer, including storage media, monitors, input devices (keyboard and mouse), and printers. The printers are grouped separately, as shown in Figure 5-3, which is the standard configuration for the Devices and Printers window.

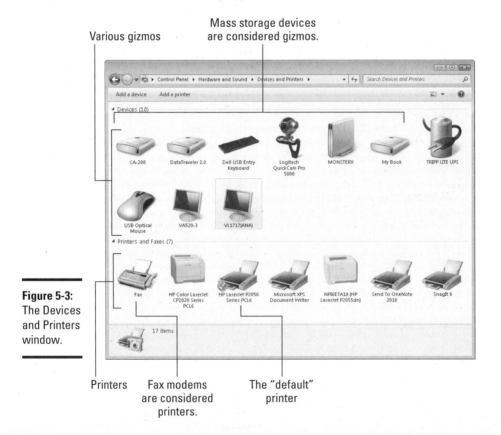

Various gizmos

Mass storage devices are considered gizmos.

Figure 5-3: The Devices and Printers window.

Printers   Fax modems are considered printers.   The "default" printer

To get to the Devices and Printers window, choose Devices and Printers from the Start button menu. Or, from the Control Panel, choose the link View Devices and Printers, found beneath the Hardware and Sound heading in the main Control Panel window.

In Windows Vista, printer activity has its locus in a window named, logically, Printers. The window contains a handy toolbar with buttons, as shown in Figure 5-4. In Windows XP, the window is called Printers and Faxes, and the relevant printer commands appear on the taskbar on the left side of the window.

Toolbar   "Show more" button

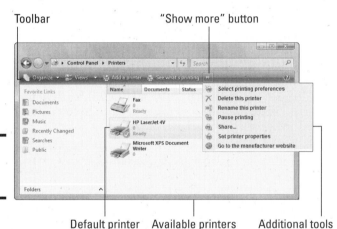

Figure 5-4:
The Printer
window.

Default printer Available printers Additional tools

The buttons and menu, or the various printer tasks, appear in the Printers window only when a specific printer is selected.

The easiest way to summon the Printers window in Windows Vista or Windows XP is by choosing either the Printers or Printers and Faxes command (respectively) from the Start menu. Either command is available, however, only when the Start menu is configured to show it. Follow these steps:

1. **Right-click the Start button and choose Properties.**

2. **In the Taskbar and Start Menu Properties, click the Customize button.**

3. **In Windows XP, click the Advanced tab.**

4. **Scroll the list and put a check mark by Printers (in Windows Vista) or Printers and Faxes (in Windows XP).**

5. **Click OK and then click OK again to close the open dialog boxes.**

If you desire a desktop shortcut icon for the Printers window in Windows Vista or Windows XP, open the Control Panel and right-click either the Printers or Printers and Faxes icon. From the pop-up menu that appears, choose Create Shortcut. In Windows XP, click Yes to confirm that you want a shortcut icon placed on the desktop.

✦ You use the Printers window to install a new printer on your PC. Use the Add a Printer button or link and then work the steps in the wizard to configure the printer.

✦ Some printers (hello, HP!) require that you run special software to install them, and not just use the Add a Printer button in Windows. The truth is that you can go either way. If you choose not to use the special software that comes with the printer, however, you miss out on some printer features that Windows alone cannot access, such as detecting ink levels or being able to print on both sides of a sheet of paper.

✦ You also use the Printer window to remove printers from your computer. Although you physically unplug the printer, you remove the Printer icon by deleting it from the Printers window: Click to select the icon and then press the Delete key on the keyboard.

✦ If your printer doesn't appear in the window, it may not have been installed or it could have been accidentally removed. Check the printer's USB cable and power cord.

✦ A network printer must be connected to the network, turned on, online, stocked with paper and ink, and ready to print before it works as a printer.

✦ I recommend *not* removing the printer drivers (software) when you disconnect a printer. That way, the job of reinstalling the printer later is easier.

✦ For more information on adding and setting up a printer, refer to my book *PCs For Dummies*, first published on the planet Earth 21 years before the Zaglaxian invasion.

Checking the printer driver

Like most things in a computer, your printer requires both hardware and software to function in a sane manner. The printer itself is the hardware. The software is a *printer driver* that controls the printer, helping Windows talk to the printer and cajole it into printing things in a pleasing manner.

The printer driver is installed when you first set up or add the printer. To check on the printer driver, follow these steps:

1. **Open the Printers window or Printers and Faxes window where printers dwell.**

It can be the Devices and Printers window in Windows 7, the Printers window in Windows Vista, or the Printers and Faxes window in Windows XP.

2. **Right-click a printer icon.**

3a. **In Windows 7, choose Printer Properties from the menu.**

Windows 7 also has a Properties command for your printer, but it's not the command you want.

3b. **In Windows Vista and Windows XP, choose Properties from the short-cut menu.**

4. **In the printer's Properties dialog box, click the Advanced tab.**

The Advanced tab in the printer's Properties dialog box lists the current driver associated with the printer, similar to the one shown in Figure 5-5.

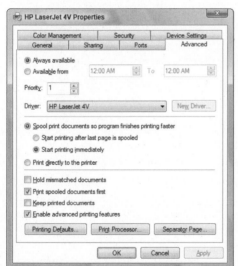

Figure 5-5:
Checking on the printer driver.

The name of the printer driver should match your printer. If not, you can reset the driver by choosing another one from the Driver drop-down list button in the middle of the dialog box.

5. **Close the printer's Properties dialog box when you're done.**

If the driver is all screwed up, the best solution is to delete the printer: Choose its icon in the window and choose Delete This Printer from the toolbar or task list. Then use the Add As Printer button or link to add the printer again.

Changing or updating a printer driver is one surefire way to cure those frustrating, otherwise-impossible-to-solve printer problems.

Working with print jobs

When you print something in Windows, you're creating a *print job*. That's a good, general name for anything you print: Printing is handled by the operating system and not by individual programs. Therefore, what you print becomes a duty, or "job," for the operating system, and not for the application you used to create the document.

Print jobs are associated with whichever printer you're using. In Windows, to view print jobs, you open the icon for the printer you're using; the icon is found the appropriate window, as described in the earlier section "Dealing with printers."

By opening the printer's window, you see any current or pending print jobs, as shown in Figure 5-6.

Figure 5-6:
Print jobs
waiting in
the queue.

Print jobs don't wait in a line. No, they wait in a *queue*. In fact, the term *printer queue* is an ancient computer term, dating back to before the French and Indian war. I believe Benjamin Franklin coined it.

You can adjust items in the queue or cancel or pause printing.

To adjust an item, simply drag its icon up or down. That changes the order in which the item prints.

To pause or cancel an item, click to select it. Then from the Document menu, choose Pause or Cancel, respectively. Other items on the Document menu include Resume, which continues printing a paused job, and Restart, which can be used to reprint a document from the beginning.

Canceling a print job

About the only real reason to use a printer's window is to cancel something sent to the printer. Sadly, the Print window, covered in the preceding section, isn't effective for this task: You probably won't see a full printer queue window. Today's printers pack lots of memory, so the jobs slip off into the printer's memory rather than wait in the computer's memory.

If you see a print job looming and you want to cancel it, choose Document⇨ Cancel. Even so, doing this doesn't unsend any information inside the printer's memory. Some printers can hold dozens of pages, so canceling a print job may not immediately abort the printing. That can be frustrating.

To best cancel a print job, go to the printer itself. If your printer sports a Cancel button, use it. It stops the printing almost immediately.

For a printer that lacks a Cancel button, try taking the printer off-line: Press the On-line or Select button. A few lines or pages may continue to print, but eventually the printer stops. Remove the last sheet of paper if necessary. Then reset the printer or, if the printer lacks a Reset button, turn it off.

By resetting or turning off the printer, you erase any remnants of a document in memory. That way, the unwanted print job doesn't continue to print when you put the printer back on-line.

Using the Printing Troubleshooter

The Windows Help system contains a number of useful troubleshooting tools, which can often guide you to a quick solution by asking step-by-step questions.

In Windows 7, the Printer Troubleshooter is attached to every printer in the Devices and Printers window, courtesy of a pop-up menu. Follow these steps to troubleshoot a printer in Windows 7:

1. **Open the Devices and Printers window.**

   Directions are found earlier in this chapter.

2. **Right-click on the icon representing the printer you want to troubleshoot.**

   It can be any printer in the Devices and Printers window, though if Windows 7 detects a printing problem, it flags the printer with a yellow alert icon, as shown in Figure 5-7.

3. **Choose the Troubleshoot command.**

4. **Work your way through the Troubleshooter, answering questions and such in an effort to resolve the issue.**

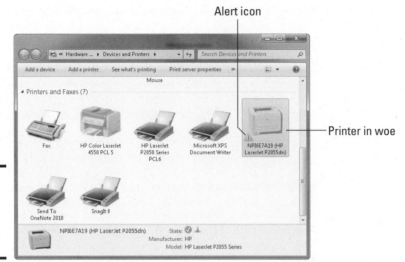

Figure 5-7:
A printer
in need
of trouble-
shooting.

To visit the Printing Troubleshooter in Windows Vista, follow these steps:

1. **Pop up the Start menu and choose Help and Support.**

2. **In the Windows Help and Support window, type** troubleshoot printer problems **and press Enter.**

3. **Choose the first item in the list.**

   The item is titled Troubleshoot Printer Problems.

4. **Work through the troubleshooter by choosing the questions that apply to you and then following the answers.**

In Windows XP, obey these steps:

1. **Open the Printers and Faxes window.**

2. **From the links on the left side of the window, choose Troubleshoot Printing.**

3. **Follow the steps in the wizard to help solve your printing conundrum.**

The wizards are generally good, but also refer to the later section in this chapter, "General Printer Problems."

Visiting the Print Management window

Windows 7 and Windows Vista feature the Print Management console, shown in Figure 5-8. This central location for printing has more features than the Printers window, but it's not really a secret or powerful place that only the gurus know about.

Figure 5-8: The Print Management console in Windows Vista.

To visit the Print Management console, obey these steps:

1. **Open the Control Panel window.**

2. **Choose System and Security.**

3. **Choose Administrative Tools.**

4. **Open the Print Management item.**

5. **In Windows Vista, you click Continue or type the administrator's password to continue.**

   The Print Management console can quickly help you reference jobs that your PC is printing on multiple printers: Choose the Printers with Jobs item on the left side of the console window. You can control multiple jobs across all printers by canceling or pausing those jobs in bulk in the Print Management console window.

6. **Close the Print Management console window when you're done.**

The sad truth of the Print Management console is that there's little you can do there unless you're printing a lot of stuff.

General Printer Problems

The first step in diagnosing printer problems is to determine whether the problem lies with the printer itself or with the application you're using. Generally speaking, the Print Preview command helps you determine whether your software is up to snuff or the printer has gone hinkey. The information in this section also helps determine the source of the problem and potential solutions.

Print Preview lies

Yes, I wrote that Print Preview can help determine whether the problem is with the printer or specific to your software. Although this statement is true for the most part, in some situations the Print Preview command *lies*.

First, remember that your printer cannot print on one edge of the paper. For the other three edges, the margin may be all the way up to the edge of the page, or it might be a half an inch or so away from the edge. The fourth edge, however, is required by the printer to feed the paper. Regardless of what Print Preview says, you can't print on that edge of the page. The solution: Draw in the document's margins.

Second, some features have problems being implemented properly. I'm thinking specifically of Microsoft Word's annoying page border feature. The problem is with Word, not with the printer, but it's difficult to determine because the Print Preview window shows the border present.

To fix the page border on a page in Word, set the border from the *text*, not from the edge of the paper.

Finally, ensure that you haven't set your application or the printer itself to print in *Draft mode*. This mode is used for quickly printing a document without fancy text formatting or graphics. If you need these types of features, disable Draft mode in your application or in the printer's Properties dialog box.

Wrong colors, streaks, madness

For the content of your document or even its formatting, when the printed page looks ugly, chances are that the printer itself is to blame. The chief motivator of the ugly printing demon is your printer's ink supply.

Weird or faded colors indicate that a color ink cartridge is low. Some printers inform you of this fact, and others don't. Sadly, if you use an ink cartridge that contains multiple ink colors, you must replace the entire thing. Yep, that's how they make their money!

Dark streaks down the page might indicate that ink or another gunky substance got on the printer's paper-feeding mechanism. But for a laser printer, the streaks often mean that the toner is old. Replace the toner cartridge.

✦ Replace the ink cartridges in an inkjet printer when they're empty. Obey your printer! Using ink cartridges that are too low on ink can damage some printers.

✦ It's possible to extend toner life in a laser printer. The first time you see the Toner Low warning, remove the cartridge and gently rock it from side to side. Replace the cartridge and the warning message should no longer appear. When it does, replace the cartridge at once!

Weird characters on the page

Unless you're writing science fiction and the weird characters are part of your narrative, the characters I refer to as *weird* appear to be random letters, numbers, or symbols that appear on printouts. Typically, the characters appear at the top of every page. They may be the same on all pages, or different.

First, confirm that you didn't screw up the document's header by using the Print Preview command. Some documents print with an automatic header. For example, your Web browser or the Windows Notepad program may automatically insert a header in your document. But its text doesn't exactly look *weird*.

Second, update the printer software driver. Refer to the section "Checking the printer driver," earlier in this chapter, to confirm that the proper printer driver is chosen. If not, directions in that section explain how to delete and then add your printer again — hopefully, with the proper driver.

You can also visit the printer manufacturer's Web site to check for new or updated driver software.

Page after page of gobbledygook

I've seen a printer spew endless pages of nonsense — and I'm not just speaking about the time I did consulting work for a particular political cause, either. I'm talking pages of junk. It often happens for one of two reasons.

The first reason is that printing was somehow interrupted. The stream of data flowing from the computer to the printer had a hiccup, so the printer is misinterpreting the information. The solution is to stop the printer, cancel the print job, and then restart the printer and resend the print job. (Print again.)

The second reason for seeing the junk may be an improper printer driver. See the section "Checking the printer driver," earlier in this chapter, for instructions on how to check the printer driver and change it to a better one.

Printer jams

The number-one cause of printer jams is, of course, paper. Paperless printers seldom jam, but, sadly, they just don't sell well. You probably have a printer that uses real paper, so it may jam someday.

The first solution to a printer jam is to find the jam and remove the paper. If the printer is smart enough to tell you where the jam occurred, heed its advice. Otherwise, follow the paper's path from tray to output, by opening various printer hatches and covers to find the errant sheet. Remove the jammed sheet and then resume printing.

◆ If the page that jammed needs to be printed again, use the Print dialog box to print only the single sheet that jammed. See the earlier section "Printing in Windows" for details.

◆ Some printers may not recover from a paper jam until you open and close the cover.

◆ I don't recommend turning off a printer to recover from a jam; when you do, you often have to reprint the entire document.

◆ Some printers are smart and recover well from a jam, reprinting the page that was jammed.

◆ Sometimes the printer says it's jammed but has merely experienced a misfeed from the paper tray. Remove the paper and fan it out, to puff some air between the pages. Then try printing again.

◆ Avoid using overly thick paper in your printer, because it tends to jam.

◆ If you must use thick paper, check to ensure that your printer doesn't have a straight-path option, where the paper simply moves from the front of the printer to the back without making too many turns.

Page orientation

Consider yourself fortunate when the printer has on its paper tray a little icon or hint that explains how the page feeds through the printer. This icon comes in especially handy when printing on letterhead or the back side of a sheet of paper. Figure 5-9 explains how the icons work, though the icons you see on your printer may be subtly different.

If your printer lacks this informational icon, feel free to create your own. Or, write a hint and tape it to the printer. For example, on my laser printer, where I print checks, it says, on the paper tray, "Checks go in face down, top toward you." (That's the lower right example from Figure 5-9.)

Similar icons can be made to illustrate how an envelope feeds into the printer. Unlike when you use a sheet of paper, you have *eight* ways to insert an envelope because your printer may feed the envelope longways or "end-ways."

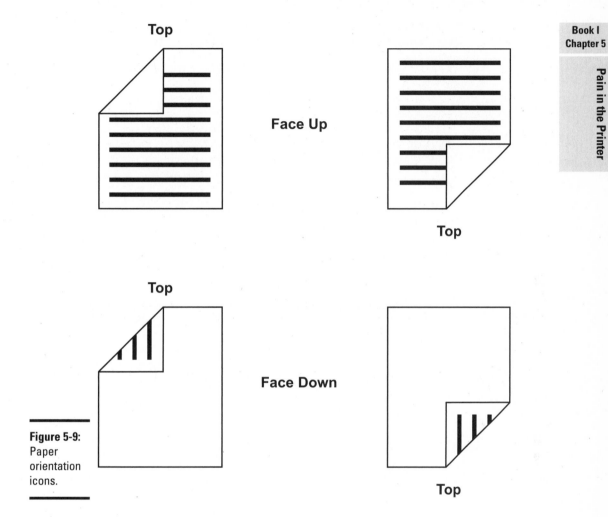

Figure 5-9:
Paper
orientation
icons.

Envelopes must eat, too

Most printers have an envelope slot, feeder, or tray. The better printers even let you stack up envelopes for mass mailings. Finding the tray is the first step in printing an envelope. The second step is to ensure that the envelope is properly oriented.

If the printer has icons for envelope orientation, heed them. If not, refer to the preceding section and create your own envelope icons. (Curiously, the envelope icon on my printer is backward, so I made my own icon with a Sharpie.)

When the printer lacks icons, print a sample envelope and see where the address shows up. This trick helps you determine how to orient the envelope, though you may have to complete one or two more sample runs before you get the orientation just right.

After working through envelope orientation, your next task is getting your software to print an envelope. It's not as difficult as it sounds: An envelope is merely a sheet of paper; one of a specific size. Use the Page Setup dialog box to choose the envelope size from the list of paper sizes. *Ta-da!* Just format the envelope "document" accordingly and then print.

✦ High-end printers often feature an envelope-feeder option, which allows a massive number of envelopes to be shot through the printer at a time.

✦ Some applications feature an Envelope command, which can be used to print a single envelope or more. In Microsoft Word, use the Envelopes button in the Create area on the Mailings tab. (In older versions of Word, you use the Tools⇨Envelopes and Labels command and click the Envelopes tab in the dialog box.)

✦ Those peel-and-close envelopes work best in a laser printer. Because a laser printer uses heat to fuse the toner to the paper, the heat can also seal an empty envelope.

Chapter 6: Seeing Trouble

In This Chapter

✓ Understanding the video system

✓ Getting info about the display adapter

✓ Using a second monitor

✓ Swapping out parts

✓ Adjusting the display

✓ Installing new driver software

✓ Using the video troubleshooter

*I*t's surprising to some people that the monitor is not the computer. I can see where the confusion comes from: You look at the monitor, you manipulate things on the screen. It's an important gizmo. Even so, the monitor is merely an output device, a peripheral part of the computer system. As the computer's face, and the PC's primary output device, the monitor must be kept in tiptop condition, and you must know what to do when this most important peripheral fails to do its job.

The PC Graphics System

The monitor is only one part of your PC's graphics system. It's the most important part as far as your eyeballs are concerned because you see the monitor. What you *don't* see, however, is the most important part: the *display adapter*. This section explains what these terms mean and when to use them. Knowing these terms is an important first step to troubleshooting the PC's graphics system.

Terms to describe what you see

When speaking about that TV-like thing connected to your computer, you use three words: *monitor, screen*, and *display*. Here's how and when to use them:

Monitor: A monitor is a chunk of computer hardware. It's the gizmo that displays images created by the computer's display adapter, which is located inside the console.

Screen: The screen is the part of the monitor that displays an image: text, graphics, Windows desktop, games. All this information shows up on the screen part of the monitor.

Display: The display is the image you see on the screen. For example, the display may show you the Windows desktop, some icons, and a window with a picture of Megan Fox frolicking in the surf.

Here are some more points that may help clarify the differences:

✦ When you clean the monitor, you're cleaning the entire thing: base, back, top, and screen — unless you're a teenage boy, in which case you clean only the top part.

✦ Cleaning the screen doesn't clean the display; by cleaning the screen, you're removing dust, fingerprints, and sneeze globs. See Book III, Chapter 4 for information on cleaning an LCD monitor; refer to Book VI, Chapter 4 for information on cleaning a CTR (glass screen) monitor.

✦ When you clean the display, you're basically clearing off windows, icons, and other graphical information. It's a software thing.

✦ Yes, the nerds like to say "Clear the screen." They really mean "Clear the display."

Graphical system overview

The key to understanding, and therefore troubleshooting, computer graphics is to know that the brains of the operation lie in the *display adapter,* which is inside the computer console. Figure 6-1 illustrates a typical PC graphics system.

The image is generated inside the PC by using the display adapter hardware. The image is then sent to the monitor, which displays the image. Technically, all the action takes place inside the console, with the display adapter. That gizmo determines the graphics abilities of your computer.

The monitor's main contribution to your PC's graphics system is its screen size. It also has some technical aspects, which are covered later in this chapter.

✦ Figure 6-1 shows the PC's display adapter as an expansion card, which is common for high-end graphics. Most PCs, however, use a display adapter that's built into the computer's motherboard.

✦ The display adapter might also be called the *graphics adapter.* This term hearkens back to an era when PC monitors displayed mostly text. To display graphics, you had to buy special graphics hardware: the graphics adapter.

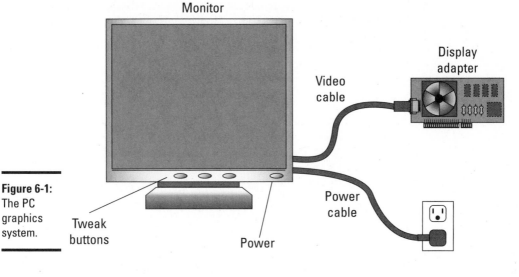

Figure 6-1:
The PC
graphics
system.

The display adapter

The only visual part of the display adapter you see on your PC is the spot where the monitor's video cable plugs in. Well, if you have a translucent computer console, you might be able to see the display adapter inside. Regardless, the two common types of video connectors are illustrated in Figure 6-2: VGA and DVI.

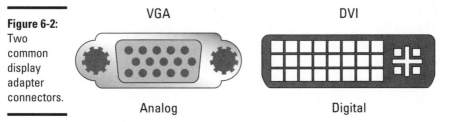

Figure 6-2:
Two
common
display
adapter
connectors.

Other information about the display adapter must be gathered from within Windows. You can look in two places: the Adapter's Properties dialog box, which is covered in the next section, and the Device Manager, covered elsewhere in this minibook.

✦ The best way to ensure that you're properly using your PC's display adapter is to keep its software (the device driver) up-to-date. See the section "Updating drivers," later in this chapter.

✦ DVI stands for Digital Visual Interface. It's also called the *digital* connector.

✦ The DVI connector shown in Figure 6-2 is a *female* connector. The male connector (found on the video cable) may not have a pin for every hole in the female connector. No, the pins aren't missing: There are several types of DVI connector, by design. The female connector accepts every type of DVI male connector and uses the differences to help the hardware identify and properly use the monitor.

✦ A mini-DVI connector is also often found on laptop computers. See Book III for more information.

✦ Some monitors accept a signal by using an HDMI (High-Definition Multimedia Interface) connector. These monitors also double as TV sets and are typically large and expensive.

✦ Other monitor interfaces exist as well, such as Display Port.

✦ VGA stands for Video Gate Array, and commonly (though incorrectly), Video Graphics Adapter.

✦ The VGA connector might also be known as the *analog* video connector.

✦ The VGA connector is similar in size to the old PC serial port. Note that the VGA connector, however, sports 15 holes rather than 9.

✦ Adapters are available for connecting VGA and DVI monitors to DVI and VGA adapters, respectively. A bonus with the DVI-to-VGA adapter is that it might also let you easily attach a second monitor to your PC. See the section "That second-monitor thing," later in this chapter.

Display adapter info

Video performance is based on two factors. The first is the graphics processor. A nice, beefy graphics processing unit (GPU) makes your PC's graphics shine. A nice, 3D physics engine makes all the difference when playing games.

The second factor that affects the PC's video system is the amount of dedicated video memory available. A display adapter with 256MB of video memory is a good baseline for computer games. More memory makes things better, but the cost also comes into play: More memory is expensive, and unless your PC has a beefy GPU and a 3D physics engine to help out, more memory isn't worth it.

Sadly, both the GPU and video memory are factors you cannot change after buying the graphics card. You can replace a graphics card, but rarely can you upgrade an existing card the way you can, say, add memory to your PC.

To discover which type of display adapter is in your PC, as well as how much memory it sports, you view the display adapter's Properties dialog box. You have various ways to get to that dialog box, depending on which version of Windows you have.

In Windows 7, view the display adapter's information by following these steps:

1. **Right-click the desktop.**

2. **Choose Screen Resolution.**

3. **In the Screen Resolution window, click the link Advanced Settings.**

Information about the display adapter is shown in the Properties dialog box, similar to Figure 6-3.

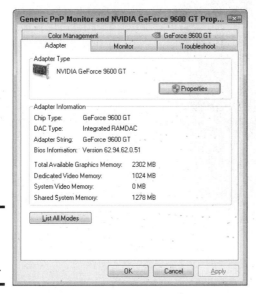

Figure 6-3:
Display adapter information.

To view some basic information about your PC's display adapter hardware in Windows Vista, abide by these steps:

1. **Right-click the desktop and choose Personalize from the shortcut menu.**

2. **Choose Display Settings in the Personalization window.**

The Display Settings dialog box appears.

3. **Click the Advanced Settings button.**

The display adapter's Properties dialog box is shown.

4. **If necessary, click the Adapter tab.**

The display adapter's information appears, looking a lot like Figure 6-3.

For Windows XP, follow these steps to see information about your PC's display adapter:

1. **Right-click the desktop and choose Properties from the pop-up menu.**
2. **In the Display Properties dialog box, click the Settings tab.**
3. **Click the Advanced button.**
4. **In the display adapter's Properties dialog box, click the Adapter tab.**

The information that's displayed looks similar to the dialog box shown in Figure 6-3, but some of the more detailed information is missing.

Although the dialog box doesn't say whether the display adapter sports a GPU or 3D physics engine, it tells you an important piece of information: the name of the adapter. In Figure 6-3, it's NVIDIA GeForce 9600 GT. This information comes into play when updating graphics drivers, as covered later in this chapter. More revealing, however, is the video memory information displayed in the dialog box.

In Figure 6-3, the adapter has 2302MB of video memory available. That's a total figure: 1024MB (1 gigabyte) of video memory dwells directly on the adapter card. That's a good thing. The rest, 1278MB of video memory, is shared with the main computer memory.

Close the dialog box and any other open windows when you're done absorbing the information.

✦ You see the least measure of performance from a video adapter that shares all its memory with the computer's main memory. For basic computer use, however, that's okay: Beyond e-mail, word processing, and the Internet, you don't need truly beefy graphics to run a PC.

✦ In Windows XP, a display adapter that shows 0MB or another low value is doubtlessly sharing main memory. If you want better video, you need to upgrade with a new display adapter.

✦ A great improvement in the visual presentation of video games can be had by replacing the PC's display adapter with a newer model that sports at least 256MB of video memory. (More memory is better.) Refer to Chapter 8 for information on replacing a video adapter.

The monitor

The PC's monitor merely does what the display adapter tells it to do, but I'm not implying that the monitor is lacking in smarts. Fortunately, most of the stuff the monitor does is automatic, such as self-adjusting to whichever resolution the display adapter demands.

The monitor sports two tails: one for power and the other to connect to the computer — specifically, to the display adapter.

There are two flavors of monitor: LCD and CRT. The LCD is now more popular because of its size and because it's flat and lightweight. It also consumes less power. CRT monitors — the older, bulkier glass monitors — might still be around, but they aren't that popular any more.

On the monitor, you find a power switch plus a series of adjustment buttons. Sometimes the buttons are real, as in physical buttons you press, but some monitors feature touch controls, where you simply touch part of the monitor to turn it off or on or to activate a feature.

Most monitors sport four adjustment buttons, which are used in combination to help manipulate an onscreen menu. Using the menu is covered in the section "Adjusting the monitor," later in this chapter.

A monitor is gauged by its size. As on a television set, the monitor's size is measured diagonally on the screen. In addition to its diagonal size, the monitor's aspect ratio is used to determine the relationship between the screen's horizontal and vertical sides. Figure 6-4 helps you understand the ideas behind monitor size and aspect ratio.

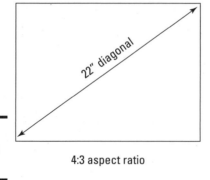

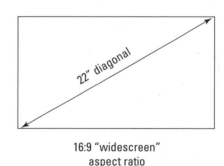

Figure 6-4:
Measuring
a monitor.

4:3 aspect ratio

16:9 "widescreen"
aspect ratio

Here are some additional, trivial details about a computer monitor, without getting too technical:

Backlit: An extra light on LCD monitors that makes the screen brighter. Can also be called a *backlight.*

Contrast ratio: The difference between the monitor's brightest white and darkest black. Some monitors get extra points for showing truly rich blacks.

Dot pitch: The distance between a monitor's pixels as measured in millimeters (mm). The closer the distance, and the smaller the dot pitch value, the sharper the image on the monitor. A relationship exists between the dot pitch and screen size as far as resolution is concerned.

Luminance: The monitor's brightness.

Refresh rate: The number of times per second that the monitor's image is displayed. The refresh rate is measured in hertz, which is why you may see the term displayed on the screen when the monitor changes resolution. Refresh rate might also be referred to as *frequency*.

Resolution: Images displayed on a monitor using tiny, colored dots, or *pixels*. The monitor displays images by using a given number of pixels horizontally and vertically, which is referred to as the *screen resolution.* The resolution is set by the display adapter and controlled via software (in Windows).

Viewing angle: The angle that determines how well the monitor can be seen when you're not staring straight at it, which is an angle of 0 degrees; an important concept for LCD monitors. The closer the viewing angle is to 180 degrees, the easier it is to see the monitor.

One key issue with monitors is *glare,* or the reflection of light off the monitor and into your eyeballs. The best way to reduce glare is to position the monitor so that bright lights aren't reflected on the screen. Don't compute with your back to a bright window. When you can't move the monitor or remove the glare, buy an antiglare screen for the monitor.

+ Another monitor type is *plasma*, though it's less trendy for computers than it is for large, widescreen televisions.

+ Pixel is a combination of the words *pic*ture *el*ement. It's the smallest dot of color that can be displayed on a monitor. Images on the screen are composed of thousands of individual pixels.

+ LCD monitors may have a limited set of resolutions they can adapt to. For example, the monitor may accept resolutions of only 1280 x 1024 or 1600 x 1200 pixels. Other resolutions may not render properly and can damage the monitor. The only way to know for certain is to check the documentation that comes with the monitor.

+ LCD stands for liquid crystal display.

+ CRT stands for cathode ray tube.

+ CRT monitors are still preferred by graphic designers. That's because the analog nature of the CRT monitor better reproduces colors that match the real world (because the CRT monitor is analog, not digital).

✦ Aspect ratios other than 4:3 and 16:9 are used, though they're not as common.

✦ A widescreen monitor doesn't share the same amount of screen real estate as a traditional 4:3 computer monitor. Despite identical diagonal measurements, a monitor with a 4:3 aspect ratio has more square inches of screen space than the widescreen monitor at the same diagonal screen size. That's one reason why 4:3 monitors are a bit more expensive than the widescreen versions (and why monitor manufacturers push the widescreen format).

✦ Some monitors feature dual inputs. For example, the inputs allow a single monitor to be used with two computers or perhaps to input two different types of signals. A problem with this type of monitor is that it may appear to be broken when it's simply not receiving a signal through the proper input. The solution is to change inputs by using the monitor's controls.

✦ The nerdy term for a computer monitor is *VDU,* or *visual display unit.*

✦ See Book III, Chapter 4 for information about cleaning an LCD monitor and screen; Book VI, Chapter 4 describes how to clean a standard or CRT monitor.

That second-monitor thing

Certain editions of Windows can power two monitors. All you need to complete the picture are two monitors plus two display adapters or one display adapter that can handle two monitors.

The easiest way to tell whether your PC has this ability is to check the spot in Windows where screen resolution is set. In Windows 7, it's the Screen Resolution screen, as shown in Figure 6-5. In Windows Vista and Windows XP, it's the Display Properties dialog box, as shown in Figure 6-6. When a second monitor shows up in either of those places, your PC's display adapter has the ability to use two monitors.

To use the second monitor, select it in the Screen Resolution window or Display Settings dialog box. What you do next depends on your version of Windows:

Windows 7: Choose an option from the button My Multiple Displays. Choosing Extend These Displays creates one large desktop across both monitors.

Drag monitor
around.

Primary monitor   Secondary monitor

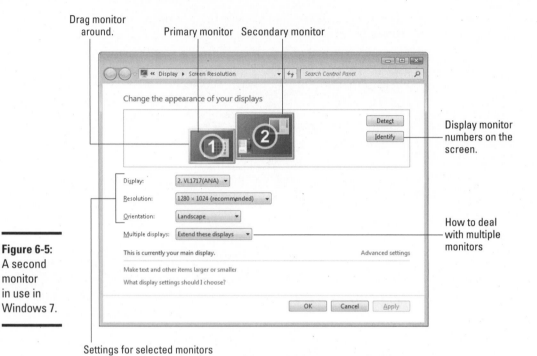

Display monitor
numbers on the
screen.

How to deal
with multiple
monitors

Figure 6-5:
A second
monitor
in use in
Windows 7.

Settings for selected monitors

Windows Vista: Choose the option Extend the Desktop Onto This Monitor, as shown in Figure 6-6.

Windows XP: Choose the option Extend My Windows Desktop Onto This Monitor.

The taskbar shows up on only one monitor. To see which monitor is which, click either the Identify Monitors or Identify button.

The option you choose in order to set the main monitor (the one on which the taskbar appears) is titled differently, depending on your version of Windows. To switch main monitors, click the monitor that you want to be the primary monitor and then choose one of the following options:

Windows 7: Make This My Main Display

Windows Vista: This Is My Main Monitor

Windows XP: Use This Device As the Primary Monitor

Primary monitor

Display monitor
numbers on the screen.

Secondary monitor   Drag monitor around.

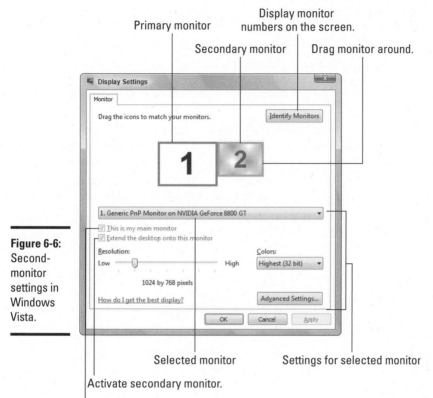

Figure 6-6:
Second-
monitor
settings in
Windows
Vista.

Selected monitor   Settings for selected monitor

Activate secondary monitor.

Identify main monitor.

Every monitor has its own resolution and color settings. To change the settings, choose the monitor from the menu in the center of the dialog box and
then set its resolution and colors. Changing the resolution changes the monitors' relative sizes in the window. You can then drag the second monitor
around to adjust how they relate to each other.

Drag a window between the two monitors to see how their positions relate.
In fact, you can use either the Display Settings or Display Properties dialog
box for that test.

Click the OK button when you're done arranging the dual monitors.

✦ The easiest way to set up dual monitor hardware is to buy a dual monitor adapter. It comes in VGA and DVI flavors.

✦ A display adapter with a digital connector can drive two VGA monitors.
  You need to purchase a DVI-to-dual-VGA adapter to set things up.

+ Most laptops have the second-monitor ability built in. They can easily use external monitors and video projectors for making presentations. See Book III for more information on troubleshooting laptop computers.

+ To swap the Windows Vista Sidebar to the other monitor, open the Windows Sidebar icon in the Control Panel. In the Windows Sidebar dialog box, choose the monitor number from the menu by the item titled Display Sidebar on Monitor.

+ Changing the main monitor doesn't change its number. To change the numbers, you have to swap the monitors' display adapter connectors on the PC.

+ Do not remove a monitor while the computer is in hibernation. Doing so can prevent the logon screen from showing up when the computer restarts.

+ Monitor *mirroring* occurs when you display the same image on both monitors. This feature is used in laptops for presentations. See Book III.

Captain Video the Troubleshooter

Sometime in the future, heroes of freedom will swoop down from distant mountaintops, ably assisting computer users with their PC's video system troubles. Until then, you have the information in this section to help you.

Seeing nothing

When you see nothing, the first thing you should try is opening your eyes. That often solves the problem right away.

When you see nothing on the computer monitor, check the basic hardware first: Is the monitor turned on? Is it plugged in? Is the monitor properly connected to the display adapter on the console? If the monitor has dual inputs, is the proper one selected?

A computer or monitor in Sleep (low-power) mode shows its power-on LED in an amber color rather than in the normal green. If you still don't see anything on the monitor after you wake it up, the problem is with the video signal not reaching the monitor.

Press the monitor's menu button, as described in the later section, "Adjusting the monitor." If the monitor's menu appears, the monitor is fine and the problem is with the display adapter.

+ When a monitor has dual inputs, be sure that the proper input is selected. This type of checking is the same as my general "check to see whether it's plugged in" advice, but usually you need to press a button or switch on the monitor to ensure that the input is coming from the proper connection.

+ Sometimes it helps to unplug the monitor cable and then plug it back in. When the issue is a power-supply issue, such as when the monitor's power light doesn't come on, unplug the power cord and plug it in again.

+ A monitor is never something you should try to fix on your own. Never open a monitor's case.

+ When a monitor is dead, throw it out. Do so properly, according to whatever rules govern the disposal of computer equipment for your locale.

Seeing only the mouse pointer

I've encountered this problem a few times on both Windows 7 and Windows Vista PCs: After your computer awakens from Sleep mode, you see only the mouse pointer and not the Windows desktop. You can move the mouse pointer but not see anything to click.

Two solutions work for the mouse-pointer-only screen. The first is to press Ctrl+Alt+Delete, which displays a special Windows screen. If this solution works, press the Cancel button to return to your Windows session.

The second solution, unfortunately, is to turn off the computer: Press and hold the Power button until the PC turns off. When the computer starts again, go ahead and start Windows normally.

You might consider updating the display adapter driver. See the later section, "Updating drivers."

Swapping solutions

Because the PC's video system contains two parts, you have to check two hardware items for the source of the trouble: the monitor and the display adapter. To do forensic troubleshooting, it helps to swap out the parts to determine specifically where the trouble lies.

Obviously, you cannot swap out a monitor and a display adapter unless you have spares lounging about. But when you have a spare monitor or display adapter, you can use them to help troubleshoot.

Start with the monitor:

1. **Turn off the computer and monitor.**

2. **Unplug the monitor and disconnect it from the console.**

3. **Attach the replacement monitor.**

4. **Turn on the computer.**

Assuming that you know the replacement monitor works, the computer should display an image on the screen. If not, the problem lies with the display adapter.

You can use similar steps to troubleshoot a display adapter. Heed the directions in Chapter 8 for installing a display adapter, but instead replace the current adapter with one that you know works. If this trick fixes the problem, you know that you need to buy a new display adapter.

+ The replacements you use for swapping must be working in order for the swap to be an effective troubleshooting tool.

+ This trick still works when the display adapter is part of the motherboard: Simply plug a video adapter into one of the PC's expansion slots. If it works, the problem is in the video circuitry on the motherboard. Buy a new display adapter.

Adjusting the monitor

No monitor is perfect, and the manufacturer recognizes that statement. So every monitor features its own adjustment menu, along with a set of confusing buttons you can use to access and manipulate the menu, thereby honing your monitor's screen to graphical perfection.

The typical monitor has five buttons: one Power button and then four buttons to manipulate the onscreen menu. Usually, two buttons have arrows or triangles on them, and two other buttons manipulate the menu commands. The types and designs of the buttons differ from monitor to monitor.

Generally speaking, pressing one of the buttons (or the button labeled with a Menu icon) displays the onscreen menu. A menu example is shown in Figure 6-7. You then use the arrow or triangle buttons to select a menu item. The other two buttons are used (somehow) to manipulate the item and adjust the monitor.

The onscreen menu eventually disappears after a period of inactivity. Or, sometimes it disappears when you press the Main Menu button while viewing the main menu.

+ One key feature found in many onscreen monitor menus is Auto Tune or Auto Adjust. Use this feature to quickly have the monitor adjust to the image the display adapter is sending.

✦ If the LCD monitor has regions on the screen that twinkle or appear fuzzy, the monitor hasn't properly grasped the graphics information being sent to it. If the monitor sports an Auto-Adjust feature on its menu, try it. If it doesn't work, turn off the monitor, wait, and then turn it on again.

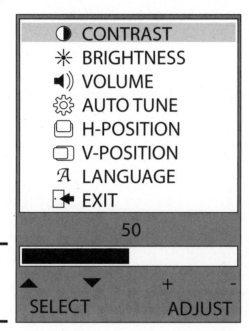

Figure 6-7:
A typical
monitor
menu.

✦ Some monitors feature a Save option on their menus. Use this option to save your favorite settings. A corresponding Recall option restores the settings you saved.

✦ Laptop keyboards have function buttons that let you adjust the monitor's brightness and contrast. Beyond that, laptop monitors lack the specific adjustments that desktop monitors have, mostly because the laptop's monitor is dedicated to the laptop and therefore requires no additional configuration.

Dealing with dead or stuck pixels

A situation unique to LCD monitors is the dead or stuck pixel issue. Being dead and being stuck are similar problems.

A *dead* pixel is one with its red, green, or blue element off, or "dead." The only way to find dead pixels is to display solid colors on the screen and scour the territory for any "holes," or missing spots.

The sad news is that you cannot fix a dead pixel; it's a manufacturing defect. Your only hope is to find enough dead pixels to be able to use the warranty. On most LCD monitors, you must find more than ten dead pixels to justify a replacement. Check your monitor manufacturer's warranty, to be sure.

A *stuck* pixel is one that stays a certain color despite signals from the display adapter requesting it to change. Unlike a dead pixel, a stuck pixel can be corrected: Using a diagnostic program, or sometimes something simple, like Windows Paint, you can "shock" the stuck pixel back to life by displaying various colors rapidly on the screen. Sometimes this technique works, sometimes it doesn't.

✦ A higher-priced monitor has less chance of sporting a dead pixel. One of my early LCD monitors has three dead pixels, but I rarely notice them.

✦ Pixels get stuck because they literally remember which colors they're displaying. By rapidly switching colors on the screen, it's possible to unstick the stuck pixel.

✦ A stuck pixel that cannot be unstuck becomes a dead pixel.

✦ No amount of hand clapping can bring a dead pixel back to life.

Saving the screen

There's no reason to run a screen saver program for its intended purpose: to prevent the perils of phosphor burn-in. Back in the old days, a computer was often used for a single task, especially in an office setting. Because the same image was displayed pretty much all the time on the screen, the image burned the CRT's phosphor, making an image visible even when the monitor was turned off.

To help "save" the screen, screen saver software was born.

At first, screen savers merely blanked the display after a period of inactivity. Later screen savers added graphical images. Screen savers are now mostly toys, though they can also serve a security function by locking the computer after a period of inactivity. But phosphor burn-in is no longer considered a serious computer maintenance issue.

✦ To configure a screen saver in Windows 7 and Windows Vista, right-click the desktop and choose Personalize from the pop-up menu. In the Personalization window, click the Screen Saver link to show the Screen Saver Settings dialog box.

✦ To configure a screen saver in Windows XP, right-click the desktop and choose Properties from the shortcut menu. Click the Screen Saver tab in the Display Properties dialog box.

✦ To have the screen saver lock the computer (for security), place a check mark in the box by On Resume, Display Logon Screen (Windows 7/Windows Vista) or On Resume, Password Protect (Windows XP). This option can be found in either the Screen Saver Settings or Display Properties dialog box.

✦ Be careful when downloading screen savers from the Internet. Many so-called free screen savers can be malware programs that turn out to be more trouble than they're worth. See Book IV, Chapter 4 for more information on malware.

✦ Back in the olden days, the primary culprits of the phosphor burn-in peril were Lotus 1-2-3 and WordPerfect, both text-based DOS programs. Although phosphor burn-in was noticeable when the monitor was turned off, it wasn't that noticeable when the program that caused the burn-in was being run. The burn-in was terribly noticeable when other programs were run.

Saving power

Your computer monitor is most likely energy efficient. That means it has a low-power mode designed to save energy. This mode is activated by a loss of signal from the PC's display adapter. You can confirm the mode in one of two ways:

First, the screen goes blank and a message appears. The message indicates that the signal from the computer is no longer available. The text varies from "Missing signal" to "No input" to any of a variety of terse and confusing messages. (In fact, the message may also appear when you simply disconnect the monitor from the display adapter.)

Second, the monitor's power-on lamp changes from green to amber in color.

The monitor is only a dumb partner in the power-saving scheme. The true mastermind is the operating system, which directs the display adapter to stop sending the monitor a video signal. You can configure your computer to save monitor power based on a period of inactivity. To set the period of inactivity — the sleep timeouts for the monitor — follow these steps:

1. **Open the Control Panel.**

2a. **In Windows 7 and Windows Vista, choose Hardware and Sound and then choose the link Change When the Computer Sleeps, found beneath the Power Options heading.**

2b. **In Windows XP, open the Power Options icon and in the Power Options dialog box, ensure that the Power Schemes tab is selected.**

3. **Use the Menu button to set the timeout value for the monitor.**

The option is titled either Turn Off the Display or Turn Off Monitor.

4. **Click Save Changes or the OK button.**

Optionally, close any other windows left hanging open.

I set my monitor to have a 45-minute timeout. (At that point, I'm most likely done.) The screen saver kicks in at 30 minutes.

If you're using a screen saver, it also sports a timeout value. When the monitor's sleep timeout is *less* than the screen saver timeout, you never see the screen saver in action. Therefore, I recommend setting the monitor's sleep timeout to a value that is several minutes (or hours) greater than the screen saver's timeout.

✦ If the monitor's power lamp is green and the screen is still blank, you might simply be looking at a blank screen saver image.

✦ The monitor also goes into power-saving mode when the computer is turned off, though for true power savings, I recommend that you just turn off the monitor as well as the computer.

Adjusting the resolution

Computer monitors display images by lighting up various pixels, or picture elements, on the screen. The pixels are arranged in a grid, where the number of pixels horizontally and vertically is referred to as the display's *resolution*.

To check or set the display's resolution, you need to use the Screen Resolution window, the Display Settings dialog box, or the Display Properties dialog box. Examples of these windows and dialog boxes are shown earlier in this chapter, in Figures 6-5 and 6-6.

In Windows 7, you summon the Screen Resolution window by right-clicking the desktop and choosing the command Screen Resolution.

In Windows Vista, conjure forth the Display Settings dialog box by right-clicking the desktop and choosing the Personalize command. Choose the Display Settings link in the Personalization window.

In Windows XP, right-click the Desktop and choose Properties to behold the Display Properties dialog box. Click the Settings tab.

Set the resolution by using the Resolution menu button in Windows 7. Available resolutions are listed from lowest to highest, from the top down. Any resolution that's ideal for your monitor features the text *recommended* after it.

In Windows Vista and Windows XP, you set screen resolution by using the slider gizmo in the dialog box: Right is higher resolution, left is lower resolution. You're essentially increasing or decreasing the number of pixels displayed, as well as the display's aspect ratio (horizontal to vertical pixels).

Use the preview screen to determine how the resolution affects things.

To check the new resolution, click the Apply button. The display changes to reflect the new settings, and you're allowed the option of clicking Yes or No to make the change permanent. If you don't see anything, just wait and the previous settings are restored.

Click OK to confirm the settings and close the window or dialog box.

✦ When the resolution seemingly and without explanation switches to very low (things look comically large on the screen), the problem is most likely a lost or improperly installed video driver. Simply reinstall the current driver; see the section "Updating drivers," later in this chapter.

✦ Only a given number of preset resolutions are available. The variety depends on the abilities of the computer's display adapter.

✦ Safe mode uses 800 x 600 pixels as its resolution, which is about as low as you want to use in Windows.

✦ A common resolution is 1024 x 768 pixels.

✦ Widescreen monitors with the right display adapter can employ the ultimate 1600 x 1200 resolution. I've also heard rumors of a 2560 x 1600 resolution, and such a thing makes me lust for technology more than I'm willing to admit.

✦ The higher the resolution numbers, the smaller things appear on the screen. When you have trouble seeing the screen, use a lower resolution.

✦ Some LCD monitors display only a handful of resolutions well. Using resolutions not recommended by the manufacturer may damage the monitor.

✦ If you have two monitors, the resolution is set for both of them. Choose the monitor from the list in the dialog box and then make the resolution settings.

✦ A humongous difference exists between the display resolution and the image resolution. The *image resolution* is the number of dots per inch (dpi) used to render the image. The amount can vary. PC monitors are set at about 96 dots per inch, which is why some images appear small on the screen and others appear huge. See the section "Setting the dpi," later in this chapter.

Changing the icon size

When a lower resolution doesn't help you see the screen, you can also try resizing the desktop icons, as well as the icons in various folders, on the taskbar, and on the Start menu.

Desktop icons

To resize desktop icons in Windows 7 and Windows Vista, right-click the Desktop and choose View⇨Large Icons from the pop-up menu.

In Windows XP, take these steps to show larger icons on the desktop:

1. **Right-click the desktop and choose Properties from the pop-up menu.**

2. **In the Display Properties dialog box, click the Appearance tab.**

3. **Click the Effects button.**

4. **Place a check mark by Use Large Icons.**

5. **Click OK and then click OK again to close the Display Properties dialog box.**

Folder icons

You can change the size of icons in the folder windows in Windows 7 and Windows Vista.

In Windows 7, use the Change Your View toolbar button to set the icon size. The button is the third button from the right on the toolbar.

In Windows Vista, use the Views toolbar button to choose either the Large Icons or Extra Large Icons command.

Taskbar icons

Icons pinned to the taskbar in Windows 7 have two sizes: large and small. To set the size, follow these steps:

1. **Right-click the Start button and choose the Properties command.**

2. **Click the Taskbar tab in the Taskbar and Start Menu Properties dialog box.**

3. **To use smaller icons, place a check mark by the item Use Small Icons.**

Or, conversely, by removing the icon, you set the taskbar to use larger icons.

4. **Click OK.**

In Windows Vista and Windows XP, the Quick Launch toolbar is used to store frequently accessed programs. To change the icon size for the Quick Launch toolbar (or any toolbar on the taskbar), follow these steps:

1. **If necessary, unlock the taskbar: Right-click in a blank part of the task-bar and choose Lock the Taskbar from the pop-up menu.**

Remove the check mark by Lock the Taskbar to unlock the taskbar.

2. **Right-click the toolbar's handle.**

The handle is located on the left end of the toolbar. (It shows up only when the taskbar is unlocked.)

3. **From the menu, choose View⇨Large Icons.**

4. **Adjust the taskbar's height to properly show the larger icons.**

Point the mouse at the edge of the taskbar, between the taskbar and the screen. Drag the mouse toward the center of the screen to set the task-bar's height.

5. **Relock the taskbar if necessary: Right-click the taskbar and choose Lock the Taskbar.**

Start menu icons

To change the size of the icons on the Start menu, follow these steps:

1. **Right-click the Start button and choose Properties from the pop-up menu.**

2. **Click the Customize button.**

3a. **In Windows 7 and Windows Vista, scroll the list to find the item Use Large Icons; place a check mark by that item.**

3b. **In Windows XP, choose the option Large Icons.**

4. **Click OK and then click OK again to close the Taskbar and Start Menu Properties dialog box.**

Setting the dpi

Dpi, which refers to dots per inch, is a key concept to using computer graph-ics. Your PC doubtlessly uses a resolution of 96 dpi on the monitor. This value can be changed to 120 dpi or any dpi value.

Changing the dpi value of your monitor isn't something you need to do; 96 dpi is fine for using a PC. In fact, most programs and web pages assume that your PC's monitor is set to 96 dpi; that's close to 100 dots per inch. When viewing the screen is difficult, however, selecting 120 dpi works better. And, for graphics artists who need a more realistic representation of information on the screen, different dpi resolutions might fix some problems.

To set the dpi in Windows 7 and Vista, start with these steps:

1. **Right-click the desktop and choose the Personalize command.**

2. **In Windows 7, click the Display link, found in the lower-left corner of the Personalize window.**

3. **From the list of tasks on the left side of the window, choose Set Custom Text Size (DPI) or Adjust Font Size (DPI).**

4. **In Windows Vista, click the Continue button or type the administrator's password when prompted to do so.**

   At this point in Windows Vista, you can choose either Default Scale (96 DPI) or Larger Scale (120 DPI). Instead, be more flexible, like Windows 7, and continue with this step:

5. **In Windows Vista, choose Custom DPI.**

   The DPI Scaling dialog box appears, as shown in Figure 6-8. You can use the menu to choose a custom DPI scaling or drag the ruler left and right, as shown in the figure.

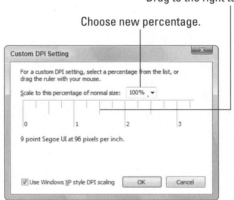

Figure 6-8: Setting a custom DPI.

6. **Click the OK button to lock in your new DPI setting.**

7. **Close the remaining open dialog boxes, windows, and whatnot on the screen.**

To set the dpi in Windows XP, obey these steps:

1. **Right-click the display and choose Properties from the pop-up menu.**
2. **Click the Settings tab in the Display Properties dialog box.**
3. **Click the Advanced button.**
4. **Choose either 96 dpi or 120 dpi, using the drop-down menu.**

   You may have to restart the PC to see the results, though if you're done, click the OK button and obey the directions. Otherwise, choose Custom DPI from the drop-down list and continue with Step 5 to set up custom dpi settings.

5. **Use the Custom DPI dialog box to configure the screen's dpi.**

   Figure 6-8 illustrates how you can work the dialog box: You can choose a percentage from the drop-down menu or use the mouse to drag the ruler larger. Sadly, you cannot reset the dpi to a value less than 100 percent.

6. **Click the OK button to confirm your settings, or click Cancel if you were just messing around.**

   Obey any additional directions given, such as restarting the computer. Oh, and close any other dialog boxes or windows you may have opened.

Windows may have to install or configure new fonts and, possibly, restart when the dpi is changed.

Setting color depth

The richness of the image on a computer monitor is determined more by the number of colors available than by the number of pixels (the resolution). Lower resolutions with more colors look better than higher resolutions. In fact, most computer games use lower resolutions simply because more colors are available.

Windows 7 sets the color depth to maximum, no matter what. Windows Vista and Windows XP should do the same, but instead they give you options.

The place to set color depth for Windows Vista and Windows XP is the same location where screen resolution is set: either the Display Settings or Display Properties dialog box, which looks similar to Figure 6-6. This dialog box has two settings for color depth: Highest (32-bit) and Medium (16-bit). Choose the highest setting available at the preferred resolution for the monitor.

Of course, setting the number of colors doesn't ensure that the screen accurately depicts the colors displayed. Every monitor has variations. You can adjust the way colors are displayed, or *rendered,* by using the Windows Color Management tool, covered in the next section.

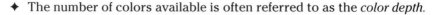

✦ The number of colors available is often referred to as the *color depth.*

✦ A relationship exists between resolution and colors. Lower resolutions can have more colors; higher resolutions sport fewer colors. The key is video memory. Lots of colors require lots of memory, which leaves less memory available for resolution. Conversely, higher resolutions require more video memory, which leaves less memory available for color depth. It's a twisted graphical circle!

Configuring color management

The idea behind color management isn't to match colors on a computer monitor with colors in the real world. Instead, strive to match colors in a way that satisfies your needs. For example, match the colors on the monitor to the colors produced by a specific printer or another output device. To make it happen, you use the Windows Color Management tool.

The Windows Color Management tool isn't something you mess with casually. My advice is to use it only when you receive instructions on which profiles to select. This information may be found in a graphics application's reference or in your PC's printer reference.

To use the color management tool in Windows Vista, follow the steps in the earlier section, "Display adapter info," to display your PC's display adapter Properties dialog box (Figure 6-3). Then continue with these steps:

1. **Click the Color Management tab.**

2. **Click the Color Management button.**

   The Color Management window appears. Yes, it's quite a complex place. There's no need to wander about aimlessly.

3. **Choose a hardware device from the Device menu button.**

   Most likely, the PC's monitor and current display adapter are chosen as the device. If you want the display to match the output of, say, a color laser printer that's available to the computer, choose it from the list.

4. **Place a check mark by the option Use My Settings for This Device.**

5. **Click the Add button to choose a profile.**

   This is the step where it helps to know what you're doing: No additional information is provided for the profiles listed in the Associate Color Profile dialog box.

6. **Select a profile from the ones that are listed.**

7. **Click the OK button.**

   The profile is now associated with the device you chose in Step 4.

8. **Repeat Steps 5 through 7 to add profiles for the device.**

9. **Click the Close button and then close the other open dialog boxes and windows as necessary.**

Windows XP isn't as sophisticated as more recent versions of Windows when it comes to using the color management tool. Follow these steps:

1. **Right-click the desktop and choose Properties from the pop-up menu.**

2. **In the Display Properties dialog box, click the Settings tab.**

3. **Click the Advanced button.**

4. **In the monitor and display adapter's Properties dialog box, click the Color Management tab.**

   Unlike in Windows Vista, the only device available for configuring is the monitor. You can add a color profile to the monitor, but again it helps to know which profile you need as opposed to just randomly choosing a profile.

5. **Click the Add button.**

6. **Choose a color profile in the Add Profile Association dialog box.**

7. **Click the Add button.**

   The profile is now associated with the device.

8. **Repeat Steps 5 through 7 to add more profiles.**

   You can highlight a single profile and use the Set As Default button to choose your favorite profile from several.

9. **Click the OK button when you're done, and, optionally, close the Display Properties dialog box as well.**

Windows installs color profiles as you add color devices to the computer. For example, when you're installing a color laser printer, Windows automatically installs the necessary color profiles.

   ✦ The PC's display adapter may have come with special utilities that set the colors better than the Windows Color Management tool.

   ✦ The monitor may have color temperature settings in its control panel. See the section "Adjusting the monitor," earlier in this chapter. Check the monitor's menu for a color temperature or other color settings.

Calibrating color in Windows 7

There's a color calibration utility that's unique to Windows 7. The utility can be used to ensure that your monitor is accurately displaying colors. To run the utility, follow these steps:

1. **Right-click the desktop.**

2. **Choose the Personalize command.**

3. **From the list of tasks on the left side of the Personalization window, choose Display.**

4. **From the list of tasks on the left side of the Display window, choose Calibrate Color.**

   You need to work with your monitor's controls (discussed in the earlier section, "Adjusting the monitor") in coordination with the images displayed on the screen to best calibrate colors for your monitor in Windows.

5. **Work through the Display Color Calibration Wizard, obeying the directions on the screen and clicking the Next button to continue.**

6. **Click the Finish button when you're done.**

There's no such thing as perfect calibration — only what you can perceive as being perfect. As long as everything looks good enough for your own eyeballs, it's perfect!

Updating drivers

Updating the video driver can solve most video woes. Two companies develop most PC display adapter technology: Intel (formerly ATI) and NVIDIA. They routinely make new graphics drivers available, ensuring that your PC remains compatible with all the latest graphical software out there.

To manually check for a new driver, visit the display adapter's Properties dialog box; follow the steps listed earlier in this chapter, in the section "Display adapter info." After your PC's display adapter Properties dialog box is displayed, follow these steps:

1. **Click the Properties button in the display adapter's Properties dialog box.**

2. **In Windows Vista, type the administrator's password or click the Continue button when prompted by the User Account Control dialog box.**

   The display adapter's Properties dialog box appears.

3. **Click the Driver tab.**

   Before wasting any time, check the date. Figure 6-9 shows the Driver tab in my computer's display adapter's Properties dialog box. The date is old, so it's worth your time to check for an updated driver.

4. **Click the Update Driver button.**

Figure 6-9:
The display
adapter's
Properties
dialog box —
Driver tab.

5. **In Windows 7 and Windows Vista, choose the option Search Automatically for Updated Driver Software.**

   You can choose Browse My Computer for Driver Software in those times when the screen resolution randomly gets low — when Windows has lost the current driver — or when you've uninstalled a display adapter and then reinstalled the same adapter later.

   It may take some time for the driver to be found and downloaded from the Internet. If nothing is available, you're told so. That's fine — you're up-to-date. Otherwise, you're told that a new driver was installed, and you're ready to go.

6. **Close any open dialog boxes or windows when you're done.**

7. **If prompted, restart your PC.**

If you update the driver and — oops! — things are even worse, you can roll back the driver. The easiest way to do this is with System Restore. A prompt for System Restore appears when you first start the PC (refer to Chapter 2). Or, you can use the Roll Back Driver button from the Driver tab in the display adapter's Properties dialog box (refer to Figure 6-9).

✦ The best way to ensure that your PC has updated drivers is to use the Windows Update service. Refer to Book II, Chapter 1.

✦ Windows XP suffers from a problem where the current video driver might become "lost." In that case, you need to reinstall a driver that's already on the computer. After following Step 5 in the preceding step list, simply use the driver that's already available on the computer's hard drive. The driver fixes the low-resolution issue.

✦ You can also check for a driver by visiting the developer's web site and looking for the Support link or Drivers link. Confirm which display adapter you have by following the directions outlined earlier in this chapter; see the section "Display adapter info."

✦ Don't forget to check for updated software for a second display adapter if your PC sports this hardware.

Using the troubleshooting helpers

As you might expect, some troubleshooters are lurking in Windows to assist you with video problems.

In Windows 7 and Windows Vista, the troubleshooter can be found in the display adapter's Properties dialog box, which was introduced in the section "Display adapter info," earlier in this chapter. After opening the display adapter's Properties dialog box, click the Troubleshoot tab (refer to Figure 6-3). If you're able to, click the Change Settings button; obey the directions on the screen. (Not every adapter lets you troubleshoot via the Properties dialog box.)

Windows XP has a video troubleshooter that's a bit more interactive. Here's how to get to it:

1. **Right-click the desktop and choose Properties from the pop-up menu.**

2. **In the Display Properties dialog box, click the Settings tab.**

3. **Click the Troubleshoot button.**

The Help and Support Center's Video Display Troubleshooter appears.

4. **Answer the questions and work through the troubleshooter to (hopefully) remedy your situation.**

5. **Close the open dialog boxes and windows when you're done.**

Another alternative to the Windows way of doing things is to see whether specific troubleshooting software is available from your display adapter's manufacturer. This type of software might be accessible by right-clicking the desktop and looking for a special command on the pop-up menu. On my PC, I see the NVIDIA Control Panel command, which opens a window full of interesting settings and options.

You can also consider typing **video help** into the Windows Help system to see whether any helpful information is available, or whether a specific video troubleshooter can be found.

Chapter 7: Peripheralitis

In This Chapter

- ✔ Understanding hardware problems
- ✔ Adjusting the keyboard and mouse
- ✔ Dealing with Sticky Keys
- ✔ Checking audio connections
- ✔ Fixing the silent PC
- ✔ Using the Device Manager
- ✔ Updating device drivers

Peripheralitis (pe·rif·er·al·i·tis) n. 1. From the word *peripheral*, meaning something outside the center, and the Greek suffix *-itis*, meaning disease or the failure to place a space between the words *it* and *is*. A computer with peripheralitis is said to have a problem with one of its peripheral devices, a gizmo attached to, but outside of, the computer console. Issues surrounding peripheralitis can be addressed by information covered in this chapter.

General Hardware Troubleshooting

The only way to avoid hardware trouble in a computer is to never turn the thing on. That's a safe bet, but for most of us, it makes our computer investment useless. I believe there's a better way to go around dealing with trouble than avoiding it.

Understanding how hardware trouble happens

The key to understanding all troubleshooting in a computer is to remember that *change causes problems*.

Change the hardware and you open the door for new hardware issues. The same theory applies to software changes. As long as you can remember what recently changed in a computer, you can narrow the number of possible solutions by eliminating what hasn't changed.

Of course, one thing that can change is that hardware fails. Because a hard drive spins, it wears down bearings. That's change, and, fortunately, a change you can hear coming. (A hard drive with old bearings squeals like an iron safe being dragged down the street by an inept burglar's getaway car.)

One solid way to confirm that hardware is causing woe is to follow my old adage: When in doubt, swap it out.

A bum keyboard or mouse is easily detected by turning off the computer, removing the suspect device, plugging in a device that you know works, and then turning on the computer again. If the problem is gone, just blame the bum gizmo. Buy a new one, or simply don't return the thing you borrowed.

✦ When swapping out doesn't fix the problem, the problem lies elsewhere. Check the usual suspects: power supply, cable connections, outdated drivers, and robots from Venus, for example.

✦ Moving things around is part of the "change" equation I mention earlier. My neighbor lost his computer sound after moving the speakers so far back that they disconnected from the console.

✦ Also see the section "Your Pal, the Device Manager," later in this chapter. Windows Device Manager is knowledgeable about your PC's hardware and can quickly alert you to any malfunctioning doodads.

✦ Chapter 8 covers information on opening the PC's case. Loose cables have been known to happen inside the PC.

Diagnosing problems in Windows 7

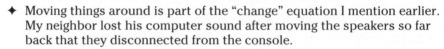

Windows 7 features many troubleshooting and diagnostic tools, all carefully hidden in the Control Panel. You can use those tools to quickly determine what's wrong with your PC and, hopefully, fix it. Most of the time, the tools lie dormant until Windows detects a problem. When that happens, you're presented with the troubleshooting options.

You can manually run the hardware troubleshooter if you like. If nothing is wrong, the troubleshooter actually lies to you and says that the problem has been fixed, so I don't recommend randomly running the troubleshooter. Before then, visit the Devices and Printers window: Choose Devices and Printers from the Start menu.

In the Devices and Printers window, skim the list of gizmos to see whether any of them is flagged with a yellow alert triangle. If so, Windows has detected a problem with that device and it's in need of troubleshooting: Right-click the device's icon and choose the command Troubleshoot.

When you suspect hardware trouble of a general or unknown nature, you can take a stab at running the generic hardware troubleshooter. Follow these steps:

1. **Open the Control Panel.**

2. **Beneath the System and Security heading, click the link Find and Fix Problems.**

   The Windows 7 Troubleshooting window opens.

3. **Beneath the Hardware and Sound heading, click the link Configure a Device.**

   Windows attempts to diagnose and fix whatever recent hardware woe you're experiencing.

4. **Obey the troubleshooter; read the screen and click the Next button if necessary.**

5. **Close the various windows when you're done.**

The troubleshooter may or may not fix the issue. If not, peruse other information in this chapter to help you determine a more specific cause and then go after a more specific solution.

Also see Book II, Chapter 1 for more information on the Windows 7 troubleshooter, as well as the Action Center, which can also help you diagnose and fix whatever ails your PC.

Keyboard and Mouse

Our future ancestors will no doubt be fascinated by computer antiques, maybe to the point of collecting old input devices, similar to the way my mother collects antique clocks and coffee grinders. I can imagine some future abode decorated with computer mice and keyboards. That should impress the neighbors because future humans will innately understand the importance of input and output, or I/O.

I/O is one of the computer's basic functions, and a vital one at that. For input, you (the human) rely on the keyboard and mouse. When those two items malfunction, the PC becomes stubbornly ignorant of your intent. This section helps you clear up some keyboard and mouse issues.

Troubleshooting basic input dilemmas

Before slamming the mouse into your computer desk or slapping your palms wildly on the keyboard, do some basic troubleshooting.

First, ensure that the computer is turned on. If the tiny power light is illuminated, the computer is on. When the computer's power supply fan is whirring, it's on. If the computer isn't on, refer to Chapter 2 for help.

Second, check the connections. Is everything plugged in? Is it plugged in properly? The old PS/2–style keyboard and mouse connectors look identical; your keyboard doesn't work when it's plugged into the mouse port, and vice versa.

Do not plug in or unplug the computer keyboard or mouse to a PS/2 connector while the computer is on. Doing so may damage the computer's motherboard. Always turn off the PC before connecting the (old-style) PS/2 keyboard or mouse. This warning doesn't apply to a USB keyboard or a USB mouse.

Third, test the keyboard or mouse for signs of life. For the keyboard, press and release the Caps Lock key. The Caps Lock light should illuminate, or switch off and on as you press the key repeatedly. When the light is active but the keyboard doesn't work, it might be defective. Restart Windows or turn the computer off and on again to confirm whether there's a one-time glitch or the keyboard is deceased.

Optical mice also feature a light, one that's used to read mouse movement. When the light is on, the mouse should function. If the light is on but the mouse isn't working, restart Windows or turn the PC off and then on again. Also consider cleaning the mouse (see Book VI, Chapter 4).

Don't worry when the keyboard or mouse dies. You cannot fix it — just buy a replacement.

Taming the wild mouse

That mouse, that mouse!

It's tracking so bad!

It zaggles, it stalls,

It's driving me mad!

A mouse that doesn't track well on the screen is dirty. Literally. Clean the mouse as described in Book VI, Chapter 4.

When you find the mouse jumping around too much, consider removing the check mark by the Snap To option, officially titled Automatically Move Pointer to the Default Button in a Dialog Box. This option is found in the Mouse Properties dialog box, on the Pointer Options tab, as discussed in the next section.

Making the mouse faster or slower

Speed is a relative thing. For the computer's mouse, you can adjust its speed faster or slower by using the Mouse Properties dialog box. Here's how:

1a. **In Windows 7 and Windows Vista, open the Control Panel, choose Hardware and Sound, and then choose Mouse.**

In Windows 7, the Mouse link is found beneath the Devices and Printer heading. In Windows Vista, choose the Mouse heading.

1b. **In Windows XP, open the Control Panel's Mouse icon.**

The Mouse Properties dialog box is displayed.

2. **Click the Pointer Options tab in the Mouse Properties dialog box.**

The Pointer Options tab, illustrated in Figure 7-1, contains a slew of useful tools for dealing with the mouse pointer in Windows.

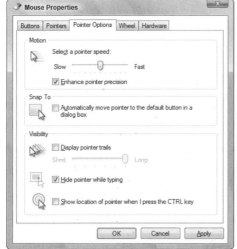

Figure 7-1:
The Mouse
Properties
dialog box —
Pointer
Options tab.

3. **Use the slider gizmo below Select a Pointer Speed to throttle the mouse pointer on the screen.**

Pick a setting faster or slower than where the gizmo is positioned.

4. **Click the Apply button.**

5. **Practice moving the mouse pointer.**

Gauge the speed.

6. **If necessary, repeat Steps 3 through 5 until you find a speed you like.**

7. **Click OK to confirm the settings.**

Close the Control Panel window.

The Enhance Pointer Precision option adds a modicum of intelligence to the mouse pointer's speed. When you accelerate the mouse quickly, Windows moves the mouse pointer in a greater leap. When you're moving the mouse slightly, for minute movements, Windows increases the mouse's sensitivity to help you navigate. It's a good feature to have active.

✦ A faster speed works best for larger displays or displays with high resolution. If you find yourself "palming" the mouse to move the pointer from one side of the screen to another, increase the mouse speed.

✦ Some computer mice use a custom Mouse Properties dialog box, different from what's shown in Figure 7-1. In that case, adjusting the mouse speed may take place in a different part of the dialog box, or specific speed tools for the mouse may be available beyond the ones Windows offers.

Making the mouse pointer more visible

The Pointer Options tab in the Mouse Properties dialog box contains a host of options to help you make the mouse pointer more visible. The options are clustered in the aptly named Visibility area (refer to Figure 7-1). Here's a quick review:

Pointer Trails: The Display Pointer Trails option "ghosts" the mouse pointer to form a cometlike tail wherever the mouse wanders. When activated, this feature makes it easy to *follow* the mouse pointer on the screen, but not necessarily easier to *find* the mouse pointer.

Mouse Ping: I call this feature *mouse ping,* but it's named Show Location of Pointer When I Press the Ctrl Key, where Ctrl means *Control.* By activating this feature, you can quickly locate any errant mouse pointer by pressing either Control key on the keyboard. Using a sonarlike (albeit visual) ping from the old *Voyage to the Bottom of the Sea* television series, this feature zeroes the mouse in.

Another option for making the mouse more visible is found on the Pointers tab of the Mouse Properties dialog box, as shown in Figure 7-2. The settings you make on the Pointers tab affect how the mouse pointer looks. You can choose a goofy animated pointer, if it pleases you, or for more visibility you can choose a larger mouse pointer or a set of large mouse pointers.

Windows doesn't have just one mouse pointer; it has mouse pointers for specific things that Windows does, and things that you do with the mouse. The list is shown in the dialog box (refer to Figure 7-2).

For example, Normal Select is the name of the standard mouse pointer. To choose a larger pointer image, double-click Normal Select in the scrolling list. Use the Browse dialog box that appears in order to choose a new, larger pointer. The Preview window in the lower-left corner of the Browse dialog box shows you the exact size of the new pointer you select; click the Open button to choose that pointer.

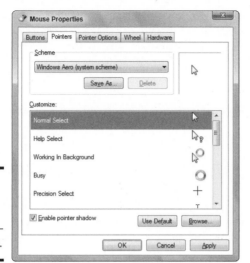

Figure 7-2:
The Mouse
Properties
dialog box —
Pointers tab.

You can select a slew of pointers all at once by using the Scheme button menu. For example, you may find that the Windows Black (Extra Large) scheme works well for your eyeballs. If so, choose it from the list.

Click the Apply button to test your choices.

If you're unhappy, choose the standard mouse pointer schemes from the Scheme button menu: In Windows 7 and Windows Vista, choose Windows Aero; in Windows XP, choose Windows Default.

Looking southward

If you're one of the 10 percent of humanity who prefers using its left hand rather than the right, there's hope: Manufacturers make left-handed computer mice. You can also direct Windows to reverse the role of the main mouse buttons so that left and right buttons are swapped to match your southernmost paw. Follow these steps, using either hand:

1. **Open the Mouse Properties dialog box.**

Refer to Step 1 in the section "Making the mouse faster or slower."

2. **Click the Buttons tab (if necessary).**

3. **Put a check mark by the option Switch Primary and Secondary Buttons.**

4. **Click OK.**

You can now use your left index finger to click the mouse's right button and get all that good left-click action.

All the manuals, web pages, computer books, and other documentation on planet Earth assume that the main mouse button is the *left* button. When you switch buttons as described in this section, the main mouse button is the *right* one. Also, when the directions say to right-click, you're doing a *left-click*. Remember that!

Honing the keyboard

The computer keyboard may be just a slab of buttons, all basically innocent little On–Off switches. But you can control a few keyboardy things. Two of them that are most crucial — especially for fussy touch-typists — are the repeat delay and the repeat rate:

Repeat delay: When you press and hold a key on a computer keyboard, the key eventually repeats itself, spewing out characters across the screen like bullets from a machine gun. The pause between pressing the key and when it starts repeating is the *repeat delay*.

Repeat rate: After you press and hold down a key on the keyboard, the key starts repeating itself. The speed at which it repeats is the repeat rate, which can be fast or slow.

The best way to understand how the rates work is to mess with them:

1a. **In Windows 7, choose Devices and Printers from the Start button menu, and then right-click the Keyboard icon and choose Keyboard Settings.**

1b. **In Windows Vista, open the Control Panel and choose Hardware and Sound, and then choose Keyboard.**

1c. **In Windows XP, open the Keyboard icon in the Control Panel.**

 The Speed tab, shown in Figure 7-3, is where you set the repeat delay and delay rate values.

 2. **Use the sliders beneath Repeat Delay and Repeat Rate to speed things up or down.**

 3. **Click the Apply button.**

 4. **Click in the text box.**

 5. **Press and hold a key on the keyboard to check the rates.**

 6. **Repeat Steps 2 through 5 to hone the settings.**

 7. **Click OK when things are set up just so.**

 Close the Control Panel window.

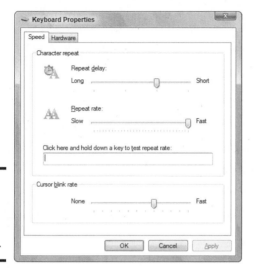

Figure 7-3:
Setting the
keyboard's
repeat and
delay rates.

When a key gets stuck, it repeats like crazy, no matter what. A stuck key indicates a mechanical problem with the keyboard, not anything that software can fix. You can try washing the keyboard as described in Book VI, Chapter 4, though buying a new keyboard may be the best solution.

Undoing the Sticky Keys warning

A common problem, especially for idle hands or video game players, is the Sticky Keys warning, as shown in Figure 7-4.

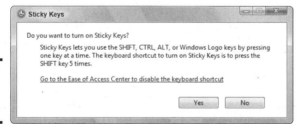

Figure 7-4:
Sticky Keys
pesters you.

Sticky Keys is one of the Windows accessibility features, designed for folks who have trouble using a computer keyboard. The feature is activated whenever you press the Shift key five times in a row. It can be unexpected and startling, but it can be switched off.

In Windows 7 and Windows Vista, heed these steps:

1. **Click the link Go to the Ease of Access Center to Disable the Keyboard Shortcut.**

   If you already dismissed the Sticky Keys window, follow these substeps:

   a. *Open the Control Panel's Ease of Access Center.*

   b. *Click the link Change How Your Keyboard Works.*

   c. *Click the link Set Up Sticky Keys.*

2. **Remove the check mark by the option Turn On Sticky Keys When SHIFT Is Pressed Five Times.**

3. **Click the Save button.**

4. **Close the window.**

In Windows XP, follow these steps to disable the Sticky Keys warning:

1. **Click the Settings button in the Sticky Keys dialog box.**

   If you banished the Sticky Keys dialog box, open the Control Panel's Accessibility Options icon. Click the Keyboard tab (if necessary) in the Accessibility Options dialog box.

2. **Click the Settings button in the StickyKeys area.**

3. **Remove the check mark by the option Use Shortcut.**

4. **Click the OK button and then click OK to dismiss the Accessibility Options dialog box. (Optional) Close the Control Panel window.**

Sticky Keys helps people use a computer keyboard with only one hand, but it would be sweet if Microsoft turned it *off* as opposed to leaving it on and having it shock people unexpectedly.

Speaking of Trouble

Computers are silent beasts. Blame two things for relating noise to computers. The first thing is Hollywood, where for some reason they believe that text displayed on a computer screen somehow makes noise. Trust me: No one would use a computer if text on the screen made noise as it was displayed.

The second thing to blame is the early teletype machines, which were used as the first computer terminals. (And hence the term *TTY* to describe a computer terminal.) A teletype contained a bell to alert the operator about an incoming message, a priority message, or an error. Early computer terminals came equipped with a single tiny speaker for the same reason.

Fast-forward several dozen years and today's computers have not only internal speakers but also an extensive set of external, state-of-the-art, surround sound speakers and a digital sound system to match. This section is where you turn when those speakers suddenly go mute on you.

Testing the speakers

Your PC console has one, internal speaker. It's okay for beeps and boops, but to make sound that scares the neighbors, you want a little more oomph. That means external speakers. Or, if you don't want to scare the neighbors, you can use headphones with your computer.

The easiest way to ensure that noise is coming from the speakers is to use the volume control in the notification area: Click the Volume Control icon, as shown in Figure 7-5. You should hear an audible "beep" (or another amusing tone) when you click the control as shown in the figure.

Adjust volume.

Click to hear something.

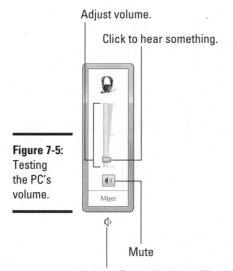

Figure 7-5:
Testing
the PC's
volume.

Mute

Volume Control in the notification area

Windows 7 and Windows Vista feature a more thorough way to demonstrate how the speakers are set up, including a stereo test. Follow these steps:

1. **Right-click the Volume icon in the notification area.**

2. **From the pop-up menu, choose Playback Devices.**

   The Sound dialog box appears, listing the gizmos on your PC that produce sound.

3. **Select a playback device, such as your PC's speakers.**

4. **Click the Configure button.**

   The Speaker Setup dialog box appears.

5. **Click the Test button.**

   You should hear tones from the left speaker and then the right speaker. (If the right speaker plays first, you have the speakers reversed; swap them.)

   You can continue to work through the Speaker Setup dialog box if you desire to further configure the computer's speakers.

6. **Close the various dialog boxes; you passed the test.**

When you don't hear a sound, there's a problem. Keep reading in the next section.

+ You can, of course, use the volume control to set the PC's speaker volume.

+ To mute the speakers in Windows, click the Mute button in the volume control's pop-up window. In Windows XP, place a check mark by the Mute option.

+ Headphones don't show up in the Windows 7 or Windows Vista Sound dialog box unless you're using USB headphones.

+ Your PC's sound hardware may have its own icon in the Control Panel, which you can use to test the audio system.

+ See the later section, "Fixing silence," for information on determining whether the speakers are broken.

Connecting the speakers

O, PC! How can I hear you? Let me count the ways!

Internal speaker: Most PCs have a speaker inside the console. It's a cheap, tiny speaker, and you don't want to use it.

Rear speaker jacks: The standard PC setup is to plug a set of stereo speakers into the audio output jacks on the I/O panel, located on the back of the typical PC.

S/PDIF: High-end audio systems might employ the Sony/Phillips Digital Interconnect Format. It requires special optical cables and equipment used only by serious audiophiles and has separate S/PDIF connectors: one for input (S/PDIF in) and another for output (S/PDIF out).

DVD speaker jacks: An older PC may require that you connect its speakers to the DVD adapter card instead of to the PC's I/O panel. A PC without a specific DVD adapter doesn't have this requirement.

Front speaker jacks: For convenience, many PCs duplicate the speaker and microphone jacks on the front of the console. You can easily connect a set of headphones, though not every PC lets you use both the headphones on the front of the console and speakers on the back.

USB speakers: You can plug USB speakers or headphones into any USB port on the computer.

Monitor speakers: LCD and other types of flat-panel monitors that come with built-in speakers plug into either the rear speaker jacks or the USB port. (The speaker connection is in addition to the monitor connection.)

Traditional audio connectors are color-coded on your PC. The three colors used match the purposes of the three connectors, as shown in Table 7-1. Ensure that you plug the speaker into the proper hole! (It's the green hole.)

Table 7-1	PC Sound Jack Color Codes
Color	*Connection*
Black	S/PDIF output
Black	Surround sound left or right
Brown	Surround sound center or subwoofer
Gray	Line-in jack (for audio equipment)
Lime	Speakers or headphone
Pink	S/PDIF input
Red	Microphone
White	S/PDIF input

✦ Obviously, you cannot hear sound from the speakers when you plug them into the microphone jack. Likewise, the microphone may seem undermodulated when it's plugged into the line-in jack.

✦ Speakers require power! Avoid using speakers that need batteries. Instead, use speakers with a power adapter. Speakers can also draw power from a subwoofer, or from the PC's USB port.

✦ A bit beyond the standard stereo speakers are speakers that come with a subwoofer. In this configuration, it's usually the subwoofer that connects directly to the console. The stereo speakers then connect to the subwoofer.

✦ At the pinnacle of computer speaker technology is *surround sound*. It involves multiple speakers situated around the computer to create realistic, 3D sound. Setting up such a thing requires a degree in audio engineering, though enthusiastic and motivated computer users can often handle the task.

Fixing silence

The biggest issue with computer sound is not hearing anything. It happens often. The solution is to follow a step-by-step process for eliminating the cause. Here's how I do it:

1. **Test the speakers as described in the section "Testing the speakers," earlier in this chapter.**

   The computer merely makes the sound. It's up to the speakers to produce the sound.

2. **Ensure that the speakers are connected to the computer.**

   Are the speakers plugged in? Are they plugged into the right jacks? If a subwoofer is connected, is it plugged in? Is it getting power? Is it even working?

   Most speakers need power to make noise.

3. **Check to see whether the speaker's volume control is turned up enough or that a hardware switch doesn't mute the speakers.**

4. **If you have another set of speakers, swap them out with the current set to see whether the speakers themselves haven't died and left behind a silent shell.**

5. **Check the Windows volume control (refer to Figure 7-5).**

   Is the volume high enough? Is the volume control muted?

6. **Check the volume mixer or volume control to ensure that individual audio devices haven't been muted.**

   The volume mixer or volume control allows you to set levels for various sound-generating items in the computer, such as the MIDI player or built-in synthesizer.

   To display the volume mixer in Windows 7 and Windows Vista, choose the Mixer link from the pop-up volume control; refer to Figure 7-5.

   To display the volume control in Windows XP, right-click the Volume icon in the notification area and choose the command Open Volume Control. The volume control is shown in Figure 7-6.

Figure 7-6:
The volume
control.

Ensure that individual devices haven't been muted; check the buttons at the bottom of the screen. Also confirm that the slider for a device isn't *bottomed out,* where the sound from that device is very low.

Close the volume mixer or volume control when you're done.

7. **Check the sound hardware configuration.**

Some PCs with speaker jacks on the front and back have to be configured to allow audio input from either place. For example, your PC may allow speakers to be plugged in the rear jacks but not in the front jacks at the same time. When your PC has this type of configuration, use the special sound software that came with the computer to confirm that all the sound jacks are working as you expect. (It's not a Windows-specific solution.)

8. **Confirm that the sound device is working properly.**

Use the Device Manager to confirm whether the sound hardware is hinkey. The Device Manager is covered later in this chapter.

9. **Check newly installed software that produces sound, such as games and sound utilities.**

Some programs may interfere or override Windows' own sound settings.

10. **Update the audio device drivers.**

Updating audio device drivers is also covered under the Device Manager topic, later in this chapter.

If all else fails, check your ears. Are other things making noise in the room? If so, the problem is probably the computer.

Things go wrong in a computer when something changes. If the sound just went out, try to recall what you just changed. It may help lead you to the solution.

✦ If you have trouble listening to an audio CD, the optical drive may have a problem. Some older CD-ROM drives had a separate cable for carrying the audio signal. You might want to open the case to ensure that the cable hasn't become disconnected. See Chapter 8 for details.

✦ Some speakers use both the green audio jack and the USB connector. That's because power is drawn from the USB connection. (The audio signal comes from the audio jack.) These speakers are mute when either the audio or USB connection isn't made.

✦ If the computer has never made sound, by all means contact its manufacturer or dealer.

Testing the microphone

For a microphone to work on your computer, it must be plugged into the proper audio jack. Table 7-1 says it's the pink jack. Plugging a microphone into any other audio jack results in less-than-satisfactory results. Well, unless it's a USB microphone, which simply plugs into the USB port.

After plugging in the microphone, test the thing. Testing works differently depending on your version of Windows.

To test the microphone in Windows 7 and Windows Vista, heed these steps:

1. **Ensure that the microphone is properly connected and stuff.**

2. **Open the Control Panel and choose Ease of Access.**

3. **Choose the link Set Up Microphone, found beneath the Speech Recognition heading.**

   The Microphone Setup Wizard materializes.

4. **Choose the type of microphone you're using: the headset, cheap-o desktop microphone or the they-saw-you-coming microphone that the guy at the music store sold you.**

5. **Click the Next button, and so on.**

   After seeing a few meaningless screens, you eventually approach the Adjust the Microphone Volume screen — pay dirt.

6. **Speak away.**

   Say: "Enunciation is the prestidigitation of audio infatuation." Or be a wienie and say, "Test, test."

   Watch that green bar go! Basically, by seeing the visual feedback, you confirm that the microphone is working.

7. **Continue working through the wizard or just click Cancel.**

   If you're satisfied with the results, you can bail out on the wizard. Otherwise, keep clicking Next and eventually you arrive at the Finish button.

To confirm that your microphone works in Windows XP, follow these steps:

1. **Plug in the microphone all nice and snug.**

   And stuff.

2. **Open the Control Panel's Sounds and Audio Devices icon.**

3. **Click the Voice tab.**

4. **Click the Test Hardware button.**

   The Sound Hardware Test Wizard appears.

5. **Click the Next button.**

   Hum a jaunty tune while the hardware is tested.

6. **Speak into the microphone to test the volume.**

   The volume meter on the screen should dance up and down as you vocalize.

7. **Click the Next button after confirming that the microphone works.**

8. **Click the Finish button.**

Your computer may not be configured to use the specific microphone jack that your microphone is plugged into. If your PC came with specific audio software, use it to configure the audio jacks to accept microphone input.

✦ Some applications may mute the microphone. Refer to Step 6 in the first set of steps in this section for information on using the volume mixer or volume control to unmute the PC's microphone.

✦ You don't want to spend too much or too little on a PC microphone. Cheap microphones don't work well, record poorly, and are annoying to hear for audio chat and online communications. Expensive microphones may require a mixer or pre-amp to work properly.

✦ Good microphones can be found in any computer or office supply store.

✦ I use a microphone headset, which provides both headphones and a microphone. It's perfect for online communications and gaming. And I'm not implying that I've been playing computer games when I should have been writing this book. No, sir!

Your Pal, the Device Manager

Windows features a central location for all the hardware in your PC. It's the Device Manager.

The *Device Manager* is that nerdy buddy you don't want to be seen with yet whose company you desperately need in times of digital peril — like MacGyver, but without a trace of personality or good looks. It's not a secret: The Device Manager merely provides a central location for accessing the various device Properties dialog boxes.

This section covers using the Device Manager as a PC hardware trouble-shooting tool.

Though the Device Manager lists every iota of hardware inside your PC, Windows 7 also has the Devices and Printers window, which lists the major hardware goodies in your computer system. As with the Device Manager, malfunctioning devices are flagged for troubleshooting in the Devices and Printers window.

Starting the Device Manager

To summon the Device Manager window in Windows Vista, heed these steps:

1. **Open the Control Panel.**

2. **Choose Hardware and Sound.**

3a. **In Windows 7, beneath the header Devices and Printers, choose Device Manager.**

3b. **In Windows Vista, choose View Hardware and Devices; click the Continue button or type the administrator's password to continue.**

The Device Manager window is shown in Figure 7-7.

In Windows XP, the steps to summon the Device Manager window are subtly different:

1. **Open the Control Panel's System icon.**

The keyboard shortcut for the System Properties dialog box is the Win+Break key combination, which is also a punch line somewhere.

2. **Click the Hardware tab in the System Properties dialog box.**

3. **Click the Device Manager button.**

The Device Manager window in Windows XP looks similar to the one shown in Figure 7-7.

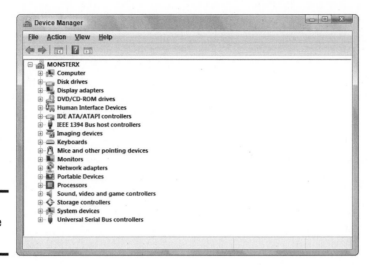

Figure 7-7:
The Device
Manager.

The Device Manager window lists all the hardware available to your PC by category. Opening a category lists specific devices, such as the PC's display adapter, shown in the Display Adapters category.

To open a category, click the + (plus) button next to the category name. The + button turns into a – (minus) button, which you can then click to close the category.

Double-click a device name to display the device's hardware Properties dialog box.

Close the Device Manager window when you're done.

Finding errant hardware

Compared with other operating systems, Windows is rather forgiving. For the sake of compatibility, Windows tolerates hardware that may not be working properly — hardware that would choke the Linux operating system into apoplexy. But rather than be ignorant of the damage, Windows alerts you to the troublesome hardware in the Device Manager.

Open the Device Manager per the instructions from the preceding section. Peruse the list. When you see either a small icon flagging a device or a category that's "open" (displaying its devices), you may have trouble.

 In Windows 7 and in Windows Vista, errant devices are flagged with a yellow-triangle warning icon.

In Windows XP, wayward devices are flagged with a yellow-circle warning icon.

The naughty device is shown open beneath its category heading. To see what's wrong (or what Windows believes to be wrong), double-click the device to display its Properties dialog box. In the Device Status area of the dialog box, you read a description of what the problem might be and potentially discover a solution.

Troubleshooting a gizmo in Windows XP

Windows XP features a special Troubleshoot button for devices in the Device Manager window. To access the button, double-click to open a device in the Device Manager window. Click the Troubleshooting button in the dialog box's General tab, as shown in Figure 7-8.

Figure 7-8: The special Troubleshooting button in Windows XP.

The Troubleshooting button opens a special troubleshooter window for the device, part of the Windows Help system. Follow the directions on the screen to answer questions about problems you're having and to view potential solutions.

Updating driver software

One vital thing you can do to keep your PC in shape is to ensure that your hardware always has the best, latest software. For many of the computer's gizmos, that means doing a software update. Here's how:

1. **Open the Device Manager window.**

Directions are found earlier in this chapter.

2. **Open the category containing the device.**

For example, Network Adapters for networking hardware.

3. **Double-click to open the device you want to update.**

4. **Click the Driver tab.**

The Driver tab in the device's Properties dialog box, which is beautifully depicted in Figure 7-9, contains several buttons dealing with updating the software that "drives" the device. (Windows XP lacks the Disable button.)

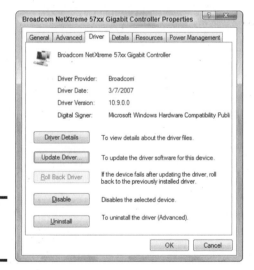

Figure 7-9:
Driver
control.

5. **To update a driver, click the Update Driver button.**

6a. **In Windows 7 and Windows Vista, choose the option Search Automatically for Updated Driver Software.**

6b. **In Windows XP, choose the option Install the Software Automatically (Recommended) and then click the Next button.**

Windows searches the computer and then the Internet for the latest or most current software to control the device. If a newer drive is found, it's automatically installed and updated; heed any directions given on the screen (such as to restart your computer).

When no new driver is found, you can assume that the driver is up-to-date.

7. **Close the window when you're done.**

It might be necessary to restart the computer after a software update. You're alerted to whether you need to restart after you close the device's Properties window.

The driver update procedure isn't foolproof. Sometimes, newer drivers are available but not found. In that case, you should go to the manufacturer's web site to check for new drivers.

If you don't know the manufacturer, use the device name at the top of the Properties dialog box (refer to Figure 7-9) as the search term for the Internet search engine of your choice. Peruse the results for a web page with *Download, Support,* or *Driver* in its title.

Chapter 8: Deep Inside the Computer Case

In This Chapter

✓ Opening the console

✓ Exploring inside your PC

✓ Maintaining basic goodies

✓ Adding an expansion card

✓ Upgrading your PC with more memory

✓ Adding an internal disk drive

*O*ne of the scariest things you can do as a computer owner, even scarier than letting your 13-year-old computer-genius nephew "check something for you," is to open the computer case. Yes, it's possible. Yes, it's sometimes a necessary operation for computer maintenance and troubleshooting. Yes, it's covered in this chapter.

Into the Case

Here's one vital piece of information you need to know before you take screwdriver in hand and attempt PC brain surgery: The computer case is the *console*. It's not "the box" or "the case," and it's especially not "the CPU." It's the *console*. Know that, and you're well on your way to computer hardware maintenance success.

Oh, and there are also a few safety issues I should mention, as covered in this section.

Opening the case

Before you can fix things inside the computer console, you must open the case. Here are some steps to take:

1. **Back up the computer's data if you haven't done so recently.**

You should have a backup copy of your computer's data fresh and available in case the most dreadful thing in the universe happens when you perform computer brain surgery.

2. **Set a system restore point in Windows.**

   See Book II, Chapter 8 for the details.

3. **Turn off the computer.**

4. **Unplug the computer.**

   This step may seem unimportant because the computer is turned off, right?

   Actually, the computer isn't turned off. It's still using power. Look at the PC's rump and you'll probably see the network adapter light blinking. Yep, there's still power a-flowin' inside Mr. PC. Unplug it.

   I recommend unplugging the power cord from the computer, not from the wall. If you unplug from the wall, some dutiful person may plug it back in "to help you out." Nope. Unplug the cord from the computer. When that's not possible, unplug from the wall and coil up the cord near you. Make snake-hissing noises if anyone trying to help you approaches the cord.

5. **Remove the console case cover.**

   Traditionally, computer cases are screwed shut; you find several screws on the rear of the case. Remove the screws with a screwdriver, though when they're the large-and-knobby type of screw, you can twist them with your thumb and fingers.

   If the screws are removable, set them aside and don't lose them.

   Some computers lack screws and feature a case-release mechanism. You may see a button to press or a bar to lift. The case then slides or lifts open.

   After the case cover is released, remove it. Sometimes the whole cover comes sliding off, and at other times you may be removing just a side panel.

6. **Behold the computer's guts!**

   Keep reading in the following section, though the later section, "The PC Console Adventure Map," describes where to find various things inside the computer.

Is the console dirty inside? Computers both blow and suck air, so dust is bound to accumulate. When the dust gets super thick, you can clean it off. Refer to Book VI, Chapter 4 for information on how best to clean the inside of the console.

✦ Watch Video 181 to see a demonstration of how to open the computer console:

   www.dummies.com/go/troubleshootingandmaintainingyourpcaio2e

✦ Refer to Book VI, Chapter 1 for more information on backing up your computer.

✦ Don't forget to close the case when you're done! See the later section, "Closing the case."

Grounding yourself

Any electrical device plugged into the wall socket commands respect from you, the human. As a soft and mostly water-based biological life-form, you're sensitive to mass quantities of electrons. Protection is vital.

The console is designed to keep the scary electronics on the inside, away from your probing fingers and dangling body parts. By unplugging the console, you ensure that the danger is minimized, but only from the console. As a human being, you pose a threat to the computer's electronics in the form of something called electrostatic discharge.

Electrostatic discharge can be a shocking experience. What happens is that the electrical potential between you and whatever you touch is great enough that a spark jumps out. The spark is the electrostatic discharge. It can damage delicate electronic components. That's a bad thing.

To help prevent electrostatic discharge, you must ground yourself.

In addition to having strong moral beliefs and a hardy stalk of ethics, you need to neutralize the electrical potential between yourself and the computer case. To easily accomplish this task, always keep one hand touching the computer's metal casing while you're working. By touching both the casing and whatever doodad you're installing or removing, you reduce the chance of an electrical-component-killing electrostatic discharge.

Electrostatic discharge is most likely to happen when it's dry outside. Be extra careful about grounding yourself when the humidity is low.

Closing the case

After meddling with your computer's delicate components, you need to close the case and turn the system back on, the whole time praying to your favorite deity that not only will the sucker work but also the problem will be fixed.

After installing or replacing or checking whatever prompted you to open the case, follow these general steps to close 'er up:

1. **Ensure that your job is complete.**

Check for any spare parts, screws, wrappers, eyeglasses, or electronic detritus remaining from whatever operation you performed.

Check any cables you might have loosened.

Ensure that every latch, screw, and cover you removed has been properly replaced.

Double-check to confirm that the installation was done properly.

2. **Replace the outside case, side, or lid.**

   Do you remember how the thing was removed? Whether it slid off or swung up? Sometimes, a metal lip or some notches must be aligned to properly position and then slide the case back on. Don't get frustrated! Don't force anything.

3. **Don't screw the lid shut just yet.**

   Of course, if the lid lacks screws, do whatever it takes to latch it shut.

4. **Plug in the console.**

5. **Turn on the computer.**

   It should come up right away. Refer to later sections in this book for troubleshooting individual hardware upgrades.

6. **If you haven't yet screwed the lid shut, do so after confirming that the computer works just fine.**

The reason I have you wait to screw the thing shut is that the upgrade might not have worked. If you need to go right back into the console, you save a step by not screwing the thing shut right away.

✦ A computer's case must be properly shut for the system to meet radio frequency interference (RFI) standards. These standards, monitored by the FCC in the United States, help keep the electronic noise generated by a computer inside the case from messing with other radio signals.

✦ Watch Video 182 to see the author of this book attempt to close a computer case in a proper and dignified manner.

www.dummies.com/go/troubleshootingandmaintainingyourpcaio2e

The PC Console Adventure Map

Don't be alarmed, but opening a computer case takes you one step closer to becoming a true computer nerd. In fact, after the fourth or fifth time you open the case, you might find yourself wanting to wear a pocket protector or feeling the urge to visit the back part of a Fry's Electronics store. Such thoughts may paralyze you.

After you overcome the Geek Factor fear, you'll recognize that maintaining your computer is no more difficult than maintaining your car. In fact, it's easier! You rarely, if ever, need to change the oil in your computer. And, a memory leak? Keep that bucket in the garage!

Not every computer looks the same inside, but every PC has similar components. Before you rummage around inside the console, get to know the territory. Figure 8-1 shows a typical PC's innards the way you might behold them after removing your PC console's lid.

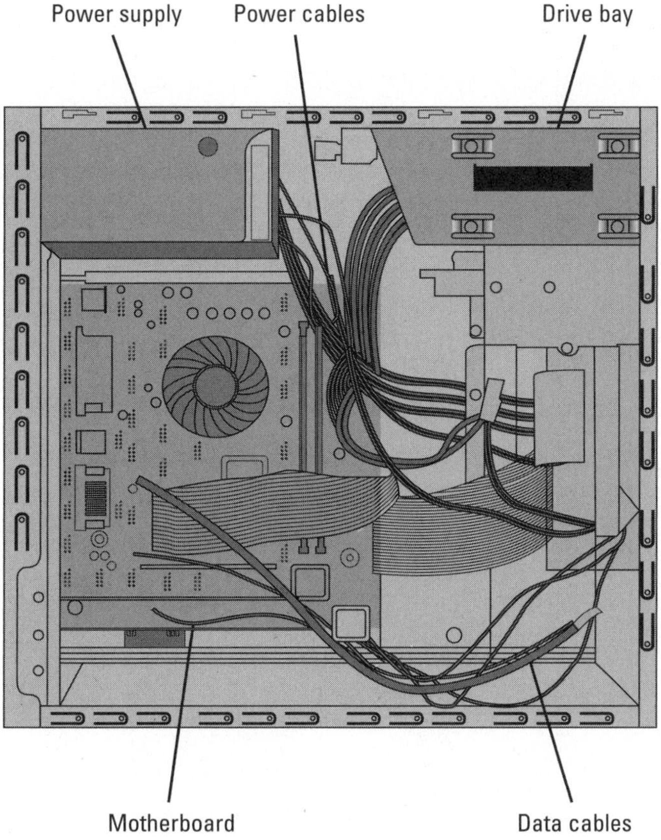

Figure 8-1:
A typical
PC's guts.

Get to know and identify these major items inside a PC console:

Power supply: The power supply converts the alternating current (AC) from the wall into direct current (DC) inside the computer. The easiest way to find it is to look for the location where the power plug connects to the console (usually, on the back). The power supply is right inside the case at that spot.

Cables: The power supply's colorful cables snake from the power supply outward. One or two clusters go to the motherboard, and others go to the mass storage devices — the disk drives. The majority of cables, however, may just hang in space to wait for future internal expansion. In addition to the power cables, various data cables run hither and thither. The smaller your PC, the more the cables obstruct your view of the items inside the console.

Drive bay: Also known as the *disk drive cage,* the drive bay occupies a lot of space inside the console. The bay contains the hard drive and optical drive; plus, it has room to add other drives. The front side of the drive bay is the front of the console, where you can access removable storage.

Motherboard: The motherboard is the main circuitry board dwelling inside the console. It's probably difficult to see because it can be obscured by cables or the drive bay or both. Figure 8-2 illustrates a motherboard that has been freed from the confines of its console prison.

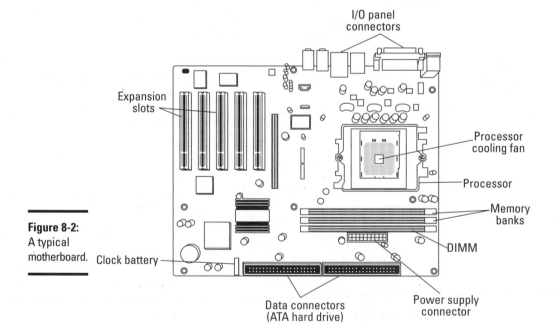

Figure 8-2: A typical motherboard.

The following items are found specifically on the motherboard and illustrated in Figure 8-2:

I/O panel connectors: The I/O panel is where you connect peripherals to the PC, including USB gizmos, the keyboard and mouse, the monitor, speakers, and other things of that ilk. Sometimes, the I/O panel is right on the motherboard (refer to Figure 8-2), or a cable may connect the motherboard to the I/O panel elsewhere in the console.

Processor cooling fan: You may not see the processor directly. That's because today's processors run very hot, and they require direct cooling. So what you see rather than the processor itself is the tiny heat hat it wears, which is really a cooling fan (not shown in Figure 8-2). Some processors also use elaborate *heat sinks*, which are metal gizmos shaped like high-tech flowers that help dissipate the high temperatures.

Processor: The processor rests beneath the cooling fan. You cannot see the processor unless you remove the fan, though I recommend that you not remove the fan just to see the processor. Trust me: It's there.

Memory banks: A typical PC sports anywhere from two to eight memory banks on its motherboard, or sometimes on a tiny expansion card jutting from the motherboard. Memory banks are always in pairs of two. Essentially, they're tiny expansion slots into which memory cards, or *DIMMs,* are inserted.

DIMM: Your computer's memory comes on tiny, comb-size expansion cards called DIMMs, or Dual In-line Memory Modules. I cover DIMMs in detail later in this chapter.

Power supply connector: The motherboard needs power, so a specific connector exists on the motherboard for the power supply.

Data connectors: The motherboard is also home to various places where data cables connect. It may have a place to plug in cables for the disk drives, speaker, I/O panel, console lamps, and other things I can't think of right now.

Clock battery: The clock battery helps the PC keep track of time when the computer is unplugged. The battery, found somewhere on the motherboard, looks like a large coin. In Figure 8-2, the clock battery is mounted vertically, which makes it difficult to see.

Expansion slots: To help customize your computer, expansion slots allow bonus circuitry in the form of *expansion cards* to be plugged in. An expansion card can add features such as a new display adapter, more USB ports, fancy audio, wireless networking, and a whole host of options. You may not see the expansion slots inside your PC when expansion cards are plugged into them.

The inside of your computer may look scary. It should! Electronics are intimidating. They command respect. Still, the reason you're using a PC and not a Commodore 64 today is that the PC was designed to be upgradable. It's part of the PC's success: Anyone with relatively basic knowledge can update, fix, or maintain their computer.

✦ View Video 183 to see a visual exploration of the insides of a PC:

  `www.dummies.com/go/troubleshootingandmaintainingyourpcaio2e`

✦ Older PCs sport a floppy drive or perhaps even a Zip drive in the drive cage.

✦ PC disk drives come in two *form factors,* or dimensions. A larger size is used by optical drives, which is about 5¼ inches wide. A smaller form factor is used by most hard drives, which is about 3½ inches wide. Either you see a different-size drive bay for every type of form factor or adapters can be used to put the smaller drives into the larger bays.

✦ Sometimes, the disk drive cage can be quite extensive. High-end PCs may have room for four or more optical drives and four or more hard drives.

✦ It's not necessary to remove the motherboard from your PC. I don't recommend it. I don't even recommend replacing a motherboard.

✦ Another term for the processor is *CPU,* or *central processing unit.* Too many people confuse the CPU with the console, so for clarity's sake, I refer to the CPU as "the processor" in this book, and to the console as "that box-thing the computer lives inside of" (which is improper English, but I use it to drive my editor nuts).

✦ In the olden days, the hard drive's face stuck out the front of the PC, just like the optical drive. The blinking hard drive light you saw on a PC from the early 1990s was, in fact, the lamp on the hard drive itself. Today's hard drives, however, are strictly internal beasts. The hard drive interface communicates the blinking light information to the console, which then flashes a hard drive lamp for the human to behold.

Common Problems and Solutions

Some frustrating issues can arise out of problems that are rather simple to fix. Here's a quick list of some things to look for inside the computer case for general troubleshooting purposes.

Checking for loose cables

Two types of cables are inside the console: power and data. Some gizmos, like disk drives, require both.

To ensure that cables are properly attached, follow these steps:

1. **Follow the steps earlier in this chapter for opening the console.**

2. **Locate the spot where the cable attaches.**

3. **Give the cable a little tug.**

   If the cable is loose, it falls out. If it does, reattach it.

4. **Gently press the cable so that it's snugly attached.**

Cables have two ends. You need to check both ends.

When you find a free cable, one that isn't plugged in anywhere, do some hunting to figure out where it goes. When the cable was plugged into a device, you can guess where it goes by looking in its general vicinity (or remembering which gizmo isn't working).

Cables that connect to the motherboard have multiple issues. Sometimes, you luck out and the cable can plug into only one location and in only one orientation. That's good. When you have multiple opportunities to plug in a cable, don't guess: Plugging a cable into the wrong spot may have no ill effects, but then again you can damage the computer by guessing.

If you need to detach a cable while working on the PC, use a pair of colored, sticky dots to label both the cable you unplugged and the connector from which you unplugged it. For example, place a blue sticky on the cable end and a blue sticky on the socket. Use different colors for each set of cable ends and connectors. When you're done, you'll know where to reconnect everything. Sticky dots can be found at any office supply store.

✦ Cables don't normally pop out by themselves. They can work loose, but they normally don't spring out of their connectors.

✦ Often cables bend and twist, and thanks to Mother Nature, they stay in those positions. You can use the bends and twists to help you locate where cables go and in which orientation they were set originally.

✦ Power cables can often be tough to attach. Sometimes they require a lot of push to get them all the way in the connector.

✦ Also refer to the section "Reseating expansion cards," later in this chapter, for information on securing a loose expansion card.

Dissipating heat

The biggest issue, and the cause of most console problems, is heat. The computer enjoys a cool environment. Electronics *love* the cold. But all that high-tech madness taking place inside your computer makes for a lot of heat. A major part of the console's design goes toward removing heat from the computer.

A typical PC has two cooling fans. One fan is atop the processor. A second fan is located inside the power supply.

The processor's fan is designed to keep the processor cool, but it just pumps air into the console.

The power supply's fan is designed to draw air out of the console. Air slots on the front of the console draw in (supposedly) cool air from the room. You can easily find the front air slots when you have a dog or cat, because the slots are lined with ample quantities of your pet's hair.

A third fan might also be found on the display adapter. Just as with the processor on the motherboard, the display adapter's graphics processor (GPU) needs to be kept cool. A fan on the display adapter expansion card serves this cooling purpose.

High-end computers offer additional console fans. You can also purchase upgraded power supplies with better fans, as well as additional fans for the console. The extra fans, which use the bonus power-supply cables inside the console, help circulate the air.

At the extreme end of the console-cooling fixation are various liquid contraptions. The so-called water-cooled computers use liquid (often, water) to cool a PC in the same way as water cools a car engine. Usually, you have to buy a specific water-cooled case to get this feature.

Another heat-dissipating doodad is the traditional *heat sink,* a piece of metal designed to draw off heat and use the air to keep components cool. Heat sinks aren't as efficient as fans or water cooling.

Upgrade, Replace, Maintain

Your computer was built for expandability. Most of it is conveniently located *outside* the console: Thanks to the ubiquitous USB port, you can instantly attach a number of hardware goodies to your computer — no fuss. But your computer has options for internal expansion. Not only that, but you may also occasionally need to perform open console surgery on a PC to fix a problem. If so, you've come to the right part of this book.

✦ For tools, you need a medium-sized Phillips screwdriver. You might need a small Phillips screwdriver, but it's the most you need. Some computer cases are designed so that you don't need any tools.

✦ Because I do a lot of upgrading and other electrical work, I have a power screwdriver. You can see me use it in some of this book's videos.

✦ One good thing: There's no way to accidentally plug in anything backward on your PC. All its connectors are *keyed,* which means that you can plug in items in only one way.

✦ Another term for a connector you can't plug in wrong: *idiot-proof.* I didn't make it up.

✦ Give yourself plenty of time to work on your computer. Don't rush. Have lots of room. If you prefer to work uninterrupted, inform others that you don't want to be disturbed. Do so in a loud voice so as to drive the point home.

✦ Laptops aren't built for expandability, not like PC desktops are. Refer to Book III for more information on expanding laptop computers.

✦ It took me an hour to add an expansion card to my first computer. The computer wasn't supposed to be upgraded by a user, but I did it anyway. Yes, I voided the warranty by doing so. I enjoyed the task so well, and enjoyed not paying someone else to do the work, that I did many upgrades afterward. I even swapped out a CRT monitor tube, which is something I wouldn't recommend — or attempt again.

Buying replacement parts

Gone are the days when you had to search for places that sell computer parts. In the old days, I scoured the back of computer magazines for mail order places. When you know what you want, you can easily buy the stuff cheap from a catalog. The web has replaced this method, though.

The first step to buying replacement parts or upgrades is to know what you want. I leave it up to you to do the research, though I offer some advice in the following sections. Ordering the right part means that you don't have to mess with returns or get stuck with something you'll never use. (Visit my web site for a view of my SCSI adapter collection: `www.wambooli.com/fun/dang/scsi`.)

The second step is to know where to buy. You have, in reality, only two choices left: a real store or the Internet.

Real stores are helpful in that you have the opportunity to ask someone a question (count yourself lucky when they know the answer), take the item home right away, and avoid shipping charges — and you have a spot to return the item if it doesn't work.

The Internet is nice because you can find the cheapest prices and a wide variety of vendors. Internet stores also seem to carry more stock than local computer outfits do. You pay for shipping, and you have to wait for your stuff to arrive. When you need the part in a pinch, that sucks.

The final step is to purchase your stuff with a credit card. I recommend using credit cards because they offer consumers the highest level of protection when it comes to fraud. If you pay cash, you get ripped off. No one pays cash. Check? Same thing. Credit card charges can be reversed if the merchant doesn't fill your order or when you get something you didn't order or that doesn't work. Use a credit card.

Too many dealers are out there for me to recommend specific places to go. If you want recommendations, ask your friends. I like Fry's Electronics. I've bought stuff at Best Buy, Office Max, Office Depot, Staples, and Costco. Online, I use ZipZoomFly.com, shop4tech.com, and the old standby Amazon.com.

✦ Choose a dealer that's been around a while. It's a plus when the dealer has a real location.

✦ Never buy from a dealer in a print ad, such as in a magazine, when the dealer doesn't list a phone number.

✦ Always, always, always check for the product return policy. Some stuff cannot be returned. Be aware of that before you order. (It's another reason to always order the right item the first time.)

✦ Though too many of my friends swear by them, I don't recommend buying computer parts at a swap meet. Only if the "dealer" is a consistent vendor and has a real-world address or a web page that's been up for a few years would I trust them. I've just heard too many stories of junk being sold, or of disreputable people reselling stolen merchandise, to feel comfortable with computer swap meets.

Replacing the power supply

If the power supply is dead, it needs replacing. You can have this done by a professional in a white lab coat or simply note the power supply's product number and search for a replacement unit locally or on the Internet. But the key is knowing the part number. For that, you have to remove the power supply:

1. **Open the computer's case as described earlier in this chapter.**

2. **Lay the computer on its side.**

The open end of the console should be facing up. You don't want to work on the power supply when the console is in a vertical position because it's more difficult to remove it that way.

3. **Detach all the power cables from all the devices in the console.**

Disconnect power cables from the disk drives and the motherboard, plus any other devices they're attached to.

4. **Remove the power supply screws.**

The screws can be accessed from the back of the console case. Be sure that you're removing the screws that anchor the power supply, not anything else.

Some power supplies use four screws; some use three.

5. **Confirm that nothing is in the power supply's way.**

   Some smaller consoles may have things that need to be removed before the power supply can be freed. I've had to pull out a DVD drive to get a power supply out. I've also had to remove the entire console case to remove a power supply from a PC from the top rather than from the side.

6. **Liberate the power supply!**

   When you cannot remove the power supply, you forgot one or more screws.

After the power supply is free, you can search it for its part number or ID. You can search the Internet by using the part number along with the key words *power supply*. Or, you can visit the manufacturer's web site to order a spare if that's an option. Most power supplies are fairly standard gizmos.

Consider getting a replacement power supply that packs more wattage or perhaps has extra cooling power. But remember that the replacement must still fit into (or be compatible with) your PC's console. If possible, take the old power supply with you to the parts store to ensure that its dimensions — especially the cable lengths — are identical.

To install the replacement, follow these steps, which are generally the reverse of the preceding steps, so I've numbered them backward:

6. **Unpack the new power supply.**

   If it came with specific instructions, follow them.

5. **Ensure that the PC case is open and ready to receive the new power supply.**

   If you had to remove anything to get the power supply out, you need to remove those same things to put the new power supply in (unless you just left your PC hanging open in the interim).

4. **Anchor the power supply by screwing it back into the case.**

3. **Reattach all the power cables from all the devices in the console.**

   Every disk drive needs power. The motherboard needs power. Anything else?

2. **Set the computer upright again.**

1. **Close the computer's case as described earlier in this chapter; remember not to tighten the screws until you know that the computer powers up.**

Refer to Video 184 for a visual example of removing and then reinstalling a PC's power supply:

www.dummies.com/go/troubleshootingandmaintainingyourpcaio2e

Replacing the clock battery

Computers keep track of time, but not reliably. A typical computer's clock can be off by as much as several minutes a day, depending on what the computer is doing. The reason for the delay is that the computer's internal clock suffers from a lack of attention.

For example, a busy computer often "borrows" time from the clock. The computer becomes so obsessed with a task that the basic job of updating the PC's ticker just doesn't happen. Those missing seconds add up.

Computers connected to the Internet can update the time by using the Internet Time feature in Windows. This feature fixes those missing minutes every day. But when the computer is turned off, the time is kept ticking by a tiny battery attached to the computer's motherboard. When the battery goes, you see weird start-up messages and potentially other problems.

To fix the clock battery problem, you replace the motherboard's battery: Open the computer's case as described earlier in this chapter. Locate the battery on the motherboard. It's often a lithium battery, one of those coin-size jobs you can buy anywhere that watch or hearing aid batteries are sold.

Be sure to close the computer case when you're done replacing the battery. Directions for both opening and closing a computer's case are offered earlier in this chapter.

Motherboard batteries last for years. When the battery goes, it's often a sign that the computer is ancient and needs to be replaced. Although you can merely replace the battery, I highly recommend that you consider a new PC eventually.

The Miracle of Expansion Cards

To help add hardware to your console, the PC comes with a set of internal *expansion slots*. You plug *expansion cards* into the slots, adding new abilities and superpowers to your meek and mild computer.

Common expansion card goodies include video adapters, high-end sound cards, networking adapters, port adapters, and more! But this section wasn't written to sell expansion cards — merely to explain how to upgrade your PC by using those cards.

Exploring expansion slots

After you know which kind of expansion card you need, the next and most difficult decision is to determine which slot it plugs into on your PC's motherboard. Each standard has a bunch of different expansion slot standards and variations.

The two most common slots available on today's PCs are PCI and PCI-Express:

PCI: The Peripheral Component Interconnect type of slot is the most popular and widely available expansion slot on today's PCs. It's normally colored white, though often beige is used. The expansion slots shown on the motherboard in Figure 8-2 are standard 32-bit PIC expansion slots. There are also 64-bit versions of the slots, which are longer than those shown in Figure 8-2.

PCI-Express: The latest rendition of the PCI standard is PCI-Express, which features a different type of slot than the one shown in Figure 8-2. PCI-Express slots are generally colored black or dark gray or sometimes even yellow. They also feature a variety of sizes, as illustrated in Figure 8-3.

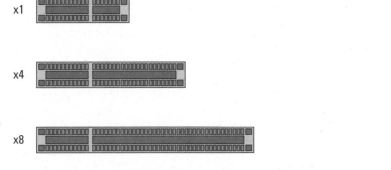

x1

x4

Figure 8-3:
Different
types of
PCI-Express
slots.

x8

x16

Older expansion standards include

PCI-X: The PCI *Extended* standard was developed to improve on PCI, but as a standardPCI-Express superseded it. Some older PCs may still feature the PCI-X slot, which looks like a standard PCI slot but is considerably longer.

Be careful not to confuse PCI-X with PCI-Express! They're different standards, different slots, and different expansion card types.

AGP: The Accelerated Graphics Port slot was designed specifically to handle high-end graphics adapters. It may still be found on older PCs, but today's systems use PCI-Express expansion slots to handle high-end graphics adapters. AGP slots were often colored maroon and had a hinged hook on one end to help anchor the AGP card.

ISA: The original expansion slot for the PC family was ISA, which simply stood for Industry Standard Architecture (because the expansion slot lacked an official and suitably technical-sounding name). It had two varieties: 16-bit and a longer 16-bit version. An older Windows XP system may still sport an ISA slot, but few (if any) relevant ISA expansion cards are available today.

Sadly, there's no solid way to determine what type of slots are present on your PC's motherboard, let alone whether the slots are available (or empty). The only way to know for certain is to open the case and have a look.

✦ When the PC's motherboard features a variety of slots, and you have a choice, choose a PCI-Express expansion card first.

✦ Expansion slots are *keyed:* The edge connector on the expansion card cannot be plugged in backward. Of course, most expansion cards feature a rear slot mount, which means that you have to be determined to plug an expansion card in backward in the first place!

✦ You can look on the back of your PC and examine the slot covers to determine whether a slot is empty. A blank slot cover, however, may not indicate that an expansion slot is available, because some expansion cards may not use the slot cover. Also, some expansion cards are double-wide and may render useless any empty expansion slots next to them.

✦ Even though the expansion slots are all standardized, expansion cards come in different lengths. You can find full-length cards, half-size cards, and others. Smaller PC consoles may have room for only smaller expansion cards, or perhaps some expansion slots are limited to hosting only shorter expansion cards. Knowing this type of information before you buy an expansion card will prove to be a boon to your self-esteem.

✦ PCI-X also featured two sets of voltages for expansion cards: 5 volts and 3.3 volts. Special notches in the expansion cards prevented the wrong slot from being used, but the differing voltages were still an issue for choosing the proper PCI-X expansion card.

Inserting an expansion card

Expansion cards are almost tinketoy simple to insert into a computer. Here are my general steps for updating your PC with a new hardware feature via an expansion slot.

These steps assume, of course, that you have bought the proper gizmo you need, that it's compatible with your computer, and that it's of the correct expansion slot type for the motherboard:

1. **Study the instructions that came with the expansion card.**

They're more detailed than what's written here, or they may have important notes such as whether to install any needed software and when to install the software (before or after adding the expansion card).

2. **Follow the directions earlier in this book for opening the computer case.**

Don't forget the part about backing up your data! Don't forget to set a system restore point!

3. **Locate an available expansion slot.**

Hopefully, you've already done this, or are at least aware of where the open slot is and that it's available and you've further purchased an expansion card designed to fit into said slot.

4. **Remove the slot cover associated with the expansion slot.**

The slot cover is part of the console, on the back of the PC. It not only anchors the back half of the card but also provides access for any connectors the card may sacrifice to the outside world. Figure 8-4 illustrates the slot-and-slot-cover relationship.

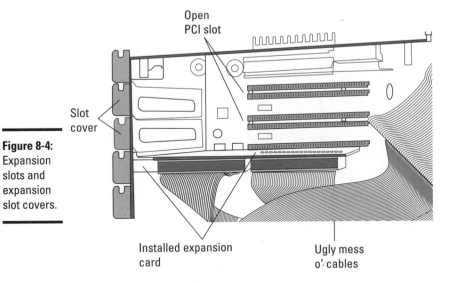

Figure 8-4:
Expansion slots and expansion slot covers.

The slot cover is anchored in a number of ways. Most commonly, it's a single screw on top. You might also find that the entire row of slot covers is held in place by a swinging latch (the latch is open in Figure 8-4). Some slot covers are punch-out covers and must be twisted or popped out by pressing with your thumb.

Save the screw you removed to take off the expansion slot cover.

5. **Eyeball the expansion slot to ensure that you can easily place the expansion card inside the console.**

   Check for any obstructing cables (refer to Figure 8-4) and gently shove them out of the way or disconnect them temporarily if necessary. You may have to remove another expansion card or perhaps even a disk drive to reach the expansion slot in question.

6. **Remove the expansion card from its protective, antistatic enclosure.**

7. **If the expansion card requires configuration, do so now.**

   The manual that came with the expansion card should explain in poor English whether you need to configure it further, and how to do it.

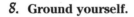

8. **Ground yourself.**

9. **Insert the expansion card into the expansion slot.**

   Two things help keep the expansion card in place: the slot itself and the slot cover. Gently press the card into the slot. Ease 'er in! Only when the slot cover is flush with the back slot (where it's supposed to be) is the card fully in place.

   When the back cover doesn't line up, you most likely removed the wrong slot cover. Go back to Step 4 and find the slot cover properly associated with the given slot.

10. **Check everything.**

    Does the expansion card look right? Is the slot cover flush? Don't force anything! If the card isn't inserted properly, you most likely plugged it into the wrong expansion slot.

11. **Reattach any cables you disconnected or reinsert anything you removed to get the card in place.**

12. **Attach the slot cover to the case.**

    Use the same screw you removed in Step 4, if need be.

13. **Close the case as described earlier in this chapter.**

14. **Turn on the computer.**

    At this point, installation continues but is different depending on whichever device you installed.

Most likely, Windows starts up and instantly recognizes the new hardware. If the drivers weren't already installed, Windows installs them automatically or asks for a disc containing the drivers.

✦ Watch Video 185 for a demonstration of how to add a new expansion card to your PC:

   www.dummies.com/go/troubleshootingandmaintainingyourpcaio2e

✦ You may need to reactivate or validate your copy of Windows after performing a major hardware addition, such as adding a new expansion card. Windows alerts you to this necessity. As long as you have a legitimate copy of Windows, you can easily activate or verify your copy over the Internet.

✦ Discard the old slot cover you removed. There's no need to keep it. I have a drawer full of them. Having a single spare is okay if you ever decide to retire an expansion card, but the odds of doing so are rare.

✦ Technically, it's not okay to keep a slot uncovered. The computer manufacturer receives its RFI certification based on the case's full design, which includes expansion slot covers. Radio interference generated inside the computer blasts out of an open slot cover.

Updating a display adapter

Adding a new display adapter to your PC works just like adding any expansion card. But beyond the physical installation, I'd like for you to be aware of a few things when performing this type of operation.

When updating a display adapter, you're either removing an adapter card or simply replacing the video adapter supplied by the computer's motherboard. Either way, there's nothing extra you need to do on the hardware side. The computer recognizes the new display adapter when you turn on the PC again.

By the way, turning the computer on again results in a generic, low-resolution display. Don't let it alarm you! Windows doesn't know anything about the new display adapter, so it returns to using the generic, low-end video adapter driver. After you install the new drivers, you can reselect your favorite display resolution.

✦ Yes, by switching to the low-resolution driver, Windows juggles any icons you have pasted to the desktop. You can restore the icons to their previous positions after updating the display adapter software.

✦ There's no need to disable the motherboard's display adapter hardware. You still see it show up in the list of display adapters in the Device Manager (see Chapter 7).

✦ You can also install a second display adapter and use two display adapters in Windows. Refer to Chapter 6 for more information on running two monitors.

Removing an expansion card

Rarely, if ever, do you need to remove an expansion card, but it happens. The last card I removed was an internal modem from one PC so that I could install it in another computer.

To remove an expansion card, follow these general steps:

1. **Turn off the computer, and remember to back up your data (if necessary) and set a restore point, all as described earlier in this chapter.**

2. **Open the PC case.**

3. **Locate the expansion card to remove.**

4. **Move any cables or other obstacles out of the way.**

   If necessary, detach cables or remove disk drives. After the procedure is complete, be sure to remember how to reinstall them.

5. **Free the expansion card's slot cover: Unscrew the screw or release the latch holding the slot cover in place.**

6. **Ensure that no cables are attached to the expansion card or in its way.**

7. **Gently pull out the card.**

   Pinch the card with your fingers and thumb and gently ease it out. If necessary, rock the card from front to back.

8. **Replace the screw or slot cover.**

   If you kept an old slot cover around, put it back over the hole so that the console case is intact.

9. **Close the console as described earlier in this chapter.**

10. **Turn on the computer.**

Windows may alert you to the device's absence. If so, follow whatever directions are given on the screen.

Store the card in a safe place, where it won't be squished, bent, or broken or come into contact with liquid, metal, or humans under the age of 9.

As with adding new hardware, when you remove hardware from a PC, you may have to revalidate or reactivate Windows. Do so when prompted after you upgrade and start your PC.

Reseating expansion cards

It's possible, though rare, for an expansion card to wiggle out of its socket. Blame the heat: Turning a computer off and on changes the console's internal temperature. That can have the effect of wiggling an expansion card free of its roost.

To reseat an expansion card, simply press it down firmly but gently into its socket. Ensure that the card's rear bracket is properly attached. (Some consoles use screws, and others may use a hinged bracket to keep the expansion cards in place.)

Your PC Wants More Memory

One of the cheapest and easiest ways to deal with a slow PC is to add more memory. For a computer, more RAM is like the best Christmas ever! This section explains how to upgrade your PC with more memory.

This section refers to memory expansion options using the term DIMM, or Dual In-line Memory Module. Laptops and some older PCs may use different options, such as SIMM, SIP, SODIMM, or others. See Book III for more laptop information.

Understanding memory banks

Your computer's motherboard sports slots into which memory is plugged. I call the slots *memory banks*, simply because I've been trained to use the term by such great television shows as *Star Trek*, *Lost in Space*, and *The Time Tunnel*. In fact, I believe computer science today owes quite a lot to the 1960s television genius of Irwin Allen.

How many memory banks your PC may have depends on what the manufacturer deemed best. What's important is how those banks are filled with memory; you can't just plug memory into the motherboard willy-nilly.

In Figure 8-5, you see several ways that a motherboard with four memory banks can host two common amounts of memory: 1GB or 2GB. Because DIMMs come in different memory sizes, memory can be set up in a variety of ways inside any PC, as shown in the figure.

You may have many reasons for choosing different arrangements of memory in a PC, but the number-one reason is that memory can be expensive. A single 2GB DIMM (refer to F in Figure 8-5) can cost ten times as much as a 256MB DIMM. So, though you probably didn't know it at the time, one reason your PC was offered at a given price was its memory configuration.

Another reason for using, say, two 1GB DIMMs (refer to E in Figure 8-5) rather than four 512MB DIMMs (refer to D in Figure 8-5) to get 2GB of memory is expandability. Upgrading memory is easier later, when memory banks are available.

   ✦ Some PCs have a pairing requirement. The memory banks are organized in pairs, and every pair must have the same DIMM size. For example, you can have 3GB of memory in a PC with four memory banks. That's two 1GB DIMMs in two slots and two 512MB DIMMs in the other two slots.

   ✦ Yes, when you make a poor choice in buying your computer, you may end up throwing away memory to upgrade. If your PC is configured with 1GB of memory (refer to A in Figure 8-5) and you want 2GB of memory total, you have to throw away all the 256MB DIMMs and replace them with a combination of DIMMs (refer to D, E, or F).

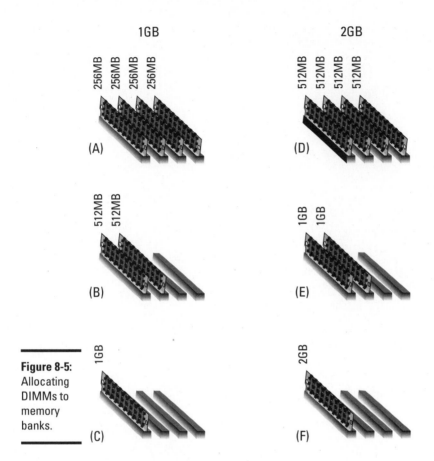

1GB   2GB

256MB 256MB 256MB 256MB   512MB 512MB 512MB 512MB

(A)   (D)

512MB 512MB   1GB 1GB

(B)   (E)

1GB   2GB

(C)   (F)

Figure 8-5:
Allocating
DIMMs to
memory
banks.

Getting the right DIMM

Not all DIMMs are alike. Things can get confusing when you're picking out a DIMM. Too bad you just can't thump them like you thump melons in the grocery store.

First comes *memory type*. There are several common types, as shown in Table 8-1. Consider all that to be technical information, however. Your computer uses only one memory type, and you must pick a DIMM that matches the type. One way to know which type of memory your PC uses is to examine the invoice — if you still have it. Otherwise, other methods are available, as described in the next section.

Second, after memory type, is the memory chip's *speed*. Oh, I could wax on about memory chip speed and how it ties into this or that technical thing. Unless you knew a lot about memory, I could probably make it all up and you'd nod your head knowingly, wanting to rush through it and not understand it (despite my making it all up). But like the memory type, the speed isn't something you pick; it's something the PC's designer chose when building the motherboard. You merely have to ensure that you buy the correct memory speed that your computer is designed to accept. Again, look on the invoice or refer to the next section.

Table 8-1	PC Memory Types
Type	*Description*
DRAM	The official name of a RAM (Random Access Memory) chip: Dynamic Random Access Memory
DDR	A Double Data Rate RAM chip, also known as DDRRAM, which is an improvement on SDRAM
DDR2	Another implementation of the DDR type of SDRAM chip
DDR3	Yet another implementation of the DDR type of SDRAM chip
EDO	The Extended Data Out RAM chip
FPM	The Fast Page Mode type of DRAM chip
SDRAM	A type of DRAM chip, Synchronous Dynamic Random Access Memory

Third, and seriously most confusing, is the *type* of DIMM. Not all memory bank slots are created equal. Each slot uses a different number of connectors, or *pins*. Some are 100-pin, some are 184-pin, and others are 200-pin. It varies. To know how many pins the DIMMs need for your PC, you can check the invoice or you can bother to open the PC and count all the connectors. But rather than do that, just refer to the next section.

Yeah, I didn't need to explain all this. It's a bother. But if you ever tried to upgrade PC memory, as I have, and you didn't pay attention to the details, you ended up with a drawer full of DIMMs that you cannot use in any computer. Instead of wasting money building a fun yet technologically obscure mobile, it helps to know a little bit about what you're doing.

Adding memory

You must discover two things before you add memory to your PC: how much memory is already in your computer and how many available memory banks it has. After you know this info, it's just a matter of determining which type of DIMM, and how many, you need in order to bring your PC up to par.

The first step is to figure out how much memory you need. Your PC may be able to use only a specific amount of memory. For example, the PC I'm using to write this book can have a maximum of only 8GB of RAM. Right now, it has

2GB. If I needed 4GB, I'd have to buy . . . anyone? Yes! I'd have to buy 2GB more of memory.

The second step is to discover all the quantifications about the DIMMs you need. You can easily pay someone else to do it: Drop off the computer at the shop and let them fuss over it. But that's probably not why you bought this book.

You can also attempt to discover on your own which type of memory you need. You can open the case and yank out a DIMM. You can stare at it. You can sleep with it under your pillow. But that probably doesn't help you much.

Or, you can find some help and have a computer program determine how much memory is installed in your computer and how best to update. Computer programs can figure out this stuff without the need to open the computer case. After all, programs run inside the computer, where they can see everything.

The site I recommend using on the Internet is at `www.crucial.com`, which also, coincidentally, sells computer memory. Visit the web site. Use the Crucial system scanner tool; follow the directions on the web page. Eventually, it tells you exactly how to upgrade your PC's memory. My results are shown in Figure 8-6.

Figure 8-6:
The Crucial memory scanner tool.

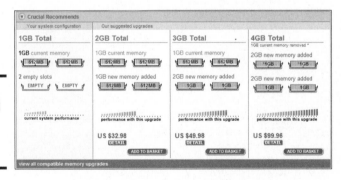

As you can see in the figure, my PC has 1GB installed using two 512MB DIMMs. It has two open slots. The rest of the figure explains various options for upgrading, including options for keeping the memory and options for removing existing memory. (On my other PCs, I discovered — much to my chagrin — that all the memory banks are full and that I'd have to upgrade to replace memory.)

The third step is to buy the memory. The Crucial web site not only tells you how much and which type of DIMMs you need, but also lets you buy the memory on the spot. It's one reason why I recommend the site. (The other is that Crucial is located in Idaho.)

The final step is to install the memory. Here are the general steps to take:

1. **Open the console as described earlier in this chapter.**

2. **(Optional) Remove any old memory if necessary.**

   a. *Locate the DIMMs you want to remove.*

   b. *Push the hooks on the ends of the DIMM.*

   By pushing the hooks out and down, you free the DIMM from the slot.

   c. *Pull out the DIMM and gently set it aside.*

   d. *Repeat these substeps for any additional DIMMs you need to remove.*

3. **Push down the clips on both ends of the memory bank slots.**

   See Figure 8-7.

4. **Remove the memory from its protective, antistatic bag.**

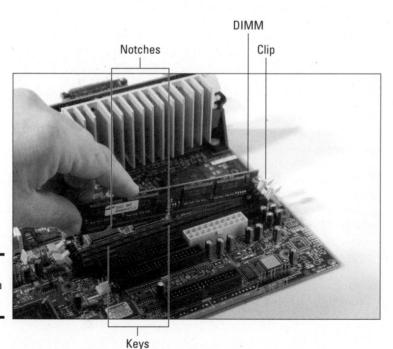

Notches   DIMM   Clip

Keys

Figure 8-7:
Upgrading a
DIMM.

Avoid touching the metal edge on the DIMM, the part that's inserted into the slot.

If you're removing DIMMs, take the ones you removed and store them in the protective bag that held the new DIMMs.

5. **Ground yourself.**

6. **Line up the DIMM with the slot.**

There are notches on the DIMM. There are keys on the slot. The notches and keys must match in order to prevent you from accidentally plugging the DIMM in backward. Use Figure 8-7 as your guide.

7. **Gently push the DIMM into the slot.**

If you're successful, the clips on either end of the DIMM automatically snap into position. Otherwise, lift the clips to complete anchoring the DIMM into its slot.

The clips *must* be in the fully upright and locked position.

8. **Repeat Steps 3 through 7 for each DIMM you're installing.**

9. **Double-check everything!**

10. **Close the console as described earlier in this chapter.**

Trepidatiously, turn the computer on. You should have no trouble, no messages, no nothing; the computer instantly recognizes and uses the extra memory. Somewhere in cyberspace, the computer is thanking you.

✦ Refer to Video 186 for a demonstration of installing and removing DIMMs:

www.dummies.com/go/troubleshootingandmaintainingyourpcaio2e

✦ DIMMs are clipped to anchor them into their memory bank slots. Unlike other internal PC expansion options, DIMMs rarely pop out and need reseating. In the olden days, however, when memory chips were manually pushed into sockets, DIMMs occasionally wiggled out and required reseating.

More Storage for You!

Beyond giving your PC more memory, another way to be nice to Mr. Computer is to upgrade its storage capacity. You can replace or add internal disk drives.

Right away, I must mention that adding an external storage device to a computer is far, far easier than upgrading it internally. I highly recommend that you choose an external hard drive or optical drive before doing an internal update. But if pressed, you can heed the advice in this section to do an internal upgrade.

Knowing the terms

Internally, you can add two types of drives to a computer console: a hard drive and an optical drive. For the purposes of installing and upgrading, consider an SSD to be the same as a hard drive.

The number of drives, and the type of drives, you add depend on how many disk drive parking spots are in your PC's internal garage.

Disk drives go into the drive bay, which you can find by using Figure 8-1. The bay must have room for whatever drive you plan to add to your PC. No room, no internal expansion. When you have one of those small-footprint PCs, or a laptop, the console probably lacks internal expansion luxury.

Beyond the issue of where it parks, the disk drive connects to the rest of the computer system with two cables. The first is a power cable. The console is probably bristling with extra power cables, enough to fully populate as much storage hardware as it can carry.

The second cable is the data cable. It's one of two types: ATA or SATA.

ATA: The daddy of all hard drive and optical drive connectors is the ATA, which stands for *AT A*ttachment. The *AT* came from the IBM PC AT computer, introduced in the 1980s. Yes, it's an old standard. It uses a flat ribbon cable and a boxy 50-pin connector.

SATA: The current and best standard for connecting disk drives inside the console is the SATA, or *Serial ATA*. It fixes some annoying issues that are present with the ATA data cable.

As with many hardware upgrades, which standard you use depends on what's inside your computer. But unlike with other internal upgrades, you can determine from the outside what's on the inside: Open the Device Manager as covered in Chapter 7. Open the item titled IDE ATA/ATAPI Controllers. That section lists for you the types of data cables available in the console: IDE or SATA or another variation.

Even though the Device Manager may cough up information about the drive interface, I highly recommend that you take a peek inside the console to confirm which type is available. When both types are available, I recommend using SATA.

✦ Other names for the ATA data cable include ATAPI, IDE, PATA, and UDMA.

✦ Variations on SATA are *eSATA*, the external version of SATA, and Ultra ATA, which is an older version of the standard.

◆ Some computers may still use the SCSI interface. You can confirm this by viewing the Device Manager (see Chapter 7) and looking under the Storage Controller category. If anything there says *SCSI,* your PC has the SCSI interface and can expand with those devices as well. SCSI stands for Small Computer Serial Interface, and it's bemusedly pronounced "skuzzy."

◆ Having the two data cable standards named ATA and SATA makes room for a slew of computer rhymes, poetry, and song lyrics. I leave it up to you to formulate your own festive literary devices.

Choosing a new hard drive

The number-one thing I look for in a new hard drive is capacity. How much more space will the hard drive give me to store my stuff? Generally speaking, for second internal hard drives, I would get a drive that's at least as big as the drive already inside the PC.

Directly related to capacity is cost, of course. The higher the capacity, the more expensive the drive. But rather than look at the bottom line, calculate the storage in terms of dollars per gigabyte.

For example, if a 320GB drive costs $60 and a 500GB drive costs $70, why pay more for the 500GB drive? Because its cost is 14 cents per gigabyte. The 320GB drive is just under 19 cents per gigabyte. Yeah, it's pennies, but the better value is in the higher-capacity drive.

Technically, you might want to pay attention to a few things in a hard drive. These details are trivial, but I list them here anyway.

Drive speed: Hard drives spin at a certain number of revolutions per minute (rpm). A speed of 7200 rpm is nice, and 10,000 rpm is better.

Buffer: In computer-speak, *buffer* means memory. On a hard drive, a buffer represents memory storage on the drive to help speed up operations. A 16MB buffer is very good, and 32MB is better.

Interface: This is either SATA (Serial ATA) or plain ATA, as discussed in the preceding section.

Hard drives may have other technical aspects, but mostly you see them listed online and in stores by capacity, drive speed, buffer size, and interface. (They also have cryptic part numbers.) Some people pay attention to the drive manufacturer. I don't. Yes, you pay more for bigger and faster, for example.

◆ When buying a hard drive to upgrade the PC's console, you want an *internal* drive.

✦ The reason the prices are so low on internal drives is that the drive doesn't come with a case, a power supply, or an interface. Also, you're installing things — and troubleshooting — on your own.

✦ The considerations for an SSD are the same as for a traditional, spinning, magnetic hard drive. Naturally, an SSDs is more expensive than a hard drive, which makes the SSD more of a novelty these days than a true alternative.

✦ Windows cannot access more than 1 terabyte (TB), or 1,000 gigabytes (GB), on a single hard drive. Fortunately, drivers larger than 1TB aren't common at this point in history. I assume that when this capacity (and larger) becomes widely available, newer releases of Windows will be able to access those huge storage spaces.

Choosing a new optical drive

A second optical drive may seem excessive, but sometimes it's necessary. For example, you might have a DVD drive and want a DVD-R/RW combo drive. Or, maybe you're a gamer and you like to keep game discs in the drives rather than swap discs all the time. Or, your needs might be as simple as wanting to replace a dead optical drive.

However you slice it, when there's room, you can upgrade the computer with another optical drive. The variety is there.

Optical drives come with two flavors: CD and DVD. You want a DVD. All DVD drives can read CDs, so there's no point in buying a plain CD drive.

The next decision is whether you want to record discs. Although several recording standards exist, most optical drives that record support all the standards. Even so, if you also want to record CDs, you need a combo drive. Be sure to check.

What about Blu-ray?

The current top-of-the-line optical drive standard is Sony's Blu-ray. A Blu-ray disc stores twice as much information as a standard DVD, but the drives are expensive. Plus, relatively few software programs are available on Blu-ray, which limit you to watching Blu-ray movies on your PC.

My prediction is that Blu-ray won't move in as the replacement for DVDs and CDs. That's because coming up fast is the solid-state drive, or SSD. Essentially large media cards, the SSDs will most likely become the removable storage media of choice, so I recommend putting off any Blu-ray upgrades for now unless you're compelled to use this standard.

Finally, there's the interface: SATA or ATA, as covered earlier in this chapter.

Remember to buy an internal optical drive. An internal drive is cheaper than an external model, which must be enclosed in a case, supply an interface, and have its own power supply.

Installing the optical drive

To shove a new drive into your computer's case, follow these general steps:

1. **If you're installing a SATA drive, ensure that you have a spare SATA cable handy.**

   SATA drives don't come with cables. You must buy a cable. But before you do, check inside the console. Some console designs feature SATA cables already in place by the locations where SATA drives are to be installed.

2. **Open the case as described earlier in this chapter.**

3. **Locate the empty spot that will accept the new drive.**

4. **Examine how the drive will be inserted.**

   Sometimes, an optical drive must be inserted from the front of the console.

5. **Move things out of the way if necessary.**

   For example, you may have to remove an expansion card to insert a hard drive. Or, you might have to slide open a cover or other internal hardware to accommodate the drive.

6. **If the drive needs attachments to be inserted, add them to the drive now.**

   Some drives need rails to fit into a drive bay. Sometimes, screws need to be attached to the drive before it's inserted. The screws help position the drive and keep it in place. Some newer systems may use drive caddies: You insert the drive into the caddy and then plug the caddy into the drive bay.

7. **Configure the ATA drive.**

   Some drives have jumpers on the back. You must properly set the jumpers so that the drive is recognized as either Drive 0, which is the first drive on the cable, or Drive 1, which is the second drive. This arrangement is also known as *master-slave,* in which the first drive is the master and the second drive is the slave. You cannot have two masters or two slaves or else the drives don't work.

   Directions for configuring the jumpers on the drive are found on the top of the drive somewhere. Figure 8-8 shows a typical drive rump, with the ATA connector, jumpers, and power connector. The jumper positions indicated in the figure are most likely different from any drive you might install.

Put jumper here
for master drive.

Put jumper here
for slave drive.

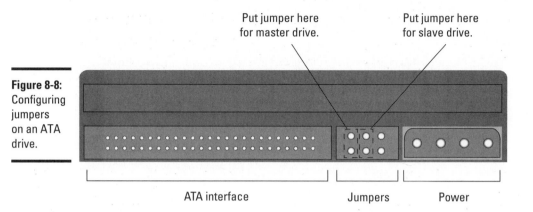

Figure 8-8:
Configuring
jumpers
on an ATA
drive.

ATA interface   Jumpers   Power

8. **Place the drive into the bay.**

9. **If necessary, anchor the drive.**

   Some drives may snap into position, and others may require screws to anchor the drive. The screws line up with tiny holes on the side of the drive bay.

10. **Connect the power cable.**

    It plugs in only one way.

    When you cannot find a power cable that matches the drive's connector, you need a power cable adapter. These adapters can be found at computer stores (*real* computer stores, not warehouses) or ordered over the Internet.

11. **Connect the data cable.**

    It plugs in only one way. If you're adding an ATA slave drive, you connect it to the middle connector in the 50-pin ribbon cable. SATA cables plug in only one way — one end on the drive and the other on the motherboard.

12. **Replace anything you needed to remove.**

    For example, reinstall an expansion card if necessary, or redo whatever you needed to undo to place the drive into its spot.

13. **Close the case per the directions offered earlier in this chapter.**

    When you turn on the computer, Windows should instantly recognize the drive, giving it a drive letter and adding it to the list of drives in the Computer or My Computer window.

✦ Video 187 covers installing a new disk drive into a PC:

   www.dummies.com/go/troubleshootingandmaintainingyourpcaio2e

✦ For further information about disk drive configuration, refer to Book VI,
Chapter 2. You can reformat the drive if necessary. Or, you can assign
the drive a new letter, which is often needed because the new hard
drive may shift all the other drive letters in the computer. That can be
bothersome.

✦ To help locate the SATA connections on the motherboard, follow the
SATA cable from an existing drive. Available SATA connections will be
near wherever any existing SATA cables attach.

Book II

Software

The 5th Wave   By Rich Tennant

"We should cast a circle, invoke the elements, and direct the energy. If that doesn't work, we'll read the manual."

Contents at a Glance

Chapter 1: Windows Gone AWOL

*W*hen you want to keep your computer working well, and keep your sanity in check, you need to ensure that Windows runs in a proper and predictable manner. After all, as the main piece of software in the computer system, the program in charge, Windows is the key to everything. When Windows misbehaves, you can turn to this chapter to get it back in line.

Windows 7 Troubleshooting

Apparently Microsoft has realized the importance of PC troubleshooting and maintenance. Windows 7 features two locations to help you do both: the Action Center and the Troubleshooting window — a special window that contains all sorts of troubleshooting tools.

Accessing the Action Center

The Action Center window displays a list of pending problems, situations, and potential disasters that might be looming — well, as far as Windows is concerned.

Your first hint of the Action Center's existence is its notification icon, which looks like a tiny flag. Clicking the Action Center notification icon displays a pop-up list of items that need attention, similar to the one shown in Figure 1-1. To act on one of the messages, click it.

Figure 1-1:
The Action
Center
notification
icon pop-up.

You can also visit the Action Center window, shown in Figure 1-2, which lists more detailed information about problems that could be ailing your PC. Important issues are flagged in red, with security issues (the most important) appearing at the top of the window. Less important issues are flagged in orange or yellow.

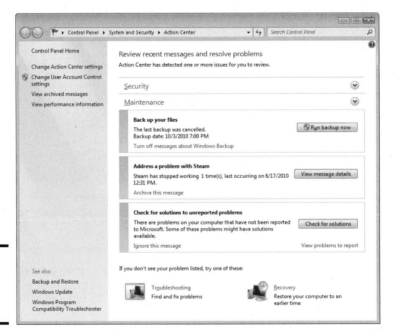

Figure 1-2:
The Action
Center
window.

To visit the Action Center window, follow these steps:

1. **Open the Control Panel.**

2. **Click the link Review Your Computer's Status, found under the System and Security heading.**

To act on an item in the Action Center window, click the button associated with the item, such as Run Backup Now, View Message Details, or Check for Solutions, all shown earlier, in Figure 1-2.

✦ When something requires serious attention in Windows, the Action Center notification icon turns red. Click the icon or visit the Action Center to see what's up. Or down.

✦ You can quickly get to the Action Center window by right-clicking the Action Center icon in the notification area and choosing the command Open Action Center.

Using the Troubleshooting window

For troubleshooting in Windows 7, nothing beats the Troubleshooting window, as shown in Figure 1-3. To display the Troubleshooting window, follow these steps:

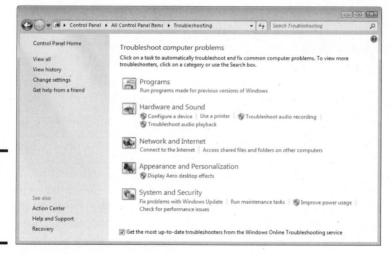

Figure 1-3:
The Trouble-shooting window.

1. **Open the Control Panel.**

2. **Choose the link Find and Fix Problems, found under the System and Security heading.**

Though the Troubleshooting window is truly something to behold, it's not a harbor for secret and otherwise unobtainable solutions in Windows 7. Nearly all the options presented in the Troubleshooting window can be accessed from other parts of Windows, most often by right-clicking an item and choosing the Troubleshoot command or by accessing the Troubleshooting tab in a Properties dialog box.

Problems and Solutions for Windows Vista

Nope, wise guy — the problem isn't Windows Vista. The Windows 7 Action Center and Troubleshooting window were built upon the foundations of the Windows Vista Problem Reports and Solutions tool. Truly, it's a godsend, not a punch line — a helpful utility for troubleshooting your PC.

The Problem Reports and Solutions window is shown in Figure 1-4. That's where the troubleshooting happens. To open the window, heed these steps:

Figure 1-4:
The Problem
Reports and
Solutions
window.

1. **Open the Control Panel window.**

2. **Choose System and Maintenance.**

3. **Choose Problem Reports and Solutions.**

The first thing to do in the Problem Reports and Solutions window is to review any pending solutions or current problems. When no solutions or problems are reported, you see the text `No Solutions Found`; otherwise, current solutions and problems are displayed.

For example, on my screen (refer to Figure 1-4), I see an update for DirectX as well as problems about the game *Half-Life 2,* which I rarely play because, as I swear to my editor, I spend most of my days writing computer books. Regardless, clicking a link displays a solution window with suggestions on what do to. Mostly, you see a web page link or perhaps the name of the program's publisher, and the rest of the solution is something you need to pursue.

Some solutions listed are the results of problems you checked on, as discussed in the next section.

Checking on new solutions

Just to ensure that everything is up to snuff, you can use the Problem Reports and Solutions window (refer to Figure 1-4) to confirm you're not going crazy. To do so, open the Problem Reports and Solutions window as described in the preceding section. Click the link on the left, Check for New Solutions. Windows reviews various issues that are logged for your computer.

If you're prompted to send information to Microsoft, click the Send Information button. It may help.

Finally, when any solutions are found, you see them listed in the window. Click a solution to see the advice that's offered. Oftentimes, you find a link to a web site where new drivers can be downloaded or where you can review the issue on a support page.

**Book II
Chapter 1**

**Windows Gone
AWOL**

Perusing recent issues

Things may happen in your Windows Vista computer — bad things — and you may be completely unaware of them. Just to be sure, you can check the Problem Reports and Solutions window to see what's up: Click the link View Problem History. The list you see works like a miniature log of issues with certain programs.

To see more details on a certain issue, double-click the item in the list. A report is shown in Figure 1-5. The report may list things you can do or try to remedy the situation.

Figure 1-5:
Details from
a problem
report.

Be sure to close the Problem Reports and Solutions window when you're done using it.

Windows Needs a-Fixin'

I'm certain that historians 200 years from now will look back upon our culture in awe. (Whether it's respect or disgust remains to be determined.) They will marvel at Windows, the operating system used by more than 80 percent of the humans who are bold enough to use computers. And they will marvel, not at how we used computers that tended to get weird all of a sudden but, rather, at how the computers were ever considered normal in the first place.

This section covers the overall situation of Windows going weird — and it does so in a variety of ways. Not only this chapter but also eight other chapters in this book mull over strange things in Windows.

When you truly need to fix Windows, visit Chapter 8. There, you discover why I recommend that you don't reinstall Windows and instead look into System File Checker as a solution.

Restarting Windows

Writing this book is quite a major project for me. A book of this size would be a big deal for any author. During the course of writing this book, I experienced many of the problems this book mentions. I also used one general tried-and-true solution to most of them: Restart Windows.

I'm not saying to log out. I'm not saying to close a few programs. Sometimes, to fix something truly odd in Windows, you must restart the entire computer. When Windows returns, the problem will most likely be gone. I would say, nine times out of ten, the restart-Windows solution works like a charm.

✦ See Book I, Chapter 3 for details on how to restart Windows if you're unfamiliar with the procedure, or if you've never, ever, restarted Windows.

✦ Restarting Windows may fix other programs as well. For example, my webcam software was acting screwy and wouldn't start or recognize the camera. After I restarted Windows, however, the problem was mysteriously resolved.

✦ There's no need to restart Windows every so often "just in case."

✦ If you have to restart Windows all the time to fix problems, a better solution probably exists. Refer to Chapter 3 for information on Safe mode to determine whether the problem is specific to Windows. Also see Chapter 4 for information on discovering a memory leak.

Deciphering error codes

There's a difference between an error code and an error message. An error message says "The printer is jammed." An error code says "Error 20."

Don't fall prey to the folly of trying to understand error codes. Whether you see the error code in Windows or in an application, the code number is useless. In fact, the code number was written by the programmer *for* the programmer. Unless you're being paid to write the program, the error code probably won't help you much.

Sure, you can use the Internet to search for the error code. Sometimes, you may find the code listed, along with a definition of what it means. When you're *really* lucky, you may find a solution. Most of the time, you won't.

Book II
Chapter 1

Windows Gone AWOL

The best location to search for Windows error codes on the Internet is Microsoft's Knowledge Base. Visit this site to start your error code search:

```
http://support.microsoft.com
```

Error codes are for the programmer, not the user, even when your error code search renders useful information. A programmer who truly wants you to know what's going on would use an error message rather than an error code.

Peeking at that debug information

Another useless feature offered by many programs is the so-called *debugging information*. It works like this: You see an error message in a dialog box or window. The error message is useless, but you see a button titled Details or More Info. So you click the button and see something like this:

```
17A7:0000  CD 20 FF 9F 00 9A EE FE-1D F0 4F 03 0B 12 8A 03
17A7:0010  0B 12 17 03 0B 12 41 07-01 01 01 00 02 FF FF FF
17A7:0020  FF FF FF FF FF FF FF FF-FF FF FF FF AF 11 4E 01
AX=0000  BX=0000  CX=0000  DX=0000  SP=FFEE  BP=0000  SI=0000  DI=0000
DS=17A7  ES=17A7  SS=17A7  CS=17A7  IP=0100    NV UP EI PL NZ NA PO NC
```

Yeah, right. It's definitely debugging information. Specifically, it's information about the computer's state when the program crashed. The information is highly detailed and extremely useful — but only to the programmer who wrote the code.

The moral of the story: Unless you want to do the programmer's job and fix what's wrong, there's nothing you can do.

Windows Updates, Doesn't It?

Maybe this update thing is getting out of hand. It's a noble idea: Software is never truly "done." Because of their very nature, software programs have bugs that just won't be found — sometimes, for decades. Not only that, but engineers also love to add features. This *creeping elegance* is something that only management can stop.

Regardless of the disease, the symptoms are that your PC's software needs to be updated. The process not only ensures that the computer is running the best possible version of Windows but also provides patches for security holes that may be found. Those updates are important, so like it or not, Windows needs updating. This section discusses Windows Update.

Understanding Windows Update

The Windows operating system comes with the feature Windows Update. It uses the Internet to phone home into the Microsoft mother ship and check for any available new files or patches and to relay information about which naughty web sites you visited. (Just kidding.)

Windows Update was originally found on top of the Start menu, nestled on the main Programs or All Programs menu. Choosing that item whisked you off to the official Windows Update web page, where you followed a series of convoluted steps to bring the PC's operating system to current status.

You can still visit the Windows Update site to update your computer. I recommend this approach for Windows XP users. Visit

```
http://update.microsoft.com
```

When you visit this site in more recent versions of Windows, however, you're thrust back into local control, so there's no point to visiting the web page in Windows 7 or Windows Vista. Instead, follow these steps:

1. **Open the Control Panel.**

2. **Choose System and Security.**

3. **Beneath the heading Windows Update, choose Check for Updates.**

You don't need to perform these steps when you've configured Windows Update to automatically check for updates; see the next section.

✦ You don't have to update your computer. If you don't use the Internet and you enjoy your computer in its present state and never plan to upgrade or add anything new, there's no reason to update. Otherwise, I highly recommend running Windows Update, as described in this chapter.

✦ Windows Update may also check for updates to other Microsoft software you own, such as Microsoft Office. It doesn't check for updates to other software. Instead, you have to manually update those programs; or, they may feature their own update options. For example, Adobe Acrobat Reader routinely checks the Internet to see whether a new version if available and, if so, prompts you to update.

✦ Windows XP features a Security Center icon in the Control Panel. You can open the Security Center icon to view the Security Center window and find therein an Automatic Updates item. There, you can turn Automatic Update off or on, but I still recommend visiting the Windows Update web site as a more complete way to keep Windows up-to-date.

Configuring updates

Windows Update can be set to run in one of three ways:

✦ **Fully automatic:** Windows downloads and installs critical updates as they appear. You can schedule the updates, but otherwise this is the "blind obedience" choice.

✦ **Semiautomatic:** You're alerted to updates, and you're given the choice of whether to download them. Updates are installed only when you choose to install them. This option is named "It's my computer, and though I may begrudgingly choose to install the updates, I'll do it on my own damn time."

✦ **Not at all:** Updates are neither checked for nor installed. You can still manually check for and install updates, but Windows Update doesn't do it automatically for you, not even a tiny bit. This option is the one for most hill people.

In Windows 7 and Windows Vista, you configure Windows updates by following these steps:

1. **Open the Control Panel.**

2. **Choose System and Security in Windows 7, or Security in Windows Vista.**

3. **Choose Windows Update.**

The Windows Update window appears, as shown in Figure 1-6. Though you can't tell by the picture, the top part of the window is shown in a happy green color. When Windows Update is turned off, the angry red color is used instead.

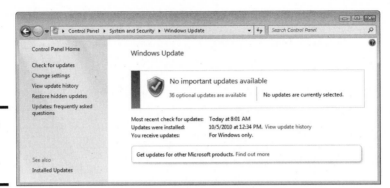

Figure 1-6:
Windows
Update is
happy.

4. **On the left side of the window, click the Change Settings link.**

5. **Use the Change Settings window to specify how often Windows Update works.**

   For example, choose Install Updates Automatically (Recommended) to have the computer do everything for you. If you experience problems updating, or you're just suspicious, choose Download Updates but Let Me Choose Whether to Install Them instead.

   When you choose Updates Automatically, be sure to set a time for the updates when the computer will be on and can connect to the Internet.

6. **Click OK to confirm the new settings.**

7. **In Windows Vista, type the administrator's password or click Continue to proceed.**

   You may close the Windows Update window now, if you're done.

In Windows XP, you turn on Automatic Updates from the Security window; open the Security icon in the Control Panel.

✦ Windows Update may not install all available updates. Figure 1-6 lists 36 optional updates. Click the link to view and, optionally, choose to install those updates.

✦ Many optional updates involve installing language packages for your version of Windows. Installation of these language packages is completely optional, though they continue to be displayed as optional updates until you install them.

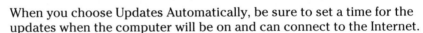

✦ Choose the weekend for performing Automatic Updates. That way, if the computer needs to automatically restart, you don't lose any work documents you may leave open.

✦ Windows Update may also show driver updates, indicating that new software is available for certain peripherals or hardware components inside your PC. Also refer to Book I, Chapter 7 for information on updating drivers for various gizmos in your computer.

Book II
Chapter 1

Windows Gone
AWOL

How much updating is enough?

When in doubt, choose every update, but sometimes it helps to be critical. I prefer to review updates rather than automatically install them all. I recommend always installing security and critical updates. As for optional updates, such as add-ons or bonus files, feel free to deny them at your whim. Especially if you read the update description and discover that it doesn't apply to your situation, you don't need to install the update.

Also, keep in mind that updates don't vanish. When you decline an update, it continues to show up on the list of available updates. If you choose to, you can install the update in the future.

Permitting an update

When you postpone an update for Windows, you're reminded of it. Again and again. Ceaselessly. A notice appears in the notification area, sometimes with a pop-up bubble that says `New updates are available`. You'll probably see it every time you log in to Windows. It will tick you off.

 In Windows 7 and Windows Vista, some automatic updates require restarting Windows. If you've configured Windows Update to download *but not install* the update, you'll notice a Shield Flag icon, shown in the margin, appear on the Shutdown or Software Power button on the Start menu. Shutting down or restarting the PC at that point installs the update.

✦ Some updates can be installed only by restarting Windows.

✦ Continue using the computer while an update downloads. If restarting Windows is necessary, you're alerted. You can choose to restart immediately, have the computer remind you about restarting every so often, or just tell the computer to shut the heck up. But remember to restart eventually.

✦ If you'd rather not install an update when shutting down Windows XP, click the link that says Click Here to Turn Off without Installing Updates. The link appears in the Shut Down window.

✦ There's no way to disable the pop-up Windows Update alert (the "balloon tip") from the notification area. Solutions are mentioned on the Internet, but I've found that they generally don't work.

✦ Naturally, folks who disable Windows Update aren't reminded of anything — not even their birthdays.

Reviewing the updates

Come take a look at what Windows Update has done to your PC! Observe the updates! See what they've done!

In Windows 7 and Windows Vista, peruse updates by following these steps:

1. **Open the Control Panel.**

2. **In Windows 7, choose System and Security; in Windows Vista, choose Security.**

3. **Beneath the Windows Update heading, click the link View Installed Updates.**

   You see a list of installed updates.

4. **Click OK when you're done, because the window is a look-only type of thing.**

In Windows XP, obey these steps:

1. **Open the Add or Remove Programs icon in the Control Panel.**

   The Add or Remove Programs window shows up.

2. **Put a check mark by Show Updates.**

   The list becomes populated with updates; you may have to scroll down a bit to find them.

3. **Close the window when you're done.**

See the following section for information on removing an update.

Undoing an update

If you install a Windows update and it makes things worse, you can easily get your computer back. In Windows 7 and Windows Vista, follow these steps:

1. **Follow Steps 1 through 3 in the preceding section to display the list of recent updates.**

   You can sort the list by date when you click the Installed On column heading. The Installed On column is located on the far-right side of the list (unless you dragged it elsewhere).

2. **Choose the update you want to undo.**

3. **Click the Uninstall button that appears on the toolbar.**

4. **Follow the directions provided on the screen.**

   If prompted to restart Windows, do so.

In Windows XP, remove an update by following these steps:

1. **Open the Control Panel's Add or Remove Programs icon.**

2. **Place a check mark by the Show Updates option at the top of the window.**

3. **Choose the update to remove.**

   The update's entry expands to offer more information, including a link titled Click Here for Support Information.

4. **Click the Remove button.**

5. **Follow the directions and steps provided.**

   If necessary, restart Windows when prompted to do so.

The update should be removed successfully and your system restored. When the operation doesn't work, try again in Safe mode. Refer to Chapter 3.

Fixing update problems in Windows 7

A troubleshooter available in Windows 7 deals specifically with Windows Update woes. The troubleshooter is a much better solution for dealing with an update problem than trying to wade through and uninstall a recent update.

To troubleshoot a Windows Update problem in Windows 7, follow these steps:

1. **Open the Control Panel.**

2. **Beneath the System and Security heading, choose Find and Fix Problems.**

   The Troubleshooting window appears (refer to Figure 1-3).

3. **Choose the link Fix Problems with Windows Update, found beneath the System and Security heading.**

4. **Work through the wizard to resolve the issue.**

Update issues in Windows 7 are also flagged in the Action Center. See the section "Accessing the Action Center," earlier in this chapter, for more information on the Action Center.

Files Missing and Found

For those times when you experience It Was Just Here syndrome, or anytime you're alerted to the absence of something that must be found, turn to this section for answers.

Searching for files

The lesson to be mastered when you misplace a file is to keep your files organized in the first place: Create folders. Give the folders names, like categories in a library. Use subfolders. Organize! Organize! Organize! When you forget, use Windows to help you quickly find a file.

In Windows 7 and Windows Vista, use the Search box on the Start button menu. Type the information you're looking for. You can type a filename or type some text that you're looking for inside a file. The results appear right on the Start menu.

Windows XP has a bit more involved form of search. Here are the steps to take:

1. **Choose Search from the Start button menu.**

2. **In the Search window, choose a category from the left side of the window.**

   For example, to search for a picture file, choose Pictures, Music, or Video. When you're unsure, choose All Files and Folders.

3. **Fill in the dog's balloon, coughing up as much detail as you can about the topic you're searching for.**

   The more details you can offer, the more exact the search.

4. **Click the Search button.**

   The results are displayed in the window.

When the file you're looking for cannot be found, you need to boost your searching skills, as covered in the next section.

You might find a shortcut file rather than the original. Shortcuts may still exist even though an original has been deleted. Therefore, search the Recycle Bin next. See the later section, "Searching the Recycle Bin."

Really searching for files

The Search command is designed to search only your own files. When you need to search outside your personal area, you need to boost the Search command with more muscle.

In Windows 7, obey these steps:

1. **Press Win+F to summon a Search window.**

2. **Type the name of the file you're looking for, or some of the file's contents, into the Search text box.**

   Some results are displayed, but you want more.

3. **Scroll to the bottom of the Search Results window.**

4. **Choose Computer from the list of icons displayed.**

   By choosing Computer, you expand the search to include all locations on your computer. The search takes a long time, but it truly looks everywhere.

In Windows Vista, follow these steps:

1. **Press Win+F to display a Search window.**

2. **Click the chevron to reveal advanced search options.**

3. **From the Location button menu, choose a specific location.**

   The broadest location is Computer. To search a specific hard drive, choose it from the list.

4. **Fill in as much information as you can about the missing file.**

5. **Put a check mark by the box labeled Include Non-Indexed, Hidden, and System Files (Might Be Slow).**

6. **Click the Search button.**

In Windows XP, heed these steps:

1. **Press Win+F to conjure forth a Search window.**

2. **Choose the All Files and Folders link.**

3. **Fill in as much information as you can about the file you're searching for.**

4. **From the Look In drop-down list, choose a specific location.**

   To search everywhere, choose the Computer option; otherwise, pick a disk drive or choose Local Hard Drives to search all hard drives inside of or attached to your PC.

 5. **Click the chevron to display more advanced options.**

6. **Ensure that a check mark appears by the items Search System Folders, Search Hidden Files and Folders, and Search Subfolders.**

7. **Click the Search button.**

By following these steps, you're directing Windows to look everywhere for the file, including places outside the normal locations where you save your files. Using this technique helps you locate files you might see referenced in error messages or in other files you need to access for troubleshooting purposes.

Searching the Recycle Bin

The Recycle Bin isn't normally searched by the Windows Search command. I mean, honestly: How many times have you searched your office trash for your car keys? So I recommend that you take a peek in the trash, er, Recycle Bin whenever the regular version of the Search command comes up empty.

Book II
Chapter 1

Windows Gone AWOL

To best search the Recycle Bin, follow these steps:

1. **Open the Recycle Bin icon on the desktop.**

   If the icon isn't available on the desktop, choose Recycle Bin from the Address bar of any Windows Explorer window.

2. **Choose Details from the Views button menu on the toolbar.**

3. **Ensure that the list is sorted by filename.**

   An upward-pointing triangle appears next to the Name column heading. If not, click the Name column heading until you see the triangle. (The upward-pointing triangle indicates an ascending, or A-to-Z, sort.)

4. **Scroll the list to look for the misplaced, and wrongly deleted, file.**

   You can quickly scroll to a specific point in the list by pressing a letter key on the keyboard. For example, to find the file `Secret Plans`, press the S key.

5. **After you find the file, click to select it.**

6. **Take heed of the information in the Original Location column.**

   The information is the pathname to the folder where the file will be restored. That's where you need to look in Step 9.

7a. **In Windows Vista, click the toolbar button Restore This Item.**

7b. **In Windows XP, choose the link Restore This Item from the task panel on the left side of the window.**

8. **Close the Recycle Bin window.**

9. **Open a Windows Explorer window (press Win+E) and navigate to the folder where the file has been restored.**

   I hope you paid attention in Step 6.

If you're unfamiliar with pathnames, treat them like road maps that tell you where files are located. You can view Video 211 to see how it's done:

www.dummies.com/go/troubleshootingandmaintainingyourpcaio2e

Here's a pathname example:

`C:\Users\Public\Pictures\2011\Vacation\Disney`

This path directs you to the Disney folder: Open Drive `C` and then the `Users` folder. Open the `Public` folder and then the subfolders `Pictures`, `2011`, `Vacation`, and, finally, `Disney` to locate the file you just restored.

You cannot search file contents inside the Recycle Bin. Windows compresses deleted files, and there's no way to look inside the file contents unless you first restore the file to its original location.

Really, really searching for files

A truly nerdy way to search for files is ignored in the graphical portion of Windows. By opening a command prompt window, you can search for files that Windows truly doesn't want you to know are there.

The following steps are technical. Yes, this is a *For Dummies* reference book, but when you really, *really* need to find a file, the method described in the following steps does the job:

1. **From the Start menu, choose All Programs⇨Accessories⇨Command Prompt.**

2. **Type** CD \ **and press Enter.**

   That's **CD**, a space, and then the backslash character. This command propels you to the root directory (folder) on the main hard drive.

3. **Type DIR and a space.**

4. **Type the name of the file you're looking for.**

   For example, if you're looking for the file secret.doc, type **secret.doc**. You can type upper- or lowercase letters.

   When you don't know the full name, replace the part you don't know with an asterisk (which is a *wildcard*). For example, you type secret* to search for all files beginning with the word *secret*.

   Don't type any spaces, because the command prompt has special ways of dealing with them and this section isn't a lesson on using the command prompt. If you must type a space, use the ? (question mark) character instead.

5. **Type another space and then** /S, **a space, and** /P.

   The complete command line to look for the file secret.doc appears like this:

   ```
   dir secret.doc /s /p
   ```

   The /s option directs a search of all folders on the hard drive; the /p option pauses the display after each screen of text. Double-check everything!

6. **Press the Enter key.**

   The results display one screen at a time.

7. **Peruse the screen full of results.**

8. **If you find a file that matches, you can open a Windows Explorer window to display the file's folder.**

Press Win+E to open a Windows Explorer window. Use the directions from the preceding section to hunt down a file by its pathname, or use Video 211 to help you.

The pathname is found above the filename in the results. The pathname reads similar to this line:

```
Directory of C:\Users\Dang\Documents\Forgotten
```

9. **If the file isn't found, press Enter to see the next screen (if necessary).**

   The prompt reads `Press any key to continue`, but the Enter key is the "any key." Repeat Steps 7 and 8 to review the results.

10. **Type the** EXIT **command to close the Command Prompt window when you're done.**

Yes, this method is not only technical — it's tedious. But the DIR command does a thorough job of scouring the entire hard drive. I've used this method many times, mostly to confirm that a file *doesn't* exist. For finding lost files I created, the steps in the earlier section, "Searching for files," always do the trick.

See Video 212, where you can watch me use these same steps at the command prompt to find a lost file.

www.dummies.com/go/troubleshootingandmaintainingyourpcaio2e

Adding items to the search index

The Windows search command doesn't actually search your stuff. Instead, it searches an index of your stuff, one that's painstakingly created at another time. That's because it's much quicker to search an index than to search everywhere. Consider this book: It's faster to look up a topic in the index than to turn every page looking for it. Search indexes work the same way.

For efficiency's sake, a search index doesn't make a note of everything everywhere in your computer. You can, however, direct the Search command to index more files in additional locations. So when you find yourself locating lost files outside the normal search locations, it pays to have Windows index those locations to make the search process faster.

The simple way to adjust search options in Windows 7 and Windows Vista is to use the Search tab in the Folder Options dialog box. Heed these steps:

1. **Open the Control Panel.**

2. **Choose Appearance and Personalization.**

3. **Choose Folder Options.**

   The Folder Options dialog box is displayed.

4. **Click the Search tab.**

5. **If you prefer more detailed searches, choose the option Always Search File Names and Contents.**

6. **When you plan to search outside your personal folders, place a check mark by the item Don't Use the Index When Searching.**

7. **Peruse other search options as well, depending on how deep you want your file searches to go.**

8. **Click the OK button to close the Folder Options dialog box and lock in your settings.**

   Optionally, close the Control Panel window as well.

As a more drastic, and technical, step in Windows 7 and Windows Vista, you can expand the locations where Windows searches by changing the search index. Follow these steps:

1. **Open the Control Panel.**

2a. **In Windows 7, choose Large Icons from the View By menu button in the upper-right corner of the window.**

2b. **In Windows Vista, choose Classic View from the task pane on the left side of the window.**

3. **Open the Indexing Options icon in the Control Panel.**

4. **Click the Modify button in the Indexing Options dialog box.**

5. **Click the Show All Locations button.**

6. **In Windows Vista, press the Continue button or type the administrator's password to continue.**

   A list of locations appears at the top of the Indexed Locations window, as shown in Figure 1-7.

7. **Choose a disk drive or folder to add to the index.**

   Browse the list (refer to Figure 1-7) to find the item you want to index. Placing a check mark in the box by the item adds the folder and all its subfolders and all their content to the index.

   Likewise, to remove an item from the index, remove the check mark by the item.

   The list on the bottom of the Indexed Locations dialog box shows which items are being indexed.

8. **Click OK when you're done adding items to the index.**

9. **Click the Close button to dismiss the Indexing Options dialog box.**

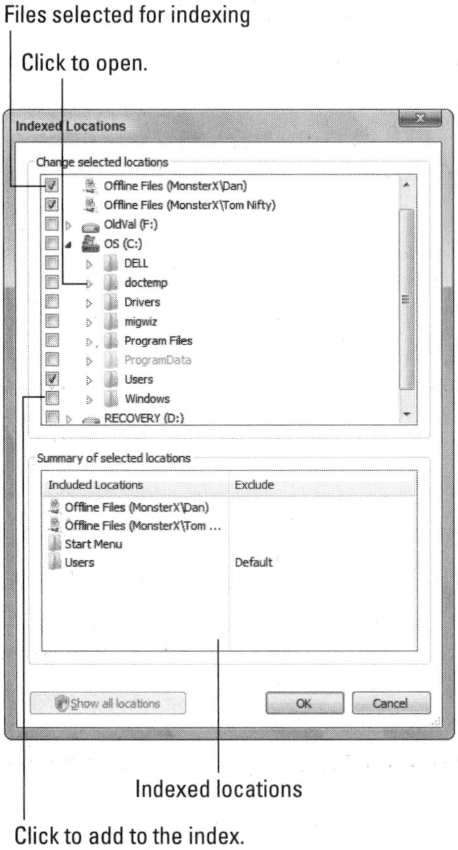

Files selected for indexing

Click to open.

Figure 1-7:
Adding new
items to the
indexed
locations
list.

Indexed locations

Click to add to the index.

10a. **In Windows 7, choose the Category option from the View By menu in the upper-right corner of the Control Panel window.**

10b. **In Windows Vista, choose Control Panel Home from the left side of the Control Panel window.**

Steps 8a and 8b are necessary to restore the Control Panel window to Category view as opposed to old-fashioned Icon view.

Windows XP doesn't have as complete a method to adjust indexing. But you should ensure that the indexing service has been activated. Do this:

1. **Press Win+F to summon a Search window.**

2. **From the list of tasks on the left side of the window, choose Change Preferences.**

3. **Choose the link with Indexing Service (for Faster Local Searches).**

4. **Click Yes, Enable Indexing Service.**

5. **Click OK.**

Windows updates the index automatically, so you don't notice it happening. You cannot disable index updating in Windows Vista, nor can you change its update schedule.

✦ Avoid the temptation to index *everything*. When you do, the index becomes useless as its efficiency drops to nil. To find files, index only the folders you frequent.

✦ *Offline* files are copies of files that exist elsewhere on the network.

✦ The Windows Search service updates the index. This process causes the computer's hard drive access light to go bonkers, and many users often wonder why the system is suddenly so busy. No, it's not a virus (at least not usually), it's the search index being updated by the Windows Search service. See Chapter 2 for more information on services in Windows.

Rebuilding the search index

If you discover that the Search command in Windows 7 or Windows Vista is behaving rather ignorantly, you can rebuild the Search command's index. Here's how:

1. **Follow Steps 1 through 3 in the preceding section to open the Indexing Options dialog box.**

2. **Click the Advanced button in the Indexing Options dialog box.**

3. **In Windows Vista, type the administrator's password or click the Continue button to proceed.**

4. **Click the Rebuild button in the Advanced Options dialog box.**

5. **Click the OK button to rebuild the index.**

6. **Close the Indexing Options dialog box.**

The time it takes to rebuild the index depends on how many files are being indexed and how busy the computer is. You can keep the Indexing Options dialog box open to view the progress, though you can still use your computer while files are being indexed.

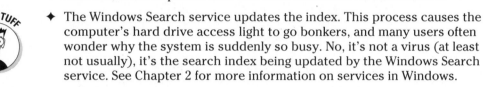

Rebuild the index after you select new locations to index, as covered in the preceding section.

A file is missing

Oftentimes, it's not you who discovers that a file has gone AWOL. Sometimes, Windows itself notices that files go missing. The missing-file message appears either when Windows starts or when you run specific programs.

The key to fixing the problem is discovering who owns the problem. To draw a line between Windows and your PC's other programs, start-up files, and device drivers, start the computer in Safe mode, as discussed in Chapter 3. When the problem persists in Safe mode, it's most likely Windows' own problem. See Chapter 8 for information on using the System File Checker to recover bits and pieces of Windows.

When the problem lies with other software, you need to turn to the other software itself to find the missing file. For example, if a start-up message indicates that an audio file cannot be found, reinstall your PC's audio software. You can find the software on a disc that was supplied with the PC or from the manufacturer's web site on the Internet.

A start-up message indicating a missing DLL or another type of file may appear because the program was sloppily uninstalled. The key is to remove the reference to the file in whichever part of Windows is starting the file. This problem tends to happen mostly in Windows XP.

In Windows XP, follow these steps to remove an unwanted start-up file error message:

1. **Take note of the error message.**

For example, if the message is `Unable to locate boogus.dll`, note the name `boogus.dll`.

2. **Press Win+R to bring up the Run dialog box.**

3. **Type** `msconfig` **to start the System Configuration Utility.**

4. **Click the SYSTEM.INI tab.**

Windows Vista has no SYSTEM.INI tab, so if you see one, you didn't pay attention to my Windows XP–only admonition at the beginning of these steps.

5. **Peruse the list to look for the name of the missing file.**

6. **When you find the filename that appears in the error message, remove the check mark by the filename.**

By removing the check mark, you direct Windows not to locate the file when it first starts.

7. **Click the WIN.INI tab and repeat Steps 5 and 6 to see whether the filename appears there.**

8. **Click the Startup tab and look for the filename there; repeat Steps 5 and 6 as necessary.**

The filename appears as part of a pathname, as shown in Figure 1-8. Be sure to check the last part of the pathname.

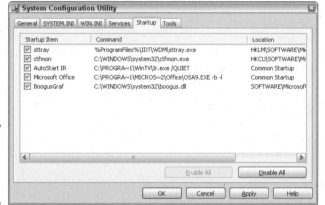

Book II
Chapter 1

Windows Gone
AWOL

Figure 1-8:
Locating
files that no
longer exist.

9. **Click OK to close the System Configuration Utility window.**

10. **Choose whether to restart the computer now or later.**

The changes don't take effect until you restart the computer.

If the message doesn't appear when you restart Windows, you fixed the problem. When it still appears, you have to check into other solutions, such as reinstalling any recently installed software. Remember to reactivate whatever you disabled in the System Configuration Utility window.

✦ The missing file may also be due to damage to the hard drive. See Book VI, Chapter 2, on disk maintenance. If the hard drive is suspect, though, other errors will occur in addition to a missing file.

✦ When you use the System Configuration Utility to modify a start-up file, you may see a warning displayed when Windows restarts. You can dismiss the warning — be sure to put a check mark in the box so that the warning doesn't appear again.

A Smattering of Annoying Things in Windows

Despite my admonition in this book's Introduction, I shall now devote the following few pages to some items that lie on the border between troubleshooting and annoying. I'm writing this section because I'm a nice guy, not because I tend to go back on my word when writing computer books.

The following items are specific to Windows as a trouble source. If an item isn't listed here, it can probably be found elsewhere in this book.

The blue screen of death

One troublesome item is so loathed that it has its own acronym: Blue Screen of Death, or BSOD. Fortunately, Mr. BSOD isn't as common as he was in years past, but he's still around. Offend Windows in an extreme way and see the BSOD for yourself. If the computer could make a sound at that point, it would be the sound of a gag.

The possible causes of a BSOD are numerous:

+ Malfunctioning RAM

+ Overheating

+ Bad voltage supply

+ Faulty hardware

+ Overclocking or another extension of system abilities

+ Poorly written software — specifically, device drivers

+ Operating system bugs and other types of bugs

+ Hyperventilating

In most cases, you can do nothing but restart the computer.

Some BSOD error messages you can recover from, such as removing media that is in use by the computer. In that case, you can restore the media to (you hope) remedy the situation.

If possible, you can check the Microsoft Knowledge Base for information about the BSOD. If you see an error number, you can refer to it by using the Microsoft web page; for example:

```
Stop 0x00000001e
```

This line of text might be part of a BSOD message. In that case, visit the Microsoft Knowledge Base at `http://support.microsoft.com` and search for the text *Stop 0x00000001e*.

The BSOD is often thought of as a Windows-only issue, but other operating systems and even game consoles use similar techniques. The most humorous examples of the BSOD appear on advertising displays and public video terminals. Microsoft engineers once gave a demonstration when the computer malfunctioned and a huge BSOD appeared on the projection screen. Oh, how I laughed.

Silence the sounds

Windows plays a host of musical ditties as you go about your day. Sometimes, the sounds serve as important reminders or warnings. At other times, the sounds annoy the heck out of you. Disabling them can be done without muting the entire sound system. Here's how:

1a. **In Windows 7 and Windows Vista, open the Control Panel, choose Hardware and Sound, and then click the link Change System Sounds beneath the Sound heading.**

1b. **In Windows XP, open the Sound and Audio Devices icon in the Control Panel and, in the dialog box that appears, click the Sounds tab.**

You see a list of all events and activities in Windows that have sounds associated with them, as shown in Figure 1-9.

Book II
Chapter 1

Windows Gone
AWOL

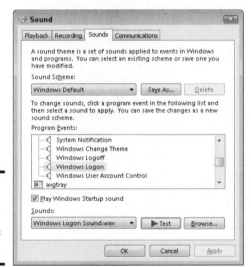

Figure 1-9:
The Sound dialog box in Windows Vista.

2. **Choose an event to silence.**

For example, choose the Windows Logon sound that plays every silly time you log in to Windows.

If you're unsure of the event but remember the sound, use either the Test or Play button in the dialog box to preview the sound for a selected event.

3. **From the Sounds drop-down list, choose (None).**

Multiple sounds are available from the Sounds drop-down list. The top option, however, is (None), which is blissful silence.

4. **Repeat Steps 2 and 3 as often as necessary.**

5. **Click OK to cement your choices, and close the window.**

6. **Close the Control Panel window.**

One sound that may not be obvious is the Windows Startup sound. To disable it in Windows 7 and Windows Vista, remove the check mark by the box Play Windows Startup Sound in the Sound dialog box (refer to Figure 1-9). In Windows XP, assign the (None) sound to the item titled Start Windows.

Anchor the taskbar

In several versions of Windows, the taskbar was highly mobile. I suppose that the programmers considered taskbar mobility high on the list of user desires. I mean, Microsoft enjoys throwing way too many options at users. Regardless of the reasons, it was too easy to move the taskbar to any side of the display.

All versions of Windows covered in this book come with the taskbar locked. The taskbar doesn't move unless you first unlock it.

To unlock the taskbar, right-click a blank part of the taskbar and choose the command Lock the Taskbar. The command has a tiny check mark by it whenever the taskbar is locked. When the taskbar is unlocked, its appearance changes. Toolbars grow visible "handles," and in Windows XP the taskbar grows a fat upper lip.

Move the taskbar

The taskbar can be moved only when it's unlocked. After it's unlocked, you can drag it to any edge of the screen: top, left, right, or bottom. Note, however, that most documentation assumes that the taskbar is on the bottom of the screen. This position implies that the Start button is in the lower-left corner and that the notification area is in the lower-right corner.

Some people cannot get the hang of moving the taskbar. If that's you, watch Video 213 to see me demonstrate it onscreen.

www.dummies.com/go/troubleshootingandmaintainingyourpcaio2e

Resize the taskbar

The taskbar can be taller or shorter, but you cannot resize it unless you unlock it first. See the earlier section, "Anchor the taskbar," for details.

After the taskbar is unlocked, you can resize it by pointing the mouse at the taskbar's top edge. Drag the mouse in toward the center of the screen to make the taskbar fatter; drag the mouse outward to make it thinner.

Review Video 214 to see a taskbar resizing demonstration.

www.dummies.com/go/troubleshootingandmaintainingyourpcaio2e

Lock the taskbar when you're done setting its size.

In Windows Vista and Windows XP, the taskbar size is also affected by the size of the icons on the Quick Launch bar. To set the icon sizes, follow these steps:

1. **Unlock the taskbar.**

   Refer to the directions in the section "Anchor the taskbar," earlier in this chapter.

2. **Right-click the Quick Launch bar handle.**

   The handle is the graphical gizmo that appears on the left end of the Quick Launch toolbar.

3. **Choose View⇨Large Icons to set the icons to a larger size, or choose View⇨Small Icons to set the icons to a smaller size.**

4. **Relock the taskbar when you're done.**

Hide the taskbar

I've gotten quite a few e-mails over the years that I can sum up in one panicky sentence:

> Where the heck did the taskbar go!

It's there. The taskbar has two ways of hiding from you. First, the taskbar is going nowhere if you lock it. See the earlier section, "Anchor the taskbar," for more information.

Second, the taskbar can be resized to be very, very thin — nearly invisible, but only in Windows XP. To find the taskbar, move the mouse to each edge of the screen. The taskbar's presence is noted by the mouse pointer changing to a tiny arrow head. That's your clue: Drag the mouse in toward the center of the screen to resize the taskbar.

Finally, the taskbar has Autohide mode. To enable or disable this mode, follow these steps:

1. **Right-click a blank part of the taskbar.**

2. **Choose Properties.**

   The Taskbar and Start Menu Properties dialog box appears.

3. **Add or remove the check mark by Auto-Hide the Taskbar.**

4. **Click OK.**

In Autohide mode, the taskbar appears only when you move the mouse pointer to the bottom of the screen (or whichever screen edge the taskbar is docked to) or when you press the Win key on the keyboard. The taskbar autohides whether you locked the taskbar or not.

See all icons on the Quick Launch bar

Windows Vista and Windows XP feature a Quick Launch bar on the taskbar. (In Windows 7, the Quick Launch bar is replaced by the ability to pin icons to the taskbar.) Some programs give you the option to add their icons to the Quick Launch bar, yet other programs add their icons without letting you know. Eventually, you discover that the Quick Launch bar gets busy, full of icons.

When the icon squatting becomes a problem, a "show more" chevron appears on the Quick Launch bar to help indicate and display hidden icons, as shown in Figure 1-10.

Figure 1-10: Quick Launch bar bloat.

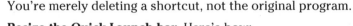

You have two options for fixing the situation:

✦ **Remove icons from the Quick Launch bar.** Right-click an icon and choose Delete from the pop-up menu.

You're merely deleting a shortcut, not the original program.

✦ **Resize the Quick Launch bar.** Here's how:

 1. *Unlock the taskbar.*

 See the earlier section, "Anchor the taskbar," for details.

 2. *Drag the handle to the right of the Quick Launch bar to the right.*

 The handle on the right is the handle for the next toolbar over, usually the taskbar. By sliding the handle to the right, you make the Quick Launch bar longer, allowing more room for the icons.

 Slide the handle over until all the icons appear on the Quick Launch bar and the little chevron thing disappears. Move the handle over a wee bit more, just to be sure.

 3. *Relock the taskbar.*

Set notification area icons in Windows 7

Why does the notification area bug some people? I'll never know. Since the notification area first appeared in Windows 95, back when it was called the system tray, it's been a pain in the taskbar. In Windows 7, however, that pain can easily be controlled or eliminated.

To lord it over regular notification area icons, follow these steps:

1. **Right-click the date-and-time part of the notification area.**

2. **Choose Customize Notification Icons from the pop-up menu.**

A window appears, which lists all potential icons that can appear in the notification area.

3. **To pick and choose which icons appear, or to hide all icons, remove the check mark by the item Always Show All Icons and Notifications On the Taskbar.**

4. **For each item in the Icon column, choose a behavior.**

The Behavior menu button lists three options:

- *Only Show Notifications:* The teeny icon appears only when it needs attention or it's active.

- *Show Icon and Notifications:* The teeny icon appears all the time.

- *Hide Icon and Notifications:* The teeny icon never shows up.

To hide all icons, choose the option Hide Icon and Notifications. You also have to hide Windows own notifications, which is covered next.

5. **When you're done, click OK.**

For adding or removing Windows own notification icons, obey these steps:

1. **Right-click the date-and-time part of the notification area.**

2. **Choose Properties.**

The System Icons window appears, which lists the five different icons that Windows itself tosses into the notification area: Clock, Volume, Network, Power, and Action Center.

3. **For each icon, choose On or Off from the button menu.**

4. **Click OK when you're done.**

Set notification area icons in Windows Vista

To show or hide the wee li'l icons in the notification area in Windows Vista, heed these steps:

Book II
Chapter 1

Windows Gone
AWOL

1. **Right-click the date and time on the taskbar and choose Properties from the pop-up menu.**

   The Taskbar and Start Menu Properties dialog box appears, with the Notification Area tab forward.

2. **To keep all icons visible, remove the check mark by the item Hide Inactive Icons.**

   I keep all icons visible on my computer. When you want to be choosy and select which icons show, keep the check mark by the item Hide Inactive Icons and then use the Customize button to select which icons show up.

3. **Place or remove check marks in the System Icons area to show or hide the icons Windows itself places in the notification area.**

4. **Click OK.**

Retrieve a window that slid off the screen

It seems like such a simple problem, yet I've received email from readers who were told by tech support people to reinstall Windows just to place a window back on the desktop. What a silly, stupid thing to say.

To move a window back on the screen, a window that may have slid off so far that you can't pinch it with the mouse, follow these steps:

1. **Click to select the window.**

2. **Press Alt+spacebar to summon the window's shortcut menu.**

3. **Press M to choose the Move command.**

4. **Use the keyboard's arrow keys to move the window.**

5. **Press Enter when you're done moving the window around.**

See Video 215 for a visual demonstration of recovering a window that has woefully slid to one side of the screen.

www.dummies.com/go/troubleshootingandmaintainingyourpcaio2e

Windows appear at odd sizes and positions

Windows remembers the size and location of the windows you open. Theoretically, the windows appear at the same size and position as they were when last opened. Theoretically.

When the window doesn't remember its size, you must manually resize it. Use the mouse to drag out the window's edges or corners.

✦ Windows doesn't remember a window's maximized size. When you *maximize* a window, you set its size to be the same as the display.

✦ Sometimes, Internet Explorer windows are automatically resized, usually to display advertising.

✦ You can instantly maximize a window by double-clicking its title bar. (Double-clicking the title bar of a maximized window restores it to its previous size and position.)

Book II
Chapter 1

Windows Gone
AWOL

Change the image viewer

I'll bet that when you open a graphics file, the program you want to use for viewing it isn't the program that opens. That's fine — you can change the image viewer to whichever program you prefer. Here's how:

1. **Locate a graphics file.**

Actually, these steps work for any file type. Technically, you're changing what's known as the *default association.*

2. **Right-click the file and choose Open With⇨Choose Default Program.**

In Windows XP, the command is Open With⇨Choose Program.

3. **Select the program to open the file from the list of programs provided.**

4. **Ensure that a check mark appears by the item Always Use the Selected Program to Open This Kind of File.**

5. **Click OK.**

Folders and icons change position

One reason that you may find folders or icons jumping around in a window is that Windows is automatically sorting them for you. Confirm whether that's true by following these steps in Windows Vista and Windows XP:

1. **Right-click in the window (or on the desktop).**

2a. **In Windows Vista, display the View menu.**

2b. **In Windows XP, display the Arrange Icons By menu.**

3. **Ensure that no check mark appears next to the Auto Arrange command.**

4. **If you see a check mark, choose Auto Arrange to remove it.**

Line up icons on the desktop

Maybe you like the desktop icons all lined up in a grid, and maybe you don't. You can make the choice for yourself. Here's how:

1. **Right-click the desktop.**

2a. **In Windows 7, choose View⇨Align Icons to Grid.**

2b. **In Windows Vista, choose View⇨Align to Grid.**

2c. **In Windows XP, display the Arrange Icons By⇨Align to Grid.**

When the icon alignment option isn't chosen, the icons rest wherever you put them.

Clear the desktop

In Windows Vista, you can hide all icons on the desktop by following these steps:

1. **Right-click the desktop.**

2. **Choose View⇨Show Desktop Icons.**

Poof! The icons are gone.

Get rid of the Desktop Cleanup Wizard

After recognizing the quandary of icon clutter, Windows XP introduced the Desktop Cleanup Wizard. It was a disappointment. First, it annoyed you to death. Second, it failed to draw the attention of people who truly clutter the desktop with hordes of icons. The wizard was retired and isn't available in Windows Vista.

To disable the Desktop Cleanup Wizard, follow these steps in Windows XP:

1. **Right-click the desktop and choose Properties from the shortcut menu.**

2. **Click the Desktop tab in the Display Properties dialog box.**

3. **Click the Customize Desktop button.**

4. **Remove the check mark by the option Run Desktop Cleanup Wizard Every 60 Days.**

5. **Click OK to close the Customize Desktop dialog box.**

6. **Click OK to close the Display Properties dialog box.**

Turn off the Documents/Recent Items menu on the Start menu

If you don't like a list of recently opened files appearing on the Start button menu, you can disable the list. Here's how in Windows 7 and Windows Vista:

1. **Right-click the Start button and choose Properties from the pop-up menu.**

2. **Remove the check marks by both items in the Privacy area of the Start Menu tab.**

3. **Click OK.**

In Windows XP, follow these steps:

1. **Right-click the Start button and choose Properties from the pop-up menu.**

2. **Click the Customize button.**

3. **In the Customize Start Menu dialog box, click the Advanced tab.**

4. **Remove the check mark by the item List My Most Recently Opened Documents.**

5. **Click the Clear List button.**

6. **Click OK and then click OK again to close the dialog boxes you opened.**

See the Windows Explorer menus in Windows 7 and Windows Vista

Windows Vista began a trend where the program design shies away from menu bars. Windows 7 continues that trend. The menu bars aren't gone; they're just hidden.

✦ To see a menu bar in a Windows Explorer window, press the F10 key.

✦ You can also press the Alt key to summon the menu bar.

✦ Some newer programs lack menus entirely, such as Paint and WordPad in Windows 7. In those programs, pressing the F10 key doesn't display a hidden menu. Instead, by pressing the F10 key, you see any keyboard shortcuts that may exist for the application's Ribbon interface.

Update a window

Occasionally files change, especially on network drives or removable media, and the Windows Explorer window fails to reflect the changes. This isn't a problem in Windows Vista as much as it was a problem in earlier versions of Windows: The solution is simple: Press the F5 key, which is the Refresh command.

Yes, it's the same F5 key you can use to update a web page. The concept is similar: The page contents have changed, and the Refresh command updates what you see with the actual contents of the folder.

Read-only files and folders

Read-only is a file *attribute,* or a characteristic that the operating system assigns to a file. In this case, *read-only* means that the file can be only opened or read; you cannot delete, change, or rename any file that's been flagged read-only.

To change the read-only attribute, follow these steps:

1. **Right-click the file or folder icon.**

2. **Remove the check mark by the Read Only item in the file's Properties dialog box.**

   The attributes are found at the bottom of the General tab.

3. **Click OK.**

Likewise, you can set the read-only attribute by placing a check mark in the box. This ensures that the file cannot be changed or deleted. Well, it can't be changed or deleted until someone removes the read-only attribute again.

✦ Files and folders you copy from an optical disc may inherit the read-only status. That's because a CD-ROM or DVD-ROM is Read-Only (RO) media. After a file is copied from the optical disc, however, you can change its read-only status as described in the steps.

✦ The solid Read-Only check box in Windows 7 and Windows Vista refers to the file's or folder's permissions. The box may indicate that read-only permissions are set for other users on the same computer. See Book V, Chapter 3 for more information on permissions.

The message "Your activation period has expired" appears

Windows is software, and Microsoft doesn't give it away. To ensure that you're using a copy of Windows that wasn't stolen or illegally reproduced by a disreputable dealer, Windows must be activated to remain functional.

Normally, activation is automatic: If you ordered the PC directly from the factory, or the dealer might do it for you. Activation might be done when you initially configure Windows. If not, you're reminded.

You can activate Windows over the Internet or by phoning the telephone number displayed on the screen.

You *must* activate Windows to continue using your computer. There's no work-around. If you don't activate in time, the operating system ceases to function. It's not an error — it's Microsoft protecting its interests.

Icons go missing

As long as you know you haven't deleted the icon, it's probably still where you left it. Sometimes icons overlap. One icon may be hidden behind another. To fix the problem, you can either autoarrange the icons in the window or align the icons to a grid.

See the earlier section, "Folders and icons change position," for information on using Auto Arrange.

See the earlier section, "Line up icons on the desktop," for information on aligning icons to a grid. (Those directions also apply to a window: Just right-click in the window rather than on the desktop in Step 1.)

What file is this?

Some people have a temptation to peek around in a computer. I do it all the time. I even did it when I was new to computers. But there's also a danger.

The danger is that it's a bad thing to delete or change any file you didn't create yourself. Just because you don't understand a file or you feel that you can delete the file and don't see any immediate change doesn't mean that the computer is okay. So my first piece of advice is this:

> *Don't delete any file you didn't yourself create.*

Likewise, don't rename, move, or modify any file you didn't create.

To sate your temptations, you may occasionally try to open a file just because you're curious. If the file is a program, the program runs. Generally speaking, any program that can foul up a computer gives you a warning before it starts up the virtual chain saw. Other files, you may try to open and see a dialog box. But I don't want you to get ahead of yourself.

First thing to note: The reason the file doesn't open is that your computer lacks the software to open it. That's a fact. If someone emailed you the file, email them back and explain that you cannot open the file. Your situation isn't your own fault; the other person needs to send the file in the proper format.

Second thing to note: Some files aren't worth opening. Don't even try. The file may just be binary code that a human wouldn't understand or appreciate anyway.

When the mood hits you, however, you do have a choice: In Windows XP, you see a dialog box with an Open With button. Click the button. It opens the same type of dialog box displayed immediately by Windows 7 and Windows Vista and shown in Figure 1-11.

**Book II
Chapter 1**

Figure 1-11:
Windows is
concerned
about the
file you
opened.

In the dialog box shown in the figure, you can choose the option Use the Web Service to Find the Correct Program, but the odds are good that the search turns up empty. I recommend choosing the second option, Select a Program from a List of Installed Programs. When you do, you see the Open With dialog box, as shown in Figure 1-12.

Figure 1-12:
The Open
With dialog
box.

The Open With dialog box is used to *open* a file *with* a specific program.

The first thing to do is remove the check mark by the option Always Use the Selected Program to Open This Kind of File. When you fail to do so, you perform the process of *file association,* which probably isn't wise to do at this point.

One program listed in the window (refer to Figure 1-12) *might* open the file in a readable state. My suggestion is to try Notepad first. Notepad can easily view text files, and many mystery files are text files.

When Notepad doesn't work, you can try Internet Explorer, which recognizes a wide swath of different programs. If that doesn't work, my heartfelt advice is to give up. Really.

Chapter 2: Programs, Processes, and Services

In This Chapter

✔ Controlling programs in Windows

✔ Viewing processes and services

✔ Stopping something run amok

✔ Dealing with `svchost.exe` and `rundll32.exe`

✔ Halting start-up programs

✔ Understanding blocked start-up programs

*I*n the Mighty Battle of Engineers, the hardware side enjoys blaming the software side for all its woes. With equal gusto, the software side relishes pointing its virtual finger of discontent at the hardware people. As someone in the middle, it's your job not to take sides, but merely to know when to duck. For those times when you need to venture over to the software side for some troubleshooting, this chapter serves as your guide. Just keep in mind that it's the software you're trying to fix here; hardware is covered in Book I.

What's an Application? What's a Process? What's a Service?

When you get into software troubleshooting in Windows, you discover that the term *software* is too general. Sure, you can use the word *program* to describe files that contain code or computer instructions. But to trouble-shoot, you need to know some weird terms, how those weird terms are used, and where those weird things are controlled. That's what you find in this section.

Don't let the technology baffle you! Although this material can get a bit nerdy, you must keep in mind that you, the human, are in charge of your computer.

Understanding the weird terms

Generally speaking, the kingdom of software includes all computer programs. A computer *program* is simply a file that contains instructions telling the computer's hardware to do something. But when it comes time to understand how programs work in Windows, you need to understand three terms:

Application: An application is something that you, the user, start in Windows. Microsoft Word, for example, is an application. Internet Explorer is an application. Even a game or utility is an application. If you started it, Windows calls it an application.

Process: A process is a program that Windows runs, or that runs automatically as part of the start-up procedure. Unlike applications, which show up on the taskbar and appear as windows on the screen, a process may not have a window. It runs invisibly. Some processes, however, appear as tiny icons in the notification area.

Service: A service is a task carried out by either an application or a process. A single process can sponsor multiple services. For example, an antivirus program may run as a process (because it's started automatically), and it may sport several services that monitor your computer for signs of infection.

Basically, applications and processes are the same thing — the only difference is whether you started it or Windows started it. Services can belong to either applications or processes. Pretty much everything is interconnected.

Most people become confused by the difference between processes and services. Just remember that a process is a program and a service is what the program does — its task.

To better understand these strange terms, you can visit the Windows Task Manager, as covered in the next section.

Visiting the Task Manager

Windows is a *multitasking* operating system: It can do several things at a time. In fact, the typical Windows PC is running about three dozen processes when it's just sitting there. Yes, modern computers are busy pretty much all the time. Most processes sit and wait, but they're in there.

Every program that's running is referred to as a *task;* hence, the term *multitasking.* To view the tasks taking place in your computer, the Task Manager window is used, as shown in Figure 2-1.

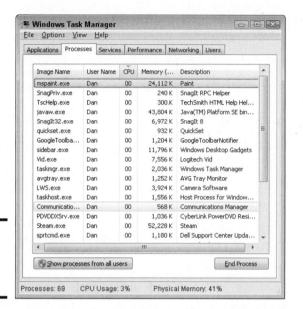

Figure 2-1:
Windows
Vista Task
Manager.

To summon the Task Manager, press Ctrl+Shift+Esc.

In the Task Manager window, if necessary, click the Applications tab. The
programs that are listed are programs you started or windows you opened.

Click the Processes tab to display all programs running in Windows, including the applications you opened (shown on the Applications tab) and processes being run by Windows itself. (Refer to Figure 2-1 for an illustration of
the Processes tab.)

✦ Each window you open in Windows Explorer appears as its own entry
  on the Task Manager's Applications tab. Likewise, when you have multiple windows open in a single application, such as Excel, each window
  appears as its own entry. In a way, items on the Applications tab merely
  echo buttons found on the taskbar.

✦ The only window that doesn't appear in the Application window is the
  Task Manager itself.

✦ In Windows XP, you can also summon the Task Manager by pressing
  Ctrl+Alt+Delete.

✦ The Windows XP version of the Task Manager lacks the Description
  column on the Processes tab. Also, the Task Manager dialog box in
  Windows XP lacks the Services tab.

✦ You can configure the Task Manager window to float over every other window on the screen: Choose Options⇨Always On Top from the Task Manager's menu bar.

✦ The nerdy way to open the Task Manager is to type **taskmgr** in the Run dialog box. Press Win+R first to summon the Run dialog box.

Understanding the application/process relationship

A connection exists between the items on the Task Manager's Applications tab and the items on the Processes tab. The applications are superficial; the process does the work in Windows. Follow these steps:

1. **Open the Task Manager.**

Refer to the preceding section for directions.

2. **Press Win+E to open a Windows Explorer window.**

Don't worry if you can't see the window behind the Task Manager; this is just a demonstration.

3. **Click the Applications tab in the Task Manager window if necessary.**

4. **Right-click either the Computer or My Computer window item, which represents the Windows Explorer window you opened in Step 2.**

5. **Choose Go to Process from the shortcut menu.**

The Task Manager window switches to the Process tab, highlighting the program `explorer.exe`, which is the name of the Windows Explorer program. Windows Explorer "runs" the Computer or My Computer window that you opened.

6. **Switch back to the Applications tab.**

7. **Click to select the Computer or My Computer window you opened in Step 2.**

8. **Click the End Task button.**

The Computer or My Computer window closes.

The End Task button sends the "You are done" signal to a program, just as though you closed the program's window — same thing.

Viewing the whole mess o' processes

Windows runs a lot of processes. Normally, the Task Manager window displays only the processes that relate to your account in Windows. To see the whole lot of them, including processes that Windows runs but doesn't want you to mess with, do this:

In Windows 7 and Windows Vista, click the button Show Processes from All Users. If prompted, click the Continue button or type the administrator's password.

In Windows XP, place a check mark by the item Show Processes from All Users.

The length of the list of items shown on the Processes tab grows slightly. You see a few more items in the list. Here are some things you can do:

✦ To sort the list by process name, click the Image Name column heading.

✦ Sort the list by the CPU column to find out how much processor time is being used by various processes. (To see the most time-consuming processes listed first, ensure that the triangle at the top of the CPU column is pointing upward.)

✦ Don't freak out because the System Idle Process might be using a vast amount of the CPU's time — sometimes up to 99 percent. That's normal. Running the System Idle Process is what the computer does when it's not doing anything else. That's probably because the computer doesn't have access to cable television.

✦ The process list is also one way you can discover viruses and Trojan horses in your computer. But don't go hunting now. Refer to Book IV, Chapter 4 for directions on how to properly rid your system of nasty programs.

✦ Yes, the End Process button is used to kill off a highlighted process. Don't use this button randomly because it adversely affects your PC.

Enjoying the services

The Task Manager window in Windows 7 and Windows Vista features a Services tab, something that the Task Manager in Windows XP lacks. Of course, it doesn't mean that Windows XP lacks services; it means only that you need to look elsewhere to find them.

To view services running on your PC, follow these steps:

1. **Open the Control Panel.**

2a. **In Windows 7, choose System and Security and then choose Administrative Tools.**

2b. **In Windows Vista, choose System and Maintenance and then choose Administrative tools.**

2c. **In Windows XP, open the Administrative Tools icon.**

3. **Open the Services icon.**

4. In Windows Vista, click the Continue button or type the administrator's password to continue.

The Services console is shown in Figure 2-2.

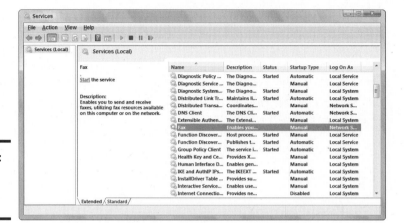

Figure 2-2:
The
Services
console.

5. Click a service to select it.

A description of the highlighted service is displayed in the console window (refer to Figure 2-2). Some services can also be started or stopped when they're selected.

6. Double-click a service to view detailed information in its Properties dialog box.

The General tab in the service's Properties dialog box has options for starting, stopping, and pausing the service. It also contains a Path to Executable entry, which references the process (program) that's responsible for running the service.

7. Close the service's Properties dialog box.

8. Close the Services window.

In Windows 7 and Windows Vista, you can quickly display the Services console by selecting the Services tab in the Task Manager window and then clicking the Services button.

✦ One key issue with services is that your PC probably doesn't need to run all of them. Running unnecessary services only slows down your PC. Chapter 4 discusses which services to disable; disabling services can not only improve performance but also reduce some security risks.

✦ In Windows 7 and Windows Vista, you can right-click a service shown on the Task Manager's Services tab and choose the Go to Process command to see which process is running that particular service.

Ending a stuck program

In a victory for hardware engineers, it happens often that computer programs die. Of course, the software factions can gleefully point out that when certain software dies, other software can help remedy the situation. (When hardware dies, other hardware often doesn't help.)

A variety of terms are used to describe the act of a program biting the digital dust: *crash, hang, torque, die,* and others too foul to mention. The term used in the Task Manager window is Not Responding, as shown so disappointingly in Figure 2-3.

Book II
Chapter 2

Programs, Processes, and Services

Figure 2-3:
Stuck
programs.

Seeing the Not Responding text in the Status column is a surefire bet that the program has achieved an unrecoverable state of existence. You can dispense with the problem as follows:

1. **Summon the Task Manager window (if necessary).**

2. **Click to select the program that isn't responding.**

3. **Click the End Task switch.**

4. **If necessary, click the End Now button if another dialog box appears.**

5. **Close the Task Manager window.**

Sometimes, Windows itself may detect and halt whacked-out programs for you. When that happens, you see a disappointing dialog box, like the one shown in Figure 2-4.

Figure 2-4:
Windows
auto-
matically
killed a
suspect
program.

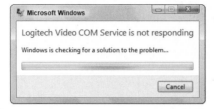

After killing the program, you may be allowed to send an error report back to Microsoft. Whether you do is up to you; sending the report doesn't fix the program, nor does it guarantee that anyone will ever look at the report.

Halting a process

A process isn't something you should randomly stop, especially for the time-honored reason "I wonder what this does?" Instead, sometimes you're directed to stop a process, or perhaps you're motivated to end a process to troubleshoot problems with your computer. When those needs arise, follow these steps to stifle a process by using the Task Manager:

1. **Summon the Task Manager window as described earlier in this chapter.**

2. **Click the Processes tab.**

3. **Select the process you want to eradicate.**

   It helps if you click the Image Name heading to sort the processes alphabetically.

4. **Click the End Process button.**

   A warning dialog box appears; ending a process isn't to be taken lightly.

5. **Click the End Process button in the Windows Task Manager warning window.**

   The process is slain.

6. **Close the Task Manager window.**

A good example of following these steps is to kill off a program that runs an icon in the notification area. For example, an icon in the notification area might control special display features. You cannot find that program on the Applications tab, but it exists on the Processes tab.

The trick to discovering which process belongs to an icon in the notification area is to somehow get the icon to display a window. For example, right-click the icon to use a Show or Display menu command. After it's open, you can follow these steps in the Task Manager window to locate the given process:

1. **Right-click the application's name on the Application tab.**

2. **Choose Go to Process from the shortcut menu.**

3. **Click the End Process button in the Task Manager window, and then again to confirm the process's demise.**

The process is gone, as is the notification area icon. (Remember that most notification area icons have Exit as a command on their pop-up shortcut menus.)

Randomly killing processes can render your PC inoperable. It's not a Terrible Thing, but you need to restart Windows (or reset the entire PC) to regain control.

Stopping or disabling a service

Windows starts up *way too many* services for your computer. My favorite is the Fax service, which is ridiculous on my PC because it lacks an internal modem and cannot fax anything. But sometimes you may be directed to disable or end a service. During those times, refer to these steps for the proper procedure:

1. **Open the Services console.**

   Refer to the section "Enjoying the services," earlier in this chapter, for details.

2. **Double-click the service you want to stop or disable.**

   The service's dialog box appears.

3. **Ensure that the General tab is selected.**

4. **To stop the service, click the Stop button.**

   If the Stop button isn't available (it's *dimmed*), the service hasn't started. Good.

5. **To prevent the service from starting when Windows starts, choose Disable from the drop-down menu next to Startup Type.**

6. **Click OK to confirm the new settings.**

7. **Close the Services console window.**

It's often not enough to stop a service (refer to Step 4), so you have to disable it as well (refer to Step 5). By disabling the service, you prevent it from restarting. Of course, if you need to merely suspend a service for troubleshooting, don't disable it, because it might not be the cause of your misery.

Later sections in this book discuss specific services worthy of stopping or disabling.

Services that rely on other services cannot be stopped willy-nilly. To stop them, you must halt them as Windows starts. That's a job for the System Configuration Utility. Here's what to do:

1. **Press Win+R to bring up the Run dialog box.**

2. **Type** MSCONFIG **to start the System Configuration Utility.**

3. **In Windows Vista, type the administrator's password or click the Continue button.**

4. **Click the Services tab.**

5. **Remove the check mark by the service you want to disable.**

   By removing the check mark, you prevent the service from being started the next time Windows starts.

   As an example, my desktop computer has no Bluetooth wireless hardware, yet I see that the Bluetooth Support Service is checked. Removing the check mark disables the service, which I don't need (and can't even use).

6. **Click OK to close the window.**

7. **Click the Restart button to restart Windows.**

   Or, you can click the Exit without Restart button. Just remember to restart Windows in the future.

Also be sure to check out the section "Using MSCONFIG to set start-up stuff," later in this chapter.

Understanding svchost.exe

A process in Windows named svchost.exe is often a source of anxiety and woe among PC troubleshooters. That's probably because the single process svchost.exe is responsible for running a plethora of services in Windows. Yes, a plethora.

The svchost.exe process can run multiple copies (or *instances*) of itself in Windows. Therefore, you may find several svchost.exe entries listed on the Task Manager's Process tab. (You have to show processes from all users in order to see the svchost.exe processes.)

In Windows 7 and Windows Vista, you can home in on which services an instance of svchost.exe is controlling by right-clicking a svchost.exe entry and choosing the Go to Service(s) command from the pop-up menu.

To review the full horde of services run by svchost.exe, you can follow these nerdy command prompt steps:

1. **Start a command prompt window.**

   From the Start button menu, choose All Programs⇨Accessories⇨Command Prompt.

2. **Type the following command:**

   ```
   tasklist /svc /fi "imagename eq svchost.exe"
   ```

   Type the command exactly as written. Yes, it's nerdy. I said that.

3. **Double-check your typing.**

4. **Press the Enter key.**

   Quickly, text spurts onto the command prompt window. The details show which services are being run by the various instances of svchost.exe, as detailed in Figure 2-5.

```
Image Name                      PID Services
============================ ======== =============================================
svchost.exe                    1028 DcomLaunch, PlugPlay, Power
svchost.exe                    1128 RpcEptMapper, RpcSs
svchost.exe                    1228 Audiosrv, Dhcp, eventlog,
                                    HomeGroupProvider, lmhosts, wscsvc
svchost.exe                    1272 AudioEndpointBuilder, Netman, PçaSvc,
                                    SysMain, TrkWks, UxSms, WPDBusEnum, wudfsvc
svchost.exe                    1316 AeLookupSvc, Appinfo, AppMgmt, BITS,
                                    Browser, gpsvc, IKEEXT, iphlpsvc,
                                    LanmanServer, MMCSS, ProfSvc, Schedule,
                                    SENS, ShellHWDetection, Themes, Winmgmt,
                                    wuauserv
svchost.exe                    1472 EventSystem, fdPHost, netprofm, nsi,
                                    WdiServiceHost
svchost.exe                    1612 CryptSvc, Dnscache, LanmanWorkstation,
                                    NlaSvc
svchost.exe                    1768 BFE, DPS, MpsSvc
svchost.exe                    1924 FDResPub, FontCache, SSDPSRV, upnphost
svchost.exe                    2060 Net Driver HPZ12
svchost.exe                    2100 Pml Driver HPZ12
svchost.exe                    2464 StiSvc
svchost.exe                    3292 PolicyAgent
svchost.exe                    4648 p2pimsvc, p2psvc, PNRPsvc
svchost.exe                    3628 SDRSVC
```

Figure 2-5: Wonderfully trivial and befuddling information on svc host. exe.

You can scroll back through the command prompt window to review the list or simply resize the window vertically.

5. **Type the** exit **command to close the command prompt window.**

The information displayed at the command prompt window is just a quick summary, but it's not the big issue with svchost.exe. No, the big issue is that many of the Bad Guys out there like to name their bad software svchost.exe just to confuse and anger you.

To determine whether svchost.exe, or one of its services, is malware, refer to Book IV, Chapter 4.

Peeking at that rundll32.exe thing

Another problem child in the Windows pantheon of processes is something called rundll32.exe. Like svchost.exe, it draws a lot of suspicion.

The rundll32.exe program exists to run programs held in DLL files. A DLL is a *Dynamic Link Library,* a common set of routines used by a number of programs in Windows. To run one of these routines directly, the rundll32. exe program lives up to its name and runs the dll program file.

The problem with rundll32.exe is that it can easily be spoofed by the Bad Guys or can run a process that's secretly malware. Book IV, Chapter 4 has more information on malware and its removal. For now, here's the command you can type at the command prompt to review the list of processes being run by rundll32.exe:

```
tasklist /m /fi "imagename eq rundll32.exe"
```

Refer to the preceding section for information on how to run this command, and substitute the text from Step 2. (It's nearly the same command.) A sample of the command's output is shown in Figure 2-6.

As with the svchost.exe program discussed in the preceding section, the information that's displayed only tells you some nerdy things about what the rundll32.exe program is up to. Only when you know which nasty programs to look for can you confirm that rundll32.exe is running them. Book IV, Chapter 4 has the details for you.

✦ The rundll32.exe program is merely the messenger. Although it can be abused to run nasty software, or you may occasionally see rundll32.exe in an error message, the program itself is most likely not the problem child. No, it's probably one of the DLLs that rundll32.exe is running that's causing you strife.

✦ Don't be surprised in Windows 7 not to find any tasks using rundll32. exe. It's an older technology, and you'd have to be running older applications or games to see any active rundll32.exe tasks.

✦ The original program to run DLL files was named rundll.exe. That was the filename used with the Windows 95, 98, and Me editions. Because Windows XP is a 32-bit operating system, the filename was changed to rundll32.exe.

```
Image Name                   PID Modules
==========================   ====   =====================================
rundll32.exe                 2072   ntdll.dll, kernel32.dll, USER32.dll,
                                    GDI32.dll, ADVAPI32.dll, RPCRT4.dll,
                                    msvcrt.dll, imagehlp.dll, ShimEng.dll,
                                    apphelp.dll, AcLayers.DLL, SHELL32.dll,
                                    SHLWAPI.dll, ole32.dll, OLEAUT32.dll,
                                    USERENV.dll, Secur32.dll, WINSPOOL.DRV,
                                    MPR.dll, IMM32.DLL, MSCTF.dll, LPK.DLL,
                                    USP10.dll, comctl32.dll, NvMCTray.dll,
                                    COMCTL32.dll, nvapi.dll, SETUPAPI.dll,
                                    uxtheme.dll, tvtpwm_windows_hook.dll,
                                    tvt_passwordmanager.dll, PSAPI.DLL,
                                    WTSAPI32.dll, NETAPI32.dll, css_banner.dll,
                                    csswait.dll, comdlg32.dll,
                                    cssuserdatadispatcher.dll, VERSION.dll,
                                    CRYPT32.dll, MSASN1.dll, WINTRUST.dll,
                                    css_dlgcustompolicy.dll, tvttsp.dll,
                                    tcsrpc.dll, WS2_32.dll, NSI.dll,
                                    rsaenh.dll, tvt_think_res.dll,
                                    css_think_res.dll
rundll32.exe                 2124   ntdll.dll, kernel32.dll, USER32.dll,
                                    GDI32.dll, ADVAPI32.dll, RPCRT4.dll,
                                    msvcrt.dll, imagehlp.dll, ShimEng.dll,
                                    apphelp.dll, AcLayers.DLL, SHELL32.dll,
                                    SHLWAPI.dll, ole32.dll, OLEAUT32.dll,
                                    USERENV.dll, Secur32.dll, WINSPOOL.DRV,
                                    MPR.dll, IMM32.DLL, MSCTF.dll, LPK.DLL,
                                    USP10.dll, comctl32.dll, NVSVC.DLL,
                                    POWRPROF.dll, WTSAPI32.dll, uxtheme.dll,
                                    CLBCatQ.DLL, wbemprox.dll, wbemcomn.dll,
                                    WS2_32.dll, NSI.dll, rsaenh.dll,
                                    wbemsvc.dll, fastprox.dll, NTDSAPI.dll,
                                    DNSAPI.dll, WLDAP32.dll, PSAPI.DLL,
                                    NETAPI32.dll, tvtpwm_windows_hook.dll,
                                    tvt_passwordmanager.dll, css_banner.dll,
                                    COMCTL32.dll, csswait.dll, comdlg32.dll,
                                    cssuserdatadispatcher.dll, VERSION.dll,
                                    CRYPT32.dll, MSASN1.dll, WINTRUST.dll,
                                    css_dlgcustompolicy.dll, tvttsp.dll,
                                    tcsrpc.dll, tvt_think_res.dll,
                                    css_think_res.dll, nvapi.dll, SETUPAPI.dll,
                                    WINSTA.dll
```

Figure 2-6:
Processes
being run by
run
dll32.
exe.

Start-Up Programs

At some point in the start-up process, computer hardware gives way to the software that eventually controls everything. Windows barges in first. As Windows loads, and afterward, more programs are loaded. They include start-up programs you configured to run automatically, such as an antivirus program or a webcam, and then programs you want to run every time you start Windows, such as an email program or a calendar. To keep things thrilling for you, problems with that software can happen anywhere on the line.

To determine that a start-up software problem is Windows' own doing, you use Safe mode, which is covered in Chapter 3. For disabling other programs during start-up, refer to the following section.

Disabling start-up programs

Windows starts lots of programs. They can be device drivers for special hardware, processes run by utilities, or even programs you run every time

Windows starts. To determine whether a program is causing a problem, you have to be a PC troubleshooting sleuth.

The first thing to do is to *pay attention.* Problems with device drivers or processes that load initially are often flagged by start-up error messages. For example, the error message in Figure 2-7 describes the name of a program that's not working. That's a big clue.

Figure 2-7:
A start-up
program
is having
issues.

After you determine which program is causing anguish, you can try to fix it. In Figure 2-7, the keyword is Sonic Focus, which is a trademark and therefore obviously some type of hardware or software program. Another keyword is Intel, found in the window title. My guess is that an audio problem exists — most likely, software related. A quick search of the Internet indicates perhaps a source for new Sonic Focus drivers or perhaps online support.

The second thing to do is to guess. It's not a bad thing to guess; when the computer doesn't cough up any solid information for you, guessing is the next logical choice. But to be successful, you have to guess methodically.

You guess by systematically disabling various start-up processes or programs, one at a time. Disable, restart, check for the problem. Eventually, you experience a time when the computer starts without the problem. When it happens, you've found the troublemaking start-up program and can continue to look for support or find an updated version of the file.

The next few sections discuss various ways to disable start-up programs in Windows.

+ Keeping your computer software up-to-date is one key way to ensure that certain problems are avoided. Developers address common problems, and newer versions of programs with those fixes are made available on a regular basis. (See Chapter 1 for more information on Windows Update.)

+ Yes, it's tedious to disable the many, many start-up programs in your computer, restart, check, and then reenable. That's the way to do it, though.

Using MSCONFIG to set start-up stuff

Some people refer to it by its proper name, which is the System Configuration Utility. But because you start the program by typing MSCONFIG, I prefer to say that it's the MSCONFIG program. What it does is provide a central location for controlling things that happen when you start your computer.

The MSCONFIG program window has several tabs:

General: This tab contains basic start-up options, including settings to go into Safe mode or disable certain start-up files.

Boot: This tab controls the operating system start-up process, including the multiple operating system selection menu and other start-up menus and options. The Boot tab isn't found in the Windows XP version of MSCONFIG.

Services: This tab lists all the services run in Windows, allowing you to disable them. (Services are covered earlier in this chapter.)

Startup: This tab lists all processes started by Windows, as well as processes started for your account. (Processes are covered earlier in this chapter.)

Tools: This tab lists shortcuts to handy troubleshooting tools in Windows.

In addition to these tabs, the Windows XP version of MSCONFIG shows two legacy tabs from previous versions of Windows:

SYSTEM.INI: This tab lists items found in the old system initialization file used in Windows 95.

WIN.INI: This tab lists items found in the old Windows initialization file, also dating from Windows 95.

Items found on the SYTEM.INI and WIN.INI tabs are start-up items that are included for compatibility purposes with older programs. Few, if any, of your PC start-up problems are caused by settings in SYSTEM.INI or WIN.INI.

You can use MSCONFIG to disable certain start-up items, such as items causing problems or for troubleshooting. Those items are found on the Startup tab. To bring up the MSCONFIG window, heed these steps:

1. **Bring forth the Run dialog box.**

   Press Win+R on the keyboard to summon it forth.

2. **Type** MSCONFIG **and press Enter.**

3. **In Windows Vista, click the Continue button or type the administrator's password to proceed.**

4. **In the System Configuration Utility window, click the Startup tab.**

   The Startup tab lists all the programs that Windows starts stealthily.

5. **Disable a start-up item by removing its check mark.**

Unless you know which item is causing the problem, I recommend removing one check mark at a time.

6. Click the General tab.

Note that the start-up selection has changed on the Startup tab. The Startup Selection has changed to Selective Startup, and the option for Load Startup Items is shaded. These are your clues that the start-up process is no longer the same. It's not bad news; you can reverse your choices easily.

7. Close the MSCONFIG window.

8. I recommend clicking the Restart button to test your changes.

9. Wait while the computer restarts.

After your computer starts up again, you may see a warning such as the one shown in Figure 2-8. More important, note whether you still have start-up problems or issues with the thing you're troubleshooting. If not, you found the culprit; you're done.

Figure 2-8:
A friendly reminder from MSCONFIG.

System Configuration Utility

You have used the System Configuration Utility to make changes to the way Windows starts.

The System Configuration Utility is currently in Diagnostic or Selective Startup mode, causing this message to be displayed and the utility to run every time Windows starts.

Choose the Normal Startup mode on the General tab to start Windows normally and undo the changes you made using the System Configuration Utility.

☐ Don't show this message or launch the System Configuration Utility when Windows start

[OK]

When problems still prevail, continue:

10. Start the MSCONFIG utility again.

Refer to steps 1 through 3.

11. Click the Startup tab.

12. Replace the check mark by the item you previously disabled (in Step 5).

13. Set a check mark by the next item you're testing.

14. Repeat Steps 7 through 10 to test that next item.

The idea is to work through all start-up programs until you find the one that's causing you trouble.

After the start-up item is disabled, the computer should start without any problems. I recommend that you search out the program's developer for an update. Use the program's Startup Item name and other information as displayed on the MSCONFIG window's Startup tab to help search for a solution on the Internet.

By disabling a start-up item, you're placing the PC into selective start-up or diagnostic mode. You may see warnings reminding you about it when you start the computer.

What about looking for start-up programs in the Registry?

The Windows Registry is a central configuration cache of weird and wonderful things. Many users innocently attribute magical and mysterious powers to the Registry. But it's nothing special. Despite that, interest and curiosity persist, often unnecessarily so.

Several locations inside the Registry list start-up programs and processes. You can visit them if you like; Chapter 9 deals with the Registry. But there's no point in wasting your time: The MSCONFIG utility lists all start-up files you find in the Registry. When you click the Startup tab in the MSCONFIG window, you're looking at a summary of every start-up file that's relevant to your account. There's nowhere else you need to go.

Finding start-up programs for your account

Like many people, you may have configured certain programs to automatically start when you log in to Windows. These start-up items appear on the aptly named Startup menu, found on the All Programs menu.

Many programs automatically put items on the Startup menu for you. You can also copy and paste the items yourself. Be careful to note that the files can be found in *two* locations. Follow these steps to train your brain:

1a. **In Windows 7 and Windows Vista, pop up the Start menu and right-click the All Programs item.**

1b. **In Windows XP, right-click the Start button.**

2. **Choose the Open command.**

A folder window appears, showing the Programs folder. This is your account's private edition of that folder. It lists only those items set up on the computer that are specific to your account.

3. **Open the Programs folder.**

4. **Open the Startup folder.**

Behold the start-up items specific to your account. Well, yes, the folder might be empty. That's because most users don't know any better and they tend to install programs for everyone. That's the "default," actually.

5. **Close the Startup folder window.**

Now you can find where everyone's start-up programs are located.

6a. **In Windows 7 and Windows Vista, pop up the Start menu, right-click the All Programs item, and choose Open All Users.**

6b. **In Windows XP, right-click the Start button and choose the Open All Users command.**

7. **Open the Programs folder.**

8. **Open the Startup folder.**

   Aye, there's the meat! Shortcut icons in the Startup folder window represent programs automatically started by your computer.

   To disable a program, continue with Step 9; otherwise, you're done, so you can close the Startup window.

9. **Select icons for the programs you no longer want started.**

   Hold down the Ctrl key while clicking multiple icons to select each one.

   Rather than have you delete the icons, I recommend copying them into a NotStartUp folder.

10. **Press Ctrl+X to cut the icons.**

11. **Press the Backspace key to return to the main Programs folder.**

12. **If necessary, create a new folder and name it** NotStartUp.

    Here are the steps necessary to create that folder, in case you're rusty in your Windows folder management knowledge:

    a. *Click the New Folder button on the toolbar, or choose Organize⇨ New Folder or File⇨New⇨Folder.*

    b. *In Windows Vista, click the Continue button, and then type the administrator's password or click Continue to give yourself permission to create the new folder.*

    c. *Type the name **NotStartUp** for the new folder and then press Enter.*

    d. *Again, click the Continue button in Windows Vista and blah-blah-blah to continue.*

13. **Open the NotStartUp folder.**

14. **Press Ctrl+V to paste in the icons you cut in Step 10.**

    You effectively moved the icons from the Startup folder, where they start programs every time you log in, to the NotStartUp folder, where they don't start them every time you log in.

    Yes, in Windows Vista, you need to click the Continue button and grant yourself administrative powers to proceed with the pasting operation.

15. **Close the window.**

My reasoning behind creating the NotStartUp folder is that it's good to keep a copy of those files that once lived inside the Startup folder. That way, if you want to restore them at a later date, it's merely a matter of cutting and pasting them from the NotStartUp folder back into the Startup folder.

   ✦ You can also create a NotStartUp folder for your own account. Create the new folder in the Programs folder you open by following Steps 1 through 4 in this section.

◆ Like other items on the All Programs menu, the items on the Startup menu are all shortcuts to files dwelling elsewhere on your PC's storage system.

◆ The reasons for all the permissions and Continue buttons in Windows Vista is that by modifying the All Users Startup folder, you're changing things for other users on the computer. Because evil software might try that trick, Windows needs your confirmation in order to proceed.

◆ Watch Video 221 for an onscreen walk-through of the procedure outlined in this section.

www.dummies.com/go/troubleshootingandmaintainingyourpcaio2e

Dealing with blocked start-up programs

Here's one that will bother you until you read this section and figure out what needs fixing. Have you ever seen the `Windows Has Blocked Some Startup Programs` notice, as shown in Figure 2-9?

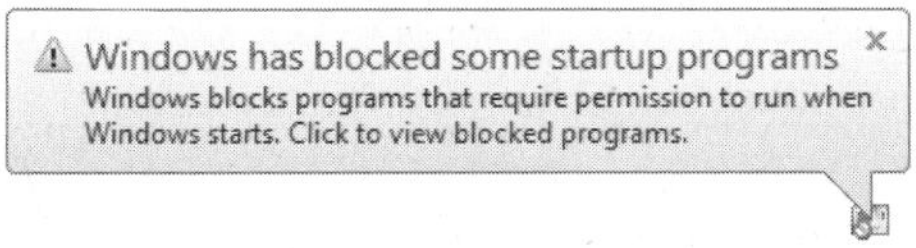

Figure 2-9: The annoying blocked-programs balloon.

⚠ Windows has blocked some startup programs ✕
Windows blocks programs that require permission to run when
Windows starts. Click to view blocked programs.

Try as you can to dismiss the sucker, it doesn't go away until you deal with the situation.

Here's how to deal with the situation in Windows Vista and Windows XP. (It doesn't appear to be a problem in Windows 7.)

1. **From the Start button menu, choose All Programs⇨Windows Defender.**

   Windows Defender comes standard with Windows Vista, but it's an optional upgrade for Windows XP. (See Book IV, Chapter 4 for details.)

2. **Click the Tools link at the top of the window.**

3. **Choose the Software Explorer tool.**

4. **Ensure that Startup Programs is chosen from the Category drop-down list.**

   You see a list of all programs that attempt to start when the computer starts, as shown in Figure 2-10. I say "attempt to start" because programs of an unknown type can be blocked. That explains the message you see when the computer starts (refer to Figure 2-9).

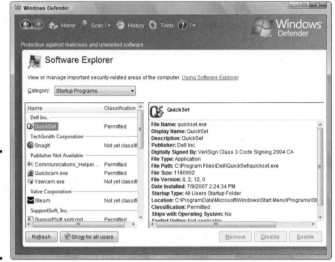

Figure 2-10:
Perusing
the start-up
programs
in Windows
Defender.

You can remove or block a program in the list: Simply click the Remove or Disable button when the program is selected. Most likely, a program that's been blocked appears in the Quarantine area.

5. **Click the Tools link at the top of the window.**

6. **Choose Quarantined Items.**

   If any items are listed, they have been blocked — and most likely for good reason.

   You can remove the quarantine by selecting an item and choosing the Restore button. But do so only if you're positively certain that the blocked program is safe.

7. **Close the Windows Defender window when you're done.**

For more information on Windows Defender, refer to Book IV, Chapter 4. The program is primarily a spyware removal tool, which is why it's covered in that chapter.

Other software on your computer might also be blocking certain start-up programs. For example, an antispyware or antivirus utility might scan your computer's files for signs of malware. Start-up files can be quarantined or blocked by those utilities as well.

Chapter 3: The Safe Mode Chapter

In This Chapter

✓ **Starting Safe mode**

✓ **Getting out of Safe mode**

✓ **Diagnosing problems**

✓ **Troubleshooting start-up files**

Safe mode is one of the most curious things Microsoft has chosen to put into Windows. The name alone is odd. Why is it called *Safe mode*? The official answer is that Safe mode is used for troubleshooting, to help you track down problems. In my mind, however, Safe mode implies an *unsafe mode*, which is apparently the normal way of using the computer. Despite the terminology, you can effectively use Safe mode to help troubleshoot your computer, as discussed in this chapter.

Safe Mode to the Rescue

It is my wish that you never need to use Safe mode. First of all, it's not fun. It reminds me of the old days of low-resolution graphics and limited computer abilities. Using Safe mode can also mean that something is terribly wrong, which is seldom amusing. This section describes Safe mode as a trouble-shooting tool for those times when you really need it.

✦ Safe mode is available for a number of operating systems, not just Windows. Some portable gizmos, such as MP3 players and cellphones, also feature Safe mode.

✦ In Mac OS X, Safe mode is called *Safe Boot*. But Apple uses the term *Safe mode* to refer to a computer that has been started with Safe Boot.

✦ Some applications have Safe mode. Microsoft Office applications all feature a safe mode of operation, used for troubleshooting. The most common reason for using Safe mode in an application is to disable cus-tomized features that may not be properly implemented.

Using Safe mode

Safe mode happens in one of three circumstances:

✦ A problem looms in your PC, one that Windows detects at boot time. The computer then automatically starts in Safe mode so that you can deal with the problem.

✦ You direct Windows to start in Safe mode from the F8 menu when the computer first starts up.

✦ You direct Windows to start in Safe mode by using the MSCONFIG utility.

Starting the computer in Safe mode works similarly to the normal start-up process. First you log in, and you may notice that the screen resolution is lower than normal.

Next, you see a start-up splash screen. It might be the Help System page that explains Safe mode, a dialog box explaining that the computer hard-started in Safe mode, or something similar. Dismiss the notice to begin using Safe mode.

When you finally arrive, you see Windows in Safe mode operation, as shown in Figure 3-1. The screen resolution is low because the standard video drivers (often a source of anguish) aren't loaded. The words *Safe mode* appear in all corners of the display.

Figure 3-1:
Safe mode.

Safe mode is three different things. You can choose which flavor of Save mode you want to use from the F8 start-up menu:

✦ **Safe Mode:** The standard version of Safe mode. Only the basic processes and services necessary to start Windows are loaded. Some hardware (external drives, audio, power management, and networking) don't work in Safe mode, and the functionality of Windows is limited.

✦ **Safe Mode with Networking:** The same mode as Standard mode, but with networking abilities enabled. Use this mode if you need to access the Internet for any reason.

✦ **Safe Mode with Command Prompt:** The most limited mode, reserved for people who know how to use the command prompt. This mode is the one to use when the video adapter is acting weird, though you need to know how to use the command prompt to be effective at troubleshooting.

Later sections in this chapter divulge the details of how to get into Safe mode and how to use it to resolve issues.

✦ Other messages may appear as you start your computer in Safe mode. For example, you may see a notice that the network is unavailable or network drives were unable to connect.

✦ MSCONFIG is the name I use for the System Configuration Utility. See Chapter 2 for more information, though the utility is also covered in this chapter.

✦ You may notice a bonus administrator login account available in Windows XP when you start the computer in Safe mode. That's the hidden administrator account, and it's visible only when you start the computer in Safe mode. The password is the same as for the main user account.

✦ In Windows XP, you can click the No button when you see the opening dialog box to do a quick System Restore. That's a good tool to use when Safe mode is encountered unexpectedly. Often, System Restore fixes the problem. See the section "Entering Safe mode unexpectedly." Oh! Here it is:

Entering Safe mode unexpectedly

Safe mode isn't intended to be your computer's main operating mode. When your computer starts in Safe mode automatically or unexpectedly, it's a sign that something is wrong. Do not continue working. Instead, fix the problem.

Often, an error message appears when Safe mode starts out of the blue. Address the issue as described on the screen.

**Book II
Chapter 3**

**The Safe Mode
Chapter**

If you recently updated hardware or software, the appearance of Safe mode most likely indicates a problem. Use System Restore to recover from a software upgrade (see Chapter 8). Shut down the computer and remove the hardware if Safe mode suddenly appears after a hardware upgrade. Restart the computer and if it returns as normal, the software or hardware upgrade was the problem.

✦ Do not use applications in Safe mode! Sure, you can get work done, but don't! Something is wrong with your computer. Fix it.

✦ Don't reinstall any new hardware you've added to your PC, hardware that may have caused Safe mode to appear. Instead, contact the manufacturer for tech support.

✦ Also be sure to check whether MSCONFIG is ordering the computer to restart in Safe mode, as covered in the section "Restarting in Diagnostic mode with MSCONFIG," later in this chapter.

Getting into Safe mode at boot time

To ensure that the computer starts in Safe mode, you can use the F8 menu, which is covered in Book I, Chapter 2: Just after the computer first starts (or is reset), repeatedly jab the F8 key. Eventually, you see the F8 start-up menu in Text mode.

Choose a Safe mode command from the text menu; refer to the previous section for a definition of each command, though the top one, Safe mode, is probably the one you want.

✦ You have to be quick with the F8 key. When you wait too long, Windows starts normally.

✦ If a bootable disc is in the optical drive, wait until the message `Press any key to boot from the CD/DVD` disappears. Then immediately press the F8 key to see the text menu.

Restarting in Diagnostic mode with MSCONFIG

You can configure Windows to start in Diagnostic mode, which is similar to Safe mode. Diagnostic mode basically works like Safe mode, but you set it as a start-up option in Windows. Pay attention to these steps:

1. **Press Win+R to bring up a Run dialog box.**

2. **Type** msconfig **into the box and press the Enter key.**

3. **In Windows Vista, click the Continue button or type the administrator's password.**

4. **Ensure that the General tab is upfront in the System Configuration window.**

Figure 3-2 shows the System Configuration Utility, which I call MSCONFIG because everyone else calls it that.

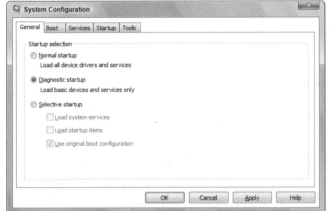

Figure 3-2:
The System
Config-
uration
Utility,
MSCONFIG.

5. **Choose Diagnostic Startup.**

6. **Click OK.**

   The System Configuration dialog box appears.

7. **Click the Restart button.**

   The computer shuts down and immediately restarts in Diagnostic mode.

If, in Step 7, you choose to exit without restarting, the computer starts in Diagnostic mode the next time you restart it or turn it back on again.

As in Safe mode, no extra drivers are loaded in Diagnostic mode. The screen you see is low resolution because the video drivers aren't loaded. What you have is, just as in Safe mode, a good troubleshooting platform. All the same tests and procedures for Safe mode work in Diagnostic mode. In fact, I call it Safe mode just to avoid typing the longer word *diagnostic*.

✦ I believe that you'll find the Diagnostic mode troubleshooting method described in this section more reliable than trying to desperately stab at the F8 key during boot time.

✦ In Windows 7 and Windows Vista, you can start the computer in Safe mode by using the MSCONFIG utility: Click the Boot tab and then click to place a check mark by the item Safe Boot. Instead of starting in Diagnostic mode, the computer truly starts in Safe mode when you select that option.

✦ Refer to Chapter 2 for more information on using MSCONFIG to disable start-up programs.

✦ When you make the change described in this section, the computer always starts in Safe mode. The only way to undo the operation is to select the Normal start-up option (refer to Figure 3-2). Directions are in the next section.

Ending Safe mode

When you're done using Safe mode to troubleshoot, you simply end your Windows session as you normally do: Choose the proper shutdown command from the Start button menu. The computer should restart normally.

When a hardware problem persists, you may find the computer once again starting in Safe mode. That means you have more work do to. Try something else. Use the suggestions in the later section, "Safe Mode Troubleshooting," to assist you.

Ending Diagnostic mode

Just as you used MSCONFIG to direct the computer to start in Diagnostic mode, you must use MSCONFIG to restart the computer normally again. Repeat the steps found in the earlier section, "Restarting in Diagnostic mode with MSCONFIG," though in Step 5 you choose Normal Startup. When the computer restarts, it once again returns to normal operation (well, as long as you resolved whichever issue urged you into Diagnostic mode in the first place).

Safe Mode Troubleshooting

Don't blame Windows! True, some things may be the operating system's fault. Bugs happen. Windows gets updated. But most of the time, the blame for any software woe in your PC can be laid squarely on the shoulders of device drivers. The way to best determine that situation is to use Safe mode. This section tells you how.

Understanding Safe mode

Safe mode tells you one thing best: whether the problem is with Windows. In Safe mode, only Windows itself is loaded: the basic parts of the operating system. Any other software — including device drivers, start-up processes, and other programs — aren't loaded in Safe mode. This leads to one immediate, solid conclusion:

When the computer runs fine in Safe mode, the problem you have is not caused by Windows.

I might add that when the computer performs flawlessly in Safe mode, the problem is also not caused by your computer hardware. No, the problem lies in some program being loaded after Windows itself starts.

Your job in Safe mode is to determine which piece of software is causing the problem and to either update that software or disable it to keep the computer running properly.

✦ When the problem persists in Safe mode, it's most likely a Windows issue. (See Chapter 8 on various ways to repair Windows.)

✦ In some circumstances, Windows doesn't cause a problem that continues in Safe mode. These problems are hardware related. The most common one is overheating. Check the power supply. Other hardware may also be screwing up. (Refer to Book I for various hardware troubleshooting methods and solutions.)

Knowing the three problem sisters

Odds are very good that the problem motivating your PC into using Safe mode was caused by one of three things:

✦ Video

✦ Power management

✦ Networking

These three areas are known as the problem sisters. The problem most likely lies with the software — the *device driver* — used to control the specific hardware. Especially if you recently upgraded the hardware or software in any of these three areas, problems can occur that thrust the PC into Safe mode.

The first thing to try is waiting. Just let the computer sit. Or, if possible, try to re-create the situation that caused the computer to crash. If the action can be repeated in Safe mode, the problem lies with Windows, not with the device.

The second thing to try depends on what happened recently. If you recently updated software, run System Restore to return the computer to a point *before* the update. Refer to Chapter 8 for more information on System Restore, though be aware that System Restore is an option available on the F8 boot menu (see Book I, Chapter 2).

Finally, check for new software. Use the Device Manager as covered in Book I, Chapter 7. If there's known trouble with the gizmo, its Properties dialog box in the Device Manager tells you so. If not, click the Update Driver button to find a new driver. Also consider contacting the hardware manufacturer to see whether an update is available. (You have to use Safe mode with Networking to access the Internet in Safe mode.)

Disabling start-up files

The most frustrating problems to solve are related to start-up files. You can use Diagnostic mode to help determine which start-up files are causing trouble. The way it works is described in Chapter 2: You systematically disable one start-up process after another by using the MSCONFIG utility.

If the problem persists after disabling a start-up process (or the problem gets worse), you disabled the wrong process. Reenable that process, and restart again in Diagnostic mode with the next process disabled.

Yes, it's tedious.

I used this method to determine that my PC's sound software was causing random crashes; the problem wasn't present in Safe mode and ceased to happen after I disabled the sound drivers.

See Chapter 2 for more information on disabling start-up files.

Chapter 4: Putting the Pep Back into Your PC

In This Chapter

✔ **Know why your PC is slow**

✔ **Fixing common problems**

✔ **Improving performance with ReadyBoost**

✔ **Ensuring that proper settings are made**

✔ **Configuring services for optimal performance**

Your PC is no longer a puppy. It lacks that zip, that endless energy. Now, your PC acts more like an old, droopy dog. You don't take your PC for a walk — you take it for a drag. The pep and vigor are gone. Yes, it happens to both dogs and cats, as well as to people and PCs. In our culture, we seem to admire things that are snappy, upbeat, and full of life. When your computer starts to lack those qualities, turn to this chapter for reinvigorating.

Man, Your PC Is Slow!

Do computers run more slowly over time? The answer is no. Performance can suffer, but electronically, a computer out of the box runs just as fast as the same computer years later. What changes, however, is the computer's *experience.* As Indiana Jones once said, "It's not the years, honey — it's the mileage." This section shows you some tricks to help roll back your PC's odometer.

Understanding slow

Slow is relative, which doesn't explain why Cousin Alfie is still at Community College. No, slow is a measurement of time, and time relies heavily upon human perception.

A modern computer runs many processes and services. Those things take time. Today's software uses a lot of the hardware's capability. That consumes time. You add more software to your computer. That takes even more time. Unless you buy the most expensive and powerful computer available — and buy a new computer every six months — things take longer over time.

Although a slow computer can be acceptable, what should be alarming is the onset of *suddenly slow*. I call it this-stupid-thing-wasn't-this-slow-last-week syndrome. It's a situation that needs to be addressed because it spotlights a problem you can fix.

✦ Sadly, when your computer is more than 5 years old and you know it's getting slow, that's just time catching up with it. People e-mail me and complain that their 10-year-old Windows 98 computers are impossibly slow. There's nothing you can do about it, other than buy a new computer. Old computers are slow.

✦ See Chapter 2 for more information on processes and services.

✦ Newer technology is faster than the old stuff; the design, the processor's power, the speed of memory, and the bus — all of these combine to make a newer computer definitely faster than your current computer. But over time, that new computer decreases its performance as well.

✦ Windows XP was sold as the "current" version of Windows until late 2006, when Windows Vista slouched out of its cell. As such, any PC that shipped with Windows XP as its preinstalled operating system is getting long in the tooth. My advice is to back up your Windows XP computer frequently and plan now for its replacement.

Testing multiple tasks

It's been written that U.S. President James Garfield could simultaneously write something in Greek with his left hand and in Latin with his right hand. That's *multitasking,* and it's a rare feat for a human being. Most of us have trouble walking while chewing gum. But when it comes to your computer, multitasking is a snap.

Sure, the more programs running at the same time, the slower they run. But the speed decrease should *not* be noticeable, especially when you switch applications. If it is, your PC may not have enough memory installed. Try this simple test:

1. **Start up a few programs.**

Some programs are memory hogs, especially the larger applications, such as anything in Microsoft Office or Adobe Photoshop, or perhaps a video editing program, such as Windows Movie Maker. Start up some programs and don't close them. You want to have a host of programs running all at once (which Windows easily handles).

2. **Press Ctrl+Esc to switch to a running program.**

Like the Alt+Tab key combo, Ctrl+Esc methodically plods through each program window you have open. Keep pressing Ctrl+Esc to cycle through the clutch of programs you opened.

3. **Observe any delay in the program switching.**

   When you experience a delay or you can hear the hard drive crunch away, your PC doesn't have enough memory to properly multitask all those applications.

4. **Close the applications you opened for the test.**

What you're experiencing is the computer making up for a lack of RAM. Windows avoids the `Out of Memory` error message by swapping out chunks of memory to mass storage (the primary hard drive). That's the delay you experience when switching programs.

There's nothing wrong with chunks of memory being swapped to disk and back. It's a clever solution, and it even has a name you've probably heard: *virtual memory.* It's covered in the next section. Keep in mind that virtual memory is a software workaround for a hardware problem.

To truly resolve the issue, pack your PC with more memory. Refer to Book I, Chapter 8 for information on adding RAM to your computer. A more convenient solution, however, is to use ReadyBoost. See the section "Putting ReadyBoost to work," later in this chapter.

Book II
Chapter 4

Putting the Pep Back into Your PC

✦ Windows 7 requires 1GB of memory in its 32-bit version, but 2GB of memory for the 64-bit version.

✦ Windows Vista requires at least 1GB of memory.

✦ Windows XP requires at least 512MB of memory to function at a minimum level.

✦ Obviously, the more memory your PC has installed, the happier Windows is and the more efficient your computer runs. Oh, and you'll probably be happy, too.

✦ Beyond Windows, the applications you run also require memory. The amount that's needed is listed on the side of the software box. I advise you to use the recommended value as opposed to the minimum suggested value.

Checking virtual memory

Virtual memory is disk storage that's used to supplement the actual memory (RAM) in your PC. As described in the preceding section, when memory resources get low, chunks of memory are quickly written to disk. The memory that's written is then freed for other purposes. Windows manages virtual memory, so it's not something you have to fuss over.

Okay, so you want to fuss over it anyway. Follow these steps:

1. **Press Win+Break to quickly summon the System window or the System Properties dialog box.**

2. **In Windows 7 and Windows Vista, click the Advanced System Settings link.**

3. **In Windows Vista, click the Continue button or type the administrator's password to proceed.**

4. **Click the Advanced tab in the System Properties dialog box.**

5. **In the Performance area, click the Settings button.**

   The Performance Options dialog box appears.

6. **Click the Advanced tab in the Performance Options dialog box.**

   Information about virtual memory appears near the bottom of the dialog box. The *paging file* is the disk image of your computer's memory. Windows sets its size for optimal performance based on your computer's configuration.

   Honestly, you have nothing further to do, but because you really don't believe me, follow Step 7.

7. **Click the Change button.**

   The Virtual Memory dialog box appears, as shown in Figure 4-1. Again, Windows creates the settings shown in the dialog box; you don't need to change a thing.

8. **Quickly, before the urge to screw things up overwhelms you, click OK and close all open dialog boxes and window.**

   Do it now!

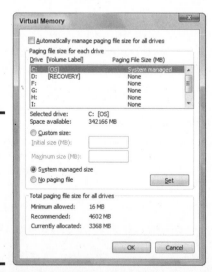

Figure 4-1:
You can resist the urge to change virtual memory settings here.

The virtual memory paging file is most likely set to be about 1 percent of your PC's hard drive size. So, if you have a 200GB hard drive, you probably have a 2GB paging file. That's fine; it's what Windows probably set for you. If the paging file setting is smaller, you might be able to improve performance by setting the paging file to be approximately 1 percent of the hard drive's size.

✦ Virtual memory was once an issue in older versions of Windows. People still think it's something they can mess with to improve performance. Although that was once true, it's no longer the case.

✦ You must remove the check mark by Automatically Manage Paging File Size for All Drives to set the paging file size in Windows 7 and Windows Vista.

✦ Having a larger paging file doesn't improve system performance. If you needed a larger paging file, Windows would allocate one for you. Trust me: The system works.

✦ Yes, if you configure the computer with No Paging File (refer to Figure 4-1), you may see those `Out of memory` error messages and experience extremely poor computer performance.

✦ Having a larger paging file doesn't make up for a PC with an insufficient amount of memory. To fix that problem, buy more memory!

Problems That Slow Down Your Computer

Your computer may be getting slow on purpose. It's not your fault. Instead, it's probably the fault of some software you have running — problem software that requires your attention. This section covers ways to deal with the slowdown-causing software.

Unclogging the spyware

The number-one reason your computer has slowed down over the past several weeks or days is most likely spyware. Hands down, that's the reason.

Without wasting your time, the solution is simple: Install antispyware software. For more details, refer to Book IV, Chapter 4.

✦ My preferred method of obtaining spyware solutions is to go to the software store and buy an antispyware package. That's because some of the solutions you download from the Internet may not be legitimate antispyware solutions.

✦ More information on antispyware software can be found in Book IV.

✦ Spyware is classified as *malware,* or *mali*cious soft*ware.* It isn't a virus, but it most likely arrived innocently from the Internet.

Finding a memory leak

Another way that bad software can slow down your computer is when that software leaks memory. Don't bother putting a pan below the PC — a memory leak has nothing to do with digital ooze seeping from the console.

Memory leaks happen when a program you run fails to release memory it has used. Normally, when you quit a program, it says to Windows, "I'm done with this memory." Windows then lets other software use that memory. It's kind of like returning a towel to the hamper at a resort swimming pool: A program with a memory leak just keeps taking the towels, and soon there are no towels left for anyone.

You can identify a memory leak by monitoring the computer's resources. When you see resources dwindling over time, it's the sign that a program is leaking memory like a towel-snatching tourist at a summer resort.

To monitor resources, you can use the Task Manager window. The graphs should generally remain steady, shown in Figure 4-2, especially the one labeled Physical Memory Usage History. When this line ramps up slowly over time and you haven't opened any new programs or done anything on the computer, you have a memory leak.

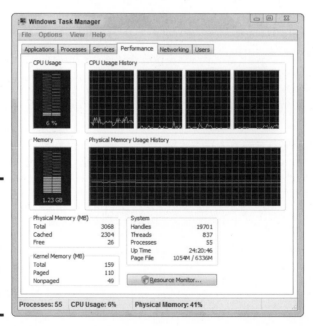

Figure 4-2: Monitoring resources by using the Task Manager in Windows Vista.

It's not your job to fix the memory leak; only the program developer can address the issue. For your part, you can narrow down which program is leaking memory all over the inside of the computer. As when you diagnose problem programs at start-up, you must use the process of elimination.

The first thing to do is to start the computer, open the proper memory usage monitor window (such as the one shown in Figure 4-2), and watch. Walk away from the computer. Let it sit. If the line doesn't rise over time, the memory leak exists in one of the programs you're running after the computer starts.

Next, you need to open — one by one — the programs you commonly use and keep the monitor window open. Watch the monitor over time as you use the program. More important, ensure that when you close the program, the memory usage goes down. The most obnoxious memory leaks are caused by programs that don't quite close completely.

Finally, don't run the culprit program again. Look for an update or alternative. If running the program is important, recognize that you most likely need to restart the computer after you run the program. Until the developer fixes the code, that's the best thing you can do.

✦ Windows XP lacks a Physical Memory Usage History graph in the Task Manager window. Instead, it has a Page Memory Usage History graphic, which may or may not indicate a memory leak.

✦ The best way to check for a memory leak is to use the performance monitoring tools covered in Chapter 7.

✦ Refer to Chapter 2 for information on diagnosing start-up program problems.

**Book II
Chapter 4**

**Putting the Pep
Back into Your PC**

Speed Up Your PC

The old joke goes that you can greatly increase your PC's speed by plugging it into a power source with a higher voltage. Although seeing images of a computer blowing up and spewing sparks amuses some people, plugging a PC into a higher-voltage socket doesn't do anything for the computer; either the PC power supply handles it or the power supply dies. Internally, nothing runs faster. Sorry.

You can, however, try a few things to get a PC up to speed. Refer to the sections earlier in this chapter for ways to solve slow-PC issues. After you get those strategies out of the way, refer to this section for other things you can do.

Performing regular maintenance

Your computer becomes sluggish over time, especially its hard drive. To help keep the hard drive spinning light and happy, don't forget regular maintenance — especially a disk defragmentation program.

Windows regularly schedules disk maintenance. It's automatic. Programs such as ScanDisk and Defrag run on a regular schedule. Even so, you might consider getting replacement programs for those utilities.

✦ Do not run Defrag on an SSD. An SSD doesn't need defragmenting, and running this utility decreases the lifespan of the drive.

✦ Refer to Book VI, Chapter 3 for information on scheduling tasks.

Putting ReadyBoost to work

Windows 7 and Windows Vista users can employ the ReadyBoost tool to improve system performance. ReadyBoost works by supplementing system memory and mass storage access with a portion of fast flash memory from a flash drive, such as a USB thumb drive. It's painless and simple, as these steps confirm:

1. **Plug the flash drive into a USB port on your PC.**

Yes, you must have a flash drive that plugs directly into a USB port. For that reason, you cannot use a media card reader with ReadyBoost, even when the media card reader is part of the PC console.

2. **In the AutoPlay dialog box, choose Speed Up My System.**

The flash drive's Properties dialog box appears, shown in Figure 4-3, with the ReadyBoost tab upfront.

Figure 4-3: ReadyBoost is ready to boost.

3. **Choose the Use This Device option.**

4. **Click OK.**

Your PC immediately starts using the flash drive to improve performance. Supposedly, the best performance increase is noticed in PCs with less than 1GB of RAM. Even so, whether you experience any speed improvements or not, scientists in white lab coats have promised me that ReadyBoost is working.

✦ ReadyBoost isn't available in Windows XP.

✦ The thumb drive must be removed properly when you're done with it. (See Book I, Chapter 4.)

✦ ReadyBoost can use only as much as 4GB of memory on a flash drive.

✦ The minimum size for a ReadyBoost-compatible flash drive is 256MB.

✦ The best flash drive size to use with ReadyBoost is a flash drive with the same amount of memory as your PC. For example, if your PC has 2GB of RAM, get a 2GB thumb drive.

✦ The option Dedicate This Device to ReadyBoost (refer to Figure 4-3) isn't available in Windows Vista. When you choose this option, the flash drive is automatically configured for use with ReadyBoost every time you add it to your Windows 7 computer.

✦ Windows technology allows for only one flash drive to be used for ReadyBoost at a time.

✦ Flash memory is designed with a limited number of read/write cycles. Eventually, flash memory wears out. Don't fret about wearing out a thumb drive with ReadyBoost, however: Microsoft estimates it would take about ten years of normal use for a typical thumb drive to be exhausted by ReadyBoost.

Setting the number of CPUs

Your PC most likely sports a processor that has multiple cores. Or, it may have more than a single processor. You should confirm that Windows is taking advantage of the extra processing power. Sadly, this trick isn't available for Windows XP.

Follow these steps to set the number of processors that Windows uses in your PC:

1. **Press Win+R to bid the Run dialog box.**

2. **Type** msconfig **and press Enter.**

3. **In Windows Vista, click the Continue button or type the administrator's password.**

4. **In the System Configuration window, click the Boot tab.**

5. **Click the Advanced Options button.**

The BOOT Advanced Options dialog box appears, as shown in Figure 4-4.

Figure 4-4:
Set the
number of
CPUs here.

6. **Place a check mark by Number of Processors.**

7. **Choose the highest number from the menu button.**

   The highest number is coincidentally the number of processor cores inside your PC.

8. **Click OK to close the BOOT Advanced Options dialog box.**

9. **Click OK to close the System Configuration window.**

10. **Click Restart Now because the changes don't take place until you restart the computer.**

    Or, you can choose Exit without Restart, in which case the changes take place the next time you restart the PC.

The performance boost in your PC from setting the proper number of processors may not be noticeable, at least not dramatically. But at least by following these steps, you ensure that Windows is using the PC's hardware better than it did before.

See Video 241 (the Windows 7 video or the Windows Vista video) to observe this section's steps in action.

www.dummies.com/go/troubleshootingandmaintainingyourpcaio2e

Using the Windows 7 Performance Troubleshooter

One way you can evaluate PC sluggishness in Windows 7 is to use the performance troubleshooter. Though this tool exists as an option for Windows 7 users, my experience with the troubleshooter has been less than stellar. Still, why not give it a try? Obey these steps:

1. **Open the Control Panel.**

2. **Beneath the System and Security heading, choose Find and Fix Problems.**

   The Troubleshooting window is displayed.

3. **Choose the link Check for Performance Issues.**

   The link is found beneath the System and Security heading at the bottom of the dialog box.

4. **Click the Next button in the Performance Wizard window.**

   What happens next depends on what the troubleshooter finds.

5. **If the troubleshooter recommends that you check programs to improve start-up performance, click the Next button.**

   Don't bother with the Start System Configuration button. Clicking it brings up the MSCONFIG utility to let you disable various start-up programs, a topic that's covered in Chapter 2 of this book.

6. **Click the Next button.**

   The wizard attempts to find other problems, which it probably fails at doing.

7. **If you feel that there's still something the wizard can do, click the Explore Additional Options button; otherwise, click the Close button.**

For more information on the Troubleshooting window, refer to Chapter 1.

Disabling unnecessary services

A *service* is something a program does in Windows — specifically, a program that starts automatically whenever the computer starts. Most services are things that Windows does, and most of those services are tasks that you don't need to have running in your computer.

Table 4-1 lists a bunch of services that you might be able disable to help improve your computer's performance.

Table 4-1		Services You Can Disable
Service Name	*Windows Version*	*Effect of Disabling*
Desktop Window Manager Session Manager	7, Vista	The desktop looks less pretty.

(continued)

Table 4-1 *(continued)*

Service Name	Windows Version	Effect of Disabling
Error Reporting Service	XP	Your computer no longer sends system error reports to Microsoft (which it doesn't do anyway, unless you click the Send Error Report button after an error occurs).
FAX	Vista	You can't send faxes, but if you don't send them in the first place, there's no point in wasting resources on this service.
Function Discovery Provider Host	7, Vista	Windows Media Center doesn't function properly.
Internet Connection Firewall (ICF)	XP	Your system runs faster.
Internet Connection Sharing (ICS)	All	You cannot share your computer's Internet access with another computer. If you don't know what I mean, disable this service.
Messenger	XP	None; this isn't the same as the Windows Messenger program.
Offline Files	Vista	You can't access the offline files if you're using offline files, and you probably aren't.
Parental Controls	Vista	Parental control features don't work, which is okay if your children don't use the computer, you have no children, or you don't act like a child.
Portable Media Serial Interface	XP	You cannot use a Windows Media Player–only MP3 player.
QoS RSVP	XP	A handful of programs no longer run or function properly.
Remote Access Connection Manager	Vista	You cannot use dialup virtual private networking (VPN).
Remote Desktop Help Session Manager	XP	NetMeeting users cannot access your PC.
Remote Procedure Call (RPC) Locator	7, Vista	None that I'm aware of.

Service Name	Windows Version	Effect of Disabling
Remote Registry	Vista, XP	You cannot modify your computer's Registry over a network.
Secondary Logon	XP	You cannot use a Limited account, but because most users are administrators in XP, it makes no difference.
Smart Card	Vista, XP	You cannot use a smart card to authenticate computer access. This service requires a smart card slot on your computer. (A smart card isn't a memory card.)
Smart Card Removal Policy	Vista	You cannot use a smart card for computer access.
Tablet PC Input Service	Vista	You cannot use a stylus to write on your Tablet PC.
TCP/IP NetBIOS Helper	All	None, unless you're certain that you're using legacy NetBIOS networking programs. (You probably aren't.)
Telephony	Vista	Your dialup networking may not work.
Terminal Services	Vista	Remote Desktop, Media Center, and other programs may not work.
Themes	All	You use Windows in a rather plain, old-fashioned view. Fancy desktop features are disabled (transparency and shadows, for example).
Uninterruptible Power Supply	XP	Your UPS cannot use Windows power management. It still works if you use the UPS's own software to control the power.
WebClient	Vista	The FrontPage web design program may not work.
Windows Firewall	7, Vista	Windows Firewall doesn't run, but if you're using other firewall software or hardware, that's okay.
WMI Performance Adapter	XP	Who knows? Honestly, no one knows what this service does.

To disable a service, follow these steps:

1. **Open the Control Panel.**

2a. **In Windows 7, choose System and Security and then choose Administrative Tools.**

2a. **In Windows Vista, choose Security and then choose Administrative Tools.**

2c. **In Windows XP, open the Administrative Tools icon.**

3. **Open the Services icon.**

4. **In Windows Vista, click the Continue button or type the administrator's password.**

5. **Locate a service to disable.**

Use Table 4-1 to help you decide which services to disable.

Click the Name column heading to ensure that the services are sorted alphabetically.

6. **Double-click the service to open its Properties dialog box.**

7. **Choose Disabled as the Startup type.**

By choosing Disabled, you prevent the process from starting when the computer starts.

Make a note of the service's original state: Automatic or Manual. Just in case you need to reenable the service, you should know how it was configured before you changed it.

8. **Click OK to confirm your choice and close the dialog box.**

When you're concerned about compatibility, or that your computer may work improperly after disabling a service, restart Windows. When the system starts up, try it out for a while to ensure that things are working well. Then continue or, if there's a problem, reenable the service to Automatic or Manual or whatever the previous setting was.

9. **Repeat Steps 4 through 7 as necessary.**

10. **Close the Services window when you're done.**

You can also, optionally, close the Control Panel window.

The services shown in Table 4-1 comprise only part of the entire list of services running in your computer. You may be able to safely disable other services that, specifically, would have no negative effect on your PC. It all depends on what you do with your computer.

Of course, the possibility always exists that disabling a service has no effect on the computer and causes no improvement in performance. That's the case with many services, which is why you don't see more of them listed in Table 4-1.

✦ Video 242 on the companion DVD shows you how to disable a service in Windows Vista, though it also applies to Windows 7:

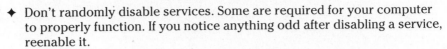
www.dummies.com/go/troubleshootingandmaintainingyourpcaio2e

✦ If disabling a service causes your PC to run more slowly or programs to function improperly, reenable the service.

✦ Don't randomly disable services. Some are required for your computer to properly function. If you notice anything odd after disabling a service, reenable it.

✦ See Chapter 2 for more information on services.

**Book II
Chapter 4**

Putting the Pep
Back into Your PC

Chapter 5: User Accounts

In This Chapter

✔ Using the user profile

✔ Managing user accounts

✔ Modifying the Windows XP logon

✔ Using parental controls in Windows 7

✔ Protecting your password

✔ Modifying the Windows Vista UAC

✔ Setting a new UAC warning sound

*O*nce upon a time, computers ran one program at a time, for one person at a time: One person, one program, one user. Today's computers not only run several programs at a time — they can also accommodate multiple users. That way, everyone in the family can use a single computer, keeping all their personal files, email messages, favorite web sites, and other information separate and sane. When things get weird — specifically, when things get weird on the computer — this is the chapter you turn to for help.

The User Account

Here's a computer joke for you:

> You: Knock-knock.

> Computer: Logon.

The computer wants to know who you are. Its reasons are many; first and foremost is security. Being able to confirm that you're the user you say you are means that your stuff in the computer is safe.

Second, the computer demands ownership. Whenever you log in to a computer, your account "owns" the programs it runs. Every program must belong to a user. To see how it works, look at the Task Manager window, as shown in Figure 5-1.

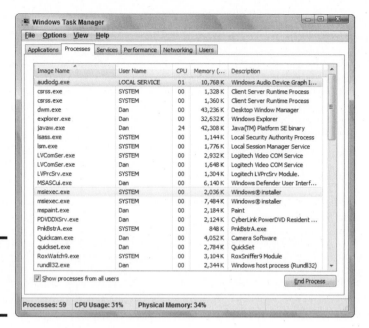

Figure 5-1:
Tasks from
multiple
users.

The user Name column in the Task Manager window, on the Processes tab, lists the user associated with a specific task. Three users are listed in this column, as shown in Figure 5-1:

Dan: That's me — my account on the computer. Processes belonging to Dan-the-user are programs that I've started or that started when I logged in to Windows. On your PC, you see your own user account name listed.

SYSTEM: The system account is Windows itself, programs that Windows has run or that require a higher priority and access than would otherwise be provided by my user account.

LOCAL SERVICE: This one is another system account for programs that Windows runs itself.

NETWORK SERVICE: It's similar to the LOCAL SERVICE user, but for use on the network.

Other users: Others who are logged in to your computer and running tasks appear in the list as well.

To see all the processes from other users and in Windows, you click the button Show Processes from All Users in the Task Manager dialog box. In Windows Vista, click the Continue button or type the administrator's password to continue.

The third reason for having your own user account is to keep your stuff separate from other stuff inside the computer. That way, your files, email messages, settings, and other items cannot be accessed or changed by anyone else who has a user account on the same computer. Not only that, but keeping all your stuff in one spot also makes it easier to back up your documents and settings and to transfer them to another computer for an update.

Having separate user accounts is a Good Thing.

- ✦ It's also important — nay, vital — to keep a password on your account. Only by having a password do you truly protect your personal files from being spied on by others.

- ✦ It still surprises me that two people (usually, a married couple) use the same computer yet do *not* keep separate accounts. Especially with email, you should set up a separate account. No, not so that you can cheat on your spouse; it's just to keep your stuff and the other person's stuff separate. It's a sane thing to do.

- ✦ The computer industry and the illegal drug trade are the only two industries that prominently refer to their consumers as *users*.

Understanding the user profile

Along with your account comes your *user profile*. That's the official name of the folder in which your files and account settings are held in Windows. The name comes from an internal variable used by Windows to help locate your files and settings whenever you're logged in to the computer.

The user profile folder is given the same name as your user account name. So, if you log in as *Frank,* your user profile folder is named `Frank`.

In Windows 7 and Windows Vista, the user profile folder is stored on the main hard drive (drive `C`, usually), in the `Users` folder.

In Windows XP, the user profile folder is stored on the main hard drive, in the `Documents and Settings` folder.

Other necessary folders branch off beneath your user profile folder. Some folders are visible, which is where you keep your stuff. Other folders are hidden, which is where Windows keeps settings and other information.

- ✦ The user profile folder is created when you first configure your account in Windows.

- ✦ A user profile exists for every user account on the computer. A general-purpose user profile is also available, which Windows uses to configure all accounts.

✦ In Windows 7 and Windows Vista, a public user profile is available for sharing documents between users on the same computer. This folder can also be shared over a network (see Book V, Chapter 3).

Configuring your account

You can modify your user profile from the User Accounts window, as shown in Figure 5-2. The User Accounts window looks similar in Windows 7 and Windows Vista. To display the window, follow these steps:

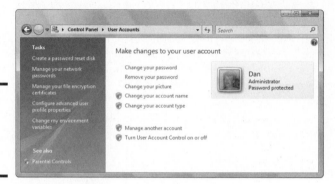

Figure 5-2:
The Vista User Accounts window.

1. **Open the Control Panel.**

2a. **In Windows 7, choose the heading User Accounts and Family Safety and then choose User Accounts.**

2b. **In Windows Vista, choose the heading User Accounts and then choose User Accounts.**

2c. **In Windows XP, open the User Accounts icon.**

In Windows 7 and Windows Vista, the User Accounts window lets you manage your own account, as shown in Figure 5-2.

In Windows XP, the User Accounts window provides an overview of tasks for all user accounts on the computer. To get to your account, choose its icon at the bottom of the window.

✦ The quick way to see information about your account in Windows 7 and Windows Vista is to click the account picture at the top of the Start menu.

✦ Most user account stuff involves basic Windows operation, which isn't covered in this book.

Changing to an administrator-level account

If you tire of typing the administrator's password, you can reset your account level to a higher one. Technically, you're resetting the account level from Standard or Limited to Administrator.

Here's how to set your account to Administrator level in Windows 7 and Windows Vista:

1. **Display the User Accounts window.**

Follow the steps listed in the preceding section.

2. **Choose Change Your Account Type.**

3. **Type the administrator's password (for the last time) to continue.**

4. **Choose Administrator.**

5. **Click Change Account Type.**

6. **Close the User Accounts window when you're done.**

In Windows XP, follow these steps for the Administrator account upgrade:

1. **Open the Control Panel's User Accounts icon.**

2. **Click your account's icon, found at the bottom of the window.**

The window changes to display detailed information about your account.

3. **Choose Change My Account Type.**

4. **Choose Computer Administrator.**

5. **Click Change Account Type.**

6. **Close the User Accounts window.**

Yes, I know: Microsoft recommends that you run the computer as a Standard or Limited user. That's a joke, especially when you're the only one using the computer. In Windows Vista specifically, using a Limited account adds a level of complexity that is utterly unnecessary for a typical user.

On the other hand, when other people use your computer, such as family members and, specifically, children or teenagers with their own accounts, set their accounts to Standard or Limited. The level of security offered by making their accounts non-administrator-level may be enough to protect your PC from being accidentally infected with malware and helps prevents others from unintentionally changing basic computer settings.

✦ You cannot downgrade your account from Administrator. To do that, you have to create a new Standard or Limited account, copy over your files, and then delete your original Administrator account. I don't recommend doing that.

✦ The whole idea behind account levels is to limit access to key computer functions to only authorized users. The history of DOS and then Windows demonstrates that Microsoft doesn't understand how necessary the function is. Rather than have a key, *superuser* account, as with the root account in Unix, you have Standard/Limited and Administrator accounts in Windows. These account types do relatively little to protect the system, though Microsoft continues to move in the right direction.

Deleting a user account

Unused user accounts take up space on the hard drive, but you can easily remove them. For Windows 7 and Windows Vista, follow these steps:

1. **Open the User Accounts window.**

Refer to the steps in the section "Configuring your account," earlier in this chapter.

2. **In Windows 7 and Windows Vista, choose Manage Another Account.**

3. **In Windows Vista, type the administrator's password or click the Continue button.**

4. **Choose the account to remove.**

5. **In Windows 7 and Windows Vista, choose Delete the Account.**

6. **Click the Delete Files button.**

7. **Click the Delete Account button.**

8. **Close the User Accounts window.**

The account is gone.

Also, see Book VI, Chapter 2 for information on increasing disk storage space.

Disabling the Guest account

For security reasons, I highly recommend that you disable the Guest account and guest access on your PC. Here's how:

1. **Open the User Accounts window in the Control Panel.**

See the section "Configuring your account," earlier in this chapter, for information on displaying the User Account window.

2. **In Windows 7 and Windows Vista, choose Manage Another Account.**

3. **In Windows Vista, type the administrator's password or click the Continue button if prompted.**

    If you see that the Guest account is already off, there's nothing else for you do to; go to Step 5.

4. **Choose the Guest account.**

5. **Click the link Turn Off the Guest Account.**

6. **Close the User Accounts window.**

The Guest account is normally turned off. Even so, I don't recommend that you turn it on to have Cousin Dave or Aunt Wilma use your computer while visiting you. Direct anyone wanting to use your computer to buy a laptop computer, and especially to get a copy of my book *Laptops For Dummies* (Wiley). Thank you.

Finding the secret Administrator account

Your computer has a secret Administrator account that's set up when Windows is first installed. The secret Administrator account is used only for troubleshooting. You see it available in Windows XP when you start the computer in Safe mode. Otherwise, the secret Administrator account appears whenever you use the Recovery Console or start the computer in Repair mode.

See Chapter 3 for details on Safe mode. See Chapter 8 for more information on repairing Windows.

Changing the Windows XP logon

Windows XP has two types of logon screens. The standard one uses the graphical images, which you click and then (optional) enter a password. A second, more technical prompt is available, as shown in Figure 5-3.

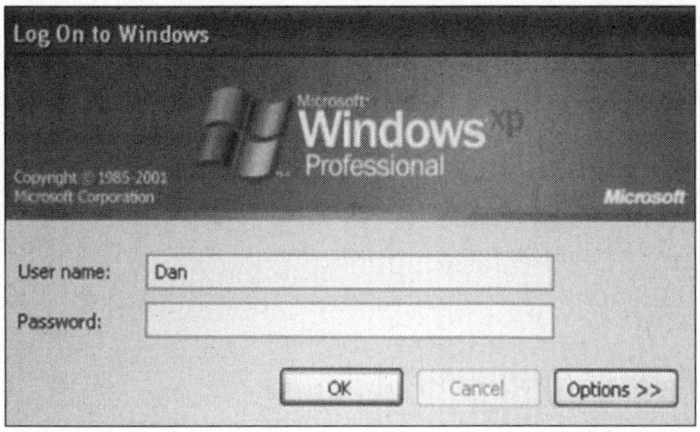

**Book II
Chapter 5**

User Accounts

Figure 5-3: The nerdy Windows XP logon.

Some say that the technical prompt is more secure. In a way, it's just as secure as putting a padlock on something wrapped in cellophane. Regardless, here's how to change the Windows XP login prompt:

1. **Open the User Accounts icon in the Control Panel.**

2. **Choose Change the Way Users Log On or Off.**

3. **Remove the check mark by the Use the Welcome Screen option.**

   When the check mark is removed, the nerdy Windows XP logon is used (refer to Figure 5-3).

4. **Click the Apply Options button.**

5. **Close the window.**

The changes take effect the next time you need to log in to Windows.

Avoiding the Windows XP Logon

It's possible to start Windows XP without ever seeing the logon screen or having to enter a password. I don't recommend using your computer that way. Passwords are important. Computer security is important. But, if you insist:

1. **Open the User Accounts icon in the Control Panel.**

2. **Choose your account.**

3. **Choose the link Remove My Password.**

4. **Type your account's password.**

5. **Click the Remove Password button.**

6. **Close the User Accounts window.**

The next time you restart the computer, Windows XP immediately displays the desktop.

✦ This trick works only when yours is the only account on the computer.

✦ I don't recommend removing your account password. Not using a password for a computer is a relic from the low-tech, low-security type of computing of the past. If you plan to buy a new computer, you *will* use a password and you *will* log in.

Windows 7 Parental Controls

Another good reason to have multiple accounts on your PC is that you can control how your kids use the computer. By using the parental controls on user accounts in Windows 7, you can ensure that your kids safely and properly use their computer time.

The parental controls covered in this section are available only in Windows 7. You can limit and control your child's computer time and access in additional ways, using third-party software such as Net Nanny and Cybersitter, for example.

Activating parental controls in Windows 7

The key to using parental controls is to properly configure multiple accounts on your PC. Specifically, your account must be at the administrator level, or you must have access to an administrator-level account. For Junior, you set up a standard user account. Only standard user accounts can have parental controls applied.

To extend your parental fingers into the PC, and better regulate Junior's computer use, you must activate the parental controls in Windows. Here's how it's done:

Book II
Chapter 5

User Accounts

1. **Open the Control Panel.**

2. **Choose Set Up Parental Controls for Any User beneath the heading User Accounts and Family Safety.**

   The Parental Controls window appears, listing all accounts on the computer.

3. **Choose the account to control; click its icon.**

   The account must be a Limited account. If your kid doesn't have a Limited account, change the account type to Limited using the Manage Another Account link in the main User Accounts window.

4. **Close the Windows Live Family Safety Filter window if it appears.**

   Windows Live offers additional protection for your computer, but that service isn't covered in this book.

5. **In the User Controls window, choose On, Enforce Current Settings.**

   After the settings are enforced, you can apply the parental controls to the account you're modifying.

The next several sections cover all the individual controls you can apply to the account.

You need to repeat the steps in this section for each kid's account on your PC.

Setting time limits

You can control when your kids can access the computer by placing time limits on their accounts. That way, they can log in and use the computer only during the hours you specify — and the computer logs them off when their time runs out.

To set time limits, summon the User Control link for your child's account by following the steps in the preceding section. Choose Time Limits to see the Time Restrictions window, as shown in Figure 5-4. Drag the mouse over the time slots when you don't want Junior to access the computer. Click OK.

Time blocked

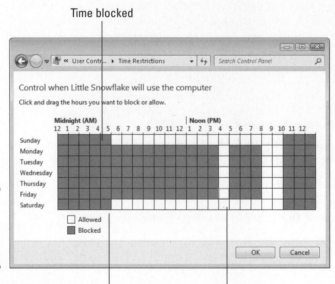

Figure 5-4:
Setting an
account's
access time.

Drag mouse over hour slots to select.   Time allowed

Controlling game access

The Windows 7 parental control features can work with the Entertainment Software Rating Board (ESRB) game rating system to control which computer games Junior plays on the family computer. You can restrict access to games by the game name, its rating, or the contents of the game (violence or adult theme, for example).

To restrict access to certain games, follow Steps 1 through 5 in the section "Activating parental controls in Windows 7," earlier in this chapter, to bring up the User Controls window. Choose the Games link to view the Game Controls window.

Choose the Yes option in the Game Controls window to restrict game access.

Block games by their ESRB ratings by clicking the Set Game Ratings link. Additionally, you can choose to block specific games by clicking the Block or Allow Specific Games link.

Click OK to lock in your choices.

✦ The ESRB defines and sets ratings for computer games similarly to the way the Motion Picture Association of America (MPAA) rates movies.

✦ Visit the ESRB web site at www.esrb.org for more information on the ratings system.

Blocking programs

You also limit Junior's ability to access any program that runs on your computer, such as a personal finance program, a communications program such as Skype, or whatever else you choose or that they could potentially abuse. Heed these steps:

1. **Open the User Controls window.**

Refer to the earlier section, "Activating parental controls in Windows 7," for information on displaying the User Controls window.

2. **Choose Allow and Block Specific Programs.**

The Applications Restrictions window appears.

3. **Choose the option *User* Can Only Use the Programs I Allow.**

It takes a while, but eventually a list appears, showing all programs found on your computer.

4. **Place a check mark by the programs you want your child to run.**

5. **Click the OK button.**

Some program names in the list may be unfamiliar to you; a program's filename often doesn't match up with the name you commonly call the program, such as winword, which is the real name of the Microsoft Word application. My advice is not to place a check mark by any program name you don't recognize.

Ode to the Password

Oh, I could rant on and on about how passwords are important and all that jazz. If you appreciate the value of a password, you do. If you don't, if you're one of the millions who casually use the password password or one that's equally silly, skip this section at your own peril.

Creating a strong password

Embrace the password! Don't try to avoid it. Instead, concentrate on creating and using a slew of good, strong passwords. Here are the three requirements your password must meet to make it nice and strong:

✦ The password has to be at least eight characters long, and preferably longer.

✦ The password must contain a combination of both letters and numbers.

✦ The password must contain at least one uppercase letter and one lower-case letter.

Additionally, you should use a separate password for each account you have: Windows, Internet, e-mail, web pages, and so on. Using the same password for everything means that if you slip up, or you have to release that password, you need to change *all* your accounts.

It's recommended that you change passwords at least once every three months. Although I don't change all my passwords every three months, I do change my online banking and financial passwords often.

To assist you in creating a strong password, this web site, provided by Microsoft, helps you check whether any given password is strong:

`www.microsoft.com/protect/yourself/password/checker.mspx`

I recommend creating your password by using two common words separated by numbers, or perhaps two common numbers separated by a word. Capitalize one of the letters, and you should be set with a good, strong password.

✦ Some passwords can contain characters other than letters and numbers. For example, the Windows logon password can contain just about any symbol you can type on the keyboard.

✦ I recommend writing down your password. Nope, not in a computer file. Instead, write down the password somewhere near your computer — in this book, for example. A better location is in a place with another type of writing, such as a recipe folder or an address book. A password innocuously stuck in the middle of your favorite recipe is obvious to you but not to anyone else.

Changing your account password

To change your account password in Windows, adhere to these steps:

1. **Open the Control Panel.**

2a. **In Windows 7, choose User Accounts and Family Safety and then User Accounts again.**

2b. **In Windows Vista, choose User Accounts and then User Accounts.**

2c. **In Windows XP, open the User Accounts icon and choose your account from the bottom of the window.**

3. **Choose Change Your Password.**

It's titled Change My Password in Windows XP.

4. **Type your current password.**

5. **Type the new password.**

6. **Type the new password again to confirm that you can, indeed, type the same thing twice.**

7. **Enter a password hint.**

You can't securely make the hint the same as the password or place the password into the hint text.

8. **Click the Change Password button.**

9. **Close the User Accounts window.**

REMEMBER

You probably use passwords all over the place in your computer and on the Internet. The methods for changing these passwords vary. For programs on your computer, such as your email program, use the program's Options or Setup window to configure the email account password.

Recovering your password

Honestly, forget it: If you lose your password, you're screwed. Write down the password if you tend to forget it. Refer to the section "Creating a strong password," earlier in this chapter. A password is something you should never lose.

Windows 7 and Windows Vista offer a tool where you can create a Password Reset disk, though it's a thumb drive. Although the tool doesn't recover your password, it lets you reset it, which lets you back into your account. Here's the lowdown for creating the Password Reset disk:

1. **Plug the USB thumb drive into your PC console.**

It can be any USB drive, or even a media card. Attach it now. Do it! Don't delay!

2. **If an AutoPlay dialog box appears, dismiss it.**

3. **Pop up the Start menu and click your account picture icon in the upper-right part of the menu.**

The User Accounts window appears.

Book II
Chapter 5

User Accounts

4. **Choose Create a Password Reset Disk.**

    It's one of the tasks listed on the left side of the window. If you don't see it, you're using Windows XP and you haven't read this entire section — now, have you?

5. **Click the Next button to proceed through the wizard.**

6. **Choose the storage device for the gizmo you inserted in Step 1.**

7. **Click the Next button.**

8. **Type your current password.**

9. **Click Next.**

10. **Click Next.**

11. **Click Finish.**

12. **You can safely remove the gizmo you inserted back in Step 1 if need be.**

    See Book I, Chapter 4 for instructions for removing a mass storage device.

See Video 251, where I walk you through creating a Password Reset disk:

www.dummies.com/go/troubleshootingandmaintainingyourpcaio2e

Windows creates a teensy file on the USB device. The file is named `user-key.psw`. It helps you only when you need to use the Password Reset disk, as you would when following these steps:

1. **Try logging in to Windows.**

    The logon prompt is where you use the Password Reset disk.

2. **Choose the link Reset Password.**

3. **Ensure that the Password Reset disk is attached to the computer.**

4. **Click the Next button.**

5. **Choose the drive containing the media used for the Password Reset disk.**

6. **Type a new password.**

7. **Type the new password again.**

8. **Click Next.**

9. **Click Finish.**

10. **Log in to Windows.**

11. **Don't forget the new password.**

I strongly recommend creating a new Password Reset disk immediately, just in case.

✦ Biggest password tip of this chapter: Don't forget your password.

✦ The biggest problem with typing passwords occurs when you accidentally have the Caps Lock key on. Fortunately, Windows reminds you when Caps Lock is set.

✦ You must create a new Password Reset disk when you change your password in Windows. Just repeat the steps in this section; though, after Step 9, you may be required to confirm that you're overwriting the original password backup information.

✦ You can use the Password Reset disk for anything in addition to holding the password. For example, on my PC, I also use the Password Reset disk as my ReadyBoost drive. (See Chapter 4 for more information on ReadyBoost.)

✦ You might be able to recover information from your account by using the Windows Recovery Console, as covered in Chapter 8. You may not be able to recover all your files or restore the password, but it's one thing to try.

✦ Avoid using those password-cracking utilities found on the Internet. Sure, some of them work; Windows doesn't store passwords completely securely. But many password-recovery tools are Trojan horses that will damage your computer or, at minimum, recover a password and then share it with thousands of hackers across the globe. Caveats abundant.

✦ See Book IV, Chapter 4 for more information about computer Trojan horses.

**Book II
Chapter 5**

User Accounts

Protecting folders with a password

You have no way in Windows to password-protect a folder or an individual file. In fact, you have no way to do that in Unix, either. Some older computer operating systems had this feature, and I know darn well that many people want and request it, but it's not available.

The closest thing to password-protecting a file or folder is to compress the folder. In Windows XP, you can assign a password to a compressed folder (or Zip file archive). Windows 7 and Windows Vista lack password protection on compressed folders.

Third-party utilities might be able to apply password protection to your files, but I have nothing to recommend.

The User Account Control

The author would like you to read this paragraph: Cancel or Allow?

Ha-ha. That's a Windows Vista joke. This section, in fact, is about one of the biggest Windows jokes: the User Account Control, which I want to abbreviate as UAC because *User Account Control* takes too long to type.

Windows 7, too, features UACs, but they aren't as obnoxious as in Windows Vista. Still, the UAC is one feature that made Windows Vista tremendously unpopular.

The UAC is Windows Vista's attempt to ratchet up security. Anytime you click a link or button flagged with the Windows security logo (see the margin), you should expect a UAC to appear. When one appears unexpectedly, you choose Cancel or Deny because it might be a sign that something is trying to compromise your computer's security.

For an administrator, the UAC in Windows Vista looks like Figure 5-5. When you use a Standard account, however, the UAC looks like Figure 5-6.

Figure 5-5: The administrator's UAC.

Figure 5-6: A Standard user's UAC.

The UAC also comes in various flavors. Don't bother licking the screen — Table 5-1 lists the variety.

Table 5-1	UAC Levels
Level	*What It Means*
Red	A program has been blocked and cannot run. You may even see an option to run the program, but with a strict warning against doing so. This UAC, the most serious one, is colored red with a red alert shield.
Blue green	You're about to change a setting that affects all users on the system. Generally speaking, it's okay to proceed.
Orange exclamation point	A nontrusted application is attempting to control the computer. It's only Windows that assumes the application is "nontrusted." If you trust the program, it's okay to proceed.
Orange question mark	A program on the Internet wants to run a program or somehow access your computer. This warning is less serious than the one with the orange exclamation point. You may see this warning, for example, when you open a PDF on a web page or try to view a document by using Microsoft Word or Notepad.
Silver	Windows recognizes the program's publisher and is simply asking you to proceed. This less serious but still necessary UAC is basically the safe version of the warning with the orange exclamation point.

Try to avoid the temptation to blindly proceed through any UAC.

A UAC should be expected. It should somehow relate to something you're doing in Windows or on the Internet. When you don't expect a UAC is when you can safely cancel the operation.

Disabling the UAC

Here's something I don't recommend doing: Disable the UAC warnings. Yeah, yeah: They're annoying. You don't like them. But after you configure Windows to your liking, they shouldn't show up that often. In fact, as long as you remember that whenever you see the shield icon, you should also expect a UAC warning, they shouldn't surprise you.

Regardless, you're probably still reading for a reason. Here are the steps:

1. **Pop up the Start menu and click your account's picture in the upper-right corner.**

The User Accounts window opens.

2. **Choose Turn User Account Control On or Off.**

3. **Type the administrator's password or click the Continue button.**

    Whoa! You were expecting that, right?

4. **Remove the check mark by the option Use User Account Control (UAC) to Help Protect Your Computer.**

5. **Click OK.**

6. **Click the Restart Now button.**

    Your computer restarts.

When the computer starts up again, *things are different.* Passwords entered automatically for you no longer show up. You may see other things that are unusual. These are the consequences of disabling the UAC. If you like that, cool. If not, repeat these steps, but in Step 4, put the check mark back.

In Windows 7, you can throttle back the amount of nuisance the UAC gives off. Follow Steps 1 and 2 in the preceding set of steps to see the User Account Control Settings window. Use the slider in the window to set the degree of annoyance you want for the UAC warnings in Windows 7. Click OK when you're done.

Disabling UAC Secure Desktop mode

The UAC tends to dominate the desktop. It not only beeps — it also places the screen into Secure Desktop mode: The screen goes dark and, in fact, no other program can use the display until you dismiss the UAC. Here's how to disable this feature:

1. **Open the Control Panel.**

2. **Choose System and Security or System and Maintenance and then choose Administrative Tools.**

3. **Open the Local Security Policy icon.**

4. **In Windows Vista, click the Continue button or type the administrator's password to proceed.**

5. **On the left side of the window, choose the Local Policies folder.**

6. **Open the Security Options folder.**

    A list of settings is shown on the right side of the window.

7. **Double-click the setting titled User Account Control: Switch to Secure Desktop When Prompting for Elevation.**

8. **Choose Disabled.**

9. **Click OK.**

10. **Close the Local Security Policy window and the Administrative Tools window.**

Disabling Secure Desktop mode doesn't reduce the level of security for the UAC. In fact, it merely allows you to see the UAC without dimming the desktop. Other programs can still access the screen, such as a screen capture utility, but that's not considered a security exploit, at least not at the time this book goes to press.

Changing the UAC beep

The noise that a UAC makes is called the Windows User Account Control, and the file that makes the sound is named `Windows User Account Control.wav`. To change the sound, you modify the Windows Registry. It's technical. Proceed with caution:

1. **Locate or create a new sound file to use for the UAC beep.**

   For example, a file like `burp.wav` is ideal. Save this file in the Music folder for your account. (That's where I save my sound files.)

2. **Open the Control Panel.**

3. **Choose Hardware and Sound and then choose Change System Sounds, found beneath the Sound heading.**

   The Sound dialog box appears, with the Sounds tab forward.

4. **Select the Windows User Account Control item from the scrolling list.**

5. **Click the Browse button.**

6. **Use the Browse dialog box to locate the sound you created or saved in Step 1.**

   For example, browse to your account's Music folder.

7. **Select the sound you want to use to replace the UAC warning sound.**

8. **Click the Open button.**

   Back in the Sound dialog box, the sound you chose is now assigned as the UAC "beep."

9. **Click the Test button to confirm your sound selection.**

   The sound should play and satisfy your sense of appropriateness to the UAC.

10. **Click OK to dismiss the Sound dialog box, and close the Control Panel window.**

The new sound file replaces the old one. Now whenever a UAC warning appears, your special sound, not the traditional sound, plays.

✦ I recommend using WAV files for the replacement sound.

✦ You can find a copy of the `burp.wav` file on my web page. Go to

www.wambooli.com/help/troubleshooting

Chapter 6: Unexpected Application Situations

In This Chapter

- ✔ Installing software
- ✔ Solving installation problems
- ✔ Removing software
- ✔ Cleaning up bloatware
- ✔ Associating and reassociating file types
- ✔ Dealing with older software
- ✔ Fixing a program
- ✔ Changing a program's privileges

Your PC does not live by Windows alone. Yea, verily, neither do other programs that dwell within your computer's bosom. Like Windows, these programs can lead to insurmountable woe and gnashing of teeth. Fret not, gentle reader. I present this chapter, an epistle of gratifying gladness and tidings of good troubleshooting.

Installation Issues

I doubt that there's ever been a computer that didn't need extra software installed. Okay, some servers and dedicated computers are sold with all their programs fully installed. But for mere mortals such as you and me, installing software is part of the game. Turn to this section whenever the game runs afoul.

Adding new software

Shoving a new program into your computer is super cinchy — well, as long as the program was purchased at a store or somehow comes on an optical disc. In that case, shove the disc into the computer and wait. Eventually, the installation program pops up on the screen. Heed the directions. You're done.

✦ Read the directions that come with the software. Especially for adding software with new hardware, you must know whether to add the hardware before or after installing the software. It's important.

✦ Sometimes, installing new software requires you to restart Windows; sometimes, it doesn't.

✦ Software downloaded from the Internet is installed in the same way as software found on a disc. For details and help with downloaded software, see Book IV, Chapter 5.

✦ Inserting the optical disc doesn't automatically install the program — you need to manually motivate it. To find what to do, see the discussion about installing programs in Book I, Chapter 4.

Dealing with installation problems

When a program doesn't install properly, the first thing you need to know is this: *It's not your fault.*

When the error is a missing file, it's not your fault. When the disc cannot be read, it's not your fault. Keep in mind that you're not a software developer. It's not your job to track down missing files or repair defective discs.

So what do you do?

Before getting frustrated, try repeating the installation. Just start over. Reread the directions that come with the software. Confirm that you have everything you need. Then restart Windows and proceed as before, but perhaps this time pay real attention to the messages during installation.

Sometimes, you must uninstall the program before you reinstall it. Refer to the section "Uninstalling software," later in this chapter.

To finally and formally resolve the situation, follow the money. Who did you pay for the software? Contact the software store or software developer for assistance. They owe it to you. (Of course, visiting the developer's web site may provide you with an instant clue because you're probably not the only one experiencing the problem.)

Be sure to check the software box for updates and notices, usually found on one of those sheets of paper you're quick to throw away. I missed one of these sheets when I tried to install a program and got frustrated. When I phoned the developer, the message I heard while on hold reminded me to look through the software box for the sheet.

Resolving compatibility issues

Microsoft maintains a database of software that doesn't like Windows 7 or Windows Vista. When you attempt to install one of these programs, you receive a warning such as the one shown in Figure 6-1.

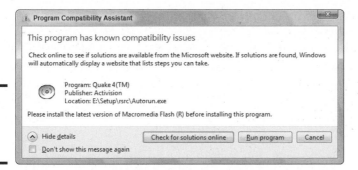

Figure 6-1:
This
program's
got issues.

If you click the Show Details button, you may see a potential solution. The details are shown in Figure 6-1, and they explain that an update for Macromedia Flash might be required before installing the program. Otherwise, you can click the button Check for Solutions Online to see what's up. Don't expect happy news, however.

My advice is to *not* install the program. Check with the publisher for an update.

Sometimes, the warning gives you happy news, such as a link to the developer's site, where you can download updates or a new version of the program.

Banish the Unwanted

Perhaps the primary reason most people remove software from their computers is to make room on the mass storage system. But even when storage space isn't a concern, you should feel free to evict any unwanted or seldom-used software on your computer. This section explains the details.

Uninstalling software

You don't just yank a program from the hard drive. That's bad. It's also nearly impossible. That's because software is installed *all over* the storage system. To remove software, you need to follow these specific directions for Windows 7 and Windows Vista:

1. **Open the Control Panel.**

2. **From beneath the Programs headings, choose Uninstall a Program.**

3. **Select the program you want to remove.**

4. **Click the Uninstall button on the toolbar.**

5. **Heed the directions on the screen.**

Follow these directions for Windows XP:

1. **Open the Add or Remove Programs icon in the Control Panel.**

2. **Select the program you want to remove.**

3. **Click the Change/Remove button that appears to the right of the selected item.**

4. **Heed the directions on the screen.**

Generally speaking, you want to remove the program — all of it. You can leave some of the data files. For example, for a game, you can leave your high score or character profiles, just in case you ever reinstall the game and don't want to earn your achievements all over again.

✦ Do not delete or remove installed applications manually.

✦ Refer to the section "Dealing with phantom removed programs," later in this chapter, for information on programs you remove that continue to be shown as installed.

✦ The Programs and Features window (in Windows 7 and Windows Vista) or the Add or Remove Programs window (in Windows XP) lists all software installed on your PC. Other programs you've installed might not show up there.

✦ Spyware and other types of malware don't appear in either the Programs and Features or Remove Programs window. See Book IV, Chapter 4 for information on removing spyware.

✦ A stubborn program may require manual deletion, but I don't recommend it. Generally speaking, only spyware is completely stubborn about being removed.

✦ If you haven't yet installed a program but you downloaded an EXE or a ZIPfile from the Internet, feel free to delete it. Also see Book IV, Chapter 5 for information on downloading software.

✦ Deleting a program's shortcut icon doesn't delete the program. Shortcut icons are found on the desktop, on the Start menu, on the Quick Launch bar, and elsewhere in Windows.

✦ Other software you installed in your computer includes Windows Updates. See Chapter 1 for information on removing recent updates.

Pruning Windows programs

Windows is technically an operating system. Despite that, it comes with lots of software, including utilities, simple applications such as Write and Paint, and games. Removing these programs is done differently between the various versions of Windows covered in this book.

In Windows 7 and Windows Vista, follow these steps:

1. **Open the Control Panel.**

2. **Choose Programs.**

3. **Choose the link below Programs and Features titled Turn Windows Features On or Off.**

4. **In Windows Vista, type the administrator's password or click the Continue button to proceed.**

   The Windows Features dialog box appears, as shown in Figure 6-2.

5. **Remove the check marks by any items to uninstall those Windows features.**

   Some items in the list have subitems, which you view by clicking their plus signs (+). When only a few of the subitems are chosen, the check boxes are filled in solid (refer to Figure 6-2).

6. **Click OK.**

   It takes a while, but eventually the items are uninstalled.

7. **Close the Programs window.**

Figure 6-2:
Removing
Windows
components.

System Restore and unexpected uninstallation

Sometimes, a System Restore operation has the unintended consequences of messing up a program you recently installed. The net effect is that a program may appear to be installed but is missing vital files that were "unhooked" by the System Restore operation.

Because you probably ran System Restore to recover from a disaster, I don't recommend undoing the System Restore. Instead, what you need to do is reinstall the program that's screwing up. Doing so reconnects the items that System Restore disconnected.

In Windows XP, obey these directions:

1. **Open the Add or Remove Programs icon in the Control Panel.**

2. **Click the icon on the left titled Add/Remove Windows Components.**

   The Windows Components Wizard window appears.

3. **To uninstall a component, remove the check mark by that component.**

   Keep an eye out for that Details button. When it's highlighted, click it and you can see various subitems. For example, choose the Accessories and Utilities item and then click the Details button. Choose Games and then click Details. Only at the lowest level can you remove individual programs (such as Minesweeper) and Windows components.

4. **Click the Next button to proceed with removing the component.**

5. **Click the Finish button when you're done.**

6. **Close the Control Panel window.**

Notice that some programs are missing from the list. Microsoft hides a few of its installed programs from you, preventing them from showing up on the list. Unless you want to get technical, in which case you can read the nearby sidebar, "Remove WordPad from Windows XP," I recommend not concerning yourself with items you're unable to remove from Windows.

+ You're warned whenever Windows cannot fully remove a component. There's nothing more you can do in that situation; Windows tries its best to remove the component, but portions may still remain.

+ Don't disable a Windows feature if you're unfamiliar with it. For example, you may think, ".NET? What's that? I don't need it!" But you do. Otherwise, you may find parts of Windows not working properly and end up having to reinstall the feature.

+ I don't recommend that you remove the Notepad text editor. All operating systems need a basic text editor.

Removing bloatware

In the early days of the PC, the computer came with its operating system preinstalled, but nothing else. Well, the BASIC programming language was available. It was provided so that you could write your own software. I'm glad those days are over.

Despite the fact that most people buy software and install it on their computers right away (or even have the software preinstalled), someone over in Marketing determined it was a crime that PCs didn't come with more software, especially demo versions and advertising. It was a crime that required immediate justice.

Remove WordPad from Windows XP

This information is technical! To unhide WordPad from the Windows XP Add/Remove Programs window, follow these steps carefully:

1. Start a command prompt window: Choose Start⇨All Programs⇨Accessories⇨ Command Prompt.

2. Type **cd \Windows\Inf** and press Enter.

3. Type **notepad sysoc.inf** and press Enter.

   The Notepad window opens with the SYSOC.INF document present.

4. Locate the line that begins with `MSWordPad=`.

5. Near the end of that line, delete the word `EDIT`. Keep the commas before and after it. On my computer, the line looks like this:

   ```
   MSWordPad=ocgen.
       dll,ocEntry,wordpad.inf,,7
   ```

6. Choose File⇨Save.

7. Close Notepad.

8. Type **exit** to close the Command Prompt window.

You now find WordPad listed in the Windows components you can remove (beneath Accessories and Utilities and then Accessories), as covered in the earlier section, "Pruning Windows programs."

Eventually, bonus software crept into the basic PC configuration. The programs accumulated into what is now known as bloatware. Basically, *bloatware* is any software preinstalled or available on your PC that you don't want. You're free to remove the software at any time, which generally frees up disk space and potentially speeds up your computer.

Removing bloatware is done just like uninstalling any PC software: Refer to the section "Uninstalling software," earlier in this chapter.

✦ Some bloatware arrives uninstalled. For example, online Internet services generally avail themselves by using Install icons in a special folder or on the Start menu. Just delete those icons if you don't plan to use any of the services or programs.

✦ Be careful! Some of the bonus software on your PC might seem to be bloatware but isn't. Software such as custom utilities or BIOS upgrade tools for your PC or laptop may be required. Other items, such as error reporting programs or manufacturer advertising, aren't needed.

✦ To help you determine which manufacturer bloatware you need or don't need, *disable* programs before you uninstall them. (Refer to Chapter 2 for information on disabling programs.)

✦ No, you don't have to live with the antivirus software preinstalled on your PC. You can remove it, but I recommend doing so only after any "free" or prepaid term has been completed.

Dealing with phantom removed programs

The situation isn't as common as it once was, but because of sloppy installation programs, some software refuses to leave the list of installed programs. Despite your efforts to remove it, and even if the program no longer exists on your PC, its name continues to show up in the list.

Before hurling the keyboard into the monitor, take one last stab at a technical way of solving the problem. Follow these steps *only* when a program has been removed but its name remains in the list of installed programs:

1. **Just in case, set a restore point by using System Restore and then back up the Registry.**

Refer to Chapter 8 for information on System Restore; see Chapter 9 for information on backing up the Registry.

2. **Follow the directions in the earlier section, "Uninstalling software," for bringing forth the window that lists installed programs on your PC.**

3. **Make a note of the name of the program that appears in the list and shouldn't appear in the list.**

4. **Press Win+R to bring forth the Run dialog box.**

5. **Type** regedit **into the box and click the OK button.**

The Registry Editor window appears.

6. **In Windows Vista, type the administrator's password or click the Continue button.**

7. **Press Ctrl+F to bring up the Find dialog box.**

8. **In the Find dialog box, type the exact text of the program's name — the program that says it's installed but isn't.**

9. **Click the Find Next button.**

The Registry is scoured for the matching text. Most likely, it's found in the HKEY_CLASSES_ROOT\Installer part of the Registry.

10. **Press the Tab key to select the folder containing the Product Name key.**

The folder is given a complex number as a name. This number is Microsoft's way of making the Registry user hostile.

11. **Press the Delete key to remove the item.**

12. **Click the Yes button to confirm the deletion.**

13. **Press the F3 key and repeat steps 10 through 12 to remove any additional entries if found.**

14. **When no more entries are found, you can close the Registry Editor window.**

See Chapter 9 for more information on the Registry Editor as well as the Windows Registry.

Cleaning up the crud

It's most disappointing after removing software to see a message along the lines of `Some elements of the program were not removed`. Ugh. Thanks for the letdown, Mr. Computer. Imagine trying to pull something like that on your mom when you were a kid: "Mom, I finished cleaning my room, but some parts of the floor remain unvacuumed."

Some programs don't uninstall all their pieces because other programs might use them. That's only polite. After all, when you're done eating, you don't remove the salt, pepper, butter, ketchup, and other items from the table when others might still be using them.

My advice: Don't sweat it. The program is gone and that's what you wanted.

Book II
Chapter 6

Unexpected
Application
Situations

The Good and Evil of File Association

File association is the operating system magic that makes an icon look the way it does. The icon takes on its appearance because the operating system believes that the icon *belongs* to a program. This scheme works well, for the most part. When it doesn't, turn to this section for desperate assistance.

Understanding file association

There's more to opening an icon than double-clicking the mouse.

Every icon is a file. A *file* is merely a chunk of information stored on disk. Boring. But the last part of the file's name, the *filename extension,* is used by Windows to identify the file. The filename extension clues Windows in to the file's type.

The *file type* tells Windows how to open the file, which program to use to display the file's contents, whether the file is a program, or whether the file doesn't belong to anything. The official term for all this nonsense is *file association.*

For example, the file named `My plans to kayak the storm drain.doc` has the filename extension `.doc`, which is short for *doc*ument. On your computer, `.doc` files are associated with a program, such as Microsoft Word. The association means that the file's icon looks like a Word document icon and that opening the file opens the file inside Microsoft Word. That's how file association works.

✦ Windows keeps track of dozens of filename extensions, noting which programs open those files.

✦ The filename extension is the final part of a filename. It begins with a period and is followed by one or more characters. Most extensions are three or four characters long.

✦ Files without extensions cannot be associated with any program. Likewise, not every extension is known to Windows. See the later section, "Creating an association for unassociated files."

✦ A file may appear to not have an extension, but it's there. See the later section, "Hiding or showing file extensions."

✦ File association can be overridden manually. So you can choose, on the fly, another program to open a file. Or, you can change the file association permanently, as discussed in this section.

✦ One major problem with filename association is that installing a new program may reassociate existing files on your computer. For example, programs opened by Paint may suddenly be opened by Photoshop Elements. To prevent this problem, most programs ask before they make the reassociation. If not, you can reassign files to associate with any program; see the section "Changing file association (the easy way)," later in this chapter.

✦ File association based on filename extensions isn't a good system. It's relatively easy to change a filename's extension, which changes the association without changing the file's contents. This can cause trouble, which is why you're warned in Windows whenever you attempt to rename or change a file's extension.

Hiding or showing file extensions

As it comes out of the box, Windows is loath to display filename extensions. Typically, only unassociated files reveal their extensions. Otherwise, when you peer into a folder window, you don't see the extensions for files that are associated with programs.

Because I'm more of a technical-minded person, I prefer to see all the filename extensions. To direct Windows to be more forthcoming about filename extensions, heed these steps:

1. **Open the Control Panel.**

2a. **In Windows 7 and Windows Vista, choose the Appearance and Personalization heading and then choose Folder Options.**

2b. **In Windows XP, open the Folder Options icon.**

3. **Click the View tab in the Folder Options dialog box.**

4. **Remove the check mark by the item Hide Extensions for Known File Types.**

5. **Click OK.**

6. **Close the Control Panel window.**

Filename extensions are now displayed in every folder window. That makes them easier to see but also adds another dimension to the filename: You now see the extension as you save and open files.

Don't change a file extension when you use the Save As dialog box to save something to the PC's storage system.

Reviewing associations

In Windows 7 and Windows Vista, you can easily review all known file associations on your PC. (Windows XP lacks this convenient feature.) Heed these directions:

1. **Open the Control Panel.**

2. **Choose Programs and then, beneath the Default Programs heading, choose Make a File Type Always Open in a Specific Program.**

   After a spell, a list appears in a window, as shown in Figure 6-3. The list is populated with all known filename extensions on your computer, along with descriptions and their associated programs.

   To change a filename extension, continue with these steps:

3. **Select the extension or file type description you want to change.**

   For example, .bmp represents a Windows Paint file.

4. **Click the Change Program button.**

   The notorious Open With window appears. It lists programs recommended for opening the file type — programs known to be compatible.

5. **Choose the proper program from the list.**

   I prefer that .bmp files open in Paint, not in the Windows Photo Viewer, Windows Photo Gallery, Picture Viewer, or whatever.

   If the program you want to use isn't listed, you can employ the Browse button to hunt it down. Be careful! You must be certain that the program you browse to can open files of the type you've selected. Don't make me wag my finger at you!

6. **Click OK.**

   The file type is reassociated.

7. **Close the Set Associations window when you're done.**

You can change associations in other ways, as covered in the next few sections.

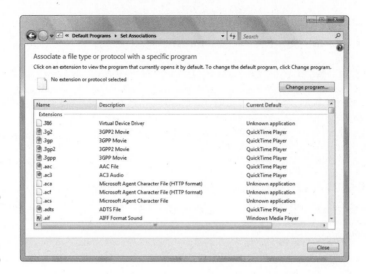

Figure 6-3:
Filename
associations.

Opening a file with a different program

When you want to open an icon by using a specific program, you need to take advantage of the Open With command. It's simple:

1. Right-click the icon you want to open.

2. From the shortcut menu, choose the Open With submenu.

Figure 6-4 illustrates the Open With submenu.

3. Choose the program to open the file.

The file opens in that program.

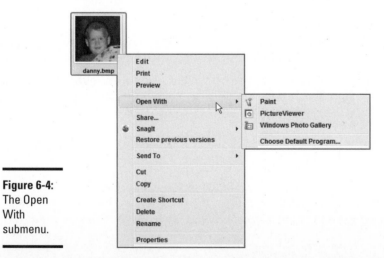

Figure 6-4:
The Open
With
submenu.

Associations at the command prompt

Windows maintains two lists to do the file association tango. The first list, the file association list, contains filename extensions and their related file types. The second list, the file type list, links file types to the programs that open those files. This system may seem like a lot of work, but it's not.

For example, consider that HTM and HTML are both filename extensions for web pages. Their file type is htmlfile. So you have

```
.htm=htmlfile
.html=htmlfile
```

The file type htmlfile is associated with the web browser, such as Internet Explorer:

```
htmlfile="C:\Program Files\
    Internet Explorer\iexplore.
    exe"
```

By associating both filename extensions with the htmlfile file type, you make it easy for the computer to reassign the file type to another web browser; only the htmlfile entry needs to be changed. Otherwise, Windows would

have to pluck out every file extension that might be opened by a web browser. So the dual lists save some time.

To review file associations at the command prompt, the assoc command is used. Typing assoc at the command prompt lists all file associations — the filename extension followed by the type. To see the type for a specific extension, type assoc followed by that extension. (The extension must start with a period.)

To see which programs are associated with a file type, use the ftype command. Typing ftype alone displays all file types and their programs. Following ftype with a file type shows which program opens that type.

You can also use assoc and ftype to create or reassign file types and associations, though it's a technical booger way beyond the scope of this book; you need to know about pathnames and the exact locations of programs, which is a bother. Instead, use the methods for file association that are described in the main text.

If the program you want to use isn't on the Open With submenu, choose the last command on the submenu — either Choose Default Program or Choose Program. You can then browse for a program to use for opening the file.

Remember to remove the check mark by the item Always Use the Selected Program to Open This Kind of File! If you fail to remove this item, the association is changed for all files of the same type — forever.

✦ You can also open any icon by using drag-and-drop. The only limitation is that you need to see both the icon you're opening and the icon for the program file. Just drag one icon onto the other and the file opens, using that program. (That's one reason I keep an icon for the Notepad text editor on the desktop, because many text files can be quickly opened and viewed by dragging and dropping them into Notepad.)

✦ You can use the Open or Preview button on the toolbar in Windows 7 and Windows Vista to choose a program for opening a file, or to change file associations.

Changing file association (the easy way)

To reassociate any file with a new program, follow these steps:

1. **Right-click the icon representing the file type you want to reassociate.**

2. **From the shortcut menu, choose the Open With submenu and then choose either Choose Default Program or Choose Program.**

An Open With dialog box appears.

3. **Choose the program to open the file.**

4. **Ensure that a check mark appears by the item Always Use the Selected Program to Open This Kind of File.**

5. **Click OK.**

All files of the type represented by the icon you clicked in Step 1 are now reassociated with the program you selected.

Dealing with unknown file types

Attempting to open an unassociated file causes Windows to get all flustered and maybe even wet itself. But instead of showing actual embarrassment, Windows displays a warning dialog box, shown in Figures 6-5 and 6-6 for Windows 7/Windows Vista and Windows XP, respectively.

Figure 6-5:
An unknown file type encountered in Windows 7/ Windows Vista.

Figure 6-6:
Windows XP
is bereft of
ideas about
a file type.

Book II
Chapter 6

**Unexpected
Application
Situations**

Here's what you do:

1. **Click Cancel.**

I'm serious. If the file isn't associated with anything, your computer cannot open it. If you received the file as an email attachment, reply to the message and request that the sender resend the attachment in a common file format. That's all you can do.

You can try to search the web for the file by choosing that option (if it's presented). This action might lead you to a web site where you can download, say, the Microsoft PowerPoint reader or perhaps a version of the Adobe Acrobat Reader. Mostly, searching the web doesn't work. Give up.

The option Select a Program from a List of Installed Programs (Windows 7 and Windows Vista) or Open With (Windows XP) displays the standard Open With type of dialog box, where you can attempt to make an association. I don't recommend it.

Creating an association for unassociated files

Some files don't belong to any program. They're plastered with a generic icon. These icons aren't intended to be opened by mere mortal computer users.

If you're desperate to try an association or you know that file has a weird name or no extension, you can give it a try. Here's what I do in Windows 7 and Windows Vista:

1. **Double-click the nettlesome icon.**

Yes, you may have tried this step. The annoying dialog box shown in Figure 6-5 shows up; ignore my advice from the preceding section.

2. **Choose Select a Program from a List of Installed Programs.**

3. **Click OK.**

4. **Pick a program from the list.**

No help from me here, though if you're just stabbing in the dark, the Notepad program is generally a good choice.

5. **Remove the check mark by Always Use the Selected Program to Open This Kind of File.**

   You don't want to make a permanent file association.

6. **Click OK.**

In Windows XP, I generally obey these steps:

1. **Double-click the vexatious icon.**

2. **Click the Open With button.**

3. **Choose Select the Program from a List.**

4. **Click OK.**

5. **Select a program.**

   I don't recommend that you pull a best guess here. My advice is to choose Notepad and cross your fingers.

6. **Ensure that no mark appears by the item Always Use the Selected Program to Open This Kind of File.**

7. **Click OK.**

If you're lucky, the file is a text file and you see its contents. If you're unlucky, the file is gibberish, containing random bits of text or just unrecognizable junk. That's okay; it was worth a try.

Close the Notepad window when you're done.

Yes, it might be worth your while to choose the option for checking the web, but don't count on any miracles happening.

What file extension is that?

As long as you've directed Windows to display filename extensions, there's hope for the unknown file type. Visit the web site `www.filext.com`. Type the extension and see what the database tells you.

For example, I just received a file with the extension ODT. A quick visit to `filext.com` confirmed that the ODT extension belongs to Open Office documents. Because I don't have Open Office installed on my PC, I'm unable to open the file. Even so, knowing what type of document it is helps me to either convert it (which I did not) or ask the person who sent me the file to send it in another format, such as RTF or plain text (which I did).

Common Problems and Solutions

After all my years in troubleshooting, I know that people have a clutch of common questions regarding applications. Without getting overly specific and prattling on for far too many pages, in this section I give you some solutions for common software problems that I've experienced over the years.

Running older software

Microsoft tries hard to keep the current version of Windows compatible with older versions. In fact, one reason that Windows Vista is so slow is that it takes great pains to ensure that older software still runs. Hopefully, that goes off without a hitch. If not, you can try a few tricks to get older software to run. The first one is to follow these steps:

1. **Right-click the program's icon.**

It can be the program itself or a shortcut icon. But if you choose a shortcut icon, the effect takes place only when you start the program by using that shortcut.

2. **Choose Properties from the pop-up menu.**

3. **Click the Compatibility tab.**

You see compatibility options, as shown in Figure 6-7.

4. **Place a check mark by the top item, Run This Program in Compatibility Mode For.**

5. **Choose a Windows version from the drop-down list.**

Book II
Chapter 6

Unexpected
Application
Situations

Figure 6-7:
Forcing a program to be compatible.

6. **Set other options.**

   For example, some older games may require that you set the monitor to 256 colors.

7. **Click OK.**

When you try running the program, Windows loads older, more compatible versions of itself to make a good try at being compatible. It may work, it may not. What matters more than what Windows does is how the software behaves; older Windows programs were notorious for being less than compatible, even with older versions of Windows!

Yes, at some point you should just give up. Some older software, especially DOS programs or applications for Windows 95, just aren't compatible with today's version of Windows.

Using the Windows 7 program compatibility troubleshooter

One of the many troubleshooters available in Windows 7 is designed specifically to look for issues with older programs. As with any software troubleshooter, sometimes it's brilliant and sometimes it's silly. Here's how to try it out:

1. **Open the Control Panel.**

2. **Choose Programs and then, beneath the Programs and Features heading, choose the link Run Programs Made for Previous Versions of Windows.**

   The Program Compatibility troubleshooter appears.

3. **Click the Next button.**

   A list of installed programs appears. Your job is to pluck from the list the program with which you're having issues.

4. **Choose a bothersome program from the list.**

   If the program isn't listed, choose the top item in the list: Not Listed. Use the Browse button on the next page to locate the program. The Browse dialog box isn't forgiving; to proceed, you need to know exactly where the file is located and its filename.

5. **Click the Next button.**

   You're next asked to either test or troubleshoot the program.

6. **Click the button Try Recommended Settings to test the program; if you already tried this option, choose Troubleshoot Program and skip to Step 12.**

   Compatibility options are applied.

7. **Click the Start The Program button to confirm that the fixes worked.**

8. **Close the program window.**

9. **Click the Next button.**

10. **Choose an option that describes the experience you had when running the program in Step 7.**

    Assuming that everything works just fine, you can continue:

11. **Choose the option No, Try Again Using Different Settings.**

12. **Place check marks by the options that describe your experiences with the program.**

13. **Click the Next button.**

14. **Continue to work your way through the wizard.**

The wizard continues to ask you questions about your experiences and problems with the program, which help customize how the program will be run, which options will be set, and which version of Windows the program works best under.

✦ Don't expect miracles. Some programs are just too old to run in Windows 7.

✦ See Chapter 1 for more information on the various troubleshooters in Windows 7.

Repairing a program

Some programs have built-in repair features. Just as you can repair Windows (covered in Chapter 8), you can often repair programs installed on your computer.

The first place to check is the Help menu. Often, a Diagnose or Repair command can be found lurking there.

A repair option may also be available in the Control Panel:

1. **Open the Control Panel.**

2a. **In Windows 7 and Windows Vista, beneath the Programs heading, choose Uninstall a Program.**

    Yes, the option is named Uninstall a Program.

2b. **In Windows XP, open the Add/Remove Programs icon.**

3. **Select a faulty program from the list.**

4. **Click the Change button on the toolbar or, if available, click the Repair button.**

5. **Heed the directions on the screen.**

When repairing a program doesn't work, your last resort is simply to reinstall it. The installation program may recognize that you're reinstalling and attempt a fix. It may even ask you to uninstall the program before it's reinstalled. That's okay: Reinstalling a program doesn't erase your files. It may just fix the problem.

Opening a Word document in an oddball format

In one Word *feature* (I won't call it a bug), the Open dialog box remembers the file format you chose the last time you opened a file. Most of the time, the Open dialog box's memory isn't an issue. That's because you open Word documents. But when you choose to open a file as plain text or in another format, you may experience a problem.

When you open a Word document and notice that the formatting is strange, or perhaps that Word tells you something is wrong with the document, immediately close the document. Summon the Open command again and note the File Type option at the bottom of the Open dialog box. Ensure that the file type matches the type of file you're opening. This usually fixes the problem.

For more information on troubleshooting Word, refer to my book *Word For Dummies* (Wiley), which contains an entire chapter on fixing Word and your documents.

Eliminating personalized menus

Some older versions of Microsoft Office had the *personalized menus* feature. Rather than use reliable, consistent menus, Office would hide seldom-used menu items. The result was a shorter menu, but one that was frustrating because some commands were missing.

I recommend that you disable the personalized menu feature in Microsoft Office versions 2000, 2002, and 2003. Here are the general steps:

1. **Choose Tools⇨Customize.**

2. **In the Customize dialog box, remove the check mark by the item Menus Show Recently Used Commands First.**

3. **Click the Close button.**

The menus should now display all the commands.

Getting rid of recently opened file lists

Even though the file may be gone, deleted, and dead with no possibility of recovery, its name still stubbornly appears in one of those recently opened files menus. For some reason, this problem annoys folks more than anything else!

The official name for the list of recent files is the *MRU list.* MRU stands for *m*ost *r*ecently *u*sed, and Windows has a lot of MRU lists.

The easiest way to purge the list is to set the number of entries to zero and then reset the number of entries to whatever it was before. For example, in Office 2007, the general steps to follow are these:

1. **From the Office Button menu, click the Options button.**

   It says *Word Options* in Word, *Excel Options* in Excel, and so on.

2. **Choose the Advanced item on the left side of the Options window.**

3. **Under the Display heading, set the number of recent documents to zero.**

4. **Click OK.**

5. **Repeat Steps 1 through 4 and set the number of recent documents back to 17, or whatever it was before you zeroed it out.**

6. **Click OK.**

Although this action effectively eliminates the list, it isn't picky. To be picky, you have to get technical and use the Registry Editor to find and eliminate specific filenames from the MRUs. Here are the steps to take:

1. **Make a note of the filename you want to purge from an MRU.**

2. **Press Win+R to summon the Run dialog box.**

3. **Type** regedit **and press Enter.**

4. **If prompted, click the Yes button, type the administrator's password, or click the Continue button.**

   The Registry Editor runs.

5. **Press Ctrl+F to summon the Find dialog box.**

6. **Type in the Find box the filename you want to purge, and press Enter.**

   The Registry is searched for that filename.

7. **When the filename is found, delete the entry from the Registry: Highlight the filename on the right side of the window and press the Delete key.**

8. **Close the Registry window.**

The change doesn't appear until you restart the application that listed the missing file.

If the text isn't found, it's probably listed in the Registry with its full path-name and not just the filename. To aid your search, you can look for MRU lists in the Registry locations shown in Table 6-1.

Table 6-1	Registry Places to Find MRU Lists
Application	*Registry Location*
Kodak Imaging	HKEY_CURRENT_USER\Software\Kodak\Imaging\Recent File List
Media Player	HKEY_CURRENT_USER\Software\Microsoft\MediaPlayer\Player\RcentFileList
Microsoft Office	HKEY_CURRENT_USER\Software\Microsoft\Office*version**application*\File MRU
	HKEY_CURRENT_USER\Software\Microsoft\Office*version**application*\Recent Files
Paint	HKEY_CURRENT_USER\Software\Microsoft\Widnows\CurrentVersion\Applets\Paint\Recent File List
Photoshop Elements	HKEY_CURRENT_USER\Software\Adobe\Photoshop Elements*version*\Common\settings\Elements MRU
Run dialog box	HKEY_CURRENT_USER\Software\Microsoft\Windows\CurrentVersion\Explorer\RunMRU
WordPad	HKEY_CURRENT_USER\Software\Microsoft\Windows\CurrentVersion\Applets\Wordpad\Recent File List

Also see Book IV, Chapter 1 for information on removing AutoComplete entries that may embarrass you when typing web page addresses.

The Registry Editor is also covered in Chapter 9.

Running a program with elevated permissions

Sometimes, you need to run a program as the administrator in Windows 7 or Windows Vista. Running a program as administrator means that the program has more access to the computer when it runs: It has *elevated privileges.* Yeah, that sounds weird, but it's often necessary to do in Windows to ensure that certain programs run properly.

To run a program with elevated privileges, follow these steps:

1. **Right-click the program or shortcut icon.**

2. **Choose the Run As Administrator command from the shortcut menu.**

You see a User Account Control (UAC) warning appear.

3. **Type the administrator's password or click the Yes or Continue button.**

The program then runs with elevated privileges.

To make the change permanent and have the program always run under elevated privileges, follow these steps:

1. **Right-click the program or shortcut icon.**

2. **Choose Properties from the shortcut menu.**

3. **Click the Compatibility tab in the program's Properties dialog box.**

4. **Put a check mark by the item Run This Program As an Administrator.**

5. **Click OK.**

Every time you run this program or open its shortcut icon, you're prompted with a UAC warning; type the administrator's password or click the Continue button to run the program.

A program flagged for elevated privileges appears with the Shield icon superimposed on its regular icon. The Shield icon is your reminder that you need to click the Allow button or type the administrator's password to use the program at the elevated level.

You don't need to slap every program with elevated privileges. I did this only two times — once to run an administrator command prompt, which is occasionally necessary for troubleshooting, and another to run an Internet communications program. The program needs to access the keyboard no matter which other program I'm running. To get that keyboard access, elevated privileges are required.

Chapter 7: Reporting for Duty

In This Chapter

✔ Culling information from Mr. PC

✔ Checking recent logs and events

✔ Finding specific events

✔ Diagnosing problems

✔ Using the Memory Diagnostic tool

There's no point in asking a child, or a politician on the witness stand, why they did something. The answer is either "I don't know" or "I don't remember." That's because children, as well as politicians, don't like to be held accountable. Your computer is neither a child nor a politician. As such, it dutifully keeps records of what it does, when it does it, and how it turned out. The computer is also brutally honest about reporting its activities. You can use that information to help troubleshoot and maintain your PC if you follow the advice and information presented in this chapter. Honestly!

The Joys of System Resources

Information is organized data. Without organization, data can be accurate, but not necessarily useful. For example, you might ask a doctor what's under your skin. The doctor might reply, "Meat." The answer would be accurate but useless information. This section helps you appreciate the difference between the meat in your computer and the specifics that make it work.

Understanding resources

Basically, *resources* are bits and pieces of computer hardware that help the computer do its thing. That thing, of course, is I/O, or input and output, which is basic computer-science stuff.

Resources include memory, mass storage, network access, processor power, and so on. When your program needs more memory or needs to access the Internet, it makes a request to the operating system. Windows then tries to fulfill the request and provide the software that the resources requested. If it doesn't, a severe hissy fit ensues, and you'll find using your computer difficult.

Although Windows tries to make the best of things, computer resources are finite. Your PC has only so much memory. The operating system does the best it can with what's available, but resources may run low. When that happens, the computer slows down — or stops. That's why monitoring resources is a necessary part of troubleshooting.

Getting system information

I remember, back in the bad old days of computers, that an installation program had the audacity to ask me whether my PC had a color monitor. It did, but I found the question offensive. After all, the installation program was running inside the computer — couldn't it just check for itself to see whether a color monitor was installed?

Of course, it could! The computer knows itself. Every time the PC starts, it takes inventory of its hardware. The operating system knows this information — not only when the computer starts but also as you add or remove components. You can see that information for yourself by using the System Information tool.

To start the System Information tool, from the Start menu choose All Programs⇨Accessories⇨System Tools⇨System Information. The System Information window opens, as shown in Figure 7-1. You see a quick summary of nerdy details about your computer, such as the type of processor installed, total memory, Windows version, and other technical tidbits.

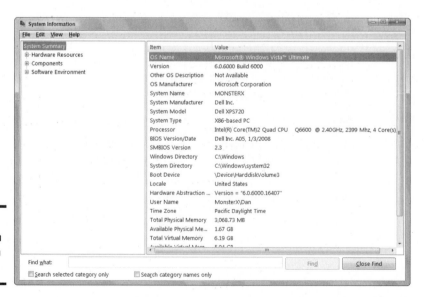

Figure 7-1:
The System
Information
tool.

To see specific information, choose a category from the left side of the window. The information is detailed and, by itself, useless. But when you need that specific information, you know where to find it.

The information shown by the System Information tool is static — it's just a report. For more dynamic information, you use one of the Windows resource monitors, covered in the next section.

✦ The final entry in the System Information window, beneath the heading Software Environment, is Windows Error Reporting. It's a quick way to review recent mishaps in your computer. Also refer to the "Reviewing events" section, later in this chapter, for information on the Event Viewer.

✦ You can also type a command at the command prompt to get system information. The command is `systeminfo`, though if you want to use it, I recommend that you type the following line:

```
systeminfo | more
```

Follow `systeminfo` with the pipe (|) character and then the word `more`. This command pumps the output through the `more` filter, which pages each screen of information. (Yes, this information is technical, which is why its icon is in the margin one paragraph back.)

Monitoring system resources

Although there's little you can do about system resources, you can monitor their consumption. The easiest way to do so is from the Task Manager window, on the Performance tab, as shown in Figure 7-2.

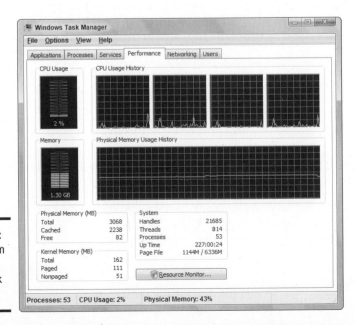

Figure 7-2:
The system resources in the Task Manager.

Summon the Task Manager by pressing Ctrl+Shift+Esc. Click the Performance tab to view some simple resource information.

In Figure 7-2, and on your computer's display, you see CPU and memory usage. (Windows XP displays page file usage, which is similar.) Information listed at the bottom of the window details other vital stats.

To see more detailed information, you can summon a resource monitor window. Follow these steps:

1. **Open the Control Panel.**

2a. **In Windows 7, choose System and Security and then choose Administrative Tools.**

2b. **In Windows Vista, choose System and Maintenance and then choose Administrative Tools.**

2c. **In Windows XP, open the Administrative Tools icon.**

After displaying the Administrative Tools window, your next step is to open the resource monitor window. This step is different in every version of Windows:

3a. **In Windows 7, open the Performance Monitor icon.**

3b. **In Windows Vista, open the Reliability and Performance Monitor icon; click the Continue button or type the administrator's password when prompted.**

3c. **In Windows XP, open the Performance icon.**

Windows XP has a rather limited display in its Performance window, as shown in Figure 7-3. To view a similar window in Windows 7, choose Performance Monitor, found beneath the Monitoring Tools folder on the left side of the window. In Windows Vista, choose Performance Monitor from the Reliability and Performance Monitor window.

You can add or remove items to the monitor by clicking the toolbar's Add button (the green Plus Sign icon). The new items appear as a new line on the chart, allowing you to review that resource. But that's about it for Windows XP; skip ahead to Step 7.

4a. **In Windows 7, choose Performance from the left side of the window and then click the Open Resource Monitor link, found in the center of the window.**

4b. **In Windows Vista, choose the item Reliability and Performance from the left side of the window.**

The window you see, Resource Monitor in Windows 7 or Resource Overview in Windows Vista, looks similar, though the Windows 7 version is shown in Figure 7-4. (The Windows Vista version lists the graphs horizontally.)

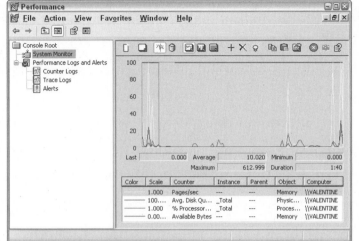

Figure 7-3:
The
Performance
window in
Windows XP.

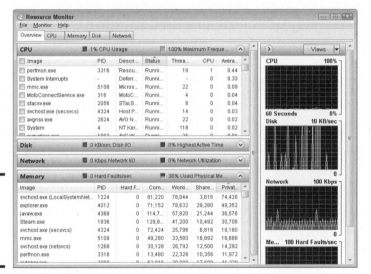

Figure 7-4:
The
Windows 7
resource
overview.

The performance window lists lots of graphical information about basic resources: CPU, disk, network, memory, and more. To see additional information for a specific resource, click the downward-pointing arrow button to reveal the details.

5. **In Windows 7, close the resource monitor window and any other open window.**

That's about all you can do to monitor the system in Windows 7. But Windows Vista has one additional window:

6. **In Windows Vista, from the left side of the Reliability and Performance Monitor window, choose Reliability Monitor.**

   Perhaps the most interesting item to check is the Reliability Monitor in Windows Vista, as shown in Figure 7-5. The monitor lists events that have occurred in the computer that may affect overall performance and reliability.

   Figure 7-5 shows a graph detailing the system's reliability. To see details about an event, click the icon. As the figure shows, you see details about what occurred. It's a helpful way to spot troublesome software that may require updating or disabling.

7. **Close all the windows you've opened when you're done.**

One key thing you can do with the resource information is to track down a memory leak (see Chapter 4).

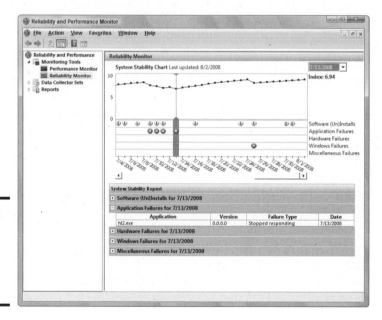

Figure 7-5:
The Windows Vista Reliability Monitor.

What Has Gone On Here?

Sophisticated operating systems keep track of all their details in *log files*. Just about anything that goes on in the computer — from a user logging in (get it?) to programs crashing to routine tasks being scheduled — is noted in a log somewhere. Because Windows has recently joined the ranks of sophisticated operating systems, it, too, keeps detailed logs. This section discusses where to find those logs, how to review them, and what to do with the information found in the logs.

Reviewing events

The first place to check for your PC's recent activities and happenings is the Event Viewer. Obey these steps:

1. **Open the Control Panel.**

2a. **In Windows 7, choose System and Security and then Administrative Tools.**

2b. **In Windows Vista, choose System and Maintenance and then Administrative Tools.**

2c. **In Windows XP, open the Administrative Tools icon.**

3. **Open the Event Viewer icon.**

4. **In Windows Vista, click the Continue button or type the administrator's password to get beyond the UAC warning.**

5. **In Windows 7 and Windows Vista, open the Windows Logs folder on the left side of the Event Viewer console window and choose the item Application.**

Finally, all versions of Windows display the same type of information, as shown in Figure 7-6. In Windows XP, only the list of events is shown; Windows 7 and Windows Vista show more detailed information.

Table 7-1 describes the event categories. Not every event is a nasty one; most are informational, which means that something happened and was noted in the log. All event types are listed in Table 7-2.

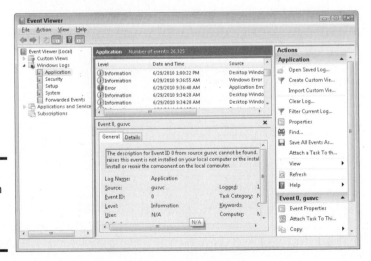

Figure 7-6:
Information
shown in
the Event
Viewer.

6. **Double-click an event to view its details.**

In Windows 7 and Windows Vista, you can either double-click or just click as the details are shown in the bottom center of the Event Viewer window.

7. **Close the Event Viewer window when you're done.**

Table 7-1		**Event Categories**	
Log	*Windows 7 / Vista*	*Windows XP*	*Type of Events That Are Monitored*
Application	Y	Y	Third-party programs; anything that's not Windows itself
Forwarded Events	Y	N	Events on network computers (with a subscription set up in order to see these types of events)
Internet Explorer	N	Y	Problems with Internet Explorer
Security	Y	Y	Logon/logoff events, file deletions, and events pertaining to resources
Setup	Y	Y	Events relating to application setup and configuration
System	Y	Y	Things that go on in Windows itself, such as start-up events and device driver failure

Table 7-2	**Event Types**
Type	*Description*
Error	Something bad happened, such as a service failed or data was lost.
Failure Audit	Something was attempted that didn't work, such as an illegal login or an attempt by a non-administrator to access administrator-level features.
Information	Something happened successfully.
Success Audit	Something was attempted and worked out, such as logging in to a remote PC; the opposite of a failure audit.
Warning	An event occurred that is worth noting but isn't specifically an error.

Yes, some of the details shown in the Event Viewer window are technical. Heck, some are downright boring. Later sections in this chapter describe how to filter events to better see only the ones that interest you.

Using the Event Viewer

Windows 7 and Windows Vista employ a more richly detailed event viewer that goes beyond the one available in Windows XP. Follow Steps 1 through 5 in the preceding section to conjure up the Event Viewer window.

The key difference between the Event Viewer in Windows 7/Windows Vista and the Windows XP version is the Overview and Summary portion, as shown in Figure 7-7. (It's the main screen.) For example, in the figure, you see that five errors occurred in the past 24 hours. You can easily expand the Error category by clicking the plus sign (+) before the Error heading to expand that section and quickly review the error events; double-click an event to see its fine details.

By double-clicking an error event, you create a custom view. Essentially, you make an event filter (covered in the next section) that shows information about the error or another event.

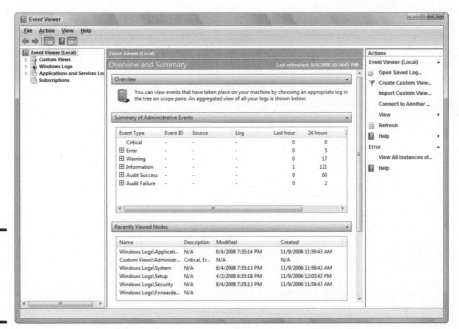

Figure 7-7:
The
Windows
Vista Event
Viewer.

Figure 7-8 shows the details of an error shown in Figure 7-7. As you can see by the message, it's an ACPI BIOS error message. (ACPI is the Advanced Configuration and Power Interface, or the computer's power management hardware.) The message explains that I would contact the system vendor for an update. (In this case, it would mean looking for an ACPI BIOS update from Dell Computer.)

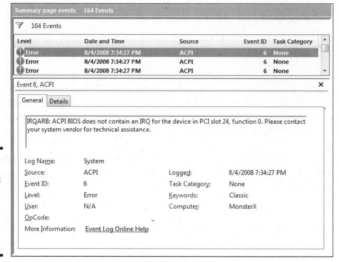

Figure 7-8: Error details in the Windows Vista Event Viewer.

Filtering and searching events

The true power of reviewing an event log is to be able to quickly filter out the information you need. Most log entries are rather mundane events. That's okay when you just want to confirm that something is happening that should happen. But the key to reviewing logs for troubleshooting is to look for pesky events. To help in your search, you need to employ a filter.

A *filter* is nothing more than a search through the logs. It's more like a data-base search-and-sort than a file search; you specify the event type, time, and other information. Then using the Power Of The Computer, you can quickly see relevant events.

To use the event filters in Windows 7 and Windows Vista, follow these steps:

1. **Bring up the Event Viewer window.**

   Directions are found earlier in this chapter, in the section "Reviewing events."

2. **From the list of actions on the right side of the window, choose Filter Current Log.**

   The Custom View Properties dialog box appears, as shown in Figure 7-9.

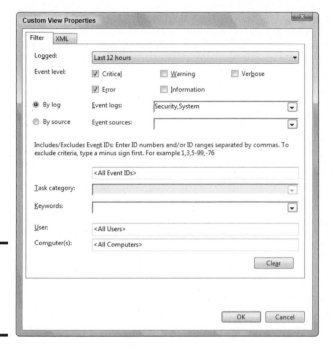

Figure 7-9:
Filtering
events in
Windows
Vista.

You can make the report permanent by choosing the Create Custom View link rather than Filter Current Log in this step. The rest of the steps in this section remain the same, but the filter you create is saved under the Custom Views folder on the left side of the window.

3. **Choose a time frame from the Logged button.**

4. **Select the event levels you want to view by selecting check boxes.**

5. **Choose By Log and then select specific logs from the drop-down list, or, if you have a device to monitor, choose By Source and then select the device or driver from the list.**

   The items By Log and By Source are dimmed when you select a sub-category in the Windows Logs folder. To enable both items, select the Windows Logs folder before you begin setting up the filter.

6. **Choose other items as necessary, though unless you know the details, there's little need to fill in the rest of the dialog box information.**

7. **Click OK.**

8. **Peruse the results.**

   Any logged events that match your filter are displayed.

In Windows XP, you can sift through the events in a specific category by following these steps:

1. **Summon the Event Viewer window.**

   See Steps 1 and 2 from the section "Reviewing events," earlier in this chapter.

2. **Right-click an event category.**

   For example, pick System.

3. **Choose Properties from the shortcut menu.**

4. **On the category's Properties menu, click the Filter tab.**

   The Filter part of the dialog box, shown in Figure 7-10, lets you sift through and sort the events.

Figure 7-10:
Filtering events in Windows XP.

5. **Choose the type of events you want to view.**

   Place a check mark by each event type you want to monitor.

6. **Select a source.**

   Choosing a source works best when you want to monitor a specific source or you suspect a certain piece of hardware or device driver to be causing trouble.

7. **Select a category.**

8. **The item's event ID, user, and computer can generally be left blank.**

9. **Use the From and To settings to narrow the time frame if necessary.**

10. **Click OK.**

    The results are displayed in the center portion of the Event Viewer window.

If no matching events show up, no events of the specified types have occurred. That might be good news because it means that no events relating to whatever concerned you have taken place. But if you want to be a stickler, consider broadening your search to find those events. Or, you can just forgo filtering and review the logs manually.

See Video 271 for a visual walkthrough of the steps outlined in this section.

www.dummies.com/go/troubleshootingandmaintainingyourpcaio2e

Finding logs

You find logs mostly in a forest, but that's not the subject here. Nope, when you talk about logs in a computer, you talk about *information*.

The Event Viewer is a tool that collects information from various logs and places it in a central place. The log files themselves exist elsewhere in Windows and are maintained and updated as your computer treads through its day.

Most vital logs have their information displayed by the Event Viewer. Many log files, however, dot the PC's hard drive. Most of them are found in the `Windows` folder. Some might inhabit the root directory of the boot drive (usually, drive `C`). Others are found all over the place.

Two files you might concern yourself with are the *boot log* files. These files are created when you specify boot logging as a start-up option. The files are named either `ntbtlog.txt` or `bootlog.txt`, depending on how old your PC is. These files, found in the `Windows` folder, list the success or failure of various pieces of Windows as it's loaded into memory from the PC's mass storage system.

You can enable or disable boot logging by using the MSCONFIG utility. Follow these steps in Windows 7 and Windows Vista:

1. **Press Win+R to summon the Run dialog box.**

2. **Type** msconfig **and press Enter.**

3. **In Windows Vista, type the administrator's password or click the Continue button.**

4. **Click the Boot tab.**

5. **Place a check mark by the item Boot Log.**

6. **Click OK.**

7. **Click the Restart button to restart now. Otherwise, click Exit without Restart.**

   The logging doesn't take effect until you restart Windows, and you have no reason to do so immediately unless you *really* want to see the boot log.

In Windows XP, you must enable boot logging by editing a text file, `boot.ini`, on disk. That's nerdy, and the file `boot.ini` may not exist on your computer. Instead, I recommend pressing the F8 key when Windows first starts (see Book I, Chapter 2) and choosing the item Enable Boot Logging.

The boot log is overwritten every time you start Windows. And, the log is produced only when you turn on the boot logging option.

What can you do with the boot log? You can check for the failed installation of certain pieces of Windows or device drivers. The drivers or files are obviously flagged in the log. Because you know the filename, you can then either disable it from loading or look for an update. (Also see Chapter 8, on repairing Windows.)

✦ See Book I, Chapter 2 for more information on PC start-up issues.

✦ Activating the boot log in Windows 7 or Windows Vista means that you configured your PC for a custom start-up. If that bothers you, disable the boot log after you cull whatever useful information you need from the boot log file; repeat the steps from this section, but in Step 5, remove the check mark.

✦ Traditionally, computer logs are all text files. They may have the filename extension `log`, or they may use `txt` instead.

✦ You can search for log files by using the Windows Search command, covered in Chapter 1. Simply look for files named `*log*` anywhere on the hard drive, including system, hidden, and nonindexed locations.

✦ Most log files are in plain text, but the text may be organized by using the XML, or Extensible Markup Language. *XML* is merely a way to organize information, and although XML files are readable as text, to get the most from the information, you should use an XML reader, such as the Event Viewer program.

✦ If you find the file `boot.ini` on your Windows XP computer, you can enable boot logging by modifying the file. Open it in Notepad and look for the line that contains this text:

```
Windows="Windows XP
```

(That's only a portion of the line; in the file, it's longer). Add the text `/bootlog` to the end of the line. Save the file. When you restart Windows, boot logging takes place automatically.

Diagnostics

Contrary to popular belief, a diagnostic isn't someone who doesn't believe in two gods. Nope, a *diagnostic* is a computer tool you can use to help diagnose (get it?) something that happened in your PC. This section details your options.

Understanding diagnostics

Next to the terms *plasma inducer* and *phase inhibiter*, *diagnostic* was one of the most common terms used in the old TV series *Star Trek: The Next Generation.* But unlike those other terms, *diagnostic* is a real word that applies to a real computer tool that you can use for troubleshooting.

A diagnostic comes in two flavors: report and check.

A report type of diagnostic simply inventories what's available. For example, the System Information window, covered elsewhere in this chapter, is an inventory type of diagnostic report. Its value lies in telling you what's up with the computer. Oftentimes, an internal hardware conflict or a malfunctioning device is obvious on this type of diagnostic report.

The check type of diagnostic is to computer hardware what a physical examination is to a human being: The hardware is tested. For a video display, it might mean that colors are displayed and various graphics modes reviewed. For a hard drive, information may be written to and read from the hard drive repeatedly to ensure reliability. This type of testing is a check type of diagnostic.

Star Trek, of course, showed various diagnostic "levels." Supposedly, the Level 1 diagnostic was the most intense, apparently forcing such introspective self-examination that the starship itself struggled with the process. The Level 3 diagnostic was more casual. All this is silliness compared to the realistic diagnostics you can perform on your PC for troubleshooting purposes.

Book II
Chapter 7

Reporting for Duty

Diagnosing DirectX

Microsoft introduced DirectX in the 1990s to help game programmers better use the PC's hardware muscle. The results were good: Today, the PC remains a superior gaming platform. By allowing game programmers access to components such as memory, video, sound, and input devices, DirectX has proven to be a success.

You can use the DirectX diagnostic tool to check on not only how the DirectX system is working but also whether you have problems with video, sound, and other basic PC components. Here's how:

1. **Press Win+R to bring forth the Run dialog box.**

2. **Type** dxdiag **and press Enter.**

3. **If prompted, click the Yes button to confirm that you want to proceed.**

   Behold the DirectX diagnostic tool as it peruses your PC's system, as shown in Figure 7-11. Wait until it's done before you proceed.

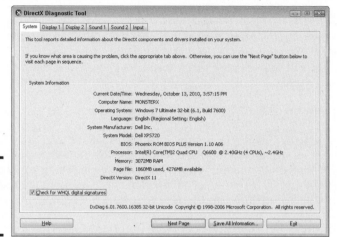

Figure 7-11:
The DirectX
diagnostic
tool.

4. **Click the Next Page button to view information about each different part of your PC, those various things controlled by the DirectX software.**

   Check the Notes section, at the bottom of the window, to see whether any problems are reported.

5. **Close the DirectX Diagnostic Tool window when you're done.**

   Click the Exit button.

Your PC most likely has the best version of DirectX for whatever software you use. The only time you need a DirectX update is when you install new software that requires it. For example, when installing a new game, you may be prompted to upgrade to the latest version of DirectX. Do so at that time.

DirectX is smart enough that an older version cannot overwrite a more current version.

DirectX versions 10 and later are available only for Windows 7 and Windows Vista, not for Windows XP.

Using the Memory Diagnostic tool

Windows 7 and Windows Vista come with a Memory Diagnostic tool, and it's one of those memory-testing diagnostics, not just a diagnostic that says "You have this much memory." Here's how to use the Memory Diagnostic tool:

1. **Save everything.**

   Your computer is restarted by the memory diagnostic procedure, so save your stuff, close windows, and get ready for a restart.

2. **Open the Control Panel.**

3a. **In Windows 7, choose System and Security and then choose Administrative Tools.**

3b. **In Windows Vista, choose System and Maintenance and then choose Administrative Tools.**

4. **Open the Memory Diagnostic Tool icon.**

5. **In Windows Vista, click the Continue button or type the administrator's password to continue.**

6. **In the Windows Memory Diagnostic Tool window, choose the option Restart Now and Check for Problems.**

    Wait until the computer restarts. When it does, the Memory Diagnostic Tool screen appears almost immediately. Wait while memory is checked thoroughly. Don't get bored; the display entertains you.

    When the test is over, the PC restarts again.

7. **Log in to Windows as you normally do.**

    The test results are displayed from a pop-up bubble in the notification area.

Because the Memory Diagnostic Tool is a serious diagnostic, I don't recommend using it unless you suspect your PC of falling victim to memory issues, such as random errors, system crashes, and other weird activities. (Well, "weird" is typical for a computer, so look for activities weirder than normal.)

Windows cannot properly detect memory malfunctions on its own because Windows itself must dwell in the same foul RAM that's causing the problem. But the Memory Diagnostic tool can get to the bottom of the situation as it starts up as its own operating system.

If problems are detected, the only true solution is to find and replace the bad memory. It can be a pain in the butt, unless you just want to replace *all* the memory in your PC. And, as long as you're going to do that, you might as well buy your computer even more memory than it had.

Doing a hardware diagnostic

Windows doesn't come with specific hardware diagnostic tools. Even so, when you add new hardware to your PC or the manufacturer installs it, diagnostic tools or programs may be available.

For example, the PC's display adapter software may include a diagnostic tool: Look for the adapter name, such as ATI (Intel) or Nvidia, on the Start menu's All Programs submenu. Or, you might find the diagnostic tool accessible from the notification area: Right-click the manufacturer's icon and choose the diagnostic tool from the pop-up menu.

Likewise, the network adapter may have its own diagnostic tool or a suite of tools available. The only way to know for certain is to look. (See Book V for information on troubleshooting networking issues.)

If you own a utility suite, such as Norton Utilities, you may find hard drive diagnostic tools as well as other utilities for checking various PC components. (Check out Book VI, Chapter 2 for things you can do in Windows to maintain the PC's disk drives.)

✦ Yes, using one of the many hardware diagnostic tools can be time consuming.

✦ Video diagnostics can be something to behold: The colors are fascinating. Watching the display adapter change between various text and graphics modes can be fun to watch. But mostly the diagnostic performs repeated tests that have no effect on the display.

✦ The best diagnostics usually come on bootable discs. That's because, in order to truly ensure that the hardware is being examined, the program must have direct access to the PC's guts. You can't do that through Windows. Even so, few diagnostic tools available to the general public take the boot disc approach. Only professional diagnostic tools come on boot discs. Even then, few PC technicians use them because it's just cheaper to replace parts than it is to undertake a true, deep level of troubleshooting.

Chapter 8: Recovery Options

In This Chapter

- Recovering previous versions
- Working with System Restore
- Using the System File Checker
- Starting the Recovery Console
- Repairing a master boot record
- Using a recovery disc
- Determining whether to reinstall Windows

There's no need to resort to complete despair when you experience computer woe. As a special gift to you, Windows offers quite a few disaster recovery options. From a single file to parts of Windows to the entire operating system, a method often exists to restore what you once had and to recover your computer system. This chapter shows you where those recovery and restore options are buried.

Windows Time Travel

Both Windows 7 and Windows Vista sport a feature that I have named Previous Versions. It uses System Restore technology, as well as any backups you've made of your computer stuff, to rescue older versions of a file. For example, if you massively change a file, or if it's overwritten, you can restore it by using the Previous Versions feature. Here's how:

1. **Right-click the file or folder.**

2. **Choose Restore Previous Versions from the shortcut menu.**

The file or folder's Properties dialog box appears, with the Previous Versions tab upfront, as shown in Figure 8-1.

When no previous versions exist, you see the message `There Are No Previous Versions Available`. That's it. You're done: Go to Step 5. Otherwise, you see a list of older copies of the file.

3. **Choose a previous version from the list.**

Ideally, you should select the most recent version, though if you're after an ancient version of the file or folder, you can pluck it from the list instead.

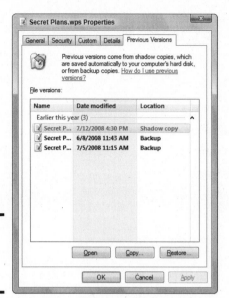

Figure 8-1:
Previous
versions of
a file.

4a. **Click the Open button to open the file and review its contents.**

The Open button is best used when you just want to peek. In fact, I've used the Open button to open a file, copy a swath of text (or an image), and then close the file without ever restoring it.

4b. **Click the Copy button to copy the file or folder to a specific location in your PC's storage system.**

The Copy option is useful when you don't want to overwrite the existing version of the file.

4c. **Click the Restore button to overwrite the existing file or folder with the previous version; click the Restore button in the warning dialog box to confirm this choice. Click OK.**

5. **Close the file or folder's Properties dialog box when you're done.**

Previous Versions works best when you frequently back up your files; plus, the System Restore utility must be active. If you disabled System Restore, you cannot use Previous Versions.

✦ See Book VI, Chapter 1 for more information on Backup.

✦ System Restore is covered in the next section.

✦ The Previous Versions feature isn't a substitute for recovering a file from the Recycle Bin; if you delete a file, you need to recover it from the Recycle Bin.

✦ The Recycle Bin doesn't contain older versions of files, nor can it help you restore a file that's been overwritten with new data. Only the Previous Versions feature can bring back a file that's been changed.

✦ You cannot use the Previous Versions feature on Windows files or your programs. To recover bad Windows files, see the later section, "The System File Checker." For bad program files, reinstall the program.

✦ To restore a previous version of a file that has been renamed, use the Previous Versions feature on the folder containing the file. Click the Open button to open the folder's previous version, and then copy the old file from the folder to its new location.

✦ To disable the Previous Versions feature, you simply turn off System Restore. (See the section "Disabling System Restore," later in this chapter.)

**Book II
Chapter 8**

Recovery Options

Restore the System, Restore Your Sanity

The first — and best — trick you should try when Windows goes awry is a restart. Simple. Effective. Works most of the time.

When restarting Windows fails to cure the PC's ills, the next instant cure you should try is *System Restore*. This tool has been around since Windows 98, where it was tucked away in a command line utility. But, starting with Windows XP, System Restore gained full graphical popularity as a way to recover from common goofs, such as wrong settings or improperly installed software or hardware. This section explains how to use System Restore.

✦ System Restore isn't a miracle worker. For example, it cannot restore files you deleted. For that job, see the section on missing files in Chapter 1. Also refer to the section "Windows Time Travel," earlier in this chapter.

✦ When disk space runs tight, you can create more room by removing old restore point data. Refer to Book VI, Chapter 2 for information on Disk Cleanup.

✦ The best way to restore your system is to use Backup. See Book VI, Chapter 1.

Using System Restore

It happened. Something weird. A driver made things worse. The hardware update conflicts with something already in your computer, and now *two* things don't work. Or, perhaps your 13-year-old "computer genius" nephew decided to trick out your PC. Regardless of the foul, you want to recover your PC to The Way Things Were.

When should you reinstall Windows?

Short answer: *Never.*

I'm serious. Most problems in Windows can be fixed. This chapter tells you how to address what I would estimate are 98 percent of the major issues that most too-busy tech support people and amateur computer consultants would tell you requires a major reinstallation of your PC's operating system. Before you succumb to their good-natured yet ill-informed suggestions, consider a few points of my own:

Most problems in Windows can be fixed. This chapter covers some marvelous tools you can use to help recover, restore, and return Windows to an operable state. *Remember:* The reason most tech support people claim that reinstalling Windows is a solution is that their motivation is to get you off the phone and not truly address your problem. Sad but true.

There's no need to reinstall Windows to "refresh" the computer. Some wag once said that it's a "good idea" to reinstall Windows to keep the computer fresh — or some such nonsense. I say "Poppycock!" Computers are continually changing beasts. If you reinstall Windows, you also have to spend lots of time online reloading updates and patches. The benefits are nil, especially given that disk tools exist to remove the problems that reinstalling Windows supposedly solves.

The only time you truly need to reinstall Windows is when the operating system has been horribly damaged. For example, some doofus might delete a given number of files in the Windows folder, or perhaps a computer virus or corrupt program deletes a swath of files necessary to Windows. That kind of damage can only be fixed by reinstalling Windows.

Avoid the temptation. Shun those who claim otherwise. A computer's operating system is its soul, and rarely do you have a need or a reason to replace the thing, especially for trivial or passing reasons. Trust me.

Follow these steps to use System Restore in Windows 7 and Windows Vista:

1. **Save all your stuff.**

   The System Restore operation restarts your computer. Save your files; close your programs. Do it now.

2. **From the Start button menu, choose All Programs⇨Accessories⇨ System Tools⇨System Restore.**

3. **In Windows Vista, click the Continue button or type the administrator's password.**

   System Restore's main window appears. That is, unless you've recently restored the system, in which case you see an option to undo the System Restore. See the later section, "Undoing a System Restore."

4. **Click the Next button.**

   A list of recent restore points appears, as shown in Figure 8-2. The most recent restore point is selected, which is most likely the one you want.

If you don't see recent restore points, shown in the figure, and instead see another screen, choose the Recommended Restore option.

5. **Click the Next button.**

A screen detailing which hard drives to restore is shown. Again, the one you need is most likely already selected, so there's nothing else to do.

6. **Click the Next button.**

You may not have a second Next button, in which case you just:

7. **Click the Finish button.**

8. **Click Yes to restart Windows.**

Wait while Windows restarts.

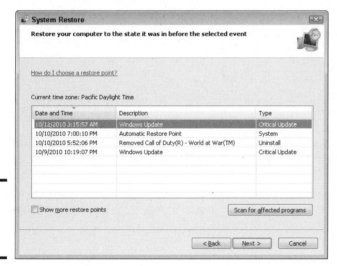

Figure 8-2:
System
Restore in
action.

Follow these steps to use System Restore in Windows XP:

1. **Save everything.**

Because System Restore restarts your computer, I recommend that you save files, close open programs, and get ready for a restart.

2. **From the Start button menu, choose All Programs⇨Accessories⇨ System Tools⇨System Restore.**

You see the main System Restore window, which is boring, so I don't illustrate it here.

3. **Choose the option Restore My Computer to an Earlier Time.**

4. **Click the Next button.**

5. **Choose a restore point from the cute calendar-like thing.**

   The most recent date is chosen by default, and I recommend using it unless you already tried it and experienced problems.

6. **Click the Next button.**

7. **Read the scary warning.**

   Ooo! Scary! Red text! They must be *serious* this time! Just kidding: You're good to go.

8. **Click the Next button.**

   It should be named *Finish* because it's the last step: System Restore does its magic. Windows restarts itself.

After you log in again, you need to wait a bit more. Eventually, you see a confirmation message explaining that Windows has been restored: In Windows 7 and Windows Vista, you see (after a seemingly endless amount of time) a dialog box explaining how the System Restore operation went; click the Close button. In Windows XP, you see a window that details what happened; click OK to close the window.

Any problems you were trying to fix should be fixed. If they're not, continue reading other sections in this chapter for additional solutions.

✦ Restoring the system is also a start-up option, as described in Book I, Chapter 2. Choose the option Last Known Good Configuration, which is more or less the last system restore point.

✦ You can also perform System Restore in Safe mode. That's a good choice, especially when the computer is unusable otherwise. See Chapter 3, on Safe mode.

Restoring to a specific date and time

Windows naturally chooses the most recent system restore point, which is generally a safe bet. Sometimes, you may want a less recent restore point. For example, when I managed to botch a system upgrade *and* a software addition, I needed to restore my computer to a point from several days earlier.

To restore to an earlier point for Windows 7 or Windows Vista, refer to the steps in the preceding section. After Step 4, choose the proper restore date. To restore to an earlier time, place a check mark by the option Show Restore Points Older than 5 Days. Complete the rest of the steps.

In Windows XP, follow the steps in the preceding section, but in Step 5 choose an earlier restore point from the cute, calendar-like thing. Then work through the rest of the steps.

✦ Choosing an older restore point increases the likelihood that the restore won't be successful. If possible, you can try to incrementally restore by choosing a more recent restore point and then running System Restore again with an increasingly older restore point.

✦ When you restore to an older restore point, you remove any software and hardware updates installed in the "between time," where some programs and certain hardware don't work and require reinstallation after the System Restore operation is complete.

Setting a restore point

System restore points are set automatically in Windows Vista, usually just after midnight (assuming that you're up that late or leave the PC on all the time). They're also set before you install new software, as part of the Setup program. But, for other times, and for Windows XP all the time, you must set a manual restore point.

For example, just before installing new hardware or perhaps before you take a stab at configuring wireless networking for the first time, manually set a restore point.

Restore points are set automatically in Windows 7. In fact, because the option to set a restore point is hidden, you can assume that Microsoft doesn't want you to manually set them. Even so, I've found where the option is hidden. To manually set a restore point in Windows 7 and Windows Vista, follow these steps:

1. **Press Win+Break to summon the System window.**

2. **From the list of tasks on the left side of the window, choose System Protection.**

3. **In Windows Vista, click the Continue button or type the administrator's password to continue.**

The System Properties dialog box appears, with its System Protection tab forward.

4. **Click the Create button, found near the bottom of the dialog box.**

5. **Type a descriptive name for the restore point.**

Describe the restore point in terms of the item you're installing or changing on the computer — for example, *Massive hard drive cleaning binge* or *Adjusting new monitor.*

6. **Click the Create button.**

Eventually, a System Protection dialog box appears, confirming that the restore point was created.

7. **Click the Close button, and close any dialog boxes or windows you've opened.**

Following these steps sets a restore point in Windows XP:

1. **From the Start button menu, choose All Programs⇨Accessories⇨ System Tools⇨System Restore.**

   You see the main System Restore window, which is boring, so I don't illustrate it here.

2. **Choose the option Create a Restore Point.**

3. **Click the Next button.**

4. **Type a descriptive name.**

   Use your writing skills to create a name that reflects the reason for creating the restore point. Examples include *About to do something utterly foolish, My cousin Ralph is visiting,* and *I do everything I read in a computer book.*

5. **Click the Create button.**

   The restore point is created and described in scary, bold, red text.

6. **Click the Close button.**

After creating the restore point, proceed with whatever modifications you plan on making to your computer. You now have peace of mind, knowing that a restore point looms in the past, in case you need it.

✦ You must manually set restore points in Windows XP!

✦ You can review the schedule for automatic restore points in Windows 7 and Windows Vista by visiting the Task Scheduler. (See Book VI, Chapter 3.)

✦ My challenge in writing this section was to use the phrase *peace of mind* (which I just heard on the television). I succeeded.

Undoing a System Restore

In Windows 7, you can undo a System Restore operation immediately after it's done: Simply rerun System Restore and choose the Undo option that appears in the System Restore window. The System Restore is undone and your system is re-restored to the way it was before you ran System Restore.

Windows Vista? It apparently has no Undo command for System Restore.

To undo a System Restore in Windows XP, heed these steps:

1. **Save your stuff!**

   The undo operation restarts your computer. Save now. Close open programs.

2. **Start System Restore: From the Start button menu, choose All Programs⇨Accessories⇨System Tools⇨System Restore.**

3. **Choose the option Undo My Last Restoration.**

4. **Click the Next button.**

   Scary! Red! Text!

5. **Click the Next button, which, honestly, should be relabeled the Undo button.**

   Windows undoes the System Restore operation. Your computer restarts. You log in.

6. **Click the OK button in the System Restore window after the computer restarts.**

   You can then use the computer as it was before you shamefully attempted to use System Restore.

Obviously, the sooner you can undo after using System Restore, the better.

Disabling System Restore

Some people believe that System Restore is a security risk. For example, you can effectively restore a virus with System Restore, or System Restore can be taken over by hostile software. In Windows Vista, System Restore also maintains information about nonsystem files that may contain data you don't want others to access. Regardless of the reason, you can disable System Restore.

Disable System Restore in Windows 7 by following these steps:

1. **Conjure up a System window by pressing Win+Break.**

   The Break key is the same key as Pause, though Win+Break has a more devious sound to it than Win+Pause.

2. **From the list of tasks in the upper-left part of the window, choose System Protection.**

3. **In the System Properties dialog box, click the Configure button.**

4. **Choose the option Turn Off System Protection.**

5. **Click OK.**

   A nasty warning appears.

6. **Click the Yes button.**

7. **Click OK to close the System Properties window, and then close the System window.**

To turn off System Restore in Windows Vista, heed these steps:

1. **Press Win+Break to quickly summon the System window.**

2. **Choose the link System Protection on the left side of the window.**

3. **Type the administrator's password or click Continue.**

4. **Remove the check mark by all disk drives in the Automatic Restore Points portion of the dialog box.**

5. **After being shocked by the warning dialog box, click the button Turn System Restore Off.**

6. **Click OK and then close the System window.**

To stop System Restore in Windows XP, follow these steps:

1. **Press Win+Break to bring forth the System dialog box.**

2. **Click the System Restore tab.**

3. **Click the check box by the option Turn Off System Restore.**

4. **Click OK.**

5. **Click the Yes button to confirm that you want System Restore turned off.**

To reactivate System Restore, repeat the steps in this section for your version of Windows, but choose the option that turns on System Restore.

If you're going to disable System Restore, please back up your data. (See Book VI, Chapter 1.)

The System File Checker

One of the most useful yet overlooked tools in Windows is the *System File Checker*, fondly known by its initials, *SFC*.

You can use the powerful SFC tool to ensure the integrity of the Windows operating system as well as to effectively restore broken parts of Windows without having to completely reinstall the operating system. Is SFC not the Windows-fixer-upper tool you've been waiting for?

✦ SFC may prompt you for the Windows disc, which is either the disc you used to install or upgrade Windows or the system recovery disc provided by your computer manufacturer. Have the disc handy!

✦ When SFC cannot fix the problem, you should try additional recovery options, as described in the section "Windows Recovery," later in this chapter.

Running SFC in Windows 7 and Windows Vista

The System File Checker (SFC) is a command line utility in the more recent editions of Windows. Furthermore, you have to start an administrator command prompt to run SFC and have it work its magic.

Before heading into the operation, be aware that running SFC takes time. It's not a quick-check-before-you-do-something-important type of operation.

Here are the steps to take to scan and repair Windows by using SFC:

1. **Save all your stuff and close any other programs you're running.**

   SFC isn't a light or casual utility. It does major repair. Don't blow it by losing information in an open program window. Save now!

2. **From the Start menu, choose All Programs⇨Accessories.**

3. **Right-click the Command Prompt menu item.**

4. **From the pop-up menu, choose Run As Administrator.**

5. **Click the Yes or Continue button or type the administrator's password.**

   The administrator's command prompt window appears on the screen.

   You run SFC by typing **sfc** at the command prompt, but don't do it yet. After SFC, you can type various options that let it do its magic. Table 8-1 lists all of them, but the key is /scannow.

6. **Type** sfc /scannow **and press the Enter key.**

   You see text:

   ```
   Beginning system scan. This process takes some time.

   Beginning verification phase of system scan.
   Verification 26% complete.
   ```

7. **Wait.**

   SFC fixes what it can. Mostly, it plods through and displays the results, like this:

   ```
   Verification 100% complete.
   ```

   What you see after this line depends on the results of the operation. When nothing is wrong, you see this text:

   ```
   Windows Resource Protection didn't find any integrity
      violations.
   ```

   When problems have been found and repaired, you see this:

   ```
   Windows Resource Protection found corrupt files and
      successfully repaired them. Details are included in
      the CBS.Log windir\Logs\CBS\CBS.log. For example C:\
      Windows\Logs\CBS\CBS.log
   ```

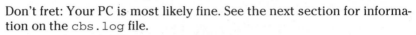

When things go awry, you see this text message:

```
Windows Resource Protection found corrupt files but was
    unable to fix some of them. Details are included in
    the CBS.Log windir\Logs\CBS\CBS.log. For example C:\
    Windows\Logs\CBS\CBS.log
```

Don't fret: Your PC is most likely fine. See the next section for information on the cbs.log file.

If you're prompted to insert the Windows disc, do so. Corrupt files must be replaced by fresh ones.

8. **Close the administrator's command prompt window.**

You've done the best you can. Hopefully, by running SFC, you've thumped Windows back into shape. If not, read the later section, "Windows Recovery," to see what else you can do.

Table 8-1	Windows 7 and Windows Vista SFC Command Options
Option	*What It Does*
/offbootdir	Specifies the location of boot files when they cannot be found on the current PC
/offwindir	Specifies the location of Windows files when they cannot be found on the current PC
/scanfile	Scans and (optional) repairs or replaces the named file
/scannow	Scans all Windows operating system files, repairing or replacing any that are defective or the wrong version
/verifyfile	Scans the named file but doesn't replace the file
/verifyonly	Scans all Windows operating system files but doesn't repair or replace any bad files and saves information in a long, huge log file

Reviewing the cbs.log file

The SFC utility keeps track of its actions in a log file named after a major American television network. Don't bother reviewing the log; it's massive. On my PC, the file ended up at 39MB. Massive.

Obviously, the entire log isn't what you want to read, unless you need the sleep. The idea is to find out which files can't be repaired. To do that, you can follow these steps in Windows 7 and Windows Vista:

1. **From the Start menu, choose All Programs➪Accessories.**

2. **Right-click the Notepad menu item.**

3. **Choose Run As Administrator from the pop-up menu.**

   You must run Notepad as an administrator to access a log file located beneath the Windows folder.

4. **Type the administrator's password or click the Continue button.**

5. **Choose File⇨Open.**

6. **In the File Name box, type** %windir%\logs\cbs\cbs.log

   As you type, a drop-down list of matching folders and files appears, which is your clue that you're doing it correctly.

   Don't type a period after the word *log!* You're typing a filename, not a sentence.

7. **Click the Open button.**

   The log file cbs.log appears in Notepad — though it may take some time to load because the sucker is huge.

   Yes! The log contents are complex. No need to fuss:

8. **Choose Edit⇨Find to summon the Find dialog box.**

9. **Type the text** cannot repair **into the box and click the Find Next button.**

   You see a log entry highlighted in the Notepad window, telling you which file SFC wasn't able to fix and why. The filename appears in double quotes along with a lot of gobbledygook about what's wrong.

10. **Click the Find Next button to look for the next file in the list that SFC couldn't fix.**

    Or, you can dismiss the Find dialog box and press the F3 key as the keyboard shortcut for the Find Next command.

11. **Close Notepad.**

What do logs tell you? Well, not much. If SFC cannot fix the file, there may be nothing further you can do — other than repair Windows, as discussed later in this chapter.

You might also try searching the Microsoft Knowledge Base for information about the filename. Visit http://support.microsoft.com and type the name of the file that befuddles SFC.

Running SFC in Windows XP

Windows XP comes with the command line utility SFC, or System File Checker. You can use SFC to check for corrupt or missing Windows files and have them instantly fixed or replaced. It's a miracle!

Follow these steps to run SFC on your Windows XP computer:

1. **Close open windows and save your stuff.**

I recommend saving things because SFC may necessitate restarting your computer. In any case, you should never be working on your computer while you're troubleshooting.

2. **Pop up the Start button menu and choose All Programs⇨Accessories⇨Command Prompt.**

The lovely command prompt window appears.

The System File Checker runs when you type sfc at the command prompt, followed by one of six options. Those options make SFC do its thing, so at least one of them is required. All options are described in Table 8-2. The option you use is /scannow.

3. **Type** sfc /scannow **and press the Enter key.**

A graphical window appears, monitoring the System File Checker's progress.

You may be prompted to insert the Windows disc. Do so!

4. **Wait.**

When everything is okay, you don't see anything; the graphical window disappears and you're left at the command prompt window.

5. **Close the command prompt window.**

The System File Checker can do only so much. If it fails, I recommend that you use more drastic means to repair Windows, as covered in the aptly named section "Windows Recovery."

Table 8-2	Windows XP SFC Command Options
Option	*What It Does*
/cachesize	Sets the size of the cache used by SFC for storing backups of system files
/purgecache	Removes backups of Windows system files, which is something you don't want to do
/revert	Undoes the boot scanning activated by the /scanboot switch
/scanboot	Directs SFC to perform a (time-consuming) system file check every time you start Windows
/scanonce	Directs SFC to scan all system files the next time you restart Windows
/scannow	Scans all Windows operating system files, repairing or replacing any that are defective or the wrong version

Windows Recovery

Having ample recovery options for Windows isn't a dismal admission that Windows is worthy of having them. Believe me — back in the Cro-Magnon days of computing, I yearned for a recovery disc or a special mode for repairing the operating system. You should consider yourself fortunate. This section explains the various available options.

Understanding the Recovery Console

One of the most useful tools for fixing problems in Windows is the Recovery Console. It's a nerdy thing. Unlike Windows in its graphical glory, the *Recovery Console* is a text-mode operating system, similar to the old MS-DOS. Indeed, many of your old favorite DOS commands can be used in the Recovery Console, making it popular with nostalgic nerds.

The Recovery Console isn't DOS, however. It's a tool used to troubleshoot your computer. It's run either from a recovery partition on your PC's hard drive or from any Windows or system recovery disc. Later sections in this chapter explain the methods.

Table 8-3 lists some Recovery Console commands of note. I don't have the space in this book to go into complete detail; documenting the Recovery Console and doing it well would take an entire book unto itself.

**Book II
Chapter 8**

Recovery Options

Table 8-3		Recovery Console Commands
Command	*Windows Version*	*What It Does*
bcdedit	7, Vista	Boots configuration editor, used in Windows Vista rather than the older bootcfg utility
bmrui	7, Vista	Runs Windows PC Complete Restore (can also be run from the System Recovery Options menu; see Figure 8-3, later in this chapter)
bootcfg	XP	Edits the boot.ini file, used to set start-up and other configuration options for older PCs. (This command is available in Windows, but it merely runs the bcdedit utility.)
bootrec	7, Vista	System start-up and repair utility
chkdsk	All	Checks a volume for errors and repairs them if it can
exit	All	Closes the Recovery Console window in Windows Vista and restarts the PC for Windows XP

(continued)

Table 8-3 *(continued)*

Command	Windows Version	What It Does
fixmbr	XP	Writes a new master boot record on the named device
format	7, XP	Formats a disk drive, preparing it for use
mbr	Vista	Starts graphical utility to manage the master boot record
recover	7, Vista	Reads information from a troublesome disk
reg	All	Lets you edit the Registry
sfc	7, Vista	Runs the System File Checker, covered earlier in this chapter

In addition to the commands available for Windows repair, all standard command-prompt commands and utilities are available in the Recovery Console. They include tools for file manipulation, such as copy and ren, the network configuration tool net, and commands for general system management.

The following sections describe how to start the Recovery Console for your version of Windows.

✦ Yeah, you probably don't have any "old favorite" DOS commands, either.

✦ The Recovery Console is just one of many tools available for repairing Windows.

✦ You can glean more information about any text-mode Recovery Console command by following the command with a space and then /?. For example, to read all options for the chkdsk command, type

```
chkdsk /?
```

To see all options displayed onscreen at one time, add the pipe character and then the more command, as in

```
bcdedit | more
```

✦ You can run and manage any Windows computer by using the command prompt alone. Most of the technical setup and configuration of your PC was most likely done by a command prompt script at the factory.

✦ Of course, all this command prompt stuff is *nerdy*. One reason that most technicians don't bother using the Recovery Console is that it's just faster and cheaper to reinstall Windows. (See the earlier sidebar, "When should you reinstall Windows?")

✦ On the subject of reinstalling Windows: *Don't*. You do not have to reinstall Windows to fix minor problems.

Getting to the Recovery Console in Windows 7 and Windows Vista

The Recovery Console in Windows Vista is available from either the F8 start-up menu or any Windows installation or recovery disc. Here are the steps to take for starting the Recovery Console from the F8 boot menu:

1. **Restart the computer.**

2. **After the start-up message appears, press the F8 key.**

You must press F8 before Windows starts. See Book I, Chapter 2 for some helpful hints.

3. **Choose the option Repair Your Computer.**

At this point, your computer may start a custom recovery program, such as the Rescue and Recovery tool available on Lenovo PCs. If so, you should either attempt to access the Recovery Console by using this utility or refer to the second set of steps in this section.

4. **Click the Next button.**

You may be prompted to choose a keyboard layout and language. You usually have no need to change these options.

5. **Choose your username.**

If you know the administrator's password, you can choose Administrator. The password should be the same as on your own user account, though it may not be.

Select only an account that has administrator access.

6. **Type your password and click OK.**

A window appears on the screen, listing several repair and recovery options and tools, similar to the ones shown in Figure 8-3. Your PC may not have these same options. For example, *Dell Factory Image Restore* appears only on Dell computers. (On other computers, you may find the Recovery Manager option, which is pretty much the same thing.)

7. **Choose the option Command Prompt.**

The command prompt window opens. You're now ready to use the Recovery Console commands, as covered in the rest of this chapter.

8. **When you're done using the command prompt, close its window.**

9. **Choose the option Restart from the System Recovery Options window.**

The computer restarts.

Figure 8-3:
Windows
Vista system
recovery
options.

In some cases, the preceding steps may not get you to the Recovery
Console. You may instead find a special recovery program or another utility. Don't give up! It's still possible to access the Recovery Console by using
a Windows installation or update disc or the recovery disc that came with
your computer. Follow these steps:

1. **Insert the Windows or system recovery disc into your PC's optical
drive.**

2. **Restart the computer.**

3. **Choose the option to boot from the CD or DVD.**

Refer to Book I, Chapter 2 to set up this option if it's not available.

4. **Work your way through the installation process until you find the
option Repair Your Computer.**

Don't worry: Nothing is changed on your computer until you choose to
reinstall Windows. But you're not doing that.

5. **Press the R key to choose the option Repair Your Computer.**

6. **If prompted, don't choose to repair any start-up or boot issues or errors.**

You can return to fix any errors later.

7. **Choose the Windows Vista installation from the list.**

8. **Click the Next button.**

   The System Recovery Options window appears (refer to Figure 8-3).

9. **Choose the Command Prompt option.**

   Say hello to the Recovery Console.

10. **When you're done using the command prompt, close its window.**

11. **Choose the option Restart from the System Recovery Options window.**

    The computer restarts.

The Recovery Console isn't a friendly place. Go there only when you know what you're doing or when you're following directions, such as those provided in this book.

Starting the Recovery Console in Windows XP

To start the Recovery Console in Windows XP, follow these steps:

1. **Stick a Windows disc in the optical drive.**

   Yes, you need a Windows installation disc to make this procedure work. The system recovery disc might also work.

2. **Restart the computer.**

3. **Ensure that the system attempts to start from the Windows installation disc.**

   You must boot from the optical drive; press Enter when you see the prompt Press any key to boot from optical drive (or whatever the message says).

4. **Proceed with the "installation" of Windows.**

   Trust me: Just follow along with the directions on the screen. You're not really installing Windows, but you must complete the initial steps to get where you need to go.

5. **When prompted, choose the option to start the Recovery Console.**

   For example, the prompt may say to press the **R** key to start the Recovery Console, similar to what's shown in Figure 8-4. Do so.

6. **Select a Windows installation if prompted.**

   The Windows installation may be the only one. If you fail to select a Windows installation and, for example, just press Enter, Windows cancels the operation and you have to start over.

7. **If prompted, type the administrator's password.**

   Finally, you should see the text-mode command prompt, which looks something like this:

   ```
   C:\WINDOWS>
   ```

   You're ready to work.

8. **When you're done, type** exit **to restart your computer.**

   The exit command closes the Recovery Console and reboots the PC. If it doesn't, press Ctrl+Alt+Delete to restart the computer.

```
Windows XP Professional Setup
==============================

   Welcome to Setup

   This portion of the Setup program prepares Microsoft(R)
   Windows(R) XP to run on your computer.


      •  To set up Windows XP now, press ENTER.

      •  To repair a Windows XP installation using
         Recovery Console, press R.

      •  To quit Setup without installing Windows XP, press F3.
```

Figure 8-4:
One way
to start the
Recovery
Console.

The Recovery Console is a command prompt window, in Text mode. If you don't see a console window, choose whatever option is available to present you with the command prompt window or the Recovery Console window. If you still don't see the Text mode Recovery Console, you have to restart the computer and begin these steps again.

✦ You should also look into starting the computer by using a recovery partition, as discussed in the section "Booting into a recovery partition," later in this chapter. The recovery partition might also have the Recovery Console option.

✦ The exit command restarts the computer only when you're using the Windows XP version of the Recovery Console.

✦ See Book I, Chapter 2 for more information on your PC's start-up options.

Fixing the master boot record

One useful and often necessary thing you can do in the Recovery Console is fix a corrupt or damaged master boot record (MBR). Chapters 1 and 2 in Book I discuss how the MBR plays a role in starting your PC and what happens when it's damaged. Recovery is entirely possible if you can access the Recovery Console and you know which command to type for your version of Windows.

In Windows 7 and Windows Vista, type the following command at the Recovery Console prompt:

```
BOOTREC /FIXMBR
```

Type the command exactly as written: BOOTREC, a space, a forward slash, and then FIXMBR *not* followed by a period. Press Enter.

In Windows XP, you type the following command to fix the master boot record at the Recovery Console prompt:

```
FIXMBR
```

Press the Enter key and then press Y and Enter to confirm.

For all versions of Windows, this command works instantly. You see another command prompt displayed. Type exit to quit the command prompt, and then restart the PC if it doesn't restart automatically.

When the computer restarts, whatever problems afflicted the MBR should be gone. For example, if you were removing a boot manager program, it no longer appears when the PC first starts.

No danger is involved in fixing the MBR; if it wasn't damaged, running the FIXMBR command doesn't screw anything up (well, unless something else is wrong with the boot drive).

Booting into a recovery partition

PC manufacturers now often partition a computer's primary hard drive into two volumes. *Drive C* is the computer's main hard drive, the one on which Windows is installed. A second, smaller drive — *drive D* — is created on the same physical hard drive. It's given the name *Recovery,* and it can be used to help rebuild, restore, re-create, or just troubleshoot Windows problems.

Figure 8-5 illustrates a typical Computer window found in Windows Vista. You see two hard drives: C and D. Drive D is labeled *Recovery.* To use this drive for starting the computer and troubleshooting, you access the computer's Boot menu.

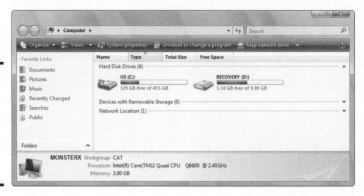

Figure 8-5:
The
Recovery
drive, found
in the
Computer
window.

A prompt describing which key to press to access the Boot menu appears when the computer first starts; see Book I, Chapter 2 for the details. On some computers, it's the F10 key, though on my Dell computer, it's F12.

When the Boot menu appears, notice that one of the options presented is to boot into the recovery volume. Choose that option to start and use the recovery volume.

What happens when you start the recovery partition depends on the computer manufacturer. You may see a custom operating system loosely based on Windows but geared toward troubleshooting and maintenance. Sometimes you see the System Recovery Options window (refer to Figure 8-3). The tools you find available can be used to help fix the main Windows volume (drive C), access special utilities, or even restore the PC from a backup.

✦ Another way to use the recovery partition is to choose the Repair Your Computer option from the F8 boot menu, described earlier in this chapter. (See the earlier section, "Getting to the Recovery Console in Windows 7 and Windows Vista.")

✦ Some computers may feature a special button, such as the ThinkVantage button on Lenovo laptops, that boots the computer into the recovery volume.

✦ Not every PC has a recovery volume. In this case, I recommend that you use a recovery disc, as mentioned in the next section.

Using a recovery disc

Welcome to the Drastic Measures Department. Here at the DMD, the object is to fix things by wiping them out and then rebuilding them. Have a problem with your plumbing? The easy DMD solution is to level your home and rebuild it from scratch, just the way it was the first day you moved in. Problem solved! Ditto for your computer!

Most PCs sold today come with recovery discs, or sets of discs. The purpose of the discs is to let you restore your computer to the same condition it was in when you bought it. As far as a recovery solution goes, this one is indeed *drastic.* Basically, it works like this:

1. **Insert the recovery disc into your PC's optical drive.**

2. **Restart the computer (or turn it on).**

3. **Boot from the optical disc.**

4. **Obey the directions on the screen for restoring your PC.**

When you're done, the PC exists just as it did when you first bought it: Windows is restored, as is any additional software supplied with your computer (though some software might not be included on the main recovery disc).

**Book II
Chapter 8**

Recovery Options

✦ The recovery disc works best only for fixing *software* problems — specifically, massive damage to the Windows operating system. The disc is ideal for recovering after a virus or another type of malware is found.

✦ The recovery disc doesn't work to fix hardware problems. If the hard drive is kaput, the recovery disc doesn't help you. It *does* help if you buy and install a replacement hard drive. See Book I, Chapter 8.

✦ Before using a recovery disc, consider running the System File Checker (SFC), as covered earlier in this chapter.

✦ A recovery disc is also part of a backup-restore operation. After recovering the computer to its pristine state, restore your backup files. That recovers your computer fully, bringing it back to the state it was in when the last backup was performed.

✦ Sometimes, you must use several discs to restore your PC. First, you restore Windows. Then you use subsequent discs to install drivers for your PC's hardware.

✦ Don't forget about updates! After you restore your computer, immediately use Windows Update to install all necessary updates. You may need to install updates in a series, which can take some time. See Chapter 1.

✦ See Book VI, Chapter 1 for information on Backup and Restore.

✦ See Book IV, Chapter 4 for more information on malware.

Making a recovery disc

You've looked and looked and you can't find the Windows recovery disc. Before making an angry phone call (useless) or writing an angry email (meaningless) or even hurling a brick through a glass window (illegal but satisfying), know that a secret command, available in Windows 7 and Windows Vista, lets you create a recovery disc.

The command works only when your PC has a recovery volume, as described in the section "Booting into a recovery partition," earlier in this chapter. In this case, you can use the secret command to create a recovery disc, which you can then use as described elsewhere this chapter. Follow these secret steps:

1. **Place a blank DVD-R or DVD+R disc into your PC's optical drive.**

   I recommend using the +R format for creating optical data discs.

   The optical disc must be blank. If it's not blank, the operation fails.

2. **Dismiss the AutoPlay (or any other) dialog box that pops up, asking what to do with the disc.**

3. **Press Win+R to summon the Run window.**

4. **Type** recdisc **and click the OK button.**

5. **In Windows Vista, click the Continue button or type the administrator's password to continue.**

   A window appears, prompting you to select an optical drive in which to create the recovery disc.

6. **Choose your PC's recordable optical drive from the menu button.**

7. **Click the Create Disc button.**

8. **Wait.**

   I probably didn't need to make you "wait" a step, but the process takes some time.

   After the disc has been created, a new dialog box appears on the screen. You deal with the dialog box soon enough, but for now:

9. **Remove the disc from the PC's optical drive.**

10. **Label the disc with the information listed on the screen, and then add the name of the computer, the date, and the words** *System Recovery.*

    Use a Sharpie or another permanent marker to label the disc.

11. **Click the Close button and then the OK button to close the open windows and dialog boxes.**

    You can also close the AutoPlay dialog box that may have appeared.

Place your copy of the System Recovery disc into a secure place, such as a firesafe or another spot where it won't get lost or damaged.

This trick works only when your PC has a Recovery drive; refer to Figure 8-5. When your PC lacks this drive or the drive has become corrupted, the operation to create a recovery disc dies after Step 5 (in the preceding step list).

Reinstalling Windows

Just as you can reinstall any software program, you can reinstall Windows. It's a relatively easy operation: Start your computer with a Windows disc — either a system recovery disc or any Windows disc. Obey the directions on the screen to install Windows.

If you have a backup disc handy, you don't need to reinstall Windows: Simply restore the data from the backup. You might have to start the computer with the Windows installation disc and then choose an option to run the Restore program. For example, the System Recovery Options window (refer to Figure 8-4) contains an item for running System Restore; see the earlier section, "Getting to the Recovery Console in Windows 7 and Windows Vista," for more information on opening this window.

Chapter 9: Registry Fixes

In This Chapter

✔ Appreciating the Registry

✔ Editing the Registry

✔ Creating a backup of the Registry

✔ Adding a new Registry key or value

✔ Searching the Registry

✔ Cleaning the Registry

*W*indows stores all its important information, settings, choices, options, preferences, and the combination to Bill Gates's secret vault in a giant repository called the *Registry*. It's supposed to be a place that mere mortal users fear to tread, yet by hanging out a digital No Trespassing sign, Microsoft sparked legions of curious PC users to prod, probe, and ponder the Registry's mysterious depths. This chapter exists to sate your Registry curiosity, by answering necessary questions and providing tips for keeping that forbidden place safe and solid.

Behold the Registry

In the merry old Land of Oz, Windows is the Wizard. It works its magic mostly behind the scenes, projecting a false image to those who dare to confront it. But if Toto were to pull back the curtain a tad, you would behold the wonders that make Windows work. One of those wonders is the *Windows Registry*. It's a central part of the operating system's personality. This section explains, first in black and white and later in full Technicolor, how the Registry fits into the PC troubleshooting picture.

The Registry doesn't hold secrets. Settings made in the Registry can just as easily be viewed or changed by using Windows itself. A few items hidden in the Registry, however, require you to delve into its depths. Just don't expect anything to overwhelm or thrill you.

Needless historical Registry information

The Registry has been around since the early days of Windows, but it took on prominence only in Windows 2000 and later. It was created to solve the problem of having too many configuration files.

Back in the early days of Windows, programs used text files to load their options, settings, and other memorable information, such as the high scores for *Minesweeper.* Those files had the extension .ini and were called "innie" files, though ini was short for *ini*tialization.

The problem was that Windows soon grew cluttered with multiple ini files. The two main ini files that governed Windows, system.ini and win.ini, soon grew cumbersome and unwieldy. Programs abused those files. Problems erupted. Civilization almost collapsed.

As a solution, Microsoft created the Registry. It did so with two goals:

✔ The first goal was to create a central repository for vital system and program information. The Registry would have rules, and programs would have to follow specific guidelines to modify or create entries in the Registry.

✔ The second goal, honestly, was to make the Registry a foreboding and inhospitable place. The reason was to keep casual users from poking around and messing things up. On that front, Microsoft failed miserably: The Registry is a source of curiosity for many users who believe that it holds hidden secrets.

Understanding the Registry

The Registry contains information used by Windows and your programs. The Registry helps the operating system manage the computer, it helps programs use the computer's resources, and it provides a location for keeping custom settings you make in both Windows and your programs.

For example, when you change the Windows desktop, the changes are stored in the Registry. When you see a list of recently opened files, that list is stored in the Registry. And, changes you make to the status bar in Word — yep, they're kept in the Registry, too.

The Registry is essentially a database. Its information is stored on disk for the most part, though *dynamic* information also exists in the computer's memory. (That dynamic information concerns the computer's hardware and operating state.) All the information is organized by using a structure similar to folders in the file storage system.

The top level of the Registry contains *hives,* each of which starts with the curious word HKEY. Table 9-1 describes the visible hives in the Registry. (The Registry has other hives that are used internally and not of significance, despite your disbelief. Honestly, you should get it out of your head that secret things dwell in the Registry!)

Table 9-1		Registry Hives
Name	*Abbreviation*	*Contents*
HKEY_CLASSES_ROOT	HKCR	Information used by programs for file association and for sharing information.
HKEY_CURRENT_USER	HKCU	Settings and configuration for the current user.
HKEY_LOCAL_MACHINE	HKLM	Settings and configuration for all users.
HKEY_USERS	HKU	Settings and configuration for all users on the computer; the information in HKCU is copied from this hive when the user logs in.
HKEY_CURRENT_CONFIG	N/A	Hardware information about the PC's resources and configuration.

**Book II
Chapter 9**

Registry Fixes

Beneath the hives are folders, or *keys*. Keys can also have *subkeys,* just as folders have subfolders. The name of the game is organization.

Keys contain *values*. Every value has a name and data. Unlike the old ini files, the data can be something other than text, including numeric values and binary information. You can find several values in a single key, or a key can be empty or contain only subkeys.

As with files and folders, values stored in the Registry are found by following a *pathname* that gives the location of a specific key or value. For example, the following pathname to the key gives the location where Adobe Acrobat Reader 8.0 is installed on the computer:

```
HKCU\Software\Adobe\Acrobat Reader\8.0\InstallPath
```

I used the abbreviation HKCU for HKEY_CURRENT_USER in the preceding line. It's followed by the subkeys Software, Adobe, Acrobat Reader, 8.0, and, finally, InstallPath. In the InstallPath key is a value that holds data in the form of text. The text is the pathname for the storage system location where Acrobat Reader 8.0 is installed.

Keys, like pathnames to files, can get long. Sometimes, a key name that's too long to fit on a single line must be wrapped, such as

```
HKCU\Software\Microsoft\Windows\CurrentVersion\Explorer\
   VisualEffects\CursorShadow
```

This key contains a binary value that determines whether Windows displays a shadow on the mouse pointer. The line is too long to fit on the page, so it wraps.

Incidentally, the CursorShadow key helps demonstrate a point I will continue to drive home: You can easily turn the mouse pointer shadow on or off by using the Pointers tab in the Mouse Properties dialog box. You don't have to delve into the Registry, nor is there any benefit to doing so.

✦ To view or modify the Registry, the Registry Editor program is used, as covered in the next section.

✦ Some keys may be empty, though they still contain a *Default* value. That's because all keys must contain a value or a subkey.

✦ The Registry concept exists in all modern computer operating systems. In Unix, for example, custom settings are kept in the /etc directory. In Mac OS X, settings are kept in a Library folder.

Using the Registry Editor

To view, modify, or create information in the Registry, you use the *Registry Editor* program. It's also known by its filename, regedit.

To run the Registry Editor, follow these steps:

1. **Press Win+R to summon the Run dialog box.**

2. **Type** regedit **and press Enter.**

3. **In Windows 7 and Windows Vista, click the Yes or Continue button or type the administrator's password.**

Behold the Registry Editor window on the screen, as shown in Figure 9-1.

Figure 9-1:
The Registry
Editor.

The Registry Editor window works a lot like Windows Explorer does for navigating folders on the PC's storage system: Open a key, or click the triangle next to it, to display the key's contents. Values appear on the right side of the window, as shown in Figure 9-1.

A pathname appears on the Registry Editor window status bar (at the bottom of the window), which helps you better determine which key is selected.

4. Close the Registry Editor window when you're done.

The next several sections describe various things you can do in the Registry Editor.

All the information organized into keys and values is vitally important to Windows. Don't experiment with the Registry by modifying values to see what happens. Doing so can have adverse effects on your computer.

✦ Nerds like me also point out that you can run the Registry Editor by popping up the Start menu and typing **regedit** in the Search box. Then click the Registry Editor icon that appears on the menu. This trick doesn't work, however, on every PC.

✦ You can explore the Registry, view things, waste time there. But don't view the Registry as a playground or an opportunity to discover more about your computer. Use the Registry only when you need to, such as when directed to do something by documentation or technical support people.

✦ Once upon a time, the program `regedit32` was used to edit the Registry. That's no longer the case. A program named `regedit32` still exists in Windows, but it merely runs the regular Registry Editor program, `regedit`.

Backing up the Registry

A healthy thing that any sane user does before messing with the Registry is to back it up. Back up! Back up! Back up! I shan't be sick of screaming this mantra!

Follow these steps to back up the Registry:

1. **Summon the Registry Editor, as described earlier in this chapter.**

2. **Choose File⇨Export.**

The Export Registry File window appears. It's basically a specialized version of the typical Save As dialog box.

3. **Choose a location for the backup.**

   Windows automatically selects the `System32` folder beneath the `Windows` folder. Saving the backup there works, but I recommend that you choose instead your `User Profile` (or "home") folder or save to an external device, like a media card.

4. **Type a name for the backup.**

   I name the backup based on the reason for backing up — for example, `Removing files from MRU lists`.

5. **Click the Save button to save.**

6. **Proceed with whatever you plan on doing in the Registry.**

7. **Close the Registry Editor window when you're done.**

To restore a Registry backup, choose File⇨Import in the Registry Editor.

A backup of the Registry is made when you set a restore point in Windows. In fact, a quick way to restore the Registry is simply to run System Restore. But, as with backing up the Registry, you need to ensure that you set a restore point before you modify the Registry. (See Chapter 8 for more information on System Restore.)

Modifying the Registry

You can do a number of things with the Registry:

✦ Add a new key.

✦ Add a new value.

✦ Rename a key or value.

✦ Change an existing value.

✦ Delete a key or value.

I strongly recommend that you take any of these actions only upon direction from a higher authority. The Registry isn't a playground or a place to experiment — even on your spouse's laptop.

Here are the general steps you take to modify the Registry:

1. **Start the Registry Editor.**

   Refer to the directions found earlier in this chapter.

2. **Back up the Registry.**

   See the section "Backing up the Registry," just before this section.

3. Open the key containing the item you want to modify.

The higher authority tells you the key's pathname. For example:

```
HKCU\Software\Microsoft\Windows\CurrentVersion\
    Explorer\Advanced
```

Start at the top level, the *hive*. Then open successive folders until you find the key you're looking for. The key just mentioned contains numerous settings for Windows.

4. To create a new key, follow these substeps:

a. Choose Edit⇨New⇨Key from the menu.

The new key appears, with its name (New Key #1) selected for editing.

b. Type the key's name and press Enter.

The key is created, but it's empty; it contains no values. The next step is probably to create a value for the key.

5. To create a new value, follow these substeps:

a. Choose Edit⇨New.

b. Select the data type from the New menu.

The higher authority you're referencing should specify which data type to choose. After you choose the data type, the new value appears in the key. Its name is selected, ready for renaming.

c. Type the value's name.

Creating a value doesn't set the value's data. (Well, actually, it sets the data to zero.) See Step 7 to set a value.

6. To rename a key or value, follow these substeps:

a. Select the key or value to rename.

b. Press the F2 key.

F2 is the Rename keyboard shortcut in Windows.

c. Type the new name and press Enter.

7. To change a value, follow these substeps:

a. Double-click the value to summon an editing dialog box.

The Edit dialog box that appears is customized for the type of data the value stores. Sometimes, it's a simple numeric value or string, as shown in Figure 9-2, but the Edit window can be quite complex when editing raw binary data. Again, the Registry isn't a place to tread lightly.

b. Type the new data.

c. Click OK.

**Book II
Chapter 9**

Registry Fixes

Figure 9-2:
Editing a
value in the
Registry.

8. **To delete a key or value, follow these substeps:**

   a. *Select the key or value.*

   b. *Press the Delete key on the keyboard.*

   Deleting a key deletes all the key's values and all the subkeys and all
   their values.

   c. *Click the Yes button to confirm.*

9. **Close the Registry Editor window when you're done.**

The changes you make to the Registry may or may not take effect right away.
Sometimes, you need to restart Windows to test the changes.

   ✦ See Table 9-1 for a list of common abbreviations used to describe the
   Registry hives.

   ✦ The Registry Editor window remembers which keys were open the last
   time it was used. Because of that, you may have to scroll to the top part
   of the left pane and close the top-level hives to better get around the
   various keys.

   ✦ You must be precise when creating or renaming a key or value! A mis-
   named key or value may not harm Windows, but then again it has no
   effect whatsoever.

   ✦ I don't consider web pages or advice from an Internet chat room a
   "higher authority" for modifying the Registry.

   ✦ Only when you can confirm directions from two separate sources on the
   Internet should you consider following those directions to modify the
   Registry. Even then, be sure to check that the two sources aren't just
   duplicate copies of the same information.

   ✦ One of the best sources for Registry information is the Microsoft
   support site: http://support.microsoft.com.

TIP

Test your Registry-editing prowess

If you desire to mess with the Registry, here's a tip for you: You can add to the Registry a value that suppresses the balloon tips that pop up from the notification area in Windows Vista. This value is one of those rare ones that cannot be set from within Windows itself; only by editing the Registry can you fix this annoying issue. Follow these steps:

1. **Open the Registry Editor.**

2. **Navigate to this key:**

```
HKCU\Software\Microsoft\
   Windows\CurrentVersion\
   Explorer\Advanced
```

3. **Choose Edit➪New➪DWORD (32-Bit) Value.**

4. **Name the new value** EnableBalloonTips.

That's it. Because the data for the value is automatically created at zero, the Balloon Tips feature is disabled. To enable it, you reset the value to 1 or just delete the value.

**Book II
Chapter 9**

Registry Fixes

Finding stuff in the Registry

Occasionally, you know that something exists in the Registry but you don't know *where* it exists. In these instances, you summon the power of the Registry Editor's Find command to help you locate the text or information tidbit you desire. Here's how:

1. **Start the Registry Editor.**

   Refer to directions found elsewhere in this chapter.

2. **Back up the Registry.**

   "Oh, but I'm just finding something." Sure you are. Back up anyway. Directions are found earlier in this chapter, in the section "Backing up the Registry."

3. **Scroll to the top of the left side of the window and click the word *Computer*.**

   By selecting Computer, you ensure that your search starts at the beginning of the Registry.

4. **Press Ctrl+F.**

   The Find dialog box appears, as shown in Figure 9-3.

   Enter the text you want to find — for example, the name of a file that appears in a most recently used (MRU) list.

5. **Click the Find Next button.**

6. **Review the key or value to ensure that it's the one you're looking for.**

   Depending on how detailed you were, some false positives might occur in the search.

7. **Click the Find Next button, if necessary, to locate the next tidbit in the Registry.**

8. **Do whatever task needs completing when you find what you're looking for.**

9. **Close the Registry Editor window when you're done.**

Figure 9-3:
Use the Find
dialog box
to locate
tidbits in the
Registry.

Indeed, the Registry is huge. Sometimes, a search can take a long time to complete. Yet that's why the Find command exists.

✦ I generally close the Find dialog box after the first find result. You don't have to close the dialog box, but it does get in the way.

✦ You can press the F3 key to repeat the last Find command. The F3 shortcut is handy because it lets you repeat a search without reopening the Find dialog box.

Registry Cleaning

Oh, how many times do I need to say that you don't need to mess with the Registry? I shouldn't even bother repeating myself, but I do. To bring the message home, I'd like to address the issue of cleaning the Registry. In a word: Don't.

Sure, some third-party utilities claim that they can somehow miraculously scour the Registry and remove redundant entries and unused keys and values or purge the Registry of nasty things. Although that statement might be true, it's probably not. Therefore, I don't recommend using a Registry cleaner or even attempting to do so on your own.

✦ Many of those free Registry cleaners that you download from the Internet are really spyware or some other form of malware. They serve only to slow down your computer, making the problem worse.

✦ Honestly, it would be impossible for any third-party program to know which Registry keys are useless and whether they can be deleted. To assume that any program would know that information is ridiculous.

✦ Cleaning the Registry may do more damage than good.

✦ No evidence exists that any Registry cleaning utility provides any improvement in performance.

✦ I can, however, recommend antispyware programs or other utilities that purge spyware and other nasty programs from the Registry. These programs know what to look for and, therefore, do something useful. (See Book IV, Chapter 4 for more information.)

Book III

Laptops

The 5th Wave   By Rich Tennant

DANGER
HIGH VOLTAGE
POWER LINES

"Hurry, Stuart! The power bar's almost on zero!"

Contents at a Glance

Chapter 1: Laptop Asleep, Laptop Awake, Laptop Dead

In This Chapter

✔ Dealing with start-up problems

✔ Fixing a snoozing laptop

✔ Controlling what happens when you close the lid

✔ Dealing with hibernation

✔ Fixing the power management system

✔ Checking the battery

✔ Setting battery alerts

✔ Keeping the battery happy

Consider the laptop computer. It lives a carefree existence, untethered by the wires that bind its desktop cousin. Despite its portable and wire- less benefits, the laptop suffers the same slings and arrows of outrageous misfortune as its location-consistent brethren. Even worse, because of its compact and lightweight nature, the laptop has its own, special quirks. Most of them involve the laptop's amazing ability to run on its own power, which is this chapter's subject.

Laptop Start-Up Issues

Perhaps the number-one issue that vexes laptop owners is the problem of turning on a laptop and experiencing the dread of nothing happening. Nothing. No power. No blinking lights. Nada. This section addresses those start-up issues.

✦ A computer, even a laptop, suffers problems because of a change. Did you add or change anything recently — hardware or software? Did you drop or damage the laptop? Or, perhaps the machine is suffering from the greatest change of all: time. Old laptops fail.

✦ The abbreviation *AC* is used in this section. It stands for *a*lternating *c*urrent, the type of power that comes from a wall socket, as opposed to the *d*irect *c*urrent (DC) supplied by a laptop's battery.

✦ Also see Book I, Chapter 2 for general start-up issues.

Laptop just won't start

A laptop has several phases of "just won't start." The problem with not being able to start is compounded because a laptop has two power sources: When AC isn't available, electricity is drawn from the laptop's battery. So you know immediately that when the laptop doesn't turn on right away, you have a power supply issue.

✦ If the laptop appears dead, you have a power supply issue. Check to ensure that the laptop is plugged in.

✦ Check to ensure that the battery is properly installed.

✦ Try removing the battery to run the laptop from just the AC power. If it works, you may have a defective battery that needs replacing.

✦ If you have a second battery, use it instead.

✦ Check the power brick on the AC cord. Is it the right adapter for your laptop? Other portable devices may have similar-looking adapters, but unless they match the volts and amps for your laptop, the laptop doesn't work. (Not that this has ever happened to me.)

✦ Volts and Amps would be great team names. Imagine them playing each other. It would be electric.

✦ When the laptop's power lamp is on, it shows that the laptop has some life. It means that the laptop's hardware is recognizing that it has power. The problem could then lie with the laptop's hardware, not with the power supply.

✦ When your laptop has separate lamps for the AC power and battery, you can check both to see where the problem lies. If the AC lamp lights but the battery doesn't, it's a battery issue. When the battery lamp is lit but the AC lamp remains dark, the AC power brick might be dead or the AC power from the wall might be messed up or you might have a connection issue.

✦ If you consider yourself to be technically proficient, you can try testing some hardware. For example, if the laptop has removable disk drives, check to ensure that they're properly connected: With the laptop's power off, take out the drives and put them back in again. Ditto for the PC's memory card: Turn off the laptop, remove the memory, and then put the memory back.

✦ Laptops don't start when they're broken. I'm not being flip, either: Laptop hardware can fail. Failed electronics are covered by most laptop warranties. You need to get support by contacting the laptop manufacturer.

Why you need a laptop warranty

In my book *Laptops For Dummies*, I recommend buying at least a three-year warranty on a laptop. No, you're not paying to pad the manufacturer's bottom line; you're simply taking out insurance on a product you need.

Long-term warranties are necessary for laptops because of their miniaturized nature. It's not that the manufacturers need Oompa-Loompas to fix the little gizmos; it's that, unlike on desktop PCs, laptop components cannot easily be replaced or repaired. To fix a problem with your laptop's wireless connection, for example, the entire motherboard may need to be replaced. That ain't cheap.

If you can afford a warranty longer than three years, buy one. Many manufacturers offer long-term warranties. I buy five-year warranties for my laptops, as long as I plan to use them for that length of time.

You do not, however, need to buy extended service plans. They're sold by dealers and don't provide extra coverage of laptop hardware. If you sleep better at night with an extended service plan, buy one. But, for most people, buying at least a three-year warranty serves them well.

Laptop is slow to start

Time issues are subject to perception, so the issue of "slow" is always relative. Windows Vista, for example, is notorious for looking like it finished starting up but in fact has several more seconds of gyrations to complete before you can smoothly use the laptop.

The finger of slow-start blame can be pointed equally at hardware and software. Alas, you can do little for hardware problems other than return the laptop to the shop.

On the software side, I recommend that you check the system for spyware or other types of nasty software. See Book IV, Chapter 4 for more information. Also consider defragging the hard drive, as covered in Book VI, Chapter 2.

The solution for the Windows Vista startup slowness is easy: Upgrade to Windows 7. Though the upgrade process works well, you need to ensure that your laptop has the entire state of Windows 7 drivers, or special software designed to run your laptop's power management system, touchpad, fingerprint reader, and any other type of special software that's installed. Unless you can get all those drivers, don't bother with the upgrade.

**Book III
Chapter 1**

**Laptop Asleep,
Laptop Awake,
Laptop Dead**

You have control over how much the laptop does when it starts. Running a host of start-up programs — instant messaging, webcams, Windows 7 screen gadgets or the Windows Vista Sidebar, as well as other utilities — add time to the computer's start-up process. Most of those programs can be started as you need them. Consider reconfiguring that software not to start automatically when the laptop starts.

Laptop won't wake up

A wake-up problem isn't really a start-up problem, but is, rather, a failure of the laptop's power management system. This situation arises when you put the laptop to sleep (in Stand By mode) or hibernate it. When you rouse the laptop, nothing happens.

First, try screaming at the laptop. Loudly say, "Get up!" I've found, surprisingly, that this method doesn't work.

Second, try pressing the Ctrl key on the laptop. That should rouse it out of Sleep mode. I assume, however, that you probably tried that one already.

When pressing a key on the keyboard doesn't work, press the laptop's Power button. Sometimes, that simple action thrusts the laptop back to life.

Check for a separate Sleep button on your laptop. The Sleep button may be required in order to wake up the machine, as ironic as that sounds.

Finally, press and hold the Power button until the system turns off. After it's off, restart the laptop. Of course, that fixes the symptoms but not the disease.

To fix the laptop-won't-wake-up disease, confirm that the laptop is using the most current version of the power management software. See the section "Updating power drivers," later in this chapter.

✦ Try not to scream "Get up!" in public libraries. I will not explain further why I believe this to be a bad idea.

✦ The laptop won't wake up when it's on battery power and the batteries are low or drained dry.

✦ The laptop's power lamps should be on when the laptop is in Sleep mode. If the lamps are off, the laptop has been turned off.

✦ A laptop's power lamps are often on when the laptop is plugged in. It simply means that — duh — the laptop is plugged in. Unplugging the laptop should cause the lights to turn off.

Check the display

Sometimes, the power lamps are lit but the laptop still appears to be dead or sleeping. As long as the power lamps are up, there may still be hope.

First, just as with a crashed desktop, press the Caps Lock key. The Caps Lock lamp on the laptop should blink on and off as you press the key. If so, the laptop is functioning, but the display may have a problem.

Second, check the display's brightness settings. If the brightness level is turned down too much, the screen will be dark, especially in a bright room. In that same vein, LCD displays don't work well outside or in direct sunlight. Some displays may not be backlit and may not even show up in low light.

Third, look at the screen closely to ensure that it's not working. You're looking for any signs of digital life: a flicker, a pixel. Try turning up the brightness all the way to see whether the screen glows.

Finally, plug an external monitor into the laptop's monitor port. Today's laptops are designed to instantly recognize and use these external monitors, though you may have to press a special Fn (Function) key combination to make sure. If the external monitor works, the problem is with the laptop's display only, not with the laptop's display adapter or other internal hardware.

Sadly, you cannot go to the store and buy another "laptop monitor." Because the laptop and monitor are the same thing, fixing the monitor (or the display adapter) involves replacing major laptop components. You must return the laptop to the dealer for repair.

Laptop starts and then turns off

As on a desktop PC, a laptop that starts up and shuts down right away has a hardware issue. You can try starting it in Safe mode (see Book II, Chapter 3) to see whether the problem continues. If so, it's hardware.

Another possibility is that the laptop's battery needs replacing. Even with modern battery technology, the laptop's battery wears out over time. When the battery can't be recharged, it's gone. Yes, that statement is true even when the stupid battery meter says that you have 100 percent power. If the laptop is more than three or four years old, consider getting a new battery. See the section "A Battery of Issues," later in this chapter.

✦ Is the laptop too hot? Heat and electronics do not mix! Consider getting a cooling pad for your laptop as a solution.

✦ Also refer to restarting problems in Book I, Chapter 3.

Book III
Chapter 1

Laptop Asleep,
Laptop Awake,
Laptop Dead

Laptop turns off and then immediately starts

Sometimes, a laptop demonstrates its disdain for being turned off by refusing to turn itself off. There are two causes: human error and power management problems.

Before blaming the hardware, try to remember whether you chose the Shutdown command or the Sleep command. If you chose Sleep instead, it might explain why the laptop is turning on again.

Sometimes, a laptop restarts when it's installing updates. If so, try shutting it down again.

If the laptop continually restarts, it's a problem with the power management hardware. Take the laptop into the shop.

Laptop won't stay asleep

Unlike small children, laptops must obey you when you send them to Sleep mode. But keep in mind that a computer wakes up when you press a key or move the mouse. I've even found that pounding the table next to a sensitive mouse can jar it enough to wake a PC. So, no table pounding!

When the mouse or touch pad is overly sensitive, you can check the system settings to see whether you can disable the mouse to keep it from waking the computer. See Book I, Chapter 2 for information on checking into the computer's BIOS settings. Note, however, that not every laptop has settings for Sleep mode that monitor the mouse (or keyboard).

You might consider checking the BIOS settings to ensure that the laptop isn't waking up because of network activity.

Before sending the laptop into the shop

Coming in first in the category of painful departures, second only to sending a child off to college, is sending your laptop away for fixin' at the factory. Time for some comfort food! But before you indulge, I recommend doing several things — if possible.

Back up the laptop: Your data is important to you. Your data is *not* important to the factory that fixes your laptop. Before sending any computer away, back up your stuff if you can possibly do so. This process may involve removing the hard drive and connecting it to a PC or to another laptop by using an external hard drive case to pull off the data. See Book VI, Chapter 1.

Document the problem: The people fixing your laptop need to know as much as possible about the situation. For example, is the problem predictably repeatable? Double-check what you're doing to ensure that an easy or overlooked fix isn't available.

Contact tech support: Sure, let them have fun with it. Maybe they can help you, but most likely they'll give you a case number and authorize a warranty fix.

Put the laptop in its original packaging: In my book *PCs For Dummies* (Wiley), I recommend keeping all your original computer boxes. Shipping the laptop in its original box is necessary for returning it. The original box is also good to have when you move or otherwise need to store the laptop long term.

When you're ready to send off the laptop, send it by following whatever directions you're given. Many manufacturers have web pages that help you track the laptop's progress and diagnosis. Don't expect any miracles, though: The factory will probably merely confirm that the laptop is broken, swap out the parts, and then send it back to you. Or, it may send you another laptop as a replacement. It all depends on the warranty.

What Happens When You Close the Lid

I don't have any hard data, but my guess is that a laptop computer gets started and stopped more often than a desktop computer. It's the lid. Because you can close the lid on a laptop, you can quickly pick it up and get on the road. Closing the lid, however, raises an important question: What happens when you close your laptop's lid? To find out, follow these steps:

1. **Open the Control Panel.**

2a. **In Windows 7, choose the Hardware and Sound heading and then Power Options.**

2b. **In Windows XP, open the Power Options icon.**

3a. **In Windows Vista, click the link labeled Choose What Closing the Lid Does.**

3b. **In Windows XP, click the Advanced tab.**

You see a screen that shows options for the laptop's Power button, Sleep button, and lid, similar to the ones shown in Figure 1-1.

4. **Choose a power option for the lid.**

Your choices are

Do nothing: Closing the laptop's lid does nothing; when the laptop is on, it stays on.

Hibernate: The laptop goes into Hibernation mode, saving the contents of memory and then turning off the system.

Shut down: The laptop turns itself off.

Sleep/Stand By: The laptop goes into a special low-power state.

5. **(Optional) Set the lid's function for times when the laptop is plugged in or running from battery power.**

6. **Click either the Save Changes or OK button.**

Figure 1-1:
Power
options for
closing the
laptop's lid.

When I'm on the road, I prefer to have my laptop enter Hibernation mode whenever I shut the lid. That way, it doesn't lose battery power. (I generally shut the lid when I'm done working.) At home, my laptop turns itself off when I shut the lid.

✦ If nothing happens when you close the laptop's lid, Do Nothing is probably the selected option. To change this predicament, follow this section's set of steps.

✦ Putting the laptop into Sleep mode when you shut the lid drains the battery over time. Sleep mode is fine for short durations, and the laptop recovers quickly from being in Sleep mode. But if you close the lid, put the laptop into Sleep mode, and then stick it into your backpack or laptop case, the battery drains. Nothing is more disappointing than opening your laptop on the road and finding the battery dead.

✦ Windows 7 and Windows Vista use the term *sleep;* Windows XP uses the term *Stand By*. Both refer to what's commonly called *Sleep mode*.

✦ Windows XP lacks separate Power button settings for times when the laptop is plugged in.

✦ Similar power options exist for desktop PCs, but not the "close the lid" options, for obvious reasons.

✦ The Do Nothing option might seem useless for closing the laptop's lid, but it can come in handy. For example, when using the laptop with an external monitor or keyboard, having it do nothing when you close the lid means that you can keep using the computer while keeping it in a smaller location.

Power Management Issues

The laptop's power management hardware is one of the Three Sisters of Despair when it comes to computer problems. Officially known as the Advanced Configuration and Power Interface (ACPI), it's the hardware and software specification that allows your computer to go into Sleep mode, hibernate, manage power consumption, and shut itself off. This section explores potential ways to deal with laptop power management problems.

✦ The other two sisters in the Despair trio are the display adapter and networking hardware.

✦ See Book I, Chapter 3 for general information on PC power management issues. All those issues apply to a laptop as well as to a desktop computer, in addition to the laptop-specific issues mentioned in this chapter.

✦ See Book I, Chapter 6 for information on troubleshooting PC display issues.

✦ Refer to Book V for network troubleshooting.

✦ You can see my books *Laptops For Dummies* or *PCs For Dummies* (Wiley) for an explanation of the various computer-power-saving options. If you can't decide which to buy, buy both.

✦ See my book *Laptops For Dummies* for information on customizing a power plan for your laptop.

Speeding up hibernation

Sometimes, getting into Hibernation mode can be time consuming. Be patient. The laptop will get there, but you can pull one trick to try to accelerate the process: Defragment the hard drive.

Because hibernation copies information from mass storage to memory, it pays to keep the hard drive maintained. By defragmenting the drive, you ensure that ample space is available to quickly copy swaths of memory to disk. That helps expedite not only hibernation shutdown but also start-up.

✦ Never defragment an SSD, or solid-state drive. If your laptop features one, do not defragment it!

✦ Refer to Book VI, Chapter 2 for more information on defragmenting the hard drive.

Book III
Chapter 1

Laptop Asleep,
Laptop Awake,
Laptop Dead

✦ The laptop's hard drive light may flicker as the system enters hibernation. That's normal. Expect to see the lamp lit until the system turns itself off.

Testing the power management hardware

There's no direct way to confirm that you have a boo-boo in the computer's power management software. When you try, the result is the same: You have to turn over the laptop to the manufacturer (or wherever) to get it fixed. Even on a desktop PC, the power management hardware is part of the motherboard and not something you can fix, like replacing a Lego brick.

The good news: The laptop's ACPI hardware has its own BIOS, which means that, like other BIOSes in the system, it does its own testing and diagnostics when you first start the machine. So the first place to look for power management hardware trouble is the PC's start-up screen, where you may find various power management, or ACPI, start-up error messages.

Another way to test the power management hardware is to use the System Information utility. Because some laptop manufacturers poorly implement the ACPI standard, conflicts may occur that the System Information utility would detect. Follow these steps:

1. **From the Start menu, choose All Programs⇨Accessories⇨ System Tools⇨System Information.**

2. **Click the plus sign (+) to expand the Hardware Resources list on the left side of the System Information window.**

3. **Choose Conflicts/Sharing.**

You see a list of items displayed, as shown in Figure 1-2.

The items in the list are both conflicts *and* sharing. What you probably see, shown in Figure 1-2, are shared hardware resources, which aren't a problem. But:

4. **Scan the list for any mention of power management hardware — specifically, the acronym ACPI.**

Finding something wrong with the ACPI hardware merely confirms your suspicion. Again, there's no way to fix the problem, especially by using the System Information window.

5. **Close the System Information window.**

Hardware issues, especially IRQ conflicts, aren't as prevalent in today's laptop hardware as they once were, and then primarily with PC desktops loaded with expansion cards. Even so, checking the System Information display may explain why you're having power management issues.

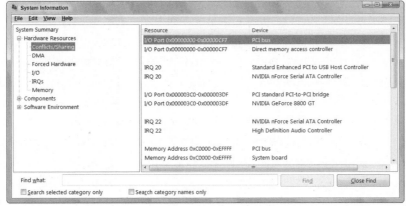

Figure 1-2:
Scanning for potential power management hardware trouble.

For example, if the power management hardware is being shared with an internal modem, you may notice power management issues when the modem is being used. That's the type of conflict the System Information window highlights. Resolving the issue involves reconfiguring the conflicting hardware, which might be possible in the BIOS/Setup program.

✦ Refer to Book 1, Chapter 1 for more information on the PC's start-up process. The details described in that chapter apply equally to desktop and laptop computers.

✦ Troubleshooting power management issues in Safe mode is difficult. That's because the power management software isn't loaded in Safe mode, which means that even if the power management hardware is broken, you have no way to test it. See Book II, Chapter 3 for more information on Safe mode.

✦ The System Information window is covered in Book II, Chapter 7.

Updating power drivers

Most often, power management issues are resolved by obtaining the latest version of your laptop's ACPI power management software, or *device driver*. Ensuring that you have the latest version is something you should do; the Windows Update program may not look for new power management software for you.

The easy way to check for new power management software is to follow these steps:

1. **Press Win+Break to quickly summon the System window or System dialog box.**

Book III
Chapter 1

Laptop Asleep,
Laptop Awake,
Laptop Dead

2a. **In Windows 7 and Windows Vista, click the link on the left side of the window: Device Manager.**

2b. **In Windows XP, click the Hardware tab in the System Properties dialog box, and then click the Device Manager button.**

3. **In Windows Vista, click the Continue button or type the administrator's password.**

The Device Manager window appears on the screen.

4. **Open the System Devices item by clicking the plus sign (+).**

5. **Right-click Microsoft ACPI-Compliant System.**

6. **Choose the shortcut menu item Update Driver Software.**

7. **Heed the instructions onscreen.**

You might also try repeating these directions, but use the item titled Microsoft ACPI-Compliant Embedded Controller in Step 5. (Indeed, you can choose any item with ACPI in it if it seems to be the source of trouble, such as the ACPI Lid item when you're having issues with the laptop not sleeping when you close the lid.)

The automatic method described in these steps may not work. In that case, you must visit the laptop manufacturer's web site. Search the Support section for your PC's make and model for any new power management drivers.

✦ Some web sites offer a scanning utility that can confirm whether the laptop's software is up-to-date. Use these tools!

✦ Do not remove any ACPI entries, because doing so may disable some of your laptop's power management features, such as the ability to sleep the laptop by pressing the Power button. Also, it's a *real pain* to reinstall these features after they've been removed.

✦ See Book II, Chapter 1 for more information on Windows Update.

✦ See Book I, Chapter 7 for a discussion of the Device Manager.

A Battery of Issues

The key to unlocking the door of laptop freedom is the battery. You must care for the laptop's battery with loving affection. This section has some tips and suggestions.

Monitoring battery life

Your laptop may be fortunate enough to provide you with *two* battery meters, and perhaps more. You're the lucky one, indeed. Imagine a car with two fuel gauges.

No, a car with two fuel gauges doesn't work the same. Unless the car has two gas tanks, having two fuel gauges is obsessive and sad. No, laptops are special.

The first battery meter is found on the laptop's case, along with other fancy lamps: power, hard drive, Caps Lock, Num Lock, and wireless activity, for example. The lamp may be solid, or it might fade over time or change colors. Although such a thing is handy, it's only for show. You need more information, which is why Windows provides you with a second software battery meter.

The second battery meter is found in Windows, in the notification area, as shown in Figure 1-3. The tiny icon appears in two ways: one when the laptop is plugged in or charging and another when the battery is being used. In the latter case, the icon drains as the battery is used.

Figure 1-3:
The battery
meter.

Book III
Chapter 1

Laptop Asleep,
Laptop Awake,
Laptop Dead

In Windows 7 and Windows Vista, click the Battery/Power Plug icon to display the battery meter; the Windows 7 version is shown in Figure 1-3. In Windows XP, point the mouse at the battery meter and a pop-up balloon appears, detailing battery life.

The battery meter is supposed to show up in the notification area on all Windows laptops. If you don't see it, you can twist some arms to get it to show up.

In Windows 7 and Windows Vista, follow these steps to show the battery icon in the notification area:

1. **Right-click the date and time on the far right end of the taskbar.**

2. **Choose Properties from the pop-up menu.**

   In Windows 7, the System Icons window appears, listing the notification icons that belong to Windows with an On/Off menu button by each item.

   In Windows Vista, the Taskbar and Start Menu Properties dialog box appears, with the Notification Area tab forward. The check mark items in the bottom of the dialog box control Windows own notification icons.

3a. **In Windows 7, choose On from the menu button by the Power item.**

3b. **In Windows Vista, place a check mark by the Power item.**

4. Click OK.

In Windows XP, obey these directions to make the notification area (well, the system tray) Battery icon appear:

1. **Open the Control Panel's Power Options icon.**

2. **Click the Advanced tab.**

3. **Place a check mark by the item Always Show Icon on the Taskbar.**

4. **Click OK.**

Your laptop may feature, in addition to the hardware battery meter and the teensy Battery icon in the notification area, a third meter. Some laptops feature a manufacturer's battery meter. It might be a toolbar, an extra icon in the notification area, or another tool or feature.

✦ If you're a fan of the onscreen gadgets in Windows 7 or the Windows Vista Sidebar, various battery-power gadgets are available.

✦ Good meters show both battery percentage remaining and time remaining.

✦ The length of battery time remaining is an estimate. Don't bet the bank on it.

✦ The battery meter lies. Generally, the meter skews toward being full more than it shows a steady decline representing the battery's true power. So don't be surprised when the battery power drops quickly as it gets low; when the meter claims that you have 15 minutes left, you probably have more like 7 minutes until the laptop runs out of juice.

Setting low battery warnings

Windows can be configured to assault you with various low-battery warnings. Furthermore, you can configure Windows to automatically hibernate or shut down your laptop when the battery gets *way* too low.

In Windows 7 and Windows Vista, follow these nimble directions to set the low-battery-power warnings:

1. **Open the Control Panel.**

2. **Choose Hardware and Sound, and then choose Power Options.**

3. **By the selected power plan, click the Change Plan Settings link.**

4. **Click the Change Advanced Power Settings link.**

The Power Options dialog box shows up.

5. **Click the plus sign (+) by Battery.**

You see five items for consideration, each with settings available for when the laptop is plugged in or on battery power. The items are in chronological order:

Low Battery Notification: Turns on a warning for when the battery power gets low, as set by the Low Battery Level item.

Low Battery Level: Determines at which percentage the Low Battery Notification warning appears. The value is set as a percentage of battery life.

Low Battery Action: Specifies what happens when the battery reaches the Low Battery Level warning. Options are Do Nothing, Hibernate, Sleep, and Shut Down.

Critical Battery Level: Determines at which percentage the critical battery action takes place. Values are set as a percentage of battery life and must be lower than the Low Battery Level values.

Critical Battery Action: Specifies what happens when the battery reaches the percentage set by the Critical Battery Level. Options for On Battery are Hibernate, Sleep, and Shutdown. The additional option of Do Nothing is available for when the laptop is plugged in.

Additional items might be available, which would be specific to your laptop. For example, my Lenovo laptop has a Reserve battery level, which sits between the Low and Critical levels.

6. **Set the values for the various warnings, levels, and actions.**

7. **Click OK and (optional) close the Edit Plan Settings window.**

In Windows XP, obey these directions to set various battery warnings:

1. **Open the Control Panel's Power Options icon.**

2. **Click the Alarms tab.**

3. **Place a check mark by the item Activate Low Battery Alarm When Power Level Reaches.**

4. **Use the slider to set the battery percentage level for the Low Battery alarm.**

   Ten percent seems like a good level.

5. **Click the Alarm Actions button.**

6. **Choose what happens when the alarm kicks in.**

   For example, specify Sound Alarm or Display Message. Add an action, such as Hibernate, Sleep, or Shut Down.

7. **Click OK to close the Alarm Actions dialog box.**

8. **Repeat Steps 3 through 7 for the Critical Battery alarm.**

9. **Click OK to close the Power Options Properties dialog box.**

The visual warnings you specify appear as shown in Figure 1-4. Obey them!

Figure 1-4:
A low-
battery-
power
warning.

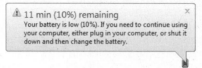

It might make no sense to have options for low and critical battery levels when the laptop is plugged in, but consider what happens when the battery is charging: If you plug in a laptop when its battery is low and the Plugged In setting for Critical Battery Action is set to Shut Down, the laptop turns itself off even when it's plugged in.

Swapping batteries

Unlike flashlights, toys, and television remotes, laptops don't share a common battery size and shape. They may in the future (let's hope), but for now — nope. So, although you cannot swap batteries with another laptop user (unless they have *exactly* the same kind of battery), you can buy your laptop a second battery and use the battery to prolong battery life.

Whether your laptop came with two batteries or you purchased one after the fact, swapping batteries works simply:

1. **Charge the spare battery.**

   No point in swapping in a dead battery. . . .

2. **Save all your stuff before the swap.**

3. **Have the spare battery at hand.**

4. **Eject the laptop's battery.**

5. **Insert the spare.**

6. **Continue working.**

Your laptop has the ability to keep itself alive while the batteries are being swapped. As long as you do so immediately, you should be able to remove the battery and replace it with no interruption in computing (though the screen may go blank).

   ✦ Use a Sharpie to label batteries. Name them A and B or Fred and Ethel. That way, you don't mistakenly swap in the same battery. Avoid using tape or any sticky substance to label a battery, because the sticky stuff is adversely affected by the battery's heat.

✦ If you discover that your laptop cannot survive swapping, shut down or hibernate the laptop first. After swapping batteries, turn the laptop on again.

✦ Laptop batteries are charged in the laptop. After charging the first battery in the laptop, remove it and charge the second.

✦ Some laptops come with external battery chargers. If your laptop has one, use it. Some companies may have a rack charger for a whole host of batteries. If you're obsessive, you can buy one for your house. Put it in the "sewing room" that no one uses.

✦ Be sure to store the extra battery properly. I put mine into a Ziploc bag and then into my laptop case.

✦ I hope that the nice people at Johnson & Johnson see my Ziploc plug in this book and send me a whole crate of Ziploc bags.

✦ As this book goes to press, keep in mind that you aren't allowed to pack spare laptop batteries in your checked luggage, only in your carry-on baggage. Furthermore, the Transportation Security Administration (TSA) prefers that you cover the spare battery's terminals with electrical tape and store the battery in a clear plastic bag.

Prolonging battery life

There are many things you can do to get the most from your laptop's battery. Aside from not turning on your laptop, here are my suggestions for prolonging the laptop's battery life:

✦ Craft yourself a viable power management program in Windows. See *Laptops For Dummies* (which I wrote) for steps and suggestions.

✦ Turn down the laptop monitor's brightness level when it's using battery power. Some laptops do this automatically, as part of the power management system.

✦ Create a power plan that spins down the laptop's hard drive after a few minutes of use.

✦ Avoid using the optical drive while on battery power. The battery drains faster than when you're watching a movie on your laptop.

✦ Mute the speakers.

✦ Avoid accessing the network while on battery power.

✦ Disabling the wireless networking adapter also saves power.

✦ Try to use the laptop's dialup modem only when the laptop is connected to a power source. Modems drain battery power, and usually when you're near a phone jack, you can find a wall socket nearby. Use it.

✦ Battery usage statistics are calculated under ideal circumstances. Though your laptop manufacturer may boast that the battery lasts for a full three hours, expect less time.

Maintaining the battery

Your laptop's battery isn't immortal. No, I'm referring not to its ongoing ability to drain as you use it but, rather, to its demise over time. Eventually, even the smartest smart battery becomes useless.

There's nothing extra you need to do to maintain a laptop's battery. You don't even need to remove it regularly to clean its terminals. Except on laptops where I have two batteries available, I don't think I've ever removed a battery from my laptops.

Bottom line: Maintaining the laptop's battery is easy.

✦ When you're storing a laptop for a long time (say, more than a month), remove the battery and store it separately. That way, if the battery leaks, it doesn't wreck the laptop.

✦ When storing a battery, put it in a dry location where it won't be disturbed or come into contact with metal.

✦ A battery not used or stored for a period of time loses its charge. Blame the planet earth. (I hear a lawsuit is in the works.)

✦ Do not throw away old batteries! Always dispose of a computer battery properly, according to the hazardous waste regulations for your locality.

✦ Never drop a laptop battery, get it wet, open it, or place it in a fire.

✦ Generally speaking, don't do anything to the battery that an intoxicated person would do, especially just before they would say, "Hey, check this out."

✦ Don't manually drain a battery by shorting it. For example, don't connect the battery terminals by using a wire. That causes fires.

✦ Keep the battery's temperature even. Avoid situations where the battery may get too hot or too cold. Like Goldilocks, your laptop battery likes temperatures that are *just right*.

✦ The longer you own the laptop and use its battery, the less performance you'll see from it. After about three years, buy your laptop a replacement battery and use it. Dispose of the original battery in the manner proper for your locale.

Chapter 2: A More Usable Laptop

In This Chapter

✔ Creating a laptop base station

✔ Choosing devices for a stationary laptop

✔ Keeping the laptop cool

✔ Making the screen larger

✔ Typing with the On-Screen Keyboard

At first glance, today's laptop resembles yesterday's laptop in almost every way. The newer laptop is faster and lighter, has better graphics, and lasts longer between charges. Beyond that, the limitations of a laptop are based on human qualities: Your eyeballs, fingers, and lap aren't getting smaller, to keep up with ever-shrinking technology. Yeah, especially the lap. To help you deal with the laptop computer's unique constraints, this chapter offers some suggestions for making the laptop a more usable gizmo.

A Home for the Laptop

The laptop may be a merry wanderer of the earth, but eventually it comes home to roost. Just where does it roost? This section is about creating that useful place for your laptop.

Making the laptop feel at home

When you're out on the road all the time, you might settle on keeping the laptop in its case when you're home. That works. It's handy. I've done it — snaking the power cord out of the case and into a handy wall socket. But, for many of us road warriors, the laptop shares a place of prominence when it returns home or to the office. Do your laptop a favor and make its laptop lounging location feel like home.

♦ I recommend that you have a home for your laptop — a place to put it for recharging, connecting to the local network, and perhaps even adding some big-boy desktop toys, described in the next section.

♦ As with a desktop computer, make your laptop's home in a sturdy, well-ventilated place — maybe even have a vase of flowers nearby, to add some cheer.

+ Yes, you have to get new flowers when the old ones turn all crumbly and dead.

+ Keep the laptop out of the sun or anywhere else it might get too hot.

+ If the laptop must be in the sun, do not apply sunscreen to the laptop.

+ If you're using a security device to anchor the laptop, find a home for your laptop near a permanent item to which you can attach the security cable.

+ Even though the laptop is anchored by a security cable, you still need to protect your laptop's data. Use a password on your account! (Students in college dormitories seem to forget this point.)

+ Allow plenty of room around the laptop's home for adding external devices, as described in the next section.

+ Although you can use a laptop on a coffee table or kitchen table or anywhere in your home, these locations do not make good permanent places for Mr. Laptop. Think *dedicated* laptop home.

+ When the laptop arrives home after an arduous journey, offer it some cookies or a beer. When the laptop refuses, ask whether you can have the snacks and beverages yourself. Most laptops silently concede.

Selecting devices for the laptop

Of the many types of gizmos you can buy for your laptop, I like to lump them into two categories: portable and stationary. The difference between the two categories has to do with bulk and power requirements. Not only that, but some devices are also better suited for a laptop's permanent abode.

Portable devices are the gizmos you take with you on the road. My book *Laptops For Dummies* (Wiley) lists a slew of them. For the laptop at home, consider some devices that are not only less portable but can also boost the laptop's potential at a single location. Here's a rundown of some gizmos to consider:

Monitor: Every laptop features a handy way to connect an external monitor. Normally, the connection is used for a video projector to make presentations. But you can still connect a normal, stand-alone PC monitor, such as a widescreen LCD monitor.

Full-size keyboard: I must confess that PC laptops sport nice keyboards that serve the devices well. As a typing snob, I enjoy the larger PC keyboard, with its roomier layout and separate numeric keypad. Honestly, giving a laptop a full-size keyboard at its home location gives you the best of both desktop and portable PC worlds.

Mouse: I believe that every laptop, portable or stationary, benefits from having a real mouse. Some smaller-than-normal wireless mice prove ideal for road use. Back home, however, having a good, palm-size mouse with a wide assortment of buttons and an ominous, glowing LED is better.

Printer: I suppose that if your laptop is your only computer, connecting a printer to it when you get home is a good idea. The printer may be an optional item, however: For most folks, accessing a printer is done through the network. As long as the laptop is connected to a network at home (either wired or wireless), you can access and use any printer available on the network.

External storage: As a huge fan of backups, I recommend buying your laptop a hefty external hard drive for its at-home base. Furthermore, if you have a lighter laptop (a *subnotebook*) without an optical drive, get your laptop a nice optical drive for its at-home resting place.

Powered USB hub: Most external gizmos you add to your laptop are USB devices. Just plug them into the laptop's USB port — until you run out of laptop USB ports. In that case, set up a powered USB hub. By *powered,* I mean that the hub plugs into the wall. A powered USB hub accepts a wider variety of devices than does a portable, nonpowered USB hub.

Arranging these goodies works just like setting up a desktop PC, but you leave everything in place and awaiting the arrival of the laptop. Yeah, it's kind of like a shrine awaiting an idol. When the laptop arrives, plug, plug, plug everything in and you're ready to go. Well, *stay.* Okay, you know what I mean.

**Book III
Chapter 2**

A More Usable Laptop

TIP

✦ A great way to set up a laptop shrine is to perch the thing atop a tiny riser or shelf. That way, the laptop's screen is at eyeball height when you work. People who fix bad backs and necks tell me that having a computer monitor at eyeball height is ideal.

✦ Getting an external optical drive is a must for a laptop without an optical drive, especially for installing software.

✦ Obviously, if your laptop has a widescreen monitor (as many of them do), you would have no need to connect an external monitor. That is, unless you want to use two monitors at a time. See the second-monitor info in Book I, Chapter 6.

✦ If all you need is a numeric keypad, you can forgo a separate, full-size keyboard and get just a numeric keypad. Many of them are USB-powered and highly portable.

✦ You need a USB keyboard in order to expand your laptop. Nearly all keyboards sold today are USB.

✦ You can also add a desktop scanner to the list of stationary items, though I found some nifty portable scanners that are worth looking into.

Some of them not only are light and skinny but also run off the laptop's USB port. That makes them helpful for a swift scan when on the road.

✦ Newer laptops come with mini-VGA connectors, which are smaller than standard VGA monitor jacks. The mini-VGA has the advantage of being able to communicate with more optical devices, though you need to keep a stock of adapters to hook up the variety.

Cooling Mr. Laptop

A lot of hardware problems are caused by heat, and nothing turns up the heat like a laptop. Therefore, I suggest that you bless your laptop with a breath of fresh air by giving it a cooling pad, such as the one shown in Figure 2-1.

The cooling pad makes an ideal place mat on which to set your laptop. Even better, most cooling pads are USB powered, which means that they work by plugging into a USB port. That makes the thing portable — a bonus.

Laptops get hotter than desktops because of their diminutive size. A smaller case makes it more difficult to keep hardware cool. Furthermore, the laptop's processor just oozes heat. Although the laptop is designed to deal with the heat, using a cooling pad makes things better. It may also prolong the laptop's life by keeping its electronics at a more even temperature.

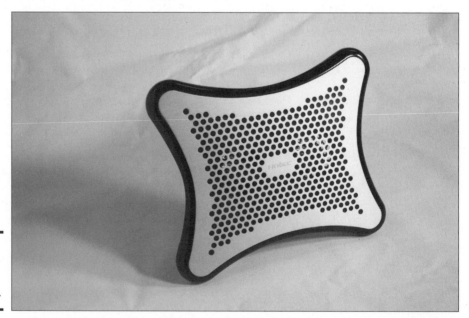

Figure 2-1:
A typical
laptop
cooling pad.

Handy Laptop Utilities

Portable computing has always had its drawbacks. As mentioned earlier in this chapter, a keyboard can be only so small before human fingers cannot use it. Some laptops feature lovely widescreen monitors, but at a trade-off with battery life and weight. Where compromises can't be made, you can find software solutions. They come in the form of utilities that help make using your laptop a tad easier.

The tools and utilities described in this section are part of the Ease of Access tools in newer versions of Windows. These tools aren't available in Windows XP.

Using the Windows Mobility Center

A handy keyboard shortcut to know for your laptop is Win+X, which is the Windows key and the X key on the keyboard. Pressing this key combination conjures forth the Windows Mobility Center, similar to the one shown in Figure 2-2.

Figure 2-2:
The
Windows
Mobility
Center.

**Book III
Chapter 2**

**A More Usable
Laptop**

The Windows Mobility Center offers quick access to popular laptop features in Windows, including battery status, wireless networking, external monitor, and other features, as shown in Figure 2-2.

Your laptop may come with additional items in the Windows Mobility Center — items added and customized by your laptop's manufacturer. For example, on my Lenovo laptop are keyboard lighting options, a screen magnifier, hardware stability protection, and other items I never use.

The biggest problem with the Windows Mobility Center is remembering that it's there. Also, having the weirdo Win+X keyboard combination doesn't help: What's up with the letter *X?*

Magnifying the screen

One of the Windows Ease of Access features is the Magnifier program, as shown in Figure 2-3. It has two parts: a control window where you can set various options and the main magnifier window.

The magnifier window is what you use to better see a portion of the display. The window follows the action — either the mouse pointer or the location where you're typing. That part of the screen appears as much as 16 times larger, which can make using a small laptop screen more bearable.

To start the Magnifier, from the Start menu choose All Programs⇨Accessories⇨Ease of Access⇨Magnifier. The screen blinks and blanks for a second, and then you see the two windows (refer to Figure 2-3). Or, if you've used the Magnifier before, the control window may not appear.

To use the Magnifier, first make settings in the control window. In Windows 7, summon the window by clicking the mouse in the Magnifier. Click the Gear icon to see more options and settings.

Magnifier window

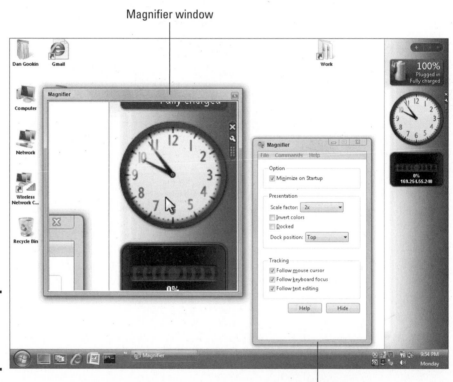

Figure 2-3:
The
Magnifier in
action.

Control window

In Windows Vista, the control window (shown in Figure 2-3) might be minimized to the taskbar; click its button, named Magnifier, to restore it. After making any necessary adjustments, you can minimize the control window to better use the magnifier window.

To close the magnifier window, right-click its toolbar button and choose the command Close Window or Close from the pop-up menu.

✦ The magnifier window remains on top of all other windows, allowing you to see what you're doing, but in a larger size.

✦ I recommend undocking the magnifier window. To do so, remove the check mark by the Docked option in the control window. Then you can resize and move the magnifier window just as you can mess with any window on the display.

✦ You cannot move the magnifier window when it's docked, but you can make it wider or taller.

✦ You can increase the magnification size by choosing a new value from the Scale Factor button in the control window.

Typing on the On-Screen Keyboard

Unless you have one of those aircraft-carrier-size laptops with a wide screen, your portable puppy probably lacks a full-size keyboard. For most purposes, you can get by with using a standard laptop keyboard just fine; it has an embedded numeric keypad; plus, smaller keys ring the main typewriter keys along with an Fn key for doing various and useful things.

At those times when you're desperate for a full-size keyboard, however, you can summon the On-Screen Keyboard utility, fondly called "the OSK" and shown in Figure 2-4.

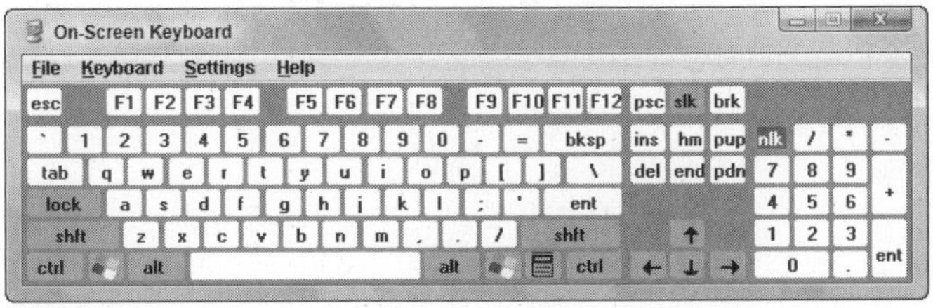

**Book III
Chapter 2**

A More Usable Laptop

Figure 2-4:
The
On-Screen
Keyboard.

The OSK gives you mouse pointer access to full-size keyboard luxury right there on your laptop's screen. Because it's really an Ease of Access tool, it's not a rapid or sneaky way of doing things. Nope, it's just a handy alternative.

To view the On-Screen Keyboard, choose All Programs⇨Accessories⇨Ease of Access⇨On-Screen Keyboard from the Start menu. The On-Screen

Keyboard window shows up, floating atop all other windows on the screen (refer to Figure 2-4).

Use the On-Screen Keyboard by plucking out keys with the mouse pointer. Clicking a shift key (Shift, Alt, or Ctrl) locks the key for one keystroke. "Pressing" Ctrl+S, for example, is done by clicking either Ctrl key and then clicking the S.

You can still use the laptop's keyboard while you use the On-Screen Keyboard. In fact, you can press and hold a shift key on the laptop's keyboard to affect the OSK display.

✦ You can view a smaller version of the OSK by choosing Keyboard⇨Standard Keyboard from its menu.

✦ To ensure that the OSK window always stays on top of other windows, choose Settings⇨Always On Top.

✦ Tablet PCs feature a special input mode, using something called the Input Panel. For more details on using it, as well as on using a stylus for input directly on the tablet screen, see my book *Laptops For Dummies*.

✦ In the battle to be Top Window on the Screen, the Magnifier kicks the On-Screen Keyboard's butt. You can bring the OSK forward, however, by clicking its window. Hovering the mouse pointer outside the OSK window pops the magnifier window upfront again.

Chapter 3: Out on the Road

In This Chapter

- ✓ Finding the perfect laptop bag
- ✓ Putting stuff into the laptop bag
- ✓ Checking things before you go
- ✓ Breezing through airport security
- ✓ Using your laptop on a plane

*I*t's difficult to believe, but a few people who own laptop computers never take them anywhere. I find that odd. Well, I suppose that others may take their desktop computers everywhere, though I've never seen anyone on a transcontinental flight retrieve a full-size PC from the storage area beneath the seat in front of them. Regardless, this chapter is the one you turn to for advice and help when you take your laptop on the road.

The Elsewhere Laptop

It's entirely possible to disconnect your laptop from the wired world and prance merrily out the door with it. Well, maybe not *prance*. The notion is that portable computing involves several degrees of freedom.

A few times, I've quickly yanked my laptop from its home office perch and gone out on the road. A few times, indeed. Most often, before you leave, a few things are worthy of preparation. Those things are covered in this section.

Choosing a proper laptop bag

I highly recommend that you find a dedicated case or bag for your laptop. It *needs* one. Nothing fancy, nothing expensive. The variety is out there, and most backpacks and briefcases these days are designed to accommodate laptop computers.

Ensure that your laptop bag comfortably fits the laptop. The last thing you want is your laptop bouncing around inside an empty space. Worse, you don't want to waste space and weight for filler foam and pads. Likewise, avoid a case where the laptop fits too snugly; your future laptop may be smaller or larger and when you plan ahead, you can continue to use the same laptop bag.

Find a case that has room for the laptop's power brick and various cables and portable goodies, plus a smattering of office supplies.

Don't go too big! The ideal laptop case size is one that fits easily beneath an airline seat.

Finally, look for protection. The case should be soft enough that minor abuse doesn't damage the laptop. I prefer zippers on the case because the laptop is less likely to slide out or to be damaged by snaps.

✦ My favorite laptop case is a soft Eddie Bauer briefcase. Second to that model is a standard, though rugged, backpack. The backpack is nice for those trips when I need a lot of accessories that don't fit into the Eddie Bauer case. Also, I can hoist the backpack over my shoulders, which keeps my hands free: one for the coffee and another for the airline ticket.

✦ The manufacturer's case may not be your best choice. I'm not saying that it's a *bad* choice — just that you should review other options and decide for yourself.

✦ Avoid any laptop case that has the manufacturer's name or the word *laptop* emblazoned on the outside. A backpack with a laptop inside is just another backpack, but a laptop case with the word *laptop* or *Dell* in a bold font on it is a target for thieves.

Packing the laptop bag

In addition to the laptop itself are a few things you should put into the laptop bag. Here's a list of stuff to consider:

✦ Power brick and cord

✦ Spare battery

✦ Ethernet cable

✦ Portable mouse

✦ Headphones

✦ Lock or cable

✦ Screen wipes

✦ Phone cord, if you plan to use the laptop's modem

✦ Media items (thumb drives, media card reader, or optical discs, for example)

✦ PC Cards and other types of adapters (such as cellular modems) you plan to use

I list the portable mouse, but it shouldn't be the only USB gizmo you toss into the bag. The variety of small, portable USB devices is almost endless, so consider putting a few of your favorites into the laptop bag.

Additionally, have a smattering of office supplies in your laptop bag. You know: pens, paper, sticky notes, paper clips, highlighters, stress toys, or anything else you'd find handy while you use the computer.

If you have a video projector, you can pack it in your laptop case or use its own case. (I put my video projector in my checked luggage when I travel.)

Checking stuff before you leave

With your laptop at the ready, go on the road boldly, but be prepared. Here's a checklist of things to peruse before you leave:

✦ Back up. See Book VI, Chapter 1.

✦ Charge the battery.

✦ Charge the spare battery.

✦ Check with the Windows Update service to ensure that you have the latest updates. Install them before you leave. See Book II, Chapter 1.

✦ Synchronize files between the desktop and laptop if necessary. Refer to my book *Laptops For Dummies* (Wiley) for the details.

✦ Ensure that you have copies of necessary passwords, either in your head or "hidden in plain sight" in your laptop bag.

✦ If you're traveling overseas, remember to take a power adapter.

**Book III
Chapter 3**

Out on the Road

Regarding Windows Update, you must not allow the laptop to automatically install updates when you're on the road, or anywhere on the go. Especially in more recent editions of Windows, updates install when you shut down the laptop. The updates not only keep the laptop on longer than expected but can also screw things up if the battery dies in the middle of an update.

After you install any available Windows updates, I recommend that you reset the Windows Update options. Select the setting that checks for, but doesn't download or install, the updates. By doing so, you prevent surprise updates.

When you return from the road, or whenever you're in a place where you have a solid Internet connection and a power supply, you can install updates. Allow yourself plenty of time because some updates tend to take several minutes to download, and perhaps a restart or two.

See Book II, Chapter 1 for details on how to configure Windows Update.

Resuming life after you travel

After returning your laptop to its home (covered in Chapter 2), you have a few things to accomplish. The two main things you need to do are charge the laptop again and resync your files.

Charging the laptop is easy: Plug it in.

Resyncing files can be a rather complex issue. In fact, I believe that Windows makes it more complex than necessary, whether you're using the older Briefcase application or the newer Windows Sync program. Other alternatives exist, however, as discussed at the end of this section.

One thing you might want to avoid after coming home is reconnecting to the network if the laptop is coming out of hibernation. Because the laptop was hibernated, it retains its previous network connection settings. In a wireless network, no issues should crop up. But, for a wired network, your laptop may still cling to its previous IP address, which can wreak havoc with the current network. Disconnect the laptop from the network, restart it, and then reconnect.

✦ The topic of synchronizing files between desktop and laptop computers is covered in depth in my book *Laptops For Dummies*.

✦ I prefer not to use the crazy Windows synchronization schemes. Instead, I use the network to copy to the laptop any files I need, and then I copy them all back when I'm done.

✦ Projects that I keep bouncing between laptop and desktop find a good home on a thumb drive instead. That way, I don't need to worry about synchronization, though I do remember to back up the thumb drive from time to time.

✦ Let me rant on synchronization some more: One thing that Windows doesn't synchronize is your email folder. To resolve this conundrum, I recommend leaving your email on the server when you're on the road. See Book IV, Chapter 3 for details.

✦ To fix the IP issue, do not connect your laptop to a wired network when you first bring it back home or to the office — specifically, when rousing the laptop from hibernation. Instead, shut down the laptop, connect the network, and then start up the laptop again. That should resolve any network conflicts.

✦ See Book V for network troubleshooting.

Life in the Air

I always get a teeny thrill when I whip out my laptop above the 10,000-foot level in an airplane. I get an even bigger thrill when I actually get work done and don't end up playing *Spider Solitaire* the whole time. This section has some tips for using your laptop whilst traveling aloft. Sadly, it doesn't feature any suggestions that will motivate you toward working rather than playing or watching a movie on your laptop.

Getting through security

I suppose the airport security people somehow got wind of the news that laptop PCs, just like all computers, will *crash*. That information alarmed the security people. They're naïve about technology, so it would be easy to believe that laptop computers are a security threat. Whatever. I'm not going to debate the government here (as much as I'm tempted).

The airport security situation is a fact of life. Well, unless your life is *really* good, in which case you don't fly commercial airlines and there is no security issue. Then again, you probably have a well-dressed minion toting your laptop and a paid tech staff to advise you. So I don't waste time with you, especially because you're probably not even reading this book anyway. For the rest of us, the laptop presents a special issue in the airport security line.

A laptop must dwell in its own bin. To be x-rayed, the laptop must be placed in a bin by itself (though I also put my cellphone in the same bin). Put your shoes, laptop bag, keys, coat, hand grenades, and other personal items in a separate bin.

Laptops must be x-rayed. The x-ray machine doesn't harm the laptop, nor does it "erase" any digital memory cards.

Grab your laptop from the bin *first* when you exit the metal detector. Place the laptop immediately back into your laptop bag. Then gather your phone and keys and other items. You don't want someone pilfering your laptop while you're desperately struggling to put on your shoes at the security gate.

As this book goes to press, the Transportation Security Administration (TSA) is allowing laptops to traverse the x-ray machines in their own bags, as long as the bags meet certain criteria. How do you know? The bag says so when you buy it. If the bag doesn't say it's approved, it's not. Simple.

✦ Send your laptop through the x-ray machine last. First, send your luggage, shoes, coat, and other items. Then send the laptop last, and in its own bin. That way, you can gather your belongings and then be ready for the laptop when it arrives on the exit side of the security area.

✦ The key to successfully navigating security is to *pay attention*. Don't chat it up with others, and don't be distracted. Focus on your immediate task, and recognize that the short, annoying experience and suspension of your Fourth Amendment rights will soon be over.

✦ A laptop occupies a separate bin because it helps the security people identify the laptop as a laptop. It also helps you better keep track of it.

✦ The bins used by the TSA in the United States remind me of the old *bus tubs* I used when I was a busboy at a restaurant long, long ago.

✦ Typically, the TSA-approved bag style is flat — either a pouch or sleeve design or a folding flat bag. The bag lacks pockets, and the TSA prefers that no other items be inside it but the laptop, which in my opinion makes for a lousy laptop bag. Even then, security personnel may ask that you remove the laptop from the TSA-approved bag if they cannot see a clear image on the scanner.

✦ Way back when laptops weren't commonplace, the airport security people required that you open and turn on the laptop — to prove that it was a laptop and not an empty laptop case filled with C4 explosives. I remember opening a laptop for airport security in the early 1990s and discovering that its battery was dead. The security guy waved me through anyway. The fool.

Storing the laptop

Earlier in this chapter, I recommend getting a laptop bag. If you travel by air, I must *insist* that you get a laptop bag. Furthermore, I'm making this admonishment:

Do not put your laptop in checked luggage.

The risk of putting your laptop in checked luggage is not that it might be stolen. Although it's always a possibility, the odds are greater that your laptop will be damaged in checked luggage. Rough handling and the weight of other bags can crack the screen. Spilled liquids can render your laptop useless. Nope, it's just better to put the laptop in its own bag.

When onboard, put the laptop bag under the seat in front of you. Placing the laptop bag at your feet gives you quick access to the laptop and all the goodies in your laptop bag; you don't have to stand up or have others move when you need to retrieve or store the laptop.

✦ Keep the laptop bag with you. Do not lose sight of it. (You know that I'm serious here because I wrote *do not* rather than the friendlier *don't*.)

✦ Obviously, when you plan to use your laptop on an airplane, try not to get a bulkhead seat. These seats have no storage space beneath the seats in front of them because there *are* no seats in front of them.

✦ Don't ask the pilot to store the laptop under his seat.

✦ Never put your laptop in the seatback pocket. You will forget it. Plus, who knows what gloopy evil lurks in the seatback pocket?

Using your laptop in the air

The most important thing you need to do when using your laptop in the air is to *disable the wireless network*. That is, unless the airplane offers wireless network access and you don't mind paying through the nose for it. If not, I still recommend turning off the wireless network because it consumes battery power.

Turning off the wireless network is cinchy on most laptops — specifically, the type that features a hardware On-Off switch for wireless networking. In that case, slide the switch to the Off position. You're set.

When your laptop lacks a wireless networking hardware switch, you have to disable the wireless networking software. I recommend that you do so before you get on the plane, but I've had to make the switch in the air and lived to tell about it, so I assume that you'll be given a little slack as well if you forget.

To disable wireless networking in Windows 7 and Windows Vista, follow these steps:

1. **Press Win+X to summon the Windows Mobility Center.**

2. **Click the button labeled Turn Wireless Off.**

3. **Close the window.**

**Book III
Chapter 3**

Out on the Road

In Windows XP, you have to follow a different set of steps when there's no hardware wireless switch:

1. **Open the Control Panel's Network Connections icon.**

2. **Right-click the wireless network connection.**

3. **Choose Disable from the shortcut menu.**

4. **Close the Network Connections window.**

After you're certain that the wireless networking hardware has been disabled, it's time to work! Using your laptop in the air works just like using it anywhere, though it's less comfortable and the milieu sucks.

✦ Use your laptop only when the flight crew announces that it's okay to do so. Likewise, when they tell you to turn off the laptop, don't hesitate.

✦ You most likely want to reenable the wireless networking hardware after you're back in civilization. To do so, flip the hardware switch. If you used the software method described in this section, repeat the preceding set of steps but choose Turn Wireless On in Step 2 for Windows 7 and Windows Vista, or Enable in Step 3 for Windows XP.

✦ Some laptops feature Airplane mode. Use it.

✦ I recommend getting a window seat if you plan to use your laptop aloft. The main reason: You have control over the window shades. When it's too bright outside, it makes seeing the laptop screen impossible.

✦ You can buy screen filters that prevent other passengers on the plane from peering into the laptop screen. Get one.

✦ If you're lucky, the airplane cabin features EmPower, which allows you to plug in your laptop and use it without sacrificing battery life. You need an EmPower adapter to make the connection work.

✦ If your laptop doesn't have a wireless networking hardware switch, peruse the keyboard for a special key combination that disables the wireless network.

✦ The keyboard combination to disable the wireless networking adapter on Lenovo laptops is Fn+F5.

✦ Pay heed to those low-battery-power warnings! Even when your laptop is fully charged, it will poop out eventually. See Chapter 1 for more information on setting battery warnings and timeouts.

Chapter 4: Laptop Maintenance

In This Chapter

✓ **Cleaning the laptop case**

✓ **Cleaning the screen**

✓ **Cleaning the keyboard**

✓ **Understanding laptop hardware upgrades**

*J*ust as there are two parts to a computer's personality, there are two types of maintenance on a computer: hardware and software. The software side rules the hardware side, and, indeed, there's more you can do maintenance-wise with software than with hardware. For software maintenance, I recommend reading Book VI, which applies to all PCs, including laptops and tablets. For maintaining your laptop's hardware, you have this chapter.

A Sparkling Laptop

All computers require cleaning, and laptops even more so. That's because you end up handling a laptop more than you do a normal computer. A laptop can also wind up in exotic environments, so it can suffer from gunk and debris that would make a mere desktop computer blanch. Cleaning the thing involves more care than putting your laptop in the dishwasher (which I don't recommend). Instead, follow the handy, helpful cleaning advice in this section.

Making the case beautiful again

Here are the ingredients for maintaining your laptop case:

Sponge: Any household sponge will do, especially the kind my kids call a SpongeBob sponge.

Cleaning liquid: Mix one part standard dishwashing detergent with five parts water.

Lint-free cloth: This item can be found anywhere that cleaning supplies are sold.

Cotton swabs: You can use the standard Q-tip, though I prefer medical swabs because they're better made and wrapped a little tighter.

Cleaning is a standard operation:

1. **Turn off the laptop.**

   Don't clean a laptop while it's on. In fact, unplug it. Here, let me make it a step:

2. **Unplug the laptop.**

   There.

3. **Mix the cleaning liquid.**

4. **Soak the sponge in the cleaning liquid.**

5. **Wring out the sponge until it's dry.**

6. **Gently wipe down the laptop's case.**

7. **Use the swab to reach into the nooks and crannies.**

   Do not insert the swab into any ports, jacks, or holes on the laptop. There's no need to clean inside those places.

8. **Finish the job by wiping the case again with the lint-free cloth.**

   Use the cloth to sop up any excess moisture.

Now prepare to take your laptop on the road again and get it dirty all over!

Unlike desktop PCs, laptops are designed to be out in the wild. You may notice that your laptop's case has a more rugged feel to it than does a standard desktop computer. That's a good thing. Indeed, you probably don't need to clean your laptop unless it's *really* dirty. Then again, everyone's idea of *really dirty* is different. I remember disagreeing with my mother on that point many times when I was younger.

✦ The laptop case is the *outside*. On the inside, where the thing hinges, you find the keyboard and screen. Cleaning those items is covered in the following two sections.

✦ Okay, I lied. You can also use the sponge and swabs to help clean up the touch pad. It lives near the keyboard.

✦ Medical swabs can be found at any pharmacy or medical supply store.

✦ Never spill any liquid inside the laptop!

✦ Isopropyl, or "rubbing," alcohol makes a good cleaning liquid. *Do not* use it to clean the monitor.

✦ Avoid using any detergent that contains strong chemicals, such as ammonia or bleach.

✦ Check out Video 341 to see me work the steps of cleaning a laptop case:

www.dummies.com/go/troubleshootingandmaintainingyourpcaio2e

Washing the screen

Things are better since the mayor cleaned up the downtown coffee bistros. I remember when smelly bums from the street used to walk in. They'd just start cleaning everyone's laptops with these filthy rags. Guilt would obligate you to pass the helpful hobo a dollar or your "spare change" and then thank him. You'd smile, wait for him to leave, and then clean the screen all over. Thankfully, those days are over.

When you feel like cleaning the laptop screen, you have three options (in addition to waiting for a vagrant to do it for you):

Use a lint-free cloth to dry-clean the screen. All laptops use LCD monitors. These monitors are *very* fussy about liquids. A lint-free cloth helps get the dust off the screen and can also help remove finger smudges and some (but not all) sneeze globs.

Use a damp sponge to wipe the screen. Use only water to make the sponge damp. Wring out *all* the moisture from the sponge before you wipe the screen. Rub gently, lovingly.

Get an LCD monitor cleaning kit. By getting a cleaning kit, perhaps the best option, you receive a lint-free cloth as well as a package containing a damp towelette moistened with the official LCD monitor-cleaning solution. I use and recommend the Klear Screen brand:

```
www.klearscreen.com
```

As with cleaning the case, you should turn off the laptop, and even unplug it, before you clean the monitor. In fact, you can more easily see what you're cleaning when the screen is off.

After the screen is clean, let it dry before you close the lid or use the laptop again.

Unlike cleaning the case (see the preceding section), you'll most likely end up cleaning the laptop's monitor more often. I do. So don't believe that you're becoming obsessive or turning into your own mother just because you clean the laptop's monitor more often than you clean the case.

✦ Never, ever, under any circumstances, use alcohol or ammonia cleaners on an LCD screen. Just don't.

✦ If you're curious: Alcohol and ammonia can damage the laptop's LCD display to the point where the image becomes unreadable. Further, if you have a Tablet PC, the screen's ability to detect input is greatly diminished by the use of harsh chemicals.

+ Tablet PCs require more screen cleaning than do standard desktops. That's because you touch the screen more often when using the laptop in Tablet mode.

+ The monitor should be completely dry before you close the laptop's lid.

+ Yes, for some extra cash, you can dress down and wander the cafés and clean laptops. Remember not to shower for several days before attempting this task. I cannot, however, recommend being a laptop-screen-cleaning tramp as a way to pay for college.

+ Refer to Video 342 to watch how I clean my laptop's monitor:

www.dummies.com/go/troubleshootingandmaintainingyourpcaio2e

Kleaning the keyboard

The best way to clean the laptop's keyboard is by using a small, portable vacuum. Using the vacuum's tiniest attachment, gently suck the hair, scone flakes, and crud from between the laptop's keys. *Thwoop!*

To clean the laptop's key caps, turn off the laptop and then use a pencil eraser to rub off the crud and buildup. Afterward, use the vacuum again to clean out any eraser stubble and crud between the cracks.

+ I don't recommend using a can of compressed air to clean a laptop's (or desktop PC's) keyboard. The air may clear away the debris, but it may also blow it deeper into the laptop. After the gunk is inside, there's no way to clean it out.

+ Unlike on a desktop PC keyboard, you do not wash a laptop keyboard by using liquid. In fact, if you spill anything into a laptop keyboard, you're pretty much screwed. I pray that you followed my advice (in *Laptops For Dummies*) and originally purchased a nice warranty for your laptop.

+ Watch Video 343 to witness the author deftly cleaning a laptop keyboard.

www.dummies.com/go/troubleshootingandmaintainingyourpcaio2e

Hardware Upgrades

You just can't upgrade laptop hardware the same way you can upgrade a desktop PC. That's one reason why we're not all using laptops exclusively these days.

The desktop PC system is built on upgradable, swappable, easy-to-replace-and-fix parts. That aspect of the PC's design was the key to its success back when it first came out, and continues to be one of the best reasons to buy a PC desktop today. On a laptop, you have three ways to upgrade the hardware:

Not at all: Some laptops are entirely shut out of the hardware upgrade path. On those systems, the laptop is a closed box. You can get a new battery. You can add USB gizmos and PC Cards. But you cannot upgrade any other hardware.

Limited, factory upgrades: A few laptop models allow upgrades, but they're limited to the manufacturer's whim. For example, your laptop may have a swappable drive bay, where you can add an extra hard drive, an optical drive, or a media card reader. But that additional hardware is available only from the manufacturer. You can't just drive to a big-box store and buy a new hard drive, as you can with a desktop.

Slightly flexible upgrades: Finally, a smattering of laptops have both upgradeable memory and permanent storage options. Some even allow for a new video card to be installed. But those laptops are few and generally not as portable or lightweight.

Bottom line: You have to look into your own laptop's potential for hardware upgrades to see what's available and how the upgrade works.

+ Most people don't buy laptops to upgrade them. When buying a laptop, I recommend that you buy *all* you need.

+ My best advice for any hardware upgrade — when one is possible — is to add more memory. Windows 7, for example, needs 2GB RAM at minimum. If you're working with graphics on your laptop, more memory helps tremendously.

+ I recommend buying laptop memory from Crucial (www.crucial.com.). Its web site features a memory configuration utility you can use to determine how much RAM is installed in your laptop and which type of memory and how much more you can install.

+ Some types of laptop hard drives are standard and can be removed easily by using a tiny screwdriver and some patience. I've ordered spare hard drives for my laptops and have had no trouble swapping them out.

+ If you plan to buy a larger-capacity hard drive for your laptop, ensure that you have a set of system recovery discs. You need the discs in order to reinstall your laptop's operating system and control software after initializing the new drive. Furthermore, you need a backup from which to reinstall your personal files and programs.

+ You can add external storage to your laptop. An external hard drive makes for a useful home-location addition to any laptop, especially for backing up.

Book IV

Internet

The 5th Wave   By Rich Tennant

SOMEWHERE IN THE CITY, SASQUATCH, BIGFOOT AND ELVIS SPEND ANOTHER WARY NIGHT.

©RICHTENNANT

"Look—all I'm saying is every time they come out with a new browser with an improved search function, it's just a matter of time."

Contents at a Glance

Chapter 1: Internet Malaise

In This Chapter

✔ Checking the Internet connection

✔ Setting timeout values

✔ Dealing with call waiting

✔ Confirming that the Internet is out there

✔ Selecting primary Internet programs

✔ Cleaning up history

✔ Eating cookies

✔ Fixing AutoComplete's memory

For some people, being without the Internet is like having a day where the sun doesn't shine. A reminder: Mankind has survived for thousands of years without the Internet. Until just recently, reading a book was considered a popular and enjoyable pastime. In some parts of the world, folks do their social networking in person, face to face. And, as far as I know, the post office still hand-delivers written correspondence. Despite these and many other interesting tidbits, the Internet remains a core part of our daily existence. When that's not the case, turn to this chapter for troubleshooting.

Problems Getting (and Staying) Online

Sometimes the Internet seems like the high-wire act at a circus: Despite any skills you may have, your balance depends not so much on your skill as it does on other factors you cannot control. I mean, who would perform a high-wire act when, at any time, the wire itself may vanish? That's the kind of struggle the typical Internet user faces. The answers to these common Internet connection problems are covered in this section.

Before proceeding, don't troubleshoot something that isn't there. This book isn't about setting up an Internet connection for the first time. If you've never connected to the Internet, you have nothing to troubleshoot. Instead, get your system set up and then get on the Internet. Your Internet service provider (ISP) should be your primary source of assistance.

Using the Windows 7 Internet Connection troubleshooter

Don't get your hopes up: Windows 7 features a slew of troubleshooters and one of them just happens to be an Internet Connection troubleshooter. Knowing that such a thing exists is reassuring. Having such a thing solve your Internet connection problem is amazing.

Whether it actually helps or not, running the Windows 7 Internet Connection troubleshooter is worth a try. Obey these directions:

1. **Open the Control Panel.**

2. **Beneath the System and Security heading, choose the link Find and Fix Problems.**

   The Troubleshooting window appears.

3. **Beneath the Network and Internet heading, choose the link Connect to the Internet.**

   Contrary to its name, clicking the link doesn't connect you to the Internet. Instead, the Internet Connection troubleshooter starts.

4. **Click the Next button.**

5. **Choose Troubleshoot My Connection to the Internet.**

   The other option, Help Me Connect to a Specific Web Page, is useful for when you have trouble accessing a web page. See Chapter 2.

6. **Continue to heed the directions and advice given by the troubleshooter.**

7. **Click the Close button when you're done.**

For broadband Internet access, many of the connection problems are caused by your local network — the modem and router, specifically. In addition to the solutions suggested in this book (specifically, the next section), consider reading Book V.

Testing broadband Internet

At the dawn of the 21st century, connecting to the Internet seems to be routine. Being on the Internet all the time is more or less the norm: always on, always available, generally high speed. Well, until something goes wrong.

When you experience problems getting or staying online, check these items:

Power source: Confirm that you have power — when the power goes out, the Internet goes out.

Other signals: If you're using cable Internet access, for example, check the cable TV. If the TV signal is out, your problem is with the cable system. On a DSL connection, check the phone line: No dial tone means no Internet.

Modem lights: Broadband modems, illustrated in Figure 1-1, feature several pretty lights that do more than just look impressive. Ensure that your modem's lights are on, have the proper color, and, if appropriate, are blinking.

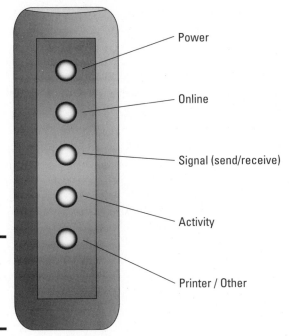

Figure 1-1: Typical broadband modem lights.

Table 1-1 explains what the lights can mean and how they factor into checking the Internet connection. Not all modems have the variety of lights listed, but the lights are there for a reason: They help you troubleshoot the Internet connection.

Table 1-1	Broadband Modem Lights
Lamp Name	*What the Modem Is Doing When the Lamp Is Lit*
Power	Receiving power and operating normally.
Online	Letting you know that it's connected to the service, but not necessarily to the Internet.
Signal	Sending information to, and receiving it from, the Internet.
Send	Sending information to the Internet.
Receive	Receiving information from the Internet.

(continued)

Table 1-1 *(continued)*

Lamp Name	What the Modem Is Doing When the Lamp Is Lit
Activity	(Flashing) Sending communications to, or receiving it from, the computer or local network.
Status	Working or having issues. The lamp may change color, depending on the modem's condition or connection.

The variety of lamps on a broadband modem is endless. My cable modem, for example, features a USB lamp that flashes whenever the USB port is being used (for a printer or a network disk drive).

First, check the power light. Is the modem turned on? Check the power connection from the modem to the wall socket. No power means no Internet.

Second, check the modem's signal or receive light. When the light is off, blinking, or colored red or orange, the Internet connection has a problem. Specifically, a signal isn't being broadcast. You can phone your ISP for assistance or, as I recommend instead, wait a few seconds to see whether the problem clears itself.

Disable the standby or loopback switch. Some modems feature a diagnostic switch, which can be labeled Standby or Loopback. Ensure that the switch is in the proper position for the modem to communicate.

Check physical connections. Is the modem connected to a router? Is the router plugged in and functioning? Are the network connections working? Can your computer access other computers on the local network? Can you *ping* the router? (See the later section, "Checking to see whether the Internet is really out there," for more information on ping.)

Restart the modem. Turn the modem off, and turn it on again. If the modem lacks a power switch, unplug it and plug it back in. Restarting the modem is perhaps the most common trick for getting a broadband connection back up and running. In fact, you may want to perform these official, desperate modem-restart steps:

1. **Unplug the modem.**

2. **Wait 30 seconds.**

3. **Plug the modem back in.**

If this trick doesn't work, you need to restart the modem and the router. Follow these steps next:

1. **Unplug the modem.**

2. **Unplug the router.**

3. **Wait 30 seconds.**

4. **Plug in the modem again.**

5. **Plug in the router again.**

If the Internet is still inaccessible, try these two suggestions:

Restart the computer. The problem might be in your computer, and the generic trick for fixing just about any computer problem is to restart the PC.

Restart the entire network. The modem may be fine. Your computer might be fine. The problem may lie in the network betwixt the two. See Book V for more information about restarting the network.

If the problem continues, perhaps the modem needs replacing. If you're renting the broadband modem, have your ISP supply you with a replacement . Otherwise, you have to buy a new one (or borrow one) to see whether the modem has gone hinkey.

✦ Also refer to the section "Checking to see whether the Internet is really out there," later in this chapter.

✦ Broadband Internet access over a cellular modem (known as *tethering*) doesn't disappear when the power goes out. If your laptop is so equipped, you can still use the Internet during a blackout.

✦ Checking connections may also involve checking outside your home or office. Usually, the ISP (cable or phone company) can test the line all the way up to your modem. That should determine whether the problem is the ISP's or yours.

✦ The broadband connection relies heavily on computer networking to function properly. When the local network connection is down, you cannot access the Internet. See Book V for more information on network troubleshooting.

✦ *Broadband* is the generic term that describes cable, DSL, satellite, and other high-speed connections to the Internet.

Checking dialup connections

Well, say hello to the 20th century. Using a dialup connection is slow, and I hope you recognize that it's the antique way to access the Internet. Still, my Aunt Eva claims that coffee heated in a saucepan stays hot longer than coffee zapped in a microwave. ("Takes the same time, too," she wants me to add.) Though the philosophy is quaint, there's nothing charming about a dialup Internet connection.

**Book IV
Chapter 1**

Internet Malaise

I know: You often have no choice when using dialup. You might not have broadband out where you live. Or, you don't see the point in spending extra money for broadband (or a microwave oven). Or, you don't use the Internet much anyway (or drink coffee). Fine. That doesn't mean the dialup connection won't be without problems.

The first place to look when you have dialup connection conundrums is on the Connections tab in the Internet Properties or Internet Options dialog box, as shown in Figure 1-2. Here's how to get there:

Figure 1-2:
Checking dialup settings.

1. **Open the Control Panel.**

2a. **In Windows 7, choose Network and Internet and then Internet Options.**

2b. **In Windows XP, open the Internet Options icon.**

3. **Click the Connections tab.**

4. **Select the dialup connection from the list.**

   In Figure 1-2, it's named Booga, which isn't my ISP but is one of my favorite made-up names (next to *Wambooli*).

5. **Choose a new setting for the dialup connection (if necessary).**

   You choose from three settings:

   Never Dial a Connection: Choose this option if you don't want your computer to automatically dial into the Internet.

   Dial Whenever a Network Connection Is Not Present: This standard option is the one you select to be prompted whenever an Internet connection is requested by a program on your PC.

Always Dial My Default Connection: This option may seem like the best one, but it's not. Do not choose this option.

6. Click OK.

7. Close the Control Panel window.

The number-one dialup issue is dialing up at seemingly random times. Choosing the option Never Dial a Connection (refer to Step 4 in the preceding step list) solves this annoying issue. Of course, you may need to manually connect to the Internet in this case. If so, refer to the later section, "Dialing in manually," for the details.

✦ Contrary to what the Never Dial a Connection option says, it doesn't mean that you'll never be connected to the Internet. It should be renamed Never *Automatically* Dial a Connection.

✦ When you don't hear a dial tone when the dialup modem starts to connect, there's most likely a problem with the phone system.

✦ Also check the phone cable to ensure that it's plugged in at both ends.

✦ Some options in various email programs allow dialing into the Internet — or not. See Chapter 3 for details.

Remembering your dialup Internet password

Why tire of continually typing your Internet password when you can have the computer remember it for you? Here's how:

1. Open the Control Panel.

2a. In Windows 7, choose Network and Internet and then choose Internet Options.

2b. In Windows XP, open the Internet Options icon.

3. Click the Connections tab.

4. Select the dialup connection from the list.

5. Click the Settings button.

A Settings dialog box for the dialup connection appears.

6. Type your Internet username.

7. Type your password.

8. Click OK.

9. Click OK to close the Internet Properties or Internet Options dialog box.

By typing your username and password, you allow Windows to supply them automatically whenever you summon a dialup connection.

◆ Your Internet username and password are most likely different from your other usernames and passwords, such as the ones you use to log in to Windows or collect your email.

◆ Passwords are a fact of life in the modern computer. See Book II, Chapter 5 for more information and suggestions about using and keeping passwords on your PC.

Dialing in manually

When starting an Internet program doesn't automatically connect you to the Internet, you need to manually summon a connection. The procedure is different among all versions of Windows covered in this book.

In Windows 7, you have several easy ways to access a dialup connection if you've configured Windows 7 to display the Connect To item on the Start menu or the Networking icon in the notification area. When that item isn't displayed, you can access a dialup connection by following these steps:

1. **Open the Control Panel.**

2. **Click the link Connect to the Internet from beneath the Network and Internet heading.**

3. **Choose from the list the dialup connection you want to use.**

4. **Click the Next button.**

5. **If prompted, input your username and password and click the Dial button to connect.**

In Windows Vista, follow these easy steps:

1. **From the Start menu, choose Connect To.**

2. **Choose your ISP's Connection icon from the list in the Connect to a Network window.**

3. **Click the Connect button.**

4. **If prompted, enter your username and password.**

5. **Click the Dial button.**

Wait until the modem connects you and you're online.

In Windows XP, follow these convoluted and complex steps:

1. **From the Start menu, choose Network Connections.**

2. **Double-click to open your ISP's connection icon.**

3. **Click the Dial button.**

Wait until the modem makes the connection, and then you're online.

To configure Windows 7 to display a Connect To item on the Start menu, right-click the Start button and choose Properties. Click the Customize button in the Taskbar and Start Menu Properties dialog box. In the Customize Start Menu dialog box, put a check mark by the Connect To item. Click OK.

Speed is relative. When I first used a modem (way before the Internet existed), I had to dial a phone myself. After waiting for the answering modem to wail, turning on my PC's external modem, and hanging up the phone, I was online. The modem communicated at 300 bits per second (bps), which is slow enough for anyone to be able to keep up with the text as it appears. Today's dialup modems are more than 150 times faster.

Dialing randomly

As long as you can hear the modem, you may notice that it occasionally decides — with no apparent motivation — to dial up the Internet. It may happen at random times, or it may be predictable, such as when you first log in to Windows.

Nothing that happens in a computer is truly random, so there has to be a program somewhere trying to phone up the Internet for some reason, legitimate or not. My general advice is to click the Cancel button. If you're lucky, you may see a message displayed that can help you identify the disgruntled program and, hopefully, configure it to either not dial in to the Internet or at least understand why it tries to do so.

✦ If you're not prompted, or you do not see a Cancel button, when the PC dials into the Internet, change the dialup settings. See the earlier section, "Checking dialup connections," for information.

✦ Most Help programs, such as those for Windows or Microsoft Office, now rely on the Internet to supply relevant information. When you click the Help button, or press the F1 key, you may experience the computer trying to connect to the Internet.

✦ A common reason for the seemingly random dialups is that Windows confuses the Internet with your local network. For example, Windows may dial into the Internet when you try using a network printer or accessing a network computer. Sadly, there's nothing you can do about that; the computer is just being dumb.

Dealing with dialup timeouts

An annoying and preventable reason for being disconnected from the Internet is that your dialup account has *timed out*. The dropped line can happen for two reasons.

First, noise on the line can drop the connection. It can be as simple as someone else picking up a phone extension or as complex as sunspots.

Poor-quality phone lines cause frequently dropped connections. The biggest culprit, however, is call waiting. (See the later section, "Disabling call waiting," for more information.)

Second, *you* timed out. Both the PC and the ISP monitor the dialup Internet connection. When your connection fails to send any information after a set amount of time, the line is dropped. That's because it's assumed that you left the computer, fell asleep, or perhaps were even shot from behind by a jealous lover.

To prevent a timeout disconnection, review the timeout settings in Windows. Three of them are buried in two separate locations. Here's how to find the lot:

1. **Open the Control Panel.**

2. **In Windows 7 and Windows Vista, switch the icon view: In Windows 7, choose Large Icons from the View By menu in the upper-right corner of the window; in Windows Vista, choose the Classic View link, found on the left side of the window.**

3. **Open the Phone and Modem Options icon.**

In Windows 7, the icon is called Phone and Modem.

If you see the Location Information window displayed, the modem hasn't yet been configured for your computer. Configure the modem by setting a location, and then start these steps over. Refer to my books *PCs For Dummies* and *Laptops For Dummies* (Wiley) for details on setting up and using a modem.

4. **Click the Modems tab.**

5. **If necessary, select the PC's modem from the list.**

6. **Click the Properties button.**

7. **If you're using Windows XP, skip to Step 10.**

8. **Click the Change Settings button, found on the General tab.**

9. **In Windows Vista, click the Continue button or type the administrator's password to continue.**

10. **Click the Advanced tab in the modem's Properties dialog box.**

11. **Click the Change Default Preferences button.**

12. **Set the modem's timeout values in the modem's Default Preferences dialog box.**

The dialog box you see, shown in Figure 1-3, contains some generic settings for the modem — stuff you might not otherwise give a rip about. But one item in particular is the Disconnect a Call If Idle for More Than value. This setting controls the modem's maximum timeout value; after that period of inactivity, the modem disconnects.

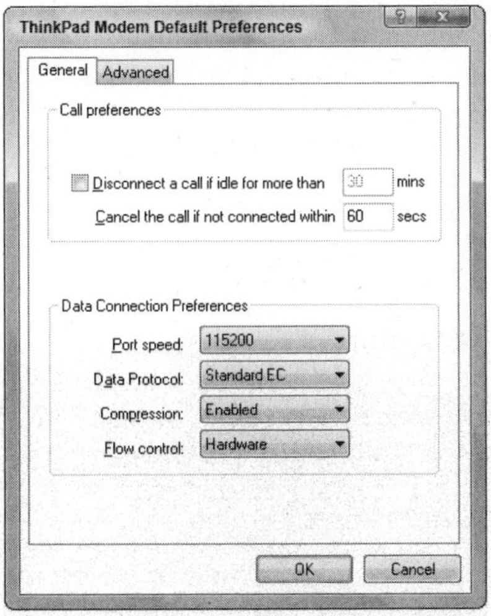

Figure 1-3:
Setting the modem's timeout values.

Place a check mark by the item Disconnect a Call If Idle for More Than and select a timeout value.

There's no way to set an "unlimited" timeout. The maximum value is 42 minutes.

13. **Click OK to lock in the new timeout for the modem, and keep clicking OK to close the various dialog boxes you opened.**

Meanwhile, back in the Control Panel, which should still be in Icon view for Windows 7 and Windows Vista, you can begin the steps for setting the second timeout value:

14. **Open the Internet Options icon.**

15. **Click the Connections tab in the Internet Options dialog box.**

16. **Select a dialup connection from the list.**

When you have more than one dialup connection, you need to repeat these steps for each one.

17. **Click the Settings button.**

18. **Click the Properties button.**

19. **Click the Options tab in the ISP's Properties dialog box.**

20. **Use the menu button to set the value for Idle Time Before Hanging Up.**

Your choices are limited to those on the menu.

21. **Click OK.**

If you're using Windows 7, you're pretty much done; skip to Step 27. Otherwise:

Book IV
Chapter 1

Internet Malaise

22. **Click the Advanced button.**

    The final timeout setting is made in the Advanced Dial-Up dialog box, as shown in Figure 1-4.

Figure 1-4: The final timeout setting.

23. **Place a check mark by the item Disconnect If Idle for XX Minutes.**

24. **Set the number of minutes to have an automatic disconnect.**

25. **Click OK.**

26. **Close the other dialog boxes by clicking OK until you see no more dialog boxes with OK buttons.**

27. **In Windows 7 and Windows Vista, restore the Control Panel to Category view.**

    In Windows 7, choose Category from the View By menu; in Windows Vista, click the Control Panel Home link.

28. **Close the Control Panel window.**

Indeed, there appears to be an abundance of locations where you can set timeout values for a dialup account. Perhaps one of them was set too low, which explains why you unexpectedly disconnected from the Internet.

Your ISP can also drop your connection when it detects that your dialup connection has been idle for too long. You have to check with the ISP to see what the timeout value is.

Disabling call waiting

One of the most abrupt and preventable ways to get knocked offline is by the call-waiting signal. It's the bane of dialup Internet users.

You may want call waiting turned on. After all, you have the service for a reason. But being kicked offline is annoying. Therefore, the phone company allows you to stifle the call-waiting feature on a per-call basis: You just dial a special code before making a call. The code suspends the call-waiting feature for the duration of the call. Because your computer's modem works like a telephone, you can have it "dial" the call-waiting suspension code for you. Follow these steps:

1. **Display the Phone and Modem dialog box.**

   Refer to Steps 1 through 3 in the directions in the preceding section.

2. **Click the Dialing Rules tab.**

3. **Choose your current location from the list.**

   The setting to disable call waiting is available only when you set up a location. If you don't have a location set up, click the New button to create one.

4. **Click the Edit button.**

   The Edit Location dialog box shows up.

5. **Place a check mark by the item To Disable Call Waiting, Dial.**

6. **Choose the proper code to disable call waiting from the menu button.**

   If the code you need to dial isn't listed, type it in.

7. **Click OK to close the Edit Location dialog box.**

   You can also close the Phone and Modems Options dialog box and the Control Panel window.

You have better alternatives than disabling call waiting. If you prefer to have call waiting as a feature while you're using the modem, you can look into specialized software. For example, AOL users can use the AOL Call Alert feature.

Internet Troubleshooting Tools

Troubleshooting the Internet is a big task, so my initial advice is not to bother with it. After all, highly paid black-belt nerds work for the major communications companies already, and it's their job to troubleshoot the Internet. Let them. On your end, you can choose from a smattering of general networking tools to determine whether an Internet problem lies locally or far away. This section tells you how.

+ The information in this section is general to the Internet. For specific help on the web, see Chapter 2. Email miseries are ameliorated in Chapter 3.

+ Most of these tips and tricks are technical in nature. Because they arose from basic networking and the early, text-only days of the Internet, many of them run in a command prompt window. Scary.

Checking to see whether the Internet is really out there

The Internet's immediate ancestor was built to survive nuclear war. So, in theory (because no nuclear attack has occurred — yet), the Internet is always with us. The question is, however, whether the Internet is available to your computer.

You may have a solid Internet connection. The modem's lights indicate that everything is sending and receiving hunky and dory. But something leads you to believe that the Internet is not "up": The online game you're playing may not respond. Web pages may not open. Email refuses to be sent. Although the problem may not be something you can fix, it's something you can check by using the ping command.

Ping stands for *packet Internet groper*. The program sends a chunk of information (the packet) to a network address. The computer at that address echoes the packet back. The ping command then reports information about the packet sent and received, such as the total length of time taken by the round trip.

You can use ping to confirm that a specific domain or IP address on the Internet is up and available. Follow these steps:

1. **From the Start menu, choose All Programs⇨Accessories⇨Command Prompt.**

   A command prompt window appears.

2. **Type** ping wambooli.com **and press the Enter key.**

   The word `ping` is followed by a space and then the name of a server or an IP address. In this example, I'm using `wambooli.com`, which is my own web site. In practice, you can use the name of any domain or server on the Internet, such as `yahoo.com`, `google.com`, or `microsoft.com`.

   You should see output similar to the output shown in Figure 1-5.

3. **Type** exit **to close the command prompt window.**

Figure 1-5:
The ping command confirms that the Internet is up and available.

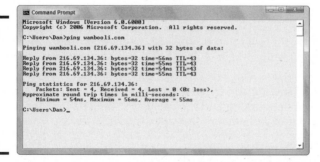

```
Command Prompt

Microsoft Windows [Version 6.0.6000]
Copyright (c) 2006 Microsoft Corporation.  All rights reserved.

C:\Users\Dan>ping wambooli.com

Pinging wambooli.com [216.69.134.36] with 32 bytes of data:

Reply from 216.69.134.36: bytes=32 time=56ms TTL=43
Reply from 216.69.134.36: bytes=32 time=55ms TTL=43
Reply from 216.69.134.36: bytes=32 time=54ms TTL=43
Reply from 216.69.134.36: bytes=32 time=55ms TTL=43

Ping statistics for 216.69.134.36:
    Packets: Sent = 4, Received = 4, Lost = 0 (0% loss),
Approximate round trip times in milli-seconds:
    Minimum = 54ms, Maximum = 56ms, Average = 55ms

C:\Users\Dan>_
```

When the ping command is successful, the Internet is up. Specifically, it means that the domain or IP address you typed is accessible. You should see results such as those shown in Figure 1-5. The information displayed indicates a successful, round-trip ping adventure.

When ping isn't successful, it can mean any number of things.

When you see the response `Destination host unreachable`, the web site or domain isn't available, or "up," on the Internet. That message may also mean that the Internet isn't available. So, despite your having an Internet connection, something else that's out there on the Internet is preventing you from accessing information. (Think "backhoe.")

The message `Request Timed Out` means that the host is out there but cannot be reached. It's probably busy, although the message may also indicate that some or all of the Internet isn't available.

In all cases, there's really nothing you can do; the ping command merely confirms whether the Internet is reachable. When ping reports that something isn't available, you can just sit and wait, knowing that the problem isn't related to your equipment.

+ The backhoe is the natural enemy of the Internet.

+ *Domain* is short for a *fully qualified domain name*. It's the official name of a computer or network on the Internet. The domain includes the hostname, such as `wambooli` or `yahoo` or `google`, followed by a top-level domain like `com`, `net`, or `edu`. The domain is simply a word related to an IP address. It's easier to use the Internet by typing a domain name rather than a long, complex, easy-to-forget number.

+ You can also use ping to troubleshoot the local-area network in your home or office. See Book V for more on network troubleshooting.

+ The IP address for most — but not all — routers is `192.168.0.1` or `10.0.0.1`. Try pinging them to ensure that your router isn't having the issue.

+ Just because the ping command is successful doesn't mean that a web site is available. The web server on a domain might be down or busy, in which case ping reports that everything is fine even though your web browser is still unable to view the site. My advice is to try again later.

+ Another reason that ping may not work is that the router or the firewall (or both) is configured to deny all ping requests, both incoming and outgoing.

+ There's a condition when ping sometimes falsely reports that a web site that isn't available appears to be available. Some ISPs redirect bad domain requests to a special search page. So rather than see an `unknown Web page` message in a w browser or a `Destination host unreachable` message from the ping command, you see the ISP's redirection page instead.

**Book IV
Chapter 1**

Internet Malaise

✦ The term *ping* is often used as a noun in online computer gaming. It refers to the speed at which a remote server makes a connection. High pings are bad, indicating a slow connection (or long-distance connection). Low pings are best.

✦ Beyond gaming, ping time is also used to determine which servers are closest to your location. For example, when given the choice of multiple servers for downloading a file, choose the server that reports a fast ping time. To determine the fastest ping time, every server must be pinged and its average ping time noted.

✦ Ping is also used in Internet denial-of-service (DOS) attacks. A vast number of infected or compromised computers send a huge number of ping requests to a specific server on the Internet, which effectively shuts down all other traffic to the server.

✦ The ping command was named after the sound made by a submarine sonar. Later, the term *packet internet groper* was retrofitted to make *ping* an acronym. The result of using this method is commonly called a *backronym*.

Confirming that an Internet location exists

Visiting certain locations on the Internet for the first time is like trying to find an address in an unknown part of town: You can easily get lost and, worse, you might be in the wrong location, looking for an address that doesn't exist. Using a computer, however, you can easily confirm a few things before you give up.

The first thing to try when you're told that a web site or another Internet location doesn't exist is to check your typing. Especially for those `Web page 404` errors, which tell you that a web page doesn't exist, odds are pretty good that you incorrectly typed the address. (You may also have clicked a bad link, but there's nothing you can do to fix that.)

The second thing to try is to reload. In most web browsers, pressing the Ctrl+R key combination refreshes the page; refreshing a web page gives the Internet a second chance to send you the same information. It's amazing how often the reload trick works — especially for missing pictures or web pages that suffer from ugly formatting.

Finally, you can use the ping command to confirm that the web site's domain exists. But note that you can ping only a web site's domain, not an individual web page. For example, the web site `http://sports.espn.go.com/nhl/index` is part of the domain `go.com`. You would need to ping `go.com` to see whether the site is accessible. Refer to the preceding section for details.

✦ The Refresh command usually has a shortcut icon or toolbar button on the browser's main toolbar.

✦ The Refresh command is also used to order a new version of a web page. Because many web pages are updated frequently, by refreshing you always see the most recent version of the page.

✦ When the web site is `http://sports.espn.go.com`, you can ping `go.com` or `sports.espn.go.com`. But you cannot ping `sports.espn.go.com/nhl/index` because it's an "unknown host."

Choose Your Internet Programs

There's more than one way to skin a cat, but save kitty for a moment and recognize that you can also browse the Internet or pick up your email in more than one way. You may have several email programs on your computer, plus a browser or two. You can let each of them fight it out for your favors, or you can advance to a more civilized state and pick your top programs in a calm and less brutal manner.

To specify which programs are set up in Windows 7 and Windows Vista, follow these steps:

1. **Open the Control Panel.**

2. **Choose Programs, and then beneath the heading Default Programs, click the link Set Your Default Programs.**

The window probably should read Set the Computer's Default Programs because you, a human, have no default programs.

The Set Your Default Programs window is shown in Figure 1-6. Though the default programs inventory isn't specific to Internet programs, you will find Internet programs in the list.

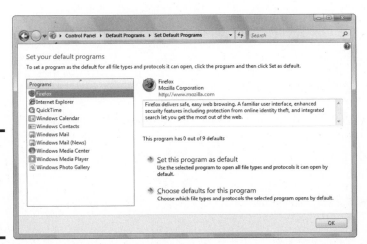

Figure 1-6: Choose the computer's Internet programs here.

3. **Choose from the list the program you want to use as your web browser.**

    One example is Firefox, as shown in Figure 1-6.

4. **Choose the option Set This Program As Default.**

5. **Repeat Steps 3 and 4 for your email program.**

6. **Click OK.**

In Windows XP, follow these steps to set the programs used for Internet access:

1. **Open the Control Panel's Internet Options icon.**

2. **Click the Programs tab.**

3. **Choose an email program from the E-Mail drop-down list.**

4. **Add the check mark by the item Internet Explorer Should Check to See Whether It Is the Default Browser.**

    The option is at the bottom of the dialog box. When the option is selected, Internet Explorer begs you to make it the default web browser when it starts. You can then switch browsers, but only between Internet Explorer and another web browser.

5. **Click OK.**

6. **Close the Control Panel window.**

Whenever you install new Internet software, such as a new email program or web browser, it typically asks whether you want it to be the "default." Answering Yes at that time sets the new software as the main program. There's no need to go through the preceding set of steps.

✦ Internet Explorer is the preferred web browser in Windows. Sometimes, it runs because Windows wants it to run, regardless of which browser you set up as the default web browser.

✦ Yes, it's silly that Windows XP lacks a better way to choose a default web browser. Various lawyers agree with you, but because Microsoft will no longer support Windows XP at an unspecified later date, the well-advised solution is to get a newer version of Windows.

✦ Some programs, such as Internet Explorer, incessantly ask whether you want them to be the defaults every dang doodle time they run, even after you specify another program as the default.

Binary Breadcrumbs

Hither, thither, or yon, where you've been on the Internet isn't a secret. Like seeing a car driving a dusty road miles away, a plume of digital dust lingers behind your every online movement. Always.

Keeping track of where you've been on the information superhighway is billed as a "feature" of the Internet programs you use. Tracking is designed to help you get back to where you once were, to quickly recall places or terms you typed. But this feature can also be a security risk, not to mention that it holds a potential for embarrassment. This section tells you how to cover your online tracks.

Revising history

All web browser programs come with a History feature. It details the web sites and pages you visited, usually for the past week or two. That way, you can quickly return to where you once were, but others using the computer can also view a trail guide of your Internet travels. When you go somewhere that you would rather not have others know about, you need to practice some good old historical revision.

For Internet Explorer 8, follow these steps to prune the history list:

1. Choose Safety⇨Delete Browsing History.

The Delete Browsing History dialog box appears, as shown in Figure 1-7. Obviously, this dialog box plays a key role in deleting digital history.

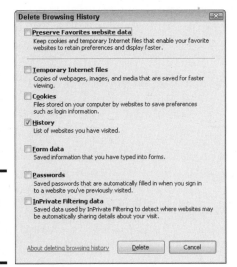

Book IV Chapter 1

Internet Malaise

Figure 1-7: The Delete Browsing History dialog box.

2. Ensure that a check mark appears by the History option.

You can check all items in the dialog box if you want to perform a more complete wipe of your web browsing history.

3. Click the Delete button.

If you'd rather just dispense with history altogether, you can disable it as a feature by following these steps:

1. **Choose Tools⇨Internet Options.**

2. **Click the Settings button in the Browsing History area of the dialog box's General tab.**

3. **Set the Number of Days to Keep Pages in History value to zero.**

   It's at the bottom of the Temporary Internet Files and History Settings dialog box.

4. **Click OK.**

5. **Click OK to close the Internet Options dialog box.**

Keep in mind that the History feature continues to track recent web sites, even when you disable it. Setting the Number of Days to Keep Pages in History value to zero merely erases the history list every day, not every second.

If you desire simply to pluck out specific unwanted remnants of where you've been, follow these steps:

1. **Press Ctrl+H to summon the History window in Internet Explorer.**

   The web page history is categorized by day, web site, and, finally, web page.

2. **Right-click a day, web site, or web page to remove from the History list.**

3. **Choose the Delete command from the shortcut menu.**

4. **Click the Yes button to confirm the deletion.**

   And the offending entry is gone.

You have to repeat all these steps to delete additional entries; after you delete an entry, the History panel/window/thing closes.

You can use the preceding technique to clear out the history when you set the Number of Days to Keep Pages in History value to zero, as described earlier. Simply delete the items you don't want to keep, and know that the rest of history will be zapped at the end of the day anyway.

✦ To clear the history for Internet Explorer 6 and earlier, click the Clear History button, found on the General tab of the Internet Options dialog box.

✦ To set the Number of Days to Keep Pages in History option in Internet Explorer 6, open the Internet Options dialog box and set the value on the General tab.

✦ In the Firefox web browser, you can remove what's called "personal information" by using the Clear Private Data command: Choose Tools⇨Clear Recent History.

Removing cookies

I'm not one to believe that web page cookies are evil, but I recognize that a lot of people prefer to lose their cookies as they travel the Internet. Here's how to purge those digital biscuits in Internet Explorer:

1. **Choose Safety⇨Delete Browsing History.**

The Delete Browsing History dialog box shows up (refer to Figure 1-7).

2. **Place a check mark by the Cookies item.**

3. **Click the Delete button.**

Sadly, there's no way to delete specific cookies in Internet Explorer; you're given only an all-or-nothing choice. You can, however, remove individual cookies — if you can find the secret location where they're stored.

In Windows 7 and Windows Vista, here's where the cookies are hidden:

`%USERPROFILE%\AppData\Roaming\Microsoft\Windows\Cookies`

In Windows XP, the Cookies folder is found here:

`%USERPROFILE%\Cookies`

To see the Cookies folder, summon a Windows Explorer window (press Win+E) and type one of these pathnames. Press Enter and you see the contents of the Cookies folder, as shown in Figure 1-8.

**Book IV
Chapter 1**

Internet Malaise

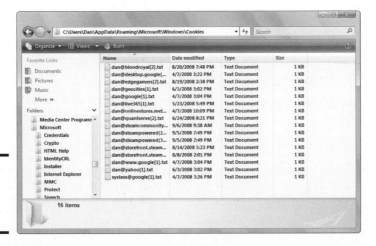

Figure 1-8:
The secret
Cookies
folder.

Cookies are given names based on your Windows username, followed by the at-sign (@) and then the name of the web site that planted the cookie on your computer.

You can view the cookie's content by double-clicking any Cookie icon; cookie files are text files. The content isn't really useful, however, it consists mostly of numbers that have meaning only to the web site that created the cookie.

Delete a single cookie the way you delete any file: Select the icon and press the Delete key on the keyboard.

+ Cookies are re-created when you visit the same web site again.

+ Cookies saved by web browsers other than Internet Explorer are stored elsewhere in your user profile folder.

+ You can disable cookies altogether in most web browsers, but by doing so, you render some web pages useless. My advice is to not bother with disabling cookies.

Purging temporary files

As you surf the web, your web browser picks up all sorts of stuff. Primarily, it collects media — pictures, sounds, videos — but also other information you see on any web page. All those items are known collectively as *temporary files*. You might also hear them referred to as the *cache*.

Normally, you have no reason to worry about temporary files. They exist to help web pages you frequent load faster. But temporary files also serve as digital fingerprints of places you visit. To remove these remnants, you can purge your computer of temporary files. Here's how to do so in Internet Explorer version 8:

1. **Choose Safety⇨Delete Browsing History.**

The Delete Browsing History dialog box pops up (refer to Figure 1-7).

2. **Place a check mark by the item Temporary Internet Files.**

3. **Click the Delete button to confirm.**

The files you deleted accumulate again as you revisit web pages. It's nothing you can prevent — temporary files are part of the web browsing process. But you can delete those files every so often.

+ Yep, anytime you see porn on a web page, even if you visited the site "accidentally," a copy of that image is retained on your PC as a temporary file. That is, until you delete the temporary files.

+ You can also delete temporary files by using the Disk Cleanup utility. See Book VI, Chapter 2 for more information.

✦ There's a way to eliminate temporary files. You can configure the web browser to not display any media files. Then you see only text when you visit a web page — no graphics, sounds, videos, or other types of files. On some web sites, you can still view the information because most of it is text. But making this type of change renders a number of popular web sites unreadable. To suppress the media display in Internet Explorer, click the Advanced tab in the Internet Options dialog box and remove all check marks under the Multimedia heading.

Dealing with AutoComplete

The *AutoComplete* feature is the handy tool that quickly summons stuff you previously typed, saving you from spending time typing it all over again. Whenever you type a web page address or fill in a form, AutoComplete displays a list of options or previously typed text. The feature is a blessing, but it can also be a curse — especially when things you don't want others to see keep popping up on the screen.

To utterly disable AutoComplete, follow these steps:

1. **Open the Control Panel.**

2a. **In Windows 7 and Windows Vista, choose Network and Internet and then Internet Options.**

2b. **In Windows XP, open the Internet Options icon.**

3. **Click the Content tab.**

4. **Click the Settings button in the AutoComplete area.**

For Internet Explorer 6, click the AutoComplete button.

5. **Remove all check marks to utterly disable AutoComplete.**

Or, you can be selective and remove the check marks by only the items that bug you, such as Web Addresses to remove those previously typed web page addresses that keep popping up on the Address bar.

In Internet Explorer 6, you can also click the Clear Forms and Clear Passwords button at this time. Doing so removes any stored information that AutoComplete has collected.

6. **Click OK.**

It might be a good idea to clear the history after you have disabled AutoComplete. See the section "Revising history," earlier in this chapter.

If you want to further check whether items have been properly purged from the AutoComplete repository, get technical and peruse the Registry for those entries. See Book II, Chapter 9 for information on searching the Registry — but be aware that a search works only when you know the text of the AutoComplete item you want to remove. For URLs, look in the following Registry key:

`HKCU\Software\Microsoft\Internet Explorer\TypedURLs`

Watch Video 411 to see a demonstration of how to purge AutoComplete information in Internet Explorer 8.

www.dummies.com/go/troubleshootingandmaintainingyourpcaio2e

Chapter 2: Woes on the Web

In This Chapter

✔ **Setting up toolbars**

✔ **Fixing Internet Explorer**

✔ **Working offline**

✔ **Dealing with ActiveX**

✔ **Fixing pop-up problems**

✔ **Adjusting a web page's display**

✔ **Printing problems**

✔ **Resurrecting missing pictures**

The Internet was doomed to mediocre success until the web came along. The web was the first Internet tool that presented information in a familiar format. Add in all those *hyperlinks,* the connections between pages that make the web a web, and the World Wide Web exploded. To keep yourself safe from any shards, debris, or smoke from that explosion, I offer you this chapter on troubleshooting the web.

✦ Many web woes are caused by malware or evil software. It's a big category, so it gets its own chapter; see Chapter 4. Go there for information on malware as well as phishing attacks.

✦ Files are also downloaded from the Internet, which may seem to you like a web page issue, but it's really a file transfer issue. Therefore, it's covered in Chapter 5.

Internet Explorer Hates Your Guts

Microsoft decided to name its official web browser Internet Explorer. Back in the early days, I enjoyed calling it Internet Exploder. Oh, such mirth makes me tingle. But after eight iterations, Internet Explorer continues to be the bane of many web surfers. This chapter covers some common issues in Internet Explorer and how to deal with them.

✦ Internet Explorer isn't your only web browsing choice. A popular alternative is the Firefox web browser, which has features and powers far beyond anything Microsoft is capable of creating. Grab a free copy of the Firefox web browser at `mozilla.com`.

✦ I don't cover Firefox specifically in this book. After all, this isn't a web browser troubleshooting book. Where appropriate, I mention some things that Firefox is capable of doing.

Showing the menu bar

After the menu bar enjoyed a good 20 years as a computing paradigm, Microsoft decided to dispense with it in many of its programs. For the purposes of this section, the menu bar has apparently vanished from Internet Explorer. But not really.

To see the good ol' familiar menu bar in Internet Explorer, press the F10 key.

Indeed, the F10 key is an *old* paradigm itself. Pressing F10 in Windows programs selects the menu bar, which reveals menu bar shortcut keys in a traditional sense or reveals the entire menu in a modern sense.

Alas, the F10 menu bar trick is only temporary. To see the menu bar full time in Internet Explorer, choose Tools⇨Toolbars⇨Menu Bar, where Tools is a button on the toolbar.

Managing toolbars

The dawn of the 21st century also saw the dawn of the overabundance of Internet Explorer toolbars. Microsoft slaps one on, called the Windows Live toolbar. You can find an endless cornucopia of Google Desktop toolbars. Developers are creating Internet Explorer toolbars more rapidly than teenagers are accumulating Facebook friends.

You don't need all these toolbars. They add clutter to the web browser window. Plus, they add features you probably never use. It's your computer — you be the boss!

Manage the toolbars in Internet Explorer by following these steps:

1. **From the Tools button on the toolbar, choose Tools⇨Toolbars.**

The Toolbars submenu appears. Active toolbars appear with a check mark by their names, as shown in Figure 2-1.

2. **Choose a checked toolbar from the submenu to remove it.**

3. **Repeat Steps 1 and 2 until Internet Explorer is purged of all unwanted toolbars.**

Removing the check mark by a toolbar doesn't uninstall the toolbar. You can reactivate the toolbar at any time by choosing the toolbar from the Toolbars submenu.

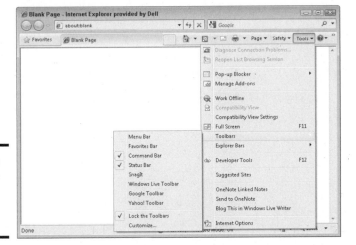

Figure 2-1: Where the toolbar controls lurk.

The Links bar is another toolbar you can remove, though I prefer keeping it active as a bookmarks menu. The status bar is also useful because it provides information about the web page you're viewing (or trying to view).

To uninstall a toolbar, you remove the program that set the thing up in the first place. See Book II, Chapter 6 for details.

Dealing with add-ons

An *add-on* is a supplemental program designed to enhance your web browsing experience.

Wow. That's good. I should write ad copy. But because you're not buying anything here, let me explain in a friendlier manner: An *add-on* is a tiny program attached to Internet Explorer, like adding chrome to a car. The add-on serves to run special web page features, like animation or video or other must-see elements on a web page. Without the add-on, these items don't function, or else you see text begging you to install the add-on.

You manage add-ons by clicking the Tools button in Internet Explorer 8. From the Tools button menu, choose Manage Add-Ons. You see the Manage Add-Ons dialog box, as shown in Figure 2-2. It displays which add-ons are loaded and whether they're enabled or disabled.

Book IV Chapter 2

Woes on the Web

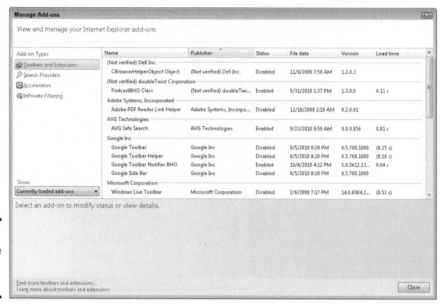

Figure 2-2:
The Manage
Add-Ons
dialog box.

To disable an add-on that's bugging you or causing Internet Explorer to crash, select the add-on from the list in the Manage Add-Ons window and click the Disable button that appears in the lower-right corner of the dialog box. Likewise, to reenable the add-on (in case it isn't the cause of your web page troubles), select it and click the Enable button that appears.

Click the Close button when you're done with the Manage Add-Ons window.

✦ I recommend installing add-ons. Most of them add flavor to the web pages you visit and are required for that "enhanced web browsing experience." Besides, you now know how to remove add-ons and controls if they displease you.

✦ You can temporarily disable all add-ons in Internet Explorer, which comes in handy for troubleshooting. To do so, from the Start menu choose All Programs➪Accessories➪System Tools➪Internet Explorer (No Add-Ons).

✦ In Internet Explorer 6, choose Tools➪Manage Add-Ons to see the Manage Add-Ons window.

✦ In Firefox, choose Tools➪Add-Ons to find and manage add-ons.

✦ Also see the later section, "Secret Ingredient: ActiveX."

Resetting Internet Explorer

Just as restarting your computer often fixes minor software ills, you can attempt to repair Internet Explorer by performing a software reset. Here's how:

1. **In Internet Explorer 8, click the Tools toolbar button and choose the menu command Internet Options.**

2. **Click the Advanced tab.**

3. **Click the Reset button.**

   The Reset Internet Explorer Settings dialog box appears. It's not an entertaining read.

4. **Click the Reset button in the Reset Internet Explorer Settings dialog box.**

   Purge! Purge! Purge!

5. **Click the Close button.**

6. **Click the OK button and then:**

7. **Close all open Internet Explorer windows to restart Internet Explorer.**

After you restart Internet Explorer, all the add-ons and customization you completed are removed. The home page is also reset to whatever it was when you first set up your PC (such as to the manufacturer's web site or to whichever MSN or Windows Live site Microsoft is pushing). It's as though you started Internet Explorer for the first time.

✦ Resetting Internet Explorer doesn't remove any of your bookmarks. But if you added a custom toolbar or reset the home page, you need to reconfigure those settings after resetting.

✦ Running the System File Checker can also repair Internet Explorer. See Book II, Chapter 8.

✦ I don't recommend repairing or attempting to fix older versions of Internet Explorer. Instead, upgrade. See the next section.

Upgrading Internet Explorer

One of the most fundamental ways to fix Internet Explorer is to upgrade it. The newer version offers features you probably want or need; plus, it fixes a lot of the bugs and security flaws of the previous edition. (The preceding sentence is eternally true for all versions of Internet Explorer — past and future.)

In fact, I recommend upgrading Internet Explorer to the latest version even when you aren't having issues with the program.

Internet Explorer upgrades are obtained simply. First, the Windows Update process installs any newer versions of Internet Explorer that are available. Second, an automatic check is done every time Internet Explorer starts. If a newer release of the program is available, you're immediately whisked to an update web site (even when your home page is set elsewhere).

Manual updates for Internet Explorer can be obtained at the Microsoft web site:

```
www.microsoft.com/windows/downloads/ie/getitnow.mspx
```

See Book II, Chapter 1 for more information on Windows Updates.

Understanding the "work offline" thing

A menu item curious to many users is Work Offline. It's on the Tools button menu in Internet Explorer, but might also dwell on the File menu in other Internet applications. The item shouldn't be a mystery: Choosing the Work Offline option tells the program not to access the Internet. Indeed, you work offline when you choose that command.

If you attempt to do something on the Internet or the web page you're viewing tries to fetch new information, you see a warning such as the one shown in Figure 2-3, which explains that you're using Internet Explorer offline.

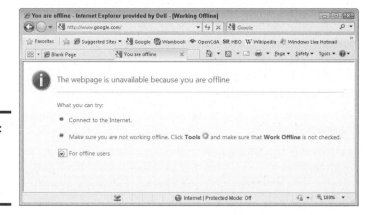

Figure 2-3:
The working-offline warning.

To disable Work Offline mode and return to normal, choose the Work Offline command again.

✦ Choosing the Work Offline command doesn't disconnect the computer from the Internet.

✦ I use Work Offline mode when I'm reading web pages on an airplane. I save the web pages before I leave and then choose the Work Offline command so that I'm not continually bothered by the PC's vain attempts to contact the Internet while I read.

Secret Ingredient: ActiveX

The letter *x* is so cool that our culture would be lost without it. Phonetically, it's useless. As long as there's a *k* and an *s* in the alphabet, *x* remains a mystery. Indeed, *x* itself often refers to an unknown value. It's this mystique that lends the *x* to so many wickedly awesome things. Could ActiveX be one of them? This section explains.

Understanding ActiveX

I'm certain I could explain a lot of technical mumbo jumbo about ActiveX, but the purpose of this book isn't to cure insomnia. Simply put, ActiveX is a software technology — a computer program to help other programs. What ActiveX does is create wee little programs that work on a web browser — specifically and solely Internet Explorer.

Anytime you visit a web page that shows a video or plays a game or lets you use a text editor, you're probably seeing an ActiveX *control*. The ActiveX program is sent from the web page to your computer, and the program "runs" in Internet Explorer.

Some folks were concerned a few years back about ActiveX being a bad thing. A security flaw in the way ActiveX was run years ago allowed the Bad Guys to send viruses and other nasty software to your computer. These issues have since been addressed.

✦ Controlling ActiveX is covered in the next section.

✦ No relationship exists between ActiveX and other Microsoft technologies using the word *Active*: Active Desktop or Active Directory, for example. Microsoft simply enjoys using the word *active* to describe things.

✦ Likewise, the technology DirectX has no relationship to ActiveX. Apparently, Microsoft also enjoys sticking the capitalized letter *X* to the end of certain words. (See Book II, Chapter 7 for a tiny tidbit on DirectX.)

✦ Web browsers other than Internet Explorer use Java and other network software technologies rather than ActiveX.

Book IV Chapter 2

Woes on the Web

Restricting ActiveX controls

Internet Explorer automatically installs ActiveX controls from the web sites you visit. If you prefer a higher level of security, you can restrict this access. Follow these steps:

1. **In Internet Explorer, choose the Internet Options command from the Tools button menu.**

2. **In the Internet Options dialog box, click the Security tab.**

3. **Choose Internet from the list of zones.**

4. **Click the Custom Level button.**

The Security Settings – Internet Zone dialog box appears, as shown in Figure 2-4.

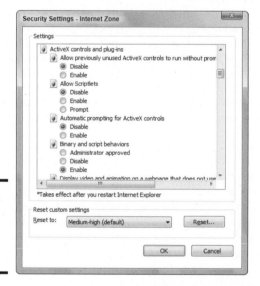

Figure 2-4: Control ActiveX in this dialog box.

5. **Scroll down to the section titled ActiveX Controls and Plug-Ins.**

The items organized in the ActiveX section deal with how Internet Explorer deals with various ActiveX situations on the Internet. Each option has two or more settings:

Enable: The ActiveX feature works automatically.

Disable: The ActiveX feature isn't allowed.

Prompt: You see a warning whenever an ActiveX control is being sent to your computer. At that time, you can choose whether to allow it.

Administrator Approved: A User Account Control warning appears when the ActiveX control tries to run.

The items in the list are set up tightly as far as security is concerned: Digitally signed and approved ActiveX controls are allowed, and you're prompted for almost everything else. Questionable ActiveX controls are disabled. However, I recommend the change in Step 6.

6. **Beneath the entry Run ActiveX Controls and Plug-Ins, choose Prompt.**

7. **Click OK to close the Security Settings – Internet Zone dialog box.**

8. **Click Yes to confirm the changes you made.**

   If you haven't made any changes, the Warning dialog box doesn't appear.

9. **Click OK to close the Internet Options dialog box.**

By making the change I suggest in Step 6, you add a higher level of security to your web browsing. But you also add a level of annoyance: the ActiveX control warning, as shown in Figure 2-5. As you soon can discover, the web pages you use are crawling with ActiveX controls.

Figure 2-5:
The ActiveX warning.

There are two solutions. The less secure one is to change the Run ActiveX Controls and Plug-Ins setting back to Enable from Prompt. That works. A more secure setting, however, is to simply add to your list of trusted sites the web sites you visit and trust. I explain how it's done later in this chapter, in the section "Adding a web site to your trusted zone."

Disabling ActiveX controls

When an ActiveX control comes floating in, it pretty much becomes part of your computer, attaching itself to Internet Explorer like a tick on an Alabama hound dog. In Internet Explorer 7, you could remove ActiveX controls by using the Manage Add-On window. That's no longer true in Internet Explorer 8.

The only thing you can do with installed ActiveX controls is to disable them, just as you disable any add-on. Follow these steps in Internet Explorer 8:

1. **Open Internet Explorer.**

2. **From the Tools button menu, choose Manage Add-Ons.**

   The Manage Add-Ons dialog box comes into view (refer to Figure 2-2).

**Book IV
Chapter 2**

Woes on the Web

3. **From the Show drop-down menu, ensure that All Add-Ons is chosen.**

   And now, the bad news: The add-ons in the window aren't sorted or even identified as individual ActiveX controls. Believe me: ActiveX controls are listed, but you have to find them individually. That takes time, unless you know the developer or specific name of the ActiveX control.

4. **Click an add-on in a list.**

   You see whether the add-on is an ActiveX control by looking at the detailed information in the bottom of the window. If the add-on type is an ActiveX Control, you've found one.

5. **Disable the ActiveX control by clicking the Disable button.**

6. **Repeat Steps 4 and 5 for every ActiveX control in the Manage Add-Ons window.**

   Of course, you don't have to disable all the controls; if you see some that you use frequently, such as Adobe Shockwave Flash player, keep it enabled. (Then again, Flash has its issues on certain web pages.)

7. **Click the Close button to dismiss the Manage Add-Ons window when you're done.**

Don't turn this exercise into a witch hunt. You'll find good ActiveX controls as well as evil ActiveX controls. In fact, if the entire issue bugs you, just use Firefox rather than Internet Explorer.

+ Also see the section "Dealing with add-ons," earlier in this chapter.

+ A good antivirus program automatically detects and removes evil ActiveX controls. See Chapter 4.

What's Up, Pop?

Advertising is as old as mankind. Those cave paintings weren't documenting a hunt — they were selling spears. As mankind has progressed, advertising has grown more effective. These days, spears are sold by using a pop-up window to assault your web browsing experience. Yeah, people hate it. This section explains how it works and what you can do about the dreaded pop-up windows.

Understanding pop-ups

The problem isn't as bad as it once was. Back, say, ten years ago or more, online advertisers virtually throttled web page viewers with an onslaught of pop-up advertising windows. Opening a single web page would often produce a flurry of three or more additional windows, each of which contained an advertisement. It was annoying.

Pop-up windows are created in several ways. Primarily, it's the JavaScript programming language that's responsible. JavaScript is built into every web browser. One of its features is that it allows for one web page window to spawn another window. Or four.

Advertisers took advantage of the spawning feature to display a new window boasting about their products every time you visited certain web pages. The window would *pop up* over or under the window you were viewing — hence the term *pop-up* to describe them.

Eventually, the situation got out of hand. Pop-ups ceased to be effective advertising and became irritating almost to the point where a negative backlash occurred. Legitimate advertisers stopped using pop-ups, and the questionable pharmaceutical dealers and porn peddlers took over. Fortunately, browser developers responded swiftly by allowing the JavaScript pop-up window feature to be disabled.

The bottom line is that pop-ups are still out there, but not as pervasively or as perversely as in days gone by. Like many web browsers, Internet Explorer has an anti-pop-up tool you can use, as described in the next section.

✦ One of the most insidious pop-up schemes was the *mousetrap*. When a pop-up advertising window appeared, you would click to close it. But by closing the window, you caused another one to open in its place. Sometimes, two windows would open every time you closed one window.

✦ Technically, a window that pops up behind the web page you're viewing is a *pop-under* window. It's still a pop-up.

✦ I should mention that many early pop-up windows featured unpleasant, hard-core pornographic images.

✦ The pop-up problem was worse years ago because Internet Explorer was directly wired into the Windows operating system; you couldn't "quit" Internet Explorer. Pop-up windows then eventually overwhelmed many users' desktops, requiring them to restart their computers (often by forcing a shutdown) to get rid of them.

Witnessing a pop-up

To see a real pop-up window in action, and to test Internet Explorer's pop-up blocking abilities, visit a special page on my Wambooli web site:

```
www.wambooli.com/help/pc/pop-up.html
```

When you visit this web page, a pop-up is programmed to appear. It's an ugly, green window with pink text! If you don't see the pop-up, your pop-up blocker is working; look for the notice just above the web page part of the window.

Avoiding pop-ups

Internet Explorer is configured to block all pop-up windows; the pop-up blocker feature is *on*. When a web page tries to sneak in a pop-up window, a warning (displayed just below the tabs and toolbar) says `Pop-up blocked. To see this pop-up or additional options click here.`

When you click the warning, a menu appears. Here are your choices:

Temporarily Allow Pop-Ups: Lets the pop-up sneak on through, but only because you gave it permission

Always Allow Pop-Ups for This Site: Lets you grant permission for the web site (and all pages on the site) to toss pop-up windows your way

Settings: Displays a submenu that allows you to change how Internet Explorer reacts to pop-ups

More Information: Displays a Help window about pop-ups

I generally ignore the warning myself by clicking the X on the right end of the pop-up blocker warning message, which dismisses the message. In fact, if you tire of the warning and just don't want to be bothered or you don't mind the warning but hate the beep, or both, you can control the pop-up blocker's settings.

To make changes to the way Internet Explorer's pop-up blocker behaves, from the Tools button menu, choose Pop-Up Blocker⇨Pop-Up Blocker Settings. You see the Pop-up Blocker Settings window, as shown in Figure 2-6.

Figure 2-6:
Controlling the Internet Explorer pop-up blocker.

You can use the Pop-Up Blocker Settings window to manually add sites for the pop-up blocker to ignore (though I prefer to add each site individually as I encounter it). Most important for me is the option Play a Sound When a Pop-Up Is Blocked. I don't like random beeps, so I turn that option off.

Incidentally, the Pop-Up Blocker Settings window is where you can remove any web sites you accidentally added to the Do Not Block list: Choose a site from the Allowed Sites list and then click the Remove button.

Click the Close button when you're done messing around with the Pop-Up Blocker Settings window.

✦ You can turn the pop-up blocker on or off by choosing the proper command from the Tools button menu's Pop-Up Blocker submenu.

✦ Pop-ups aren't always ads, of course. Some web sites use pop-ups to display information.

✦ At the custom-level settings, pop-up windows are allowed whenever you click a button or link to display the pop-up.

✦ If you set the filter level in the Pop-Up Blocker Settings window to High (refer to Figure 2-6), all pop-ups are blocked, no matter what.

✦ Blocking all pop-up windows may be a bad idea for some web sites. That's because items such as menus, slide shows, and other multimedia features on a web page may function by using pop-up windows. When you disable all pop-ups, you disable the features of the web site and decrease its usability.

✦ A new, nontraditional type of pop-up is even more annoying than the JavaScript pop-up: This Flash pop-up sometimes looks like a pop-up window but at other times appears to seamlessly float over the top of a web page. (The Internet Movie Database, at `imdb.com`, features some annoying examples.) Internet Explorer's pop-up blocker doesn't block the Flash windows. The only way to block them is to disable the Flash ActiveX component, but that would also make many videos, media, and games cease to function on the Internet.

Web Page Hell

The list is practically endless when it comes to generic web page mayhem. Things are better than they once were; today's web browser is a truly sophisticated beast that can usually handle even the most unruly web sites. When it doesn't, turn to this section for assistance.

**Book IV
Chapter 2**

Woes on the Web

Dealing with a missing web page

You *know* that a web page exists. You were there yesterday, or just an hour ago! Yet the web browser is telling you that the web site isn't found or you see a list of suggestions for alternative sites. The missing web page episode can be very frustrating, especially when it's a major site, such as Google or Facebook.

First, ensure that you're connected to the Internet; try visiting another web page.

Second, know that web pages do go down. Sometimes they go down for maintenance or for other reasons. After all, web sites are run by computers similar to the one you own and, yes, these computers have problems, too.

Third, sometimes the Internet gets busy. When this happens, the message you see in the browser window says that the web connection has timed out. Try again later, which may end up being a day later for a web page that's really, really busy.

Finally, web sites can be blocked by security software. You may see a warning displayed, or the web site may simply be nonaccessible. This situation arises most often when you're using a laptop on a public wireless network.

For all situations where security software isn't the cause, my advice is to simply wait and try again later. The problem usually resolves itself, unless the web site has gone permanently offline.

✦ One reason that web pages get busy is an overabundance of traffic. Though major web sites such as Microsoft and Yahoo! can handle a lot of traffic, smaller sites cannot. When a smaller web site gets a lot of hits, its server times out.

✦ Another tool you can try when dealing with missing web pages is the web page connection troubleshooter. See the Windows 7 Internet Connection troubleshooter discussion in Chapter 1.

Adding a web site to your trusted zone

When you ratchet up Internet security (such as by disabling ActiveX components, as discussed earlier in this chapter), you might find your once-pleasant and speedy web browsing experience plagued with speed bumps. You can fix this problem, and ensure that you're not bothered with ActiveX or other types of warnings, for web sites you trust. Follow these steps in Internet Explorer:

1. **Browse to a site you can trust.**

For example, go to any web page you visit frequently, but also one where you see warnings about security, such as ActiveX controls.

2. **From the Tools menu button, choose Internet Options.**

3. **In the Internet Options dialog box, click the Security tab.**

4. **Click the big, green check mark: Trusted Sites.**

5. **Click the Sites button.**

   You discover the Trusted Sites dialog box, as shown in Figure 2-7. The web site you're visiting is shown next to the Add button.

6. **If the web site you're adding doesn't use the** `https` **URL, remove the check mark by the option Require Server Verification (https:) for All Sites in This Zone.**

   When you forget to uncheck this option and you add a non-`https` site, a rude warning dialog box appears.

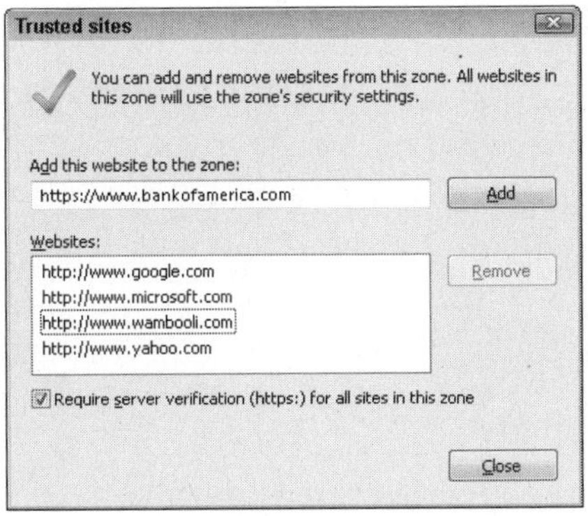

Figure 2-7:
The Trusted
Sites dialog
box.

7. **Click the Add button.**

   The web site is added to the list.

8. **Click Close.**

9. **Click OK to send off the Internet Options dialog box.**

Adding a site you frequent to your trusted zone helps expedite things that happen on the web site, without your having to compromise overall Internet security.

✦ You don't need to add individual pages within the site; add only the root part of the site. For example, adding `www.microsoft.com` provides for all web pages within the `microsoft.com` domain to be trusted.

✦ You may still be prompted for ActiveX alerts when you add a web site to the trusted zone. The alerts may not be coming from the web site directly but, rather, from frames or links to online advertising.

✦ Web sites whose addresses begin with https are *secure* web sites, established by a verification process. These sites ensure that the information you send is encrypted and cannot be lifted by a bad guy en route. I'm not implying that an http (no *S*) site is insecure, but rather that it's possible to trust a normal site that doesn't need the extra verification.

Fixing weirdly sized windows

The weirdly sized window is more appropriately an issue in Windows, not in the web browser. The problem seems to surface often in a web browser, probably because the program opens more windows than other programs do.

Some web pages automatically resize windows: The web page opens and suddenly fills the entire screen. You can do nothing to prevent it from happening (other than not visit the web site). All you can do is resize the window after it opens.

Because Windows remembers the size and position of previous windows you opened, you may experience new web pages opening in oddly sized windows. To fix the problem, manually resize the window.

✦ To manually resize a window, use the mouse to move the window's edges. You can grab the top or bottom edge of a window to make it taller or more squat. You can grab the left or right edge of a window to make it wider or thinner. You can grab a window's corner to resize the window in two directions at one time.

✦ Resized windows are most apparent when you have a nice, roomy, widescreen monitor. The newly resized window enlarges to cover the entire screen but isn't maximized.

✦ Maximizing a window isn't the same as resizing it. When you maximize the window, you do not reset the window's size and position on the desktop.

Looking bigger (smaller)

Zoom can mean to go really fast. But it can also mean to move in closer, such as by using a camera's zoom lens. The latter definition is used as the name of a command featured in just about every program. The Zoom command is used to make what you see appear smaller or larger on the screen.

In Internet Explorer, you can zoom an entire web page, making its contents larger or smaller: From the Page menu, choose Zoom and then choose a zoom size from the submenu.

When it's merely the text size that needs adjusting, you can use the Text Size submenu, also found on the Page button menu.

✦ The keyboard shortcut to zoom into a web page is Ctrl++ (the plus key).

✦ The keyboard shortcut to zoom out of a web page is Ctrl+– (the minus key).

✦ You can also zoom an image by pressing the Ctrl key and using the wheel button on the mouse: Ctrl+scroll up zooms in; Ctrl+scroll down zooms back out.

Printing a web page

The mechanics of printing a web page work like printing any document in any application: Choose the Print command from the File menu, work the Print dialog box, and then print, blah-blah-blah — you know the drill. Assuming that the printer is connected and ready to go, the web page should print. But that *is* an assumption.

My first mistake is assuming that the Print command is on the File menu. Internet Explorer has no File menu, but it has a Print button on its toolbar. Clicking the button prints the web page, or you can display a menu, as shown in Figure 2-8, that shows more printing options.

Figure 2-8:
The Print toolbar button's menu.

My second mistake is to assume that you can fit all the content of a single web page on a single sheet of paper. You can! But often, Internet Explorer shrinks the content to fit a page. Here's how to fix the problem:

1. **From the Print button on the toolbar, choose the Print Preview command.**

The Print Preview window opens, as shown in Figure 2-9. The window not only helps prevent wasting paper but also assists in ensuring that you print the web page exactly the way you want.

2. **Select the proper page orientation.**

Some web pages look better on paper when they're printed in land-scape orientation. Again, the Print Preview window helps you determine whether landscape is a better choice before you print.

Chapter 2**

Woes on the Web

Print

Portrait orientation

Landscape orientation   Change print size.   Margin adjuster

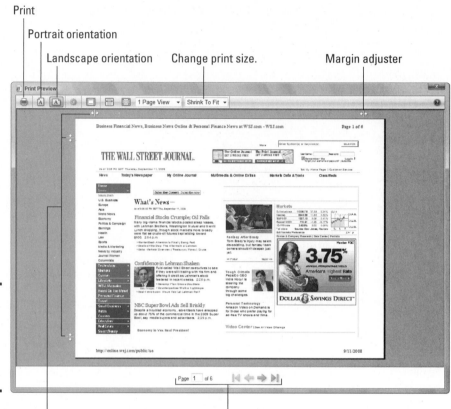

Figure 2-9:
The Print
Preview
window
for Internet
Explorer 7.

Margin adjusters   Page viewing controls

3. Set the proper zoom or shrink value by using the Change Print Size menu.

As you choose a size, use the preview image to determine whether it looks good.

4. Click the Print button to bring up the Print dialog box.

5. Work the options in the Print dialog box.

Some examples are Number of Copies and Which Pages to Print.

6. Click the Print button to print the web page.

7. Close the Print Preview window.

You're returned to the web page.

In an amazing twist of technology, a once-electronic web page is now inked to a sheet of paper. Be sure to amaze your friends with such a thing.

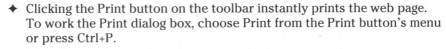

✦ Clicking the Print button on the toolbar instantly prints the web page. To work the Print dialog box, choose Print from the Print button's menu or press Ctrl+P.

✦ A single web page is often output to several printed pages.

✦ To print only part of a web page, select the part you want by using the mouse. Then press Ctrl+P and, in the Print dialog box, choose Selection. Click the Print button to print only the selected portion of the web page.

✦ Only one part of a web page can be selected at a time.

✦ Sometimes, text fails to show up when you select the Shrink to Fit option. It's a "feature" of the web page. Simply choose another size from the Change Print Size menu.

✦ You can print an image on a web page by right-clicking the image and choosing Print Picture from the shortcut menu. This trick comes in handy when the image doesn't print with the rest of the web page.

✦ For printer troubleshooting, see Book I, Chapter 5.

Disabling JavaScript error messages

It isn't your job to fix a broken web page. You may feel like it's your job. I guess that's because the web page error message, like other computer error messages, appears on the screen and blares at you. It makes you assume that it's your problem and that you must deal with it. But, for a web page, it's not your problem. Further, you can do nothing about it.

A specific error message case comes with the *JavaScript* programming language. What JavaScript does is help automate and format web pages. You'll probably never deal with JavaScript, other than to use it on a web page. But you may, occasionally, see something like the example shown in Figure 2-10.

Figure 2-10: The web page screwed up, not you.

Figure 2-10 features a JavaScript warning message. The warning is for the programmer, which can be seen when you click the Show Details button. (Don't bother.) Instead, remove the check mark by the item Always Display This Message When a Page Contains Errors.

To ensure that errors don't appear in the future, follow these steps in Internet Explorer:

1. **Choose the command Internet Options from the bottom of the Tools button menu.**

2. **Click the Advanced tab in the Internet Options dialog box.**

   You see three items to check in the list, all found beneath the Browsing heading.

3. **Place a check mark by the item Disable Script Debugging (Internet Explorer).**

4. **Place a check mark by the item Disable Script Debugging (Other).**

5. **Remove the check mark by the item Display a Notification about Every Script Error.**

6. **Click OK to close the Internet Options dialog box.**

Suppressing the error message doesn't remove the error from the page. The error is still there. But it's up to the programmer or web page designer, not you, to fix the problem.

Dealing with missing pictures

A placeholder indicates a missing image on a web page, as shown in Figure 2-11. Different web browsers use different missing-picture icons. Internet Explorer uses the red *X* in a box, as shown in the figure.

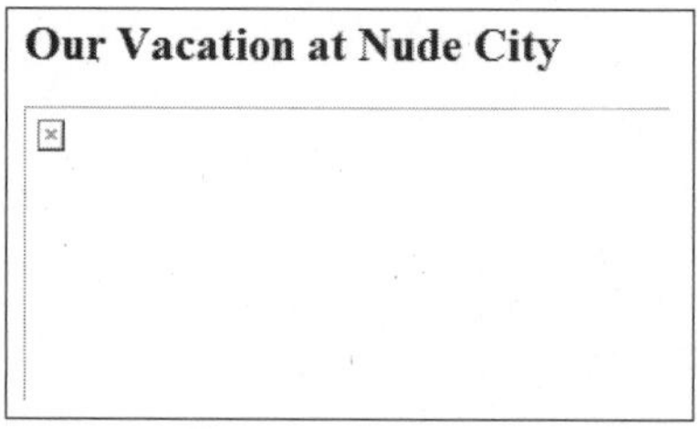

Our Vacation at Nude City

⊠

Figure 2-11: One thousand words missing.

The first trick to try making the picture appear is to refresh the web page: Press F5 or Ctrl+R. Refreshing loads a new web page from the Internet, which may pick up an image that the web server was too slow to send in the first place.

The second trick is to right-click the missing-image icon and choose the Show Picture command. Sometimes this method works, but only when you configure Internet Explorer *not* to display images, which brings up the third trick:

Ensure that Internet Explorer is configured to display images. Follow these steps:

1. **From the Tools button menu, choose Internet Options.**

2. **In the Internet Options dialog box, click the Advanced tab.**

3. **Scroll down to the Multimedia heading and ensure that a check mark appears by the item Show Pictures.**

4. **Click OK.**

Some users disable pictures on web pages, which greatly increases the speeds at which web pages load. But it also means that you have to manually load the images when you want to see them (refer to Trick 2). By completing the preceding steps, you ensure that the images are loaded.

When these tricks fail, it's simply a problem with the web site; the image file isn't present or the code that lists the image's filename is wrong. There's nothing you can do about it.

Chapter 3: Email Postage Due

In This Chapter

- Knowing how email works
- Struggling with a draft
- Working in the trash
- Dealing with repeated messages
- Fixing email program quirks
- Blocking and unblocking messages
- Using junk mail filters
- Avoiding large email attachments

I was looking the other day in the tattered old book *Mail For Dummies*, published in 1934. It had such interesting chapters as "Thank-You Notes," "Proper Salutations," and "Stamps." The troubleshooting information was fairly limited, covering topics such as folding stationery, knowing when it's okay to use pencil, and choosing which side of the stamp to lick. With today's electronic mail, there are no more stamps, but there are certainly some troublesome topics to lick. This chapter seals the envelope on those issues without your having to use your tongue.

- There's no single email program, though email works pretty much the same in all email programs. Wherever possible, I keep the information in this chapter generic.

- This chapter assumes that you already set up and configured your email program and that it has worked in the past. If you need help getting your email, my best advice is to contact your Internet service provider (ISP) for assistance.

- A big hurdle for email users to clear is the topic of email attachments. Because this process falls under the topic of file transfer, it's covered in Chapter 5.

- Your PC may be blessed with multiple email programs. To determine which one is used as the primary program, see the information on choosing Internet programs in Chapter 1.

Message for You, Sir!

Electronic mail, or email, predates the Internet. Computers back in the early 1960s were often caught sending each other mail, some of it quite salacious. Eventually, the computer operators learned how the trick worked and email was born. Email is now the number-one reason that people use the Internet. This section covers the basics of email so that you can better understand what it is that you're troubleshooting.

Understanding email

Many parallels exist between email and traditional postal mail. The biggest difference is in speed, which is why regular mail is referred to as *snail mail*. (The snail has long been a beloved mascot of the U.S. Postal Service.) Otherwise, the similarities between email and mail are numerous.

Figure 3-1 illustrates the basic email-sending concept. A message is composed on a computer by using an email program: a *client*. The email program combines the text you wrote (the *body*) with the recipient, subject, date, and time (the *header*).

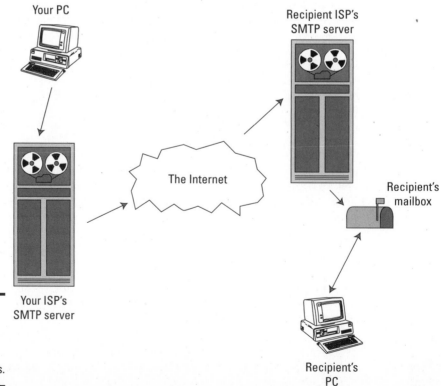

Figure 3-1: The illustration of how email works.

Your PC

Recipient ISP's SMTP server

The Internet

Recipient's mailbox

Your ISP's SMTP server

Recipient's PC

Your email program (the client) then sends the message off to an email server by using the *Simple Message Transfer Protocol*, or *SMTP*. The email server is basically a program running on another computer. For most people, the computer is located at your Internet service provider, or ISP.

At the server, the message is dissected and the recipients culled from the message's To, Cc, and Bcc fields in the header. The SMTP server then finds the host computer for the recipients. For example, if the message is being sent to `billg@microsoft.com`, the server looks up `microsoft.com` and sends the message off to that computer.

For a few nanoseconds, the message hops around the Internet as it makes the connection to the destination computer.

At the destination computer, another SMTP server fetches the message and stuffs it into a mailbox for the intended user. There, it sits and waits until the user logs in to collect his mail. But the mailbox on the server isn't the same thing as the inbox in your PC's mail program.

The recipient's mail program collects new messages from his ISP's server. The mail program uses the *Post Office Protocol (POP)* to fetch the message. POP is used instead of SMTP because the email message is no longer being sent on the Internet; it has arrived. All the POP does is fetch the message waiting on the server and transfer it back to the user's computer and his email program.

After the mail messages are on the recipient's computer, they're stored in a database. Secretly, all email programs are database programs. After your messages are received, they exist in various mailboxes organized by your email program: Inbox, Deleted Items, and Junk, for example. Messages can be read, forwarded, deleted, and so on, which is all basic email program stuff.

✦ The email methods described in this section don't apply to web-based email. They also don't apply to email systems at large organizations, such as Lotus Notes or Microsoft Exchange.

✦ In addition to POP is the *Internet Message Access Protocol (IMAP)* method of reading email. Unlike POP, IMAP doesn't delete messages from the user's mailbox on the server until the user deletes the message. Web-based email programs, such as Gmail and Hotmail, often prefer IMAP.

✦ All email is plain text — all of it. When you write a message, the message itself is text, the technical *header* information is plain text, and even the formatting you apply is plain text. If you attach a file, the file is converted to plain text and sent with the message.

✦ Your email is stored on the ISP's computer until you pick it up. Unless you retrieve those messages, your mailbox on the ISP's mail server continues to fill up until it's so bloated that no more messages can be received.

Book IV Chapter 3

Email Postage Due

+ Most ISPs limit the size of your mailbox, which means that all the messages are stored and waiting for you to pick them up. Additionally, your account may have size limits on individual messages, which often can't be larger than 5 or 10 megabytes. Contact your ISP for specifics.

+ When your mailbox gets full, the ISP *bounces* any new email you might receive. The message is returned to the sending SMTP computer, but the sender may not receive a notice that the message has bounced.

+ To fix a full mailbox, you must *read your mail!*

+ After you pick up your mail from the server, the messages are deleted from your personal mailbox on the server. When they aren't, your email client continues to pick up the same email messages repeatedly. That's why you sometimes receive multiple copies of the same message. Also see the section "Leaving mail on the server," next in this chapter.

+ The ISP keeps an archive of the mail arriving in your mailbox. Email is legally *discoverable*, which means that in a lawsuit either side can request, and receive, all the messages you've sent and received. Email is *not* private.

+ Email's lack of privacy is why I highly recommend that you never send sensitive information (bank account numbers, credit card numbers, or Social Security numbers) via email.

+ Locally, your email program puts your mail into mailboxes or mail folders. These folders work like the folders in Windows, but the mail messages in the folders aren't stored as individual files. Instead, each mailbox or folder in your mail program is a single text file on disk. See the later section, "Trashing a message," for reasons why it's important to know how email messages are stored on your computer.

Leaving mail on the server

In the standard email scheme of things, whenever your email program goes to pick up new mail, the mail is sent to your computer and then deleted from the server. One option, however, lets you elect to *not* delete the message from the server. Here's how to set up the option in Windows Live Mail, Windows Mail, and Outlook Express:

1. Choose Tools⇨Accounts from the menu.

If you're using Windows Live Mail, press the F10 key to see the menu bar, and then choose Tools⇨Accounts.

2. Choose your mail account from the list.

In Outlook Express, you can click the Mail tab to see only your mail accounts.

3. Click the Properties button.

4. **Click the Advanced tab in the mail server's Properties dialog box.**

The settings for leaving mail on the server are kept in the bottom part of the Advanced tab, as shown in Figure 3-2.

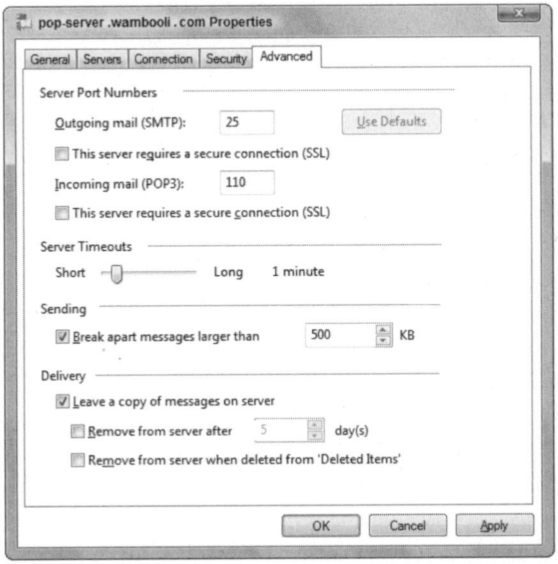

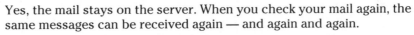

Figure 3-2:
Settings
for leaving
mail on the
server.

5. **Place a check mark by the option Leave a Copy of Messages On Server to prevent your email from being deleted after you receive it.**

Yes, the mail stays on the server. When you check your mail again, the same messages can be received again — and again and again.

When you keep receiving the same email over and over, you should *disable* this option.

6. **If you want to have messages removed after a number of days, place a check mark by the item Remove from Server after X Days, and then enter the number of days.**

You can enter values from 1 through 100 in the Days box.

7. **If instead you want the messages removed when you delete them locally, place a check mark by the item Remove from Server When Deleted from 'Deleted Items.'**

I believe this option to be the best one, which I explain in a few paragraphs.

8. **Click OK to confirm the settings and close the dialog box.**

Book IV
Chapter 3

Email Postage Due

The reason for leaving mail on the server is simple: You can pick it up again. Indeed, when you keep picking up the same email over and over, the option to leave the mail on the server is probably set. But for most folks, leaving mail on the server is done on purpose.

Suppose that you're on the road with your laptop. You don't have time to *answer* email, but you want to read it. Further, there's no coordination of e-mail between your desktop and laptop computers. The solution is to leave the messages on the server. That way, you can reply to email that requires an immediate response, and you can collect those messages again when you return to the desktop PC. (This scheme works only when the desktop PC is configured *not* to leave messages on the server.)

✦ Laptop computers, smartphones, and other portable devices are commonly configured to leave mail on the server.

✦ Other email clients have options to leave mail on the server. Generally speaking, edit your account settings (not the program settings). One option in your email account leaves messages on the server.

General Email Melancholy

For the most part, your email experiences should be pleasant and unremarkable, for the most part. For those other parts, turn to this section for help on what to do.

Dealing with drafts

Most email clients feature folders into which you can stuff your email messages. The folders are named Inbox, Outbox, Sent, Deleted Items or Trash, Junk, and Drafts. It's the Drafts mailbox that seems to vex too many users. Don't let it.

A *draft* is simply an email message you haven't yet sent. It's not the same thing as an email *waiting* to be sent. Nope, it's an email message you close by choosing File⇨Save or closing the window rather than clicking the Send button. This act places the message into the Drafts folder.

You have three choices for dealing with messages in the Drafts folder:

Do nothing. This option is always a favorite, especially for elected officials.

Open the message and send it. It's a simple solution: You open the message (double-click it in the Drafts folder), review it, edit it, and touch it up, and then click the Send button to zip the email along its merry way.

Delete the message. Click to select the message and then drag it to the Deleted Items or Trash mailbox.

That's how to deal with your drafts.

✦ Sometimes, the Drafts folder doesn't show up until you create a draft email to put in it.

✦ Messages can "suddenly appear" in the Drafts folder when you forget to send a message or you close the message window without sending. It happens. In fact, even I am surprised to find messages in my Drafts folder when I was double-dog certain that I sent them.

Trashing a message

Deleting an email message is a simple affair: In most email programs, you simply drag the message into the Deleted Items or Trash folder. Done.

The Deleted Items or Trash mail folder works like all other folders in your email program: It stores messages. The messages sit in the folder and aren't deleted until you direct the program to purge them. You have several options for purging messages:

Not at all. This option leads to the Deleted Items or Trash folder growing very large and eventually your email program becoming sluggish as it deals with the bulk.

Delete messages after a given amount of time. I like this option. I prefer setting the delete interval to one month. That way, I can fish for something urgent that I might have accidentally deleted and still be able to find it.

Delete messages when you close the mail program. This option still allows you to rescue missives from the Deleted Items or Trash folder, but only until you close the email program.

Delete at once! This option doesn't allow any recovery for deleted mail — vicious, satisfying, and permanent.

Here's how you can adjust the Deleted Items folder's behavior in Windows Live Mail, Windows Mail, and Outlook Express:

1. **Choose Tools⇨Options.**

In Windows Live Mail, press the F10 key to see the menu bar.

2a. **In Windows Live Mail and Windows Mail, click the Advanced tab in the Options dialog box and then click the Maintenance button.**

2b. **In Outlook Express, click the Maintenance tab in the Options dialog box.**

3. **Place a check mark by the item Empty Messages from 'Deleted Items' Folder On Exit.**

   By placing the check mark there, you ensure that the mail program purges all deleted messages when you exit. Otherwise, the messages are retained.

4. **Click the OK or Close button and close any other open dialog boxes.**

In Microsoft Outlook 2010, follow these steps to remove email left in the Deleted Items folder:

1. **From the File tab, choose Options.**

2. **In the Outlook Options window, choose Advanced from the left side of the window.**

3. **Place a check mark by the item Empty Delete Items Folders When Exiting Outlook.**

4. **Click OK.**

In earlier versions of Microsoft Outlook, you can control the Deleted Items folder behavior by following these steps:

1. **Choose Tools⇨Options from the menu.**

2. **In the Options dialog box, click the Other tab.**

3. **Place a check mark by the item Empty the Deleted Items Folder Upon Exiting to have the folder purged when you close Outlook.**

4. **Click OK.**

You can always purge an individual message from the Deleted Items or Trash folders by opening the folder, selecting the message, and then deleting the message.

The Deleted Items or Trash folder works like every other email message folder. It's not a real folder, but it is a long text file database stored on your PC. When you purge a message from the Deleted Items or Trash folder, or when you empty that mailbox folder, the deleted messages are gone for good!

In Windows Live Mail, Windows Mail, and Outlook Express, you can instantly purge the Deleted Items folder by choosing Edit⇨Empty 'Deleted Items' Folder.

Multiple message mayhem

Suppose that you don't use Windows Live Mail, Windows Mail, or their ancestor, Outlook Express. One day, in your email inbox, you see a series of messages from the same person. They have titles like the ones shown in Figure 3-3. Opening the messages reveals garbage. What can you do, what can you do?

	From	Subject	Received
Inbox	Al Gore	Please keep it between us!	9/16/2009 6:09 AM
Outbox	B Rodriguez	I hear you have some pix?	9/16/2009 6:12 AM
	Paris Hilton	What you wanted agnph.jpg [1/6]	9/16/2009 4:21 PM
Sent	Paris Hilton	What you wanted agnph.jpg [2/6]	9/16/2009 4:21 PM
Drafts	Paris Hilton	What you wanted agnph.jpg [3/6]	9/16/2009 4:21 PM
	Paris Hilton	What you wanted agnph.jpg [4/6]	9/16/2009 4:21 PM
Junk	Paris Hilton	What you wanted agnph.jpg [5/6]	9/16/2009 4:21 PM
Trash	Paris Hilton	What you wanted agnph.jpg [6/6]	9/16/2009 4:21 PM
	Dan's Editor	Why aren't you working?	9/17/2009 8:24 AM

Figure 3-3: Weird, multiple messages.

The cause of this problem is that the person sending the mail has configured an option in one of Microsoft's email programs to split apart long messages. There are only two things you can do:

First, you can choose to replace your email program with one of Microsoft's email programs: Windows Live Mail, Windows Mail, or Outlook Express. These programs automatically reassemble split-apart message attachments. That's the easy solution, but because the author of *Always Obey Microsoft For Dummies* is taking way too long to complete that title, I offer an alternative solution:

Second, tell the person sending the message to reconfigure the mail program *not* to split apart long messages and to resend the message. To do this, instruct the person to go out and buy a copy of this book and follow these steps in Windows Live Mail, Windows Mail, or Outlook Express:

1. **Choose Tools➪Accounts.**

In Windows Live Mail, press the F10 key to behold the menu bar.

2. **Choose your email account from the list.**

In Outlook Express, you can click the Mail tab and then choose your email account because that screen is less cluttered.

3. **Click the Properties button.**

4. **Click the Advanced tab in your mail server's Properties dialog box.**

5. **Remove the check mark by the item Break Apart Messages Larger than X KB.**

6. **Click OK and then click the Close button to dismiss the Internet Accounts dialog box.**

Ensure that the sender goes out and gets his own copy of this book. Don't loan this book to anyone, especially people who break apart long messages.

Repairing hyperlinks in Outlook Express

A problem that plagued users of Outlook Express for generations was the bad-hyperlink conundrum. Most sophisticated email programs display as a clickable link any text that looks like a web page or an email address in an email message. It's magic! But sometimes Outlook Express loses the magic.

To remedy the situation, and to try to restore links to your email message in Outlook Express running Windows XP, follow these technical steps:

1. **Open the Folder Options icon in the Control Panel.**

2. **Click the File Types tab.**

3. **Select (NONE) URL: HyperText Transfer Protocol from the list of registered file types.**

   Figure 3-4 illustrates what you're looking for.

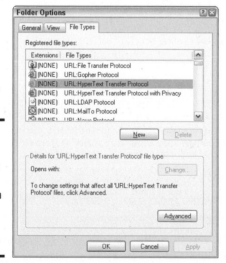

Figure 3-4: Finding the proper item on the File Types tab in the Folder Options dialog box.

4. **Click the Advanced button.**

The Edit File Type dialog box appears.

5. **Click the Edit button.**

6. **If you don't see the word *open* in the Action dialog box, type it in there.**

Type **open** (no period).

7. **Confirm that the Application Used to Perform Action text box contains the text `"C:\Program Files\Internet Explorer\iexplore.exe" -nohome`.**

If the text box doesn't contain the text, type it exactly as written:

```
"C:\Program Files\Internet Explorer\iexplore.exe"
         -nohome
```

The final option is a hyphen followed immediately by the "word" nohome (there's no space between the two).

8. **Place a check mark by the option Use DDE.**

9. **Ensure that the text `"%1",,-1,0,,,,` is written in the DDE Message box.**

If the text isn't written, type it. Here's how it looks:

```
"%1",,-1,0,,,,
```

That's %1 in double quotes, followed by two commas, and then –1, a comma, zero, and four commas. The text must be typed exactly as shown.

10. **Ensure that the text `IExplore` is typed in the Application box.**

11. **Check to confirm that the DDE Application Not Running box is left blank.**

12. **Click OK.**

No, you're not done yet. You need to confirm that a second item has also been set properly and then fix it if necessary.

13. **Back in the Folder Properties dialog box, on the File Types tab, choose (NONE) URL: HyperText Transfer Protocol with Privacy from the Registered File Types list.**

It's the item just below (NONE) URL: HyperText Transfer Protocol (refer to Figure 3-4).

14. **Repeat Steps 4 through 12 exactly.**

15. **Click OK to close the Folder Options dialog box.**

If you still have problems, repeat these steps, but modify Step 7. First, try changing the first part of the text to %programfiles%, like this:

```
"%programfiles%\Internet Explorer\iexplore.exe" -nohome
```

Book IV
Chapter 3

Email Postage Due

If it still doesn't work, add the text %1 to the end of the command. Here's how the command should look:

```
"%programfiles%\Internet Explorer\iexplore.exe" -nohome %1
```

Fixing that email disconnection urge

The Windows Mail email program may disconnect a dialup Internet connection after it receives email. It's a problem inherited from the old Outlook Express program: After the program checks for available email, it hangs up the modem. The hang-up occurs even when you're online doing something else. Here's how to fix that program in Windows Live Mail, Windows Mail, or Outlook Express:

1. **Choose Tools⇨Options from the menu.**

   Press the F10 key in Windows Live Mail to see the Tools menu.

2. **Click the Connection tab in the Options dialog box.**

3. **Remove the check mark by the option Hang Up after Sending and Receiving.**

4. **Click OK.**

That should fix the problem. If not, you can take some additional steps:

1. **Choose Tools⇨Options from the email program's menu.**

2. **If necessary, click the General tab.**

3. **Remove the check mark by the option Check for New Messages Every xx Minutes.**

4. **Choose Do Not Connect from the menu button titled If My Computer Is Not Connected at This Time.**

5. **Click OK.**

By making the changes in the last set of steps, you ensure that the mail program doesn't automatically check for messages and, hopefully, doesn't disconnect you from the Internet.

✦ By disabling the email program's automatic email checking, you must manually check for new mail. It's an easy thing to do: Click the Send/ Receive button from the mail program's toolbar to check for new messages.

✦ In Windows Live Mail, the Sync toolbar button is used rather than Send/Receive.

✦ The Send/Receive toolbar button may be labeled Send/Recv in earlier versions of Outlook Express.

"Why doesn't the address book work?"

A common email question I get, mostly from Outlook users, is that something is amiss with their address books. Names can't be recalled or used, and nothing seems to work correctly. Sadly, the problem isn't anything you can fix.

Outlook works best when it's on a network with something called Microsoft Exchange Server. This program (running on a main computer, or *server*) is responsible for controlling address book and contact information. You should consider it the "rest of Outlook."

For a small-office or home setup, it's impractical, not to mention expensive, to set up an exchange server. A better solution, and my suggestion for you, is to use an email program other than Outlook.

"I can't read your message!"

When email arrives in an unreadable state, you must first recognize this simple fact: *It's not your fault.* Your email program can deal with only what it receives, and though you use the program to read incoming mail, the program didn't compose or format that mail. How could it have?

If the message is all gibberish, one of two things has happened. The first is that the email was sent by using foreign-language characters that your PC cannot display. Most of these messages are usually foreign-language spam. (I get Russian-language spam all the time.)

The second type of message is a formatted message. For example, the text may be very small or very large. You may see bright pink text on a blue background. Animated goobers may be dancing or winking at you. It's all formatted text, similar to the way a web page is formatted.

The solution to the formatted-text problem is to ask the sender to resend the message in *plain text*, not formatted text.

When email is sent by using plain text, it's received in plain text. Your email program has no trouble displaying this type of message; the font size is fine, and it has no foreign characters or gibberish — well, unless the person is just writing nonsense, and even *that,* you cannot control!

✦ In Outlook 2010, you can compose a message in plain text by clicking the Format Text tab and choosing Plain Text from the Format group.

✦ In Outlook 2007, you create a new message in plain text by clicking the Options tab and clicking the Plain Text button in the Format area.

✦ In Windows Mail, Outlook Express, and older versions of Outlook, you compose a message in plain text by choosing Format➪Plain Text from the New Message window.

✦ For small text in an email message, you can try zooming the email message in the window by using the View⇨Text Size submenu.

Unable to send email

A problem you sometimes encounter on the road is an inability to properly send email. You may receive a validation error message from the email server or encounter a problem with the recipient's names not being recognized as valid. Welcome to life on the road.

The problem with your email is most likely that you're trying to send it by using your home SMTP server and, when you're on the road, you're using another SMTP server that doesn't appreciate your laptop's settings.

A possible solution is to fuss with the mail program's SMTP server settings and try to figure out the outgoing mail's proper SMTP server settings. But I can instantly recommend that you not bother with this process in a hotel or wireless hot spot (such as an airport or a café).

The solution I use is to pick up my email in the standard way, but to send out the email by using Hotmail, Yahoo Mail!, Gmail, or another web-based mail service. These services don't seem to have a problem with my laptop's location. You can also contact your ISP to see whether it has web-based email service.

The worst-case scenario is that you cannot even send email. Although it may be the "worst case," it's not the end of the world. Remember that phone calls also work for communications and that most serious stuff can generally wait until you have a good connection that appreciates your email server.

Email You Don't Want

Everyone loves getting email, but they don't love handling all the email. Though the problem of spam or junk email isn't quite as obnoxious as it has been in years past, unwanted messages still beach themselves like so much digital jetsam. This section describes how you can deal with those messages.

Blocking senders

The good news about bad news is that it seems to consistently come from the same sources. Whether it's unwanted email, spam, junk mail, or perhaps a persistent relative or acquaintance who won't stop sending you "cute" stuff, most email programs have an easy way to block them.

Perhaps the best, quickest way to deal with unwanted email is to use your email program's feature to place a message recipient on a Block Senders list. It's an easy thing to do, though the method varies depending on the email program.

In Windows Live Mail, Windows Mail, and Outlook Express follow these steps:

1. **Open the message you want to block.**

2a. **In Windows Live Mail, choose Actions⇨Junk E-Mail⇨Add Sender to Blocked Senders List.**

2b. **In Windows Mail, choose Message⇨Junk E-Mail⇨Add Sender to Blocked Senders List.**

2c. **In Outlook Express, choose Message⇨Block Sender.**

3. **Click the Yes button or click OK.**

Now feel free to read your email without being bothered by the sender. Then again, it probably won't be the last time you need to block a sender.

When your email program lacks a Block Sender feature, you have to use the feature that filters email or creates a mail rule. Simply create a rule that identifies the sender, or the sender's domain, and then redirect any message from that user into the Deleted Items or Trash folder. See the later section, "Junking email," for information.

Unblocking senders

The Blocked Senders tool was a welcome addition to the email programs that ship with Windows. It worked! Sometimes, it worked too well. The biggest problem people had with it was blocking people they didn't mean to block. Oops.

Here's how to unblock an accidentally blocked sender in Windows Live Mail and Windows Mail:

1a. **In Windows Live Mail, choose Actions⇨Junk E-Mail⇨Safety Options.**

You may have to press the F10 key to expose the Actions menu.

1b. **In Windows Mail, choose Tools⇨Junk E-Mail Options.**

2. **Click the Blocked Senders tab.**

3. **Select the user you want to unblock.**

Users are listed only by email address, so it helps to know their addresses.

4. **Click the Remove button.**

   Yeah, the button should read Stop Blocking or something similar, but Microsoft doesn't ask for my input.

5. **Click OK.**

In Outlook Express, you can unblock a sender by following these steps:

1. **Choose Tools⇨Message Rules⇨Blocked Senders List.**

2. **Select from the Message Rules dialog box the user you want to unblock.**

3. **Click the Remove button.**

4. **Click OK.**

Removing someone from the Blocked Senders list doesn't automatically restore any of their blocked messages. To find those, you need to dig through the junk mail or Deleted Items folders.

Junking email

Junk filters use formidable logic and magical incantations to identify the telltale signs of spam. Or, you can train them to identify email you don't want. It all depends on how your email program implements the junk mail filter.

In Windows Live Mail and Windows Mail, follow these steps to configure automatic junk-mail options:

1a. **In Windows Live Mail, choose Actions⇨Junk E-Mail⇨Safety Options.**

1b. **In Windows Mail, choose Tools⇨Junk E-Mail Options.**

   A dialog box appears, as shown in Figure 3-5. It's called Safety Options in Windows Live Mail, and Junk E-Mail Options in Windows Mail.

   The Options tab, shown in the figure, is where you make the primary settings. Other tabs are more specific, including information about blocked senders (see the preceding two sections.)

2. **Choose a level for filtering junk mail.**

   There are four settings, as described onscreen.

3. **Click OK.**

Some email programs use a mark-as-junk approach to identifying junk email. The idea is that you can train the email program to identify suspect email. Over time, the program instantly recognizes messages you don't like and automatically transfers them into the Junk mail folder.

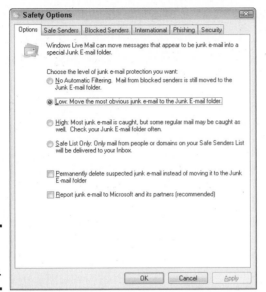

Figure 3-5:
Setting junk
mail options.

✦ Junk mail filters aren't foolproof. Odds are good that a junk email filter will capture some legitimate messages and falsely determine them to be junk.

✦ I recommend routinely checking the Junk mailbox or mail folder to determine whether real mail is inside. If so, you can remove the messages, and I also recommend toning down the junk mail filter's aggressiveness.

✦ Which is better — using a junk mail filter or training your email program? It's pretty much a draw. Most of the programs you can train, such as Thunderbird, have options to untrain or reset the training. You also have options to mark a message as "not junk," which further refines the training.

Creating a junk mail filter

Nearly all email programs feature a standard message-filtering system. You use this system to organize your email, such as by transferring business messages into a Work mailbox, but you can also use the filters to help fight spam.

A junk mail filter works simply: Identify junk email by its sender or Subject line, and then either delete the message or move it into a Junk mailbox. Here's how to implement such a thing in Windows Live Mail, Windows Mail, or Outlook Express:

1. **Open the junk mail.**

   Sorry.

2a. **In Windows Live Mail, choose Actions⇨Create Rule from Message.**

2b. **In Windows Mail and Outlook Express, choose Message⇨Create Rule from Message.**

   The New Mail Rule dialog box appears, as shown in Figure 3-6. There are four parts of the dialog box, just as there are four steps to creating a mail rule. Start in Area 1.

3. **To filter a message by subject, choose Where the Subject Line Contains Specific Words; to filter a message by sender, choose Where the From Line Contains People.**

   Suppose that you keep receiving email from a certain outfit that tries to connect you with old friends from high school. Because the site won't unsubscribe you, you decide to filter its messages. The best way to do it is to filter by the From line. On the other hand, if you want to remove messages with the words *oil change* in them, filter by subject.

   Next comes the action, set in Area 2.

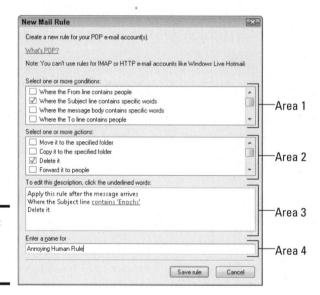

Figure 3-6: Creating a junk mail rule.

4. **Select the Move It to the Specified Folder check box.**

   Or, if you want to be vicious, you can choose Delete It. But the idea here is to filter junk, not just delete it outright.

In Area 3, you refine the rules by choosing specific parameters.

5. **In Area 3, click the specified link to replace its text with the name of a specific folder.**

   A Move dialog box appears, listing the mailbox folders used by your email program. If you don't see them, click the plus sign (+) by the item Local Folders.

6. **Choose the Junk E-Mail folder from the list in the Move box.**

   If you don't see the Junk E-Mail folder there, click the New Folder button to create it. Name the new folder **Junk E-Mail**; click OK to create it.

7. **Click OK.**

8. **In the Name of the Rule box, type a descriptive name for the rule.**

   For example, type Annoying High School Contact Junk Mail Rule for filtering email from a web site that promotes contacting old friends but gives you no way to unsubscribe from the service.

9. **Click Save Rule or OK to create the rule.**

10. **Click OK to confirm that you know you created the rule.**

Creating the rule may not instantly filter the Inbox; you still have to manually drag a junk message to the Junk E-Mail folder. But any new mail that arrives will fall victim to your mail rule, helping keep this type of message out of the inbox.

✦ You might consider not using the full message subject, as shown in Area 3. Sometimes, setting the subject to include only a keyword, like *porn* or *mortgage,* is enough to filter out the unwanted. See the next section for information on editing and refining your message rule.

✦ The idea behind junking a message instead of deleting it is to ensure that you can rescue it out of the Junk E-Mail folder *false positives.* These messages are flagged as junk but may not be junk. When you delete a potential junk message, you run the risk of having it purged from the Deleted Items folder before you have a chance to review it.

✦ Check the Junk E-Mail folder from time to time to ensure that your rules are doing their job. If not, edit the rule! See the next section.

Editing a junk mail rule

Rules may need refining from time to time, which probably explains why the U.S. Tax Code runs some 60,000 pages. New rules are necessary for unwanted email; they not only make the junk mail filters more powerful but also help them rule out false positives. On the other hand, adding rules to the Tax Code merely keeps accountants and lawyers employed.

To edit or customize a rule in Windows Live Mail, Windows Mail, or Outlook Express, follow these steps:

1. **Choose Tools⇨Message Rules⇨Mail.**

   The Message Rules dialog box appears, as shown in Figure 3-7.

2. **Choose the rule to edit from the list (refer to Figure 3-7).**

3. **Click the Modify button.**

   The dialog box you see is the same as the New Mail Rule dialog box, as shown in Figure 3-6. Basically, your job is to edit or modify the rule you originally created.

   For example, if the subject is too long or detailed, click that link in Area 3 and edit the Subject line to be more concise.

4. **Click the Safe Rule or OK button when you're done making modifications.**

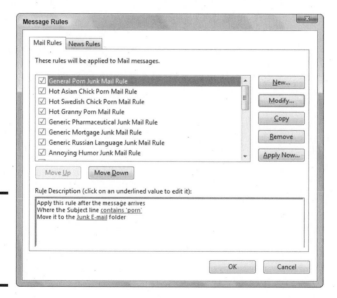

Figure 3-7:
Rules are edited in this dialog box.

Filters are executed in order, from the top down, in the Message Rules dialog box. Some rules may not be executed because earlier rules take priority. Therefore, to fix the situation, you can select a specific rule and use the Move Up or Move Down arrows to adjust the sequence.

Disabling a mail rule

If a rule isn't working, and can't be corrected by editing, consider removing it. Removing a rule doesn't delete the rule, which is a good thing if you discover that the rule was indeed working for you. Anyway, follow these steps in Windows Live Mail, Windows Mail, or Outlook Express to disable a rule:

1. **Choose Tools⇨Message Rules⇨Mail.**

You may need to press the F10 key to find the Tools menu in Windows Live Mail.

2. **Remove the check mark by the rule you want to disable.**

3. **Click OK.**

To reenable a rule, simply replace the check mark in Step 2. Otherwise, when you confirm that the rule isn't needed and the junk mail it was trying to filter has stopped, you can delete the rule by following these steps:

1. **Choose Tools⇨Message Rules⇨Mail.**

2. **Select the rule to delete.**

3. **Click the Remove button.**

4. **Click OK.**

I don't recommend deleting a rule until you disable it first. It's far easier to reenable a rule than it is to re-create it.

Skipping email over a certain size

The last chapter in the book of unwanted email dwells on the subject of huge email attachments. I hate them. What a huge email attachment tells me is that someone hasn't read my books. They're either unaware that sending a link to a web page or video is easier or ignorant of how to resize and properly send pictures as an email attachment. *Enough with them!*

To deal with my frustration, I practice yoga. But in the electronics world, I deal with large email attachments by creating an email filter to merrily skip over them. Here's how to configure Windows Live Mail, Windows Mail, and Outlook Express not to download large email messages:

1. **Choose Tools⇨Message Rules⇨Mail.**

The Message Rules dialog box saunters onto the display (refer to Figure 3-7).

2. **Click the New button.**

   The New Mail Rule dialog box appears. Because a message wasn't selected, the dialog box is blank.

3. **In Area 1, place a check mark by the item When the Message Size Is More than Size.**

   You have to scroll down to find the option. And, no, the option doesn't make literal sense, but you're replacing the second word `size` with a specific value in Step 5.

4. **In Area 2, choose the option Delete It from the Server.**

5. **In Area 3, choose the word `size` to replace it with a specific size value.**

   The Set size dialog box appears. When I had dialup Internet, I set the size to 500 kilobytes (KB). For my faster connection, I set the size to 3000KB, or 3MB.

6. **Click OK to close the Set Size dialog box.**

7. **In Area 4, type** Filter Out Large Messages.

8. **Click Save Rule or OK to create the rule.**

9. **Use the Move Up button to place the rule at the top of the list in the Message Rules dialog box.**

   You want the Filter Out Large Messages rule to come first; otherwise, the message might be downloaded to your computer, which isn't what you want.

10. **Click OK to close the Message Rules dialog box.**

When a large message comes in, you won't know about it: The message simply never arrives in the inbox. It also implies that the person who sent it will never know that the message wasn't received.

✦ See Video 431 for a demonstration of filtering large emails.

   www.dummies.com/go/troubleshootingandmaintainingyourpcaio2e

✦ The size limit on an email attachment depends on your ISP's mailbox limits. The limit can be as little as 5MB or even unlimited. Most ISPs use a 10MB limit. Contact your ISP to see what the limit is.

✦ Do not choose the option Do Not Download It from the Server (Step 4). If you do, the message continues to dwell in your mailbox on the server, taking up space and potentially leading to a full mailbox. That's a Bad Thing.

✦ Don't be part of the problem: Try not to send your friends large email messages.

✦ Rather than try to send huge file attachments in email, consider burning an optical disc and sending it in the regular mail.

✦ A more effective way of sending videos or other large files is to send a web page link instead. For example, a video link to YouTube or another video web site takes up only one line of text compared to the megabytes required for the video itself.

Chapter 4: Wicked Software

In This Chapter

- ✔ **Ridding your PC of malware**
- ✔ **Protecting against viruses**
- ✔ **Avoiding a phishing scam**
- ✔ **Clearing your PC of spyware**
- ✔ **Using a firewall**
- ✔ **Preventing Internet nasties**

By the pricking of my thumbs,
Something wicked this way comes.
Open, locks,
Whoever knocks!

—*Macbeth,* Act IV, Scene 1

*L*ike the murderous thane, there are evil plots afoot to dethrone you from the seat of power before your PC. Indeed, one of the easiest ways that wicked software oozes into your computer is by opening locks. Sometimes, the software picks the locks by itself, but most often it's you, the user, who lets in the software. It's kind of like inviting a vampire into your home: After you do, he makes himself right at home and soon you're dead — or just down a few quarts. This chapter covers software of the wicked kind.

Malicious + Software = Malware

Even though I placed this chapter in the bosom of the Internet minibook, the Internet itself isn't responsible for evil software. No, the Internet is merely the delivery system. Software of the wicked bent has been around computers since the steam-powered age. This section explains what you need to know.

Understanding malware

I suppose that people grew tired of using the terms *virus* or *Trojan* to refer to evil software. There was also a big issue about what was a virus and what was a *worm*. It got messy. Nerds extremely dislike using incorrect terms. So somewhere along the line, someone glued together the terms *malicious* and *software* and came up with *malware*.

Malware has always been a computer category, even if the term is new. Programmers often wrote self-destruct programs that would either quickly remove items from their own computers or destroy an employer's computer system in the event that the programmer was fired. With the dawn of the Internet, a distribution system became available for sending these evil programs out into the ether. It proved wildly successful.

As far as you're concerned, malware exists and you must take extra steps to fight it. Believe it or not, the first step is *not* to buy a security utility. That's Step Three. The first two steps require more effort on your part.

The first, best thing you can do to protect yourself from malware is to *find out more about your computer.* Honestly, you can't tell when something is wrong when you're unable to determine exactly what "right" is.

The second thing you can do is to not be a fool. Malware succeeds by preying on human weakness. The most successful computer virus works despite every effort by software developers to stop it. That's because you cannot program the human brain; people do things they shouldn't do because of social engineering.

Put simply, *social engineering* is the art of making people do things that they otherwise wouldn't. For example, you're fooled into opening an email attachment because the message claims that it contains a compromising picture of a celebrity or an embarrassing video of a politician. Despite the warnings, you open the attachment. Your computer is infected. The Bad Guys win.

The final thing you can do to protect yourself from the malware tsunami is to use software tools to ensure that your computer hasn't been compromised, and to repair any damage done. These tools include an antivirus program, antispyware, a firewall, plus other utilities. Windows provides a smattering of its own tools. Or, you can choose to buy everything at one time in an Internet security software suite.

Finding malware

There's no need to find malware; it will find you. That's the motivation behind the sick freaks who produce malware. Knowing that, know also that malware will enter your computer in one of three ways:

As a download from a web page: If you have the latest version of your web browser, you're alerted to any download from a web page to your computer. In other words, you must *invite* the program into your realm. If the program is malware, in it comes.

Malware malcontents

Phishing: The phishing scam masquerades as a legitimate web site or link to a site, but what it's really trying to do is "fish" for information. By fooling you into thinking that you're visiting your bank or a shopping or government web site, the scam gets you to divulge personal or financial information, which the Bad Guys then exploit.

Spyware: Like its name says, spyware monitors your movements on the Internet, sending information back to a central computer that then targets you with advertising. It sounds okay, but the category has broadened to include programs you download to your computer that monitor your activities to the point that your computer slows down to a useless state. Further, the spyware itself becomes nearly impossible to remove.

Trojan horse: The Trojan program is malware that masquerades as a legitimate program. The program may have a legitimate function, but it carries ulterior motives. Trojans can delete data, compromise security, relay spam or porn, and otherwise infect your computer.

Virus: Like its living counterpart, a computer virus infects your computer, taking control over some or all of its functions. The virus destroys data or looks for things like passwords, credit card numbers, or other sensitive data. This information is often sent to another computer. A virus can also "own" your computer, turning it into a zombie box on the Internet. The *zombie box* is used to relay spam email or pornography or to coordinate attacks against web sites on the Internet.

Worm: Officially, a worm is a virus that replicates itself over a network. Worms often arrive via email, peruse your address book, and then send a copy of themselves to others in your address book, masquerading the message as though it's from you. Worms are used to deliver viruses, or the worm itself might be a virus, because the terms are interchangeable.

As an email attachment: Malware arriving as an email attachment is the same bad stuff that comes from a web page. The difference is primarily in social engineering: The malware is most likely disguised as a message from a friend or has another tempting aspect that entices you to open it.

As a file on infected removable media: Originally the most popular method for malware distribution, inserting a strange disc or another type of media into your PC's storage system is still a way to give your computer a virus. The disc offers something enticing — a free game or software. The worst scenario is when you're required to start your PC with the disc. Bad, bad, bad.

Antivirus software can help identify malware as it arrives on your PC, but don't let it be your crutch. Just be vigilant. Remember: Even antivirus programs can be fooled. In fact, all the major viral infections of the past dozen or so years managed to slip by the antivirus programs that were then widely in use.

**Book IV
Chapter 4**

Wicked Software

✦ The key to getting malware to work is social engineering. In the case of a web page link, the web page may direct you to ignore warnings from Windows or to disable your antivirus software to continue.

✦ If the web site looks fishy, or it's offering something that cannot possibly be true, it's probably not a good idea to download any of its files or even click a link. See Chapter 5 for more information on downloading.

✦ If a file downloads automatically and you didn't request it, do not open the file. Delete it at once.

✦ If a pornography web site downloads a "video viewer," it's a virus.

✦ If the email says to disable your antivirus program before opening the attachment, don't.

✦ It's common to get malware from chat rooms. Some (bogus) user comes into the chat room and coughs up a web page link to malware, often with an enticing but wrong description of what you find when you click the link. Don't click the link.

✦ Sometimes, programs can be sent directly from an online chat room or from instant messaging software. Whatever you do, however you're tempted, do not click the link or open the file.

Protecting your PC

There exists something called *PC survival time*. It's the average length of time an unprotected Windows computer spends on the Internet before malware takes over and controls the entire system. The current PC survival time is about 16 minutes.

Your PC doesn't have to fall prey to the PC survival-time challenge. As long as you know what to do, your computer can last for months on the Internet with no problems whatsoever. But you must take steps to protect the system from the Bad Guys.

Windows features a central location for protecting your PC. In Windows 7, it's the Action Center, which is discussed in Book II, Chapter 1. Specifically, the top part of the Action Center window, shown in Figure 4-1, deals with security issues on your PC.

To open the Action Center window, follow these steps:

1. **Open the Control Panel.**

2. **From beneath the System and Security heading, choose the link Review Your Computer's Status.**

The Action Center window appears, listing any current issues for your PC.

3. **Click the down-pointing arrow button in the Security heading to reveal its contents.**

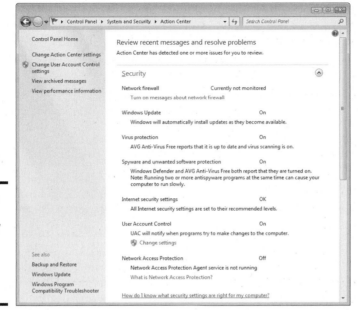

Figure 4-1:
The
Windows 7
Action
Center,
security
info.

In Windows Vista and Windows XP, the location for protecting your PC is the Windows Security Center, as shown in Figure 4-2. It provides an information summary of your PC's security state, plus quick access to the vital items you need in order to keep your PC safe.

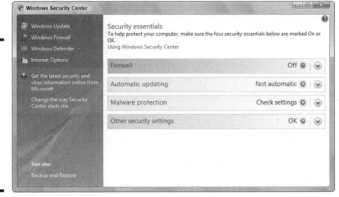

Figure 4-2:
The
Windows
Vista
version
of the
Windows
Security
Center.

To open the Windows Security Center window in Windows Vista or Windows XP, follow these steps:

1. **Open the Control Panel window.**

2a. **In Windows Vista, choose the link Check This Computer's Security Status, found beneath the Security heading.**

2b. **In Windows XP, open the Security Center icon.**

The settings you see may look different from the ones shown in Figure 4-2; your options may appear in green, yellow, or red, depending on the settings.

There are several items to check for your PC's security. These items appear in the windows shown in Figures 4-1 and 4-2:

Firewall: The firewall is designed to protect your PC from unwanted network traffic moving both into and from your computer. See the later section, "Life Behind the Firewall," for more information.

Automatic Updating: Keeping your copy of Windows up-to-date ensures that any known threats are being dealt with. Indeed, the most common reason for the PC's short survival time on the Internet is that many users don't update their software. See Book II, Chapter 1 for more information on updating Windows.

Malware Protection: The general category of malware protection includes services that defend your computer against viruses and spyware. For virus protection, see the section "When Mr. Virus Comes Calling," next in this chapter. Using the Windows Defender program can fight Spyware and other software nasties. See the section "I Spy, with My Little Eye," later in this chapter.

Other Security Settings: The most generic category in the Windows Security Center covers two topics: Internet security settings (see Chapter 2 in this minibook) and the Windows Vista User Account Control (covered in Book II, Chapter 5).

✦ Windows XP sports a different version of the Security Center that replaces the Malware Protection and Other Security Settings areas with a single area titled Virus Protection.

✦ The Windows Firewall window mostly serves as a gateway to other, specific locations in Windows. Various sections in the rest of this chapter discuss how you can use these locations to help protect your PC.

✦ The PC survival time is so short primarily because the computers that are tested are *not* behind a *firewall*. The firewall protects you from a great majority of the Internet attacks. See the section "Life Behind the Firewall," later in this chapter.

✦ The Windows Security Center is available only after you update your copy of Windows XP to the latest release or service package (SP2 or SP3).

When Mr. Virus Comes Calling

The first computer virus was created back in the 1970s. Curiously enough, the second computer virus was created to track down and delete copies of the first computer virus. As the personal computer revolution caught fire in the mid-1980s, computer viruses broke out all over. It was the perfect storm of people who failed to understand their computers, pirated software, and human weakness.

Viruses continue to thrive, and the need to fight them is still present. Unlike in the early days, however, today's computers offer a better line of protection against the viral scourge. This section explains the details.

Inoculating your computer

To properly fight viruses, you should get an antivirus program. That's because Windows itself doesn't come with antivirus software. If your PC came supplied with antivirus software, it was most likely a trial version. Still, because Windows lacks a specific antivirus utility, the antivirus information in this chapter is generic and applies to all antivirus programs.

The antivirus program you choose should have two modes of operation:

Interactive: In this mode, the program lurks in the background and monitors the computer's activity. Specifically, the interactive mode looks for a virus coming in from the Internet (a download or an email attachment) or delivered on removable media.

Scan: In this mode, the antivirus program probes all parts of the computer's memory and storage system, looking for signs of infection. You can direct the program to scan your PC at any time, though traditionally an antivirus program scans the computer when it first starts.

When a virus or sign of infection is found, the antivirus software alerts you to its presence. The virus may be destroyed or the file quarantined for later examination. Either way, whatever operation the virus was set out to perform is thwarted.

✦ It's possible to be vigilant and avoid using antivirus software. But that big, looming monster called Doubt plays a role in how you use your computer. Nasty software exists. Even if you don't run an interactive antivirus program, I highly recommend that you use antivirus software to scan your computer routinely for signs of infection.

✦ Antivirus software requires frequent updating. Normally, you subscribe to the antivirus developer's web site, allowing downloads of new virus definitions and protection information. Only by keeping your antivirus software up-to-date do you ensure that your computer can battle new and malevolent threats.

✦ Yes, those subscriptions cost money. But consider that the cost is far less than the cost of taking your computer into the shop to have a professional rid your system of infection and restore your data.

✦ You can run more than one antivirus program at a time. In fact, having two antivirus programs is a great way to boost your PC's security. For example, you can run either Norton or McAfee antivirus software as your primary protection. Then, every so often, run a secondary program to perform a scan-only; the secondary program may find things that the first program misses.

✦ If you choose to run two antivirus programs at one time, place only one into Interactive mode. Running two antivirus programs in Interactive mode doesn't help fight viruses and instead merely slows down your computer.

✦ Avoid using web-based antivirus scans, because most of them are malware — either spyware or Trojan horses. It's okay to download an antivirus program from a legitimate developer on the web, but I don't recommend using any antivirus software that runs from a web page.

Disabling antivirus software

Sometimes an installation program requests that you disable your antivirus software. The reason is that the antivirus software has difficulty determining whether the program you're installing is a legitimate program or perhaps a virus taking roost in your PC's storage system.

As long as you purchase software in a store or download it from a reputable site on the Internet, you can safely install the thing. To disable your antivirus software, locate its icon in the notification area on the taskbar. Right-click the icon and choose the option to disable or exit the program.

✦ Disable your antivirus program only when installing new programs. If you downloaded those programs from the Internet, ensure that they're from a reputable source. See Chapter 5 for more information on determining what a reputable source is.

✦ After installing the software, reenable the antivirus software. In fact, it might even be a good idea to restart your PC at that point; by restarting, you ensure that the computer is scanned for new infections and that the antivirus software starts up as it should.

✦ Never disable the antivirus software when you don't expect anything to be installed or when you're prompted to do so by a web site or an email message.

✦ At times, legitimate software has been shipped from the developer with a virus lurking on the disc. Those times are extremely rare, however, and if you subscribe to an antivirus update service, you're alerted to these infected discs almost immediately.

The quarantine question

Often, when your antivirus software finds a sign of infection, it places the suspect file into quarantine. Some people are confused by the quarantine concept, so I thought I'd explain it a bit.

The normal way to deal with an infected file is for the antivirus software to ruthlessly delete it. That's good. In fact, the antivirus software may not only ruthlessly delete the infected file but also obliterate it so that no portion of the file exists anywhere on your PC's storage system. That's a good thing. But what happens if the file wasn't infected and, worse, you really need that file? That's why the concept of quarantine was created.

A quarantined file isn't deleted. It shows signs of infection, but by being in quarantine, the file has no opportunity to infect your computer. It's safe. If the file can be fixed and the infection eliminated, the file can be removed from quarantine and put back into service. Or, if the file was falsely identified as being infected, it can be removed from quarantine and reused right away.

Generally speaking, I keep files in quarantine for a few weeks or longer. Every so often, I review the list of files in quarantine and then just have them rubbed out. I figure, after a long period, I didn't need the files anyway, so they can go away and not be missed.

Hook, Line, and Stinker

Not everyone can write computer software. Fewer still can manufacture a clever virus, such as one that would rush out to your computer and find your passwords, PINs, and bank account numbers. But some ambitious people get all that information without writing a line of code. Their technique is called *phishing*, and this section tells you all about the scam.

Understanding the phishing scam

The phishing scam is so deceptively simple that you would think for a moment it could never work. Often, it starts with a phony email message. The message looks like it's from your bank, the government, an online retailer, or some outfit you would do business with. It may have graphics that look official. If may even have a disclaimer or security alert in the message.

The message requests information and implies a sense of urgency: Something bad will happen if you don't reply to the email or visit a web site. Part of your duty is to supply sensitive information: account numbers, Social Security information, credit card numbers, personal identification numbers, mother's maiden name, or passwords, for example.

First, a word of reassuring advice: Nothing legitimate ever gets passed through email. Your bank may email you, but if there's a problem with your account, someone will definitely phone or send you a regular letter — not an email message.

Second, tools available in both the web browser and email program can help you quickly identify a phishing scam. The next few sections describe how.

The phishing scam works because of social engineering. It's much easier to believe that something bad will happen if you don't do anything than it is to simply ignore what is basically a cleverly disguised scam.

Fighting phishing in Internet Explorer

Like most modern web browsers, Internet Explorer features an antiphishing filter. The filter is used to flag known phishing web sites as well as to report suspect sites. If you obeyed your computer, the filter is probably on already; there's nothing else do to.

For versions of Internet Explorer before version 8, you can confirm that the Phishing Filter is active by following these steps:

1. **Choose Tools⇨Phishing Filter⇨Turn On Automatic Website Checking.**

   If you see Turn Off Automatic Website Checking, the antiphishing filter is on already; there's nothing else for you to do.

2. **In the Microsoft Phishing Filter window, choose Turn On Automatic Phishing Filter (Recommended).**

3. **Click OK.**

When the phishing filter is on, it flags suspect web pages for you automatically. The Address bar turns red in Internet Explorer, and you see a message displayed, as shown in Figure 4-3. My advice: Choose the option Click Here to Close This Webpage.

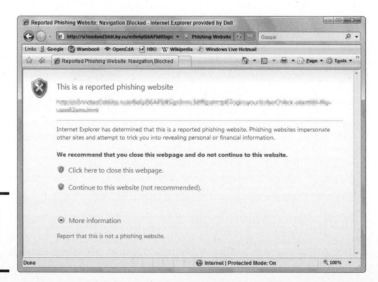

Figure 4-3:
A phishing web site is found.

You've already won!

Though not officially phishing, another popular email scam involves prize money or other free loot that you're somehow spontaneously entitled to. Often called the *Nigerian scam, 419 fraud,* or *foreign lottery scam,* it's generically known as the *advanced-fee fraud.*

The scam works like this: You get an email alerting you that money is coming. You've won a foreign lottery, or perhaps some bigwig needs help transferring money into the United States. All you need to do is forward some cash to help with processing, pay taxes, or release something from impound. Or, perhaps the scam artist merely wants your bank account number.

Don't believe a word of it.

Again, social engineering is to blame for the advanced-fee fraud. With the lure of getting something for nothing, the gullible and greedy follow along with these scams and lose millions of dollars annually to the Bad Guys. Nothing is free. And, if they claim that it's free but requires money up front, it's still not free.

The worst news is that only common sense helps you fight this type of scam. A phishing filter doesn't matter. When you get an email saying "You've won," you most likely have not. Delete the message.

When you encounter a web site you suspect of phishing but it's not flagged, you can test it and report it.

Testing a web page for something phishy

To test a web site for a potential phishing scam in Internet Explorer 8, choose Safety⇨SmartScreen Filter⇨Check This Web site. In older versions of Internet Explorer, choose Tools⇨Phishing Filter⇨Check This Web Site. You see an information dialog box asking you to confirm the web site address and to ensure that it was what you were suspecting. Click OK to dismiss the dialog box.

If the web site looks bad and wasn't reported, you can report it yourself: In Internet Explorer 8, choose Safety⇨SmartScreen Filter⇨Report Unsafe Website. In older versions of Internet Explorer, choose Tools⇨Phishing Filter⇨Report This Website. Information about the site is sent to Microsoft. If the web site is confirmed as a phishing site, the site address is added to several lists, and web browsers using phishing filters are blocked from accessing the site.

Avoiding misleading email

Most phishing scams begin with an email message. That's how they got me once: I had just bought something on eBay when a phishing scam mail came in. It looked like it was from eBay, so I replied and had almost filled in the entire form when I noticed that I wasn't on an eBay web site. Things have since changed, and your email program most likely provides protection against email phishing scams.

To confirm that Windows Live Mail and Windows Mail is configured to protect you against phishing scams, follow these steps:

1a. **In Windows Live Mail, choose Tools⇨Safety Options.**

You need to press the F10 key to see the menu bar and choose the Tools menu.

1b. **In Windows Mail, choose Tools⇨Junk E-Mail Options.**

2. **Click the Phishing tab.**

3. **Ensure that a check mark appears by the item Protect My Inbox from Messages with Potential Phishing Links.**

4. **Click OK.**

When a potential phishing email message comes in, such as one that contains a misleading web page link, you're alerted before the message ever roosts in the Inbox. The warning dialog box is shown in Figure 4-4. Simply click the Close button.

Figure 4-4:
A phishing
email has
arrived.

By clicking the Close button, you instantly stuff the suspect message into the Junk E-Mail folder in Windows Mail. Whew.

1 Spy, with My Little Eye

Look! Inside your PC! It's a virus! It's a Trojan! It's a worm! Nope. It's *spyware*, yet another type of malware, vicious and invasive. This section discusses what spyware is, what it does, and how to squish it.

Understanding spyware

How would you like to use your computer while, the entire time, people are sitting behind you, looking over your shoulder and watching what you do on the Internet? Hundreds of people are watching you. Not only that, but you also cannot get any of them to leave. If you can picture this scenario, you understand the evil concept of spyware.

It all started out innocently enough: Spyware was designed to help customize advertising on the Internet. Based on which web pages you visited, advertising was targeted specifically for you. That sounds good. But this fresh concept quickly turned sour.

Several flavors of malware all fall under the category of spyware:

Tracking: The most innocent form of spyware is merely a tracking cookie placed by a web site on your computer. The cookie is little more than a text file, though it's read by various web sites as you plod through your Internet activities. This type of spyware can easily be removed by deleting all your Internet cookies, described in Chapter 1.

Adware: As its name implies, adware is advertising software. It may not even be spyware, but, rather, software that features ads to support the program's development. Examples include free toolbars and screen savers that may have a legitimate function but also display advertising and just may also monitor Internet use or scan your email.

Piggyback: The worst spyware is the piggyback program. The spyware attaches itself to another program and may reset your web home page, redirect web site requests, flood your screen with advertising at random times, and perform other irritating acts. The worst thing is that the piggyback software is nearly impossible to remove. Indeed, the software agreement that many users innocently agree to states that the program cannot and will not be removed from their computers.

Though spyware is malware, it's not considered a virus. That's because spyware doesn't self-replicate and most of it is acquired voluntarily. Yes, it's true: Most people *invite* spyware into their computers. Irritating programs are downloaded willingly; they promise a service or claim to do something clever. Then they prove to be the piggyback type of spyware that cannot be uninstalled.

The insidious part is that spyware multiplies. Unless you keep an eye on things, the amount of spyware in your loaded PC grows larger and larger. You may not lose data, but the PC slows to a crawl because of all the spyware programs clogging the arteries.

Because spyware isn't considered to be viral, most antivirus programs don't scan for, detect, or remove spyware. To combat the scourge, use specific antispyware software, such as Windows Defender.

Book IV
Chapter 4

Wicked Software

✦ Some antivirus programs are bundled with antispyware utilities as part of an Internet security suite.

✦ Most free spyware scanners simply remove Internet tracking cookies. They don't perform a complete evaluation of your computer system for spyware infection.

✦ Some spyware programs steal credit card numbers. They fly under the banner of making your online purchases easier by storing all your payment information for you. Wrong! If you value your financial security, credit card information should never be stored anywhere.

✦ Avoid free or web page—based antispyware programs. They are often spyware themselves. The only spyware programs I trust are Windows Defender and anything they sell in a box at the software store.

Getting Windows Defender

One of the best ways to fight spyware is to use the Windows Defender program. When you can't find it in your version of Windows, you can get it as an update.

First, check to ensure that Windows Defender isn't already installed; it's found as a command on the Start button's All Programs menu.

To quickly locate Windows Defender, type **Windows Defender** into the search text box at the bottom of the Start menu. You should see the Windows Defender icon appear in the search results. If it's not there, download the program by following these steps:

1. **Browse to the following web site:**

    www.microsoft.com/windows/products/winfamily/defender

2. **Click the big, fun Get It Now button.**

Microsoft may change its web page design, so if you don't see the big, fun Get It Now button, look for another clue to how to download the program.

3. **Follow the directions onscreen to continue with the download.**

(See Chapter 5 for more general information on downloading and installing programs from the Internet.)

4. **After Windows Defender has been downloaded, work through the Installation Wizard for Windows Defender.**

5. **When prompted, click to use the recommended settings and opt for a complete installation.**

Windows Defender immediately begins scanning your computer. Continue reading in the next section.

Using Windows Defender

Windows own spyware-fighting utility is Windows Defender. Windows Defender not only scans your system for spyware but can also help you remove stubborn piggyback programs.

Start Windows Defender by choosing the Windows Defender item from the Start button menu's All Programs menu. In Windows Vista, you can also find a Windows Defender icon in the Control Panel.

After starting the program, you see the Windows Defender main screen, similar to the one shown in Figure 4-5.

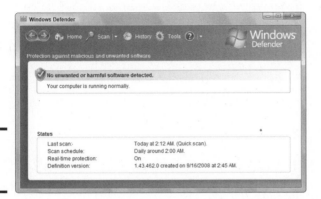

Figure 4-5:
Windows
Defender.

Hopefully, the screen you see looks a lot like Figure 4-5, where you see the message that your computer is running normally. If not, you can choose from several options to remedy the situation:

Always Allow: As long as you recognize and allow the program, Windows Defender remembers the software and flags it as okay. You're no longer bothered by the warning. The program name then appears in the Allowed Items list.

Ignore: Windows Defender gives the item a pass, allowing it to run or be installed on your computer. But the next time the program runs, you see the same warning again.

Quarantine: The item in question is placed into a special area on disk; it's not running and not in risk of harming your computer. The software remains in quarantine until you unquarantine the program or delete it.

Remove: Windows Defender obliterates the program, rubbing it out of existence. Smoldering bits puff out the back side of your PC.

Choose your option, and Windows Defender deals with the suspect program appropriately.

Windows Defender may also pop up a warning while you're using the Internet in what's called *real-time protection*. The Windows Defender Warning dialog box alerts you to the presence of known spyware. There are several alert levels for the programs that are found, as described in the remainder of this list:

**Book IV
Chapter 4**

Wicked Software

Not Yet Classified: The program is most likely okay. Many programs are unknown to the various spyware databases and therefore are "not yet classified." If you recognize the program, let it be. If you don't recognize the program, such as you did not mean to install it or don't know where it came from, remove it.

Low: The program is probably not evil, but you don't want it anyway. If the program was installed without your knowledge, remove it. Otherwise, check the publisher or source.

Medium: A medium-level program may compromise your PC's security or collect sensitive data. Review the details and decide whether to remove it, especially when you don't recognize the publisher.

High: Remove the software.

Severe: Definitely remove the software.

Click the appropriate button — Remove All or Ignore — to deal with the items that are found. Remember that if you don't recognize the publisher or you're not trying to install new software, *remove it!*

✦ Windows Defender is set up to work all the time. To disable it, refer to the next section.

✦ You can remove a program from the Allowed Items list if you discover later that it is indeed spyware. To do so, choose Tools and then choose Allowed Items from the Tools and Settings window.

✦ Review items held in quarantine by choosing Tools from the Windows Defender window and then clicking the Quarantined Items link. You can then select an item and click the Remove or Restore buttons to deal with it.

✦ It's okay to run multiple spyware checking programs, though I don't do so myself. As long as I have and trust a spyware program, such as Windows Defender, I don't see a need to add more programs to my PC or run more utilities that may slow down the system.

Scanning for spyware in Windows Defender

For the most part, Windows Defender runs automatically. You can perform a quick scan at any time by clicking the Scan button.

To perform a more rigorous scan, click the arrow next to the Scan button. From the menu, choose the Full Scan option. It goes into far more detail, but it also takes longer to complete. I recommend using it only when you suspect spyware to be bothering you.

Scheduling Windows Defender

To schedule when and how Windows Defender runs, follow these steps:

1. **Click the Tools link at the top of the Windows Defender window.**

The Tools and Settings part of the Windows Defender window appears. It lists many powerful utilities for helping pluck nasty software from your PC.

2. **Choose the Options link.**

The Options page appears.

3. **Ensure that there's a check mark by the item Automatically Scan My Computer.**

When this option is unchecked, Windows Defender is turned off. I don't recommend turning it off.

4. **Choose a frequency, either daily or a specific day of the week.**

Daily is best.

5. **Pick a time.**

Specify a time when the computer will be on (either running or in Sleep mode). Windows Defender doesn't awaken the computer from hibernation. See Book I, Chapter 3 for more hibernation information.

6. **Choose the type of scan, either Quick or Full.**

7. **Review other settings in the window.**

There are too many to list here, and none is incorrectly set by default.

8. **Click the Save button.**

9. **In Windows Vista, type the administrator's password or click the Continue button.**

A key to the success of running any malware utility is to keep it updated. Windows Defender is no exception. Updates for Windows Defender are automatically installed on your computer — if you have Automatic Updates configured that way. If you don't, you might want to reconsider your automatic update strategy. See Book II, Chapter 1.

Life Behind the Firewall

I don't expect you to use your computer without using the Internet. I tried it once: I had a PC set up that I wanted to keep *pure*. The thing wasn't connected to the Internet and I wouldn't play any games on the system or run any software other than Microsoft Word. That scheme lasted all of about 20 minutes.

It's tough to be a part of the universe while not connected to it. One way to make that connection safer is to use a *firewall*. This section explains the details.

Understanding firewalls

Consider the Internet a hole through which wonderful things can travel both to and fro. You send information to the internet, but more often gobs of information flow in from the Internet, all coming through that tiny hole you call your Internet connection.

The problem with the hole through which the Internet flows is that it's wide open. There's no guard, no monitor, not even a doorbell. That's because the Internet was designed by very trusting people, mostly scientists and researchers who appreciated the unfettered, free-flowing nature of information. The fools.

The Bad Guys soon learned that the Internet was a highway with no traffic rules. Like any eager opportunist, the Bad Guys were soon wandering unwelcomed, poking, prodding, and pilfering information as well as planting viruses and other toxic software. Obviously, a highway patrol was needed.

To help monitor the hole through which Internet information flows, software designers borrowed a concept from the construction industry: the firewall.

In construction, firewalls are rated by how long they take to burn through. A one-hour firewall theoretically will stand for one hour before the flames lick into the next room. Computer firewalls work in a similar manner, though the idea is to keep the bad guys out permanently, not just after a given amount of persistence.

What the firewall does is monitor both incoming and outgoing Internet traffic. When a firewall is properly configured, only the information you request from the Internet is allowed in. Outgoing information can also be filtered.

When information you didn't request comes in, the firewall instantly squishes it, blocking the doors and windows, so to speak. Likewise, when information tries to sneak out, you can be queried about whether it's okay for that information to be sent.

Generally speaking, the firewall prompts you with Allow or Deny types of messages. If you don't want something coming in, you can choose to deny it by blocking it temporarily or permanently. The firewall can also learn from your choices so that after a few times, you aren't bothered with the warnings.

Bottom line: To help keep your computer system secure, you need a firewall.

✦ The first line of defense against Internet-spawned malware should be a firewall.

✦ A firewall is a priority for broadband Internet users. The bad guys, who need the connection speed and storage that your compromised PC offers, covet those high-speed connections.

✦ Two types of firewall are available for your computer: hardware and software.

✦ A *hardware* firewall is an electronic gizmo installed between the broadband modem and your computer. It's often included as part of the router. (See Book V, Chapter 1 for basic information on a network router.) A hardware router monitors all incoming and outgoing Internet traffic. It's a far more robust solution than a software firewall, though not as cheap.

✦ A software firewall is a program running on your PC that monitors only the Internet traffic entering and leaving your computer.

✦ Dialup Internet users aren't at risk as greatly as broadband Internet users, but I recommend using a software firewall for dialup Internet access.

Setting up a router with a firewall

The best solution for broadband Internet users is to set up a hardware firewall. Most wired and wireless routers sold today feature one. That's good news. The better news is that the firewall is most likely configured perfectly for you; there's really little left to do.

Chapter 1 in Book V offers some basic router information, including information on how the thing is set up. Without my repeating too much of the information here, you access the router by using the PC's web browser. Figure 4-6 shows a router's firewall configuration screen, which is set similarly to the way most routers deal with firewalls.

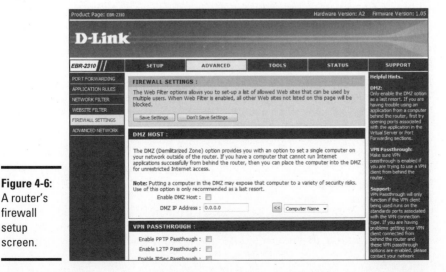

Figure 4-6:
A router's firewall setup screen.

Book IV
Chapter 4

Wicked Software

At its simplest level, the hardware firewall is an on-off type of affair. Some routers may feature an advanced firewall where you can add rules and such, but in most cases the rules are straightforward: Don't allow in any Internet traffic that wasn't specifically requested by a computer on the network. This rule pretty much blocks all the Bad Guys from getting through.

✦ When you have a hardware firewall, you don't need to use a second, software firewall.

✦ You can test your computer's firewall by visiting the Gibson Research web site and using their ShieldsUP!! program. Visit

www.grc.com

Using the Windows Firewall

Windows comes with a firewall called, remarkably, Windows Firewall. To access it, follow these steps:

1. **Open the Control Panel.**

2a. **In Windows 7, choose System and Security and then choose Windows Firewall.**

2b. **In Windows Vista, choose Security and then choose Windows Firewall.**

2c. **In Windows XP, open the Windows Firewall icon.**

You see the main Windows Firewall window, which is boring, so I don't show it here. The only thing you can do in the window is activate the Windows Firewall if it's not turned on. And I don't recommend turning it on when you have a router on your broadband connection that also features a firewall.

When you choose to use the Windows Firewall, it monitors all network traffic coming into and going out from your PC. Any suspect information, such as information you didn't request, is blocked automatically.

Sometimes, the Windows Firewall prompts you when it encounters something smelly. A firewall warning appears, and you're given three options:

Ask Me Later: Access is blocked, but only once. If the same request comes through again, you see the warning again.

Keep Blocking: Access is blocked and continues to be blocked.

Unblock: Access is allowed. Choose this option when you recognize the program making the request and everything is okay. Pat Windows Firewall on the head for being diligent.

Always choose the Keep Blocking option when you don't recognize the program or service making the request.

✦ Other software firewalls out there are better and more thorough than the Windows Firewall. I have none that I can recommend offhand, though if you have purchased an Internet security suite, you may find a software firewall included.

✦ If you use dialup networking, I highly recommend using a software firewall like the Windows Firewall.

✦ You don't need to use the Windows Firewall, or any software firewall, when your computer sits on a network behind a hardware firewall. (See the preceding section). Running redundant firewalls doesn't keep your PC any safer, but it does unnecessarily slow down the system.

✦ Software firewalls are often a cause of network woe; they often prevent you from accessing other computers on your network. See Chapter 3 in Book V for more peer-to-peer networking information.

✦ The Windows Firewall warnings aren't the same as the Windows Vista User Account Control (UAC) warnings. See Chapter 5 in Book II for more information on UAC warnings.

Disabling the Windows Firewall

To disable the Windows Firewall, you follow unique steps for each version of Windows covered in this book.

Following these steps disables the Windows Firewall in Windows 7:

1. **Open the Control Panel.**

2. **Choose System and Security and then choose Windows Firewall.**

3. **From the list of links on the left side of the window, choose Turn Windows Firewall On or Off.**

4. **Choose the option Turn Off Windows Firewall (Not Recommended).**

5. **Click the OK button.**

6. **Close the Windows Firewall window.**

In Windows Vista, disable the firewall by heeding these directions:

1. **Open the Control Panel.**

2. **Choose Security and then Windows Firewall.**

3. **Click the Change Settings link in the Windows Firewall window.**

4. **Type the administrator's password or click the Continue button.**

5. **Choose Off in the Windows Firewall Settings dialog box.**

6. **Click OK.**

7. **Close the Windows Firewall window.**

In Windows XP, follow these quick steps to disable the Windows Firewall:

1. **Open the Control Panel's Windows Firewall icon.**

2. **Choose Off in the Windows Firewall Settings dialog box.**

3. **Click OK.**

4. **Close the Windows Firewall window.**

When you disable the Windows firewall, the Action Center or Windows Security Center screen reports that "something is wrong" (refer to Figures 4-1 and 4-2). You may also find yourself bothered by its attempts to remedy the situation (such as with pop-up reminders from the notification area). That's okay: If you have a hardware firewall, you don't need to run the Windows Firewall, or any other software firewall, on top of it.

Disabling Windows Remote Assistance

Windows comes with an option to allow someone else on the Internet or a local network to access your computer. It can be done to share files, but primarily the feature exists to let someone somewhere help you fix your PC. The feature is *Windows Remote Assistance.*

For some reason, the Windows Remote Assistance feature is activated on just about every PC. I recommend turning it off because it presents a serious security risk.

Here's how to disable Windows Remote Assistance in Windows 7 and Windows Vista:

1. **Press Win+Break to quickly summon the System window.**

2. **From the list of links on the left, choose Remote Settings.**

3. **In Windows Vista, type the administrator's password or click the Continue button.**

4. **Remove the check mark by the item Allow Remote Assistance Connection to This Computer.**

5. **Choose the Remote Desktop option Don't Allow Connections to This Computer.**

6. **Click OK.**

7. **Close the System window.**

In Windows XP, follow these steps to disable Remote Assistance:

1. **Conjure forth the System dialog box by pressing the Win+Break key combination.**

2. **Click the Remote tab in the System Properties dialog box.**

3. **Remove the check mark from the item Allow Remote Assistance Invitations to Be Sent from This Computer.**

4. **If available, also remove the check mark from the option Allow Users to Connect Remotely to This Computer.**

5. **Click OK.**

If you need over-the-Internet help in the future, you can reenable Remote Assistance: Repeat these steps, but add the check mark in Step 4 for Windows 7 and Windows Vista or in Step 3 for Windows XP. Also in Windows 7 or Windows Vista, you can enable the Remote Desktop settings if you want to allow that feature.

You must respond to a request for assistance to use Windows Remote Assistance. Responding opens up your computer for remote access — but because you responded, the access is permitted through a firewall. In other words, a firewall doesn't protect you from unwanted "assistance."

Chapter 5: The File Transfer Chapter

In This Chapter

✔ Understanding files

✔ Knowing what *download* means

✔ Getting images from a web site

✔ Installing a program from the web

✔ Dealing with email attachments

✔ Sending a picture via email

✔ Using FTP

✔ Saving an FTP site

✔ Working with file permissions

Most people use the Internet, but few understand what the Internet is all about. It's simple: The Internet is about storing information and transferring that information to and fro. The information itself is stored in the form of a file. Therefore, the whole arena of "file transfer" is essentially what the Internet is all about. Files hither. Files thither. Files yon. This chapter covers all of that (though not as much on the files yon as on the files hither and thither).

What Is a File?

Before you can understand *file transfer*, you need to appreciate the entire concept of a computer file. I'm continually surprised at how many people who use computers, and who are generally smart, really don't know what a file is. Because of that, they never really get their arms around the notion of file transfer. So let me explain.

Computers store information in chunks called *files*. The file is the container. Although the information in a file consists of all those ones and zeroes you read about in computer folklore, the information itself is useful stuff. Files contain your programs, the documents you create, pictures, music, video — anything and everything you save on your computer. No matter what it is, it's stored in a file.

To help make files useful, the operating system slaps various attributes on the file. That helps the operating system deal with the files, but it also aids you in discovering which files are which. To help you connect with this process, open and view the Documents or My Documents folder on your computer; you can choose the folder from the Start menu. The Documents folder on my computer is shown in Figure 5-1.

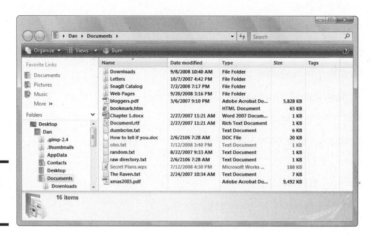

Figure 5-1:
Looking at files.

A folder window normally lists files by their icons and names, plus additional information. The additional information that's displayed depends on the view you choose. In Figure 5-1, I chose Details view. On your PC, choose Details from the Views toolbar button or menu.

You should recognize five basic attributes of a file:

Name: The filename is given when the file is created or saved to disk. Files can also be renamed after they're created. The filename is the number-one file attribute.

Type: All files have a type, which identifies either the program that created the file or the category to which the file belongs. The file type is tied directly to the last part of the filename — the filename extension.

Icon: The icon helps identify the file in the graphical environment of Windows. The icon shown is directly related to the file type.

Size: The file's size is measured in bytes, which may seem like a complex computer concept but isn't: A single *byte* is merely one character. So, if your name is 24 letters long, it takes 24 bytes to store your name in a file. Complex information such as images, sound, or video requires more storage than plain text. Regardless, the size of a file, measured in bytes, is another important file attribute.

Date: The operating system records the date and time when a file is saved, making this information part of the file's attributes. Further, the operating system also records the date a file was last opened, as well as the date a file was last modified. In Windows, the modification date is shown in the standard folder window (refer to Figure 5-1).

Every file has these basic attributes. Files have additional attributes as well, such as the read-only attribute, hidden file attribute, and a host of others (including some secret stuff they don't even tell to Bill Gates). But the basic file attributes are things you should know.

Above all, here's an important point to remember:

Everything you create on the computer is stored in a file.

When you use a program such as WordPerfect to create a document, the document is saved as a file on your PC's storage system. The document isn't "in" WordPerfect. The document is a file.

After the file is created, you can copy it to another folder or storage device on your computer, or you can copy the file to a location on the Internet or send the file to another person as an email attachment. That's the essence of the file, and that's why it's important to understand what a file is before you understand what file transfer is all about.

+ Programs are files, just like the documents you create or music you play. The difference is that programs contain instructions that tell the computer what to do.

+ You can change the number of columns displayed in a folder (in Details view) by dragging the column headings left or right. You can add or remove columns by right-clicking a column header and choosing the column types to add or remove from the shortcut menu.

+ Yes, both the type and icon file attributes are directly tied to the file's name.

+ The file's name is its most important attribute. That's why I urge readers of my other books to save their stuff by using short, descriptive filenames.

+ Refer to Chapter 6 in Book II for more information on how file types tie into the filename extension and how the weak concept of file association can lead to weird things happening on your PC.

+ Because files have sizes measured in the thousands and millions of bytes, abbreviations are used. KB represents *kilobytes,* or increments of 1,000 bytes. MB represents *megabytes*, or increments of 1 million bytes.

Book IV
Chapter 5

The File Transfer
Chapter

✦ See my book *PCs For Dummies* (Wiley) for more information on the concept of bytes in relation to file size and computer storage.

✦ A *shortcut file* is also a file, though a tiny one. The shortcut file itself merely contains a reference to another file elsewhere on the PC's storage system. So the shortcut file *is* a file, but when you open it, you're opening the referenced file.

✦ See Book II, Chapter 1 for information on finding files lost in your PC's storage system.

✦ See Chapter 4 in Book I for information on your PC's storage system, where the files dwell.

The Art of Downloading

On your computer's storage system, you work with files by creating, copying, moving, renaming, or deleting them. It's all basic file management stuff. But to work with a file on a network or on the Internet, you need to use a new term. The term is *download,* and it's the topic for this section.

Downloading the right term

I find it amusing when technical terms are used by people who don't understand the terms. A good example is the word *downloading*. What is *downloading?*

If you were to hear the brie-and-chardonnay crowd talk about downloading, you would believe that *download* is defined as any type of file transfer; sending information to any computer is a download. They say, "I'll download this to your computer" or "Download that to me." It's an incorrect use of the term, but it amuses me, so I don't bother correcting them.

The term *download* refers to transferring information from another computer into your computer. Originally, the term applied to receiving a file from a server or a mighty computer out on the Internet. I'd always imagine that computer up on a hill with my computer at the bottom of the hill. This picture helped me remember that downloading means receiving a file.

The companion term to download is *upload*, though it's not as abused as download. To upload a file is to send something from your computer to another computer. That's it. Figure 5-2 illustrates the concept.

✦ Download = Receive from the Internet.

✦ Upload = Send to the Internet.

✦ When you don't know whether you're downloading or uploading a file, you're merely doing a *file transfer*.

✦ You don't download or upload when you copy files on your own computer's storage system. For example, saving a file to an optical disc doesn't imply that you're "downloading" the file (though the term may be used regardless).

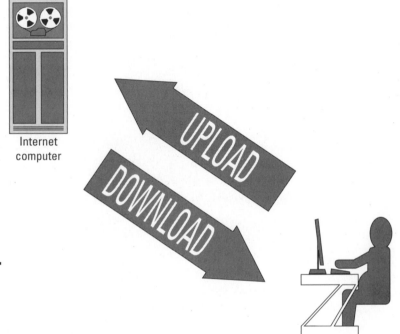

Internet computer

You

Figure 5-2:
The illustrated concept of downloading.

✦ Some sticklers out there claim that copying a file between two computers on a network isn't the same concept as downloading. No, to the purists, you download only when you fetch a file from a server, either locally or (most often) on the Internet.

✦ Sending a file as an email attachment is neither downloading nor uploading.

✦ Of course, when you're using the server or you're sending a file to a friend on the Internet, you're downloading the file into their computer. It's kind of a weird exception to the download/upload scheme of things, but then again, you could merely say that you're "transferring files" and not have to worry about any nerds snickering behind your back.

Grabbing an image from a web page

Technically, it's considered a download to snag an image from a web page. Here's the simple process:

1. **Right-click the image.**

2. **Choose the command Save Picture As.**

The command might be different in browsers other than Internet Explorer. I've seen Save Image As in addition to Save Picture As.

3. **Use the Save Picture dialog box to find a location to save the picture.**

You can rename the picture as it's saved to your computer's storage system. For example, if that saucy picture of Betty White is named DSC450013.JPG, you can rename it to Oh My Betty.jpg if you want.

4. **Click the Save button.**

The image now exists as a file on your computer.

You can also drag the image from the web page window out onto the desktop or into any open folder window. (You might be prompted to click Yes or No to ensure that dragging the image is okay, which it should be.)

✦ Windows prefers to save images in the Pictures folder, which is My Pictures in Windows XP. If you want to get more organized, you can use subfolders within the Pictures folder.

✦ Some images cannot be saved to disk. These images are protected from being copied or they're somehow created or displayed in a manner that makes copying impossible.

✦ Don't bother saving the image if you plan only to email it. Instead, choose the command E-Mail Picture from the menu instead of Save Picture As (refer to Step 2 in the preceding list).

✦ It's okay to copy and use images from the Internet, but keep in mind that many of those images are copyrighted. Under the fair-use laws, you can keep a picture for your own purposes, but you cannot reuse, sell, or otherwise profit from the image.

Downloading a program from a web site

I'll bet that nearly half the software on your computer was downloaded from a web site. Some of it's free stuff, some may be Windows updates or driver updates, and some may be programs you are trying out or have purchased online. The rest, of course, is probably stuff you stole. Or maybe not; I shan't judge you.

Downloading a program works like this in Internet Explorer:

1. Click the link that says to download the file.

It may be a button or link or a graphical image.

If prompted, choose the EXE, or executable, file option. Your second choice should be a ZIP file (Compressed Folder).

2. If you see a security warning at the top of the window (below the tabs), choose the menu item Download File.

The File Download dialog box appears, as shown in Figure 5-3. The first button in the dialog box is either Run or Open, depending on what you're downloading. If you're downloading an EXE (program) file, the button is Run; for ZIP and other files, the button is Open.

Figure 5-3:
The File
Download
dialog box.

3. Click the Save button.

You can, if you like, click the Run or Open button. The difference is that Save keeps the download on your PC, allowing you to reinstall the program later without having to download it again. The Run option downloads the file but doesn't save it for reuse later.

4. Click the Save button in the Save As dialog box.

I recommend saving the program into your account's Downloads folder. If you're using Windows XP, you can create a Downloads folder in the My Documents folder and save the file there.

If the name provided in the Save As dialog box is obscure, feel free to change it to something more memorable.

5. Wait as the download progresses.

After the download, a number of things can happen. They all depend on which type of file you received.

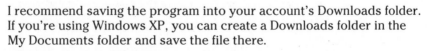

**Book IV
Chapter 5**

**The File Transfer
Chapter**

If you downloaded an EXE file, simply click the Run button in the dialog box that appears, which begins the installation. Follow the directions on the screen.

If you downloaded a ZIP file, you need to open the ZIP file to continue installation. Follow these steps:

1. **Click the Open button if one is available after the download is finished.**

2. **If prompted with a UAC, click the Allow button to allow the web site to open a folder on your PC.**

   The web site isn't opening the folder; you are.

   If there's no Open button, open the Downloads folder window and then open the Compressed Folder (ZIP) icon.

3. **In Windows 7 and Windows Vista, click the toolbar button Extract All Files; in Windows XP, click the link on the left side of the window — Extract All Files.**

4. **Work through the Extraction Wizard.**

   In Windows 7 and Windows Vista, click the Extract button. In Windows XP, click the Next button repeatedly until it turns into the Finished button and then click that button.

   When Windows is done extracting the files, you should see them in a folder window.

5. **Double-click to run the Install or Setup program.**

   If you don't see the Install or Setup program, open the Install, Setup, or Bin folder, or just open the only folder visible onscreen. Eventually, you find an Install icon or a Setup icon.

   If you still cannot find an Install program or a Setup program, open any file named `readme`. This file contains instructions for getting started, or at least more information on what to do next.

6. **Follow the directions as the installation program runs.**

   At this point, you're running the setup program; the file is being installed on your computer.

Sometimes, a download is really a *stub*, or another program loader. By running the stub, you download an even larger file from a remote server. In that case, continue following the directions on the screen that work through the setup procedure.

When the program is fully installed, it should work like any other program you installed from a disc: The program's name and icon appear on the Start button's All Programs menu, and perhaps even an annoying icon or a dozen appear on the desktop or on the Quick Launch bar.

✦ Some web sites offer you multiple links for downloading a program. They're links to various *mirror sites*, which are simply other locations on the Internet that have the same program for downloading. The idea is to pick a mirror site near you. That way, the download proceeds faster than if you choose a server located halfway around the world. Also, some sites may be busy, in which case choosing another mirror site results in a faster download.

✦ Program files listed on web sites often include the version numbers in their names. For example, version 5.6 is the sixth release of the fifth version. It's one release later than version 5.5.

✦ Typically, multiple versions of a program are made available. You can choose the most recent version or an older version that might be more stable.

✦ Prerelease, or *beta,* versions of programs are available. Don't download them unless you really need the software or feel like providing the developer with troubleshooting information.

✦ Some programs also come with their source code, which means that the files used to create the program are included. These files often use the abbreviation SRC somewhere in the name.

✦ You don't need to download the SRC version of a program. That version contains the file source code, which is useful only if you plan to do your own programming.

✦ Unless you truly need (and recognize) alternative download file formats, don't bother: Archives (GZ, TAR) are for other operating systems or those with special extraction utilities.

✦ Programs can also be received by FTP. See the section "FTP Trouble," later in this chapter.

✦ As with other installed software, you remove a program downloaded from the Internet by using the techniques covered in Chapter 6 of Book II.

Email Attachment Irritants

Yet another way email becomes desirable is as a file transfer program. In fact, the last time I printed a book and sent it into a publisher was in 1989. For a while, some publishers flirted with FTP servers. But now all the stuff I write — including every chapter in this book — is sent by email. This section explains how it all works and what to do when things go wrong.

Emailing a file

One of the simplest email operations you can perform is to send someone a file. It works like this:

1. **Compose the message.**

The primary thing you're doing is sending email. An email message has one or more recipients, a subject line, and an actual message.

2. **Click the Attach button on the toolbar.**

The Attach button commonly sports a paper clip icon, such as the example from Outlook Express, shown in the margin. You may also see a File⊅Attach command or a toolbar button labeled Attach.

3. **Use the dialog box to search out the file to attach to the message.**

The dialog box is similar to the standard Open dialog box found in any application. Use the dialog box's controls to look for the storage media, folder, and eventually the file you want to send.

You must understand the whole folder concept to be able to quickly locate files you want to attach to an email message. I recommend my book *PCs For Dummies* to help you organize files on your computer.

4. **After the file is found, click the Open or Attach button to attach it.**

5. **Repeat Steps 2 through 4 to attach additional files.**

6. **Send your message.**

In most email programs, you simply click the Send button and off the message goes, attachment in tow.

It may take longer than normal to send the message, depending on the size of the attachment. Delivery is nearly instantaneous, though keep in mind that it might take some time for the recipient to pick up the email.

✦ Avoid sending any email attachment larger than 10MB. Most online mailboxes are capped at 10MB. If you send a larger message, the recipient's mail server rejects it.

✦ See Chapter 3 for more information on general email troubleshooting.

✦ File attachments grow. Sending a 1MB file may result in the email message being 1.4MB. That's because the file attachment is converted into plain text by your email program. (All email is plain text.) The recipient's email program converts the attachment back into its original format after the recipient opens or saves the attachment on their computer.

✦ Rather than send larger files through email, burn them to an optical disc and place the disc in the regular postal mail. Yes, sending a file by *snail mail* is slower, but it's a waste of time and Internet storage to email files that might be rejected for being too large.

✦ An easier way to send multiple files is to first place the files into a compressed folder (or ZIP file archive). After they're there, you can send all the files as that single compressed folder. Of course, the recipient has to deal with the compressed folder, which is an extra step. If the person has trouble, just recommend one of my books.

✦ A compressed folder not only contains multiple files but also takes up less space than sending the files individually.

✦ Avoid using the Add Photos toolbar button in Windows Live Mail, or the Insert⇨Picture command in Windows Mail or Outlook Express. That command *embeds* an image into your email message; it doesn't attach the picture. To attach a picture, use the steps described in this section. Otherwise, the recipient might not be able to save or forward the image.

✦ In older versions of Outlook, the command to attach a file is Insert⇨File.

✦ Do not send shortcuts! Send the original file. If you send a shortcut, the recipient gets only a tiny file stub that's utterly useless.

✦ Try to send the generic version of a document file; don't send documents created in Office 2010/2007 or in WordPerfect, because not everyone has those files. The generic document file format is RTF, or Rich Text Format. You can also save the document by using the HTML format, which can be read by anyone using a computer with a web browser.

✦ Avoid sending programs. Most antivirus utilities automatically assume that a program attachment is a virus. The program file may make it, but the recipient most likely will delete it. To avoid that, send *two* messages. In the first one, explain that the next message contains a program attachment and it's legitimate. Then follow up with the email message containing the attachment.

Emailing a photo

The most common thing to email is a photo and the easiest way to do it is overlooked by far too many people. Follow these steps to email a picture file the easy way:

1. Open the folder containing the image you want to email.

Ha! Fooled you. I'll bet you were thinking that you needed to be in your email program for this task. Nope.

2. Right-click the image file to send.

3. Choose Send To⇨Mail Recipient from the shortcut menu.

An image-size-adjustment dialog box appears, as shown in Figure 5-4; in Windows XP, the dialog box offers only two choices: Make All My Pictures Smaller or Keep the Original Sizes.

4. Choose a size for the image and then click the Attach button.

The button is labeled OK in Windows XP.

**Book IV
Chapter 5**

The File Transfer
Chapter

Figure 5-4:
Adjusting
the image
size before
sending.

5. **If prompted in Windows XP, choose an email profile.**

You should be using separate user accounts for your email, not a single account on the computer with multiple email accounts.

Your email program starts, creating a new message with the image file automatically attached. Depending on the program, the Subject line may reflect the attachment and the message body may contain information about the attachment and a warning about computer viruses.

6. **Type the recipient's address.**

7. **Edit the Subject line, in case the one that's automatically used seems vague and meaningless.**

8. **Type the message body.**

Feel free to edit any text placed automatically in the body by Windows.

9. **Click the Send button.**

There's no need to close your email program after sending; only the New Message window appears; then the message is sent and you're back to doing whatever distracts you from getting real work done.

The method described in these steps helps address the biggest issue with sending photos: sending them in a convenient size.

Of course, another way to send a smaller-size image is to use an image-editing program to reset the image's size. Then again, going through those steps either alters the image's original size or gives you two copies of the same image on your PC: one small for email and the larger, original copy. That's why I recommend following the steps in this section.

✦ You can right-click any file icon to send it, similar to the way you send an image as described in this section.

✦ Although it's possible to make a large image smaller, it's not quite as easy to make a small image larger. If the image is already small, making it larger just makes it fuzzy.

✦ Store your digital photographs in a large format. The larger file format is a must for image editing. Also, larger picture files print better than smaller ones that might be better suited for attaching to an email message. Just remember to resize your images when sending them as an email attachment.

Choosing the right graphics file format

Beyond file size, discussed in the preceding section, another important factor to note when sending an image is to send it in the proper graphics file format.

Not all images stored on your computer have the same format. As computer graphics have evolved and various image editors developed, a slew of graphics file formats have come and gone. Some are well suited for sending email, and some are better suited for image editing.

The best formats for sending email photo attachments are JPG and PNG. These are also the most common formats, widely used on the web. The images look good, and the file size is small.

Among the worst formats for sending email photo attachments are TIFF and BMP. They're graphics file formats, but the file size is *huge*. In addition to these file formats, the graphics file formats native to image-editing software, such as the PSD format used by Adobe Photoshop, are inappropriate to send unless the recipient asks for such file formats and also has the software to open and edit those images.

To convert a TIFF, BMP, PSD or another type of graphics file into the JPG or PNG format, use image-editing software. Open the file and then use the File⇨Export or File⇨Save As commands to save the file using another graphics file format. Further, if you have the skills, consider resizing the image before you save it in the new file format.

✦ JPG is also written JPEG.

✦ The GIF image format is also small, but has limited resolution for photographs. PNG is a better choice.

✦ TIFF images are used primarily in applications. Although you can email them, unless the recipient requires the file in TIFF format, you're wasting time.

Receiving an attachment

People may love receiving email, but they love getting email *attachments* even more. That's my guess. It's based on the fact that so many people send me email attachments. They send pictures, music, videos, and PowerPoint presentations — all to amuse, inform, or outrage.

Book IV
Chapter 5

The File Transfer
Chapter

A good chunk of the email you receive will likely have attachments tagging along. Depending on your email program, you may see the attachments directly in the message: The images appear, and perhaps even the videos show up in their own windows, where you can watch them, right in the message.

To save the attachments, follow these general steps:

1. **Select the message or open the message in its own window.**

   Double-click a message in the Inbox to open it in its own window.

2. **Choose File⇨Save Attachments from the menu.**

   The command may be subtly different, depending on your email program, but generally it's found on the File menu.

3. **Use the dialog box to find a location for the file.**

   Use the Browse button to change the folder location.

4. **Click the Save button to save the attachment.**

The most important thing to do is follow Step 3 closely: Remember where you saved the attachment. The biggest problem with receiving attachments is that people forget where they put them.

To solve the attachment dilemma, I create a special folder for my email attachments. Inside my Documents folder, I create a subfolder named E-Mail Attachments or just Attachments. I place all attachments in this folder initially. Later, I may copy the attachments to other, more appropriate folders. But by placing all the attachments in the same folder, I always know where to find them.

✦ You don't have to open an email attachment.

✦ When you cannot open an email attachment, or when you're prompted to find a program to open the file, reply to the sender. Have the person resend the document in a common file format.

✦ If you're not expecting an email attachment, do not open it.

✦ You're never required to open an email attachment; there's no legal liability for failing to do so. Serious stuff arrives by way of postal mail, not by email.

✦ It may also be possible to save a file attachment by clicking an attachment icon in the message window. Again, all email programs handle attachments differently.

✦ Compressed folders or ZIP archives sent as attachments require a bit more work: You must first save the ZIP attachment. Then you need to open the ZIP archive or compressed folder and extract its contents.

✦ It's common for some folks to send out PowerPoint presentation files. You need to have the Microsoft PowerPoint program to view those files. When you don't have PowerPoint, you can download a free PowerPoint viewer from Microsoft's web site: Visit `microsoft.com` and type **PowerPoint viewer** in the Search box.

✦ Some types of images sent in an email message cannot be saved. These are typically embedded images, which are part of the message itself and not an email attachment. The only way to save these images is to reply to the sender and request that the images be attached. (What the person is doing is using the Insert⇨Picture or Insert⇨Image command instead of Insert⇨File Attach or File⇨Attach.)

✦ Your PC's antivirus software may add a few steps to the attachment retrieval process. That's a good thing; it's wise to be wary.

FTP Trouble

The oldest and perhaps best way to fling files between two remote computers is to use something ancient and potentially cryptic called FTP. This section discusses the to's and fro's of FTP.

Understanding FTP

FTP is one of those wonderful computer terms that's both a noun and a verb.

As a noun, *FTP* takes on its formal expansion to *File Transfer Protocol*. That's the name for a method of sending files, but also the name of the program that actually sends the files. Usage example: "Log in to my FTP server to pick up those files."

As a verb, *FTP* means to send or receive files. A proper replacement is the word *send* or *fetch*. Usage example: "FTP it to me."

Originally, FTP was developed to send and receive files in the old text-based computers and networks of the pre-graphical era of computers (before the mid-1980s). You use FTP to access a remote computer on the network to *get* or receive files, or to *put* or send files.

FTP existed as one of the original programs for accessing information on the Internet, long before HTTP became popular for accessing web pages. As such, your PC's web browser, as well as the Windows Explorer program that displays files on your computer, can be used to access FTP servers to get or put files from places remote.

✦ FTP stands for File Transfer Protocol.

✦ The term *get* is used in FTP to refer to receiving files.

✦ The term *put* is used in FTP to refer to sending files.

✦ In the modern context, using FTP in Windows is similar to opening a Windows Explorer window for a remote folder on a network computer. The next section explains the details.

✦ A computer on the Internet that offers FTP access is said to be an *FTP host* or *FTP server*.

✦ You're required to enter a username and password to access an FTP server, just like logging in to your own computer.

✦ Various public FTP servers don't require you to have an account for access. Occasionally, you may have to log in to these servers. Often, the account name is `guest` and the password is either `please` or `password`. Sometimes, you're required to give your email address as the account name and then you can type anything for the password.

✦ Web pages are uploaded to the Internet by using FTP. The web page files are created on your own computer and then sent to the ISP's web server by using FTP, either by itself or as part of the web page creation program.

✦ Windows comes with a text-based version of the FTP program, similar to the one originally found on the old Unix computers that dominated the Internet back in the early days. I don't bother covering the text-based FTP program in this book because the book is overdue already and, though it tempts me, I don't like angering my editor.

Accessing an FTP server in Windows Explorer

The first step to accessing an FTP server is to know its name. Like a web page, FTP servers on the Internet sport a unique *Universal Resource Locator,* or *URL.* It's that text thing you type into a web browser's Address bar.

Obviously, you know where you're headed in your FTP journey — personal web space, corporate file repository, or software download page. In that case, you have the name of the FTP server — the URL — already. For purposes of this exercise, I'm using the Free Software Foundation's GNU FTP server: `ftp.gnu.org`. To access this FTP server, follow these steps:

1. **Open a Windows Explorer window; press Win+E.**

You can use either Windows Explorer, which displays folder windows, or Internet Explorer. Because FTP involves working with files, I chose Windows Explorer.

2. **Click to select the Address bar.**

If the Address bar isn't visible in Windows XP, choose View⇨Address Bar.

3. **Type the FTP site's address.**

In this example, type **ftp://ftp.gnu.org**.

4. **Press Enter.**

The GNU FTP server is open to the public, using anonymous access. Most FTP servers, however, are password-protected. See the next section for more information.

In a second, you see the window populated with folders and files, just as though you were looking at storage on your own PC, as shown in Figure 5-5. Keep in mind, however, that you're using a remote computer on the Internet.

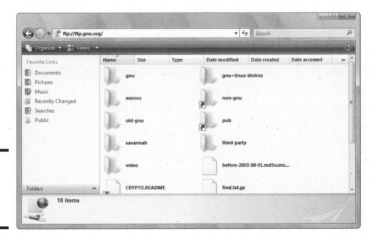

Figure 5-5:
An FTP server folder.

As an example, I show you how to download the Emacs text editor from the GNU FTP site.

5. **Open the GNU folder.**

6. **Open the Emacs folder.**

7. **Open the Windows folder.**

You're now in the location where the files to install Emacs on your computer are located.

8. **Select the icon titled emacs-xxxxx-i386.zip.**

A version number replaces the xxxxx. Otherwise, the icon represents the current version of the Emacs text editor.

Book IV Chapter 5

The File Transfer Chapter

9. **Press Ctrl+C to copy the file.**

10. **Press Ctrl+N to summon a new Windows Explorer folder window.**

If you're using Internet Explorer instead of Windows Explorer, a new Internet Explorer window appears instead. That's okay, but what you really need is a folder window, not a web page.

11. **In the new window, browse to your Downloads folder.**

Windows Vista comes with a Downloads folder, found in your account's primary folder (the User Profile folder). In Windows XP, you have to create a Downloads folder if you haven't done so already.

12. **Press Ctrl+V to copy the file to the Downloads folder window.**

It takes a few moments to copy the file because, technically, you're *downloading* it from the Internet.

After the file is copied, it exists on your own computer. You can open the icon to continue installation, or you can feel free to delete it if you don't want to use the Emacs text editor.

13. **You can close the Downloads folder window.**

14. **Close the FTP server window to disconnect from the FTP server.**

You can also break the connection by simply closing the FTP server window.

You work with an FTP server folder just like any other folder on your own computer. The three common activities are browse, get, and put:

Browse: To open a folder, double-click its folder icon. The folder takes a bit longer to open because you're working remotely over the Internet.

Get: To copy a file from the FTP server (to *download* it), choose the file and press Ctrl+C on the keyboard. Open a folder on your own PC and press Ctrl+V to paste. The file is then copied from the FTP server to your own PC.

Put: To copy a file to the FTP server (to *upload* it), choose the file on your own PC and press Ctrl+C. Click in the FTP server window and press Ctrl+V to paste, thus copying the file to the FTP server.

These techniques work on all FTP servers, including the one for your own, personal web space on the Internet. That FTP server (like many others) sports a login option. See the next section.

✦ A public FTP server allows you to copy files from its server, but you cannot copy files *to* the server. For that, you need higher access; see the next section.

✦ You can also drag to copy files between your computer and an FTP server. Both folder windows must be open and visible for the file-drag operation to work.

✦ When dragging files between a local folder and an FTP server folder window, you're always *copying* the files, not moving them.

✦ You may be denied access to any part of an FTP server, whether the server is public or not.

✦ *URL* stands for Universal Resource Locator. It's used in a web browser to identify a place to find stuff on the Internet. The most popular URL is `http` for locating web pages. There's also the `mailto` URL for sending email. `ftp` is also a URL, as is the ancient `gopher` URL, which is no longer used.

✦ You may be given a specific FTP URL, similar to a web page URL. It all works the same; type the full FTP server URL to log in to the server and use the specific folder.

Accessing a password-protected FTP site

The majority of FTP servers on the Internet require a password for access. After all, who wants the Internet rabble waltzing in, getting and putting files at random?

Accessing a password-protected FTP site works the same way as described in the preceding section. After Step 4, however, you see a password prompt similar to the one shown in Figure 5-6.

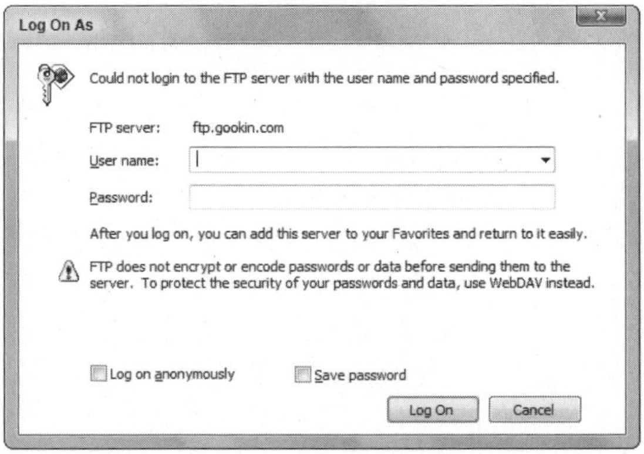

Figure 5-6:
An FTP site logon prompt.

> **Log On As**
>
> Could not login to the FTP server with the user name and password specified.
>
> FTP server: ftp.gookin.com
>
> User name: [▼]
>
> Password: [   ]
>
> After you log on, you can add this server to your Favorites and return to it easily.
>
> ⚠ FTP does not encrypt or encode passwords or data before sending them to the server. To protect the security of your passwords and data, use WebDAV instead.
>
> ☐ Log on anonymously   ☐ Save password
>
> [Log On]   [Cancel]

Type your FTP account username and password. Click Log On to connect to the site.

After you log in to a password-protected site, you can get or put files just like using a public FTP server: Copy and paste files just as you do in Windows.

One issue you encounter with password-protected FTP sites is that they have timeout values set. After several minutes of inactivity, you're logged off the FTP server; in Windows, the FTP server window is replaced with the Computer window. It's your clue that you're logged off.

- ✦ Windows automatically remembers the username you typed to access the password-protected FTP server. The name appears in the Log On As dialog box the next time you connect to the server.

- ✦ If you place a check mark by the option Save Password, Windows also remembers your FTP server password.

- ✦ Obviously, remembering your password is part of the password-protected FTP process; don't forget it!

- ✦ Automatic logouts from FTP servers are part of the system security process. Even if you could reset the FTP server timeout value to anything longer than a few minutes, I don't recommend it.

Remembering an FTP site for future access

Windows can remember the FTP sites you frequent, which saves time when accessing the same FTP site repeatedly. To save an FTP site, follow these steps:

1a. **In Windows 7 and Windows Vista, open the Computer window.**

1b. **In Windows XP, open the My Network Places window.**

You can open either window by choosing Computer or My Network Places from the Start menu or from the Address bar in any Windows Explorer window.

2a. **In Windows and Windows Vista, right-click in the Computer window and choose Add a Network Location from the shortcut menu.**

2b. **In Windows XP, choose Add a Network Place from the left side of the window.**

A wizard opens to help you add the FTP site to your computer's favorite place for remembering FTP sites: the Computer window in Windows Vista or the My Network Places window in Windows XP.

3. **Click the Next button.**

4. **Select the option Choose a Custom Network Location.**

5. **Click the Next button.**

6. **Type the FTP server address into the text box.**

   Type the full name, including the `ftp://` part.

7. **Click the Next button.**

8. **If you're accessing an anonymous (public) FTP server, keep the check mark by Log On Anonymously and skip to Step 10. Otherwise, remove the check mark.**

9. **Enter your username into the User Name box.**

10. **Click the Next button.**

11. **(Optional) Type a name for the FTP server.**

    For example, type **Work Server** or **Picture Uploads**. The name appears in the My Computer window, under the FTP server's icon.

12. **Click the Next button.**

13. **Click the Finish button to connect to the FTP server and finish the wizard.**

After you complete the wizard, the FTP server opens in its own window. If you need to log in with a password, you're prompted (refer to Figure 5-6).

After the FTP server is added, you can quickly access it by opening its icon in the Computer window. In Windows XP, you find the icon in the My Network Places window.

Setting file permissions

When uploading to the Internet, certain attributes for files are stored on an FTP server that you might consider setting. They include Read, Write, and Execute permissions for your own account as well as others who may visit the FTP site. By not setting the proper permissions, you may prevent access to the files by other users or inadvertently allow unknown users access to your stuff.

To set permissions for a file, follow these steps:

1. **Open the FTP server and browse to the folder containing the file you want to modify.**

   You can also modify a folder itself.

2. **Right-click the file icon and choose Properties from the shortcut menu.**

   You see the FTP Properties dialog box, as shown in Figure 5-7.

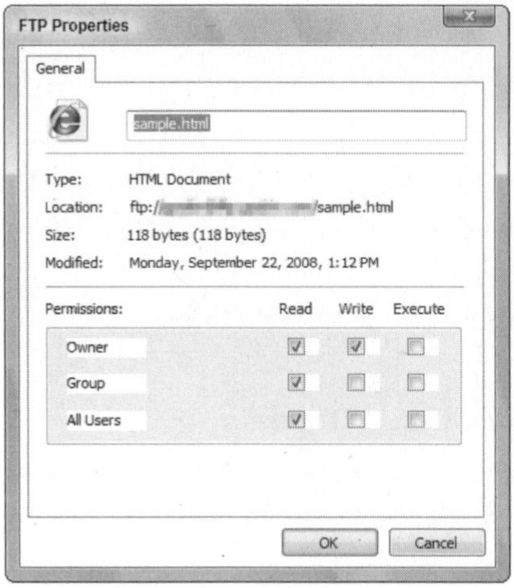

Figure 5-7:
The FTP
Properties
dialog box.

The dialog box shows you details about the file and gives you the ability
to change the file's permissions. There are three permission settings:

Read: Files can be opened or copied from the server.

Write: Files can be changed. For a folder, Write access means that
files can be added to the folder.

Execute: Files can run, like programs. Folders can be opened.

These permissions are set for three different types of users:

Owner: The person who created the file or folder — you or whoever
created the folder on a public server.

Group: Used to apply permissions to a whole mess of people, such as
a guest or public group.

All Users: Everyone.

3. **Set the permissions as necessary.**

For example, to allow only your own account to access the file, set the
Read and Write permissions for only the Owner. To let others access the
file but not change it, set their Read permission, but don't set the Write
permission.

4. **Click OK.**

The file or folder's attributes are now changed.

You can repeat these steps for other files in your FTP folder that require
special permissions.

✦ Generally speaking, the attributes are properly set for you. Normally, a file is set with Read and Write permissions for the Owner and then Read permissions for the Group and All Users.

✦ It's silly to not give a file any access. At minimum, your own files should have both Read and Write access for the Owner.

✦ All folders require Execute access if you're to open them. Normally, the Execute attribute is set for all users automatically.

✦ Beyond folders, don't set the Execute attribute unless you know that it needs to be done; having executable files on an FTP server can be a security risk.

Book V

Networking

Open the computer window.

Open a web browser.

Nifty links

Open the network window.

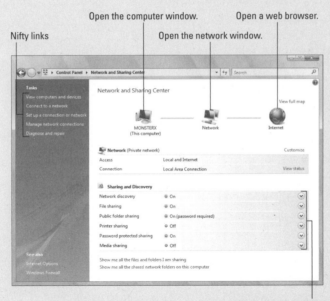

Local network settings

Access networks from the Network and Sharing Center.

Contents at a Glance

Chapter 1: Network Hardware Help

In This Chapter

✓ Configuring a basic network

✓ Dealing with router problems

✓ Checking network connections

✓ Testing the PC's network adapter

✓ Restarting the modem

✓ Fixing the entire network

Some people are born to network, and others have networking thrust upon them. I assume that you're in the latter class. Where once the computer network was the domain (sic) of nerds and engineers, anyone with a home computer and high-speed Internet connection is suddenly plunged into the mysterious world of networking. This chapter explains what can go wrong with the hardware part of that world.

✦ Like all elements of a computer, networking is composed of two parts: the hardware part, covered in this chapter, and the software part. See Chapter 2 for all that wonderful software information.

✦ The information in this chapter assumes that the network is set up and running. You might have done it, or someone else might have done it. But it's your job to fix things.

✦ This book covers only the basic type of PC networking, commonly known as *peer-to-peer* networking. I don't cover file servers, local domains, or other, larger types of networks. In those situations, a hired hand often deals with and fixes networking problems for you.

The Network Big Picture

To better understand the whole world of networking, you need to get the *big picture*. Know the terms. Experiment with the jargon. Read this section.

Understanding networking

Networking is about communications and the sharing of resources. Along with sunny days in May and free cake, communications and sharing are possibly the best things in the world. But cake isn't free, and it rains in May, so don't believe everything you read.

The story of networking is about the desire of yesterday's proto-nerds to move information from one computer into another computer. Oh, I suppose they started with just two computers. But then the guy with the third computer got jealous and soon, well, *everyone* wanted in on this networking gig.

Information being sent and received among various computers smacks of communications, and that's the basis of a computer network. It all happens in such a manner that information destined for one computer arrives at the computer intact and accurate, and the sending computer knows that the information was received.

The result of the communications is not that the computers start up a 1-900 cyberfriends chat line. No, the computers are more interested in the sharing of *resources*. Your PC can share several resources on a computer network:

Mass storage: Hard drives, optical drives, and other types of storage can be shared and used by others on the network. Networking provides a solution whereby you don't need to copy files to removable media and walk them between computers — the *sneakernet*.

Media files: Another resource you can share between PCs on a network is your music, picture, and video files. Windows Media Player, as well as Apple's iTunes and other media jukeboxes, can be accessed and their media libraries shared over a simple computer network.

Printers: There's no need for every PC on the network to have its own printer when you can have one key printer on the network. Everyone can then use Ed's nice color printer, even though it's in Ed's office and he's overly possessive of his stuff.

Modems: everyone on the network can share a single modem. In fact, high-speed modems must connect to your computer by using the network interface.

That's pretty much the networking philosophy. The methods by which computers are networked, however, became standardized in the early 1990s, at just about the same time the Internet exploded on the scene. Conveniently, the Internet is also a network, so the world is starting to make sense.

The protocols and methods for networking are referred to as *Ethernet*. It's the networking standard used by the Internet and by all local networks. Before that time, computer networks could use a number of different networking schemes, both hardware and software. But with Ethernet, nearly all computer networking has become standard.

✦ Mass storage resources consist of folders you can access on other computers. Additionally, there can be stand-alone network hard drives, up for grabs by anyone using the network.

✦ Windows Media Player version 11 and later can share your media files with other PCs running copies of Windows Media Player. A teensy icon in the notification area alerts you to the presence of other PCs sharing their Windows Media Player libraries.

✦ Only the folders you elect to share are available for others to use on the network. A level of security is provided by password protection as well as by read-only access. See Chapter 3 for the details.

✦ Even when you have only one computer and a broadband modem, you technically have a network set up. Don't deny it! Embrace it!

Discovering network hardware

In the beginning was the wire. And it was good. But communications doesn't live by wires alone.

To make the network work, you need some basic hardware components. Nothing is too outrageously expensive, but some things have outrageous names attached to them. Knowing what the names refer to is important to understanding the big network picture:

NIC: The first part of the network dwells inside your PC, as either part of the motherboard circuitry or an expansion card. It's a *NIC,* or "nick." NIC stands for network interface card, though I've also seen it defined as network information card. Regardless, just say "NIC" and you'll be fine.

The NIC most likely does some technical and confusing things that I don't bother describing here. Windows and a special NIC software driver control it. Most important, the NIC is where you plug in the network cable.

Ethernet cable: Named after the protocol for networking, a cable is required in order to connect your PC to other PCs on the network. This standard is referred to as *Ethernet cable*, but it has a technical name: *CAT 5,* for Category 5, not kitty cat 5.

Every computer on the network must have a NIC with an Ethernet cable attached (unless you have a wireless NIC, and that topic is covered shortly). That cable doesn't go to other computers. (They aren't daisy-chained — an older, but once popular, way to network PCs.) Instead, the computers and their Ethernet cables all tether directly to a central location, or *hub*. On a typical PC network, that hub is a *router*.

Router: The router not only manages traffic on your network but also coordinates larger network traffic, such as information coming in from and going out to the Internet. Most routers also have the smarts to deal with USB devices, like printers and hard drives.

The router is a big deal in your computer network. Therefore, specific information on routers is covered in the later section, "You Say 'Rooter,' I Say 'Router.'"

Broadband modem: The final piece of the network for most common setups is a broadband modem. It communicates with the router, so it's just another shared resource on the network. The modem is your local-area network's gateway to the Internet, which is the world's computer network.

When it comes to using the NIC with a router, there's a speed issue. Ethernet can run at speeds of 10 megabits per second (Mbps), 100 Mbps, or 1 gigabit per second (Gbps). The faster, the better.

Only older, antique Ethernet networks ran at 10 Mbps. Today, 100 Mbps is common, though the 1 Gbps, or *Gigabit Ethernet,* connections are preferred. But if you want to have a network that runs at this speed, the NIC and router and all additional network devices must be Gigabit Ethernet.

A typical small-office or home-office network setup is shown in Figure 1-1. As shown in the figure, the center of the operation is the router. It connects to three computer systems: two desktops and one laptop PC.

Assume that every PC has a NIC (not shown in the figure). The cable goes from the PC to the router.

The router has some USB ports, and Figure 1-1 illustrates the router connected to a printer and hard drive.

The router is also connected to a broadband modem. As on PCs, the modem is connected to the router by using an Ethernet cable. The modem is also plugged into a phone line or cable line or connected to a satellite dish. That's how the modem talks with the Internet.

Not shown in Figure 1-1 is the myriad of power supply cables. Routers and cable modems, plus printers and hard drives, all require power. That makes for a heck of a mess.

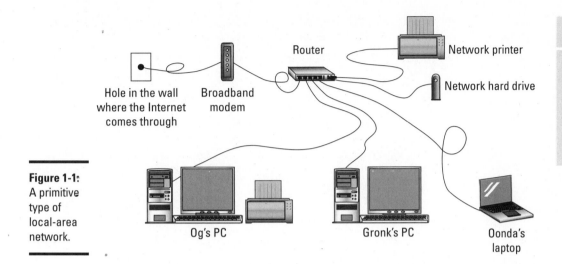

Figure 1-1:
A primitive
type of
local-area
network.

Hole in the wall
where the Internet
comes through

Broadband
modem

Router

Network printer

Network hard drive

Og's PC

Gronk's PC

Oonda's
laptop

✦ Your computer network is a *LAN*, or local-area network.

✦ This LAN is your LAN, this LAN is my LAN.

✦ Stand by your LAN.

✦ Know your network! Know what the parts are called. Know where to connect the cables at each end. Check the router connections. The more you know how your network looks now, when it's working, the better you can fix it later, when it's not working.

✦ The NIC's presence is evident by the networking cable jack on the back of your computer or the side of a laptop. The jack is often called an *RJ-45*, though that's not its official designation.

✦ Even wireless networking uses a NIC. In that case, you don't plug anything into the NIC because it sends and receives its information wirelessly. That's why they named it a *wireless* NIC.

✦ Another way to create a network is to use a simple device called a *hub*. It's basically a box into which you plug Ethernet cables so that your computers can chat with each other. Hubs are electronically stupid, so I don't recommend getting one.

✦ *Hub* is also a generic term applied to any location where network information is coordinated — for example, a wireless hub, which is really a router.

✦ One step up from a hub (and a step down from the router) is the switch. Switches are a bit better at managing network traffic and are often used to expand the number of Ethernet ports available on a network, as covered elsewhere in this chapter.

✦ The Ethernet cable features the same connections on either end. There's no way to plug in the cable backward.

✦ Like Penn & Teller, networking cable is also referred to as *twisted pair*. It provides for the cable's two-way communications and also explains why you cannot plug in an Ethernet cable backward. But it doesn't explain why an Ethernet cable is incapable of magic and is bereft of sardonic wit.

✦ It doesn't matter where you plug an Ethernet cable into the hub, switch, or router. Some older hubs, however, may have a special *uplink* connector, which is used to connect that hub to another hub or switch. See the section "Adding more Ethernet ports to the network," later in this chapter.

✦ Both the NIC and the hub/switch/router have status lights that blink when data is being transmitted over the network. These lights flicker — sometimes, often. It's nothing bad.

✦ Gigabit Ethernet gizmos are often labeled *GbE* or sometimes *1 GigE*.

✦ It's possible to connect a broadband modem directly to your PC's NIC. Don't. I could list several reasons why such a configuration is a Bad Thing, but the number-one reason is security: Your PC would be wide open to Internet attack in such a setup.

✦ Creating and configuring your own home- or small-office network is easy. You can even buy starter kits. I recommend hiding the cables as best you can. Try to avoid situations where someone can trip over them or they become snarled in a viper nest of other cables and power cords.

✦ If you plan to run network cable through the ceiling or air ducts, get *planar* cable, which is designed for such purposes.

✦ This is the last bullet point.

Putting a printer on the network

A network printer is any printer "up for grabs" on the network. Officially, it's a *shared* printer. It can be a printer connected to a PC on the network, where the computer operator has elected to share the printer, making it available for anyone else on the network to use. Or, it can be a printer directly connected to the network.

It might seem odd to have a printer out there, all by its lonesome, connected to the Internet. It happens. It can happen in one of two ways.

First, you can add a USB printer directly to the network's router, if the router features a USB connection. After connecting the printer, access the router's control program to complete its setup. See the section "Configuring the router," later in this chapter, for information on accessing the router's control program.

Second, you can add a printer directly to the network, if the printer has an Ethernet port. Simply connect the printer to the network and turn it on. Sadly, you must use Windows to hunt for the printer before you can use it on your PC. I call it a manual network connection.

After the printer is turned on and connected to the network, you can direct your PC to use the printer. The first thing to do is see whether the printer came with its own software installation disc. If so, use the disc and follow its instructions. If not, you can add the network printer for use in Windows 7 and Windows Vista by following these steps:

1. **Open the Control Panel.**

2a. **In Windows 7, choose View Devices and Printers from beneath the Hardware and Sound heading.**

2b. **In Windows Vista, choose Printer from beneath the Hardware and Sound heading.**

3. **Click the Add a Printer toolbar button.**

The Add Printer window appears.

4. **Choose the option Add a Network, Wireless, or Bluetooth Printer.**

5. **Rather than wait for the inevitable, choose the option The Printer That I Want Isn't Listed.**

6. **Ensure that the option Add a Printer Using a TCP/IP Address or Hostname is selected.**

7. **Click the Next button.**

8. **Type the printer's IP address into the Hostname or IP Address box.**

You can often find the IP address by printing the printer's configuration; check the printer documentation to find out how to use the printer's control panel to cough up its current configuration, including the IP address.

9. **(Optional) Enter the port name, if you know what it is.**

10. **Click the Next button.**

11. **Continue with the printer setup.**

I have to be vague at this point because Windows may recognize the printer, in which case setup continues rather quickly. Otherwise, you need to choose the printer make and model from the list.

In Windows XP, follow these steps to set up a sole, lonely network printer:

1. **Open the Printers and Faxes icon in the Control Panel.**

2. **Choose Add a Printer.**

The link is on the left side of the window.

3. **Click the Next button.**

4. **Choose the option A Network Printer or a Printer Attached to Another Computer, and click the Next button.**

5. **Choose the option Connect to This Printer, which is the second option.**

6. **Type the printer's IP address into the text box.**

   The IP address should be available from the printer, either on its control panel or by printing the printer's information sheet.

7. **Continue with the printer setup.**

   At this point, the setup can change, depending on how Windows recognizes the printer. As long as contact is made with the printer over the network, you can figure out the rest of the steps.

When you're done setting up the printer, print a test page. It confirms that the printer is connected and working.

✦ There's no need to make the network printer your PC's *default* printer — unless it's Ed's printer and, well, we all remember how possessive he is.

✦ Obviously, there's no need to configure a network printer when it shows up automatically in the Printers window.

✦ If the printer is connected to the network by using one of those tiny printer server dongles, you probably need to configure the printer by using the software that came with the printer server dongle. The configuration program either allows the printer to be used on the network, on your PC, or it provides you with the IP address you can use for the steps in this section.

✦ You might also be able to get the printer's IP address from the router configuration program. See the section "Configuring the router," later in this chapter, for information on accessing the configuration program. The printer's IP address is listed along with the IP addresses assigned to all devices connected to the router.

✦ The printer should set its IP address by using DHCP. You don't need to know what this term means, but you must make that setting if you're given a choice.

✦ Network printers can also be added by plugging the printer directly into the network. As long as the printer features an Ethernet connection, you can plug it into the router directly. This type of printer may not show up immediately.

Adding a network hard drive

As with network printers, putting a hard drive up for grabs on the network is done primarily by sharing folders on your computer with other computers on the network. But it's possible to connect a hard drive directly to the network — a hard drive that doesn't have a computer attached. It can happen in one of two ways.

First, you can connect an external USB hard drive to a router that features USB ports. Plug the hard drive into the wall and then connect it to the router. The hard drive may be instantly recognized, or it might require additional configuration. See the section "Configuring the router," later in this chapter, for information on accessing a router's configuration program.

The second method to connect a hard drive is directly. This method works only when the hard drive features its own Ethernet port: Simply plug the hard drive into its power supply, plug the hard drive into the router with an Ethernet cable, and you're done. The hard drive appears in the Network window along with other drives shared on the network.

✦ See Chapter 2 for more information on where you can view and access network hard drives in Windows.

✦ In Windows XP, networked hard drives appear in the My Network Places window.

✦ Not all external hard drives feature an Ethernet port. Expect to pay more for a stand-alone network hard drive.

You Say "Rooter," I Say "Router"

The heart in your computer network's circulatory system is the *router*. Yes, you need a router. Especially when you plan to use a broadband modem, a router is a must-have item. This section explains how the router fits into your networking picture and how to deal with minor router despair.

✦ Router rhymes with "powder."

✦ Don't say "rooter" unless you live in the United Kingdom.

✦ In Australia or Canada, either pronunciation is acceptable: "rooter" or "router."

Understanding the router

If you've been around high-speed Internet or have had a small network installed at your home or office for a while, you know that you have a router, but you probably don't know what the router does or why it's needed. In a normal *For Dummies* book, I'd simply say "Live with it," but this isn't a normal *For Dummies* book.

Technically, what you have in your home or office (refer to Figure 1-1) is a *gateway,* not a router. This tiny computer manages the local network traffic, sending bits and bytes between any connected computers. It also may manage a hard drive or printer.

On the other end, the router acts as your local network's connection to the Internet. It presents all local network traffic to the Internet as a single front. It further provides defense against probing attacks from the Internet, mostly by ignoring them with a firewall.

Do you need a router? Theoretically, no: You can hook up a single PC directly to the broadband modem and be online. In this type of configuration, you would need an extremely robust software firewall and a lot of Internet security software. Even so, the setup may not work because some broadband modems require a router to be present or else they cannot communicate. Regardless, though you may not need a router, you *want* one.

✦ There are wired routers and wireless routers. You can also find combination wired/wireless routers. Indeed, most wireless routers also sport a standard Ethernet cable connection.

✦ See Book IV, Chapter 4 for more information on firewalls.

Connecting the router

Though it be a technical beast, a router isn't difficult to set up. In fact, after it's set up, you rarely, if ever, have to reconfigure or mess with the router. It's a solid little gizmo.

On the hardware side, the router features connections on its rump, similar to the one shown in Figure 1-2. Refer to the directions that came with the router for specifics on how things are set up, but generally the Ethernet cables from your PCs hook into the LAN connectors. A single connector is designated for the broadband modem, which also plugs into the router by using an Ethernet cable.

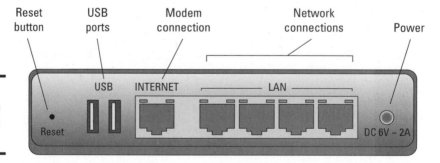

Figure 1-2:
Connectors
on a typical
router.

Some routers have On-Off switches, but mostly you just plug the thing into the wall socket to turn it on. There's no need to turn off the router unless you're troubleshooting the network or you plan on not using the network for an extended period; most folks leave their broadband modems and routers on all the time.

One important item to find on the router is its reset switch. It's probably located on the back of the router (refer to Figure 1-2). The reset switch is most likely recessed. See the later section, "Resetting the router," to find out how and when to use the reset switch.

The front of the router is less interesting than the back. The front features a few lamps that flicker as traffic flows into and out of the router, plus perhaps a status light or three. Ho-hum.

✦ You must properly plug the modem's cable into the router. Don't connect the modem into any Ethernet plug other than the one designated for the modem or for the Internet.

✦ Wireless routers have similar connectors to the wired router (refer to Figure 1-2), with the addition of one or more antennas.

✦ Not all routers feature the connections shown in Figure 1-2. Some lack USB connectors. That's okay: You can connect a printer or hard drive to the router by using an Ethernet cable, as discussed later in this chapter.

✦ Plug the modem into the Internet or Modem jack on the router. Sometimes the jack is labeled WAN, for wide-area network.

Configuring the router

Routers, like all computer gizmos, have both hardware and software setup. After you connect the router, the next step is to configure it. Primarily, and for security reasons, the most important thing is to set an administrator password for the router.

You connect to the router by using Internet Explorer (or your favorite alternative web browser). Follow these general steps:

1. **Set up the router hardware.**

Refer to the preceding section for tips on the hardware connection.

2. **Start up Internet Explorer or your favorite alternative web browser.**

The computer you're using must be connected to the router.

3. **Type the router's address into the web browser's Address bar.**

The address looks something like `http://192.168.0.1` or possibly `http://10.0.0.1`. The quick-start guide for the router gives you the proper address.

When you're successful, you see the router's login screen, similar to the one shown in Figure 1-3.

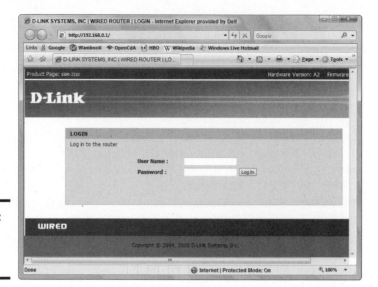

Figure 1-3:
A router's login screen.

If you cannot connect to the router, restart your PC and try again.

4. **If necessary, log in to the router.**

   You may have the preset administrator's password supplied in the documentation, or maybe no password is set yet.

   After you're "in" the router, you continue to use your web browser to set various options. The two most important are setting the administrator's password and enabling the firewall.

5. **Change the router's administrator password.**

   Please O please, pick a nice, strong password. Especially for a wireless router, you don't want to pick something obvious or easy that the hackers or neighborhood kids will figure out.

6. **Ensure that the router's firewall is active.**

   The firewall most likely is active, but check, just in case. Use the router's web-based interface in your PC's web browser to navigate to the firewall option screen.

7. **When you're done, close the web browser window.**

   You may see a logout option; if so, log out before you close the window.

The router remembers its settings, so there's no need to reconfigure it after a power outage. After it's set up, you'll probably never need to mess with it again.

And now, the shortcut. There's a quick way to connect to your router, by skipping Steps 1 through 3 in the preceding set of steps, but the trick works only in Windows Vista:

1. Open the Network window.

You can choose Network from the Start menu or from the Address bar in any Windows Explorer window.

2. Double-click to open the router's icon in the Network window.

By opening the router's icon in the Network window, you immediately open a web browser window, where you can log in and begin messing with the router.

✦ Write down the router password! Do not rely on it being in a computer.

✦ You can access the router from any computer on your local network — if you log in with the proper password.

✦ If you forget the password, you can reset the router. See the next section.

✦ Don't forget to change the password on your router. When the router comes from the factory, it has a standard — and well-known — password. Follow my advice in this chapter and immediately set a new password for your router.

Resetting the router

Perhaps the best general solution for a stupid router is to reset it. To do so, stick a bent paper clip into the Reset hole, using Figure 1-2 as your guide. Press and hold the paper clip. Release. This action should restart the router, erasing its settings and placing it into the condition it was in when you first set things up.

After resetting the router, you need to set the router's administrator password and review other settings, such as the firewall.

✦ Sometimes you need to have the router turned on for it to reset, and sometimes the reset works whether the router is on or off.

✦ You might also consider restarting the entire network to fix a router issue. See the section "Restarting the entire network," later in this chapter.

Pinging the router

The first test you need to make for a router is to *ping* it, or send it a signal that proves not only that the router is there but also that your computer is connected to the router and that all communications are taking place in a friendly manner.

To send the router a friendly ping, follow these steps:

1. **From the Start menu, choose All Programs⇨Accessories⇨Command Prompt.**

A Command Prompt window opens.

2. **To discover the router's address, type** ipconfig **and press Enter.**

The ipconfig command coughs up some information about your PC's current network configuration. You see information that includes something like this:

```
IPv4 Address. . . . . . . . . . . : 192.168.0.103
Subnet Mask . . . . . . . . . . . : 255.255.255.0
Default Gateway . . . . . . . . . : 192.168.0.1
```

The *IPv4 address* is your PC's IP address on the local network. The address is assigned by the router, using something called DHCP, discussed in Chapter 2.

The *subnet mask* is a type of filter that helps PCs on the network better see each other. (And I'm sticking with that explanation for now.)

The *default gateway* is the IP address of the router. Make a note of it.

If you see the message, media disconnected, check both ends of the Ethernet cable.

3. **Type the command** ping, **a space, and then the IP address of the router, or default gateway; press Enter.**

For example, using the output shown in Step 2, the command is

```
ping 192.168.0.1
```

After you press the Enter key, the ping command attempts to send four packets of information to the router, which should echo those results to you. You see something like this:

```
Pinging 192.168.0.1 with 32 bytes of data:
Reply from 192.168.0.1: bytes=32 time<1ms TTL=127
Reply from 192.168.0.1: bytes=32 time<1ms TTL=127
Reply from 192.168.0.1: bytes=32 time<1ms TTL=127
Reply from 192.168.0.1: bytes=32 time<1ms TTL=127

Ping statistics for 192.168.0.1:
    Packets: Sent = 4, Received = 4, Lost = 0 (0%
    loss),
Approximate round trip times in milli-seconds:
    Minimum = 0ms, Maximum = 0ms, Average = 0ms
```

The information is technical, but not complex. The key is that you want to see a mess of data, as shown in the previous example. When you see the text Destination host unreachable or Request timed out, that's when the PC has trouble communicating with the router.

4. **Type** exit **and press Enter to close the Command Prompt window.**

Are there problems? You may not seem to see any, but first confirm that the gateway address given in Step 2 is the same as the router address. If not, the PC is most likely just pinging itself in Step 3. That works, but it's not the same as communicating with the router.

When the router is unreachable, you probably need to turn off the router and then turn it on again. Because most routers lack a Power button, you need to unplug it and then plug it back in. After the power is back on, try repeating these steps to see whether you can ping the router.

If the router remains unreachable, you need to restart the entire network, as described in the section "Restarting the entire network," later in this chapter.

✦ Yes, routers can go bad. I've seen a few of them spoil in my day. The last router I had died and needed to be replaced. Fortunately, a replacement router won't break you financially. Routers are cheap.

✦ Well, *gateways* are cheap. The real routers, used by the big boys, are *not* cheap.

✦ The ipconfig command's output lists some Tunnel adapter information. Feel free to ignore it.

✦ The router is really a *gateway*, which is why the results of the ipconfig command list its address as Default Gateway.

✦ IP stands for Internet Protocol. See Chapter 2 for more information on the IP address.

✦ See Book IV, Chapter 1 for more information on using the ping command.

Adding more Ethernet ports to the network

Soon you may discover that the router has run out of places to plug in your net-junk. There's your computer, another computer, perhaps a network hard drive, a printer, and then — oops! — you're out of Ethernet ports.

The solution is to add more Ethernet sockets. You do that by buying something called a *switch,* which allows you to plug in more Ethernet cables and attach that switch to the router. An illustration of the result is shown in Figure 1-4.

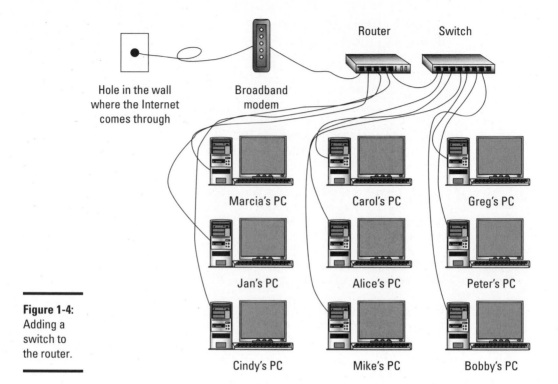

Hole in the wall
where the Internet
comes through

Broadband
modem

Marcia's PC   Carol's PC   Greg's PC

Jan's PC   Alice's PC   Peter's PC

Figure 1-4:
Adding a
switch to
the router.

Cindy's PC   Mike's PC   Bobby's PC

The operation is simple: First, buy a switch that matches the speed of the router and your PC's NIC cards. For example, if they're 1-gigabit Ethernet cards, buy a 1-gigabit Ethernet switch.

Second, plug in the switch. All switches need a power supply.

Third, connect the switch to the router. Some switches have a special jack for this task, labeled an Uplink connector. Quite a few switches, however, are "smart switches" that feature automatic uplink abilities — you can connect them to the router by using any available Ethernet socket.

Finally, plug the Ethernet cables from the various PCs on the network into the switch.

The result is that you can connect all the network gizmos you need to connect.

✦ Don't worry about order or sequence or anything; the switch is smart, but the router is smarter. All computers connected to either the router or the switch are on the same network.

✦ If the switch loses power, the computers connected to the switch lose their network connections.

✦ Buy a switch with many more Ethernet ports than you need. To drive this point home, I can tell you that I have an 8-port Fast Ethernet switch for sale right now on eBay. If I can sell it, it will offset the cost of the 16-port Fast Ethernet switch I just bought recently.

✦ Refer to the section "Restarting the entire network," later in this chapter, for information on getting a stubborn switch to work.

General Network Troubleshooting

Most of the network troubleshooting you do involves configuring a PC to talk with the network. That's a software duty, so those issues are covered in Chapter 2. Everything else is most likely a hardware networking problem. Those issues are addressed in this section.

Inspecting the NIC

Whether old St. NIC is part of your PC's motherboard circuitry or attached as an expansion card, you can sneak a peek at its status by using the Device Manager.

In Windows Vista, follow these steps to check on the NIC hardware:

1. **Open the Control Panel.**

2a. **In Windows 7, choose Hardware and Sound, and then choose the Device Manager link beneath the Devices and Printers heading.**

2b. **In Windows Vista, choose Hardware and Sound, and then choose Device Manager.**

   You need to type the administrator password or click the Continue button to proceed in Windows Vista.

3. **Expand the Network Adapters item to view all network adapters installed on your PC.**

   You most likely have only one.

4. **Double-click the Network Adapter entry to display your PC's network adapter's Properties dialog box.**

   The General tab in the Properties dialog box lists the device status. Any problems detected by Windows appear in that message box. Otherwise, the message reads `This device is working properly`.

5. **Click the Resources tab in the Properties dialog box.**

6. **Check the Conflicting Device list.**

You should see no conflicts listed. If not, the source of the conflicts must be resolved. Generally, it would mean removing whatever other device is conflicting with the NIC or reconfiguring the device. See the sidebar "Device conflicts," later in this chapter, for details.

7. **Click OK to close the Properties dialog box.**

8. **Close the Device Manager window as well as the Control Panel.**

Follow these steps to check on the NIC's hardware in your Windows XP computer:

1. **Press Win+Break to quickly summon the System Properties dialog box.**

2. **Click the Hardware tab.**

3. **Click the Device Manager button.**

   The Device Manager window appears.

4. **Expand the Network Adapters area by clicking the plus sign [+] icon.**

   You see a list of all network adapters installed in your PC.

5. **Double-click a network adapter entry.**

   The adapter's Properties dialog box appears. On the General tab, you see the device status. It should say `This device is working properly`. If not, any specific problems are noted.

6. **Click the Resources tab.**

7. **Review the Conflicting Device list.**

   No conflicts should be listed. When they are, resolve them by looking at the source of the conflict. Refer to the later sidebar, "Device conflicts," for information.

8. **Click the OK button to close the Properties dialog box.**

9. **Close the Device Manager and the Control Panel windows.**

The first solution for fixing a bad NIC is first to view the suggestions listed in the Properties dialog box. When those suggestions aren't helpful, one alternative is to use another NIC.

If you have a NIC on an expansion card, simply remove the old one and install a new one. See Book I, Chapter 8 for information on replacing expansion cards.

When the NIC is on the motherboard, your alternative is simply to install a second NIC as an expansion card.

For a laptop, get a USB NIC, either wired or wireless, when the laptop's NIC fails.

Device conflicts

Device conflicts arose more often in earlier PCs because of their limited expansion options. A network adapter, for example, had to be assigned memory space as well as something called an IRQ. The PC has a limited number of IRQs. To fix the conflict, you had to reassign the IRQ of the conflicting device, which involved some hardware marksmanship. On today's PCs, such hardware conflicts are rare.

To deal with a hardware conflict, you must reset the IRQ on one of the two conflicting devices. Or, you can remove one device. My suggestion is to see which devices can be replaced by a comparable USB device. USB devices don't have the conflicts that IRQ gizmos do.

✦ You will probably know when the NIC isn't working properly before you even open its Properties dialog box. That's because bum devices are flagged with a yellow icon in the Device Manager.

✦ When you're having network adapter problems in Windows XP, click the Troubleshoot button (after Step 5) to run the NIC Troubleshooter.

✦ If your PC came with a NIC diagnostics tool, using it would be, obviously, a better option for checking on the NIC as well as for testing the NIC's condition. Check the Start button's All Programs menu. Look for a folder (submenu) specific to the NIC manufacturer, such as Intel, Netlink, or Linksys.

✦ Yes, you can have multiple network adapters in a PC. For example, a laptop computer would have both wired and wireless NICs. When you have multiple NICs, you can repeat the steps in this section to review any problems or conflicts with each of the adapters.

✦ To disable a NIC, open its Properties dialog box by following the directions listed in this section. In Windows 7 or Windows Vista, use the Disable button on the Driver tab; in Windows XP, choose Disable from the drop-down menu at the bottom of the General tab. By disabling the device, you ensure that Windows doesn't use it and instead uses another NIC that functions properly.

Upgrading the NIC's driver

The software that controls the network hardware — specifically, the NIC — is a *driver*. Rarely do you need to update this software. In fact, a routine or security update is included with the standard Windows Update, as described in Book II, Chapter 1.

To specifically update a NIC driver, obey these steps:

1. **Set a system restore point.**

   See Book II, Chapter 8 for more information.

2. **Follow the steps in the preceding section to open the PC's NIC Properties dialog box.**

   Each version of Windows has a separate set of directions.

3. **In the NIC Properties dialog box, click the Driver tab.**

4. **Click the Update Driver button.**

5. **Follow the directions onscreen to search the Internet, or use the Windows Update service to find the best or most current driver.**

6. **In Windows XP, choose to install the software automatically.**

   What happens next depends on whether you need a new driver.

   If the driver is up-to-date, you see a message explaining as much. Otherwise, a newer driver is downloaded from the Internet and installed on your PC.

7. **Close the NIC Properties dialog box as well as any other open windows when you're done.**

You might have to restart your computer; do so, if prompted.

+ When the new driver doesn't fix the problem, my next suggestion is to replace the NIC.

+ If problems occur, restore the system: Restart the computer, and, if you can, run System Restore and choose the most recent restore point.

+ Updating the NIC driver may solve some problems. But mostly, when you have NIC problems, you should do a hardware analysis as described in the preceding section.

Disconnecting from the network

You can disconnect from the network in a hardware or software fashion.

Hardware-wise, simply unplug the Ethernet cable from the PC. Poof — the network, and the Internet, is gone. A small warning bubble may appear in the notification area, as shown in Figure 1-5. It's also your visual clue that the network has connection issues.

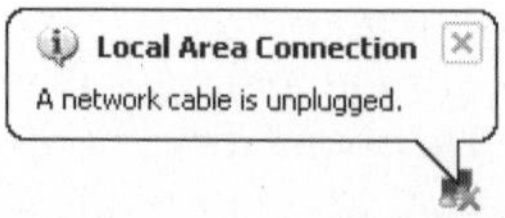

Figure 1-5:
A dis-
connected
cable!

> ⓘ **Local Area Connection** ☒
> A network cable is unplugged.

The solution to the problem is to reconnect the cable. Check both ends.

Normally, an Ethernet cable shouldn't become accidentally unplugged. When it does, it means that the cable's end is broken. Get a replacement.

Reconnecting to the network is simple: Plug the Ethernet cable back into the PC. There's nothing else you need to do. Windows instantly recognizes the network connection, as shown in Figure 1-6.

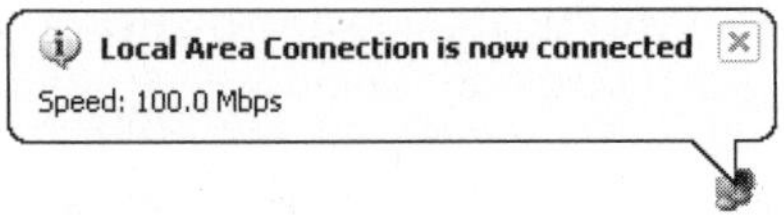

Figure 1-6:
A
reconnected
cable!

> ⓘ **Local Area Connection is now connected** ☒
> Speed: 100.0 Mbps

Cables can also go bad, in which case the cable may appear to be plugged in but no signal is coming through the cable. In that case, check the lights on the NIC or router. The lights should routinely blink as network traffic is sent and received. When the light isn't on or turns yellow rather than green, it can indicate a connection problem. Replace the cable.

✦ You can also disconnect the PC's Ethernet cable from the router (or switch). I don't recommend that approach, however; unless you're using a different color of Ethernet cable for each PC, it's difficult to determine exactly what you're disconnecting.

✦ Software-wise, you can disconnect from the Internet by using Windows. See Chapter 2 for the details.

✦ It's more common to disconnect from a wireless network than from a wired network. The common way to do that on a laptop is simply to shut the laptop's lid, but see Chapter 4 for more wireless information.

Resetting the broadband modem

Occasionally, you may lose your connection to the Internet. The local network is okay: You can still access network printers and hard drives just fine, but the Internet is unreachable.

The first things to check are the lights on the modem: Is the modem getting a signal? If not, the problem is with your Internet service provider (ISP).

Next, turn the modem off and then on again. By *cycling* the modem's power in this way, you can often wake it up and it reconnects to the Internet. (An email pal of mine who works for an ISP's tech-support center says that the power cycling solution fixes about 90 percent of broadband modem problems.)

When turning the modem off and on doesn't work, turn off the modem *and* the router. Wait a spell. Turn the modem back on. Wait. Turn the router back on. At that point, the entire system should be up and running and your PCs can see each other and access the Internet.

If, after all that, the network still doesn't work and Internet access looks like a faded memory, you have my permission to phone your ISP for tech support.

Restarting the entire network

The ultimate network fix is to restart the entire network. It's a simple thing to do — not a regular activity or routine maintenance — but a general cure-all for many network ills. The procedure works like this:

1. **Turn everything off.**

   Computers. Printers. Hard drives. Modems. Switches. Routers. Hubs. If it's connected to the network, you turn it off.

2. **Turn on the broadband modem and wait for it to start properly.**

   It takes a few moments for the modem to find a signal and chat it up with the Internet. When all the modem's status lights are on and the modem is happy, you can move on to the next step.

3. **Turn on the router.**

   Again, wait for the router to start up and get happy.

4. **If you have a switch connected to the router (refer to Figure 1-4), turn it on next.**

5. **Turn on a computer connected to the network.**

   Let the computer start up as normal. Observe network errors, if any.

6. **Log in to the computer and connect to the Internet.**

   When you can get on the Internet, the network is up and working properly. The network has been reset.

7. **Repeat Steps 5 and 6 for every computer on the network.**

8. **Start up any network printers or hard drives.**

Throughout these steps, observe any problems. When you find a problem, you find the problem hardware. Replace that hardware.

For example, I had a bum switch on my office network. Only by restarting the entire network did I locate the bad switch and replace it.

Working through these steps is necessary only when you're having trouble with the network. There's no need to restart your network every few months or so. Yes, some people do so anyway. If it makes you feel better about the network, restart it every few months or so. Otherwise, if the network is behaving normally, there's no need to restart it.

✦ There's no need to unplug the Ethernet cables when you restart the network. However, if a problem occurs with a specific device, disconnect it so that the rest of the network can operate properly.

✦ If the network remains unreachable, the problem is with one of the components — most likely, the router. If you still cannot ping the router after restarting the network, replace the router.

Chapter 2: The Soft Side of Networking

In This Chapter

- Searching out network places in Windows
- Determining your PC's IP address
- Fixing IP address troubles
- Working with DHCP
- Diagnosing and repairing the network
- Disconnecting the network

I'd be lying to you if I explained that your computer network consists of all those cables and blinky-light things. That's the hardware part of the network — the part you can pick up and hurl out a window in a fit of rage. Though tossing network hardware out the window may be emotionally satisfying, it gets rid of only half the network; the other half is software, which is much more difficult to toss out a window, but quite easy to troubleshoot, thanks to the information in this chapter.

Where Is the Network Software?

To see the storage in your computer, you open the Computer or My Computer window. You would think that, to use the network you'd open the Network window. That's only half-correct; though the Network window displays some networking stuff, it doesn't give you the entire picture. For that, you need to know exactly where Windows hides all its networking windows and dialog boxes.

Finding network locations in Windows 7 and Windows Vista

Consider yourself lucky that there aren't a billion different locations for network troubleshooting in Windows 7 and its very similar ancestor, Windows Vista. Nope. Instead of a billion places you should know about, there are only these:

- ✦ The Network and Sharing Center window
- ✦ The System window

✦ The Network window

✦ The Network Map window

✦ The notification area

✦ The Network Connections window

✦ The Setup Network Connections Wizard

Each of these locations has something to do with networking on your PC — specifically, the software side of networking. You should know how to find and open each window or dialog box and recognize what can be done in each one in regard to troubleshooting the network.

Networking and Sharing Center window

Of the horde of networking places, the central location is the Network and Sharing Center; the Windows 7 version is shown in Figure 2-1; Windows Vista, in Figure 2-2. From that window, you can open just about any other networking location in Windows.

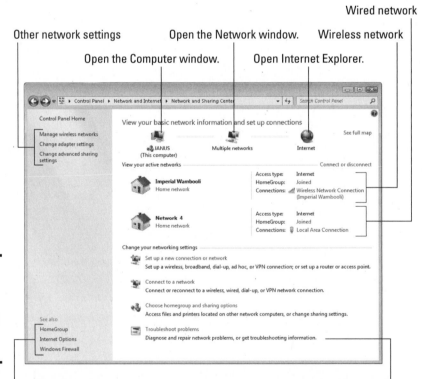

Figure 2-1: The Network and Sharing Center in Windows 7.

Open the computer window.

Open a web browser.

Nifty links

Open the network window.

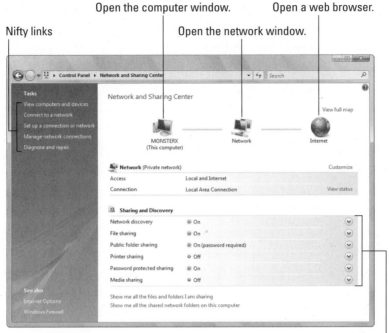

Figure 2-2:
The
Network
and Sharing
Center in
Windows
Vista.

Local network settings

Follow these steps to get to the Network and Sharing Center window:

1. **Open the Control Panel.**

2. **From beneath the Network and Internet heading, choose the View
Network Status and Tasks link.**

The list of tasks on the left side of the window lead you to other, exciting networking locations in Windows.

In Windows Vista, the Sharing and Discovery area near the bottom of the
window controls various peer-to-peer networking features. Those same settings are available, though not as obvious, in Windows 7: Click the Change
Advanced Sharing Settings link on the left side of the Network and Sharing
Center window to access them.

✦ Figure 2-1 shows a Windows 7 laptop, which features both wired and
   wireless network connections. For a typical desktop PC, you see only a
   wired connection and one "*Monopoly* house" in the window.

✦ By the way, the *Monopoly* house indicates that the network is a private
   network, which offers less security. Work networks have a wee bit more

security and use a Glass Building icon. Public networks use a Park Bench icon instead and feature more security.

✦ To change the network security type, choose the link by the Network House (or Glass Building or Park Bench) icon. In Windows 7, the link is immediately to the right of the icon; in Windows Vista, the link is on the right edge of the Window and named Customize.

✦ A network disconnection is indicated in the Network and Sharing Center window by a red X appearing over the lines between your computer and the Network icon, or between the Network icon and the Internet. When you click the red X, a network troubleshooter runs to help diagnose the problem.

✦ You can also display the Network and Sharing Center window by clicking the Network and Sharing Center toolbar button in the Network window.

System window

Though it's not listed on the fast track of networking tasks in the Network and Sharing Center window (refer to Figures 2-1 and 2-2), the System window contains a few key items of interest for creating a small peer-to-peer network. Primarily, that window is where you specify the computer and network names.

To visit the System window, press the Win+Break key combination. The area of concern with regard to networking is found in the Computer Name, Domain, and Workgroup Settings area, as shown in Figure 2-3.

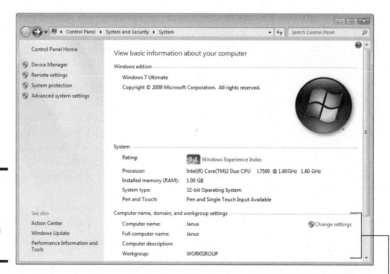

Figure 2-3:
Networky
things in
the System
window.

Networky things

You change the items in the Computer Name, Domain, and Workgroup Settings area by clicking the Change Settings link on the right side of the window. For more details, refer to Chapter 3.

TIP

The Pause key on most PC keyboards shares the Break key, so the Win+Pause key combination also works.

Network window

Honestly, the Network window has little to do with managing the network. The window is named correctly, but instead of showing you network controls on your computer, the Network window displays a list of computers and network devices available *on* the network, as shown in Figure 2-4.

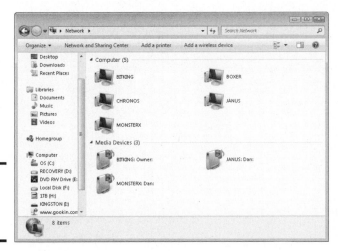

Figure 2-4:
The
Network
window.

To open the Network window, choose Network from the Start menu, open the Network icon on the desktop, or choose Network from the drop-down Address bar list in any Windows Explorer window. You can also type **Network** on the Address bar to visit the Network window.

Not much network hardware troubleshooting gets done in the Network window, but it helps you "see" other computers in a peer-to-peer workgroup. Troubleshooting the workgroup, such as when computers should shoot up in the window but don't, is covered in Chapter 4.

+ You can click the Network and Sharing Center button on the Network window's toolbar to get to the Network and Sharing Center window.

+ You can log in to the router by opening its icon in the Network window, though the icon doesn't appear in the Windows 7 version of the Network window.

✦ A variation on the Network window is the Network Map, covered later in this chapter.

✦ See Chapter 3 for information about the HomeGroup window in Windows 7. It adds a new level to organizing information on the network, but has little to do with network software troubleshooting.

✦ If I had my choice, I'd rename the Network window to Local Network and then rename the Network and Sharing Center window to Networking. Oh, I know: It's all about *me*. . . .

Network Map

The Network Map window, shown in Figure 2-5, provides a detailed look at how Windows assumes that the network is physically laid out. Yeah, it's a guess, but it's interesting to look at.

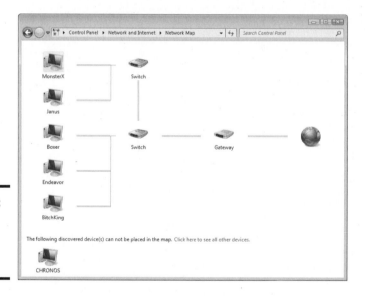

Figure 2-5:
The
Network
Map
window.

In Figure 2-6, you see the wireless version of the Network Map window. Additionally, because the laptop whose Network Map window is shown in Figure 2-6 has two NICs (wired and wireless), there's a button from which you can choose which network connection to map.

To view the Network Map window, open the Network and Sharing Center window and click the link View Full Map (refer to Figures 2-1 and 2-2).

The Network Map window may not place all computers on the network into the map. In Figure 2-5, the computer Chronos is a Macintosh, which doesn't send the proper mapping information to Windows computers. The other computers (all PCs) on the network do send that information.

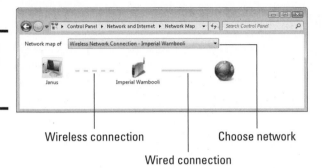

Figure 2-6:
A wireless
network
map.

Wireless connection   Choose network

Wired connection

Windows XP computers can appear in the map, but only when they're running special software that makes them visible in the map. The software is Link Layer Topology Discovery (LLTD), and it can be installed on your Windows XP PC by grabbing the LLTD update on the Windows support web site:

`http://support.microsoft.com/kb/922120`

Click the Download link in the middle of this web page to install LLTD. Having the update installed doesn't do anything else for the Windows XP computer, other than make it show up in a Network Map window.

✦ The map doesn't show a computer on the network unless the Network Discovery item is turned on. See Chapter 3 for details.

✦ The map isn't visible when you're using a public network, such as in a cybercafé.

✦ Software firewalls may also prevent PCs from appearing on the map.

✦ PCs running antique versions of Windows (earlier than Windows XP or Windows 2000) don't show up on the map.

✦ Figure 2-5 shows my PCs connected to two switches and then to the router, which is properly labeled *Gateway* in the Network Map window. Two switches are used: One is a local switch behind my desk, and the other is a main switch located in the "network cabinet" in my office. Switches are used in my office network because the router has only four Ethernet ports and I have more than four PCs or devices connected.

Notification area

Nestled among the teeny icons that pock the notification area (or taskbar, on the far-right side) is an infinitesimal icon representing the local network. When the network is on and connected to the Internet, it appears as shown in Figure 2-7.

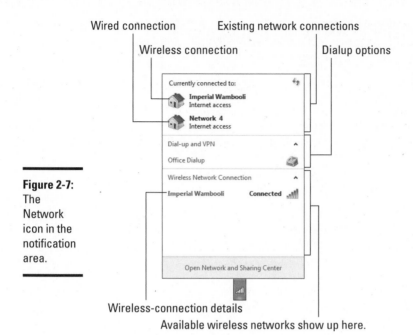

Wired connection   Existing network connections

Wireless connection   Dialup options

Figure 2-7:
The
Network
icon in the
notification
area.

Wireless-connection details

Available wireless networks show up here.

The notification area in Windows 7 and Windows Vista has different types of networking icons. Figure 2-8 shows the variety.

Figure 2-8:
Identifying
network
notification
icons.

Windows 7
wired network

Windows 7
wireless network

Windows
Vista network

Pointing the mouse at the Network icon in the notification area displays a brief pop-up window explaining the current connection status. Clicking the Network icon displays a larger pop-up (refer to Figure 2-7). Right-clicking the icon displays a pop-up menu, from which you can choose a host of networking options.

Mostly, the Network icon shows you that the network is connected. An X on the icon means that the network is unavailable. In Windows Vista, the globe part of the icon means that the local network is connected to the Internet.

Network Connections window

The most technical place to visit in the Network Land of Wonder is the Network Connections window, as shown in Figure 2-9. The window lists every network adapter connected to your PC, as well as dialup adapters you may have, such as the one shown in the figure (which is a laptop PC).

Figure 2-9:
Network
connections
are listed
here.

To view the Network Connections window, you use the Network and Sharing Center window. In Windows 7, choose the link Change Adapter Settings; in Windows Vista, choose the link Manage Network Connections.

Any problems or trouble with a network connection are flagged in the Network Connections window. It even mentions the cause, such as *Cable unplugged.* By opening a Connection icon, you can check the connection specifically and perform more troubleshooting.

Setup Network Connections Wizard

The final location for network troubleshooting nonsense is the Set Up a Connection or Network window, as shown in Figure 2-10. The window is the first step in a wizard that lets you connect to the Internet, a wireless network, a virtual private network (VPN), or any other computer with a modem.

To access the Set Up a Connection or Network window, choose the link labeled Set Up a New Connection or Network in the Network and Sharing Center window (refer to Figures 2-1 and 2-2). A description of working the steps to set up a peer-to-peer network is offered in Chapter 3.

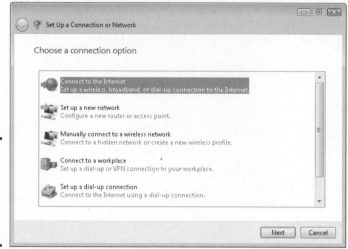

Figure 2-10:
The Set
Up a
Connection
or Network
window.

Finding network locations in Windows XP

If you thought that Windows XP keeps all its networking settings and information in only two locations, you're woefully wrong. Windows XP features a multitude of windows, dialog boxes, and wizards for gathering and setting network information. Here's the list:

+ The Network Connections window

+ The Network Connection Properties dialog box

+ The My Network Places window

+ The notification area

+ The Network Setup wizard

+ The System Properties dialog box

Each of these locations has something to do with networking on your PC — specifically, the software side of networking. You should know how to open each window and what can be done in each window in regard to troubleshooting the network.

Network Connections window

The start of the Windows XP network software journey begins in the Network Connections window, as shown in Figure 2-11. In the window, you find an icon for every network or dialup connection. If you have wired and wireless NICs on your PC or laptop, you see separate icons for those connections as well.

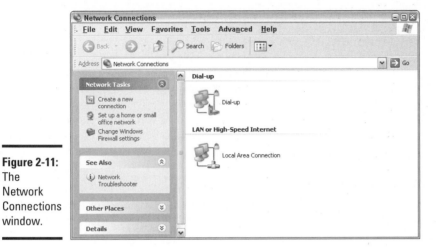

Figure 2-11:
The
Network
Connections
window.

To open the Network Connections window, open the Network Connections icon in the Control Panel. You can also display the Network Connections window by right-clicking the Network icon in the notification area. See the section "Notification area," a little later in this chapter.

Network Connection Properties dialog box

Specific network setup information is linked to the icons that appear in the Network Connections window. Each network connection features its own Properties dialog box, such as the one shown in Figure 2-12. It's the location where network settings are made regarding file sharing, as well as other configuration stuff.

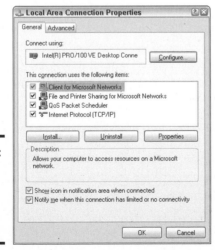

Figure 2-12:
A network
connec-
tion's
Properties
dialog box.

To see a connection's Properties dialog box, follow these steps:

1. **Open the Network Connections icon in the Control Panel.**

2. **Right-click a connection icon.**

3. **Choose Properties from the shortcut menu.**

Every network connection has different connection Properties dialog boxes. On a laptop, for example, are separate dialog boxes for wired and wireless connections.

My Network Places

It's not really a network configuration place, but the My Network Places window shows you shared folders that are available to your computers on the network, as shown in Figure 2-13.

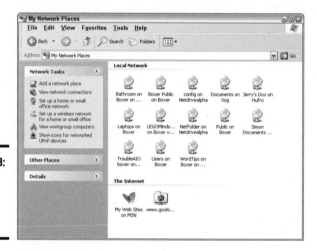

Figure 2-13: The My Network Places window.

By choosing the link View Workgroup Computers, you can see the list of computers available on the peer-to-peer network, similar to the Windows 7/ Vista Network window (refer to Figure 2-4).

Various links on the left side of the My Network Places window display other important networking locations. For example, the link Set Up a Home or Small Office Network helps you configure a new network connection. The link Set Up a Wireless Network for a Home or Small Office gets you started with a wireless network.

Notification area

One of the tiny icons dwelling in the notification area is a networking icon. I call it the Network icon. It indicates the presence of a network connection, but that's about it.

What's magical about the Network icon in the notification area is that when you double-click the icon, you see the Local Area Connection Status dialog box, as shown in Figure 2-14. That window also appears when you open a connection icon from the Network Connections window (refer to Figure 2-11).

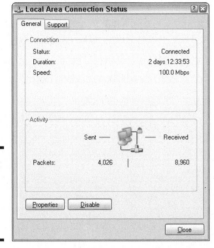

Figure 2-14:
The network's Connection window.

To ensure that the Network icon shows up in the notification area, follow these steps:

1. **Open the Network Connections icon in the Control Panel.**

2. **Right-click a network connection icon.**

3. **Choose Properties from the shortcut menu.**

4. **In the network connection's Properties dialog box, ensure that a check mark appears by the item Show Icon in Notification Area When Connected.**

5. **Click OK.**

6. **Close the Network Connections window.**

Repeat these steps for any extra connection icons appearing in the Network Connections window (refer to Figure 2-11). That way, a little Networking icon appears in the notification area for each of your network connections.

Network Setup Wizard

To connect to a wireless network, or to configure a wired network, you can use the Network Setup Wizard. Opening the Network Setup Wizard icon in the Control Panel accesses it.

You work the Network Setup Wizard like you work any wizard: Answer questions and click the Next button as necessary.

System Properties dialog box

Though it's called the System window, information is buried there that deals with networking names — specifically, your computer's network name as well as the name of the peer-to-peer workgroup you might join. That information is kept on the Computer Name tab in the System Properties dialog box, as shown in Figure 2-15.

Figure 2-15: The System Properties dialog box and its Computer Name tab.

To view the system Properties dialog box, open the System icon in the Control Panel. The quick-and-dirty way to open the System Properties dialog box is to press the Win+Break key combination. Then click the Computer Name tab and you're there.

IP Gone Wrong

I've discovered that anyone even remotely exposed to the Internet or computer networking recognizes the acronym IP. They don't know what it is, and maybe not even what it stands for, but they recognize that it plays a role in computer networking. This section explains why IP is important to your computer network and what to do with IP problems.

Understanding the IP address

IP is the acronym for Internet Protocol. It's used to describe a set of methods and procedures for sending and receiving information. It's nerdy stuff, not worthy of your attention here.

What is worth noting is that IP is sometimes followed by the word *address*. In that context, an IP address is assigned to every computer on an Ethernet network. Like the street address for your home, an *IP address* identifies network computers. It helps traffic flow between computers because each one has its own IP address.

An IP address is formatted as a series of four values separated by periods:

```
192.168.0.1
```

Each value ranges from 0 through 255.

Each period is just a period.

For your home or office network, the IP address is most likely assigned by the router, using something called DHCP (covered later in this chapter). The router keeps track of every computer's NIC and maps an IP address to the NIC every time the computer joins the network. In the end, all computers have a unique IP address, and the world is safe for local networking.

✦ The IP address assigned to your PC on a network is a *local* address. Similar IP addresses are used on the Internet to identify domains and other resources. Those are Internet IP addresses, separate from your local address.

✦ The router is assigned an IP address by your Internet service provider (ISP). That IP address is an Internet IP address. It's shared by all PCs on your network.

✦ Local IP addresses start with `192.168` and `10.0`.

✦ The IP addresses discussed in this section are IPv4 addresses. Because the number of unique IP addresses is limited, a second standard, IPv6, has been established. The IPv6 standard allows for many more addresses, which will help accommodate future growth of the Internet.

✦ If the router doesn't assign an IP address, one must be configured manually.

✦ No two computers on the network can have the same IP address.

✦ IP is often prefixed by the acronym TCP, as in *TCP/IP*. The *TCP* part stands for Transfer Control Protocol: It's simply a set of rules for transmitting information on a network. Technically, TCP/IP refers to the methods and engineering as opposed to a specific address or value.

Checking your PC's IP address

When your computer is on an Ethernet network, it has an IP address. If it doesn't, you have problems, covered later in this chapter. For now, the task is to find your PC's IP address.

To check the IP address assigned to your computer, follow these steps in Windows 7 and Windows Vista:

1. **Open the Network and Sharing Center window.**

Specific directions are found earlier in this chapter.

2a. **In Windows 7, on the right side of the window, choose the link Local Area Connection.**

2b. **In Windows Vista, on the right side of the window, click the View Status link.**

A dialog box appears, listing some brief information about the network connection. But that's not good enough!

3. **Click the Details button.**

You find the PC's IP address listed as IPv4 IP Address in the Network Connection Details dialog box.

4. **Click the Close button and close the Network and Sharing Center window.**

In Windows XP, follow these steps to discover the IP address assigned to your PC:

1. **Open the Control Panel's Network Connections icon.**

2. **Open the icon representing your PC's network connection.**

When you have more than one icon, just pick the main one.

3. **In the Status dialog box, click the Support tab.**

The Connection Status area lists the IP address.

4. **Click the Close button.**

If your PC features two network connections, each one has its own IP address. So a laptop PC that has both wireless and wired network adapters features two IP addresses when both adapters are connected to a network. Repeat the steps in this section for each network icon to check the IP address for each connection.

Understanding DHCP

Back in the early days, IP addresses were set up manually. I'm old enough to remember doing that. I had to configure each PC on my network with its own IP address, unique from all the other computers. I even wrote the IP address on each PC's monitor. I was proud of myself, but was forgetting one tiny fact: Computers exist to make life easier. Why punish yourself by assigning IP addresses when the computer can do it for you?

On a modern Ethernet network, with a robust router as overseer, IP addresses are assigned to each PC as it joins the network. The process, which is automatic, is referred to as *Dynamic Host Configuration Protocol,* or *DHCP.*

There's nothing to set up: Your router's configuration program most likely contains a page that directs the router to use DHCP to set IP addresses. You can turn off the option, but there's no reason to do so.

✦ There are two parts to DHCP: the client and the host. The *host* exists on your router, which assigns IP addresses. The *client* is on your computer. It asks the host for an IP addresses and then assigns that address to the network connection.

✦ When your computer isn't connected to a network, its DHCP client program assigns a random IP address to the computer. That IP address is useless because the PC isn't connected to a network. But the random IP address confuses some users because it appears as though the computer has a legitimate IP address. It does not.

✦ The best way to test a network connection is to ping the router. See Chapter 1.

✦ Also see Chapter 1 for more information on the router's configuration program.

✦ You can configure the router to specify which range of IP addresses to use. Again, you have no reason to change the DHCP settings for a small, home or office network.

Resolving an IP conflict

An IP conflict indicates that another computer on the same network is using the same IP address as your computer. For example, both PCs may have the address 192.168.0.104 (which seems to be a troublesome IP address for my own computer network). Obviously, such a situation cannot stand.

The first thing to do is to run the Repair and Diagnose options, as covered later in this chapter, in the section "Repairing the network." If that doesn't work, try the old standby of restarting the computer that is reporting the conflict or has no network connection.

The final thing you can try is to determine which computer is the problem child: Check the IP address of all PCs on the network to see which one is assigned the duplicate IP. If you can, turn off that PC or disconnect it from the network. Restart the computer (or reconnect it to the network) to see whether this technique can fix the issue.

Renewing the DHCP lease

The router is configured to let your PC have its IP address for only a given amount of time. After that time expires, the DHCP server must renew your use of the assigned IP address. The action is called *renewing the DHCP lease*.

The DHCP lease is renewed automatically, one would hope. If it isn't, you can try to renew it by diagnosing and repairing the network connection, as described in the section "Repairing the network," later in this chapter.

You can force a renewal by using the Command Prompt window. Follow these steps:

1. **From the Start menu, choose All Programs⇨Accessories⇨Command Prompt.**

2. **At the command prompt, type** ipconfig /renew **and press the Enter key.**

3. **Close the Command Prompt window.**

The command `ipconfig /renew` forces all network adapters on your PC to immediately request a new DHCP list from the server (the router).

Manually assigning an IP address

If you want to "go rogue," you can configure your PC to use its own IP address, DHCP be damned. Here's how to do that in Windows 7 and Windows Vista:

1. **Open the Network and Sharing Center window.**

2a. **In Windows 7, on the right side of the window, choose the link Local Area Connection.**

2b. **In Windows Vista, on the right side of the window, click the View Status link.**

3. **In the Status dialog box, click the Properties button.**

4. **In Windows Vista, type the administrator's password or click the Continue button.**

    A Properties dialog box for the connection appears. It lists the various protocols and services being used by the connection, as shown in Figure 2-16.

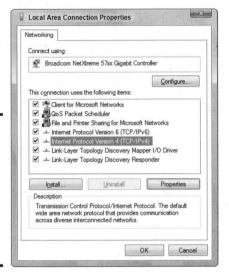

Figure 2-16:
Protocols
and
services
used by a
network
connection
in Windows
Vista.

5. **Select the service titled Internet Protocol Version 4 (TCP/IPv4).**

6. **Click the Properties button.**

   The dialog box labeled Internet Protocol Version 4 (TCP/IPv4)
   Properties appears.

7. **Choose the option Use the Following IP Address.**

8. **Type the IP address.**

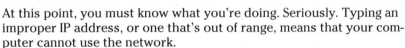

   At this point, you must know what you're doing. Seriously. Typing an
   improper IP address, or one that's out of range, means that your computer cannot use the network.

9. **Type a subnet mask.**

   For a local-area network, the value is usually 255.255.255.0, but then
   again, I'm assuming that you know what to type as a mask.

10. **Type the default gateway address.**

    The default gateway address is the IP address for the network's router.

    Because DHCP also obtains the address for the DNS server, which helps
    your computer find addresses on the Internet, you need to manually list
    those addresses as well.

11. **Type the address of the preferred DNS server.**

    This value is obtained from your ISP.

12. **Type the address for the alternative DNS server.**

13. **Click OK to close the Internet Protocol Version 4 (TCP/IPv4) Properties dialog box.**

14. **Close the other open dialog boxes and windows.**

In Windows XP, follow these steps to manually set an IP address on your computer:

1. **Open the Control Panel's Network Connections icon.**

2. **Open the icon representing your PC's network connection.**

3. **Click the Properties button in the Status dialog box.**

4. **From the list of items, choose Internet Protocol (TCP/IP).**

5. **Click the Properties button.**

   The Internet Protocol (TCP/IP) Properties dialog box appears.

6. **Choose Use the Following IP Address.**

7. **Type the IP address for your computer.**

   Well, officially, you're typing an IP address for the network adapter, but it's kinda the same thing.

   Don't randomly type an address. You need to type a value that's useful for accessing the network. Obviously, if you don't know what you're doing here, don't choose to manually assign an IP address.

8. **Type a subnet mask.**

   The value used on a local network is commonly 255.255.255.0, but it can be different, such as 255.255.255.127.

9. **Type the default gateway address.**

   The default gateway is the router, so type the router's address.

10. **Type the address for the preferred DNS server.**

    The address should be obtained from your ISP. It's used to help your computer find web pages and other addresses on the Internet.

11. **Type the address for the alternate DNS server.**

    The alternate DNS server's IP address is something that your ISP provides.

12. **Click OK to confirm the settings.**

13. **Close all other open dialog boxes and windows.**

Yes, it's kind of an ordeal to manually configure an IP address. The complex process underscores why DHCP was necessary and how it became popular.

Network Troubleshooting

As long as the network hardware is connected and the router, switches, and NICs have their lights blinking in a pleasing manner, your next stab at troubleshooting the network is to take a good look at the software that drives the hardware. This section covers various software tricks for network troubleshooting.

✦ Refer to Chapter 1 for information on network hardware troubleshooting.

✦ Any network troubleshooting involving accessing other PCs on a network is covered in Chapter 3, which deals with peer-to-peer networking.

Repairing the network

Lurking in various places around the numerous networking windows and dialog boxes are certain Repair links and buttons. Your first stab at resolving a network oddity is to grasp one of those Repair options to see whether using it helps. Here's the rundown on where to look:

Network icon: Right-click the Network icon in the notification area and choose the command Troubleshoot Problems or Diagnose and Repair from the pop-up menu.

Network and Sharing Center window: In Windows 7 and Windows Vista, click the link Troubleshoot Problems or Diagnose and Repair. (These are essentially the same commands you can choose from the Network icon in the notification area.)

Local Area Connection Status dialog box: In Windows 7 or Vista, click the Diagnose button. In Windows XP, click the Support tab and then click the Repair button.

Network Connections window: Choose a network connection icon in the window, and then click the Diagnose button in Windows 7 or the Diagnose This Connection button on the toolbar in Windows Vista. In Windows XP, click the link on the left side of the window, Repair This Connection.

No matter how you get there, the results are the same: Windows looks at the network connection and attempts to resolve some issues. For example, it may renew an expired DHCP lease or it might explain that another computer on the network is "bogarting" your PC's IP address.

If everything is okay, simply click the Close button and get on with your computer day.

✦ There may be other locations where you can access the standard network troubleshooting utilities. Generally speaking, they all do the same thing described in this section.

✦ Windows: 1,000 different ways to do one thing wrong.

Using the Windows XP Network Troubleshooter

Windows XP features a Network Troubleshooting Wizard, which includes a swath of useful diagnostic tools as well as some tests.

To run the Network Troubleshooting Wizard, open the Control Panel's Network Connections icon. In the Network Connections window, choose the task on the left, under the See Also heading, titled Network Troubleshooter. You see the Help window, as shown in Figure 2-17.

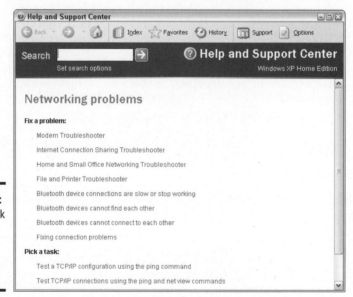

Figure 2-17: The network trouble-shooter in Windows XP.

The item of primary interest to you is probably the third one down: Home and Small Office Networking Troubleshooter. Choosing this item displays a multiple-choice review of common problems and potential solutions.

The two links near the bottom of the Help system window (refer to Figure 2-17) might appear interesting, but they're merely directions for using the `ping` command, covered in Chapter 1.

Close the troubleshooting wizard when you're done working its steps.

Disconnecting from the network

The final, and fatal, move you can make is to simply disconnect the PC from the network. You can do this physically, or you can break the connection by using software.

Here's how to disable an Ethernet connection in Windows 7 and Windows Vista:

1. **Open the Network and Sharing Center window.**

2a. **In Windows 7, on the right side of the window, choose the link Local Area Connection.**

2b. **In Windows Vista, on the right side of the window, click the View Status link.**

3. **Click the Disable button in the connection's Status dialog box.**

4. **Type the administrator's password or click the Continue button.**

5. **Close the Network and Sharing Center window.**

Follow these steps in Windows XP to disable the network connection:

1. **Open the Control Panel's Network Connections icon.**

2. **Double-click to open the icon representing the PC's Ethernet connection.**

3. **Click the Disable button.**

The disconnection is instant. In Windows 7 and Windows Vista, you see the red X marking the line between your PC and the network or Internet. In Windows Vista, the connection icon appears dimmed with the text *Disabled*.

To reconnect to the network in Windows 7 and Windows Vista, click the red X icon between your computer and the Internet (or Network) icon in the Network and Sharing Center window. Obey the troubleshooter to enable the network adapter, which reconnects you to the network.

To reconnect in Windows XP, double-click to open the disabled-connection icon in the Network Connections window.

Chapter 3: Peer-to-Peer Networking

In This Chapter

✔ Using a peer-to-peer workgroup

✔ Enabling file and printer sharing

✔ Sharing folders and printers

✔ Setting network access for your folders

✔ Searching for shared folders

✔ Setting up a private network

✔ Making the firewall network-happy

✔ Checking out who's using your PC's folders

*L*ife may not be fair, but computer networking is entirely fair. That holds especially true for the kind of small office or home network used by the typical computer. All computers on the network are friends. No lone computer is superior to any other; they're all equals. That's why the network is a *peer-to-peer* network. It's not a bully overlord client-server type of network. No, rather than have one computer in charge, everyone is in charge. They share. They live in peace. It's a simple, happy life — until something goes wrong and you need to read this chapter.

Once Upon a Time, There Was This Workgroup

The peer-to-peer network happens because all computers on the network are the same: They're peers. In Soviet Russia, the term was сеть товарищи, or network comrades. No one is in charge! Not even the KGB! All computers work happily together in one *workgroup*. This section discusses that concept.

Understanding the workgroup

When your PC joins a peer-to-peer network, it becomes part of a workgroup. The *workgroup* is simply a group of computers using the same Ethernet network. There has to be a hub, which can be merely a switch or a router. The computers don't necessarily need to be connected to the Internet — just to each other.

The workgroup can be the entire network — all the computers, connected — as shown in Figure 3-1. That's the most common setup for home or small office networks.

The key to creating a workgroup is simply to assign computers on the network the same workgroup name. So, in Figure 3-1, all computers are configured to use the workgroup FRIENDS simply because that's the workgroup name set by each computer. In Figure 3-2, half the computers are in the GALS workgroup; the rest are in the GUYS workgroup.

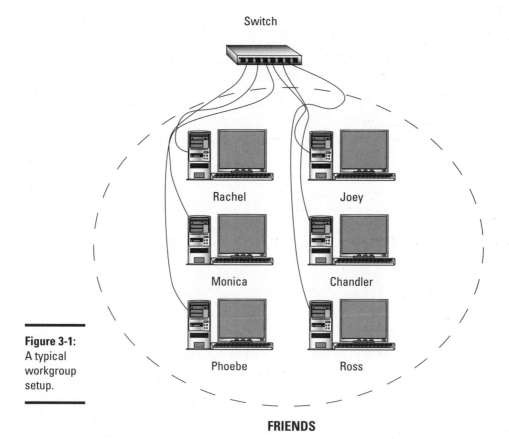

Switch

Rachel

Joey

Monica

Chandler

Figure 3-1:
A typical
workgroup
setup.

Phoebe

Ross

FRIENDS

There's no reason to split up a small network into workgroups (refer to Figure 3-2). In fact, I highly recommend that all computers on your network use the same workgroup name because it makes accessing the computers easier, especially in Windows XP. There's no advantage to having separate workgroups; no security is provided. Multiple workgroups are simply an option for classifying computers on a larger network.

✦ The workgroup name is a software thing. Setting a workgroup name has no effect on the network hardware; for example, the router couldn't care less about the workgroup name.

✦ The workgroup name has no effect on a network IP address.

✦ The workgroup still exists in Windows 7, but is shoved aside in favor of the HomeGroup concept. I complain about the HomeGroup elsewhere in this chapter.

✦ Other, non-peer-to-peer networks may have other *hierarchies,* or forms of organization, other than a workgroup, or they may feature a concept similar to the workgroup.

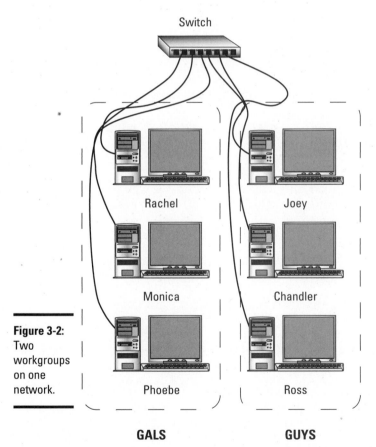

Figure 3-2:
Two
workgroups
on one
network.

GALS **GUYS**

Creating a workgroup

There's no magic to creating a workgroup. Out of the box, Windows assigns your PC to a workgroup named WORKGROUP, or possibly MSHOME. You can stick with those names. In fact, that's probably what you're doing now on your computer. Or, you can change the names of the workgroup. Here's how:

1. **Press the Win+Break key combination to summon the System window or System Properties dialog box.**

2a. **In Windows 7 and Windows Vista, click the Change Settings link in the Computer Name area.**

2b. **In Windows XP, click the Computer Name tab in the System dialog box.**

3. **In Windows Vista, type the administrator's password or click the Continue button.**

4. **Click the Change button.**

Another dialog box appears.

5. **Type a new workgroup name.**

In Windows 7 or Vista, you may need to choose the Workgroup option first.

Workgroup names should contain only letters and, possibly, some numbers. The name cannot contain any spaces, and Windows converts the name into ALL CAPS no matter what you type.

6. **Click OK.**

After a few seconds, you see a dialog box welcoming you to the workgroup.

7. **Click OK.**

Windows begs you to restart your PC, which is necessary for the computer to *really* join the workgroup.

8. **Click OK to dismiss the dialog box.**

9. **Restart your computer.**

After your computer is restarted, it belongs to the new workgroup. The workgroup affects networking on your PC as far as which network computers show up in the Network window. That topic is covered in the next section.

✦ Ensure that all computers connected to the network use the same workgroup name.

✦ To join a workgroup, enter the workgroup name as described in this section.

✦ If you have trouble joining a workgroup, check the name; it must be spelled exactly.

✦ MSHOME is "em es home," or *Microsoft home* network.

✦ There's no reason to change the workgroup name from WORKGROUP or MSHOME, though I do it anyway. More important than resetting the workgroup name is to ensure that your network is properly identified as public or private. See the section "Checking network privacy," later in this chapter.

✦ Despite my recommendation in the preceding bullet point, I change the network name for my laptop because it's more difficult to find a laptop on a different workgroup, especially at a public wireless hot spot.

Browsing the workgroup in Windows 7 and Window Vista

When it comes to workgroup names, neither Windows 7 nor Windows Vista really gives a darn. That's because, regardless of how you set up the network, all computers on the network appear in the Network window. Even computers with a different workgroup name show up. So much for workgroup name recognition.

Well, not so fast.

To see the workgroup name, just click a Computer icon in the Network window. The bottom portion of the window displays the workgroup name, as shown in Figure 3-3.

Figure 3-3:
Network computers, organized by workgroup.

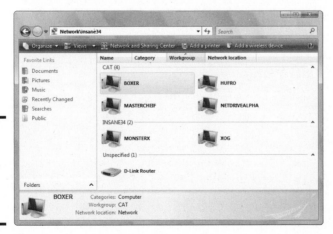

To see the workgroups, you organize the window to display Computer icons in workgroup categories (refer to Figure 3-3). To make that happen, right-click in the window and choose Group By⇨Workgroup from the shortcut menu.

To restore Normal view, right-click in the window and choose Group By⇨None.

If you don't see the information at the bottom of the window (refer to Figure 3-3), use the Organize button on the toolbar: Choose Layout⇨Details Pane.

Browsing the workgroup in Windows XP

Windows XP follows the workgroup paradigm a little more seriously than more recent versions of Windows do. When you open the My Network Places window, you first see a listing of network folders and perhaps some Internet locations. That's handy for accessing resources on the network, but it doesn't show you workgroup information.

To see the computers in the workgroup, choose the link View Workgroup Computers from the list of network tasks on the left side of the My Network Places window. The window changes to show only the computers assigned to your PC's workgroup; you see the workgroup name shown on the Address bar.

 To see all workgroups on the network, click the Up button on the toolbar. You see any additional workgroups on the network, as shown in Figure 3-4. To browse those workgroups, open their icon and you see the list of computers and other resources available.

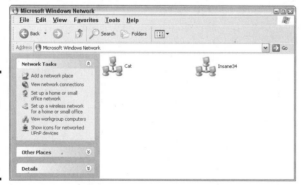

Figure 3-4:
Workgroups available on the network (Windows XP).

HomeGroup nonsense in Windows 7

Though Windows 7 still features workgroups, a greater emphasis was put on a new, and unique to Windows 7, concept called the *HomeGroup*. I can promise you that it's possible to gracefully and successfully use your computer without ever having to bother with the obscure concept of HomeGroups.

The biggest issue with HomeGroups is creating or joining one. One computer on the network should be the HomeGroup creator. The rest of the computers join that HomeGroup. After it's all set up, files can be shared and accessed by using the HomeGroup window.

The problem with the HomeGroup is that other Windows computers can't take advantage of it. So you're left using the Network window and sharing files and folders the traditional way. Because of that, I urge you to avoid using the HomeGroup in the first place.

More detail on setting up and using a Home-Group can be found in my book *PCs For Dummies,* Windows 7 Edition (Wiley).

If you click the Up button one more time, you see a window describing the entire network named, ironically, Entire Network. The icon labeled Entire Windows Network represents the peer-to-peer network your PC uses.

Don't fret over the hierarchy of the network-and-workgroup structure as presented in Windows XP. The bottom line is that you can easily access shared folders within the My Network Places window, regardless of in which workgroup those computers reside.

Everybody Share

The key issue with having a network is sharing resources: folders, modems, and printers, for example. Of the lot, the primary resource to share between computers in a peer-to-peer network is the folder. That's the topic of this section.

Making sharing possible in Windows 7 and Windows Vista

Before you run amok with sharing, you must ensure that Windows has a favorable attitude toward offering up the computer's precious resources. The place to look is the Network and Sharing Center window, shown in Chapter 2, in Figures 2-1 and 2-2.

To open the Network and Sharing Center window, open the Control Panel and beneath the Network and Internet heading, choose View Network Status and Tasks.

To set sharing options in Windows 7, you need to click the link Change Advanced Sharing Settings on the left side of the window.

 In Windows Vista, the sharing options are shown at the bottom of the window. Click the Show More arrow next to each of the six sharing categories. Each item has two settings: one to turn the item on and another to turn the item off. An Apply button confirms your choice, also displaying a User Account Control (UAC) dialog box for you to confirm administrator permission to make the change.

Here's how to set the items to allow your computer to share its resources on the network:

Network Discovery: Choose the option Turn On Network Discovery. This option ensures that your computer will find other PCs on the network, as well as find printers and shared folders. It also lets other computers on the network find your PC.

File and Printer Sharing: In Windows 7, this option provides for the sharing of both folders and printers on the network. Choose the setting Turn On File and Printer Sharing.

File Sharing: In Windows Vista, choose the option Turn On File Sharing if you plan to share folders on your PC with other computers on the network.

Public Folder Sharing: In Windows 7 there is only one "on" option; choose it. Windows Vista has three options: The first option allows read-only access and is the most secure. The second option allows full access. The third option (and this item is the only one with three options) disables Public folder sharing.

Printer Sharing: In Windows Vista only, choose the option Turn On Printer Sharing if you have a printer directly connected to your PC and you want to share it on the network.

Password Protected Sharing: Choose the option turn On Password Protected Sharing to ensure that only those with an account on your computer can access files. I recommend this setting for security reasons.

File Sharing Connections: Unless your local network uses all Windows 7 computers, choose the option Enable File Sharing for Devices That Use 40- or 56-Bit Encryption.

HomeGroup Connections: If you're choosing to ignore the Windows 7 HomeGroup thing, choose the option Use User Accounts and Passwords to Connect to Other Computers.

Media Sharing: In Windows Vista, click the Change button to control media sharing with Windows Media Player. I generally leave this option off because I'm an iTunes person.

Media Streaming: This Windows 7 option allows other computers (and even an Xbox) to access your Windows Media Player songs, pictures, and videos. Click the link Choose Media Streaming Options to mess with the settings, though I just leave everything as is.

Setting the options as described in this section merely confirms that you have sharing set up. Additional steps include joining a workgroup and ensuring that the network hardware and software are all connected and good to go. See Chapters 1 and 2 for additional instructions.

Making sharing possible in Windows XP

To configure sharing for folders and printers on your Windows XP computer, you must customize the network connection. It's normally done when you first set up the computer for networking. But it can also be accomplished by following these steps:

1. **Open the Network Connections icon in the Control Panel.**

2. **Right-click your computer's network connection icon.**

You should have only one icon for the main Ethernet connection, though laptop computers will have two — one for the wired and another for the wireless connections. Yes, that means you need to repeat these steps for both types of connection.

3. **Choose Properties from the shortcut menu.**

4. **In the connection's Properties dialog box, ensure that a service titled File and Printer Sharing for Microsoft Networks is listed.**

If it is, great. Ensure that a check mark appears by that option (which turns on the option), and you're done. Skip to Step 10. Otherwise, continue:

5. **Click the Install button to summon the Network Component Type dialog box.**

6. **Choose Service.**

7. **Click the Add button.**

8. **From the list in the Select Network Services dialog box, choose File and Printer Sharing for Microsoft Networks.**

9. **Click OK.**

10. **Click the Close button in the connection's Properties dialog box.**

If you're prompted to restart the PC after completing these steps, do so. Otherwise, your computer is all set up to share folders and a printer.

Sharing your PC's printer

To share a printer attached to your PC with other computers on the network, follow these steps:

1. **Open the Control Panel.**

2a. **In Windows 7, choose the View Devices and Printers link found beneath the Hardware and Sound heading.**

2b. **In Windows Vista, choose the Printer link beneath Hardware and Sound.**

2c. **In Windows XP, open the icon Printers and Faxes.**

3. **Right-click the printer icon.**

4a. **In Windows 7, choose Printer Properties from the pop-up menu.**

4b. **In Windows Vista and Windows XP, choose Sharing from the pop-up menu.**

5a. **In Windows Vista, click the button Change Sharing Options, and then type the administrator's password or click the Continue button.**

Because you're sharing one of the computer's hardware resources and it affects all users on the computer, you need administrator access to share the printer.

5b. **In Windows 7, click the Sharing tab.**

6. **Choose the option Share This Printer.**

7. **(Optional) Type a share name.**

Be descriptive. The name Possessive Larry's Color Laser is a good description, as is Mom's Inkjet in the Den.

8. **Click OK to share the printer.**

 Shared printers sport a tag on their icon in the Printers window. In Windows 7 and Vista, the icon looks like a man and a woman, or what I call the Sharing Buddies tag, as shown in the margin. In Windows XP, the tag is the serving hand that appears under the icon.

✦ Some types of printers, such as PDF printers or Fax printers, cannot be shared on the network. Windows bluntly tells you so when you make the attempt.

✦ A shared printer is available only when the computer it's attached to is turned on.

✦ You cannot print on a shared printer when the computer it's attached to is in Sleep mode or Stand By mode. Likewise, because Hibernation turns a computer off, you cannot use the printer attached to a hibernating PC.

✦ You can print to any printer directly attached to the network, though that printer must be turned on as well. See Chapter 1 for information on attaching a printer directly to the network.

Sharing a folder

The key to accessing information on a network is to share folders between computers. After a folder is shared, any other user on the network can access it, using its files just like any folder on their own computer. That's the gist of it.

To share a folder in Windows Vista, follow these steps:

1. **Right-click the folder you want to share.**

You have to see the folder, not be "in" the folder.

2. **Choose Properties from the shortcut menu.**

Yeah, I know: The shortcut menu has sharing commands. This type of sharing refers to sharing the folder between users on the same computer, not on the network.

3. **Click the Sharing tab in the folder's Properties dialog box.**

4. **Click the Advanced Sharing button.**

5. **In Windows Vista, type the administrator's password or click the Continue button.**

The Advanced Sharing dialog box appears, as shown in Figure 3-5.

6. **Place a check mark by the option Share This Folder.**

7. **If necessary, type a more descriptive share name.**

The folder name already appears in the Shared Name box. Additionally, when other users see this folder available on the network, they also see your computer's name after the folder's name.

8. **Click OK to close the Advanced Sharing dialog box, and then click the Close button to discharge the folder's Properties dialog box.**

Figure 3-5:
The
Advanced
Sharing
dialog box,
where the
real sharing
takes place.

You share a folder in Windows XP by obeying these steps:

1. **Find the folder you want to share.**

2. **Right-click the folder's icon.**

3. **Choose Sharing and Security from the shortcut menu.**

    The folder's Properties dialog box appears with the Sharing tab upfront.

4. **Choose the option Share the Folder On the Network.**

5. **(Optional) Type a share name.**

    Windows automatically sets the share name to the folder name.
    Although the folder name might make sense on your PC, you may need
    something more descriptive for network users.

6. **Click OK to share the folder.**

 After the folder is shared, it appears with a tag on its icon in Windows Vista
and Windows XP. In Windows Vista, the tag is the *sharing buddies*, shown in
the margin. Windows XP uses the Serving Hand tag.

Other computers can access the shared folder on your computer. At this
point, they have read-only access, which means that they can open files
or copy them from your PC but cannot add files to the folder, delete files
already in the folder, or modify the folder. See the section "Setting shared
folder permissions," a little later in this chapter, for more details on how to
modify access to a shared folder.

✦ No, you cannot share individual files — only folders.

✦ Because a compressed folder is really a file, you cannot share it unless it's inside a shared folder.

✦ Share a folder within your personal area, or your "home" folder. Do not share any other folder, such as one in the Program Files or Windows folders.

✦ Do not share your account folder. Doing so is a security risk.

✦ Although, technically, you can share an entire hard drive by sharing its root folder, don't. Sharing an entire drive is a security risk because it gives everyone on the network access to everything on that drive.

✦ Sharing a folder doesn't allow someone on the Internet to use that folder on your PC. Sharing works only with computers on the local network.

Setting shared folder permissions

Any little kid knows the difference between sharing and giving. How many times in your own life do you remember saying, "You said you only wanted to *look* at it, not take it"? The same type of playground logic applies to sharing folders on a network: Unless you explicitly say so, other users can only look at your files, not modify them, delete them, or add to their numbers.

Bottom line: Not being able to copy a file into a shared folder isn't a bug or even PC trouble; it's *permissions*.

To set folder permissions for a shared folder in Windows 7 and Windows Vista, heed these steps:

1. **Right-click a shared folder icon.**

Refer to the preceding section for information on sharing a folder.

2. **Choose Properties from the shortcut menu.**

3. **In the folder's Properties dialog box, click the Sharing tab.**

4. **Click the Advanced Sharing button.**

5. **In Windows Vista, click the Continue button or type the administrator's password.**

The Advanced Sharing dialog box shows up.

6. **Click the Permissions button.**

The shared folder's Permissions dialog box appears. You see a list of users who can access the folder, coupled with a set of access privileges at the bottom of the dialog box.

7. **Select a group or username.**

   You can add individual usernames or categories by clicking the Add button. The Everyone group lets anyone and everyone on the network gain access.

8. **Set the permissions for the selected group or user.**

   There are three types of permissions:

   > **Full Control:** Gives a user the same control over the folder as your account has
   >
   > **Change:** Lets a user change files but not add new ones or create folders
   >
   > **Read:** Lets a user open files and copy files from the folder

   For each permission, you can choose either Allow or Deny. Choosing neither option means that the user gets the same permissions as his account has for your computer.

9. **Click OK to close the Permissions dialog box.**

10. **Click OK to close the Advanced Sharing dialog box.**

11. **Click OK to close the folder's Properties dialog box.**

In Windows XP, follow these directions to set folder permissions:

1. **Right-click the Shared Folder icon and choose Sharing and Security from the shortcut menu.**

2. **Place a check mark in the box Allow Network Users to Change My Files.**

3. **Click OK.**

Yes, Windows XP has a far easier game of it when it comes to setting folder permissions. But then again, keep in mind that more recent versions of Windows are more secure.

Consider sharing the Public folder on your computer, making it "up for grabs" to any other user on the network. This way, you can easily make files available by copying them to the Public folder. This trick avoids complications that arise when sharing individual folders.

✦ If you add more specific users or groups in Windows 7/Vista (refer to Step 8 in the preceding set of steps for Windows Vista), you must select each group individually and set permissions for that user or group.

✦ Having multiple users and groups in a shared folder is often a source of woe. When you have trouble accessing a shared folder on a Windows 7 or Vista PC, it's most likely because individual users, as opposed to groups, are selected for sharing.

✦ Setting file permissions can get quite technical in Windows 7 and Vista. You can not only share files on a network but also share folders with other users on the same PC.

Accessing shared folders

Finding and using shared folders on the network happens either from Windows Explorer or within an Open or Save As dialog box. Still, considering that an Open or Save As dialog box is basically just a little Windows Explorer window, it's all the same thing, regardless.

The methods for accessing a shared folder differ between Windows 7 and Vista and Windows XP.

In Windows 7 and Windows Vista, open the Network window or choose Network from the Address bar in an Open or Save As dialog box. Open the icon representing a computer on the network. If necessary, log in to that computer by using the Connect To dialog box. Then open the shared folder that appears in the list.

In Windows XP, open the My Network Places window or choose My Network Places from the Address bar in any Windows Explorer, Open, or Save As dialog box. The list of shared folders for all computers on the network appears in the window, as shown in Figure 3-6. Just open the icon of the folder you want to use.

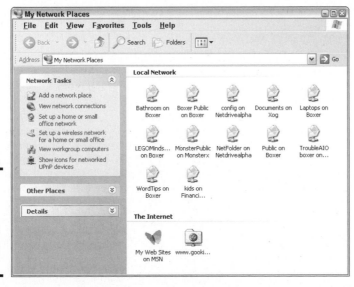

Figure 3-6:
Shared folders on the network in Windows XP.

As in Windows Vista, you may be prompted to provide login information to access the shared folder. Type your username and password to get proper access to the folder. Yes, that often means you need to have an account on the shared computer or know the username and password of an account on that computer.

✦ The Browse dialog box is essentially the same thing as the Open dialog box.

✦ Shared folders are available only when the computer sharing the folder is turned on and not in either Sleep mode or Stand By mode.

Discovering which folders you're sharing

Windows Vista has two features that clue you in to not only which folders are being shared on the computer but also which shared folders on the network your computer is using. Both tools are found at the bottom of the Network and Sharing Center window:

Show Me All the Files and Folders I Am Sharing: Choosing this link displays the Search Results window, which lists all folders you're sharing with others on your PC. These are folders that other users on your computer can access when they log in. They are *not* network shared folders.

Show Me All the Shared Network Folders on This Computer: Choosing this link displays the Network window, listing all folders your PC is sharing on the network. These aren't necessarily folders in use by other computers. (For that information, see the section "Finding out who else is using your computer," later in this chapter.)

Unsharing a folder

To stop sharing a folder, repeat the steps from the section "Sharing a folder," earlier in this chapter, and deselect the option Share This Folder (in Windows 7 or Vista) or Share This Folder on the Network (in Windows XP). This action effectively "unshares" the folder.

If someone else on the network is using the shared folder as you unshare it, you see a warning dialog box. Always try to ensure that the other user is done sharing before you cut them off; if that person is changing a file, then by halting sharing, you could damage the file. Then again, if the other user is doing so without permission, the file has already been damaged.

Workgroup Woes

Life is good on the network. I enjoy it. Moving files back and forth is a breeze. In fact, the images you see in this book were sent over the network from my test computer to my writing computer. Everything worked smoothly. When things failed to move smoothly, I took notes and then wrote this section on general workgroup woes.

What is a domain?

The term *domain* is often tossed around when referring to computer networking. Indeed, you often see options for setting a domain name or prefix for your network in Windows. You might think that it's an option you need to set, but it's not.

A domain type of network relies on a central computer or server to rule over the rest of the network. It's not democratic, like the peer-to-peer type of network that most Windows users have in their homes or small offices. When you work on a larger, domain-type of network, a central computer is responsible for your files and programs. In fact, you can log in to any computer in the domain to work on your stuff because files aren't stored on the PC you're using.

Bottom line: If you have a domain type of network, someone is probably being paid to maintain and troubleshoot it for you. Don't sweat it.

Checking network privacy

Windows Vista doesn't let you create just any old peer-to-peer workgroup. Nope, it lets you configure a workgroup to be either public or private. That may seem like a silly choice, but it's not: A public network requires more security. After all, the network is in public. Who knows where those other people's laptops have been?

A private network, however, is most likely the kind of network you have in your home or small office. The network isn't (or shouldn't be) visited by random folks driving by or stopping in for a quick porn download.

In Windows 7 and Windows Vista, you can check whether the network you're using is public or private and then reset the network type for your computer. Follow these steps:

1. **Open the Control Panel.**

2. **Choose View Network Status and Tasks from beneath the Network and Internet heading.**

   Windows Vista is upfront about whether the network is public or private: Next to the Network heading in the middle of the window, you see the text *Public Network* or *Private Network*.

3a. **In Windows 7, click the link by the Network icon.**

   The link says Home Network, Work Network, or Public Network, which is your clue about the network's security level.

3b. **In Windows Vista, click the Customize link.**

4a. **In Windows 7, choose the network type from the Set Network Location window and then click the Close button; you're done.**

The Set Network Location window for Windows 7 is shown in Figure 3-7. The most secure network is the public network (the bottom option). The least secure network is the home network, but it's the one you should use for your home or small-office network.

Figure 3-7: Setting network type in Windows 7.

4b. In Windows Vista, choose Public or Private from the Set Network Location window.

The Set Network Location Wizard appears, as shown in Figure 3-8.

Choose Public if the network is in a public location or in a situation where anyone can join the network. Choose Private when you control the entire network and only computers you know of are connected.

Generally speaking, when in doubt, assume that you're using a public network. A hotel room connection, for example, is public. Cybercafé? Public. The wireless network at your friend's apartment? Public.

5. Name your network or assign a new icon.

This step is optional.

Those settings are more for fun than for network security.

6. Click the Next button.

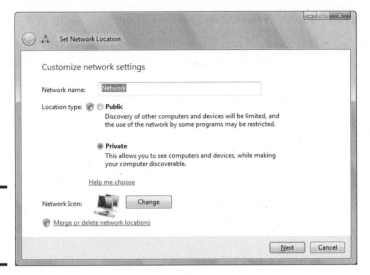

Figure 3-8:
Setting the
network
type.

7. **Type the administrator's password or click the Continue button.**

   Changing the network type is a security issue; you don't want a random program or virus making the change for you.

8. **Click the Close button.**

The changes you make don't affect the entire network. After all, if you just joined a wireless network in a cybercafé, why would your computer be allowed to lord it over all other computers on the network? No, the public/private thing merely tells Windows how to treat the network.

Reaching unreachable PCs

Perhaps the biggest problem with a peer-to-peer network is finding that a computer has suddenly gone missing. Worse, the whole network might be gone! The situation causes almost as much teeth-gnashing as a missing web page, but it's more frustrating because *you* might be the one responsible because it's your network. What to do, what to do. . . .

Here are some things to check for finding wayward network PCs:

✦ Check to ensure that the PC is turned on. A computer that's turned off cannot be accessed — don't let that surprise you!

✦ Computers that are hibernating, in Stand By mode or Sleep mode, cannot be accessed on the network.

✦ Likewise, a shared printer connected to a snoozing PC cannot be used.

✦ Conversely, you can use a computer that is on but no one is logged in to.

✦ You can, however, access a computer where only the monitor is sleeping.

✦ Check the firewall on your PC to ensure that local network traffic is allowed. (See the next section.)

✦ Check the workgroup name. The computer may not show up in the workgroup window, specifically on Windows XP, when it's using a different workgroup name.

✦ Confirm that the computer's user hasn't discontinued sharing that folder.

✦ Check the other computer to ensure that it doesn't have an IP conflict.

✦ Check a Windows 7 or Vista PC to ensure that all sharing options are properly set as described in the section "Making sharing possible in Windows 7 and Windows Vista," earlier in this chapter.

If all these solutions fail, consider restarting your PC. And if *that* fails, restart the network. See Chapter 2 for information on restarting your local-area network.

Allowing local traffic through the Windows firewall

Perhaps the number-one reason why computers don't communicate with each other on a peer-to-peer network is a software firewall. The firewall can prevent your PC from accessing other computers, as well as prevent those computers from accessing your PC. Either way, it's frustrating.

To fix the problem, you need to ensure that all local network traffic is allowed through the firewall. Because specific programs aren't accessing the firewall, you probably need to make the change manually. Here's how to check or change the local network traffic setting in the Windows Firewall:

1. **Open the Control Panel.**

2a. **In Windows 7, choose System and Security and then choose the link Allow a Program Through Windows Firewall, found beneath the Windows Firewall heading.**

2b. **In Windows Vista, choose the link Allow a Program Through Windows Firewall, found under the Security heading.**

2c. **In Windows XP, open the Windows Firewall icon.**

3. **In Windows Vista, type the administrator's password or click the Continue button.**

4. **If necessary, click the Exceptions tab in the Windows Firewall Settings dialog box.**

   The Windows XP version of the dialog box is titled Windows Firewall.

5. **Ensure that a check mark appears by the item File and Printer Sharing.**

   By enabling this exception, you ensure that all local traffic flows through the network without being blocked.

6. **Click OK and close any other open windows.**

These steps are specific to the Windows Firewall. If you're using another software firewall, take similar steps to ensure that local network traffic — specifically, file and printer sharing — isn't being blocked.

You don't need a software firewall when the network's router sports a good hardware firewall. See Chapter 1 for more information on router configuration.

Getting at multiple networks

Windows features a Bridge Connections command, which allows you to access two separate networks on a single PC. For example, if you have a laptop computer with both wired and wireless connections *and* you're using both, you can bridge those connections so that your laptop can access computers on both networks.

Yes, this type of situation might be rare. But Windows lets you do it.

To bridge connections, follow these steps:

1. **Open the Network Connections window.**

   See Chapter 2 for specific directions on opening this window.

2. **Select the network connections to bridge.**

   To select more than one connection at a time, press and hold the Ctrl key as you click each one.

3. **Right-click the selected icons and choose the Bridge Connections command.**

4. **In Windows Vista, click the Continue button or type the administrator's password if you're prompted to do so.**

5. **Dismiss the confirmation dialog box if one appears.**

There are a few times when this trick doesn't work. Windows doesn't, for example, bridge a connection between a local network and the Internet, which would be a security risk. Neither does bridging work when you're using Internet Connection Sharing, which is a way of sharing your PC's Internet connection directly with another PC by hooking the two computers together with an Ethernet cable.

To break up a network bridge, open the Network Connections window, right-click the bridge, and choose Delete from the shortcut menu.

Finding out who else is using your computer

The question is, who else on the network is using your PC? Which other computers on the local network are peeking into your folders? You may not know, but your computer does. Want to know the answer? Follow these steps:

1. **From the Start menu, choose All Programs⇨Accessories⇨Command Prompt.**

The Command Prompt window opens.

2. **Type** netstat **and press the Enter key.**

The `netstat` command displays network statistics. In its basic form (what you typed), current local connections to your computer are displayed. You see something like this if another computer is using one of your PC's shared folders:

```
Active Connections

   Proto   Local Address          Foreign Address
     State
   TCP     192.168.0.103:139      192.168.0.101:60172
     ESTABLISHED
   TCP     [fe80::e1fe:4a18:c135:883f%8]:445
     MonsterX:50209          ESTABLISHED
```

The output is, admittedly, technical. (You should expect no less from the command prompt.) What you're looking for is the other computer's network name, such as `MonsterX`, as shown in the code example.

3. **Type** exit **and press Enter to close the Command Prompt window.**

If you cannot determine another computer's name from the `netstat` command output, pay attention to the IP addresses. You have to cross-check the IP address displayed with that of other computers on the network, which can be a pain. But that's the only other way to use the command.

✦ The output also doesn't explain exactly which folder the other computer is using. In fact, the other computer may not even be using a folder. It could be using a printer or accessing something else. The mystery of it all!

✦ The `netstat` command can also be used to determine which Internet connections are active on your computer. Type **netstat -a** to see the list, which can be quite extensive.

✦ See Chapter 2 for information on discovering a PC's IP address.

Chapter 4: Networking Unplugged

In This Chapter

- ✔ Understanding wireless networking
- ✔ Setting up a base station
- ✔ Keeping the weirdoes out
- ✔ Turning on the wireless NIC
- ✔ Hunting down hard-to-find wireless networks
- ✔ Managing the wireless connections
- ✔ Using a Bluetooth peripheral
- ✔ Fixing Bluetooth problems

*T*hose network nightmares you've been having are completely unrealistic. Especially the part where you get tangled in all the cables. That's because computer networking need not involve wires. Wireless networking is all the rage, primarily for laptop computers, but desktop PCs equipped with wireless NICs can also live the untangled networking existence. When wireless woe occurs, laptop or desktop, turn to this chapter for wireless network troubleshooting.

Unwired Networking Basics

Perhaps you're one of the rare people who finds networking easy. Don't laugh: Networking isn't a constant source of trouble after the network has been configured. But that's often the case only for wired networking. With wireless networking, configuration seems to be an ongoing ordeal, especially if you're out in the real world and roaming wireless networks.

To help get your wireless networking bearings, I offer this section on the basics of wireless network.

Setting up a wireless network

There are two types of wireless networks: infrastructure and ad hoc. The *infrastructure* network is most likely the type of wireless setup you have in your home or office. It's laid out similarly to a wired network, but (surprisingly) without wires, as shown in Figure 4-1.

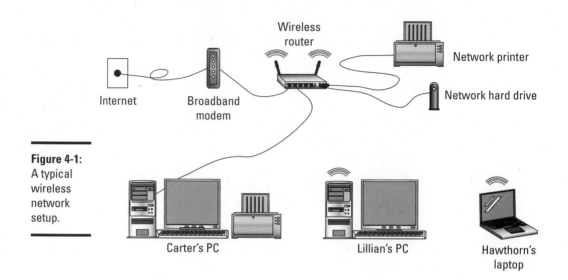

Wireless router

Network printer

Network hard drive

Internet

Broadband modem

Figure 4-1:
A typical
wireless
network
setup.

Carter's PC

Lillian's PC

Hawthorn's
laptop

The basic wireless, peer-to-peer network consists of these components:

Wireless router: The heart of the wireless network is the wireless router.
Like a wire-based network, the hub is a central location that all computers
connect to, providing the computers with network access.

The wireless hubs now available also serve as routers. Well, officially, wireless hubs are gateways, not routers, but they're called *routers.* They're also
called *access points,* so get used to that term as well.

Despite the nomenclature confusion, all you need to know is that the hub/
router/access point is a smart little beast that helps manage wireless connections and also helps connect your wireless network to the Internet.

Wire-based connections: Almost every wireless router I've seen has one or
more standard, wire-based Ethernet port. One port is used to connect the
router to a broadband modem. Other Ethernet ports might be also available,
allowing you to connect standard wire-based networking to the wireless hub
(refer to Figure 4-1).

Wireless NIC: Your computer needs a wireless network information card, or
NIC, to talk with the wireless router. A laptop comes standard with a wireless NIC, but for a desktop PC you have to get a wireless NIC as an option.
It's installed internally as an expansion card, or you can use one of the various plug-in USB wireless NICs.

That's pretty much it for the infrastructure type of wireless network.

The *ad hoc* type of wireless network is basically a group of wireless computers connected with each other. An ad hoc network has no central hub or router. Instead, all its computers can directly access the other computers' files and shared resources. They may or may not have Internet access, but that's not the point of the ad hoc network.

As long as you have all the hardware, you can quickly set up any wireless network. But that's only the hardware. The software side presents additional challenges, as covered later in this chapter.

✦ One of the beauties of a wireless network is that you can mix in wired components as needed. If you need more Ethernet ports, for example, simply add a switch to the wireless router. See Chapter 1 for more information on switches.

✦ Despite the wireless nature of wireless networking, you still need an Ethernet cable (a wire) to connect a wireless router to a broadband modem.

✦ Another advantage of a wireless network is that it's portable. It's far easier to pull up stakes with a wireless network than to pack up all the bits and pieces of a wired network. If you live in an apartment, or just move around a lot, a wireless setup a good option.

✦ See Figure 1-2 (in Chapter 1 of this minibook) for an illustration of a wired router, which has similar connections and features to a wireless router.

✦ The term *access point* is often abbreviated AP. Don't be puzzled when you see the words *wireless AP* — it simply refers to the access point, not to the Associated Press.

✦ A wireless network is often called a *WLAN,* for wireless local-area network.

✦ A wireless network is also referred to by the term *Wi-Fi*. It stands for *wi*reless *fi*delity, which is odd because *fidelity* comes from the root word for *faith*. I suppose you need a lot of faith to use a wireless network.

✦ Ad hoc networks are often used by computer gamers to gather in a single location to play games with each other.

✦ See Chapter 1 for basic network hardware information.

✦ See Chapter 3 for information on peer-to-peer networks.

Using the proper wireless network standard

If you're familiar with written music, you're probably used to seeing a lot of Italian. If you're familiar with computers, you're probably used to seeing a lot of numbers. One of them, 802.11, deals with wireless networking.

Specifically, all the gizmos on your wireless network must adhere to the 802.11 wireless networking standard.

The number 802.11 refers to the methods and protocols used to send network information without wires. But the number 802.11 isn't enough: A tiny letter suffix also determines which revision of the 802.11 standard is being used:

802.11n: The most current wireless networking standard. It can communicate with all the older standards. If you can, ensure that all your wireless networking equipment uses the 802.11n standard.

802.11g: The second most popular wireless networking standard, but one notch older than 802.11n (despite the missing letters *h* through *m*). The 802.11g wireless networking devices can communicate with the other 802.11 standards, but they don't use all the nifty new 802.11n features. Specifically, 802.11g gear lacks the range of 802.11n stuff.

802.11b: The oldest still-popular wireless networking standard. Although it can talk with the truly ancient 802.11a equipment, it can also communicate with 802.11g or 802.11n wireless hardware.

802.11a: The original wireless standard; not good for much any more.

To see which type of wireless NIC is installed in your computer, follow these steps:

1. **Press the Win+Break key combination to open the System window or System Properties dialog box.**

2a. **In Windows 7 and Windows Vista, click the link on the left labeled Device Manager.**

In Windows Vista, you also need to type the administrator's password or click the Continue button.

2b. **In Windows XP, click the Hardware tab and then click the Device Manager button.**

3. **In the Device Manager window, expand the area labeled Network Adapters.**

You most likely see two network adapters, as shown in Figure 4-2. One entry represents the wired Ethernet adapter (NIC); the other, the wireless.

One way to gauge the adapter type is by looking at its name. In Figure 4-2, the adapter's name ends with 4695AGN, which implies that the NIC might adhere to the wireless networking standards 802.11a, 802.11g, and 802.11n. But you can dig deeper:

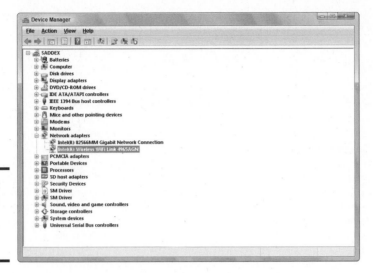

Figure 4-2:
A wireless
NIC in the
Device
Manager.

4. **Open the wireless networking adapter item.**

   The adapter's Properties dialog box appears.

5. **Click the Advanced tab.**

   If you have an 802.11n-compatible adapter, you see a couple of entries for 802.11n settings. They confirm that the adapter is 802.11n-compatible, which means that it can also talk with older 802.11g as well as with 802.11b wireless networking hardware.

6. **Click the Cancel button to close the adapter's Properties dialog box.**

7. **Close the Device Manager window and any other windows you opened.**

All your wireless network devices should be of the same standard, especially if you want to get the most performance from the wireless network. Although you can mix up the lot, such as an 802.11n hub with 802.11g NICs, things still work — although you're not getting all the 802.11n goodness from your 802.11g adapters.

When you're having trouble connecting an older PC or laptop to the wireless network, it's probably using an older wireless standard. Replace it with a newer NIC.

+ Say "eight-oh-two-eleven." Say it any other way and your geeky friends will never take you seriously.

+ If any of your computers is using an 802.11b NIC, I highly recommend replacing it with an 802.11n model or getting an 802.11n USB adapter.

✦ Yes, some letters are missing. I'm sure that there was an 802.11c standard, and who can forget that 802.11j standard? Although they probably had datasheets and prototypes, those standards were never released or made widely available to the public.

Configuring the wireless base station

Setting up a wireless base station works similarly to configuring a router for a wired network. See the section in Chapter 1 about configuring the router for a general overview.

Connecting to the router is done by setting it up according to the manual. Next, access the router by using a web browser on your computer. (The computer can be connected to the router wirelessly or connected directly with an Ethernet cable.)

To access the wireless base station's configuration menu, start a web browser on the computer connected to the base station. In the web browser's Address bar, type the router's IP address, such as

```
http://192.168.1.1
```

The exact address is found in the router manual. You're prompted for a username and password; that information is also in the manual.

You can probably set up a lot of things; a configuration tool may walk you through the basics. For security's sake, ensure that the following items are all set when you configure the wireless router:

Change the base station's administrator password. Set a new password for accessing the base station's configuration program. Too many people forget to do this part, so their wireless hub has the password *netlink* or something similar. That's too easy for the bad guys to figure out, so set a good, strong password for the base station!

Set the network name or SSID. The SSID, or service set identifier, is basically the wireless network's name. It's not the workgroup name, which can be set separately. Instead, it's the name that people see when they look to join the wireless network. Change the name to something unique — something other than *Linksys* or whatever name is preset for the router.

Suppress the SSID. It's more secure not to broadcast the SSID, so if you have the option to suppress it from being broadcast, consider setting this option. When the name is suppressed, the access point is still known, but only by typing the proper name can someone access the network.

Password-protected access. To join the wireless network, you want users to supply a password. Set a good one.

Set up a firewall. Ensure that the wireless router has its firewall settings activated. Nothing protects your computers from the nasties of the Internet like a good, solid hardware firewall.

The items listed here represent only a small taste of the vast assortment of settings and options for a wireless network — another reason why many people find wireless network setup to be a pain in the rump.

✦ Additionally, you can restrict access to only a limited set of computers, as described in the later section, "Restricting access to your wireless network."

✦ When the wireless router setup goes haywire, you can restore the router's factory settings by punching its Reset button. See the section "Resetting a base station," later in this chapter.

✦ For wireless security, use a password on your network and the WPA-/WPA2-level security. WPA, or Wi-Fi Protected Access, is a replacement for the older WEP standard. You might also see the term *PSK,* which refers to a *preshared key*, a common security method for wireless networks.

✦ The wireless network's WPA/WPA2 password is anywhere from 8 to 64 characters long. After you set it, *write it down*. The password for my office's wireless network is 28 characters long, including upper- and lowercase letters, numbers, and symbols, plus characters from the Klingon alphabet. Yes, I wrote it down.

✦ Set a nice, tough password for your wireless network. You can configure Windows to remember the password so that you don't have to type it every time you turn on the computer. But you also don't want something that one of the Bad Guys can easily guess.

✦ I used to suppress my wireless hub's SSID, but I don't do it any more. Instead, I use MAC address filtering to help restrict access. See the section "Restricting access to your wireless network," later in this chapter.

✦ My favorite local SSID is named `This Is My Network Keep Off`.

Connecting base stations

Yeah, they lied. The box probably said that your wireless router has a range of 300 feet. Perhaps that's true on the moon, but obstacles on this planet easily interfere with a wireless network signal — obstacles such as wood and brick and especially metal. If you look around right now, you can probably see lots of wood and brick or metal. That stuff is hindering the wireless signal.

If all your wireless computers are in one room, a single wireless base station works just fine. But when you have dreams of darting around your house using a laptop or having that game machine in the den access the wireless network, you're probably better served by using a second wireless base station.

The secret to using multiple base stations is to bridge the connections so that all your wireless hubs are part of the same network. This concept, creating a *wireless distribution system (WDS),* is shown in Figure 4-3.

To make WDS happen, the wireless router must have WDS capability. You can confirm it by reading it on the box or by checking the router's configuration program for a WDS settings page.

With both WDS-capable wireless routers in range, you configure the first router (the one connected to the Internet) as the WDS main router, and the second as a WDS remote. Activating WDS for both routers spreads out the wireless network, giving you more access points but keeping all wireless connections on the same network.

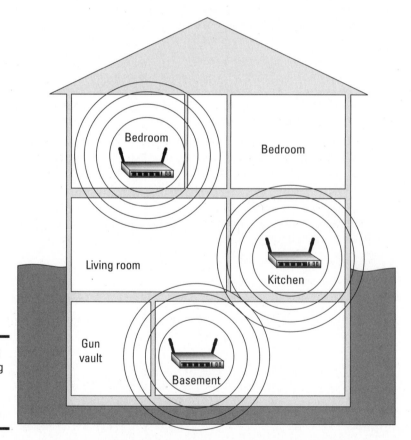

Figure 4-3:
Connecting
base
stations
with WDS.

You can even add a third WDS access point by setting up a third router as another WDS remote. It all depends on the router's signal strength and the area being covered.

✦ Creating a WDS depends on the abilities of the wireless routers. All routers involved must be able to be configured for a WDS. When there's no WDS setup page for the router's configuration, you cannot create a WDS.

✦ The wireless router's WDS configuration may require you to manually enter the other router's MAC address. Find the MAC address by contacting the router, using your PC's web browser; or, sometimes the manufacturer prints the MAC address on the bottom of the router.

✦ You might have to configure all wireless routers in a WDS to use the same network channel, such as Channel 1 or Channel 11.

✦ Some wireless routers can bridge to only one other router, and some can do "multipoint" bridging to create a larger WDS.

✦ Setting up a WDS for multiple wireless routers isn't the same thing as using the Bridge Connections command in Windows. By bridging a wired and wireless network connection on a laptop, for example, you allow network access to both networks. See the section in Chapter 3 about getting at multiple networks.

✦ By using WDS, you can have one wireless router connected to the Internet and then other wireless routers around your home or office that help distribute the connection to all the computers.

Restricting access to your wireless network

One major weakness of wireless networking is security. Your best move is to apply a good, solid network password, as described in the section "Configuring the wireless base station," earlier in this chapter. A better option is to restrict access to only those computers known to the wireless router or base station. That way, only computers you authorize can use the network, even when the network password is known.

How the technique works depends on the router. It may be called a wireless MAC filter, MAC address filter, network filter, or restricted MAC access. The idea is to supply the router with a list of MAC addresses. It works because every wireless NIC has a unique MAC address. The result is that only those PCs whose MAC addresses are known can access the wireless network.

After enabling MAC address filtering for your router, you need to enter the list of MAC addresses from the PCs that use that network. The method for obtaining this information is different between the different versions of Windows covered in this book.

In Windows Vista, follow these steps to discover your PC's wireless NIC's MAC address:

1. **Open the Control Panel.**

2. **From beneath the Network and Internet heading, choose View Network Status and Tasks.**

   The Network and Sharing Center window appears.

3a. **In Windows 7, choose the link on the left side of the window: Change Adapter Settings.**

3b. **In Windows Vista, click the Manage Network Connections link.**

   The Network Connections window appears. Every network connection, wired or wireless, appears as an icon in the window.

4. **Double-click to open the Wireless Network Connection icon.**

5. **In the Wireless Network Connection Status dialog box, click the Details button.**

   The MAC address, titled Physical Address, appears in the Property column.

6. **Close the various dialog boxes and windows.**

Follow these steps to discover the wireless NIC's MAC address in Windows XP:

1. **Open the Network Connections icon in the Control Panel.**

2. **Open the Wireless Network Connection icon.**

3. **Click the Support tab in the connection's Status window.**

4. **Click the Details button.**

   Lots of information is listed in the Details dialog box, including the MAC address, which is listed in the Property column as Physical Address.

5. **Close the various windows and dialog boxes.**

After you know the MAC address for a computer (or gizmo), you can access the wireless router and input that MAC address into the list of authorized computers. Yes, doing it is a pain, but the benefit is that only those computers you authorize can use the network. Considering that you need to input the MAC address only once for each computer, I think the security trade-off is worth it.

✦ Every NIC has a unique MAC address.

✦ MAC stands for Media Access Control. It's a Scottish thing.

✦ The MAC address is a series of six values separated by hyphens. The values include the numbers 0 through 9 and letters *A* through *F*.

Resetting a base station

As with a wired router, you reset the wireless base station by locating its teensy, tiny Reset switch, found somewhere on the back of the unit. Use a bent paperclip to push the Reset switch in, wait a sec, and then release it.

By resetting the base station, you revert it to its factory presets. These presets include the default password and configuration, essentially turning the thing into another stupid wireless router. So, after you reset the router, be sure to reconfigure it to the settings you want.

When the Hook-Up Gets Hung Up

As a human being, you're unable to see into that portion of the electromagnetic spectrum where wireless networks flit and hum. I'm certain that the wireless signals would prove an awesome sight, probably all purple and bubbly. But you'll never see it — only your PC can. Assuming that a wireless network is out there somewhere, and that your PC can see it, the next step is to connect to it. This section describes how that happens, or doesn't happen, and what to do about it.

Enabling the wireless NIC

The biggest problem with connecting to a wireless network is that you don't have your computer's wireless NIC activated. There are two places to look.

 First, check for an external switch on a laptop computer that turns wireless networking on or off. You may find a tiny wireless NIC icon next to the switch, similar to the one shown in the margin. Place that switch into the On or active position.

Second, confirm that the wireless NIC has been activated in Windows. Oftentimes, the NIC is disabled, especially when traveling by air, and there's no external wireless NIC switch.

To confirm that Windows has enabled the wireless NIC, follow these steps in Windows 7 and Windows Vista:

1. **Open the Control Panel.**

2. **From beneath the Network and Internet heading, choose View Network Status and Tasks.**

3a. **In Windows 7, choose the link on the left side of the window: Change Adapter Settings.**

3b. **In Windows Vista, click the Manage Network Connections link.**

4. **Confirm that the Wireless Network Connection icon in the Network Connections Window is enabled.**

   If so, you're done. Skip to Step 7. Otherwise, you need to enable the connection.

5. **Right-click the Wireless Network Connection icon and choose Enable from the shortcut menu.**

6. **In Windows Vista, type the administrator's password or click the Continue button.**

   The adapter is enabled.

7. **Close the various dialog boxes and windows.**

In Windows XP, obey these steps to check your PC's wireless NIC:

1. **Open the Network Connections icon in the Control Panel.**

2. **Confirm that the Wireless Network Connection icon is enabled.**

   If the icon sports the text *Enabled,* you're done. Skip to Step 4.

3. **Right-click the Wireless Network Connection icon and choose Enable from the shortcut menu.**

4. **Close the Network Connections window.**

After you enable the wireless NIC, your computer may instantly connect to one of its recognized networks. If not, you need to proceed with a manual connection, as described in the later section, "But I can't find the network!"

✦ Do not enable a wireless NIC on an airplane unless flight personnel tell you that it's okay to do so.

✦ The wireless switch might also be labeled Airplane mode.

Finding a wireless network

You can seek out a wireless network in at least two ways. The first is the common way, which is to use Windows. Boring. The second is to use any custom software that came with the wireless NIC. The custom software doesn't work better at finding the signal, but often it displays the signals it found in a better, sexier way than the traditional Windows method does.

 Connecting to a wireless network in Windows 7 happens in a number of strange and confusing ways. The easiest way is to click the Wireless Networking icon in the taskbar's notification area (shown in the margin): Up pops a list of available wireless networks, as shown in Figure 4-4; choose one from the list and click the Connect button. If prompted, type the network password.

Refresh

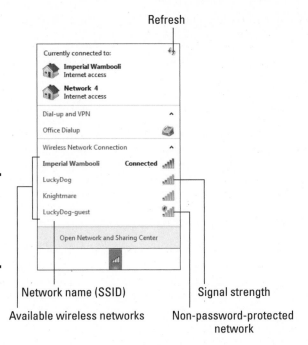

Figure 4-4:
Accessing
wireless
networks in
Windows 7.

Network name (SSID)

Available wireless networks

Signal strength

Non-password-protected
network

In Windows Vista, connect to a wireless network by choosing the Connect
To command from the Start button menu. A Connect to Network window
appears, shown in Figure 4-5, from which you can choose a wireless network.

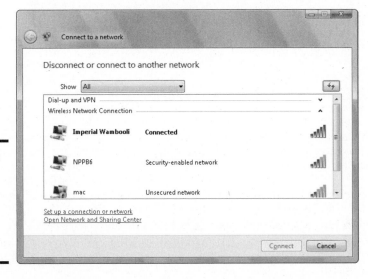

Figure 4-5:
Available
wireless
networks
seen by
Windows
Vista.

In Windows XP, you need to access the Wireless Network Connection icon in the Network Connections window: Open the Network Connections icon in the Control Panel and then right-click the Wireless Network Connection icon. Choose the command View Available Wireless Connections from the short-cut menu.

Accessing the custom wireless network connection software that came with your PC's wireless NIC depends on that software, so I can't be specific here. On my laptop, for example, I right-click a teeny icon in the notification area. Eventually, after wading through some weird dialog boxes, I can see a fancy connection window, as shown in Figure 4-6. It not only shows available wireless networks but also graphically shows the network's signal strength.

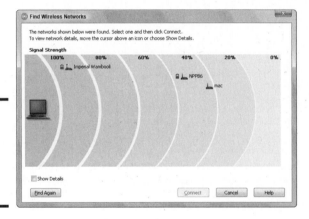

Figure 4-6:
A custom
wireless
network
access
program.

After choosing a network, the next step is to enter a password for access, unless your computer already knows the network and the password has been saved or the network doesn't use a password.

After you're connected, you see a wireless connection icon appear in the notification area. You can point the mouse at the icon to check the connection's status.

- ✦ See the later section, "Managing wireless connections," for more information about saved wireless connections.

- ✦ You may, sometime after connecting, be prompted to specify whether the wireless network is public or private. Refer to Chapter 3, the section about checking network privacy, for more information on the public/private question.

- ✦ Some of those passwords can be long and tedious to type, especially in Windows XP, where you have to type it twice.

✦ Yes, some networks have no passwords. The LuckyDog-guest network shown in Figure 4-4 has no password, which is why it's flagged with a teensy yellow shield icon. Password-less networks make for easier access, but they're also less secure.

✦ If you're using an unsecured network, definitely employ a software firewall. See Book IV, Chapter 4.

✦ Public wireless hot spots often lack passwords. You might be required to "log in" by providing your email address or a form of temporary ID.

✦ Always set to Public any wireless network you use outside your home or office. That helps boost general wireless security.

✦ Windows Vista also assaults you with various User Account Control (UAC) warnings as you connect to wireless networks. Type the administrator's password or click the Continue button to proceed.

"But I can't find the network!"

Boy, wireless networks would sure work better if there were a more substantial way to connect to them. Say, something like *wires?* But I jest. The first problem you encounter when trying to make the wireless network connection is finding the network.

Above all, have patience. Not all wireless networks show up at first blush. Remember that physical objects around you affect the signal: walls, bookcases, large partitions made from lead, and superheroes. Those things readily block the wireless signal.

Next, move around. Sometimes, moving the laptop just a few feet in one direction improves signal reception. Remember that if you cannot see the wireless hub directly, odds are good that you won't get a solid signal.

Windows 7 and Windows Vista feature Refresh buttons: Refer to Figure 4-4 for Windows 7; in Windows Vista, click the Refresh button found in the upper-right portion of the Connect to Network window (refer to Figure 4-5). Keep clicking this button to have the wireless NIC rescan for network availability.

Some wireless networks don't send out their SSIDs. Although the wireless NIC still picks up the signal, no name is given for the access point. You have to supply the name. Of course, I'm assuming that you know the SSID already. After you know it, from either the network administrator or a stained piece of paper given to you by the tattooed, pierced guy who makes your coffee, you must use that information to tell Windows how to find the wireless network.

In Windows 7, follow these steps to connect to a wireless network that's not showing its name:

1. **Open the Control Panel.**

2. **Choose the link View Network Status and Tasks from beneath the Networking and Internet heading.**

   The Network and Sharing Center window appears.

3. **Choose the link Set Up a Connection or Network.**

   The Set Up a Connection or Network window shows up.

4. **Choose Manually Connect to a Wireless Network.**

5. **Click the Next button.**

6. **Type the network SSID (name) into the Network Name text box.**

7. **Choose the security type from the Security Type button menu.**

8. **If the Encryption Type button becomes available, choose the proper type of encryption from the menu.**

9. **Type the wireless network's password into the Security Key text box.**

   Put a check mark by the option Start This Connection Automatically. That way, you don't have to input this same information again if you ever need to reconnect with the same wireless network.

10. **Click the Next button to connect with the network.**

    As long as you didn't screw anything up, and the network gods are pleased, you're connected to the nameless wireless network.

11. **Choose the Connect To option.**

    And the connection is complete.

Here's how to connect to an unnamed wireless network in Windows Vista:

1. **Pop up the Start button menu and choose Connect To.**

2. **Click the link Set Up a Connection or Network.**

   It's at the bottom of the window (refer to Figure 4-5).

3. **Choose Manually Connect to a Wireless Network and click the Next button.**

   A window appears with various fill-in-the-blanks items, helping you hone your choice of which wireless network to connect to.

4. **Type the SSID into the Network Name box.**

5. **Select Security Type from the button menu.**

6. **If the Encryption Type button becomes enabled, click it.**

   The encryption type is based on the security type.

7. **Type the security key or passphrase.**

   I prefer putting a check mark in the Display Characters check box so that I can double-check my typing.

8. **Click the Next button.**

   If all goes well, Windows presents the network as ready for a connection.

9. **Choose the option Connect To.**

   And . . . you're only half done. Now you need to use the Connect To command from the Start button menu to connect to the network.

In Windows XP, supply the SSID by following these steps:

1. **Open the Network Connections icon in the Control Panel.**

2. **Right-click the Wireless Network Connection icon.**

3. **Choose Properties from the shortcut menu.**

4. **Click the Wireless Networks tab in the Wireless Network Connection Properties dialog box.**

5. **Click the Add button.**

   It's found near the bottom of the dialog box.

6. **Type the SSID into the Network Name (SSID) text box in the Wireless Network Properties dialog box.**

7. **If required, type the Network Key — twice.**

8. **Click OK.**

   You're not connected at this point, but the network should now show up in the list of available networks. Connect to the network as you normally would.

Another cause of a dropped connection may be a timeout. For example, some for-pay wireless services give you only a limited amount of access time. After that time expires, you're no longer connected or you may see the Pay Up home page rather than the Internet.

Finally, the connection problem may simply be that the password is incorrect. A dialog box warns you about it, but keep in mind that any wireless network passwords you stored in your PC might be changed by the various networks you access. In fact, I purposely don't memorize the wireless password at the coffee shop I frequent in town because they keep changing it.

✦ You can check the connection strength by pointing the mouse at the wee connection icon in the notification area.

✦ In Windows Vista, the wireless connection strength is also displayed beneath the network's information area in the Network and Connection Sharing window.

✦ If you're using Windows 7 or Windows Vista, you can install various wireless networking gadgets for the Sidebar. Most display the wireless network's name, signal strength, and IP address.

✦ Third-party utilities can also be used to gauge signal strength, such as the wireless networking tool shown earlier, in Figure 4-6. Various *war driver* utilities, used to find wireless signals, can also be used to discover signal strength. The popular NetStumbler program can be downloaded here:

        www.netstumbler.com

Managing wireless connections

Both Windows 7 and Windows Vista feature a little black book. But unlike former dates, the black book helps you keep track of all the wireless networks your computer has gone out with. You can see the whole list of 'em by opening the Control Panel's Network and Sharing Center icon and clicking the Manage Wireless Networks link. When you do, the Manage Wireless Networks window appears, as shown in Figure 4-7.

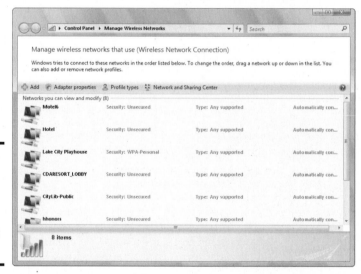

Figure 4-7:
The wireless networking black book in Windows Vista.

The Manage Wireless Networks window displays a list of wireless networks you accessed in the past. By keeping track of those connections, Windows makes it easier for your computer (okay, your laptop) to recognize and instantly connect to those networks when they're within range. It saves time.

If you have trouble connecting to one of the networks, you can enter updated information as your computer tries to make the connection. For example, you can enter a new password if the old one is rejected or has expired.

You can change any saved wireless connection by double-clicking its icon in the Manage Wireless Networks window. In the connection's Properties dialog box, click the Security tab to type the new password.

If you'd rather not have a connection made automatically, double-click the Connection icon and in its Properties dialog box, remove the check mark by the Connect Automatically When This Network Is in Range option.

To set a priority for the connections, drag the connection up or down in the window. Connections at the top of the window have a higher priority.

Windows ensures that the computer first connects to the higher-priority networks. Well, that is, unless you turned off that option in the connection's Properties dialog box. (The setting is titled Connect to a More Preferred Network If Available.)

Close the Manage Wireless Networks window when you're done messing around.

+ Even when you don't remember choosing to save a wireless network connection, don't be surprised to see it in the list.

+ Removing an item from the list is easy: Select the wireless Network Connection icon and click the Remove toolbar button.

+ I recommend removing older connections. For example, after a road trip, I just remove all the various icons for the hotel networks I connected to.

The Bluetooth Thing

The Bluetooth wireless networking standard has been around since the 1990s. I'll admit that it's not as popular on the PC as it is on the Mac, considering that a lot of PC laptops don't bother coming with Bluetooth hardware. Even so, Bluetooth exists as a wireless standard for connecting peripherals and for wireless networking. That's a brew for trouble, which this section can help you shoot.

Understanding Bluetooth

Like everything else in your computer, Bluetooth requires both hardware and software.

A Bluetooth adapter supplies Bluetooth hardware. If your PC didn't come with the Bluetooth hardware installed, you can easily add it by purchasing a Bluetooth USB dongle.

To determine whether your PC has Bluetooth hardware, check the Device Manager for Bluetooth Radio. Follow these steps:

1. **Open the Control Panel.**

2. **Choose Hardware and Sound, and then choose Device Manager.**

In Windows 7, the Device Manager link is found beneath the Devices and Printers heading; in Windows Vista, Device Manager is its own heading.

3. **In Windows Vista, click the Continue button or type the administrator's password.**

4. **Look for the item Bluetooth Radios in the list.**

If the item is there, your PC has Bluetooth hardware installed, and you can safely assume that the software has been set up as well.

5. **Close the various windows you opened.**

 The Bluetooth software is supplied by Windows, as well as by whatever installation disc comes with the Bluetooth hardware. After it's set up, you'll most likely use the Bluetooth icon in the notification area to manage various connections and settings. The Bluetooth icon is shown in the margin.

✦ The Bluetooth icon in the notification area is the means by which you do most Bluetoothy things in Windows.

✦ In Windows 7, you see the Bluetooth hardware listed in the Devices and Printers window. You can use that window, and the Add a Device toolbar button, to browse for and connect Bluetooth gizmos to your computer.

✦ Windows Vista allows you to access Bluetooth via the Control Panel. It's located in the Hardware and Sound category and has its own heading, Bluetooth Devices.

✦ Bluetooth devices are *paired*, which means that a Bluetooth gizmo is assigned to work with only one device at a time. The pairing process is part of connecting a Bluetooth gizmo, covered in the next section.

 ✦ The wireless networking used by Bluetooth isn't as robust as the Wi-Fi wireless networking described elsewhere in this chapter. For the most part, Bluetooth is a low-powered system. You can't move a Bluetooth gizmo more than 10 feet or so from its paired device without losing the signal.

Connecting a Bluetooth gizmo

Adding a Bluetooth device to your computer works like this:

1. Ensure that the device is powered on, has its Bluetooth radio on, and is discoverable.

For the simplest Bluetooth devices, you merely turn on the gizmo and push a button (often the Power button) to ensure that the device is active. Being *discoverable* means that the device is broadcasting itself as available.

2. On your computer, click the Bluetooth icon in the notification area.

3. Ensure that the Bluetooth adapter is turned on.

In Windows 7, choose the menu item Turn Adapter On; in Windows Vista, the item is named Turn Bluetooth Adapter On. If you don't see that command on the menu, the adapter is on and you're ready to go.

4a. In Windows 7, choose the command Add a Device.

4b. In Windows Vista, choose the command Add a Bluetooth Device.

The window that appears is named Add a Device in Windows 7, or Pair with a Wireless Device in Windows Vista. The Windows 7 version is shown in Figure 4-8, though both windows look similar.

If you don't see the device you want to pair with, wait a few seconds. If necessary, touch the Power button or Bluetooth button, or somehow reactivate the device as discoverable.

Figure 4-8: Hunting down Bluetooth gadgets.

5. **Choose the device from those listed in the window.**

6. **Click the Next button.**

7. **If prompted, obey the directions on the screen to enter the passkey to ensure that the devices are paired securely.**

   For example, on my wireless keyboard, I'm asked to type a number on the screen by using the Bluetooth keyboard and then press the Enter key (on the Bluetooth keyboard). For a smartphone, you may be asked to confirm that a PIN is the same on both your computer and the phone.

   Some devices, such as a wireless mouse, don't require a passkey; they simply connect and are ready to use (though the device may not be usable until you complete the next, final step).

8. **Click the Close button after the devices are paired.**

   You can now use your Bluetooth device with your computer.

After the device is paired, it effectively becomes a peripheral to your computer, just like any other peripheral — but it's wireless!

✦ Bluetooth peripherals paired with your PC can be turned on or off at any time. Turning on a paired device again instantly reestablishes the wireless connection; there's nothing more you need to do, other than start using the device.

✦ To use a Bluetooth gizmo with another computer, you must unpair it. See the next section.

✦ You'll find other Bluetooth computers listed in the Add a Device or Add a Bluetooth Device window; refer to Figure 4-8. In that figure, both SADDEX and CHRONOS are other computers you can pair by using Bluetooth. The pairing allows you to use hardware features on the other computers.

✦ An extra screen appears in the pairing process when pairing your computer with another Bluetooth computer. Use that screen to choose which of the other computer's hardware you want your computer to use, such as its microphone, speakers, Internet connection, or whatever is available.

✦ On a smartphone, you need to turn on the Bluetooth radio as well as set the phone to be discoverable. The steps for accomplishing this feat are unique and confusing for all cellphones.

✦ Pairing with a smartphone allows you to use that phone's Internet connection, to use the phone itself to make phone calls, to listen to music on the phone, or to make use of any of a bunch of interesting features, depending on the phone.

✦ Refer to Chapter 1 in Book II for information on displaying notification icons if the Bluetooth icon goes a-hiding on you.

✦ An option on the Bluetooth icon's pop-up menu is titled Join a Personal Area Network. It's possible to use Bluetooth to create a personal network or to join an existing network. For that to happen, both computers need to share similar software; so, the trick often doesn't work because the software isn't compatible. Even so, I recommend using the traditional wireless networking described earlier in this chapter because it's just easier to deal with.

Managing Bluetooth connections

To see which Bluetooth devices are connected to your computer, click the Bluetooth icon in the notification area and choose the command Show Bluetooth Devices. You see the Bluetooth Devices window, which lists every gizmo that's talking with your computer's wireless Bluetooth radio.

Manage settings for a Bluetooth device by double-clicking its icon in the Bluetooth Devices window. Some devices, such as smartphones and other computers, have more options than the simpler devices, such as a keyboard or mouse.

To unpair a device, follow these steps:

1. **Click the Bluetooth icon in the notification area and choose the command Show Bluetooth Devices.**

2. **Right-click a device in the window.**

The device doesn't need to be on to be unpaired. You'll notice that the devices show up in the window regardless of whether they're on.

3. **Choose the command Remove or Remove Device.**

4. **Click the Yes button in the Remove Device dialog box.**

5. **If prompted, type the administrator's password or click the Continue button.**

The device is unpaired and no longer appears in the Bluetooth Devices window.

You can always pair the device again, as described in the preceding section.

Bluetooth devices can be paired with only one computer at a time.

Dealing with Bluetooth woe

Like anything else you add to your computer, a Bluetooth gizmo introduces change. That change can cause problems, which is kind of the theme of this book. You can have problems with other devices that are incompatible with your Bluetooth device, you can have problems with the Bluetooth device itself, or you can have issues with the Bluetooth networking hardware. Lots of things can go hinkey on you.

To check on the status of the Bluetooth hardware, follow these steps:

1. **Click the Bluetooth icon in the notification area.**

2. **Choose the command Open Settings (in Windows 7) or Open Bluetooth Settings (in Windows Vista).**

The Bluetooth Settings dialog box appears, as shown in Figure 4-9. Use the dialog box to check the various settings for the Bluetooth hardware, to ensure that it's working properly.

For example, to check for updates to the Bluetooth driver, click the Driver tab and then click the Update Driver button.

When the adapter is acting oddly, you can click the Restore Defaults button (refer to Figure 4-9) to erase any settings you may have made that screwed things up.

3. **Click the OK button to close the Bluetooth Settings dialog box when you're done.**

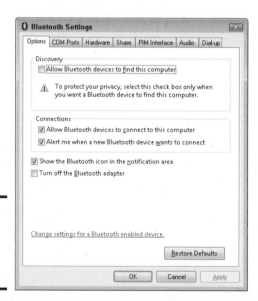

Figure 4-9:
The
Bluetooth
Settings
dialog box.

Here are some other suggestions for working with your Bluetooth gizmos, as well as general Bluetooth troubleshooting:

✦ It's possible to use Bluetooth to connect multiple devices to your computer, such as more than one mouse or keyboard — nothing wrong with that. In fact, you can connect multiple input devices by using the PC's USB ports as well. All input devices (mice and keyboards) remain active.

✦ When you can't do something on your PC, or input is acting oddly, check to ensure that a second keyboard or mouse isn't being manipulated beyond your control. For example, if a book is pressing the Shift key on the second keyboard, it may explain why all your text is in uppercase.

✦ Ensure that the wireless radio is on: Click the Bluetooth icon to confirm that it's on for your PC. Check the Bluetooth gizmo itself to ensure that it's broadcasting a Bluetooth signal.

✦ Some Bluetooth dongles feature a teensy button you can use to wake up the wireless radio.

✦ Because Bluetooth devices are wireless, they use batteries. To help preserve battery life, most Bluetooth devices have an automatic sleep or stand-by mode. You may need to wake the device before it can be used: Press or click a button on the device to wake it up.

✦ Wireless devices consume batteries. Always have fresh batteries on hand. If a device doesn't work, change the batteries. Properly dispose of used batteries.

Book VI

Maintenance

The 5th Wave   By Rich Tennant

"How's the defragmentation coming?"

Contents at a Glance

Chapter 1: Backup, Backup, Backup

In This Chapter

✔ **Making a copy of your stuff**

✔ **Using an external hard drive for backup**

✔ **Setting up the first backup**

✔ **Creating a backup routine**

✔ **Restoring files from a backup set**

✔ **Restoring personal files**

✔ **Using Windows Vista Complete PC Backup**

Most people believe it a sad fact of 21st century life that when you lose your computer's stuff, it's gone forever. Music, photos, videos, old emails, documents, financial information — all of it's just a spark away from digital non-existence because, well, that's the way things are on the computer. People accept this situation as truth, but it's absolutely not. The key is to create a backup copy, or *archive,* of your stuff. Do it often and you'll never lose a thing. Well, a digital thing.

That Emergency Copy

Nothing is better than having a good collection of stuff on a computer: work, play, music, video, pictures, email — an electronic image of your digital life. Well, actually, there's something better: having a *second copy* of all that stuff. I'm shocked at the number of people who fail to make a second, safety copy. If this idea is new and revolutionary to you, read this section to find out more.

Understanding backup

It's one of the old ones, perhaps the most ancient of computer utilities. It's commonly called *backup*, though it's had other names, such as the curious *tar*. The purpose is a vital one: to ensure that you have a second copy, or even multiple copies, of your data. Sounds good, right? Yet few people bother and end up paying the price later.

You can make a safety copy, or backup, of your computer files in three ways:

Manual copy: To back up your files, simply duplicate them on removable media: an optical disc or a media card. You use the standard file copying methods in Windows to copy the files. It's simple. Time consuming, but simple. I do it all the time.

Backup program: Employ a backup program. The program does basically the same thing as when you copy files. The advantage is that it automates and simplifies the process. Plus, the program adds features such as scheduling, the ability to manage backup *sets*, and the power to quickly restore files from the backup.

Internet backup: It's the newest kid on the backup block — a backup program, similar to what's described in the preceding paragraph, but stored on the Internet rather than on optical discs or external hard drives. Internet backup also involves ongoing fees, which is why it isn't my preferred recommendation.

No matter how you back up, the result is the same: You have a second copy of your files. You can use the copy to restore files you accidentally deleted, recover files irreparably changed, or restore portions of your system damaged by a virus or hardware disaster. Backup is good news.

And now, for the bad news:

Too many people don't back up. In the olden days, people didn't back up, because it was a chore. I remember backing up one of my early PC's hard drives to a set of about 40 floppy disks. Shuffling those disks in and out was a nightmare. That's why few people bothered back then.

Today's backup programs take advantage of high-capacity optical discs, media cards, external hard drives, network and Internet storage. There's no more disk swapping. (Well, there can be, when you use optical discs.) External storage is cheap and plentiful. Backup programs are widely available, and a good backup program comes with Windows. Despite all that, the bad news remains that few people back up.

Worse: People who don't back up seem somehow resigned to the fact that all computer data is temporary. It need not be.

You have no reason in the digital age not to keep with you copies of your digital life — pictures, videos, music, and documents — forever. You will never lose this stuff if you use backup and stick with a regular backup schedule. It's not that difficult.

✦ The process of backing up files is referred to as *archiving*. A backup copy of a file is also known as an *archive*.

✦ The key to being successful in backing up your files is to place them on *removable* media, which is a type of storage that's different from the computer's internal storage — specifically, the hard drive. Remember that the hard drive is the first location for storing files on your computer. To keep the backup copy safe, it should be on another storage media. That way, if your PC has a hardware problem, your files exist safely elsewhere.

✦ Backup is also necessary when the computer's primary storage is an SSD (see Book I, Chapters 2 and 4 for more on SSD). That's because the backup philosophy is about your stuff (data), not about the media on which it's stored.

✦ Removable media or an external hard drive (which is another form of removable media) is best for your file backups. That's because you can store the removable media elsewhere, such as in a firesafe.

✦ Yes, I strongly recommend storing your backup copies in a firesafe. You can find a small, portable firesafe for your data at most office supply stores.

✦ Backup programs can be run automatically. You never forget to back up when you schedule the backup program to run every day and make that safety copy of your stuff.

✦ Backup programs remember which files have been backed up and which files have been created or modified since the last backup. You can take advantage of this situation by directing the backup program to archive only those files that are newly created or have been modified since the last backup operation.

✦ The clutch of files that's backed up is referred to as a *backup set*. Backup programs can manage multiple backup sets.

✦ Backup programs feature a restore utility that allows you to easily recover files that have been backed up. The files can be restored individually, or the computer's entire file system can be rebuilt by using the archived copy.

✦ The tar utility still exists in the Unix operating system. This *t*ape *ar*chive relates to copies made to a tape backup machine often connected to early Unix systems. The tar utility is still used, mostly to create archive files similar to compressed folders (Zip files) in Windows. Tar archives often use the filename extension `tar` or `tar.gz` for compressed archives.

Types of backup

Backup programs don't always archive all the files on your computer. Instead, the programs can be customized to back up specific types of files (music, for example) or only files from certain folders. Additionally, different types of backups are created, which can be tuned to create an overall backup strategy:

Full backup: A n archive copy of all files on your computer's main hard drive.

Personal backup: An archive copy of all your user files on the computer's main hard drive.

The backup includes neither program files nor the Windows operating system.

Incremental backup: The name of a backup set that includes only those files created or modified since the last backup.

Image backup: An image backup copies information directly from the computer's hard drive at a very low level. It's a backup copy, but merely of raw data and not of separate files. This type of backup might also be called a *clone*.

Making that backup copy

You don't need to run a backup program to make a backup. In fact, anytime you copy a file, you're essentially making a backup; the duplicate file is a safety copy of the original. As long as the copy is saved to an external storage device or media, it's an official backup.

The following steps demonstrate how to manually create a backup copy of one or more files. These steps work for any version of Windows, and you can use them whether or not your computer has a backup program. To complete these steps, you need an external storage device, such as a media card or USB thumb drive:

1. **Open the folder containing the files you want to back up.**

If you're backing up a folder, that folder's *parent* folder must be visible. For example, to back up my Work folder, I need to be able to see the Documents folder, which is where the Work folder lives.

I don't recommend backing up your account, or user profile, folder by using the file-copy method. That's because your account folder and all its subfolders is probably larger than any storage media you have. If it isn't, that's swell. If it is, however, you'll run out of room on the backup media and won't know about it until it's too late (which is another reason to use a real backup program rather than just copy over files).

2. **Click to select the files or folders you want to back up.**

To select more than one icon at a time, press and hold the Ctrl key as you click each icon.

3. **Press Ctrl+C to copy the files.**

   The Ctrl+C key combination places the list of files (or a single file) into the Windows Clipboard, where they sit happily until you paste them into another folder, which completes the entire copy operation.

4. **Insert the removable media into your PC, or attach the media.**

   For example, plug in the USB thumb drive or stick a media card into your PC's media card reader. If the removable storage device is already attached, you're set to go.

   You can also use an optical disc as the removable storage media. Ensure that the disc has been inserted and prepared by Windows for use as a data disc.

5. **If you see the AutoPlay dialog box, choose the option Open Folder to View Files; skip to Step 8.**

   When the AutoPlay dialog box doesn't appear, manually open the external storage device by using the Computer window:

6. **Open the Computer window.**

   In Windows XP, it's the My Computer window. The window lists all storage devices attached to your PC, similar to the list shown in Figure 1-1. One device should represent the storage media you're copying the files to.

Book VI
Chapter 1

Backup, Backup, Backup

Figure 1-1:
Removable media in the Computer window.

7. **Open the icon representing the removable media.**

Which icon is it? The answer depends on the type of media and on how the drive letters are assigned. In Figure 1-1, for example, the USB thumb drive is given the letter *G* (named KINSGTON). That's the one I'm using.

8. **Create a new folder for the backup: Right-click in the media's window and choose New⇨Folder from the shortcut menu.**

Sure, you can just copy the files over, but you find life easier to deal with if you create a special backup folder.

9. **Name the folder to reflect the backup contents and today's date.**

I name my work backups with something like `work.2009-06-01.bak`. That's the name `work` for the content, and then the date, and then the letters `bak` for *backup*. This book's backup folder files are named `TroubleAIO.2009-10-10.bak` and so on, depending on the backup date.

10. **Open the folder.**

11. **Press Ctrl+V to paste in the files, which effectively copies them from your PC's hard drive to the backup media.**

12. **Properly eject the media and keep it in a safe place, such as in a firesafe.**

I admit that most people don't put backup media in a safe place. Even I let the media card stick out of the front of my PC's console, looking like a tiny diving board.

For backups to be effective, you must keep making them. You don't follow these steps only one time and then consider yourself finished. Backing up is like doing the laundry: You always have new dirty clothes that need washing. So, just like you're never really done doing the laundry (unless you wash your clothes in the nude), you should back up on a regular schedule to catch those new or modified files.

How often is enough? Once a day seems about right for people serious about their data. That's another reason to consider a real backup program instead of merely copying and pasting files.

✦ I use both techniques: a real backup program and copying and pasting files. I'm very serious about backing up my stuff.

✦ The keyboard shortcut to copy a file is Ctrl+C, and then you press Ctrl+V to "paste" the file copy into a destination folder.

✦ You can copy files in Windows in about a jillion other ways. Anytime you see a book about Windows that's thicker than your fist, it probably lists every last way to copy a file.

✦ The steps in this section work differently if you use an optical disc. The optical disc must be prepared, and then the files must be burned to the disc and, finally, the disc ejected.

✦ In Windows Vista, use the Live File System to create your backup optical discs. See my book *PCs For Dummies* for details.

✦ True, you don't need to include the current date in a filename because Windows slaps a creation date on every file it creates. I add dates to filenames anyway because the date stamp on old files doesn't always survive the transfer to newer computers or media. By putting the date in the filename, I ensure that I always know the backup date.

✦ Another advantage to placing the date in a backup filename is that you can use Windows to easily sort the file list. As long as you use the same format, such as year-month-date, the files are sorted chronologically.

✦ When you're adept with wildcards, you can use them to match groups of backup files by their names or dates. For example, `work.*.bak` matches all my work folders on the backup media.

✦ Then again, using a real backup program allows you to manage all that information automatically. It's your call.

✦ If you forget to properly name a folder, click to select it and press the F2 key. Type the new folder's name.

✦ Another, valid way to back up is to place all your file duplicates into a compressed folder. If you recall from elsewhere in this book, a compressed folder is also a Zip file, which is also an *archive*. The advantage of using a compressed folder for your file-copy backups is that it takes up less space on the backup media.

Using a backup program

Far simpler than copying files is to run a backup program. The benefits are many, as discussed throughout this program.

Windows 7 comes with a Backup program, called Backup and Restore. It's available free with Windows 7 Professional and Ultimate versions, but doesn't come with the Home versions of Windows 7.

Windows Vista comes with the backup program Windows Backup. It's available in all versions of Windows Vista.

Windows Vista Business Edition and Windows Vista Ultimate come with the backup program Complete PC Backup. Unlike the standard Windows Backup program, Complete PC Backup copies all files from your computer to external media. It's ideal for completely restoring your computer system.

Windows XP also comes with a backup program, though it might not have been installed on your PC. You may be able to locate the program by looking in the special folder ValueAdd. You can look for this folder on your PC's start-up hard drive or on drive C or on the Windows XP distribution disc. Open the Msft folder inside ValueAdd, and then open the NTBackup folder. Run the NTBackup program, NTBackup.msi, to install the Windows Backup Utility in Windows XP.

Numerous third-party backup programs are also available, including Internet backup options. Check your local or online software store for the variety. Because of space constraints, I don't cover any of those applications in this chapter.

✦ I'm just guessing at the name Windows Backup for the backup program that comes with Windows. That's because I don't see the words *Windows Backup* on any dialog boxes, windows, or wizards used by the backup program.

✦ Several programs can also back up. For example, Microsoft Word can be configured to automatically create a backup copy of any old document you modify. The Quicken money management program also urges you to create a backup copy of your financial stuff about every third time you close the program.

The Computer Backs Up for You

There's no need to fuss over backup. As long as you configure the backup program properly, things should run just fine. This section explains how to set things up for automatic, reliable backups on your PC.

Getting an external hard drive

The best way to back up in Windows is to get an external hard drive. Forget about using optical discs because you'd have to use a stack of them to back things up. That's a pain. Forget digital media because the capacity is too low. Instead, invest in an external USB or eSATA hard drive.

All the external hard drives I purchased recently require no extra setup on the software side; after plugging in the drive, it pops right up in the Computer window, and I'm ready to use the thing.

Okay, well, some programs may be preinstalled on the hard drive. In fact, the hard drive may have an *autorun* setting, in which case a configuration program may appear whenever you first turn on the drive. Whatever.

- Get an external hard drive that has a capacity equal to or greater than the capacity of your PC's internal hard drive or primary mass storage device.

- If you can afford it, get the largest-capacity external hard drive.

- Another advantage of an external hard drive is that you can easily detach it and put it into a firesafe.

- For more information on external hard drives, see Book I, Chapter 4.

- Feel free to delete any bonus programs that came on the external hard drive.

- It's *your* hard drive. If you don't plan to use the "free" programs that came with the drive, don't. Delete them. Delete anything you don't want on the external hard drive. You need the storage space more than you need those programs.

- Okay, I lied. If you plan to use Complete PC Backup, you probably need to convert the external drive's format. Information is provided in the section "Setting up an external hard drive for Complete PC Backup," later in this chapter.

Finding the backup program

Like many annoying things, Windows changes the location of its backup program with every new edition.

Locate Backup in Windows 7

Don't bother looking for the Windows Backup program on the Start button menu. In Windows 7, the Backup program is found in the Control Panel, for some reason. Here's how to bring it forth:

1. **Open the Control Panel window.**

2. **Beneath the System and Security heading, choose Back Up Your Computer.**

The Backup and Restore window appears, as shown in Figure 1-2. Unlike in Windows Vista, this window is the *only* place you need to go for backing up or restoring files on your PC.

3. **Close the window when you're done looking.**

Later sections in this chapter explain how to use the Backup and Restore window.

System Repair disc option

Full system backup

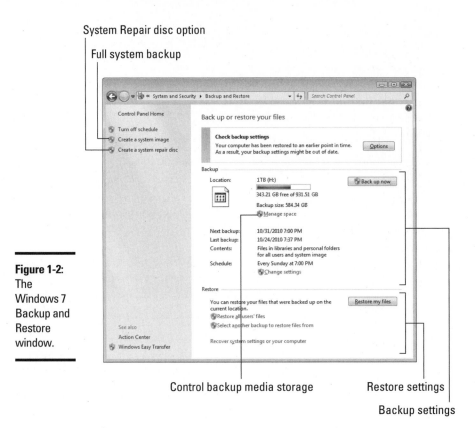

Figure 1-2:
The
Windows 7
Backup and
Restore
window.

Control backup media storage

Restore settings

Backup settings

You can also access the Backup and Restore window from the Windows 7 Action Center. A Backup and Restore link in the lower-left corner of the Action Center window takes you directly to that window. You might also see alerts in the Action Center window, reminding you to back up or alerting you that a scheduled backup failed to run.

Refer to Chapter 1 in Book II for more information on the Action Center.

Locate Backup in Windows Vista

Just to prove how unpopular the operating system is, Windows Vista has two locations for its backup operations: the Backup Status and Configuration window and the Backup and Restore Center.

Backup and Restore Center: Open the Control Panel's Backup and Restore Center icon to view the Backup and Restore Center window, as shown in Figure 1-3. The window lists information about recent backups and allows you to back up your computer or restore files.

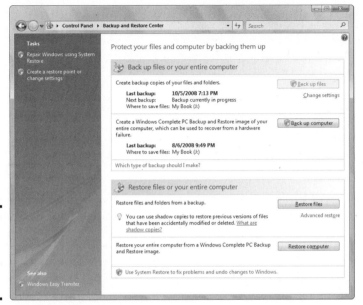

Figure 1-3:
The Backup
and Restore
Center
window.

Backup Status and Configuration: The Backup Status and Configuration window is shown in Figure 1-4. To open the window, from the Start button menu, choose All Programs⇨Accessories⇨System Tools⇨Backup Status and Configuration. The window you see looks similar to the one shown in Figure 1-3.

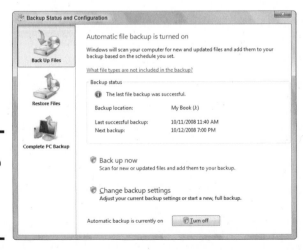

Figure 1-4:
The Backup
Status and
Configura-
tion
window.

Why do you see two locations? I don't know. It's confusing. The windows have lots of overlap, which means that you can do the same things in both of them. Yes, it's dumb and redundant, and a reminder to those who like Windows Vista why it was worthy of derision.

✦ When your version of Windows lacks the Complete PC Backup program, Figures 1-3 and 1-4 look different. The Back Up Computer and Restore Computer buttons, plus the areas they're in, are missing from the Backup and Restore Center window (refer to Figure 1-3). In Figure 1-4, the Complete PC Backup button-thing is missing from the left side of the window.

✦ Of the two locations, I use the Backup Status and Configuration window more often.

✦ Two or three large buttons are on the left side of the Backup Status and Configuration window. The top one, Backup, causes backup options to appear in the window. The second button is Restore, which deals with restoring files to your computer from a backup. See the section "Files from Days of Yore," later in this chapter, for information on restoring files.

✦ A third button that appears on the left side of the Backup Status and Configuration window is Complete PC Backup. See the later section, "The Windows Vista Complete PC Backup," for more information.

✦ You can quickly jump from the Backup and Restore Center to the Backup Status and Configuration window by clicking the Change Settings link beneath the Back Up Files button.

✦ Windows also features, in the notification area, an itsy-bitsy icon that appears whenever a backup is overdue. Clicking the icon opens the Backup Status and Configuration window. Or, is it the Backup and Restore Center window? Oh, it doesn't matter. . . .

Configuring (and making your first) backup

The first backup you make with Windows Backup is different from the rest of them, mostly because this first-time operation also configures the backup software. The following steps walk you through the process and assume that you're backing up to an external hard drive that's always connected to your PC:

1. **Start the Windows Backup program.**

Refer to the preceding section for specifics on conjuring up the proper backup window for your computer.

In Windows Vista, open the Backup Status and Configuration window, though if you haven't yet used Backup, you see a different window from the one shown earlier, in Figure 1-3.

2. Choose the option to configure the Backup procedure.

In Windows 7, choose Set Up Backup.

In Windows Vista, the button is labeled Set Up Automatic File Backup. It looks like a link, but it's a button — a *big* button.

3. If prompted, type the administrator's password or click the Continue button.

The computer desperately looks for backup devices. They include these backup destinations:

Hard Drive: The best choice, though I recommend selecting an *external* hard drive. Although an internal hard drive works, you should choose a separate, physical hard drive inside the computer, not a partition.

Optical Drive (CD or DVD): An okay choice, though if you have more information to back up than can fit on a single optical disc, you'll swap discs. Keep in mind that automatic backups require extra preparatory work.

Network Drive: Works only when the computer is connected to a server type of network. That explains why no shared network hard drive appears on the list.

4. Choose the option Hard Disk.

5. Select the external hard drive from the drop-down menu.

6. Click the Next button.

When your PC has more than one internal hard drive or disk partition, you may be prompted to select those additional disks for backup. I don't recommend doing so unless you keep important files on those drives, such as images, music, or crucial documents.

7. Choose any extra disk drives to back up if prompted.

8. Click the Next button.

The next step is to choose which types of files you want to back up. Rather than let you fuss over this decision, I recommend backing up *all* your personal information; keep all options selected.

9. Click the Next button.

10. Set a backup schedule.

Use the gizmos in the window to set a regular backup schedule. The type and variety of available gizmos depends on whether you select Daily, Weekly, or Monthly from the menu button labeled How Often at the top.

How often you back up depends on how often you use the computer and on the nature of the information it holds. For example, in an office situation, I recommend backing up daily, right after work. At home, I work every day, so I back up every day. For my kid's game computers, I have the backup program run once a week.

11. **Click the Save Settings and Start Backup button.**

Because the next thing you should do after setting up the backup program is to back up your computer, the steps are combined.

Feel free to do something else while the backup proceeds. A typical backup can take anywhere from a few minutes to several hours, depending on how much stuff is being backed up. Browse the web, check your email, play *Spider Solitaire* — you get the idea.

When the backup is completed, a pop-up balloon from the notification area alerts you (unless that feature has been disabled).

12. **Click the Close button to dismiss the Back-Up Files window.**

13. **Close the Backup Status and Configuration window.**

Now count yourself lucky, for several reasons:

First, you just backed up your computer. A second, safety copy of your personal files exists, allowing you to recover them if unwelcome fates befall you.

Second, the computer is backing up to an external hard drive that will always be there and (hopefully) take a long time to fill up. You don't need to set things up or remember to do this or that in preparation.

Third, you set up automatic backups to take place. As long as the computer is on (or sleeping) when that time rolls around, the computer is backed up.

Now you can use your computer with confidence. Files are regularly updated on the backup disk. They can swiftly and accurately be recovered if anything bad ever happens, when anything bad ever happens.

✦ To recover files from a backup disk, see the section "Files from Days of Yore," later in this chapter.

✦ You can also set the backup configuration by clicking the Options button in Windows 7, or in Windows Vista by clicking the Change Settings link in the Backup and Restore Center window.

✦ Yes, your computer must be on when the backup takes place. The computer can be in either Stand By or Sleep mode. That's okay: Windows wakes the computer and runs the backup. But an automatic backup doesn't run when the computer is turned off or in Hibernation mode (which means that it's turned off).

✦ Backing up your data consumes computer resources. Be sure to schedule a backup for when you're not doing anything else, especially something processor-intensive on the computer, such as editing video, working with images, or playing a sophisticated computer game (full screen with action).

✦ Every time you back up your files, the Windows Backup program creates a new, unique *backup set* on the external hard drive. These sets are maintained like a database for use by the Restore portion of the Backup program. That way, not only can older files be recovered, but older *versions* of those files can also be recovered as well.

Confirming that the backup worked

When you do things correctly, your computer is backed up all the time automatically. But how do you know?

In Windows 7, you can check the Action Center to confirm that the backup worked. In fact, the Action Center instantly alerts you to a failed or skipped backup.

In Windows Vista, to confirm that the backup took place, open either of the two backup windows: Backup Status and Configuration or Backup and Restore Center (refer to Figures 1-3 and 1-4). I prefer viewing the Backup Status and Configuration window (refer to Figure 1-4). Ensure that the Back Up Files button is selected (in the upper-right part of the window), and then read the information in the Backup Status area. It not only lists the last successful backup but also describes when the next scheduled backup takes place.

Because Windows Vista has no Action Center, a warning pops up from the notification area whenever an automatic backup doesn't take place. You can click the icon to open the Backup Status and Configuration window or right-click the icon to choose Backup Now and immediately run the backup procedure.

Making an immediate backup

Do you have moments of brilliance? Perhaps a burst of productivity? I do. Sometimes I seem to just churn out a lot of work in a short amount of time. When that happens, I want to make doubly sure that I have a backup copy of my stuff. I call it an *immediate* backup.

Sometimes I make an immediate backup by simply copying a file or folder to a media card. That works. But when I end up doing work all over the computer, the only way to ensure that I catch everything is to simply usurp the scheduled backup and run an instant, immediate backup. Here's how:

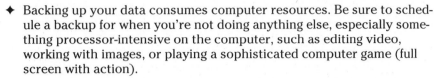

1. **Start your PC's backup program.**

   Refer to the section "Finding the backup program," earlier in this chapter, for the specifics.

2. **In Windows Vista, ensure that the Back Up Files button is selected from the left side of the Backup Status and Configuration window.**

3. **Click the Backup Up Now button.**

4. **If prompted, type the administrator's password or click the Continue button.**

   Windows starts running the backup program. While it runs, you're free to do something else, which I recommend because backing up files takes time.

5. **Click the Close button when the backup is done, and then close the Windows Backup window.**

There's no need to do an immediate backup if your computer's backup schedule is tight — say, once a day. But on those PCs where backup is a weekly or monthly routine, I recommend making an immediate backup once in a while, just to be safe.

Clicking the Back Up Files button in the Backup and Restore Center window can also start an immediate backup.

Modifying the backup routine

If you originally configured the backup properly, there's no need to change things. Then again, I suppose that they wouldn't have provided a way to modify the backup routine if people always guessed the proper ways to do things in the first place.

You have a number of reasons to modify the computer's backup routine:

✦ You want to back up more often.

✦ You want to choose a different set of files to back up.

✦ You added another internal hard drive and need to back it up.

✦ You need to reset the time to later in the day because the backup routine is causing your PC to lag while you're playing *Call of Duty*.

✦ You just bought a newer, larger external hard drive to write off as a tax expense, and you need to start using it.

✦ Other reasons I cannot think of right now.

To "recajigger" the backup routine, follow these steps:

1. **Start the Windows Backup program.**

In Windows Vista, ensure that you're using the Backup Status and Configuration window.

2. **In Windows Vista, ensure that the Back Up Now button is chosen from the left side of the Backup Status and Configuration window.**

3a. **In Windows 7, click the Options button and then choose Change Backup Settings.**

If the Options button isn't visible, click the link Change Settings, found beneath the statistical information in the center of the window.

3b. **In Windows Vista, click the big Change Backup Settings button.**

4. **If prompted by the User Account Control (UAC) warning, click the Continue button or type the administrator's password to proceed.**

5. **Work through the wizard to reset whatever backup options need resetting.**

As when you first configured the backup, you choose the external backup media, decide what to back up, set the schedule, and select other options.

In Windows 7, set the backup schedule by clicking the Change Schedule link on the final screen.

6. **In Windows 7, click the Save Settings and Exit button.**

In Windows 7, after changing the schedule, you can click the Back Up Now button to begin a new backup. Otherwise, just close the window and the backup will happen on schedule.

In Windows Vista, a backup takes place immediately after you make changes; sit back and watch. Click the Close button when the backup has completed, and then you can close the Backup window.

✦ In Windows 7, you can change only the backup schedule by clicking the Change Schedule link in the Backup and Restore window.

✦ Also see the earlier section, "Confirming that the backup worked," for information on how you can ensure later that the backup has taken place according to your wishes.

**Book VI
Chapter 1**

Backup, Backup,
Backup

Stopping a backup in progress

Why stop a backup? Primarily because the Backup program is a resource hog. If you need to use your computer and not have random pauses and stops (especially when playing *Call of Duty*), you can stop a backup.

The key to stopping a backup is to find the Stop Backup button.

In Windows 7, you find the Stop Backup button by clicking the View Details button in the Backup and Restore window while a backup is taking place. In the window that appears, you see a progress bar for the current backup as well as the Stop Backup button.

In Windows Vista, the Stop Backup button appears in either the Backup Status and Configuration window or the Backup and Restore Center window while a backup is taking place.

You're asked to confirm that you want to stop the backup after you click the Stop Backup button.

✦ There's nothing wrong with stopping a backup; it doesn't destroy any data that's already on the backup hard drive. Stopping the backup does, however, prevent the backup program from making copies of all the files in need of backing up.

✦ You can't resume a stopped backup, but you can make an immediate backup to make up for the stopped backup. See the earlier section, "Making an immediate backup."

Disabling the backup program

You have no way to postpone a backup, but you can turn off the backup program, essentially disabling automatic backup. Follow these steps:

1. **Open the Windows Backup program.**

In Windows Vista, use the Backup Status and Configuration window.

2. **In Windows Vista, ensure that the big Back Up Files button is selected on the left side of the window.**

3a. **In Windows 7, click the Turn Off Schedule link, found on the left side of the window.**

3b. **In Windows Vista, click the Turn Off button, found at the bottom of the window.**

4. **If you're assaulted by a UAC warning, click the Continue button or type the administrator's password.**

5. **Close the Backup Status and Configuration window.**

You can easily resume the backup schedule again:

In Windows 7, choose the link Turn On Schedule, found near the bottom of the Backup part of the window.

In Windows Vista, click the Turn On button, which conveniently replaces the Turn Off button in Step 3.

✦ Backup programs don't run when you turn them off.

✦ Turning off the backup program is one way to suppress the continual pop-up messages about missing the backup. For example, on my laptop, I turn off the backup program when I'm on the road because I'm away from the external backup drive. Upon returning home, I turn on backup again.

Files from Days of Yore

Backup files are nice to have, but they do no good unless it's possible to fish out one or more files from time to time, or even — in the worst-case scenario — when you lose all your files. In that case, you rely on Backup's lesser used but wonderfully opposite program, Restore. This section explains how to use Restore.

✦ Most of the information here is specific to the Backup program that comes with Windows 7 and Windows Vista. The Windows XP backup program has a similar Restore option, as do various third-party backup programs.

✦ I refer to the restore procedure as a *restore program, restore operation,* or sometimes just *restore.* It's not a different program from the Windows Backup utility — just a different part of the same program.

✦ Unlike when you use the backup program, there's no need to configure Restore.

✦ The restore operation works best when you have a recent file backup. Back up your files! Do it often.

✦ You can also restore files from a manual backup or file copy. The operation works the same as creating the manual backup: Look on the backup media for the file you want, and then copy it back to the computer's primary storage device, the hard drive.

✦ Yea verily, even when you have a backup file, you don't get everything back. All files created or modified since the last backup are lost. But it's better than the alternative of losing them all.

Restoring something from the last backup

The beauty of having a backup set of files is that you can recover a file, one that's long lost or destroyed or just a previous version of something you once had. So, although you cannot use the backup sets to restore your misspent youth, you can perform the following steps to restore a file from a backup set:

1. **Start the Windows Backup program.**

In Windows Vista, open the Backup Status and Configuration window.

2. **In Windows Vista, click the Restore Files button on the left side of the window.**

Because the Windows Vista backup window is *modal,* it shows either the backup settings or the restore settings. You want the Restore Files portion of the window to be shown.

3a. **In Windows 7, click the button Restore My Files.**

3b. **In Windows Vista, click the Restore Files button.**

Windows Vista assaults you with two additional choices:

> **Files from the latest backup:** The file you restore is the most recent version of the file that's backed up. Most often, this choice is the one you want.

> **Files from an older backup:** Use this option only when you want to recover an older version of a file, as discussed in the next section.

In Windows 7, you click the link Choose a Different Date because it assumes that you always want to restore files from the most recent backup.

4. **In Windows Vista, choose the option Files from the Latest Backup and click the Next button.**

You use the next screen to choose which files and folders you want to back up. The screen shown in Figure 1-5 is from Windows 7; the Windows Vista version is similar.

5. **Add files and folders to be recovered.**

You can use three buttons on the right side of the screen (refer to Figure 1-5) to add files to the list. The buttons are named differently for Windows 7 and Windows Vista, but they do similar things:

> *Search:* Click the Search button to summon the Search for Files to Restore window, where you can hunt down the files you want to restore.

> *Browse for Files/Add Files:* Click this button to choose individual files to restore.

> *Browse for Folders/Add Folders:* Click this button to restore an entire folder — and all files and folders in that folder.

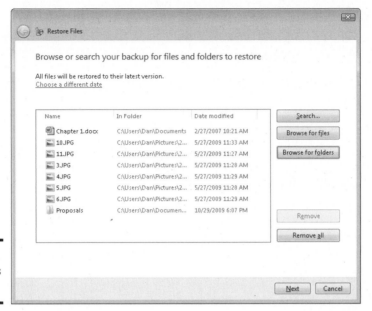

Figure 1-5:
Choose files
to restore.

After choosing a button, you see another dialog box from which you choose the files. The dialog box lists files on the backup, not on your computer.

In Windows 7, choose your user account from the list of folders on the left side of the window to locate your personal files and folders. Then browse the folders to find the files or folders you're looking for.

In Windows Vista, you use the Add Folder to Restore dialog box, similar to the Open or Browse dialog box in the window.

Keep adding the files you want to restore; repeat Step 5 and keep clicking the buttons to collect all the files and folders you want to restore. In Figure 1-5, you see a smattering of files I'm restoring on my PC.

When you need to restore only a single file, just restore that file. Don't feel pressured to restore a bunch of them just because the program lets you.

6. **Click the Next button.**

   You need to choose where to restore files. You have two options:

   In the original location: The files and folders you selected are placed back on the hard drive in the same folder where Backup found them. Most of the time, this option is the one you choose, especially for file recovery.

   In the following location: You get to select in which folder to place the restored files. This option is best for recovering an older version of a file where you don't want to overwrite the current version.

7. **Click the Restore button or the Start Restore button.**

   The files are restored.

8. **Click the Finish button.**

9. **Close the Backup window.**

The only kink in the hose happens when you attempt to restore a backed-up file and the same file still exists on the hard drive. A warning message appears, similar to the one shown in Figure 1-6.

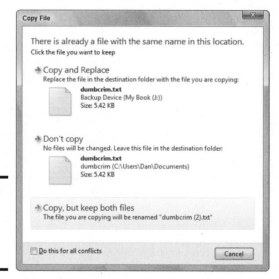

Figure 1-6: Restoring a file that already exists.

You have three options:

Copy and Replace: The backup file replaces the existing file. This option is most likely the one you want, unless you want to keep both versions of the file. In that case, choose the option Copy and Keep Both Files.

Don't Copy: The file isn't restored. Choosing this option basically undoes the restore operation for that lone file.

Copy, but Keep Both Files: The file is restored but given a new name. Both files exist in the same folder: the current one and the restored copy with a number in parentheses after its name.

If you have any doubt, please choose the option Don't Copy. You can always try to restore the file later, but you don't want to lose something unexpectedly.

+ You can also start the restore operation in the Backup and Restore Center window by clicking the Restore Files button.

+ The files you restore aren't removed from the backup set. If the need arises, you can restore them again.

+ Recovering a deleted file from the Recycle Bin is easier than recovering a file from a backup.

+ See Book II, Chapter 8 for information on the Previous Versions command in Windows 7 and Windows Vista.

Restoring from an older backup

Unless otherwise directed to do so, the restore operation looks for only the most recently backed-up file. But what about older files? What if you have a file that's evolved and you need to recover an earlier version? Maybe you want both the earlier version and the current version. Windows Backup can handle that.

To scour older backup sets, follow the steps presented in the preceding section. But rather than use the most current backup, you select an earlier one.

For Windows 7, click the link Choose a Different Date, in Windows Vista, use the dialog box that appears to choose a recent backup. You can also use the menu button to select a time period to see backups from even earlier than last week.

In Windows Vista, you choose the option Files from an Older Backup. After clicking the Next button, you see a list of recent backup sets. To see even older backup sets, put a check mark by the option Show Backups Older than 30 Days.

Choose a date and time in the window. The dates march back through time as long as you've been backing up your computer (though older backup sets are purged as the backup media gets full).

After choosing a date, click the Next button. At that point, the restore operation proceeds as described in the preceding section.

Be sure that you choose the option Copy But Keep Both Files when restoring the older version, when you do want to keep both files.

Restoring all your personal files

The restore operation works simply for restoring files or folders that get smooshed or seemingly vanish overnight. You can also restore *all* your personal files if anything nasty ever befalls them. The steps work the same as for restoring any file or folder, but you must take care to find the right folder. As you may expect, the steps are different between Windows 7 and Windows Vista.

✦ This type of restore operation doesn't recover all files on your computer. For that operation, see the section "The Windows Vista Complete PC Backup," later in this chapter.

✦ You can recover all your PC's files even when your version of Windows lacks the Complete PC Backup. You start by reinstalling Windows and then reinstalling your program files. After that, use Restore to recover your personal files as described in this section. The process isn't perfect, and it's time consuming, but it works.

Restore your files in Windows 7

The methods for restoring all your personal files in Windows 7 are pretty easy:

1. **Get to the Backup and Restore window.**

2. **Click the button Restore My Files.**

Use the most recent backup, which is presented in the Restore Files window.

3. **Click the Browse for Folders button.**

4. **From the list of folders on the left side of the window, choose the one with your account's name.**

For example, on my PC, I choose Dan's Backup.

5. **Click the Add Folder button.**

Now your account folder, and all its contents, are selected for restoration.

6. **Click the Next button.**

In the Restore Files window, the option to restore files to their original location is chosen. That's the one you want; to restore all your files.

7. **Click the Restore button.**

8. **Sit back and watch.**

The operation may take some time, depending on how much stuff you're restoring.

9. **Click the Finish button and close the Backup and Restore window.**

Restore your files in Windows Vista

To get all your personal files back in Windows Vista, follow these steps:

1. **Click the button Restore Files on the left side of the Backup Status and Configuration window.**

From the Start menu, choose All Programs⇨Accessories⇨System Tools⇨Backup Status and Configuration to open the window.

2. **Click the Restore Files button.**

3. **Choose the option Files from the Latest Backup.**

   I'm assuming that you want the most recent version of the file, which makes sense.

4. **Click the Next button.**

   The key to restoring your personal files is to choose your account's personal folder.

5. **Click the button Add Folders.**

   The Add Folder to Restore window appears.

6. **From the Address bar, choose Users.**

   The Users folder is "one folder up" from your account folder.

   You may have to click the angle-brackets thing (<<) at the left end of the Address bar to display a drop-down folder menu. From this menu, you can choose the Users folder.

7. **Click to select your account folder from the list.**

   Your account folder has the same name as your account in Windows. On my PC, the folder is named Dan.

8. **Click the Next button and continue to restore the files.**

   Follow through with Step 7 and onward in the section "Restoring something from the last backup," earlier in this chapter.

The Windows Vista Complete PC Backup

Suppose that the worst possible thing happens, and I'm not talking about that dream coming true where you're naked in public. I'm talking about that dreaded day when you lose everything on your computer: your files, music, pictures, videos, programs, all that pornography, Windows — everything. Yes, even your great American novel. Such a day of woe, but it need not be when you use the Complete PC Backup, as described in this section.

+ Complete PC Backup is a feature found only in Windows Vista Business, Windows Vista Enterprise, and Windows Vista Ultimate editions.

+ Windows 7 automatically backs up your entire PC, so there's no Complete PC Backup equivalent necessary for its version of Backup.

+ The odd thing about dreaming that you're naked in public is that no one else in the dream seems to mind that you're naked. That's because the dream isn't really about being *nude*; rather, it's about being exposed, or vulnerable. Roll that in your cigar and smoke it, Dr. Freud!

Understanding Complete PC Backup

The Complete PC Backup program is different from the regular backup program. Unlike the automatic backup, which is a file copying and archiving utility, the Complete PC Backup program is a disk imaging program. It sounds cool — and it is.

A *disk imaging* program doesn't copy individual files to a backup disk. Instead, it copies the raw information from a hard drive — specifically, the main drive partition on your PC. That's where Windows, your programs, and all your personal files and other information are stored. All that stuff is compressed and copied to an external hard drive.

Unlike when you use a regular backup, you have no way to pluck out individual files or folders from a disk image backup. Still, that's not the reason behind Complete PC Backup. No, the reason you use it is to fully restore your computer's hard drive in case of a disaster. The restore recovers everything: Windows, program files, and all your personal information. Ta-da! You get your computer back.

You access the Complete PC Backup program from the standard backup locations in Windows: the Backup and Restore Center window (refer to Figure 1-3) or the Backup Status and Configuration window (refer to Figure 1-4). Both locations launch the same program, though I prefer (as usual) to use the Backup Status and Configuration window.

Setting up an external hard drive for Complete PC Backup

To use an external hard drive for the Complete PC Backup, you must ensure that the drive is formatted with the NT File System, or NTFS. Because most external hard drives come formatted with the FAT32 standard, it means that the drive must be converted.

The conversion operation is technical, but not that difficult to work through. Here are the steps:

1. **Open the Computer window and make a note of the external hard drive letter and its volume label.**

In Figure 1-1, earlier in this chapter, you can see that the external hard drive is named My Book and is given drive letter J. You need to know this drive letter.

The drive's *volume label* is a smidgen of text used to identify the media by name. It's not used for much in Windows, except for instances that involve formatting or conversion. In the Computer window, the volume label name appears in front of the drive letter. For drive J, the label is `My Book`.

2. **Close the Computer window.**

   The next step is to open an administrator Command Prompt window.

3. **From the Start menu, choose All Programs⇨Accessories and then right-click the Command Prompt icon.**

4. **Choose the command Run As Administrator from the pop-up menu.**

   The Administrator Command Prompt window opens and displays a command prompt.

5. **Click the Continue button or type the administrator password to continue.**

6. **Type the command** convert D: /fs:ntfs, **but replace D with your PC's external drive letter.**

   For example, on my PC, the external drive letter is J, so I type this command:

   ```
   convert j: /fs:ntfs
   ```

   Double-check your typing! A colon appears after the drive letter followed by a space. A colon appears between fs and ntfs.

7. **Press Enter.**

   If you see the message Drive is already NTFS, you're fine; skip to Step 10. Also, confirm that you typed the proper drive letter in Step 6.

   You're prompted for the drive's volume label:

   ```
   The type of the file system is FAT32.
   Enter current volume label for drive J:
   ```

   To cancel the operation at this point, press Ctrl+C.

8. **Type the drive's volume label.**

   You can always reopen the Computer window if you forget what the label was, but because you made a note of it in Step 1, you won't have to.

9. **Press Enter.**

   Windows converts the drive's internal structure to the NTFS format. Again, none of the drive's files are erased.

   The process can take several minutes, depending on the drive's capacity. You see some information displayed on the screen as you wait.

   When the operation has been completed, you see the text Conversion complete and then another command prompt.

10. **Type** exit **and press Enter to close the Administrator Command Prompt window.**

To confirm that the drive has been converted, open the Computer window and select the external drive's icon. The bottom part of the window, the Details pane, should describe the file system as NTFS. (If the Details pane doesn't show up, choose Layout➪Details Pane from the Organize button menu.)

✦ Converting the drive to NTFS doesn't change how you can use the drive. As far as you're concerned, the drive still shows up and holds files just like before. Internally, however, Windows is using the drive more efficiently.

✦ Most operating systems now available understand the NTFS format and can use an NTFS hard drive just as well as they can use a FAT32 hard drive.

✦ Converting the drive is *not* the same as reformatting the drive. The reformat operation erases the drive's contents.

✦ Also see the section "Getting an external hard drive," earlier in this chapter.

✦ If you attempt to use Complete PC Backup with a non-NTFS external hard drive, you're suitably thumped with a warning. Better convert the drive before that happens.

Backing up your entire computer

I recommend running Complete PC Backup on your PC. Doing so is in addition to having a regular backup schedule, as described elsewhere in this chapter. Here's how to pull off the Complete PC Backup operation:

1. **Open the Backup Status and Configuration window.**

Choose All Programs➪Accessories➪System Tools➪Backup Status and Configuration from the Start button's menu.

2. **Ensure that the big button Complete PC Backup is selected on the left side of the window.**

The Backup Status and Configuration window appears, as shown in Figure 1-7.

3. **Click the button Create a Backup Now.**

4. **Type the administrator's password or click the Continue button.**

5. **Choose the option On a Hard Drive.**

Trust me: You *do not want* to use optical discs. The Complete PC Backup operation takes a zillion of them.

6. Select the external, NTFS-formatted hard drive from the menu button.

If the disk doesn't have enough room, you're warned; choose another disk or work in Windows to remove excess files from the disk.

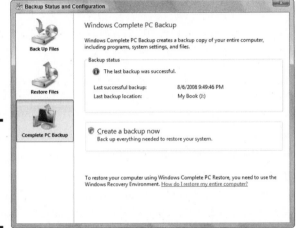

Figure 1-7:
The Complete PC Backup is done here.

7. Click the Next button.

8. If necessary, choose any additional disk drives or partitions in your computer for backing up, and click the Next button.

A summary screen appears, listing which disks will be backed up and how much space will be used.

If you already ran Complete PC Backup, you see a message describing how only newer information will be added to the backup; unlike in a traditional backup, a new backup set isn't created when you run Complete PC Backup a second time.

9. Click the Start Backup button.

10. Do something else while the program runs.

Actually, the backup may not take that long. An image backup doesn't consume as much time as a file-by-file backup.

You can continue to use your computer while the Complete PC Backup is running. Browse the web. Write a letter. Play a game of *Spider Solitaire*.

When the backup is complete, you see the message The Backup Completed Successfully.

11. **Click the Close button and then close the Backup Status and Configuration window.**

Unlike in a regular backup, you have no need to refresh the Complete PC Backup often. In fact, the thing cannot be scheduled; you can only run Complete PC Backup manually. But continue to make regular backups as described earlier in this chapter. Those backups keep your own files current, which is more important than keeping a full image of the PC's hard drive.

You can run the Complete PC Backup again, and I recommend doing so every six months or thereabouts. When you run the Complete PC Backup again, it makes a note of only the changed items on your PC, so it keeps the image backup fresh and also avoids eating up a whole lot of disk space.

Beyond a couple of times a year, there's really no reason to run the program more often.

✦ You can also start a Complete PC Backup operation by clicking the Back Up Computer button in the Backup and Restore Center window.

✦ The Complete PC Backup can be done whether or not you turned on the regular PC backup. See the section "Disabling the backup program," elsewhere in this chapter.

✦ The backup image is placed on the external hard drive in a folder named `WindowsImageBackup`. It's separate from any folders used with the standard backup program.

Restoring your entire computer

If you're astute, you probably noticed that the Backup Status and Configuration window (refer to Figure 1-7), lacks an option to do a restore operation for Complete PC Backup. There's no Restore button. I mention this because I wasn't astute and really didn't notice that the button was missing until just a moment ago. That's probably because I've never really needed to restore my entire PC. (Not yet, anyway — knock on wood.)

A Restore Computer button can be found in the Backup and Restore Center window (refer to Figure 1-3). Clicking this button is useless; a warning dialog box appears when you click it. The warning basically says:

Using the Complete PC Backup restore operation is designed only for disaster recovery. As such, it can be run only by starting your computer with a recovery disc or booting into a RECOVERY hard disk partition. For details, refer to Book II, Chapter 8. Use the System Recovery Options menu to choose Windows Complete PC Restore, and then follow the directions on-screen.

✦ The recovery option isn't one to use casually. For example, you would be silly to run the Complete PC Backup restore procedure simply to recover a lost file. Instead, use the Backup program as described in the section "Files from Days of Yore," found earlier in this chapter.

✦ Recovering your hard drive with the Complete PC Backup program erases the computer's hard drive.

Book VI
Chapter 1

Backup, Backup, Backup

Chapter 2: Pampering the Hard Drive

In This Chapter

- ✔ Grabbing more disk space
- ✔ Cleaning up the hard drive
- ✔ Using compression
- ✔ Working with disk tools
- ✔ Setting a new drive letter
- ✔ Assigning a drive to a folder
- ✔ Formatting media
- ✔ Creating a new volume
- ✔ Making a hard drive larger

The PC's hard drive is a robust little dude. Hearty and reliable, it stores the stuff that makes your computer *your* computer. It's your PC's personality. It's the primary storage device, where your precious files are stored. Obviously, taking care of the hard drive should be a top priority. This chapter explains what you can do.

- ✦ This chapter assumes that your PC's primary storage device is a hard drive.
- ✦ Eventually, the SSD will take over for the hard drive. As such, some of the regular maintenance described in this chapter will change, as noted in this text.

Free Up Some Storage Space

This section is sponsored by the word *capacity*. It's a great word, especially when applied to mass storage on a computer. The more capacity you have, the more room for storing your stuff — not just programs and your documents but also massive files, such as your music collection or videos. You need the storage space! Dwindling room on the hard drive is the number-one hard drive problem.

Looking at the storage situation

Forget files, folders, and whatnot. I'm writing about *bulk* here. The stuff you create and collect on your PC's hard drive — the primary storage device — can grow to colossal proportions. Yet while all that stuff accumulates, the hard drive itself doesn't change from its original capacity. It's like a closet: You can keep buying new clothes, but it doesn't make the closet any larger.

The hard drive is the PC's primary storage device. It's home to three vital items:

✦ The computer's operating system: Windows

✦ The software — programs and applications — that let you do things with your computer

✦ Your stuff: files, documents, media, and other things you create or collect

The ideal situation is to have a hard drive that boasts a capacity to hold all three things, not only for now but also for as long as you plan to own your computer. Most people, sadly, aren't that forward-thinking. Not only that, but the casual computer buyer also doesn't have a clue to how much storage is enough. So they buy less than they need.

Before you have a conniption fit over disk storage, you should first check on how the hard drive is doing. How much space is being used? How much space is available? How soon before you run out? These questions can be answered by following these steps:

1. **Open the Computer window.**

   In Windows XP, it's the My Computer window.

2. **Right-click the main hard drive icon and choose Properties from the shortcut menu.**

   On the General tab, shown in Figure 2-1, you see detailed information about disk usage as well as the handy purple pie chart, illustrating disk usage.

3. **Close the disk's Properties dialog box when you're done looking.**

4. **Close the Computer/My Computer window.**

The more purple you see in the disk size pie chart, the better. (Purple is the Free Space chunk of the pie.) The smaller the purple slice, the sooner you're due for a disk capacity solution. Your options are to remove files, compress files, or compress the entire disk to recover some space. Another solution is to buy a second hard drive. The most complex solution is to replace the hard drive, though that strategy can be quite technical.

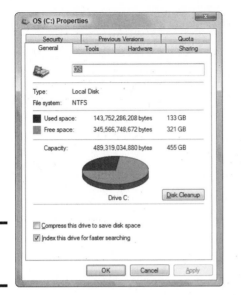

Figure 2-1:
Hmmm.
Disk pie.

The rest of this section describes methods for increasing disk capacity.

At what point do you worry? I'd say when capacity reaches 90 percent, it's a good time to start seriously cleaning up a hard drive. Even before that point, however, you should prune away things you don't need.

✦ When hard drive storage (free space) ever falls below a certain percentage, Windows displays a warning message. If you see the message, I highly recommend that you act immediately.

✦ The term *hard drive* applies to the PC's primary storage device. It's known on most PCs as drive C, though it can be another drive letter or you can have multiple hard drives inside your PC.

✦ Dwindling disk capacity is an old issue — almost as old as having hard drives in PCs.

✦ Back in the late 1980s, software solutions were devised to deal with full hard drives. The software compressed files on the hard drive on the fly, allowing for more room. But the software solution avoids the real issue, which is having a larger hard drive in the first place.

✦ See the sections "Using file compression" and "Compressing every dang doodle file on a hard drive," elsewhere in this chapter, for more information on creating room on a hard drive by using software solutions.

✦ As this book goes to press, the typical PC is sold with a hard drive capacity of about 300GB. That's fine for most usage, though more is always better.

✦ See my book *PCs For Dummies* (Wiley) for a better understanding of what a gigabyte (GB) is, as well as more information on how storage capacity is measured.

✦ Perhaps the best solution for dealing with the storage situation is a hardware one: Get another hard drive, either an internal or external model. More important, *use* that hard drive. See the section "Moving your program files," later in this chapter.

✦ Another storage space solution is to remove software you don't use. See Book II, Chapter 6 for information on uninstalling software in Windows.

✦ Ironically, the pie chart is used to show capacity on all mass storage formats, including media cards that don't use round discs for storage.

✦ Optical discs are always shown as being full. That's because they're read-only. When you're burning a new optical disc, the software you use to burn the disc reports how much space is available.

Things that gobble storage space

Back in the old days, it was computer software that grabbed the biggest chunk of disk space. Programs once asked whether you wanted to install the entire thing on the hard drive or keep portions of the program on a CD. The culprits are now your own files — specifically, media files.

Video: The most space-consuming file you can add to your computer is a movie. Feature films eat up several gigabytes. Even regular video files are very large; a 2-minute video can be 30MB or more.

Music: Expect to use about 1MB of disk storage for each minute of music you store on your PC.

Pictures: Image files can be small, such as those you find on the Internet or exchange by email. But Raw image files — those you want to keep so that you can print a 4-x-5 enlargement (or larger) — they occupy several megabytes of storage.

Programs: A typical program uses about 20MB of disk storage, though some computer games can use gigabytes of storage. But that value is *static:* After you install the program, it doesn't continue to consume more space. The documents you create in the program use space, but the size of the program itself doesn't grow.

Documents: The documents you create on your computer take up the least amount of space. A word processing document uses 100K or so, which is 0.1MB — just a thin slice of disk storage.

You can estimate how much disk storage you need on your PC. I use a formula to calculate it, though it doesn't help to know the formula after you buy the hard drive. Generally speaking, the average size of about 300GB is good enough for most uses. If space concerns you or you plan to produce videos or music, get a higher-capacity hard drive — 500GB or larger.

Removing large files

Where's that big fish? No, not a fish. A *whale*. Where are the whales located in the ocean that is your PC's hard drive? I mean, *big* files. Have you ever done a large-file search? Not a comprehensive search, but a search for large files? If you've never done this type of search and disk capacity is running low, now is the time.

In Windows 7, follow these steps to find gigantic files lumbering on your PC:

1. **Press Win+F to bring forth the Windows Search window.**

2. **Click the mouse in the Search text box in the upper-right corner of the window.**

3. **Type** size:gigantic**.**

That's **size**, a colon, and then the word **gigantic**. Do not follow *gigantic* with a period.

Instantly, you see the window populated with files larger than 128MB, which is apparently where Microsoft believes the threshold of *gigantic* to begin.

To see a wider array of files, type **size:huge** to see files between 16MB and 128MB; type **size:Large** to see files in the 1-to-16MB range.

4. **Sort the list by right-clicking in the window and choosing Sort By⇨Size.**

5. **If the file list is sorted from smallest to largest, right-click in the window again and choose Sort By⇨Descending.**

6. **Examine the search results to find hefty files ready for deletion.**

I spy some huge files in the list, mostly downloads that are larger than 1GB. Whoa. Rather than have those files consume a major chunk of storage space, I archive them to a DVD+R disc and then delete them from my PC's hard drive.

To archive a file, insert a DVD+R into your PC's recordable optical drive. Select the file you want to archive, and then click the Burn button on the toolbar. (You can do all this from within the Search Results window.)

Delete a file by selecting it and pressing the Delete key on the keyboard.

7. **Close the Search Results window when your reign of destruction is at an end.**

Obey these steps in Windows Vista to find some whale-size files:

1. **Press Win+F to summon a Search Results window.**

2. **Click the Advanced Search button.**

3. **From the Location button, choose Indexed Locations if it's not already chosen.**

4. **From the Size KB button menu, choose Is Greater Than.**

5. **Type 5000 in the Add a File Size text box.**

   You're looking for files larger than 5MB.

6. **Click the Search button.**

   Windows scours the hard drive for files larger than 5MB. The drive has a bunch of them. Of course, Windows doesn't sort them for you — it doesn't even list the file sizes in the Search Results window.

7. **Ensure that Details is chosen from the Views toolbar button menu.**

8. **Right-click any column heading in the list of found files.**

9. **From the shortcut menu, choose Size.**

   You're adding the Size column to the list of details.

10. **Locate the Size column and drag it to the right, just after the Date Modified column.**

    Refer to Video 621 for details on how to work the preceding four steps in this list.

```
www.dummies.com/go/troubleshootingandmaintaining
    yourpcaio2e
```

11. **Click the Size heading until the list of files is sorted from largest to smallest.**

    It may take two clicks to do it. The results I see on my PC are shown in Figure 2-2.

12. **Peruse the list.**

    If you're like me, you see a file you downloaded or created ages ago — something you needed once but no longer. If so, great: You can delete or archive the file.

    To delete a file, select it and then press the Delete key on the keyboard.

    To archive a file, select it and press Ctrl+X to cut it. Then open a folder window on an external drive or a media card, and move the file to that drive by pressing the Ctrl+V key.

13. **Close the Search Results window when you're done.**

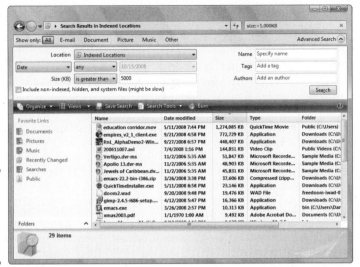

Book VI
Chapter 2

Pampering the Hard Drive

Figure 2-2:
Whopping
files found
by Windows
Vista.

In Windows XP, heed these steps to go whale-size file watching:

1. **Press Win+F to bring up the Search Results window.**

2. **Click the link on the left side of the window: All Files and Folders.**

3. **From the Look In drop-down menu, choose My Documents.**

4. **Click the chevron to expand the What Size Is It area.**

5. **Choose Specify Size (in KB).**

6. **Choose At Least.**

7. **Type** 5000 **in the Size text box.**

You're directing the Search command to scout out files larger
than 5MB.

8. **Click the Search button.**

Windows looks through your stuff, trying to find files you created or collected that are larger than 5MB. The files are listed in the Search Results
window.

To sort the files from largest to smallest, click the Size heading.

9. **Peruse the list.**

What are you looking for? Large and largely forgotten files. If you don't
recognize the file, delete it. If you recognize it and don't need it,
delete it.

To delete a file, select it and then press the Delete key on the keyboard.

You can also archive the file by moving it from the hard drive to an external hard drive, burning it to an optical disc, or moving it to a media card.

10. **Close the Search Results window when you're done.**

I use the term *archiving* to simply imply moving a file from the main hard drive, the one running out of room, to another hard drive, optical disc, or media card. The notion is that you still want the file but don't necessarily need to have it handy.

✦ You can hone the search for large files by specifying specific file types. For example, specify the filename `*.wmf` to look for all Windows Media Files (videos) on the hard drive. Additional large file formats are shown in Table 2-1, in the Type column.

✦ View the Search Results window in Details view. Choose Details from the Views toolbar button in Windows 7 or Windows Vista; in Windows XP, choose View⇨Details from the menu.

✦ If you delete the file, it merely moves to the Recycle Bin. You don't see much disk storage space savings — until you empty the Recycle Bin.

✦ You can press Shift+Delete to instantly delete a file and recover the disk space used by the file. The Shift+Delete operation isn't reversible, however. Use it with care.

✦ I prefer that you *archive* program files as opposed to delete them outright.

✦ To move a file, you cut and paste it. Cut it from its current folder window or select it from the Search Results window by pressing Ctrl+X. Then open the window where you want to move the file, and press Ctrl+V to complete the operation.

✦ You may find some compressed folders when perusing the list. Be careful! You want to confirm the compressed folder's contents before you whisk it off into oblivion.

✦ If you're using the Windows Media Center to record live TV, you should peruse the list of recorded shows to see whether any require deleting. Recorded TV takes up a *lot* of disk space. To delete a recorded TV show in the Windows Media Center, choose Recorded TV from the TV + Movies menu, select a recorded show, and choose Delete from the list of buttons that appears. Click Yes to confirm the deletion.

✦ Music files can be removed from the Windows Media Player by right-clicking the music file's icon and choosing Delete from the pop-up menu.

Table 2-1	Filename Extensions for Large Files	
Filename Wildcard	*File Type*	*Description*
*.AVI	Audio Video Interleave	QuickTime or Real Player media format
*.BMP	Bitmap Graphics	Windows Paint document, also used by Windows for wallpaper
*.EXE	Executable	A program file (don't delete — uninstall!)
*.MOV	Quicktime Movie	Apple QuickTime movie format; video files
*.MP3	MPEG Audio	Music or sound file
*.PDF	Portable Document Format	Adobe Acrobat document
*.WAV	Windows Sound	Music or sound file
*.WMA	Windows Media Audio	Windows Media Player sound file
*.WMF	Windows Media File	Windows Media Player media format; videos
*.WMV	Windows Media Video	Windows Media Player video file
*.ZIP	Compressed Folder	Zip file archive (delete carefully!)

Using Disk Cleanup

A handy way to remove lots of files you don't need on a hard drive is to employ the aptly named Disk Cleanup tool. What Disk Cleanup does is locate files that can easily be removed to free up some disk space, especially files that may not be obvious to you, such as temporary files used by Windows or when browsing the Internet.

To run Disk Cleanup in Windows 7 and Windows Vista, follow these steps:

1. **From the Start button menu, choose All Programs⇨Accessories⇨ System Tools⇨Disk Cleanup.**

2. **In Windows Vista, choose the option My Files Only.**

   I recommend that you start with your own files first. If that doesn't remove enough files, repeat these steps and choose the option Files from All Users on This Computer.

3. **If prompted, choose the mass storage device that you want to clean up.**

   The prompt appears only when you have multiple storage media on your PC. You probably want to choose drive C, the main storage device.

4. **In the Disk Cleanup dialog box, place check marks by all the items you want to remove.**

   The dialog box is shown in Figure 2-3. It's okay to place check marks by *all* items. Those things wouldn't be listed if they were crucial to the computer's operation.

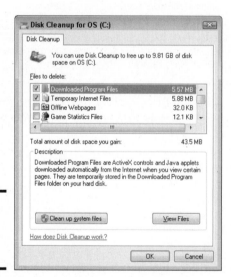

Figure 2-3:
The Disk
Cleanup
dialog box.

There's one exception to placing check marks by all the items, however: Hibernation File Cleaner. Do not remove that item if you use hibernation on your computer.

5. **Click OK.**

   You're not quite there yet.

6. **Click the Delete Files button to begin the cleanup process.**

   Wait while the disk is being cleaned. When the process is complete, the window goes away.

In Windows 7, you can click the Clean Up System Files button (refer to Figure 2-3) to remove unneeded bits and pieces of various Windows updates that may be littering the hard drive. Click the button before Step 4, and then after the system files are cleaned up, you can proceed with removing other disk detritus.

You run Disk Cleanup in Windows XP by adhering to these steps:

1. **From the Start button menu, choose All Programs⇨Accessories⇨ System Tools⇨Disk Cleanup.**

2. **In the Disk Cleanup dialog box, click the More Options tab.**

**Book VI
Chapter 2**

**Pampering the
Hard Drive**

   The Disk Cleanup dialog box's More Options tab lists additional items worthy of cleanup. Three buttons are labeled Clean Up, which take you to various other locations in Windows:

   Windows Components: Clicking the Clean Up button opens the Windows Components Wizard window, where you can remove (or add) various pieces of Windows. You can also display the Windows Components Wizard by opening the Add/Remove Programs icon and clicking the button Add/Remove Windows Components on the left side of that window.

   Installed Programs: Clicking the Clean Up button opens the Add/ Remove Programs window, which can also be opened from the Control Panel.

   System Restore: Clicking the Clean Up button by this option displays a Yes/No dialog box. Click the Yes button to remove all but the most recent restore point, which is a safe move.

3. **Click the Disk Cleanup tab.**

4. **Place check marks by all items you want to remove.**

   You can select an item beforehand to read its description. There's nothing in there to be concerned about; the Disk Cleanup program doesn't present you with options that would damage your computer or its performance — at least not on the Disk Cleanup tab.

5. **Click the OK button.**

   A Yes/No dialog box appears.

6. **Click the Yes button to begin the cleanup process.**

   Windows removes the files you specified. When it's finished, the window goes away. You're done.

Because there's no final report, I recommend that you check the hard drive's size to see any improvement in the storage situation. Refer to the steps in the section "Looking at the storage situation," earlier in this chapter.

✦ You can also access the Disk Cleanup utility from a disk drive's Properties dialog box by clicking the Disk Cleanup button on the General tab. Refer to Figure 2-1.

✦ See Book II, Chapter 8 for more information on System Restore.

Moving your program files

I'm often asked whether it's possible to move program files from the primary hard drive, C, to either a secondary internal hard drive or an external hard drive. It's a good question, but one that has a complex answer.

First, and most important, you cannot simply move a program file. In Windows, programs aren't single files. Often, they're not even found in a single folder, but rather in dozens of places on the hard drive. The file locations are referenced throughout Windows, which means that moving any of them would cause the program to fail. A simple file-move operation will be unsuccessful.

Second, I recommend using a second, internal hard drive as your PC's supplemental disk storage. The problem with an external hard drives is that it might get its drive letter suddenly reassigned when you add new media to the PC. That would be bad. An internal hard drive, on the other hand, has a solid, reliable drive letter.

Finally, the way to move a program file is to uninstall it and then reinstall it on the secondary hard drive. That's it.

You need to uninstall the program because most software doesn't let itself be installed twice on the same computer. Besides, the idea is to clean up disk space, and the original installation must be removed.

After uninstalling the program, reinstall it. Set the location for the software to be installed as the secondary drive. Often, to set the location, you must complete a customized, or "advanced," installation. Choosing that option allows you to specify where the file is installed, and you can select the second hard drive as the file's destination.

To keep your computer organized, I recommend creating a Program Files folder on the secondary hard drive. Install the programs in that folder.

After setting up the program on the new hard drive, it should run as it did before. Nothing is lost, and as a bonus, you free up some disk space.

✦ This trick works only when you remember to install all new software on the secondary drive. So the next time you run an installation program, remember to choose the secondary hard drive as its location or destination. To make it happen, you choose the Advanced or Customized installation option.

✦ If you have problems registering the reinstalled program, contact its developer. When you purchased the program, you bought the right to install it on your computer. Some program licenses prohibit reinstalling the same program, which is disappointing. But in most cases, reinstalling shouldn't be an issue.

✦ It helps if you reinstall the largest programs on the secondary drive. You can discover how big programs are by viewing the window where you uninstall software in Windows. The size of the programs installed is listed along with other information about the program. Refer to the information about uninstalling software in Book II, Chapter 6.

Using file compression

Windows comes with a feature I call *blue file compression*. It's an on-the-fly type of compression that stores files on a disk in a smaller size. When you open the file, it's decompressed to its original size. So, as a user, you don't notice the compression in any way other than that your files consume less disk space.

Oh, and I call it blue file compression because the compressed files are listed in the folder window with blue text rather than black. Here's how to blue-compress a file:

1. **Right-click the file or folder icon to compress.**

When you compress a folder, you compress all files and folders held in that folder. It's a simple way to compress a slew of files all at once.

2. **Choose Properties from the shortcut menu.**

3. **On the General tab of the Properties dialog box, click the Advanced button.**

The Advanced Attributes dialog box appears, as shown in Figure 2-4.

4. **Place a check mark by the option Compress Contents to Save Disk Space.**

5. **Click OK, and then click OK again to dismiss the Properties dialog box.**

Figure 2-4:
The
Advanced
Attributes
dialog box.

You see the name of the file or folder displayed in blue text when it's compressed. Beyond that, there aren't really any changes; the file can still be manipulated or opened as it was before. It does, however, take up less space on disk.

✦ Also see the nearby sidebar, "Compression isn't always the answer."

✦ To remove compression from a file, repeat the preceding steps, but in Step 4 remove the check mark.

✦ An option in the Windows XP version of the Disk Cleanup program lets you compress seldom-used files. It's another way to automatically reduce the file size of the documents and whatnot that you seldom use. I recommend it. See the section "Using Disk Cleanup," earlier in this chapter.

✦ The encryption attribute (refer to Figure 2-4) is available only on NTFS-formatted hard drives. See Chapter 1 for information on the NTFS format.

✦ You can also archive files into a compressed folder, which takes up less space. In fact, for seldom-used files, I recommend creating a compressed folder and moving the files into it. Although this method compresses the files, keep in mind that you cannot open a file stored in a compressed folder, nor does the Windows Search command find files (or their contents) inside a compressed folder.

Windows offers a single command that sifts through every file on a hard drive and applies the compression attribute to them. The result is that the entire hard drive is compressed and takes up less space. This strategy isn't a surefire solution to a cramped hard drive, but it can be done.

Compression isn't always the answer

Digital compression works because a file has a lot of redundant information in it — lots of bytes and chunks that repeat over and over. Compression software takes advantage of the situation by removing those repeating chunks of code. Using magic I can't begin to explain (or understand), a file that once sucked up 1MB of disk space can suddenly consume only 64KB or so. That's a lot of savings.

Compression, however, isn't a magic lozenge for curing a cramped hard drive. That's because only certain files compress well.

For example, text files can be smooshed down to become quite small. Windows Bitmap files (BMP) compress well. Most of the files on your hard drive, however, are probably already in a compressed state. Therefore, they don't benefit from additional compression. In fact, by compressing them, you might make your computer run slower because of all the overhead required to decompress the file on the fly.

Compressing every dang doodle file on a hard drive

To compress an entire hard drive, follow these steps, though I recommend that you read this entire section before you begin:

1. **Open the Computer window.**

   In Windows XP, open the My Computer window.

2. **Right-click a drive icon and choose Properties from the shortcut menu.**

3. **Place a check mark by the item Compress This Drive to Save Disk Space.**

4. **Click the Apply button.**

5. **Ensure that the second option is selected in the Confirm Attribute Changes dialog box: Apply Changes to Drive *X*:, Subfolders and Files.**

6. **Click OK.**

7. **If prompted with a UAC, click the Continue button and then type the administrator's password or click Continue (again) to continue (again).**

   If during this process, you encounter file errors, click the Ignore All button. Files get busy and are in use by other processes, for example. There's no way to compress them all.

8. **Wait.**

   It takes a long time to assign the compression attribute to all files on the hard drive. On my test hard drive, with 48GB of files, Windows is reporting that compression will take 12 hours to complete. Definitely, this is an overnight operation. (See? I told you to read this section before diving in.)

   If you grow weary, you can always click the Cancel button and resume later.

9. **Close the drive's Properties window.**

   No confirmation dialog box appears when the operation is over, which is kind of a letdown.

To confirm that the files on the drive have been compressed, open the drive icon and view the files; you discover that the files are compressed and sport blue filenames. You also note that some folders are compressed and others are left alone. That's okay: The compression being used by Windows doesn't compress everything well.

The kicker, however, is to discover whether any disk storage savings have resulted. To view this information, open the drive's Properties dialog box and take a look. (Specific steps are offered in the section "Looking at the storage situation," earlier in this chapter.)

✦ Blue file compression works on the fly. Windows decompresses files when you access them, and then it recompresses those files when you save them back to disk.

✦ Even though Windows may compress a file, it doesn't necessarily mean that the file will occupy less disk space. That's because not all files compress well. See the earlier sidebar, "Compression isn't always the answer."

✦ The type of disk compression covered in this section isn't the same as the old DoubleSpace program that came with earlier versions of Windows.

✦ To decompress the drive, repeat the preceding steps but remove the check mark in Step 3.

Disk Drive Tools

When I was so very young, I thought that the yellow oil light on my car's dashboard was the friendly reminder that the oil needed changing. After the car's engine seized, though, I recognized my error. As my friend Brad says, maintain your toys and you'll have them forever. Those who practice regular maintenance enjoy the blessings of keeping their possessions in good shape. The PC's hard drive, with all its precious data, is no exception. This section explains how to keep that spinning gizmo of digital goodness in tiptop shape.

✦ Most computer maintenance is done automatically in Windows 7 as well as in Windows Vista. Even so, you should consider manually running the programs discussed in this section, or at least becoming familiar with them.

✦ Just in case maintenance doesn't happen automatically, you can use task scheduling in Windows to set up automatic maintenance. See Chapter 3.

Understanding fragmentation

Don't believe the doomsayers: Fragmentation is natural and accepted. All storage media has some level of fragmentation. It's related to how information is stored by the operating system and, honestly, it's beneficial. It's too much fragmentation that does you in.

Fragmentation can be a tough subject to comprehend. Most people who use a computer don't even understand the concept of a file. To grasp the concept of fragmentation, which is really *file* fragmentation, you have to accept that everything stored on computer media is stored as files.

Files are stored on storage media, such as the main hard drive. The fragmentation part occurs when the file isn't stored as a single chunk of information. Instead, the file is split: Part of it may be stored in one spot on the storage media, and another part of the file might be stored elsewhere. The file isn't damaged because the operating system knows where to find it. But the file is *fragmented* or, as the nerds say, *noncontiguous*.

To help you form a picture of how file fragmentation works, think of your PC's hard drive as a parking lot surrounding a large municipal stadium. Figure 2-5 illustrates this concept; note that the stadium isn't drawn to scale and has far too few parking spaces.

A parking lot is basically asphalt. For the parking lot to function, it must be painted with spaces, as shown in Figure 2-5. A similar thing happens to the hard disk surface, though the surface material is some form of magnetic oxide, not asphalt. The painting of "parking spaces" on a disk is called *formatting*.

Both painted parking spaces and media formatting are similar concepts: Without parking spaces or formatting, cars and files wouldn't know where to go. Chaos would ensue.

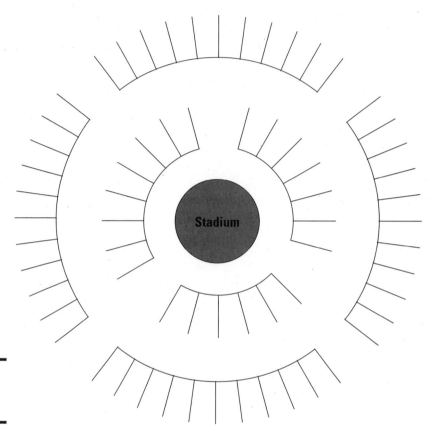

Figure 2-5:
A stadium
parking lot.

Now pretend that it's an hour before game time. The parking lot is beginning to fill. Cars come in one side of the parking lot and are directed by cheerful parking lot attendants in orange tunics to fill the empty spaces in an orderly manner. Each car is parked next to another car, as illustrated in Figure 2-6.

Your PC's hard drive fills with files in a manner similar to the way the stadium parking lot fills with files: Files are placed on the media one after the other, just like the cars illustrated in Figure 2-6.

The stadium parking lot and your PC's hard drive fill up sequentially. But the hard drive doesn't stay that way for long. On your computer, you probably delete a file now and then, or you uninstall a program. Windows itself creates and deletes temporary files all the time. If this situation were duplicated in the stadium parking lot, the picture would resemble Figure 2-7. You see empty parking spaces where cars have left because the home team is losing 52-3 and people are leaving in droves.

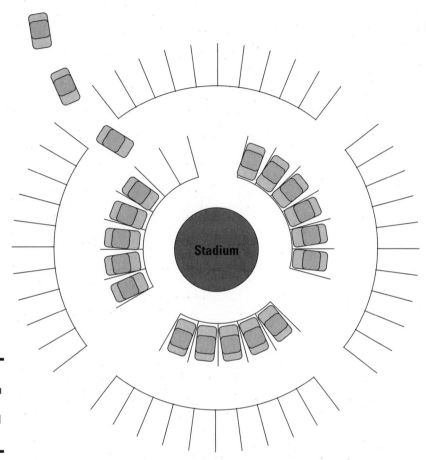

Figure 2-6:
The stadium
parking lot
begins to fill
with cars.

Is the parking lot in Figure 2-7 full? Of course not. Plenty of spaces are available. But if the cheerful parking lot attendants in orange tunics continue to fill the parking lot sequentially, they may report that the parking lot is full — despite parking spaces still being available.

That same kind of nonsense can happen in your computer. If the operating system continues to fill the disk sequentially, you might see a hard drive with half its storage space available, yet the operating system reports that it has no more room for files. Obviously, this type of situation would tick you off.

To make the best use of the available storage space, the operating system begins to split up, or *fragment,* new files stored on the hard drive. So, when a new file is added to the hard drive, the operating system fits it into the available empty space. If the file fits, great. If the file doesn't fit, the operating system splits the file into smaller chunks that do fit. That's *fragmentation.*

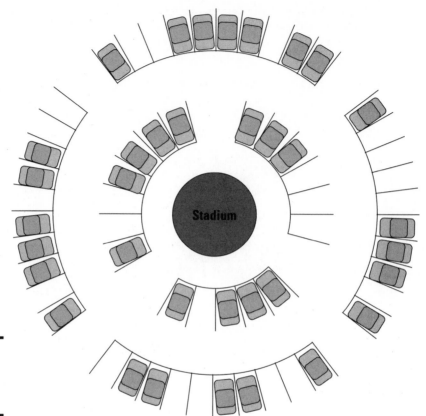

Figure 2-7:
Spaces
open up as
cars leave.

A fragmented file isn't damaged; the operating system merely reassembles the file's pieces into a single whole when the file is accessed. So information isn't lost. A tad more overhead is involved, however, in reassembling a file's fragments.

Problems arise when files are overly fragmented. As you continue to use the hard drive, more and more files are split up to take advantage of the available space. More fragments equals more overhead to reassemble the files when they're loaded or saved. The result of all that overhead is sluggish disk performance.

The solution to the fragmentation problem is to use a defragmentation, or *defrag*, utility.

A defragmentation utility does two things:

Attempts to put all files stored on disk into nonfragmented chunks: Using the parking lot example, the cheerful parking lot attendants in the orange tunics rearrange the cars so that all cars in a tailgate party are parked together.

Removes the empty spaces between the files: Files on disk are reordered, just like emptying the stadium parking lot and reparking all the cars so that it has no empty spaces. In real life, this task would be a waste of time, but because the computer can automate it, it happens quickly and efficiently. And no one complains.

Some defragmentation utilities may even do a third task: Relocate important and frequently accessed files to the start of the disk. Such a feature greatly improves disk performance.

Book VI
Chapter 2

The moral of this story is that fragmentation is a good and necessary thing. To keep your PC's hard drive working at maximum efficiency, it should be regularly defragmented.

✦ Formatting is also required for nonspinning media, such as USB thumb drives and media cards.

✦ Do not defragment SSDs, media cards, or thumb drives! Sure, they get fragmented, but their speed is fast enough that the fragmentation doesn't diminish performance. Also see the Technical Stuff note at the end of this section.

✦ Defragmentation utilities appeared early in the PC's life, at just about the time hard drives were becoming popular. (Before hard drives, PC users stored information on floppy disks.)

✦ The speed improvement from running those early defragmentation utilities was stunningly dramatic. Early tools such as Mace Utilities, Norton Utilities, and PC Tools sold defragmentation programs as a miracle cure for a sluggish PC.

✦ The PC's storage media *always* contains some fragmentation. That's just the nature of the business of storing files on a computer. Too much fragmentation, however, leads to sluggish performance. Regular hard drive maintenance must include some type of disk defragmentation.

✦ Another reason not to defragment SSDs, media cards, and thumb drives is that current technology allows for the information stored on the media to be accessed only a given number of times. The number is huge, so the device will be useable for years and years. Yet by defragmenting a media drive, you decrease its life span dramatically.

Finding the tools

Windows keeps its storage media maintenance utilities in one handy place, nestled in the storage media's Properties dialog box, on the Tools tab, as shown in Figure 2-8. Well, not all the tools: Disk Cleanup is found on the General tab in the Properties dialog box; see the section "Using Disk Cleanup," earlier in this chapter.

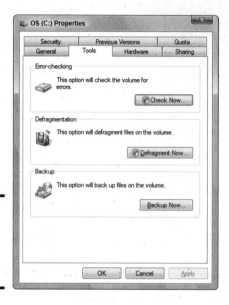

Figure 2-8:
Media
mainte—
nance
options.

You visit the Tools tab to perform routine disk maintenance, as covered elsewhere in this chapter. Here's how to get there:

1. **Open the Computer window to peruse storage devices attached to your PC.**

The window is titled My Computer in Windows XP.

2. **Right-click a storage media icon, such as the hard drive, C.**

Because you use drive C more than any other drive, it's most likely due for defragmentation.

3. **Choose Properties from the shortcut menu.**

The media's Properties dialog box appears.

4. **Click the Tools tab in the Properties dialog box.**

If you see no Tools tab, the media cannot be defragmented. Otherwise, you see media maintenance options; refer to Figure 2-8.

Error-checking: Runs a utility that checks the storage media for errors. See the section "Checking the storage media," later in this chapter.

Defragmentation: Starts the Defrag utility, covered in the next section.

Backup: Available only when Windows Backup has been installed on the PC. Refer to Chapter 1.

5. Choose a button to run a specific utility.

Running the error-checking or defragmentation utilities in Windows Vista requires that you type the administrator's password or click the Continue button to proceed. These operations affect all users on the computer.

Refer to the following sections for information on how to run the individual storage media utilities.

**Book VI
Chapter 2**

Pampering the
Hard Drive

Defragmenting a hard drive

If you haven't defragmented your PC's hard drive in a while (or ever), you're in for a treat. A freshly defragmented hard drive makes your computer seem brand new (but without that out-of-the-box smell).

REMEMBER

Your PC's main hard drive is automatically defragmented on a regular schedule when you use Windows 7 or Windows Vista. Even so, you can manually defragment media by following the steps outlined in this section.

In Windows 7, follow these steps to pull a manual defrag of the PC's main hard drive:

1. Open the Computer window.

2. Right-click the media you want to defragment, such as the main hard drive, C.

3. In the drive's Properties dialog box, click the Tools tab.

4. Click the Defragment Now button.

The Disk Defragmenter window appears. Rather than plow ahead and potentially waste time defragmenting a drive that doesn't need it, check the media's current fragmentation.

5. Click the Analyze Disk button.

6. Wait while Windows checks the defragmentation on the media.

Check the Percent Fragmented value by the disk in the Disk Defragmenter window. If it's zero, there's no point in continuing: Skip to Step 8.

Even when the drive shows 0 percent fragmented files, you can still proceed with defragmentation. No media can be fully defragmented, so the Windows Defragmenter will always find something to do.

7. **Click the Defragment Disk button.**

   Windows defragments the media. Sit back and watch, or do something else, though you shouldn't do anything on your computer while the media is being defragmented.

8. **Click the Close button, and close up any other windows you opened.**

To manually defrag the hard drive, or any media, in Windows Vista, follow these steps:

1. **Open the media's Properties dialog box and, on the Tools tab, click the Defragment Now button.**

   Steps describing how to open the Tools tab are listed in the preceding section.

2. **Type the administrator's password or click the Continue button.**

   Windows Vista is equipped to automatically defrag the computer's hard drive. Rather than see a defragment screen, you see a dialog box that lets you customize the defragmentation schedule, customize the Defragmenter utility, or just defragment anyway. Honestly, if the schedule is to your liking, there's nothing left to do. But that's probably not why you're reading this section.

   If scheduled defragmentation isn't enabled, place a check mark by the option Run On a Schedule (Recommended).

3. **Click the button Defragment Now.**

4. **Choose the media to defragment.**

   Windows automatically chooses all media that is attached to your PC and can be defragmented. If you just want to fragment the main hard drive, deselect the rest of the media.

5. **Click OK.**

   Windows begins defragmenting the drive. Unlike viewing the glorious windows of Defrag programs past (see Figure 2-9), you just get to stare at a tiny, spinning loop while the media is defragmented.

   You can use your computer while it's being defragmented.

   When the operation is complete, the spinning loop gizmo goes away. You see the Last Run item in the Disk Defragmenter window (see Figure 2-9), updated to reflect the recently completed operation.

6. **Close the Disk Defragmenter window.**

7. **Close the disk's Properties dialog box as well as the Computer window.**

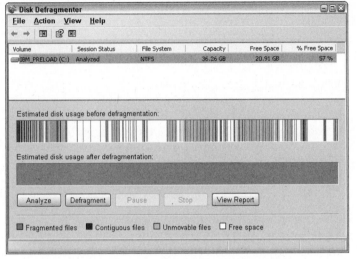

**Book VI
Chapter 2**

Pampering the
Hard Drive

Figure 2-9:
Disk
defragmen-
tation in
Windows
XP.

To run the Defragmentation utility in Windows XP, follow these steps:

1. **From the My Computer window, right-click the media's icon and choose Properties from the shortcut menu.**

2. **In the media's Properties dialog box, select the Tools tab.**

3. **Click the Defragment Now button.**

The Disk Defragmentation window appears, similar to the one shown earlier, in Figure 2-9.

4. **Click the Analyze button.**

Windows performs a scan of the drive, providing visual feedback about the fragmentation situation, which is shown later, in Figure 2-10.

You can click the View Report button to see a list of fragmented files and the number of fragments. Some files have hundreds of fragments. One file on my PC was reported to have 123,784 fragments. (I should win a prize.) Click the Close button to dismiss the Analysis Report window.

5. **Click the Defragment button.**

Depending on how large the disk is and how long it's been since it was first fragmented, defragmentation can take several hours. Be prepared to wait.

6. **Click the Close button when the operation is complete.**

7. **Close the Disk Defragmenter window.**

8. **You can also close the disk's Properties dialog box and the My Computer window.**

You may not notice any drastic improvement in disk performance, especially when the hard drive is frequently defragmented. But if you just defragmented your PC's hard drive for the first time, prepare to be stunned.

✦ You cannot defragment a network drive.

✦ Do not defragment a media card or flash drive. These drives have a limited number of "writes" available to them. That is, the media can support data being written to it a finite number of times. This number can be huge, but it's a real number; after reaching the number, the media becomes useless. By not defragmenting a media card or flash drive, you avoid accelerating the deadline.

✦ Optical drives cannot be defragmented. Though, honestly, I don't believe that optical drives can even become fragmented in the first place.

✦ Even after running the Defragmentation utility, file fragments remain on the hard drive. That's just the nature of disk storage. Please don't obsess and run the defragmentation utilities over and over, trying to get a perfectly defragmented hard drive.

✦ See Chapter 3 for more information on Task Scheduler and how to automatically schedule disk maintenance on your PC.

✦ Also see Book II, Chapter 4 for information on speeding up a slow PC.

Checking the storage media

The storage-media checking tool in Windows has its roots in the old DOS utility chkdsk, which is pronounced "check disk." That old program could fix some disk problems, but most users treated it like a lucky charm, running it whenever the computer did anything unexpected and hoping that chkdsk did some sort of magic. Ooga-booga.

You can still check the disk in Windows. The modern Check Disk program still seeks out errors on storage media, fixes them if it can, and does other routine household disk chores.

To run Check Disk, follow these steps:

1. **Open the Computer window.**

2. **Right-click the icon for the media storage gizmo you want to check.**

3. **Choose Properties from the shortcut menu.**

4. **In the Properties dialog box, click the Tools tab.**

5. **Click the Check Now button.**

6. **If prompted, type the administrator's password or click the Continue button.**

The Check Disk dialog box appears, similar to the one shown in Figure 2-10.

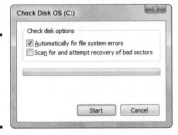

Figure 2-10:
It's not
impressive,
but it's
useful.

7. **Ensure that a check mark appears by the option Automatically Fix File System Errors.**

8. **To check more thoroughly, place a check mark in the box next to Scan For and Attempt Recovery of Bad Sectors.**

   You have no reason to choose this option when you're not experiencing disk trouble.

9. **Click the Start button.**

10. **If you see a warning regarding checking a disk in use, click the Schedule Disk Check button or the Yes button.**

    By scheduling a disk check, you place a one-time task into Windows Task Scheduler, which runs later, when you're not using the specified media. Often, that's as far as you get in this operation, especially when you attempt to check drive C, the PC's main hard drive.

    If you choose to schedule a disk check, the operation is over. The disk check takes place the next time you start Windows, so there's nothing else to do for now. Skip to Step 12.

11. **Click the Close button in the Checking Disk dialog box.**

    Hopefully, no problems were found. If they were, the dialog box explains what to do. Or not.

12. **Close the storage device's Properties dialog box.**

13. **(Optional) Close the Computer window.**

If you had to schedule a disk check, the operation takes place when you restart Windows.

If anything awry is discovered, it's fixed automatically. That's why you selected the Automatically Fix File System Errors box.

✦ Certain disk utilities are more thorough than Check Disk. Or, at least they seem to be more thorough. Honestly, if the hard drive is malfunctioning, it's probably a hardware issue. Though software cannot fix hardware problems, it can help you avoid them. Check Disk quarantines unusable portions of a hard drive, but it cannot repair them.

✦ Generally speaking, bad sectors and disk errors are signs that a hard drive needs replacing. These errors increase dramatically over time, especially when the disk is more than five years old. See Book I, Chapter 4 for more information.

✦ Check Disk is good at cleaning up *lost* files, or file fragments that exist on storage media but don't belong to any specific file. These *missing clusters* can hinder disk performance. Check Disk eliminates them automatically.

✦ The number-one cause of a missing cluster is an improper shutdown.

✦ The Check Disk routine runs automatically every time your computer recovers from a bad shutdown. For example, if you just turn off the computer without properly shutting down, Windows is smart enough to run Check Disk automatically the next time the computer starts.

✦ For a while, the Check Disk program was renamed ScanDisk. The name was retired after Windows 95.

✦ Even though the program is now named Check Disk, and its command line counterpart is chkdsk, it isn't the same program as the original DOS chkdsk.

Media Manipulation Mania

You can do a few advanced things with the storage media on your PC — specifically, the hard drives. These aren't regular, everyday types of activities but, rather, nuts-and-bolts, deep-tissue types of things. The bad news is that the overall topic is technical. The good news is that Windows gives you an amazing array of tools. This section explains what the tools are and how to use them.

✦ Few people bother working with their computer's storage media at an advanced level because they don't know that they can. Even so, the activities described in this section aren't things you do regularly.

✦ The information in this section is technical. I make a lot of assumptions. If you need a review, see Book I, Chapter 4 for some basic terms, descriptions, and explanations. I assume that you know what all the basic disk terms mean, such as *partition*, *format*, and *volume*.

✦ Be careful when you work with storage media on a technical level! You can easily and irreparably damage the media, losing data stored there. That's a bad thing, especially for your PC's main hard drive, which is why Chapter 1 covers backing up your data.

Opening the Disk Management console

The *Disk Management console* is a special location in Windows where you can manage your PC's storage devices.

To open the Disk Management console, follow these steps:

1. **Open the Control Panel.**

2a. **In Windows 7, choose System and Security and then choose Administrative Tools.**

2b. **In Windows Vista, choose System and Maintenance and then choose Administrative Tools.**

2c. **In Windows XP, open the Administrative Tools icon.**

3. **In the Administrative Tools window, open the Computer Management icon.**

4. **In Windows Vista, click Continue or type the administrator's password.**

The Computer Management window appears. It contains various *consoles*, which are kind of like miniwindows that use a specific format for displaying and controlling information.

5. **On the left side of the window, choose Disk Management.**

It's beneath the Storage heading.

When you open the Disk Management item in the Computer Management window, you see the Disk Management console. You can flip over to Figure 4-2 in Book I if you need to see an illustration. Otherwise, the following sections deal with various fun and useful things you can do in the Disk Management console.

Changing drive letters

The stars may be fixed in the heavens, but your PC's drive letters aren't fixed in the computer's universe. It's possible to change the letter assigned to a storage device. The question remains: Why would you want to?

I like to keep my external drive letters consistent. Back in the old days, I assigned the CD-ROM drive the letter *R* and the DVD drive the letter *V*. That way, if I modified the PC by adding another internal drive, the optical drive letters weren't rearranged, which would often be the source of anguish.

I don't recommend merely changing a drive letter "just because," though! Randomly reassigning drive letters can lead to unimaginable woe, especially if a program is installed on a drive and you change the drive's letter. End of warning.

Here's how to assign a storage device a new drive letter:

1. Ensure that you're not using the drive.

By *using,* I mean that no files are open on that drive and no programs are being run from the drive; not even folder windows from the drive are open. You can still change the drive letter when you ignore my device, but odds are good that things won't go smoothly for you.

2. Open the Disk Management console.

Specific steps are provided in the preceding section.

3. Right-click the storage media you want to modify.

The storage media are listed by drive letter in the upper center part of the window.

4. Choose the command Change Drive Letter or Paths from the shortcut menu.

A Change Drive Letter or Paths dialog box appears. It sports the icon and letter for the drive you selected and lists any associated drive letters and pathnames.

5. Click the Change button.

The Add Drive Letter or Path dialog box appears, as shown in Figure 2-11.

Figure 2-11:
Disk drive descriptors are manipulated here.

A warning dialog box appears if you attempt to change the system drive, such as drive C, or the drive where Windows is installed. Click OK and then Cancel, and then choose another drive.

6. Choose a new drive letter from the drop-down list.

Only drive letters not currently used by other devices or network drives are available. Because of the limitations of the Latin alphabet, only 26 drive letters are available.

7. Click OK.

An important warning appears. Some programs rely on consistent drive letters. For example, older software may always insist that the optical drive have the same letter now as it did when the program was installed. Changing the drive letter means that the program cannot find itself and will then refuse to run.

8. **If you want to proceed, click Yes to confirm that you read the warning.**

   The drive is instantly assigned a new letter. Further, a new window opens, displaying the drive's contents.

9. **Close any windows that remain opened.**

To reset the drive letter, just repeat these steps. You can assign and reassign drive letters all the do-dah day.

See Video 622 for an onscreen demonstration of changing a drive letter.

> www.dummies.com/go/troubleshootingandmaintaining
>   yourpcaio2e

✦ Review Book I, Chapter 4 for information on how drive letters are assigned as the computer starts.

✦ I don't recommend that you change the drive letter on an internal drive — including internal hard drives, optical drives, and any memory card readers you might have installed. Doing so may screw up previously installed programs.

✦ The drive used by Windows is known as the *system drive*. Its drive letter cannot be reassigned while Windows is running, nor is there really any reason to do so.

✦ Other operating systems don't use the Windows method of assigning drive letters to storage volumes. Instead, on those operating systems, the entire file system exists as a single entity; there's only one root folder. Any drives added to the system are mounted or joined to a folder, and they become part of the single file system. Perhaps a future version of Windows will take advantage of this type of file system structure and end the drive letter nonsense.

Joining a drive to a folder

It may seem silly, but it's not: You can secretly disguise storage media as folders. It makes no sense until you see how useful it can be.

Consider that your hard drive is getting full. You added a second hard drive to create more room, but you keep forgetting to use it. What if you could turn the entire hard drive into a folder on drive C? That way, it would be easier to reference, access, and use the hard drive's contents.

To map a storage device to a folder, follow these steps:

1. **Open the Disk Management console.**

   Specific steps are provided in the section "Opening the Disk Management console," earlier in this chapter.

2. **Right-click the icon representing the storage device you want to map to a folder.**

3. **Choose the command Change Drive Letter or Path from the shortcut menu.**

4. **Click the Add button.**

   The Change Drive Letter or Paths dialog box appears (refer to Figure 2-11).

5. **Click the Browse button.**

   The Browse for Drive Path dialog box appears. It's not totally unfriendly, but it assumes that you know where things are on the hard drive. Here's some helpful info:

   - Your personal folder, the User Profile folder, is located beneath the Users folder in Windows 7 and Windows Vista.

   - In Windows XP, your personal folder is found in the Documents and Settings folder.

   - Your personal folder has the same name as your account name.

6. **Use the Browse for Drive Path dialog box to locate the mounting point for the drive.**

7. **If you already set up an empty folder as the mounting point, skip to Step 9.**

8. **Click the New Folder button and create a new, empty folder.**

   The empty folder serves as the location where Windows will mount the disk drive or storage media.

9. **Click OK to set the folder you selected.**

   Back in the Change Drive Letter and Paths dialog box (refer to Figure 2-11), you see the full, technical pathname to the folder that's listed.

10. **Click OK.**

The storage media is now linked to the folder you specified. When you open the folder, you see the contents of the storage media's root folder displayed, but the pathname on the Address bar reflects the new folder you created.

You can add multiple mounting points for a single drive letter. Simply repeat the steps in this section to map the drive to another folder. A single hard drive, for example, can be mapped into several locations.

To dismount the storage media from its linked folder, repeat Steps 1 through 3. In the Change Drive letter and Paths dialog box, select a pathname and click the Remove button. Click the Yes button to confirm.

✦ Removing a disk drive's mounting point from a folder doesn't delete the folder. In fact, you can use that empty folder again to reattach the disk drive or storage media in the first place.

✦ The storage media can still be accessed from its drive letter just as before; mounting the drive (or whatever storage media) in a folder doesn't erase the drive from the Computer/My Computer window.

✦ The old word for attaching a disk drive to a folder was *join*. DOS featured a `join` command. In Windows 7 and Windows Vista, the term is *junction*.

Formatting a volume

Once upon a time, disk formatting was a regular computer chore. That's because floppy disks were all the rage and, as I often wrote, "Disks must be formatted before you can use them." PC users were intimate with (or intimidated by) the `format` command. Those were the days, and good riddance.

The only time you format something now is when you're preparing an optical disc. Even then, it's not a true format: The disc is formatted as you write to it. Hard drives come preformatted for your use and enjoyment. Floppy disks — well, God bless you if you still use them.

All computer media must be formatted before it can hold data. Think of the format operation as painting parking spaces, just like the stadium parking lot example discussed in the earlier section, "Understanding fragmentation," and illustrated in Figures 2-5, 2-6, and 2-7.

To review media formats, open the Disk Management console, as described in the section "Opening the Disk Management console," earlier in this chapter. The top-center portion of the window lists various storage devices attached to your PC. The File System column lists the formatting method for the media. Common formats are described in Table 2-2.

Table 2-2	**Media File Systems and Formats**	
File System	*Meaning*	*Description*
CDFS	Compact Disc File System	Also known as ISO 9660, the most popular optical disc format.
exFAT	Extended File Allocation Table	Also known as FAT64, designed by Microsoft for use with media cards and flash drives.
FAT	File Access Table	The original disk format used for storing files on the PC eons ago. Had many limitations.
FAT32	File Access Table, 32-bit	An updated version of the FAT that allowed access to larger hard drives. Still popular because the FAT32 is recognized by many operating systems. Not as useful as NTFS, however.
HPFS	High Performance File System	Developed for OS/2 and still used on PCs, though not as popular as NTFS.
NTFS	File System for Windows NT	The current and best disk format.
UDF	Universal Disk Format	A replacement for ISO 9660, used by DVDs. Also called ISO/IEC 13346.

Because all media comes preformatted, there's never a need to initially format storage media on a PC. You may, however, find the need to reformat media. One reason to do so is to erase all information previously stored on the media. Another reason may be to make the media compatible with another computer, such as reformatting an NTFS volume to FAT. Beyond that, honestly, I cannot think of any real reason to reformat media. Regardless, here are the steps to do so:

1. **Open the Disk Management console, as described earlier in this chapter.**

   See the earlier section, "Opening the Disk Management console."

2. **Right-click the media you want to format.**

   You can click an icon at the top or bottom of the window.

3. **Choose Format from the shortcut menu.**

The Format command is dimmed for media you cannot format, such as an optical disc. You also cannot format the media that's running Windows, such as drive C.

4. **If a warning appears, click the Yes button to continue.**

   The Format dialog box appears, as shown in Figure 2-12.

Figure 2-12:
The Format
dialog box.

5. **Type a volume label.**

   The *volume label* is merely a name that helps you identify the media.

6. **Choose a format for the drive.**

   Refer to Table 2-2.

   The rest of the options in the Format dialog box don't need to be adjusted unless you're directed to do so by a higher authority.

7. **Click the OK button to display a suitable warning.**

   A suitable warning appears, reminding you that formatting is a drastic step and erases any data stored on the media.

8. **Click the OK button to begin the formatting process.**

9. **If Windows detects that the volume is being used, click the No button.**

   Media is used when files are open, folder windows are open, or programs are accessing the drive or media card. If you're certain that nothing is accessing the card, click the Yes button to proceed with the format.

   You can watch the formatting progress in the Disk Management console; see the Status column for the media being formatted.

   Formatting takes time. The larger the volume, the longer it takes.

10. **Close the Disk Management console when you're done.**

Freshly formatted (or reformatted) media is ready for use. The media will be empty, though Windows creates the root folder. At that point, you're free to use the storage device as you see fit.

✦ The volume label is applied to the media, not to the drive. So, you can apply a label to a removable media card, which changes the card's volume label but doesn't change the name of all media you read.

✦ You cannot unformat a drive.

✦ Just as you can repaint a parking lot, you can also reformat storage media. Doing so, however, erases all information previously stored on the disk. Reformat storage media only if you truly need to.

✦ Honestly, the information isn't utterly destroyed when storage media is reformatted. Computer experts can recover information from media that's been reformatted.

✦ For information on seriously erasing media data, see the following sidebar, "Wipe out your data."

✦ Windows 7 and Windows Vista sport the Convert utility, which changes the disk format to NTFS for certain types of storage media. The Convert utility doesn't reformat the media, so no information is deleted. See Chapter 1 for more information.

✦ PC users were intimidated by the `format` command because they often typed only `format` to set up a floppy drive. But because the `format` command formatted whichever drive was being used, the result was often that the hard drive was reformatted. Even various warning prompts proved ineffective at stopping these accidental reformats. The `format` command was subsequently modified so that a drive letter had to be specified.

Wipe out your data

No one wants to throw out an old hard drive, at least no one who values their data. Even if you reformat a hard drive, or any media, information thieves can restore the data. As such, a security issue arises over information stored on old hard drives.

One solution that many folks rely on is a *disk wiping* utility. A few of them are out there. Rather than a drive merely being reformatted, random information is written and rewritten to it over and over. The result is that the random information obscures enough of the previous information written to the disk so that, supposedly, nothing can be recovered. (This type of utility is also available for erasing individual files.)

The problem with these utilities is that they don't work. They make the user feel good, but anyone with a solid knowledge of data recovery tells you that latent data is always available on the disk. In fact, one man I know has made a good living recovering data from damaged hard drives. He tells me that only an intense furnace can destroy data. I do not, therefore, recommend placing your old hard drives into an oven.

Messing with Volumes

This section has nothing to do with sound on the computer. No, the term *volume* dates back to the early days of the computer. Just as a book can be a volume, mass storage on your PC can be a volume. Indeed, Book I, Chapter 4 discusses a lot of the hard drive nomenclature, and much of it is rooted in those murky old days of the PC, where the folklore was rich and the grooming habits poor.

Both Windows 7 and Windows Vista feature a slick array of hard drive manipulation tools once found exclusively in the domain of third-party disk management utilities. These tools let you create partitions, shrink partitions, and expand drives to make them larger. This section explains the details.

**Book VI
Chapter 2**

Pampering the
Hard Drive

✦ I might suggest a refresher from Book I, Chapter 4 to get up to speed on the terms *partition* and *volume*.

✦ The techniques covered in this section apply only to hard drives.

✦ You cannot mess with the *system drive,* the hard drive from which Windows was started.

✦ Windows doesn't let you manipulate a drive that's in use. A drive is considered in use when its main window or a folder window is open, when a file on the drive is being accessed, or when a program is running from the driver or accessing the drive.

✦ In the olden days, many of the activities described in this section were accomplished by using the `fdisk` utility. But even `fdisk` didn't have the power to shrink or expand a volume on a hard drive.

Repartitioning a drive

The art of repartitioning involves several steps in Windows. The drive must first be *shrunk*. Windows uses any free space on the drive to create a new partition, which is a *volume*. The original hard drive retains all its files, but its overall capacity gets smaller.

The second step is to create a new volume, using the space made available by shrinking the drive. The volume can be created in the Disk Management console for use by Windows, or you can use another operating system's installation routine to find and then deal with the empty, or *unallocated,* volume.

To repartition the drive, heed the steps provided in the next section, "Shrinking a volume." Then follow through with the section after that, "Making use of unallocated drive space."

✦ A single physical hard drive can be divided into multiple volumes, or *partitions.*

✦ All hard drives feature one main volume. In most cases, this volume consists of the entire hard drive.

✦ You can also repartition a drive by deleting its volume outright. That destroys any information stored on the drive, but it's another way to repartition. See the later section, "Unallocating a volume."

✦ Before you move on, you should know that I do not recommend repartitioning a hard drive. The only reason I can think of for doing so is to install a second operating system. Even then, most operating systems you install come with software that does the repartitioning for you, which makes redundant a lot of the tools Windows provides. Despite that, I feel compelled to write about it anyway.

Shrinking a volume

Shrinking a volume takes advantage of a hard drive that isn't using all its space. For example, you can have a 200GB hard drive and use only 50GB of it. If so, the drive can be shrunk to, say, 100GB. That makes the remaining 100GB of disk storage available for use as another volume, such as another disk drive in Windows.

To shrink a volume, follow these steps:

1. **First, clean up some of the crap.**

To get the most space available, consider removing some unused files from the drive. Empty the Recycle Bin. And, perform other actions to ensure that you're not wasting space on the drive. See the section "Free Up Some Storage Space," at the beginning of this chapter, for some tips.

2. **Open the Disk Management console.**

Directions are found earlier in this chapter, in the section aptly titled "Opening the Disk Management console."

3. **Right-click a volume.**

It cannot be the system volume, such as drive C, or a media card, a flash drive, or an optical drive. It must be a hard drive.

4. **Choose Shrink Volume from the shortcut menu.**

Windows examines the volume to see how well it can be shrunk. Then it displays the Shrink dialog box, shown in Figure 2-13, where you can set the size of the new partition.

Figure 2-13:
Shrinking a
volume.

5. Set the amount of disk space to release.

Use the text box by the item Enter the Amount of Space to Shrink in MB
to set the new volume size. In Figure 2-13, the amount listed is 18,387MB,
or just over 18GB of storage. That's also the maximum amount that can
be shrunk; you can set the value lower, but not higher.

Set the size to whatever amount you need. Don't restrict the existing
volume too much, or else it may fill up and cause other problems.

6. Click the Shrink button to reduce the drive's size.

The computer busies itself with shrinking the volume. When the operation has been completed, you see the new unallocated volume appear
in the same slot as the current drive in the Disk Management console.
Figure 2-14 shows a before-and-after comparison of my test drive F,
which I shrunk by 10,000MB.

Before shrinking

Figure 2-14:
The before-
and-after
effects
of drive
shrinking.

After shrinking

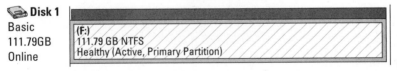

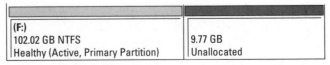

Existing volume   New volume

After shrinking an existing volume, a new volume has been created, as shown in Figure 2-14 and as you can see in the Disk Management console. Because the volume is unallocated, it's not available for use, at least not in a way that's recognizable to Windows. (Some Linux volumes might show up as unallocated.)

✦ The next section discusses what you can do with an unallocated volume.

✦ When a single physical hard drive sports unallocated drive space, you can take advantage of it to make the hard drive larger. See the section "Extending a volume," later in this chapter.

Making use of unallocated drive space

To make the unallocated portion of a hard drive useful, you must create a new volume, one that's recognized by Windows. You can create three types of volumes:

Simple: This typical hard drive is the type that most PC users have in Windows. If you're shrinking a volume to create a new logical drive, such as a new drive F (or something), this option is the one you want.

Spanned: A spanned volume combines two or more unallocated volumes, even on separate physical hard drives, creating a new drive. The new drive combines all the space of the various unallocated volumes into a single volume. Obviously, this option works only when more than one unallocated chunk of disk storage is available.

Striped: Striped volumes are used to improve disk performance by spreading information between multiple disks. The net result is that several drives are used to quickly access information, which makes all disk operations faster. You need two or more unallocated chunks of disk space to set up a striped volume.

If you're using the new volume to install another operating system on the PC, do not create another volume in Windows. Just leave the volume unallocated and let the other operating system's installation program do its thing with the drive.

To allocate the unallocated space as a usable hard drive in Windows, follow these steps:

1. **Right-click the unallocated volume in the Disk Management console.**

2. **Choose New Simple Volume from the shortcut menu.**

The New Simple Volume Wizard appears.

3. **Click the Next button.**

4. **Set the size of the new volume by using the Simple Volume Size in MB text box.**

   The size is already preset to equal the entire disk capacity, which is what I recommend. If you need to set it to a smaller size, do so. The remaining space on the drive continues to be unallocated.

5. **Click the Next button.**

   Windows lets you assign the drive a letter, or you can mount the drive on an NTFS volume as a folder. Or, you can do neither, depending on how you fill in the wizard.

6. **(Optional) Choose a letter for the new volume.**

   My advice is to use the letter that's provided.

7. **Click the Next button.**

8. **Ensure that the option Format This Volume with the Following Settings is chosen.**

9. **Ensure that the NTFS format is chosen.**

10. **Click the Next button.**

    A summary screen appears. Looks good.

11. **Click the Finish button to create the new volume.**

    Windows prepares the disk by formatting it, laying down the tracks (or parking spaces) for the files. The amount of time taken to complete the operation depends on the size of the volume. Larger disk drives take longer to format.

    The display in the Disk Management console shows the drive being formatted; you can watch its progress in the Status column at the top center of the window. The drive isn't assigned its new letter until after it's formatted.

12. **When the operation is complete, you can close the Disk Management console.**

The newly created disk drive appears in the Computer window along with the other host of drives. It's immediately available for use.

Don't be disappointed if the new volume shows up with less capacity than you wanted. The missing bytes are overhead, used by the formatting process.

Unallocating a volume

When you unallocate a volume in the Disk Management console, you're not only removing it from the storage media roster — you're also deleting all its data. In fact, the command that's used isn't `unallocate` or `de-allocate` but, rather, *delete*. After a volume is deleted, it's gone. Its status in the Disk Management console window returns to Unallocated.

By unallocating a volume, you destroy all data on that drive. You have no way to recover folders or files from a drive that's been unallocated. Proceed with these steps at your own peril:

1. Open the Disk Management console window.

Refer to the directions in the section "Opening the Disk Management console," earlier in this chapter.

2. Right-click the volume you want to unallocate.

The volume cannot be the system volume, from which Windows was started, or any volume that is in use or accessing the drive or that has files open or programs running.

3. Choose the Delete Volume or Delete command from the shortcut menu.

Despite the command name, the physical hard drive isn't deleted. Instead, the command merely removes the reference to the disk drive partition from the operating system's view and unlinks the partition from the drive's master boot record. (See Book I, Chapter 4 for more information on the master boot record.)

4. If prompted, click the Yes button in the suitable warning dialog box.

Another warning may appear if Windows believes the volume to still be in use.

5. If you're certain that the volume isn't in use, click the Yes button to de-allocate (delete) the volume.

That's it. The volume is instantly deleted, and its status in the Disk Management console window is demoted to unallocated.

The unallocated portion (all or a part) of a disk drive cannot be used by Windows. You can do three things with that chunk of disk space:

Reallocate the space. You can reallocate the partition by setting it up as another drive in Windows. Refer to the preceding section, "Making use of unallocated drive space."

Extend the volume. It's possible to use unallocated space on an existing hard drive to increase the existing drive's capacity. The steps are presented in the next section.

Use the partition for another operating system. By not doing anything, you keep the unused space available for another operating system, such as Linux. The installation program for this operating system prepares the volume for use.

You can always choose to do nothing, of course. In fact, some unallocated chunks of disk space may already be shown in the Disk Management console for your PC. That's fine. Sometimes, a chunk of disk is too small to use for anything, anyway. If that's the case, though, consider extending the volume, as described in the next section, "Extending a volume."

**Book VI
Chapter 2**

Extending a volume

Sometimes, an extra chunk of storage exists on a hard drive. For example, in Figure 2-14, you see a 9.77GB chunk of unused disk space, unallocated for drive F. You can use that unallocated portion of disk space to make a drive's main volume larger.

What may not be obvious is that you can use any chunk of unallocated storage on any drive to make any other drive larger. You can even combine unused chunks from several hard drives to increase the storage capacity of a single drive. To make any or all of that happen, follow these steps:

**Pampering the
Hard Drive**

1. **Open the Disk Management console window.**

2. **Right-click the volume you want to extend.**

The volume can be extended only when it dwells on a hard drive not currently in use and where an unallocated portion of storage is available somewhere else on the computer.

3. **Choose the command Extend Volume.**

The Extend Volume Wizard opens.

4. **Click the Next button.**

The next screen of the wizard allows you to select chunks of unallocated space on hard drives in your PC.

5. **Choose the chunks of unallocated space to add to the existing drive.**

Any unallocated space on the current drive (the one you're extending) already shows up in the Selected column (on the right side of the window). Any additional unallocated space on other drives shows up in the Available column. Use the Add or Remove buttons to choose which unallocated volumes to use.

If the Next button isn't available, the value specified by Select the Amount of Space in MB is too high. Set it to a lower value.

6. **Click the Next button.**

7. **Click the Finish button.**

As if by magic, the size of the drive instantly increases, by grabbing up all the unallocated portions.

8. **Close the Disk Management console window.**

The drive is now living large and ready for use.

Chapter 3: On Schedule

In This Chapter

- ✔ Finding where tasks live in Windows
- ✔ Creating your own tasks
- ✔ Doing a task test run
- ✔ Stopping a task
- ✔ Modifying a task
- ✔ Reviewing a task log
- ✔ Suspending a task
- ✔ Destroying a task

Sane people agree about the benefits of regular maintenance, yet it continues to be something mankind strives to attain. It's easy to forget to change the oil, which is probably why cars have low-oil lights. You computer doesn't use oil, so it lacks an oil light. Even if the computer did require oil, you wouldn't have to worry about remembering to change the stuff. That's because the computer has its own task scheduler. Your PC uses this feature to keep up with regular maintenance and other chores, all cheerfully described in this chapter.

Windows 7/Vista Task Scheduler

Unlike their predecessors, Windows 7 and Windows Vista sport a feature-rich task scheduler called, amazingly, *Task Scheduler.* It shows you all the tasks scheduled in Windows — tasks you create yourself as well as various top-secret system tasks. You can take advantage of this power yourself to set up and run your own tasks, ensuring that all the computer maintenance gets done. This section tells you how.

The Task Scheduler isn't the same thing as the Task Manager. See Chapter 2 in Book II for information on the Task Manager.

Opening the Task Scheduler

Windows keeps all its scheduled tasks, as well as the tasks you may create and schedule, in the Task Scheduler window. Here's how to get there:

1. **Open the Control Panel.**

2a. **In Windows 7, choose System and Security, and then choose Administrative Tools.**

2b. **In Windows Vista, choose System and Maintenance, and then choose Administrative Tools.**

3. **Open the Task Scheduler icon.**

4. **If prompted, type the administrator's password or click the Continue button.**

   The Task Scheduler window appears. Allow me to take you on the grand tour.

5. **On the left side of the window, select the top item, Task Scheduler (Local).**

   You see the Task Scheduler Summary, as illustrated in Figure 3-1. It provides a quick review of your tasks, including a review of which tasks have run and which are active.

Task folders   Review of recent and current tasks   Actions panel

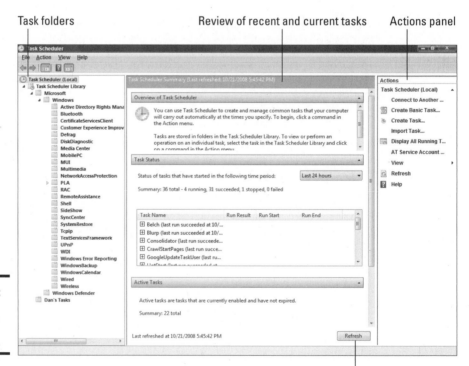

Figure 3-1:
The Task
Scheduler
overview.

Update information

6. **On the left side of the window, choose the item Task Scheduler Library.**

Tasks are organized into folders. The Task Scheduler Library folder is sort of the "root folder" for all tasks. You may see a few tasks listed there, as shown in Figure 3-2.

Additional tasks in the Task Scheduler window are organized by owner. You see a folder for Microsoft, which contains subfolders for Windows and Windows Defender, as shown in Figure 3-2. The Windows folder is open in the figure, showing additional subfolders for tasks related to specific programs or tools in Windows.

Finally, at the bottom of the window, you may see other folders. I created a personal folder for my own tasks: Dan's Tasks (refer to Figure 3-2).

The remaining steps illustrate how a task works and how information about the task is presented in the Task Scheduler window.

Book VI Chapter 3

On Schedule

Selected folder   Tasks found in selected folder   Create new task.

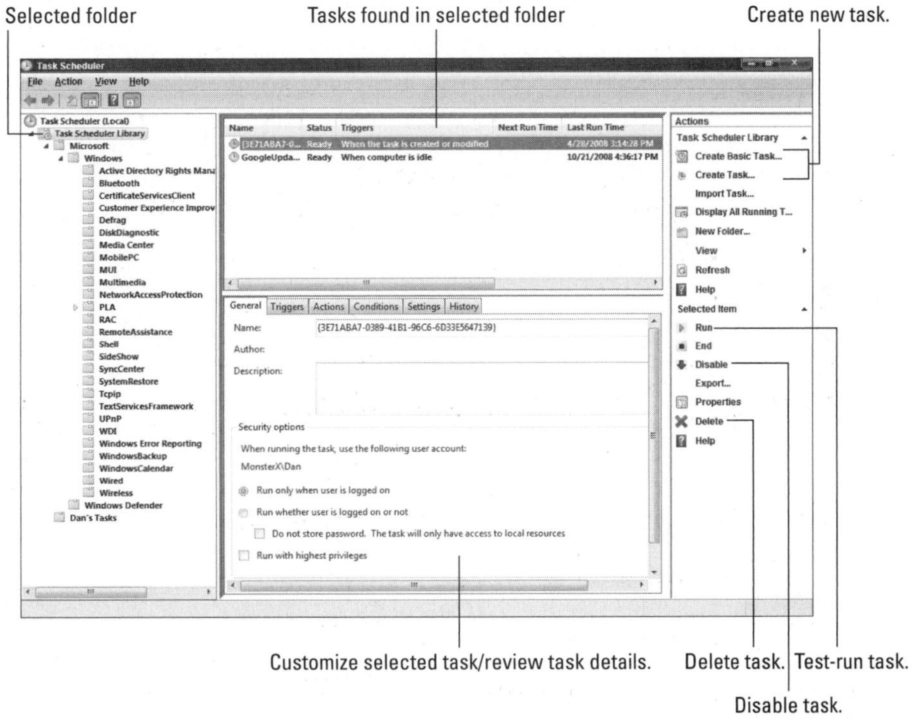

Figure 3-2: Viewing tasks in the Task Scheduler overview.

Customize selected task/review task details.   Delete task. | Test-run task.

Disable task.

7. Select the System Restore folder.

You may need to open the Microsoft folder, and then the Windows folder, to find the System Restore folder.

The System Restore folder contains tasks related to the System Restore utility — specifically, tasks that periodically create restore points for system recovery. The top part of the window describes the tasks for the System Restore folder. One task that's listed, SR, is shown as Ready (unless you disabled System Restore). You can also see the next and last run times, which verifies that the task is performing properly.

On the General tab at the bottom of the screen, you see the task's description: "This task creates regular system protection points." You can also see that the task is scheduled to run whether you're logged in or not.

8. Click the Triggers tab.

A *trigger* is an event or action that prompts a task to run. It can be a time during the day, such as midnight (which is when my computer says that a restore point is set), or it can be an action, such as system startup.

9. Click the Actions tab.

An *action* is what a task does — run a program, display a message, or make another thing happen. It's the task itself, basically, such as when you set a restore point, defragment the hard drive, or send an email message.

Yes, the action shown for setting a restore point is technical. It's gross looking. But keep in mind that you're viewing a Windows task. The tasks you set up will not be as complex. (They can be, but they probably won't.)

10. Click the Conditions tab.

The settings on the Condition tab refine when the task is run. The action, or task, doesn't run unless all the conditions are met.

11. Click the Settings tab.

The Settings tab lists further control over the task — minor things that control how and when the task is run and when to stop a task that might run amok.

12. Click the History tab.

You find on the History tab some information about when the task was last run and whether it ran successfully. That's your way to test whether your tasks are doing what you set them to do.

13. Close the Task Scheduler window when you're done poking around.

You can choose any task in any folder to study how it's set up, how it works, and whether it's run. In fact, reviewing the already-created tasks is a helpful way to find different ways to configure your own tasks, which is covered in the next section.

✦ Although the Task Scheduler window isn't the same as the Task Manager, you can use the Task Scheduler window to view any of its tasks that are running: Choose the item Display All Running Tasks from the right, Actions part of the Task Scheduler window. You see a list that shows only the scheduled tasks that are running.

✦ To see all programs and processes running in the computer, open the Task Manager window: Press Ctrl+Shift+Esc.

✦ The Task Scheduler supplies information to the Event Viewer, which can also be used to determine whether a task has run, as well as to provide information on just about everything going on in Windows. See Book II, Chapter 7 for information.

✦ Chapter 8 in Book II is on the topic of system recovery, which is where I praise the System Restore utility.

Making your own task folder

It's best to place your own tasks into a special folder in the Task Scheduler window. That keeps them organized, and if you're the kind of person who appreciates a schedule, you're most likely the same type of person who likes to be organized. Maybe not. Anyway. Here are the steps to create your own task folder:

1. **Open the Task Scheduler window.**

Specific directions are found in the preceding section.

2. **From the left side of the window, select the Task Scheduler Library folder.**

3. **From the right side of the window, Actions, choose the command New Folder.**

The Enter Name of the New Folder dialog box appears.

4. **Type a name for the folder.**

For example, you can type My Tasks. Well, because this is Windows Vista, you probably want to type just Tasks because that *My* archetype is so Windows XP.

5. **Click the OK button.**

The folder is created and ready for you to stuff with tasks.

If you plan to go nuts with tasks, you can create subfolders in your folder. Simply repeat these steps, but in Step 2 choose your own folder.

You can't rename a folder, which seems odd to me. You can, however, remove a folder by selecting it and then choosing Delete Folder from the Actions side of the Task Scheduler window. Click the Yes button to confirm the deletion.

Creating a new task

A *task* is simply something that the computer does. Sadly, you can't create a task that makes the computer do something it doesn't do already. For example, my task that tried to get my laptop to ride a unicycle while juggling USB wireless mice failed miserably.

You create a task by using one of two options in the Actions part of the Task Scheduler window: Create Basic Task or Create Task.

The Create Basic Task option lets you set up a new task quickly, especially when you're just starting out. You don't miss anything by choosing this option: Simply work your way through the wizard and answer the questions. As long as you know what you want the computer to do, and how often you need it done, the Create Basic Task Wizard works well.

At the final step, shown by the word Finish highlighted on the left side of the window, you can place a check mark by the option Open the Properties Dialog for This Task When I Click Finish. When you remember to do that, you'll see the task's Properties dialog box, as shown in Figure 3-3.

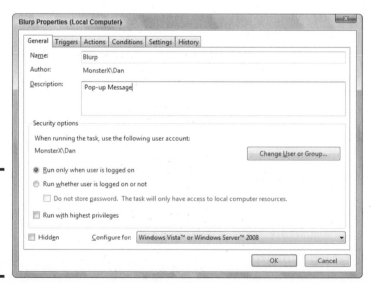

Figure 3-3:
The type of message displayed by the Task Scheduler.

The Create Task option, also found in the Actions part of the window, basically just starts the process with a dialog box that contains all the options and settings (refer to Figure 3-3). There's no walk-through, as there is with the Create Basic Task option, unless you just work through the tabs from right to left.

The key to setting up a task is scheduling when the task takes place, which is the *trigger*. Tasks can happen at given intervals or after certain events.

The intervals can be daily, weekly, or monthly and then refined to take place at a specific time, day, or week, or to even repeat. You can also schedule a task to take place when the computer starts, when you log in to Windows, or after another task has run or an event has taken place.

The final element is what the task does: the *action*. You can create only three types of tasks:

Run a program. You choose a program to run or to open a file. Windows lets you find the program, but to run some utilities, you must specify command line options, which are both confusing and difficult to discover.

Send an email message. You can send a message you compose to any email recipient. The message can contain an attachment, or it can be just text. The message content is static, however; you merely schedule when the message is being sent.

Display a message. A dialog box, similar to the one shown in Figure 3-4, appears at whatever time or after whatever event you specify.

**Book VI
Chapter 3**

On Schedule

Figure 3-4:
The type of message displayed by the Task Scheduler.

It's that time again!

You scheduled this task. Here's the message. Deal with it.

OK

You're not limited to doing only one of these tasks at a time. It's possible to stack tasks so that one executes after the other. For example, you can run a program and then send an email to confirm that the program has run.

The following sections describe how to create specific tasks and use the various features found in the Task Scheduler window.

✦ The section "Creating a task to run a program," next in this chapter, uses the Create Basic Task method of creating a task.

✦ The section "Creating a task to display a pop-up message," found later in this chapter, uses the Create Task method, which is more advanced.

✦ The *trigger* is the event that causes a task to run. It can be a certain time, an interval of time, or an event, such as starting Windows or logging in to the PC.

✦ The action is limited to only the three items mentioned in this section.

✦ One of the best ways to customize an action is to run a script, such as batch file or some type of automation routine that carries out activities in Windows. Such scripting languages can be an entire universe unto themselves, and people get wrapped up in writing scripts that do amazing things. Sadly, the topic of scripting is beyond the scope of this book.

Creating a task to run a program

Unlike previous versions of Windows, most of the utilities you can schedule are already listed as tasks in the Task Scheduler window. These utilities include Defrag, Backup, System Restore, and Check Disk. Other utilities you have might also use the Task Scheduler to set themselves up. That leaves few options available for running a task as part of general Windows maintenance.

I don't intend to make this a two-paragraph section, however. The following two sets of steps describe how to schedule a task that prints a document. It's probably nothing that you're eager to do, but the example illustrates some important points about running programs as tasks.

The first step is to create the document:

a. **Open Notepad.**

From the Start button menu, choose All Programs⇨Accessories⇨ Notepad.

b. **Type some text.**

I typed `You left the printer on.`

c. **Save the document to your Documents folder.**

Press Ctrl+S and then type a name, such as `print-sample.txt` or something else you can recognize.

d. **Close Notepad.**

Now that the text document is created, you can build a program task that automatically prints the document at a specific time or on a schedule. Follow these steps to create that task:

1. **Open the Task Scheduler window.**

Specific directions are found in the section "Opening the Task Scheduler," earlier in this chapter.

2. **Choose the folder in which to create your new task.**

I create my tasks in the Dan's Tasks folder. If you haven't yet created a folder, see the earlier section, "Making your own task folder."

3. **Choose Create Basic Task from the list of actions on the right side of the window.**

The Create Basic Task Wizard appears.

4. **Type a name for the task in the Name text box.**

For the Notepad example, type **Print Document Test.** The task name should reflect the task.

5. **Type a description in the Description box.**

Yeah, I was once one of those people who never typed descriptions. That's because I figured that I could just remember everything. Now that I'm older and wiser, I type descriptions for everything. My suggestion for the Notepad example is to type **Print a document on the printer every day at noon**, as shown in Figure 3-5.

**Book VI
Chapter 3**

On Schedule

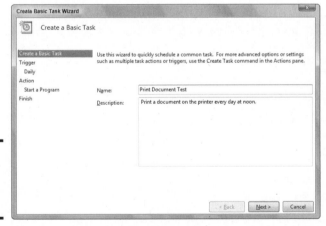

Figure 3-5:
The task is named and described.

6. **Click the Next button.**

Your next step is to decide what event must take place to trigger the task.

7. **Choose Daily.**

Basically, you're just narrowing things down for Windows. You customize the trigger in the next window.

8. **Click the Next button.**

   For time-driven triggers, you must specify the start time and interval. For event triggers, such as logging in to Windows, there's no additional step here, so you should skip to Step 11.

9. **Enter the starting date and time, plus any additional time settings.**

   For the Notepad example, set the time to noon, which is 12:00:00 PM. Set the repeat time to 1 day, to have the event trigger every day at noon.

10. **Click the Next button.**

    You need to choose an action, or the actual thing that the task does.

11. **Choose Start a Program.**

    Use the Browse button to set the program name, any options, plus the Start In folder if necessary. Yep, that's all complex stuff. For the Notepad example, the next few steps describe what to type.

12. **In the Program/script box, type** %windir%\notepad.exe.

    Do not put a period at the end of the command. Computer commands do not end in periods, though a period is specified at the end of the sentence in this step (because, otherwise, copy editors would have a conniption fit).

13. **In the Add Arguments (Optional) box, type** /p print-sample.txt.

    Do not put a period at the end of the command.

14. **In the Start In (Optional) text box, type** %userprofile%\documents.

    Do not put a period at the end of the command.

    See Figure 3-6 to confirm that you entered everything correctly.

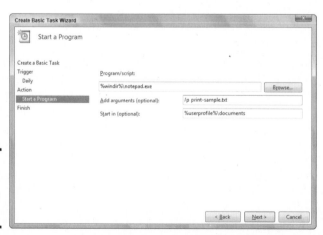

Figure 3-6:
Setting up
the program
to run.

15. Click the Next button.

The final window presents a summary of everything you did.

16. Click the Finish button.

The task has been created. Does it work? I don't know. Windows executes the task at the date and time (or event) specified. You have to review the task's History panel to confirm that it works. But there's an easier way:

With the task selected in the top part of the window, click the Run command in the Actions panel.

By clicking the Run command, you direct Windows to instantly run the task. So even though it's not on schedule, the task runs just as though the trigger event had occurred. In this case (as long as the printer is turned on), the document you created is printed.

**Book VI
Chapter 3**

On Schedule

✦ The task you created is a real task, and it runs on a schedule. If you don't want something to print every day at noon, disable or delete the task. See the section "Disabling a task" or "Deleting a task," later in this chapter.

✦ If the task was unsuccessful, you need to edit it. See the section "Editing a task," later in this chapter.

✦ There are command line options for just about every program that runs in Windows. Although that may seem like a throwback to the days of DOS, the truth is that the power in Windows relies heavily on that command line backbone. Just about every task that's run in Windows uses those command line options.

✦ Command line options are rarely documented in Windows itself. The Microsoft support page on the web can be of some help: `http://support.microsoft.com`. I happen to know Notepad's print command structure because, well, I'm a nerd. But it's also easy to remember the command `/P` to print.

✦ The word `%windir%` is the *environment variable* used by Windows to refer to the folder from which Windows was started. By using the `%windir%` variable, you ensure that the task runs on any computer with Windows installed, no matter which drive may be the system drive.

✦ The word `%userprofile%` refers to the User Profile folder, where your documents and files are stored. It works no matter which user is running the task. See Chapter 5 in Book II for more information on the User Profile folder in Windows.

Creating a task to send email

The email task is a bit silly, mostly because the email message you send is *static:* You cannot customize the message to relate any information that changes. You can add an attachment, which might be a file that's updated, such as a log file. But beyond that, the email action seems to be limited.

Use the steps from the preceding section as your guide to create an email task. Here are the specifics:

1. **Name the task** Email Test **and add your own description.**

2. **Set the trigger to Weekly and set the time as every Monday at 9 A.M.**

3. **For the action, choose Send an E-Mail.**

4. **Fill in the email message as follows:**

   From: Your email address.

   To: The recipient's email address, which can be your own email address or whoever you want to receive the message.

   Subject: The message subject.

   Text: The message text.

   Attachment: Any files you want to attach. Use the Browse button to help you locate the file.

   SMTP Server: The most important field. That's because the Task Scheduler doesn't use your PC's email program. Instead, it's the Task Scheduler itself that sends the message. As such, it requires the name of an email server to handle the request. (See Book IV, Chapter 3 for more information on what an SMTP server is and how to find out which one to use.)

   The completed screen for my computer is shown in Figure 3-7. Note that the SMTP server I specified in the figure isn't a real SMTP server; you should use your own ISP's server.

After finishing the Create Basic Task Wizard, test-run the task: Select the task at the top of the window and click the Run link, found in the Actions area on the right side of the window. If all goes well, you should receive the email message instantly.

This task continues to run until you delete or disable it. See the sections "Deleting a task" and "Disabling a task," later in this chapter.

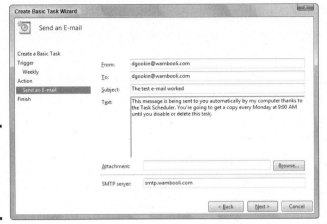

Figure 3-7:
Configuring
the mail
message to
send.

Creating a task to display a pop-up message

The simplest type of task you can create displays a pop-up message. Here
are the steps to create such a task by using the Create Task method:

1. **Open the Task Scheduler window.**

Specific directions are found in the section "Opening the Task
Scheduler," earlier in this chapter.

2. **Choose a folder for the new task.**

For example, choose a personal folder you created for all your own tasks.

3. **Choose Create Task.**

The Create Task dialog box appears. It looks similar to the task's
Properties dialog box (refer to Figure 3-3).

You start on the General tab.

4. **Type a name for the task in the Name text box.**

For this example, type **Reminder** in the Name box.

5. **Type a description in the Description box.**

For this example, type **A message that pops up and reminds you of
things way too often**.

6. **Click the Triggers tab.**

7. **Click the New button.**

How about having the message pop up every hour on the hour?

8. **Choose Daily.**

9. **Edit the start time so that the hour value ends in 00:00.**

   For example, if the current time is 10:39:19, edit it to read 10:00:00.

10. **Place a check mark by the option Repeat Task Every, and then choose 1 Hour and then 1 Day for the duration.**

11. **Click OK.**

12. **Click the Actions tab.**

13. **Click the New button.**

14. **From the Action button menu, choose Display a Message.**

   The window changes to reflect the new choice.

15. **Fill in the message title.**

   The message title appears atop the window, such as "It's that time again!" (refer to Figure 3-4). For this example, type **Gentle reminder**.

16. **Write the message.**

   The message itself appears in the dialog box. For this example, type the text **You've been gently reminded**.

   The dialog box sports only an OK button.

17. **Click OK.**

   You're pretty much done at this point. The Conditions tab provides supplemental options for refining when the task does or doesn't run. Likewise, the Settings tab provides you with more options.

18. **Click OK to create the task.**

The completed task appears in the list of tasks at the top of the window. To test-run it, select the task (if necessary) and then choose Run from the Actions side of the Task Scheduler window. The pop-up window appears, but it may show up behind the Task Scheduler window; click the Gentle Reminder button on the taskbar to see your results.

See Video 631 to see a walk-through of how to create a pop-up message task.

   www.dummies.com/go/troubleshootingandmaintaining
   yourpcaio2e

Test-running a task

To ensure that a task works, follow these steps with the Task Manager window open:

1. **From the left side of the Task Scheduler window, choose the folder containing the task you want to test-run.**

2. **Select the task from the top-center portion of the window.**

3. **Click the Run item in the Actions part of the window (on the right).**

The task goes about doing its thing.

✦ Some tasks provide no visual feedback. To confirm that the task has run, see the later section named, appropriately, "Confirming that a task has run."

✦ If the task creates a pop-up message, the message window may appear behind the Task Scheduler window.

✦ Also refer to earlier sections in this chapter that discuss creating a new task and test-running the task after it's created.

✦ The Run item isn't available when a task has been disabled. Enable the task and then test-run it.

✦ To enable a task, see the section "Disabling a task," later in this chapter.

Halting a task

Tasks are shown in the top-center portion of the Task Scheduler window. They're shown in Details view in separate columns: Name, Status, and Triggers. The Status column displays three task states:

Ready: The task is ready to go, waiting for its given triggers.

Disabled: The task has been disabled and will not run.

Running: The task is currently doing its scheduled thing.

You can disable a task that's ready. You can enable a task that's been disabled. To stop a running task, follow these steps:

1. **Select the task.**

2. **Choose the End option from the Actions list on the right side of the window.**

   A warning dialog box appears, asking whether you want to end all instances of the task.

3. **Click Yes.**

   The task is stopped.

Book VI
Chapter 3

On Schedule

Ending a task doesn't disable it. The task merely stops running — just as though you quit a program. To disable a task, preventing it from running in the future, see "Disabling a task," later in this chapter.

Confirming that a task has run

Never assume that automation takes place. Perfecting a task, test-running it, even selecting the proper goat as a sacrifice — none of these events is an assurance that the computer is behaving itself. To confirm that a task has run and run properly, follow these steps:

1. **Open the Task Scheduler window.**

Specific directions are found earlier in this chapter.

2. **From the left side of the window, open the folder containing the task.**

As an example, choose the Defrag folder, found in the `Microsoft\ Windows` folder. You can check the status of automatic defragmentation on your PC by confirming that the Defrag utility has run.

3. **Choose a task from the top-center portion of the Task Scheduler window.**

To check on the Defrag utility, choose the ScheduledDefrag task.

4. **In the bottom-center part of the window, click the History tab.**

You see a list of all recent times that the task has executed, as shown in Figure 3-8. You can click to highlight a specific event and see details toward the bottom of the window, or you can double-click an entry to see more information in a dialog box.

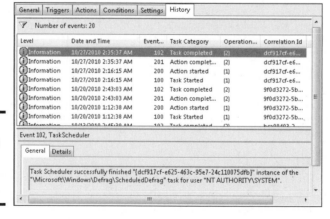

Figure 3-8:
Information about an executed task.

5. **Close the Task Scheduler window when you're done.**

When the task fails to run, an error message is displayed — hopefully, with an explanation, though often the reason a task fails to run is that the computer was turned off. In fact, the Windows Backup routine displays a notification area pop-up balloon informing you of missed backups.

✦ If you look for it, you won't find the Windows Backup program anywhere in the Task Scheduler. That's because backup schedules its own tasks. Similarly, the PC's antivirus program might do its own scheduling.

✦ Backup is covered in Chapter 1 of this minibook.

✦ If you have a problem reading the history log, the Task Scheduler displays a pop-up warning window. The warning doesn't mean that something is wrong with your task, but rather that there's a problem reading the log.

Editing a task

To review or modify an existing task, follow these steps:

1. **Open the Task Scheduler window.**

2. **Open the folder containing the task.**

   Folders are listed on the left side of the window.

3. **Select the task from the top-center portion of the window.**

4. **From the list of actions, choose Properties.**

   The task's Properties dialog box appears, similar to the one shown earlier, in Figure 3-3.

5. **Modify the task.**

   Use the various settings on the tabs to customize the task. You can reset the triggers, hone the action, or mess with any of the optional settings and controls.

6. **Click OK to save the changes.**

I also recommend that you test-run the task, just to be sure. See the section "Test-running a task," earlier in this chapter.

Disabling a task

All tasks run all the time — unless you disable them. Disabling a task doesn't delete the task (which is covered in the next section). It merely prevents the task from running again.

To disable a task, select the task in the Task Scheduler window and then choose the option Disable from the list of actions on the right.

Tasks remain disabled until you reenable them. To reenable a disabled task, select the task and choose the Enable action.

✦ Disabled tasks are flagged as such in the top part of the window, in the Status column.

✦ You must reenable a task to test-run it.

✦ Do not disable any tasks in the Microsoft folder. If you want to disable an automated activity in Windows, use the methods described in this book. Most Windows tools and utilities can be disabled by using the tool or utility program itself.

✦ You can be more precise when disabling a task. Rather than disable the entire thing, you simply disable the task's triggers. To do so, open the task's Properties dialog box, click the Triggers tab, and then edit one of the triggers. In the Edit Trigger dialog box, remove the check mark by the Enabled option (at the bottom part of the window) to disable that trigger. By disabling all triggers, you disable the task.

Deleting a task

I don't recommend that you delete a task. Instead, consider disabling it first, as described in the preceding section. If you truly want to get rid of a task, you can delete it: Select the task from the top part of the window, and then choose the Delete action from the Actions list along the right side of the window. Click the Yes button to confirm that you want the task obliterated.

✦ Deleted tasks cannot be recovered. There is no Recycle Bin for deleted tasks.

✦ Don't delete any task you did not create. Never delete any task in the Microsoft folder.

Windows XP Scheduled Tasks

Windows XP provides you with the Scheduled Tasks window. It's a place where you can create your own tasks — programs that run to do various things — automatically on a schedule. It's part of the automation thing that makes computer maintenance easy. This section explains how it works.

Opening the Scheduled Tasks window

To review any tasks you created, or to create a new task, you must visit the Windows XP Scheduled Tasks window: From the Start button menu, choose

All Programs➪Accessories➪System Tools➪Scheduled Tasks. The Scheduled Tasks window appears, as shown in Figure 3-9.

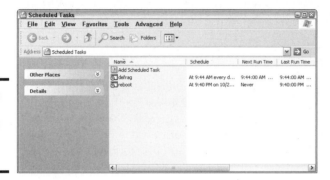

Figure 3-9:
The Scheduled Tasks window.

To ensure that you're getting the full effect of the Scheduled Tasks window, choose View➪Details from the menu. That way, you can see the schedule for each task and the next run time and last run time, as shown in the figure.

In Figure 3-9, two types of icons are shown.

 The first icon, the one that's always in the window, is the Add Scheduled Task icon. Opening this icon runs the Scheduled Task Wizard, which helps you create your own tasks.

 The second type of icon represents tasks you create. In Figure 3-9, two tasks I created are listed. The first, titled `defrag`, automatically runs the hard drive defragmentation utility, which keeps the PC's hard drives running smoothly. (Creating this task is covered in the next section.)

The second task icon is titled `reboot`. It automatically restarts the computer, but it's disabled. You can confirm by checking the Next Run Time column, which shows that the task will "never" run again. Well, unless it's reenabled.

The remaining sections in this chapter discuss how to use the Scheduled Tasks window to create, use, and modify your own tasks.

Creating a task

Not all computer maintenance is automated in Windows XP. As a prime example, consider the Defrag utility (mentioned in Chapter 2). You should run this tool often to keep the hard drive performing at top efficiency. Yet Windows doesn't automatically run Defrag by itself. Instead, you must automate the process by creating a new task. Follow these steps:

1. **Open the Scheduled Tasks window.**

From the Start button menu, choose All Programs⇨Accessories⇨System Tools⇨Scheduled Tasks.

2. **Open the Add Scheduled Task icon.**

The Scheduled Task wizard appears.

3. **Click the Next button.**

Windows presents a list of scrolling programs, along with a Browse button. You can choose a program from the list, but, sadly, the Defrag program didn't make the cut. You have to use the Browse button to locate Defrag manually.

4. **Choose the program to run and click the Next button, or click the Browse button to locate the program.**

In the example of creating a Defrag task, click the Browse button and then follow these substeps:

a. *From the Address bar in the Select Program to Schedule window, choose drive C, the PC's main hard drive.*

b. *Open the* `Windows` *folder.*

c. *Open the* `System32` *folder.*

d. *Click to select the* `defrag.exe` *program.*

The program might be called `defrag` or `defrag.exe`, depending on whether you configured Windows to display filename extensions.

e. *Click the Open button.*

5. **Type a name for the task.**

The program name is probably set up already in the wizard. If it's okay, such as `defrag`, keep it. Otherwise, you can be more descriptive and type something else.

6. **Choose the task trigger.**

The trigger is either a time interval — Daily, Weekly, Monthly — or a one-time event, such as Once, When My Computer Starts, or When I Log In.

For the Defrag task, choose Weekly.

7. **Click the Next button.**

8. **Refine the run time if prompted.**

For a weekly task, the next screen lets you choose the days of the week, start time, and repeat interval. I set up Defrag on my computer to run every Monday at 9:44 a.m. (That's because it's a Monday, and I'm probably not doing anything at my computer at 9:44 a.m.)

For a daily task, you can choose when to run the task, as well as how often a day to run it. Monthly tasks have similar options.

The One Time Only option lets you set only the day and time for the task to run.

The other two triggers, When My Computer Starts and When I Log In, are preset to run the task only at those times.

9. Click the Next button.

Your user account name is specified in the Enter User Name box. That's because all tasks in Windows must be assigned to a user. It's a security measure, though it's not that sincere.

Because your account will be running the task, you need to specify your account password.

10. Type your Windows account password in the Enter the Password text box.

11. Type your password a second time, in the Confirm Password text box.

12. Click the Next button.

A summary screen lists information about the task.

13. Click the Finish button.

And the task is created.

The task exists as an icon in the Scheduled Tasks window. But more important, the task exists in the computer's brain. Every Monday, the Defrag program will run, defragmenting your PC's hard drives automatically. That's the reason behind setting up the task and how tasks help automate maintenance on your PC.

The task doesn't run right away. In fact, your next task [sic] is to test-run the task you just created, to ensure that it works. Continue in the next section.

+ The Defrag task created in this section doesn't work as written: You need to modify the Defrag command to make it work properly. See the section "Editing a task," later in this chapter.

+ Tasks don't run when the computer is turned off. Ensure that you schedule your PC's tasks to run when the computer is on.

+ Not every activity in your PC is scheduled via the Scheduled Tasks window. For example, your PC's antivirus program probably performs automatic scans based on its own schedule. You change its schedule, or disable updates, using the antivirus program, not the Scheduled Tasks window.

**Book VI
Chapter 3**

On Schedule

Running a task

I recommend that you test-run any new task you create. Here's how it's done:

1. **Open the Scheduled Tasks window.**

2. **Right-click the icon representing the task you want to run.**

3. **Choose the Run command from the shortcut menu.**

   The task busies itself. Any feedback you see reflects what the task is doing. Some tasks have no visual feedback.

4. **Close the Scheduled Tasks window when you're done.**

You can also use these steps to run a task off-schedule. For example, when you have a task that performs a complex operation and you know that the computer will be turned off in the future, you can manually run the task at once by following the steps in this section.

Confirming that a task has run

Some tasks are like submarines: They're running, but you can't see them from shore. That's because the task whizzes away in the background, doing its thing and not bothering you or otherwise being obvious. That's okay for regular operations, but when you want to confirm that the task ran, it makes things difficult.

To confirm that the task has run, you need to check the task logs. Follow these steps:

1. **Open the Scheduled Tasks window.**

2. **Choose Advanced⇨View Log.**

   The log file is loaded into the Notepad program. The text you see in the Notepad window reflects recent log activity, though the list isn't sorted chronologically. You need to do some searching to find the most recent entries.

3. **Press Ctrl+F to summon the Find dialog box.**

4. **In the Find What box, type** most recent **and click the Find Next button.**

   You zoom to a line in the file that contains the following text:

   ```
   [ ***** Most recent entry above this line ***** ]
   ```

5. **Click the Cancel button to close the Find dialog box.**

   The log file starts at the Most recent entry line and works its way up from there.

6. **Close the Notepad window when you're done looking at the logs.**

7. **(Optional) Close the Scheduled tasks window.**

A typical task has two entries. For example, the Defrag task should show entries like this:

```
"defrag.job" (defrag.exe)
        Started 10/19/2009 9:44:01 AM
"defrag.job" (defrag.exe)
        Finished 10/19/2009 9:55:06 AM
        Result: the task completed with an exit code of (0).
```

The first entry (at the top) shows when the task was started. The next entry describes when the task has completed, as well as the results.

When a task screws up, you see something like this displayed:

```
"defrag.job" (defrag.exe)
        Started 10/12/2009 9:44:01 AM
"defrag.job" (defrag.exe)
        Finished 10/12/2009 9:44:01 AM
        Result: the task completed with an exit code of (2).
```

Your key to determining that the task screwed up is first knowing the task and checking the start and finish times. In this example, Defrag cannot run instantly: The start and finish times are the same. Sometimes, they're just very close.

Also, the `exit code 2` message usually isn't a good sign. You'd have to look it up in your online documentation to see what it means, but it's not good.

✦ The Scheduled Tasks log file is named `SchedLgU.txt`, and it's located in the Windows folder. It's a plain text file.

✦ An *exit code* is a value that all programs produce for the operating system when the program quits. It's a way for programs that run automatically (such as those run by the Scheduled Tasks window) to communicate with the operating system.

✦ Generally speaking, any exit code other than zero means that an error occurred.

✦ Every time the Task Scheduler starts, you see an entry giving the starting time.

✦ All tasks run. Whether the task was successful must be determined by examining the log.

Editing a task

Because few things are perfect the first time, you'll probably end up editing your tasks after your create them. For example, the Defrag task, created earlier in this chapter, doesn't run properly. That's because the Defrag command needs to know which drive to defragment. To specify the drive letter, you need to edit the task. Here's how:

1. **Open the Scheduled Tasks window if it's not open already.**

2. **Right-click the icon for the task you want to edit.**

For example, right-click the Defrag icon to fix the task if you find that it's not working, based on the directions earlier in this chapter.

3. **Choose Properties from the shortcut menu.**

The task's dialog box appears, as shown in Figure 3-10.

Figure 3-10: A task's dialog box.

The task's dialog box has three tabs, each of which lets you review or modify what the task does or when it runs, as well as other settings.

4. **Fix the Defrag task by editing the Run text box to include the disk drive to defragment.**

In Figure 3-10, you can see that I added C: to the line, which means that the Defrag program will defragment drive C when the task runs.

5. **Click the Schedule tab to modify the schedule.**

6. **Click the Settings tab to review various options and stuff.**

7. **Click OK to close the task's dialog box.**

8. **If prompted, type your password twice.**

   All tasks must be assigned to a user, so you need to provide the password so that the task is run by your account.

You might consider test-running the task to ensure that it's still working properly or that it's been fixed. See the section "Running a task," earlier in this chapter.

Disabling a task

All tasks shown in the Scheduled Tasks window run at their appointed times. That is, unless a task has been disabled. To disable a task, follow these steps:

1. **Right-click the icon for the task you want to disable.**

2. **Choose Properties from the shortcut menu.**

3. **In the task's dialog box, on the Task tab, remove the check mark by the item Enabled (Scheduled Task Runs at Specified Time).**

   Use Figure 3-10 as a guide.

4. **Click OK.**

A disabled task appears with a red X in its icon, as shown in the margin (though the red X isn't red). In Details view, the Next Run Time column shows the task as Disabled.

Unlike deleting a task (covered in the next section), a *disabled* task simply sits and waits. It doesn't run. It does run, however, if you reenable the task. To do so, repeat these steps, but in Step 3 place the check mark by the item Enabled (Scheduled Task Runs at Specified Time).

Deleting a task

To discard a task you never use, or perhaps a test task you created, follow these steps:

1. **Select the task icon in the Scheduled Tasks window.**

2. **Press the Delete key on the keyboard.**

3. **If prompted, click the Yes button to confirm the file deletion.**

I recommend that you consider disabling a task as opposed to deleting it outright. Unlike deleting a task, when you disable a task, it's easier to revive it, or, to *reenable* it. A deleted task has to be either recovered from the Recycle Bin or re-created from scratch.

Yes, deleted tasks are placed into the Windows Recycle Bin. The task appears by name in the Recycle Bin window. Tasks use the filename extension `job`.

Chapter 4: A Time to Clean

In This Chapter

- ✔ Obtaining cleaning stuff
- ✔ Cleaning outside the PC
- ✔ Dealing with a dirty keyboard
- ✔ Washing a keyboard
- ✔ Fixing a dirty mouse
- ✔ Making the screen sparkle
- ✔ Shining an optical disc
- ✔ Blowing the dust out of the case

The dentist reminds you to brush your teeth twice a day. You probably do the dishes at least once a day. You might wash your car once a season — usually, before it rains. But when was the last time you cleaned your computer? Probably never. No one gives a clean PC a second thought. Oh, there may be dusting to do. There may be concern over "things" on the screen. But cleaning is something you as a PC user have probably seldom considered. So read this chapter.

Your Cleanliness Arsenal

You're lucky: Some cleaning chores involve big equipment, steam generators, toxic chemicals, and maybe even high explosives. Although you can use those items to clean your PC, it's not necessary. That's because the things you need in order to clean your computer are probably items you already have around the home or office. Here's my list:

Air can: A can of air is like a can of cheese — I wouldn't recommend consuming either one. You can find cans of compressed air used for cleaning at any office supply or computer store. The air can, shown in Figure 4-1, contains pressurized gas that you can use to blow dust and crud out of the keyboard, mouse, console, and other places tiny and filthy.

Figure 4-1:
An air can.

Cleaning fluids: You don't need anything fancy to clean your computer. I use Formula 409 or Fantastic to clean the case. Soapy water works. Avoid alcohol and ammonia.

Sponge or paper towels: For wiping down surfaces, nothing beats the standard kitchen sponge, a paper towel, or even a nice software dishcloth. Don't use those moist towelette types of cleaners because they contain alcohol, which can damage certain parts of the computer.

Tweezers: Nothing beats a good pair of tweezers for retrieving specific pieces of junk from a keyboard or for pinching hair out of an optical mouse sensor.

Vacuum: I bought a tiny, portable vacuum to help clean my computer, as shown in Figure 4-2. You don't have to go that far, as long as your household vacuum sports accessories, such as a drapery cleaner, which is great for sucking the crud out of a keyboard.

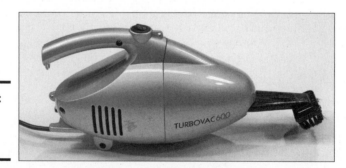

Figure 4-2:
Portable
vacuum
cleaner.

Why you should avoid cleaning with alcohol or ammonia

Along with bleach (chlorine), alcohol and ammonia are among the most popular household cleaning chemicals. They're great for cutting the grease and the grime and making dingy things all sparkly again, but they can damage your computer if you use them incorrectly.

Specifically, it's the computer's LCD monitor that's sensitive to harsh chemicals. Ammonia or alcohol can greatly reduce the monitor's clarity, giving it a dingy look over time – which

is kind of the opposite thing you want a cleaner to do. For a touchscreen monitor, those chemicals can render the mechanics that detect your finger presses and swipes, which makes the touchscreen useless.

For a computer, the bottom line is to use non-harsh cleaners on the case, and use only those cleaners approved for an LCD monitor on the computer screen.

Wipes for the LCD monitor: Cleaning the computer monitor requires special care, which is covered specifically later in this chapter. If you can, take the time to find some wipes designed specifically to clean the delicate surface of an LCD monitor. Generic wipes are available, and some pricey brand names. Just don't use alcohol- or ammonia-based wipes.

I'm not recommending that you run out and buy anything right now. Instead, follow my advice in this chapter, and if you discover anything extra that you can use to make the cleaning job easier, go out and get it.

Cleaning a PC isn't something you're going to do all the time. I clean my computers every so often, mostly when I attach something new to the console and notice how disgusting the situation is behind my computer desk. Or, I'll do an inside-the-case cleaning job when I add new hardware. But — and this is for all you moms out there — don't obsess over cleaning your PC.

✦ Air cans don't contain "air." They contain pressurized gas. I mention this fact because you shouldn't inhale the gas. Nor should you turn the can upside down to shoot out a lovely plume of white fog, which is something I've never done because it scared my cat.

✦ Although I use a can of air to clean things, I prefer to use the vacuum cleaner. Air cans tend to blow stuff around as opposed to getting rid of it outright.

✦ Avoid using strong chemicals when cleaning your PC. These chemicals include ammonia, alcohol, bleach, and acids, such as vinegar.

✦ You can still *drink* alcohol while you use your computer. But I caution you not to compose and send email while intoxicated.

✦ USB-powered vacuum cleaners are very popular with the laptop set.

✦ If you plan to use high explosives to clean your PC, be sure that someone uses a video camera to record the event. Not only will it be entertaining to watch later, but you also might win $10,000 on *America's Funniest Computer Cleaning Videos*.

Outside the Box

You may have trouble thinking "outside the box," but you shouldn't have any problems cleaning outside the computer's box. That's because the muck and grime — okay, mostly dust — that clings to the exterior of your PC is easy to locate and clean up. This section covers various things to clean on the outside of the computer system.

Cleaning surfaces and stuff

Generally speaking, I wipe down the outside of the monitor and console, using nothing more than a dry cloth. For some items, I wet a paper towel with household cleaner, such as Formula 409, and then do some rubbing to remove any buildup. But the console and monitor surfaces (not the screen) mostly collect dry dust. It's not a pain to clean.

Behind the console, and in the nest of cables beneath the computer desk, you'll probably find a lot of dust bunnies, and maybe some peanuts, paper, that old CD you thought you had lost, and other junk. Tidy up that stuff by using a portable vacuum cleaner or the hose-and-wand attachment from an upright vacuum.

You can also clean the printer with a damp cloth or paper towel. However, because the printer seldom sees as much handling as a console or monitor, it doesn't get dirty as fast.

✦ When using liquids to clean the outside of a computer, avoid spilling liquid inside the computer. Wring out that sponge!

✦ Do not spray cleaner on the computer case; instead, first spray it on a paper towel and then clean the case.

✦ There's no need to turn the computer off to clean it.

✦ Video 641 demonstrates how to clean a PC:

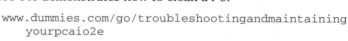

www.dummies.com/go/troubleshootingandmaintaining
yourpcaio2e

Cleaning the console vents

The most important things to clean on any computer are the air vents on the console. Air must circulate inside the box, or else the computer's components get too hot and make Mr. PC uncomfortable. That's when problems start. In fact, cleaning the air vents on your PC is probably the best way to ease the computer's woes.

The computer has two sets of air vents, shown in Figure 4-3, found on the front and back. Clean both. If the vents are clogged with pet hair, you might be able to clean them out by hand. I prefer to use a vacuum cleaner to get the gunk out. An air can works, but don't try to blow the gunk into the console.

✦ The *console* is the main PC box. The old IBM term was *system unit*. Some folks call it the *CPU,* though that term is incorrect. Nope, it's the console, the main box into which all computer goodies plug.

✦ See the section "Inside the Box," later in this chapter, for information on removing the crud from inside the PC, which is where it goes when you use an air can to clean the vents.

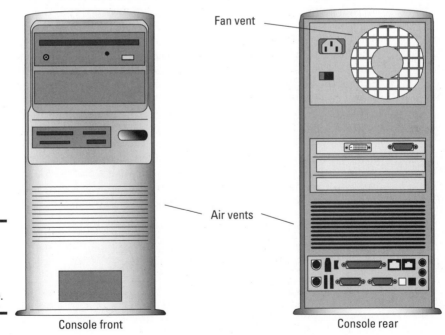

Figure 4-3: Where the vents are found on a PC console.

Fan vent

Air vents

Console front

Console rear

Cleaning the keyboard

I prefer to use a vacuum cleaner to de-crud the keyboard. I feel that the vacuum more adequately removes the debris from between the keys than a can of air does, which I think merely blows the stuff around. For intermediate crud, I use tweezers.

Sometimes, it helps to turn over the keyboard and give it a good shake. Be prepared for gross stuff to come out.

The best way to avoid a dirty keyboard is to *not eat* while you use the computer.

You can clean keycaps by using a pencil eraser. Keep in mind that the more you use a computer keyboard, the more likely it is that certain key cap labels wear off. On my keyboards, it's always the A key's label that goes first.

If you use a pencil eraser to clean key caps, take a vacuum to the keyboard immediately afterward to rid the keyboard's guts of eraser stubble.

Dealing with liquid spilled in a keyboard

The worst thing that can happen to the keyboard is water damage, such as spilled coffee or juice. This type of mishap may not ruin the keyboard, but it depends on the type of keyboard, whether it's mechanical or magnetic.

The first thing you should do after spilling liquid into the keyboard is to detach it. If you're using a USB keyboard, simply unplug it. The older PS/2 connector keyboards shouldn't be disconnected without turning off the PC first. Otherwise, by disconnecting the PS/2 connector, you may accidentally damage the keyboard connection circuitry or the PC's motherboard. That's a bad thing.

After removing the keyboard, try to give it a bath. Fill a washtub with cold, soapy water. Immerse the keyboard in the water and give it a few good shakes. Then let the keyboard drain on a towel. Let it sit overnight or until it's completely dry — typically, overnight.

The next day, after the keyboard is dry, attempt to plug it back into the PC and see whether it can be used. Often, the keyboard recovers just fine. If not, replacement keyboards are cheap.

✦ Mechanical keyboards are more expensive than their magnetic and membrane cousins. They do, however, stand a greater chance of being cleaned by using the water-immersion method.

✦ Cheaper keyboards use magnets and membranes to make the keys connect. In that case, immersing the keyboard to clean it may render the thing useless. Of course, it was probably rendered useless immediately after you spilled coffee into it, so the point is moot.

Cleaning a mouse

The mouse needs cleaning more than any other part of the computer. Optical mice especially seem to collect junk and hair on the desktop, which causes the mouse pointer to behave erratically on the screen. A good cleaning fixes the problem.

To clean an optical mouse, first position the mouse pointer on the screen in a way that, if you accidentally click the mouse, nothing "bad" happens. Then place the mouse upside down in one hand and use a pair of tweezers in the other hand to remove gunk from the mouse's optical "eye." You might also use a blast of air to finish the job.

Book VI Chapter 4

A Time to Clean

Mechanical mice rely on a rolling ball to detect movement. To clean a mechanical mouse, follow these steps:

1. **Roll the mechanical mouse over on its back.**

2. **Remove the base plate that holds in the mouse's ball.**

3. **Remove the mouse ball.**

4. **Clean the mouse ball by wiping it with a damp cloth.**

5. **Clean the sensors inside the mouse by using a pair of tweezers and an air can.**

   Rolling sensors inside the mouse detect movement of the mouse ball. Often, crud wraps itself around the rollers, which you can remove by using tweezers. (Sometimes, an X-Acto knife may be needed to scrape off the gross filth encrusting the rollers.)

   You might also consider cleaning out the cavity that the mouse ball occupies, to remove bits of fingernail, potato chip, and hair.

6. **Replace the mouse ball.**

You can now continue to use the mechanical mouse, which should be more responsive to your input.

+ Yes, a tiny hair — even a blond one — can obscure the optical mouse's ability to properly interpret movement.

+ There's no way to avoid a dirty mouse. Because mice roll on the desktop, they collect crud as you work. Fortunately, a dirty mouse manifests itself by exhibiting unreliable mouse pointer behavior. So the mouse doesn't stay dirty undetected.

Cleaning the screen

The traditional glass or CRT monitor was easy to clean. What I did was spray some standard glass cleaner on a paper towel and then rub the monitor's screen to remove the various sneeze globs and pixel dust. The key was to not get any of the glass cleaner inside the monitor. As long as you spray a conservative amount of cleaner on the paper towel, you'll meet that goal.

Cleaning an LCD monitor is trickier because not only should you not spray anything on the monitor, you also need to avoid using alcohol or ammonia to clean the thing. The best way to clean an LCD monitor is to use an LCD monitor-cleaning kit. For general cleaning, a lint-free or microfiber cloth works fine. In fact, your monitor may have come with this type of cloth.

+ For detailed information on cleaning an LCD monitor, see Book III, Chapter 4.

+ Clean a monitor when it's turned off. That way, you can best see the screen.

+ Watch Video 342 to see me cleaning a laptop's monitor. Video 642 shows me cleaning a CRT monitor:

        www.dummies.com/go/troubleshootingandmaintaining
           yourpcaio2e

Buffing an optical disc

There's no need to periodically thumb through your collection of data discs and clean them. Only when you have a problem reading the disc should you investigate cleaning it as a solution.

To clean a disc, gently wipe it with a dry, lint-free or microfiber cloth. Wipe from the center hole outward; do not wipe in a circle. That's pretty much all you can do.

+ Cracks and scratches in an optical disc render it useless. Although you can try to clean the disc as described in this section, when you continue to have problems, I recommend throwing out the disc.

+ Never attempt to clean the inside of an optical drive.

Inside the Box

Some people use a computer for years and never clean inside the thing. Perhaps if you live in a completely dust-free, sterile environment might there be nothing inside the console to clean. But most of us don't live inside a sterile environment. Some of us have pets. Worse, many of us have children. Dust, debris, and other things float inside the console. It's gross.

To clean out that stuff inside your PC's console, start by opening the case.

Never open a computer console unless you properly shut down the computer and turn it off. I recommend unplugging the computer needs before you open the case.

After you open the case, you can use a can of air to blast away the years of accumulated crust. Of course, I'm not an air can fan. When I open my PCs and shoot in a can of air, I find that all the dusty remains blow up into my face. I prefer a vacuum cleaner with the tube or drapery attachment.

Don't forget to clean the inside of the vents.

When you're done cleaning, close the case. The computer runs better because the air circulation inside the console is better without all the dust.

✦ There's no need to schedule regular cleaning inside the console. I do it only when I upgrade hardware. There are some PC's I've owned that I've never opened or cleaned. But:

✦ I would clean the inside of a PC that's experiencing the types of erratic errors that are brought on by the case being too hot. See Book I, Chapter 3 for more information on the type of random restarts created by a hot PC.

✦ Enjoy Video 643 to see how I clean the inside of a computer console:

```
www.dummies.com/go/troubleshootingandmaintaining
    yourpcaio2e
```

Book VI Chapter 4

A Time to Clean

Index

D

N

Z